The Power of Punitive Damages – Is Europe Missing Out?

Editors:
Lotte Meurkens
Emily Nordin

The Power of Punitive Damages – Is Europe Missing Out?

intersentia

METRO

Ius Commune Europaeum

Lotte Meurkens & Emily Nordin (eds.)

The Power of Punitive Damages – Is Europe Missing Out?

Intersentia Ltd
Trinity House | Cambridge Business Park | Cowley Road
Cambridge | CB4 0WZ | United Kingdom
mail@intersentia.co.uk

ISBN 978-1-78068-047-7
NUR 825

Cambridge – Antwerp – Portland
www.intersentia.com | www.intersentia.co.uk

Cover picture: © Tom Schmucker – Dreamstime.com

British Library Cataloguing in Publication Data. A catalogue record for this book is available from the British Library.

Lotte Meurkens
Emily Nordin

PREFACE

A new brush sweeps clean, but an old brush knows the corners…

Punitive damages: real plum or recipe for disaster?

Punitive damages are traditionally not awarded in Continental European legal systems. There, punishment is an exclusive power of the government that should stay part of the public law domain. The strong European view is that punitive damages should in no way be utilised to protect private law interests. Compensating the victim for his or her loss is the objective of tort law. 'American situations', especially the awarding of exorbitant amounts of punitive damages, are feared and should in the opinion of most European scholars by all means be avoided. However, since the strict difference between public and private law seems to be fading, new opportunities are created and old axioms are being reconsidered. European legal scholars have explored the American concept of punitive damages as a way to strengthen tort law and as a new means of private enforcement. For this reason, in November 2010 the Ius Commune Research School on its annual conference devoted the Liability and Insurance workshop to 'the Power of Punitive Damages' and the function that this legal remedy could serve in Europe. This book does not merely include the papers of the speakers but also other papers written in the aftermath thereof.

The book starts with an introduction into the punitive damages debate, with reference to general aspects of American punitive damages law, explanations for the absence of punitive damages in Continental Europe, and causes for the growing European interest in punitive damages (Lotte Meurkens). Further analyses of American punitive damages law are contained in the first part of this book, including four contributions by the American authors Jim Gash, Mark Geistfeld, David Owen and Anthony Sebok. This first part also includes contributions relating to the common law systems Australia (Danuta Mendelson) and England (Jonathan Morgan), as well as the mixed legal system Cyprus (Sofia Michaelides-Mateou). The second part goes into the European punitive damages debate, including contributions of Evelien de Kezel for Belgian law, Ulrich Magnus for German law, Chantal Mahé for French law, Marta Otero Crespo for Spanish law, Marta Requejo Isidro for the private international law perspective of punitive damages and Cedric Vanleenhove for European law. The third and final part contains contributions relating to punitive damages and special themes, to be precise human rights (Vanessa Wilcox), enforcement in family law (Sara Matthé), insurability (Emily Nordin and Daily Wuyts), bad faith insurers (Lodewijk Smeehuijzen), contract law (Robert Hardy), law and economics (Louis Visscher) and enforcement of EC competition law (Angela Ortega González).

In short, this book tries to promote a better understanding of the different approaches towards punishment in private law, and will give new perspectives on punitive damages.

The editors would like to thank Gerrit van Maanen for giving two young researchers the opportunity to edit this book, and Ton Hartlief, David Owen and Aloïs Van Oevelen for their advice. Our thanks also go out to the authors, whose book this is.

Lotte Meurkens and Emily Nordin
Maastricht/Antwerp, September 2011

CONTENTS

GENERAL INTRODUCTION

ABBREVIATIONS

A 2d	Atlantic Reporter, second series (preceded by volume number, followed by beginning page number)
A U L Rev	American University Law Review
ABA	American Bar Association
AC	Law Reports, Appeals Cases
Act dr Fam	Actualités du droit de la famille
AG	Advocate-General
AJT	Algemeen Juridisch Tijdschrift
Ala L Rev	Alabama Law Review
Alaska L Rev	Alaska Law review
ALER	American Law and Economics Review
ALI	American Law Institute
All ER	All England Law Reports
ALR	American Law review
Am J Comp L	American Journal of Comparative Law
Am Jur	American Jurisprudence
Am L Reg	American Law Register
Am U L Rev	American University Law Review
Ann Fac Dr Liège	Annales de droit de Liège
Ann Rev L & Soc Sci	Annual Review of Law and Social Science
Ann	Annotated
App	Appellate (Court)
APR	Algemene Praktijk Rechtsverzameling
Arr Cass	Arresten van het Hof van Cassatie
B U L Rev	Boston University Law Review
BGB	Bürgerliches Gesetzbuch
BGH	Bundesgerichtshof
BGHZ	Entscheidungen des Bundesgerichtshofs in Zivilsachen
BRH	Belgische Rechtspraak in Handelszaken
BYU L Rev	Brigham Young University Law Review
Brook L Rev	Brooklyn Law Review
BS	Belgisch Staatsblad
Buff Crim L Rev	Buffalo Criminal Law Review

Buff L Rev	Buffalo Law Review
BVerfG	Bundesverfassungsgericht
BVerfGE	Entscheidungen des Bundesverfassungsgerichts
CABG	Cahiers Antwerpen Brussel Gent
Cal Civ Code	California Civil Code
Cal L Rev	California Law Review
Cal Rptr	California Reporter (preceded by volume number, followed by beginning page number)
Cal	California
Cal Law	California Law
Cambridge L J	Cambridge Law Journal
Cass	Hof van Cassatie
CBR	Canadian Bar Review
CBR	Centrum voor Beroepsvervolmaking Rechten
CC	Spanish Civil Code
CD	Central District of United States Federal Court (followed by state abbreviation)
Chi-Kent L Rev	Chicago-Kent Law Review
CJEU	Court of Justice of the European Union
CJS	Corpus Juris Secundum
CLB	Commonwealth Law Bulletin
Clev St L Rev	Cleveland State Law Review
CLR	The Competition Law Review
CLR	Commonwealth Law Bulletin
CMLR	Common Market Law Review
cmt	Comment
Co	Company
col	column
Colo	Colorado
Colum J Transnat'l L	Columbia Journal of Transnational Law
Colum L Rev	Columbia Law Review
CoM	Committee of Ministers
Conn	Connecticut
Cornell L Rev	Cornell Law Review
CPC	Commission for Protection of Competition
CQ	The Classical Quarterly
Ct App	Appellate Court
D	United States Federal District Court (followed by state abbreviation)
DAJV	Deutsch-Amerikanische Juristen-Vereinigung (German-American Lawyers Association)
DCFR	Draft Common Frame of Reference
Del	Delaware
DePaul L Rev	DePaul Law Review
Duke L J	Duke Law Journal

EBOLR	European Business Organization Law Review
EC	European Community
ECHR	European Convention on Human Rights
ECJ	European Court of Justice
ECLR	European Competition Law Review
ECT	European Community Treaty
ECtHR	European Court of Human Rights
EC-Treaty	Consolidated versions of the Treaty on European Union and of the Treaty Establishing the European Community
Ed	Editor or edition
EEC	European Economic Community
EGBGB	Einführungsgesetz zum Bürgerlichen Gesetzbuche (Introductory Act to the German Civil Code)
EJ	Echtscheidingsjournaal
EJLE	European Journal of Law and Economics
EL Rev	European Law review
EMLR	Entertainment and Media Law Reports
Emory L J	Emory Law Journal
ERCL	European Review of Contract Law
ERPL	European Review of Private Law
EU	European Union
EWCA Civ	Court of Appeal (Civil Division)
EWHC	England & Wales High Court (Administrative Court)
f	following page
ff	following pages
FIDE	Fédération Internationale de Droit Européen
FJR	Tijdschrift voor familie- en jeugdrecht
Fla L Rev	Florida Law Review
Fla	Florida
Fordham L Rev	Fordham Law Review
Ga L Rev	Georgia Law Review
Ga	Georgia
GC	Grand Chamber
GCR	Global Competition Review
Geo L J	Georgetown Law Journal
GG	Grundgesetz
GS	Großer Senat
Hamline L Rev	Hamline Law Review
Harv J L & Pub Pol'y	Harvard Journal of Law & Public Policy
Harv L Rev	Harvard Law Review
Hastings Int'l & Comp L R	Hastings International and Comparative Law Review
Hastings L J	Hastings Law Journal
HGB	Handelsgesetzbuch
HL	House of Lords

HL Deb	House of Lords Debates
Hofstra L Rev	Hofstra Law Review
Hous L Rev	Houston Law Review
HR	Hoge Raad
HRA	Human Rights Act
I IR	International Insolvency Review
IR	Irish Reports
ICQL	International & Comparative Law Quarterly
IEHC	High Court of Ireland
IESC	Supreme Court of Ireland
Ill L Rev	Illinois Law Review
Ill	Illinois
Ilsa J Int'l & Comp L	ILSA Journal of International and Comparative Law
ILSA	International Law Students Association
Inc	Incorporated
Ind	Indiana
Indus	Industry, Industries, Industrial
Ins	Insurance
Int I LR	International Insurance Law review
Int Rev Law & Econ	International Review of Law and Economics
INT'L L Practicum	International Law Practicum
Iowa L Rev	Iowa Law Review
IPR	Intellectual Property Rights
IPRax	Praxis des Internationalen Privat- und Verfahrensrechts
IR	Irish Reports
J Am Acad Matrim Law	Journal of the American Academy of Matrimonial Lawyers
JCP (G)	JCP / La semaine juridique, Edition Générale
J Empirical Legal Stud	Journal of Empirical Legal Studies
J L & Com	Journal of Law and Commerce
J L Econ & Org	Journal of Law, Economics, & Organization
J Legal Stud	Journal of Legal Studies
J Marshall L Rev	John Marshall Law Review
J of Products Liability	Journal of Products Liability
J	Judge
JC	Jurisprudencia Civil
JDI	Journal du Droit International
JELS	Journal of Empirical Legal Studies
JETL	Journal of European Tort Law
JLE	Journal of Law and Economics
JLEO	Journal of Law, Economics and Organization
JLM	Journal of Law and Medicine
JLS	Journal of Legal Studies
JOCLEC	Journal of Competition Law & Economics

JPE	Journal of Political Economy
JT	Journal des tribunaux
JUR	Jurisprudencia Aranzadi Westlaw
JZ	JuristenZeitung
Kan	Kansas
La L Rev	Louisiana Law Review
Law & Contemp Probs	Law and Contemporary Problems
Law Com Rep	Law Commission for England and Wales, Report No 247, Aggravated, Exemplary and Restitutionary Damages, London: HMSO, 1997
Law Q Rev	Law Quarterly Review
Lawyers J	The Lawyers Journal
LC	Law Commission
LCD	Spanish Unfair Competition Act
LGSS	Spanish General Act on Social Security
LM	Spanish Trademarks Act
LOIMH	Spanish Organic Law for the effective equality between women and men
LOPHIPI	Spanish Organic Act for the Civil Protection of honour, personal and family privacy and image
Loy Consumer L Rev	Loyola Consumer Law Review
Loy L A L Rev	Loyola of Los Angeles Law Review
LP	Spanish Patent Act
LPA	Les Petites Affiches
LPI	Spanish Intellectual Property Act
LPJDI	Spanish Legal Protection of Industrial Design Act
LQR	Law Quarterly Review
MA	Massachusetts
Md	Maryland
Mich L Rev	Michigan Law Review
Minn J Int'l L	Minnesota Journal of International Law
Minn L Rev	Minnesota Law Review
Minn	Minnesota
MJECL	Maastricht Journal of European and Comparative Law
MLR	Modern Law Review
MN	Minnesota
Mut	Mutual
N Am	North America
N C L Rev	North Carolina Law Review
N Ky L Rev	Northern Kentucky Law Review
N	North
n	Note
NC	Nullum crimen: tijdschrift voor straf- en strafprocesrecht
ND	North Dakota

Nev Rev Stat Ann	Nevada Revised Statutes Annotated
Nev	Nevada
NH	New Hampshire
NH	New Hampshire Reports
NJ	New Jersey
NJB	Nederlands Juristenblad
NJW	Neue Juristische Wochenschrift
NJWB	Nieuw Juridisch Weekblad
NM	New Mexico
Nw U L Rev	Northwestern University Law Review
NTBR	Nederlands Tijdschrift voor Burgerlijk Recht
NW	North Western Reporter (preceded by volume number, followed by beginning page number
NY Int'l L Rev	New York International Law Review
NYU L Rev	New York University Law Review
NZLR	New Zealand Law Reports
OECD	Organisation for Economic Co-operation and Development
Ohio St L J	Ohio State Law Journal
OJ	Official Journal (European Union)
OJEC	Official Journal of the European Communities
Okla	Oklahoma
Or L Rev	Oregon Law Review
Or	Oregon
OUP	Oxford University Press
Oxford J Legal Stud	Oxford Journal of Legal studies
PA	Pennsylvania
Pa	Pennsylvania
Parl St	Parlementaire Stukken
Pasin	Pasinomie
PECL	Principles of European Contract Law
Pepperdine L Rev	Pepperdine Law Review
PETL	Principles of European Tort Law
PL	Public Law
QB	Law Reports, Queen's Bench
QRTL	Quarterly Review of Tort Law
R Cass	Recente arresten van het Hof van Cassatie
R	Regina
RABG	Rechtspraak Antwerpen Brussel Gent
RCJB	Revue critique de jurisprudence belge
Res Civ et ass	Responsabilité civile et assurances
resp.	respectively
Rest. (2d) Torts	Restatement of the Law, Second, Torts
RDC	Revue des Contrats
Rev Not b	Revue du notariat belge
Rev Stat Ann	Revised Statutes Annotated

RGAR	Revue générale des assurances et des responsabilités
Riv Dir Int Pr Pr	Rivista di Diritto Internazionale Privato e Processuale
RJ	Repertorio de Jurisprudencia Aranzadi Westlaw
RTC	Repertorio de Jurisprudencia Constitucional Aranzadi Westlaw
RTDF	Revue trimestrielle de droit familial
Rutgers L Rev	Rutgers Law Review
RW	Rechtskundig Weekblad
S C L Rev	South Carolina Law Review
S Cal L Rev	Southern California Law Review
S Ct	United States Supreme Court Reporter (preceded by volume number, followed by beginning page number)
S Texas L Rev	South Texas Law Review
s	section
SC	South Carolina
SD Codified Laws	South Dakota Codified Laws
SE	South Eastern Reporter (preceded by volume number, followed by beginning page number)
Stat Ann	Statutes Annotated
STC	Sentencia del Tribunal Constitucional (Spain)
Sw U L Rev	Southwestern University Law Review
SW	South Western Reporter (preceded by volume number, followed by beginning page number)
T Fam	Tijdschrift voor familierecht
T Verz	Tijdschrift voor verzekeringen
T Vred	Tijdschrift van de vrede- (en politierechters)
TBBR	Tijdschrift voor Belgisch burgerlijk recht
TBH	Tijdschrift voor Belgisch handelsrecht
Tenn L Rev	Tennessee Law Review
Tex Const	Texas Constitution
Tex L Rev	Texas Law Review
Tex	Texas
TFEU	Treaty on the Functioning of the European Union
Tit	Title
TJCE	Repertorio de Jurisprudencia del Tribunal Europeo de Justicia Aranzadi Westlaw
TJK	Tijdschrift voor jeugdrecht en kinderrechten
Tort Ins L J	Tort and Insurance Law Journal
TPR	Tijdschrift voor Privaatrecht
Tulane L Rev	Tulane Law Review
TvVP	Tijdschrift voor Vergoeding Personenschade
TvW	Tijdschrift voor wetgeving
U Chi L Rev	University of Chicago Law Review
U Colo L Rev	University of Colorado Law Review
U Mich J L Reform	University of Michigan Journal of Law Reform
U Pa L Rev	University of Pennsylvania Law Review

U Pitt L Rev	University of Pittsburgh Law Review
U St Thomas L J	University of St. Thomas Law Journal
UK	United Kingdom
UKHL	United Kingdom House of Lords
UKPC	United Kingdom Privy Council
U Pa L Rev	University of Pennsylvania Law Review
US	United States of America
US	Reporter of the Decisions of the Supreme Court of the United States (preceded by volume number, followed by beginning page number)
USA	United States of America
USC	United States Code
USF L Rev	University of San Francisco Law Review
Utah L Rev	Utah Law Review
Va L Rev	Virginia Law Review
Va	Virginia
Va J Int'l L	Virginia Journal of International Law
Vand L Rev	Vanderbilt Law Review
Vill L Rev	Villanova Law Review
vol	Volume
Vt	Vermont
Wake Forest L Rev	Wake Forest Law Review
Wash & Lee L Rev	Washington & Lee Law Review
Washburn L J	Washburn Law Journal
Wash U L Q	Washington University Law Quarterly
WC	World Competition: Law and Economics
Willamette J Int'l L & Disp Resol	Willamette Journal of International Law and Dispute Resolution
WIR	West Indian Reports
Wis L Rev	Wisconsin Law Review
Wis	Wisconsin
WL	WestLaw.
Wm Mitchell L Rev	William Mitchell Law Review
World Competition	World Competition – Law and Economics Review
WPNR	Weekblad voor Privaatrecht, Notariaat en Registratie
Yale L J	Yale Law Journal
YPIL	Yearbook of Private International Law

GENERAL INTRODUCTION

Lotte Meurkens*

THE PUNITIVE DAMAGES DEBATE IN CONTINENTAL EUROPE: FOOD FOR THOUGHT

1. The Punitive Damages Phenomenon and its (Law of) Attraction in Europe

As there is more and more attention for punitive damages in Continental Europe,[1] this book comes at the right time. The punitive damages remedy, *i.e.* monetary damages in the form of a punitive civil sanction,[2] is deeply entrenched in the American legal system where punitive damages form an established part of the legal tradition.[3] Punitive damages may be awarded to the plaintiff in a civil lawsuit apart from and in addition to compensatory damages. Several purposes have been attributed to such damages, most importantly punishment and deterrence of the wrongdoer for harming the plaintiff.[4]

The doctrine of punitive damages is originally a common law doctrine.[5] Although the remedy is alien to Continental European legal systems, European policymakers and legal scholars increasingly exchange thoughts about advantages of introducing punitive damages into their tort systems. The interest in this particular kind of damages runs parallel to changing views on law enforcement and the functions of tort law. Under the influence of law and economics theories, growing attention is paid to the preventive and instrumental function of tort law. Inspired by the American experience, it is argued that financial incentives in the form of punitive damages stimulate injured parties to file civil claims.[6] Persons who are harmed as a result of unjust behaviour of others thereby could

* PhD candidate doing research into punitive damages at Maastricht University. I am grateful to my promotor Ton Hartlief whose beneficial and critical suggestions helped me to clarify my views.

1 For example, the Institute for European Tort Law launched an interesting book on punitive damages edited by Koziol & Wilcox in 2009.

2 Mann 1992, p. 1798.

3 Blatt, Hammesfahr & Nugent 2008, p. 40.

4 Ellis 1982, p. 3.

5 For an overview on the history of punitive damages: Schlueter 2005a, p. 1 ff.; Owen 1976, p. 1262; Owen 2005, pp. 1123–1124. *Cf.* Kortmann 2009, pp. 16–19, describing that punitive damages find their early origin in ancient Roman Law and are therefore by far not alien to the Western European legal tradition.

6 A relevant example is the development in the field of EC competition law, as explained in § 6 below. The European Commission has suggested the use of damages actions in private law to fight breaches of EC antitrust rules: European Commission's Green Paper on Damages Actions for Breach of EC Antitrust

help to detect wrongful conduct and to encourage (future) wrongdoers to behave themselves.

The punitive damages remedy is typically linked to the American legal system. Therefore, in order to find out if punitive damages are suitable for Continental Europe, reference is made to the American experience with punitive damages.[7] A general idea of the American *savoir faire* with regard to punitive damages may be useful in examining the pros and cons of incorporating such damages into Continental European legal systems. Thus, paragraph 2 will provide a short description of some aspects of American punitive damages law. Paragraph 3 will give an overview of explanations for the absence of punitive damages in Continental Europe. In paragraph 4 developments from a private international law perspective will be briefly described, as this forms a good illustration of the European view on punitive damages awards. Furthermore, paragraphs 5 to 7 will give a general introduction into the European punitive damages debate: two causes for the current interest in the controversial remedy will be explained. Paragraph 8 contains some final remarks to conclude.

2. American Punitive Damages Law: in a Nutshell...

Punitive damages law is a complex area of law that cannot be described in a nutshell.[8] This paragraph only explains some general characteristics and main principles relating to it.

2.1. Nature and Theory

The Restatement of Torts' definition of punitive damages reads as follows:

> 'Damages, other than compensatory or nominal damages, awarded against a person to punish him for his outrageous conduct and to deter him and others like him from similar conduct in the future'.[9]

Thus, the theory behind punitive damages is one of punishment and deterrence and involves a combination of general societal interests with those of the harmed party in particular.[10]

It is often argued that punitive damages awards have criminal law objectives rather than tort law objectives. In this respect, they are even considered an 'anomaly' in the law

Rules (December 19, 2005), COM (2005) 672; European Commission's White Paper on Damages Actions for Breach of EC Antitrust Rules (April 2, 2008), COM (2008) 165.

7 *Cf.* Koziol & Wilcox 2009, containing a publication of Professor Sebok on Punitive Damages in the United States, pp. 155–196.

8 The following handbooks give a profound overview of American punitive damages law: Blatt, Hammesfahr & Nugent 2008; Kircher & Wiseman 2000a; Kircher & Wiseman 2000b; Schlueter 2005a; Schlueter 2005b.

9 Restatement of Torts, § 908.

10 25 C.J.S. Damages § 195.

of torts.[11] Opponents of punitive damages argue that the sanction of punishment is traditionally a matter of criminal law that should be left to the State, and that the defendant who is facing punitive damages should benefit from criminal law safeguards. Nevertheless, punitive damages are an accepted form of penal remedy in American civil law.[12]

Punitive damages are in fact a hybrid remedy that is neither completely civil nor criminal in nature, and this hybrid character indeed causes the controversy that has always surrounded the subject.[13] Questions as regards fairness, utility and constitutionality of punitive damages are a deeply politicised part of the American tort law reform debate resulting from the crises in the areas of medical malpractice and products liability in the 1970s and 1980s, which centred on liability insurance that had supposedly become unaffordable due to the increase in number and size of punitive damages.[14]

Thus, the main criticism of punitive damages relates to the confusion of tort and criminal law.[15] This is the reason why courts critical of punitive damages proclaim that punitive damages are 'not favored in the law'.[16] Punitive damages are also criticised for other reasons, such as the vagueness of liability standards – in particular the characterization of misbehaviour –, the unjustified windfall-effect to the plaintiff, the difficult point of insurance for punitive damages and whether insurance negatively influences the deterrent effect, and the unpredictability of the awards. It lies beyond the scope of this contribution to give a comprehensive overview of criticism and arguments against punitive damages.[17] What is important to remember for now is that punitive damages are a controversial, often criticised remedy. However, as always with critique, every medal has two sides. For example, as regards the unpredictability argument it has also been argued that the strength, and not the weakness, of punitive damages lies in their unpredictability.[18] Despite the criticism, punitive damages are currently available in almost every American State,[19] although there is great variety among the States as to the circumstances under which such damages may be awarded.

2.2. Purposes

The main purposes of punitive damages are threefold, *i.e.* punishment of the defendant, which should lead to specific deterrence of the defendant and general deterrence of others

11 Morris 1931, p. 1176; Schlueter 2005a, p. 79.
12 Owen 2005, p. 1122.
13 Schlueter 2005a, p. 82; Owen 2005, p. 1122.
14 Owen 1989, pp. 705–706; Owen 2005, p. 1125.
15 Owen 2005, p. 1177, providing an overview of punitive damages criticisms.
16 Owen 2005, p. 1125; Schlueter 2005a, p. 27; 22 Am. Jur. 2d Damages § 546.
17 Professor Owen gives and extensive overview of 'problems and recurring criticisms' relating to punitive damages: Owen 2005, § 18.5, pp. 1177–1200. Also: Owen 1994, pp. 382–400; Robbennolt 2002, p. 105; Schlueter 2005a, p. 33.
18 Mallor & Roberts 1999, p. 1003, referring to Rustad & Koenig 1993, p. 1277.
19 Five jurisdictions prohibit punitive damages for all civil lawsuits, namely Louisiana, Massachusetts, Nebraska, New Hampshire, and Washington. The remaining 45 States allow punitive damages to a certain extent. Kircher & Wiseman 2000a, § 4:6.

not to make similar mistakes.[20] Since these purposes are almost akin to each other, they are usually jointly mentioned.[21]

The term 'punishment' implies a retributive aim and, for that reason, a notion of desert.[22] A person who is injured by the egregious conduct of another ought to be revenged, whereas the tortfeasor deserves to be punished. This theory is justified on the basis of general notions of public morality, that it is deemed immoral to commit a wrongful act and thereby violate the rights of another person without proper justification for it.[23] The retributive function does not only protect the interests of the harmed individual, but also serves society as a whole.[24] In other words, the protection of the individual can be understood as an issue of both individual and social concern.[25] In some States, all awards of punitive damages must be supported by a finding that the public interest will be served by punishing the wrongdoer.[26]

Deterrence and law enforcement are instrumental functions of punitive damages concerning the notion of effectiveness as opposed to the notion of desert.[27] This explains the attention paid to these functions, deterrence in particular, by law and economics scholars. The aim of the instrumental functions is not so much to impose detriment on the defendant, but rather to improve safety in society.[28] Although the deterrent effect of imposing punitive damages remains questionable, it is a believed side effect of tort law and criminal law that liability or punishment does have some deterrent effect.[29] The deterrence function of punitive damages is especially interesting with regard to 'potential offenders who know that misconduct often goes undetected and unpunished'.[30] The awarding of punitive damages sends an unambiguous message that the price of getting caught is higher than the worth of committing the wrongful act. The law enforcement function is instrumental in the sense that punitive damages are a procedural mechanism which serves as an incentive for potential plaintiffs to initiate civil litigation.[31]

Compensation of the plaintiff follows from the award, but is not a primary function as punitive damages are focused on the behaviour of the defendant rather than the damage of the plaintiff, and are therefore based upon ideas of public policy rather than

20 The functions of punitive damages have been extensively analyzed in a leading article of Professor Dorsey D. Ellis: Ellis 1982, p. 4. See also: Restatement of Torts, § 908; 22 Am. Jur. 2d Damages § 542, 544; 25 C.J.S. Damages § 195; Schlueter 2005a, p. 16, 25; Yeazell 2008, p. 273; Kuklin 1989, p. 5; Mann 1992, p. 1798; Owen 2005, p. 1132 *et seq.*

21 Schlueter 2005a, p. 29.

22 Ellis 1982, p. 4; Owen 2005, p. 1133.

23 Ellis 1982, p. 5.

24 25 C.J.S. Damages § 195; 22 Am. Jur. 2d Damages § 544.

25 Harris 1989, p. 1102.

26 22 Am. Jur. 2d Damages § 542.

27 Ellis 1982, p. 8.

28 *Ibid.*

29 Owen 2005, p. 1137.

30 *Ibid.*

31 Redish & Mathews 2004, p. 2.

individual compensation.[32] Professor Owen does attach a compensatory function to punitive damages:

> '[punitive damages] have a third important function – providing victims with added *compensation*, sometimes called "aggravated damages", for the purpose of victim vindication and redress – despite the almost universal proclamation in American law that punitive damages are "non-compensatory"'.[33]

Other purposes include preserving the peace and paying the plaintiff's attorneys fees.

2.3. *Incidence and Size of Punitive Damages Awards*

As stated above, American punitive damages awards are rather controversial. Opponents of the legal remedy argue that punitive damages have 'run wild'.[34] For example, Supreme Court Justice O'Connor emphasised that the size and frequency of punitive damages awards have been 'skyrocketing'.[35] The general criticism as regards incidence and size of punitive damages awards seems a bit overstated.[36] From the 1960s onwards, several empirical studies[37] have concluded that punitive damages awards are quite uncommon.[38] On an absolute basis, punitive damages have been awarded in 2% to 9% of all cases that were won by the plaintiff.[39] The median for punitive damages awards in the 1980s and 1990s was between US$ 38,000 and US$ 52,000 per award.[40] Furthermore, a correlation between the amount of compensatory and punitive damages has been found,[41] which implies that punitive damages are not as unpredictable as often believed.

One source reveals that in 2001, 356 (6%) of the 6,504 State court civil trials – in the seventy-five most populous counties – that were won by the plaintiff resulted in punitive damages. In half of the 356 trials, plaintiffs received US$ 50,000 or more in punitive damages. In 41 (12%) of the trials with punitive damages, damages that equalled or surpassed US$ 1 million were awarded, whereas in 9 trials (3%) punitive damages of US$ 10 million or more were awarded. The 2001 study estimates the median for punitive damages at US$ 25,000.[42] Without doubt, such a median punitive damages award

32 25 C.J.S. Damages § 195; 22 Am. Jur. 2d Damages § 544.
33 In this book: D.G. Owen, *Punitive Damages as Restitution.*
34 *Pacific Mutual Life Insurance Co. v. Haslip*, 499 U.S. 1 (1991), at 18.
35 *Browning-Ferris Industries of Vermont v. Kelco Disposal, Inc*, 492 U.S. 257 (1989), at 282. Justice O'Connor's criticism was criticised on several grounds. *Cf.* Hubbard 2008, p. 395.
36 Sebok 2009, p. 156.
37 For an overview of empirical studies, see Robbennolt 2002, p. 160, fn. 262; Sebok 2007, p. 964, fn. 19.
38 Hubbard 2008, p. 361; Eisenberg *et al.* 1997, p. 633; Eisenberg *et al.* 2006; Sebok 2007, pp. 964–965, Daniels and Martin 1990.
39 Sebok 2007, p. 964.
40 *Ibid.*, p. 970.
41 Yeazell 2008, p. 273.
42 Thomas J. Cohen, U.S. Department of Justice, Civil Justice Survey of State Courts, 2001: Punitive Damages Awards in Large Counties, 2001, March 2005, p. 1, available at http://bjs.ojp.usdoj.gov/index.cfm?ty=pbdetail&iid=1132 (last visited August 2011).

disregards the very small set of extremely high awards,[43] but high amounts are not as often awarded as the public generally believes.

Punitive damages are for instance rare in legal fields that receive most public attention, such as product liability and medical malpractice.[44] Indeed, from the 1970s punitive damages awards in these legal fields have increased in number and size, and still reach fairly high amounts.[45] However, misunderstandings as regards the true size and incidence of such awards are merely caused by the fact that the extreme cases are highly publicised in national and international media.[46] A good example is the MacDonald's case.[47] It is true that the first instance court granted US$ 2,7 million in punitive damages to the plaintiff. However, the fact that the award was later reduced upon appeal to US$ 480,000 is usually ignored. To conclude, none of the empirical studies thus far seems to have revealed that the frequency or amount of punitive damages awards is 'out of control'.[48]

2.4. *Grounds for Awarding*

The foundational requirement for a punitive damages award is the infringement of a legally protected interest.[49] There is no separate cause of action for punitive damages: the plaintiff must have suffered actual damage and must produce sufficient evidence in this regard.[50] The rationale of this requirement is that conduct that caused no injury should not be punished for, which goes hand in hand with the principle that private individuals should not be encouraged to start litigation if they have suffered no injury (*damnum absque injuria*).[51] There are court decisions allowing punitive damages to be awarded even if the actual damage is small, based on the idea that this is a sufficient basis for punitive damages because the purpose of punitive damages is to punish the defendant for his egregious conduct.[52] It is indeed debatable whether the Americans argue soundly when emphasizing the punishing and deterring purpose of punitive damages on the one hand, and requiring that actual damage has to be suffered by the plaintiff – like in situations where compensatory damages are involved – on the other hand. It could be that even in the absence of damage, the behaviour of the defendant is still so remote as to justify punitive damages. In other words, if the theory of punitive damages is in fact

43 Yeazell 2008, p. 273.
44 Eisenberg *et al.* 1997, p. 633.
45 Owen 2005, p. 1125, 1129.
46 Sebok 2007, p. 962; Ryan 2003, p. 70; Robbennolt 2002, p. 159.
47 *Liebeck v. McDonald's Restaurants, P.T.S., Inc.*, 1995 WL 360309 (N.M. Dist. 1994). The punitive damages that were initially awarded amounted US$ 2.7 million, the award was later reduced upon appeal to US$ 480,000. The total award, as reduced, was US$ 640,000 consisting of US$ 480,000 in punitive damages and US$ 160,000 in actual damages.
48 Robbennolt 2002, pp. 160–161: 'These studies have common findings: although there are variations across geographical area and type of case, punitive damages are not often awarded, are rarely extreme in size, are awarded in response to egregious conduct, and are not often collected in the amounts awarded by juries.'
49 22 Am. Jur. 2d Damages § 551.
50 25 C.J.S. Damages § 197; 22 Am. Jur. 2d Damages § 551, 553; Schlueter 2005a, p. 358, 363.
51 Schlueter 2005a, p. 359.
52 E.g. *Coonis v. Rogers*, 429 S.W.2d 709 (Mo. 1968).

solely focused on punishment and deterrence of the defendant's behaviour, the award of punitive damages in a situation where there is no actual damage should perhaps be possible. However, given the general requirement of actual damage which relates to the position of the plaintiff, it is defendable that punitive damages do serve the function of compensating the plaintiff as well.

Punitive damages are in principle recoverable only for tort actions.[53] In practice, American courts impose punitive damages in all sorts of situations. For example, although punitive damages are in principle not available under contract law, punitive damages may be awarded if a breach of contract and an intentional tort are constituted by the same act, for example in certain products liability cases.[54] In the past twenty years, American courts have recognised more and more exceptions to the rule that, in the absence of statutory authorization, punitive damages are not allowed in contract cases.[55] Punitive damages are also available in property cases, provided that the defendant knowingly and wilfully infringed the plaintiff's rights.[56] Furthermore, punitive damages have been awarded in cases of medical malpractice, false arrest or imprisonment, employment law, family law, aviation litigation, aids and sexually transmitted diseases.[57] Thus, punitive damages are in fact available in an extensive number of situations, provided that the required aggravating circumstances are present. This follows from the characterization of the behaviour needed to justify a punitive damages award, for example malice or gross negligence:

> 'Something more than the mere commission of a tort is always required for punitive damages; there must be circumstances of aggravation or outrage, such as spite or malice, or a fraudulent or evil motive on the part of the defendant, or such a conscious and deliberate disregard of the interests of others that his conduct may be called willful or wanton'.[58]

The Restatement of Torts emphasises that 'punitive damages may be awarded for conduct that is outrageous, because of the defendant's evil motive or his reckless indifference to the rights of others'.[59] Therefore, besides the violation of a right and the infliction of actual damages, a certain state of mind of the defendant is needed for punitive damages to be awarded. This means that punitive damages can not be awarded in normal tort cases where there are no aggravated circumstances: a high standard of misconduct is necessary to justify the punishing and deterring purpose.[60] Whether or not punitive damages can be imposed depends on the circumstances of each individual case, including

53 22 Am. Jur. 2d Damages § 568, 569, 570; 25 C.J.S. Damages § 198, 199, 200.

54 Burnham 2006, p. 241.

55 Schlueter 2005a, p. 399; 25 C.J.S. Damages § 199.

56 Schlueter 2005a, p. 438; 25 C.J.S. Damages § 200.

57 For a list of specific tort based causes of actions, see 22 Am. Jur. 2d Damages § 570 and Schlueter 2005a, Chapters 11, 12, 13, and 14.

58 22 Am. Jur. 2d Damages § 569.

59 Restatement of Torts, § 908.

60 25 C.J.S. 2d Damages § 200. For an exception to the generally rule, see *Potter v. Firestone Tire & Rubber Co.*, 6 Cal. 4th 965, 25 Cal. Rptr. 2d 550, 863 P.2d 795 (1993), in which punitive damages were awarded on the basis of an unintentional tort action.

the relationship between plaintiff and defendant and the duties owed by them.[61] Aggravating conditions which can usually warrant a punitive damages award include misconduct, wilfulness, wantonness, malice or ill will, gross negligence or recklessness, oppression, outrageous conduct, violence, indignity or insult, fraud or gross fraud and criminal indifference.[62] Mere negligence does not justify a punitive damages award.[63] Some States allow punitive damages in cases of gross negligence, but then the negligence must be so gross that there was 'a conscious indifference to the rights and safety of the plaintiff'.[64]

To conclude, at common law the mere fact that the defendant committed an unlawful act is not, in itself, a sufficient basis for a punitive damages award.[65] The act complained of must not only be unlawful, but must also involve a certain element of aggravation.

2.5. *Assessment by Judge or Jury*

Punitive damages issues are normally decided by both trial court and jury. The court determines issues of law, whereas the jury determines issues of fact.[66] In its role as gatekeeper, the court must decide whether the question of punitive damages may be submitted to the trier of fact. This is normally the jury, but can also be the court sitting without a jury.[67] For example, the question of punitive damages is not submitted to the trier of fact when punitive damages are not recoverable for the particular cause of action, such as – possibly – a contract action. Furthermore, the court must decide whether there is sufficient evidence to support a punitive damages award before the question of punitive damages in a tort action may be submitted to a jury.[68] If so, courts normally provide juries with so-called jury instructions which are used to define applicable principles of law in a way that jurors can comprehend.[69]

The decision to award punitive damages generally lies in the discretion of the trier of fact, who decides whether the defendant's conduct was egregious enough to justify punitive damages.[70] The trier of fact is not obliged to award punitive damages, even if the evidence and pleadings justify such damages, or the defendants' acts are sufficiently egregious.[71] Besides the character of the wrongdoer's act, the trier of fact or the appellate court that reviews the punitive damages award for excessiveness may consider the nature and extent of the harm that the defendant caused or intended to cause to the plaintiff, as well as the wealth of the defendant.[72] Other factors include the nature of the wrong, the

61 25 C.J.S. Damages § 202.
62 22 Am. Jur. 2d Damages § 558.
63 25 C.J.S. Damages § 205; Schlueter 2005a, p. 162.
64 Schlueter 2005a, p. 161.
65 25 C.J.S. Damages § 204.
66 Schlueter 2005a, p. 331.
67 25 C.J.S. Damages § 196.
68 22 Am. Jur. 2d Damages § 550.
69 *Ibid.*, p. 332, 336.
70 22 Am. Jur. 2d Damages § 550; 25 C.J.S. Damages § 196; Schlueter 2005a, p. 348.
71 22 Am. Jur. 2d Damages § 550.
72 Restatement of Torts, § 908.

reprehensibility of the wrongdoing, the enormity of the wrong and the duration of the wrong, the wrongdoer's intent or motivation, the awareness of any hazard the conduct has caused, and other circumstances relating to the wrongdoer's actions.[73]

There is no fixed standard for measuring punitive damages.[74] As punitive damages primarily serve to punish and deter the defendant, the trier of fact must focus on the defendant's rather than the plaintiff's conduct when fixing an appropriate amount and should determine a proper amount without being passionate, prejudiced or biased.[75] The discretion of the trier of fact is not arbitrary or unlimited. 'Draconian' punitive damages awards are not allowed, as the amount of the award should not be disproportionate to the harm done to the plaintiff and to the defendant's ability to pay.[76] In other words, the award should be reasonable and should not go beyond what is necessary to achieve its goals.[77]

Although it is generally argued that the size and amount of punitive damages will be smaller if such claims are decided by judges instead of jurors because the decision-making of jurors tends to be more biased and emotional,[78] several empirical studies investigating decision-making of judges and jurors show that this assertion is not necessarily correct.[79] The general outcome of all relevant inquiries combined is not unfavourable for juries:

> 'Juries do not appear to make decisions that clearly differ from the decisions that judges would make, certainly not to the dramatic extent that most critics of the jury suggest'.[80]

Rather, the outcomes of these studies as regards the possible differences between judges and jurors are mixed.[81] For example, one study[82] that compared a large number of civil cases over a period of ten years reveals that in some types of cases judges awarded more damages, whereas in other types of cases juries awarded more damages.[83] Another study[84] reveals that almost one-third of 9000 punitive damages cases were awarded by judges. To the surprise of the researchers, the share of punitive damages awards by judges is rather high keeping in mind 'the overwhelming focus on jury punitive awards in the literature and policy debate'.[85] The study on punitive damages awards in large counties of 2001 reveals that in 6,504 civil trials plaintiffs received punitive damages in 6% of jury

73 22 Am. Jur. 2d Damages § 606.
74 22 Am. Jur. 2d Damages § 604; 25 C.J.S. Damages § 213.
75 Kircher & Wiseman 2000a, § 5:18; 25 C.J.S. Damages § 213.
76 22 Am. Jur. 2d Damages § 604.
77 22 Am. Jur. 2d Damages § 604; 25 C.J.S. Damages § 213.
78 E.g. Owen 1994, p. 384.
79 For an overview of empirical research on the decision-making of judges and jurors: Robbennolt, 2002, p. 146; Sunstein *et al.* 2003, p. 186 ff.; Bornstein *et al.* 2008, p. 61.
80 Robbennolt 2002, p. 158.
81 *Ibid.*, p. 152.
82 Clermont & Eisenberg 1992, p. 1137; see also Robbennolt 2002, p. 148.
83 The first types of cases were especially products liability, medical malpractice and motor vehicle cases, the second types of cases were especially marine and Federal Employer's Liability Act cases.
84 Eisenberg *et al.*, 2002, pp. 747–748; see also Robbennolt 2002, p. 149.
85 Eisenberg *et al.* 2002, p. 752.

trials and 4% of court trials. Furthermore, the median punitive damages awarded by juries amounted to US$ 50,000, whereas courts awarded US$ 46,000. Of the 260 jury trials in which a plaintiff obtained punitive damages, 14% resulted in a punitive award verdict of US$ 1 million or more. Punitive damages of US$ 1 million or more were awarded in 2% of the 79 court trials with punitive damages.[86]

These statistics seem to put criticism relating to excessiveness and unpredictability of punitive damages awarded by juries and judges into perspective.

2.6. Concluding Remarks

The above gives an insight into some general characteristics of American punitive damages law as well as the controversy surrounding the theme.

In conclusion, it is important to make clear that American punitive damages law has been affected by two developments.[87] First, the law has been subjected to legislative reforms designed to put an end to excessive and improper awards. Examples are the clarification of vague terminology and the creation of damages caps.[88] Second, punitive damages awards are extensively controlled by judicial review. Judicial review of punitive damages awards is a topic of much debate that has also attracted the attention of the Supreme Court.[89] From the late 1980s, the Court has analysed the constitutionality of punitive damages in a number of decisions[90] that give a warning to courts to review punitive damages awards thoroughly.[91] On the basis of two primary constitutional provisions, *i.e.* the excessive fines clause (Eight Amendment) and the due process clause (Fourteenth Amendment), the Court has established a framework for awarding punitive damages.[92] Thus, the American judiciary and legislator have created important additional safeguards and helpful guidelines to control punitive damages awards.

So far about the American situation. Further analyses of American punitive damages law are included in the first part of this book.

The fact that there is attention for punitive damages does not mean that the strange legal remedy is suitable for European civil law systems or consistent with its traditions. Some plausible explanations for the non-existence of punitive damages in Continental

86 Civil Justice Survey of State Courts, 2001 (fn. 42), p. 2.

87 Mallor & Roberts 1999, p. 1002.

88 Owen 2005, p. 1201.

89 Schlueter 2005a, p. 346. In this book: Anthony J. Sebok, *The U.S. Supreme Court's Theory of Common Law Punitive Damages: An Inauspicious Start.*

90 *Aetna Life Ins. Co. v. Lavoie*, 475 U.S. 813 (1986); *Bankers Life & Cas. Co. v. Crenshaw*, 486 U.S. 71 (1988); *Browning-Ferris Industries of Vermont v. Kelco Disposal, Inc.*, 493 U.S. 257 (1989); *Pacific Mutual Life Insurance Co. v. Haslip*, 499 U.S. 1 (1991); *TXO Production Corp. v. Alliance Resources Corp.*, 509 U.S. 443 (1993); *Honda Motor Co. v. Oberg*, 512 U.S. 415 (1994); *BMW of North America, Inc. v. Gore*, 517 U.S. 559 (1996); *Cooper Industries, Inc. v. Leatherman Tool Group, Inc.*, 532 U.S. 424 (2001), 121 S. Ct. 1678; *State Farm Mutual Automobile Insurance Co. v. Campbell*, 538 U.S. 408 (2003); *Philip Morris USA v. Williams*, 127 S. Ct. 1057 (2007).

91 Sebok 2007, p. 962; Ellis 1982, p. 55; Cooter 1989, p. 1145; Robbennolt 2002, p. 159.

92 Owen 2005, p. 1216; Kircher & Wiseman 2000a, § 3:1; Schlueter 2005a, p. 49; Blatt, Hammesfahr & Nugent 2008, p. 37.

Europe will be described in the next paragraph. The absence of the legal remedy will be contrasted with the relatively common use of it overseas, specifically in the United States. Therefore, some further remarks on the American setting in which punitive damages are available will be made. Although this subject matter definitely deserves to be described in an extensive analysis, paragraph 3 confines itself to a summarizing overview.

3. Why Is Continental Europe Unfamiliar with the Phenomenon of Punitive Damages?

3.1. *Punitive Damages in European Civil Law Systems: Traditional 'Fundamental Rejection'*[93]

The punitive damages remedy is not provided for under tort law in European civil law systems. The only countries in Europe that accept a restricted form of punitive or exemplary damages are England, Wales, Ireland and Cyprus, which are indeed not situated on the European continent and have a common law or mixed legal system.

Three important characteristics seem to prevent the occurrence of punitive damages in civil law systems worldwide. First, the legal remedy is inconsistent with the traditional functions of tort law (§3.2). The second point, which relates to the first, is that there is fundamental rejection in light of the division between private law and criminal law (§3.3). The last issue is that different views on the role of government might explain the absence or presence of punitive damages in a certain legal system (§3.4). These different views concern the value attached to private enforcement, responsible actors for safety in society, and the importance of other compensation mechanisms. Also, some differences between the United States and Europe relating to procedural aspects might illustrate why the two legal systems are poles apart with regard to the use of civil litigation and tort law. Although these views relating to the role of government are seen from a broader perspective and focus on the impact they have on tort litigation in general, the differences have implications for the use of punitive damages as well.

The three characteristics that form the main reason for the absence of punitive damages in Continental Europe will now be described.

3.2. *There Is the Traditional Function of Tort Law...*

The first reason for the absence of punitive damages in European civil law systems relates to the traditional compensatory function of tort law. It is said that the primary function of modern tort law is compensation of the injured person for the actual loss he has suffered.[94]

93 See Koziol and Wilcox (eds.) 2009, p. 282.
94 Deakin, Johnston & Markesinis 2008, p. 52.

The compensatory function is usually realised by the award of monetary compensation, when reparation in kind is not possible or out of place.[95] Apart from the legal remedy of monetary damages, injunctive relief and other reasonable remedies may be ordered, depending on the legal system at hand.[96] However, most tort cases are about monetary compensation.[97] Therefore, the primary function of tort law has also been described as 'one of determining when compensation is required'.[98] In all legal systems, the nature and extent of compensatory damages in tort is determined by the extent of the (estimated) actual loss.[99] No more, no less. If an injured person brings a civil action for damages and the court rules in his favour, the person held liable must restore the injured person to the status that obtained prior to the injury. This principle, known as *restitutio in integrum*, is the general principle underlying tort law which can be explained either as restoration in kind or monetary compensation.[100] Restoration in kind is defined as restoration of the *status quo ante*, *i.e.* the position in which the claimant was prior to the tort. However, as stated above restoration in kind is not always the best possible solution, whereas in most situations an equivalent in money is.[101] The liable person has a duty to repair both the material and the immaterial loss of the injured person. Against this duty of the defendant stands the duty of the claimant to mitigate damage, meaning that he should do anything that is reasonably possible to minimise the damage and to prevent the amount of damage from increasing. An example is the patient who must show that he acted reasonably when rejecting surgery contrary to medical recommendation.[102]

Other heads of damages that are available in tort law may be justified on a different basis. For example punitive damages that are not primarily awarded to compensate the victim of a tort,[103] but rather for reasons of punishment and deterrence.

The compensatory function of tort law is in fact synonymous to the function of victim protection. Victim protection is considered a function of tort law as such, which also follows from specific tort provisions that have been created to protect employees, participants of traffic, and other 'weaker' parties.[104] However, the compensatory function of tort law is not as unambiguous as one would assume at first. To strive for full

95 Van Gerven, Lever & Larouche 2000, p. 740.

96 Koenig & Rustad 2001, p. 11.

97 Rogers 2006, p. 2.

98 Hartlief 1997, p. 18, referring to Prosser and Keaton.

99 Koziol and Wilcox (eds.) 2009, p. 299.

100 Owen 1997, p. 21; Van Gerven, Lever & Larouche 2000, p. 770.

101 Van Gerven, Lever & Larouche 2000, p. 770.

102 *Privy Council Selvanayagam v. University of the West Indies* [1983] 1 WLR 585, [1983] 1 ALL ER 824; Van Gerven, Lever & Larouche 2000, p. 770.

103 However, *cf.* Owen 2009, p. 185: 'Private law is also interested in the public consequences of its rules and adjudications, but its central concern is that victims are provided redress for the harmful effects of breaches of the civil law. In cases of flagrant wrongdoing, retributive justice and deterrence are important to private law, but what drives private law's engines are the restitutionary and retributive needs of victims, not society. Thus, the essential retributive goal of punitive damages, a remedy of the private law, is to force wrongdoers to restore in full the well-being of those harmed by their aggravated misconduct. Call this "private revenge" or call it "private retributive justice," but it is, at bottom, compensatory in that it extracts money from a person guilty of flagrant wrongdoing and uses it to repair resulting damage to the victim's basket of goods.'

104 Hartlief 1997, p. 18.

compensation of all damage that falls in society would be an undesirable aim that would have paralyzing effect, as one person's right to compensation automatically restricts another persons freedom to act.[105] Therefore, compensatory damages should be allowed only if there are special reasons to do so. As long as there is no specific reason to shift the loss, the harmed person has to bear the loss.[106] Tort law points out the special reasons, in particular when the loss was caused as a result of the tortfeasor's *culpa* (fault) and *dolus* (intent), but even if the loss is accidental there may be a good reason for shifting the loss.[107] Thus, tort law lays down rules to distribute responsibility for losses.[108] The reasons that are provided by tort law to shift loss are subject to change due to varying social and political desires, as – like all law – tort law reflects its society.[109]

Unlike in common law systems, punishment has never become a recognised function of modern tort law in European civil law systems. This is the first reasonable argument that can be put forward in answering the question why punitive damages is not a recognised remedy in Continental European tort systems. The private law sanction simply does not correspond to the compensatory function of tort law. It is however important to remember that perspectives on the functions of tort law are subject to change and are always reflected by desires in society. Moreover, tort law has a 'high policy impact', which results in different views on the most favourable approach.[110] Yes, compensation undeniably is the traditional and primary function of tort law. But one should not forget that other functions have been accepted as well. Under the traditional theory, tort law has certain positive side effects such as loss-spreading, prevention, law enforcement, declaration of right and retribution. In civil law systems these are seen as *additional* side effects that cannot exclusively form the basis of a damages award.[111] Then again, it is incorrect to state that tort law has only one function.[112] Although the one function may be less apparent than the other, none of the functions 'offers a complete justification for the law':[113] tort law has a combination of functions.[114] The idea that tort law has other purposes than compensation alone is for example shown by the availability of restitutionary damages to disgorge profit, e.g. Article 6:104 of the Dutch civil code. Disgorgement of profit has the aim of preventing the tortfeasor from being unjustly enriched by his tortuous behaviour. The focus is in that way not on the compensatory function of tort law, as the harm done to the victim may be less than the profit gained by the tortfeasor.[115]

105 *Ibid.*, p. 23.
106 Hartlief 1997, p. 11, referring to Holmes, The Common Law; Deakin, Johnston & Markesinis 2008, p. 55.
107 Zimmermann 1992, p. 154.
108 Rogers 2006, p 2.
109 Hartlief 1997, p. 24; Deakin, Johnston & Markesinis 2008, p. 10; White 2003, pp. 61–62.
110 Van Dam 2006, p. 126.
111 Hartlief 1997, p. 16 ff.; Magnus 2001b, p. 185.
112 Rogers 2006, pp. 2–3.
113 Deakin, Johnston & Markesinis 2008, p. 35.
114 Hartlief 1997, p. 22; Van Gerven, Lever & Larouche 2000, p. 18.
115 Van Gerven, Lever & Larouche 2000, p. 741.

To conclude, the traditional function of tort law is seen as one of the reasons for the absence of punitive damages in Continental Europe. The next paragraph will go into the second reason, the division between private law and criminal law.

3.3. *The Strict(er) Division between Private Law and Criminal Law*

The second explanation for the non-existence of punitive damages relates to the distinction between private and criminal law. The distinction between private and criminal law traditionally weighs heavier in civil law systems than in common law systems. One of the difficulties with punitive damages in civil law systems is that the remedy does not fit into a tort system that is designed around the central function of compensation, because punishment of tortfeasors by imposing civil fines is not a legitimate function of tort law.[116] The idea in civil law systems that tort law has a compensatory rather than a punitive objective is not only based on the theoretical analysis of tort law as such, but also results from the strict division between private law and public law, which is considered 'an achievement of modern legal culture'.[117] The distinction between private and public law is considered a typical difference between civil law and common law systems.[118] While the distinction is of fundamental importance in civil law systems, common law systems are less familiar with the dogmatic belief.[119] This has to do with historical and cultural differences:

> '[...] lawyers, judges, and legislators trained in the civil law learn that law is a body of rules and are thereby better equipped to maintain the formal distinction between the two domains in the face of policy arguments for exceptions. By contrast, students of the common law study discrete cases and the facts, reasons, and distinctions courts rely on to resolve them. The history of the common law is one of endless innovation and assimilation of new ideas. General principles are always giving way, and students learn that rule-based arguments routinely lose in the battle between form and substance. The acceptance of punitive damages is an illustration of that general theme'.[120]

Obviously, criminal law and tort law have a common ground in the sense that both areas of the law deal with unlawful conduct. The difference between a crime and a tort is that the first constitutes a public wrong, a wrong to the community at large, whereas a tort is a civil wrong, a wrong to the individual victim.[121] Both areas of law have their own functions and measures, either sanctions or remedies, although we also find common

116 Behr 2003, p. 105 ff.; Koziol 2009, p. 299.

117 Koziol 2008, pp. 755–756.

118 Jurgens & van Ommeren 2009, p. 1.

119 Although common law systems seem to attach more and more value to the distinction, for example the English legal systems where there is considered to be a 'rise of the public-private divide'. On the other hand, in civil law systems the distinction becomes more and more blurred. *Cf.* Jurgens & van Ommeren 2009, p. 129; Bolt & Lensing 1993, p. 82; De Haan 1999, p. 8; Klein 1999, p. 679 ff; Redish & Mathews 2004, p. 3.

120 Wells 2010, p. 560. Also: Harris 1989, p. 1082.

121 Zimmermann 1992, p. 902.

characteristics in that regard.[122] In any case, criminal law has a punitive and deterrent function[123] which cannot principally be said of tort law. Criminal law sanctions have the character and intention of causing harm to offenders, so to punish them for the harm they have done to society. This follows clearly from the fact that criminal law is based on the idea of sanctions.[124] Available serious criminal sanctions may take the form of imprisonment, monetary fines and in some legal systems even capital punishment. In contrast to common law systems, civil law systems hardly recognise a punitive function of tort law. Some find this strange, for the reason that the idea of a sanction could be relevant for tort law as 'the legal consequences of an act are attached to a violation of a duty and faulty behaviour'.[125] Others, for example Lord Wilberforce,[126] even go further by stating that there is no reason why criminal law and private law should have exclusive functions.[127] Even so, the accepted viewpoint in civil law systems is that the primary function of tort law is compensation. The contrary is true for common law systems, where we can see that the line between criminal law and tort law is somewhat more blurred:

> '[...] the distinction in purpose between criminal law and tort is not, and has never been, entirely crystal-clear'.[128]

Common lawyers also respect the distinction, but seem not to put so much weight on it.[129] This explains – to a large extent – why there is disagreement on the issue of punitive damages.[130] In the United States, where the punitive function of tort law is traditionally not rejected, the private-criminal distinction cannot impede the imposition of punitive damages. Rather, the imposition of punitive damages is a choice of policy:

> 'Although we, too, respect the private-public law distinction, no prudent common lawyer would try to put so much weight upon it, nor would he invoke an abstract proposition like "the principle of mutual justification of legal consequences" as a decisive impediment to punitive damages. Rather, American lawyers and scholars know that they must identify substantive policies favoring limits on punitive damages'.[131]

Indeed, a major objection to punitive damages in Continental European legal systems is that punishment and retribution are objectives of the criminal law, which should be left to State authorities. Criminal law clearly is a public matter whereas tort law is a private

122 Van Gerven, Lever & Larouche 2000, p. 19.
123 E.g. Ashworth 2003, p. 18.
124 Koziol 2008, p. 751.
125 *Ibid.*
126 *Cassel & Co. Ltd. v. Broome and Another* [1972] AC 1027, 1114. See in this book: Jonathan Morgan, *Reflections on Reforming Punitive Damages in English Law.*
127 *Cf.* Wilcox 2009, p. 33.
128 Clerk *et al.* 2006, p. 6.
129 Wells 2010, p. 565.
130 *Ibid.*, p. 559.
131 Wells 2010, pp. 564–565.

matter. Some consider it unwise to transfer public powers to private individuals by means of punitive damages, because they are too much influenced by their own private interests and lack the objectivity and accountability that is needed to exercise public power.[132] In their decision making, individuals are 'free from the ethical, political, and constitutional constraints imposed on public actors'.[133] The public-private law distinction is also often used as an argument against punitive damages in the United States.[134] When we look at the European continent, it is indeed so that criminal prosecutions are instituted by the State and tort actions by individuals.[135] Because of the far-reaching powers of the State, the wrongful behaviour needs to be of such a serious nature that State intervention is justified.[136] Some legal systems, for example the Dutch, that know a strict distinction between criminal and private law have installed a monopoly for the Public Prosecutor to bring cases before the criminal court. In the Dutch legal system, which has taken a rather classical stance in that regard when compared to surrounding countries,[137] neither the citizen nor any other body has the same competences as the Public Prosecutor.[138] The prosecution monopoly is based on the principle of discretionary powers (in Dutch: *opportuniteitsbeginsel*), *i.e.* the freedom of the Public Prosecutor to select – out of a number of criminal cases – those suitable for prosecution. This policy would be frustrated if citizens would have their own private prosecution system; citizens should not be enabled to initiate prosecutions if the Public Prosecutor has earlier decided to dismiss a case in the public interest.[139] As will be shown below, objections to citizens acting as private prosecutors by filing punitive damages do not exist to that extent in common law systems. In the United States, for example, the private prosecution policy is well accepted for several reasons. It is for instance considered to contribute to law enforcement and to resolve problems relating to lack of capacity of public authorities, police forces and public prosecutors. Private prosecution, also known as *citation directe*,[140] may thus take away an important drawback of the prosecution monopoly. It could indeed be wise to reconsider prosecution policies in view of law enforcement and to look into the positive effect of private prosecution using tort law and the punitive damages mechanism.[141] Punitive damages are likely to give an incentive to claimants to initiate proceedings when harm has been done them.[142]

This brings us to the problem that private prosecution is at the expense of certain criminal law safeguards. Another important difficulty of awarding punitive damages in Continental Europe is the compatibility with such safeguards. In legal systems where there is a strict division between criminal law and private law, imposing civil fines could

132 Redish & Mathews 2004, p. 3.
133 *Ibid.*, p. 4.
134 Bolt & Lensing 1993, pp. 38–39.
135 Reed & Fitzpatrick 2006, p. 2.
136 *Ibid.*
137 Bolt & Lensing 1993, pp. 60, 82.
138 Corstens 2002, p. 51.
139 *Ibid.*
140 Bolt & Lensing 1993, pp. 60, 83; Corstens 2002, p. 72.
141 Bolt & Lensing 1993, p. 83.
142 Redish & Mathews 2004, pp. 2–3.

be considered a violation of fundamental criminal law principles underlying the constitutional State. These principles are important as they have been created to protect citizens against the far-reaching prosecuting powers of the State, and form part of each modern legal system. According to Koziol, punitive damages violate such principles.[143] A very important procedural principle that springs to mind is the principle of legality, meaning that conduct does not constitute crime and punishment is forbidden unless laid down before in the law (*nulle poene sine previa lege).* The problem with punitive damages in terms of this principle, which is also known as the 'rule of law', is that through the use of vague norms such as 'malice' or 'gross negligence' it is unclear what kind of conduct may lead to punitive damages. The Law Commission for England and Wales has therefore concluded in its report on, among other things, exemplary damages that:

> 'The 'rule of law' principle of legal certainty dictates that the criminalization of conduct is in general properly only the function of the legislator in new cases: it further dictates that there is a moral duty on legislators to ensure that it is clear what conduct will give rise to sanctions and to deprivation of liberty. Broadly-phrased judicial discretions to award exemplary damages ignore such consideration'.[144]

Just as important is the principle of double jeopardy, meaning that prosecution cannot be initiated twice for the same wrongful behaviour (*ne bis in idem).*[145] The awarding of punitive damages also forms a problem in light of this principle. As explained by the Law Commission:

> 'Defendants should not be placed in jeopardy of double punishment in respect of the same conduct, yet this would be the result if a defendant could be liable to pay both a criminal fine following conviction in the criminal courts and an exemplary damages award after an adverse decision in the civil courts'.[146]

In addition to procedural principles, one must also think of evidential safeguards that have been created for reasons of victim protection. In case of civil punishment, the defendant could easily be deprived of the high standards that apply to evidence in criminal law.[147] Starting point in a criminal proceeding is the principle that someone is innocent unless and until proved guilty, *i.e.* the presumption of innocence.[148] Furthermore, the standard of proof in a criminal proceeding is higher than in a civil case: the burden of proof is on the prosecutor who needs to collect convincing evidence

143 Koziol 2009, p. 302.

144 The Law Commission for England and Wales, Aggravated, Exemplary and Restitutionary Damages, Law. Com. No. 247 (1997), p. 99. Also: Koziol 2009, p. 302.

145 E.g. Article 7 § 1 ECHR and Article 14 § 7 ICCPR (*nulle crimen sine lege, nulle poena sine lege*); Article 6 ECHR and Article 14 ICCPR (*ne bis in idem).*

146 The Law Commission for England and Wales, Aggravated, Exemplary and Restitutionary Damages, Law. Com. No. 247 (1997), p. 98.

147 *Ibid.*

148 Ashworth 2003, p. 84.

so to show that guiltiness exists 'beyond reasonable doubt'. More in concrete, problems arise in relation to consistency of punitive damages with the European Convention of Human Rights ('ECHR'), in particular Article 6 ECHR thereof.[149] Despite the fact that the issue whether the imposition of punitive damages constitutes a *criminal charge* has not yet been solved, it is not unwise to conclude that the Article 6 ECHR safeguards should at least play a role when determining whether punitive damages are fit for Continental European legal systems.

A third explanation for the absence of punitive damages in Continental Europe, which relates to the role of government, will now be described.

3.4. *The Role of Government*

The third assumed reason for the non-existence of punitive damages relates to the view on the role of government, or governmental interference and the way in which governmental policy choices influence the view on tort law in Continental Europe. As stated above in the introduction to this paragraph, these views relating to the role of government focus on the impact on tort litigation in general. Nevertheless, without doubt different views on tort law also have implications for the use or rejection of punitive damages.

There is quite a big difference between Europe and the United States in respect of governmental influence over the well doing of citizens.[150] In Europe, the public sector is to a reasonable extent responsible for social welfare policy. In contrast, Americans have learned to protect their own interests by using legal remedies. This contrast between Europe and the United States also results in a different perception of the possible use of tort litigation. According to the German law professor Magnus who also wrote a contribution for this book,[151] the American attitude with regard to tort litigation corresponds to the idea of Von Jhering to fight for one's violated rights by means of the 'justice machinery' (*der Kampf ums Recht*).[152] According to Magnus, the American tort litigation climate is entirely different from that in Europe. In this regard, several general characteristics will be summarised in the following subparagraphs to explain something more about the tort litigation climate in the United States.

3.4.1. The Role of the American Government and Private Enforcement

A first characteristic is that Americans are used to a relatively inactive government that holds on to the theory of *laissez-faire*. In relation to tort law, this for instance means that in the United States great value is attached to private enforcement and that citizens are seen as so-called private prosecutors. Europeans are used to more active governments and do not put so much weight on private enforcement. In contrast, American individuals

149 *Cf.* Adriaanse *et al.* 2008.
150 E.g. Kagan 2007, pp. 41–70.
151 Ulrich Magnus, *Punitive Damages and German Law.*
152 Magnus 2010, p. 109.

are motivated to enforce their own rights. In so doing, they contribute to general safety in society and discharge the State from tasks relating to law enforcement and safety regulation, which is considered to be in the common interest:

> 'To a far greater extent than in the European civil law countries, tort victims in the US are accorded the task of restoring the public order which the tort has violated'.[153]

According to Carrington, private enforcement is surrounded by a certain 'mistrust of the political institutions and government officials upon whom American citizens would have to depend if private law enforcement were not available'.[154] This mistrust, Carrington continues, is supposedly reflected in the State and Federal constitutions that emphasise the weakness and ineptitude of governmental institutions other than courts, and also in the American tradition to go to court whenever an important issue is at stake.[155] The idea of private individuals pursuing the common interest by filing civil claims is less lively in Europe:

> 'The optimistic and liberal idea of giving individuals such a great (economic) incentive that they also act in the common interest finds fewer defenders in Europe. Here, the more pessimistic and paternalistic view still prevails that individuals will generally act only in their own interest and that the State has the task of pursuing the common good'.[156]

We see a great difference between the United States and Europe when it comes to law enforcement. American citizens are motivated to enforce their rights by means of the aforementioned justice machinery. In Europe, such motivation is lacking since there the State dominates law enforcement. The role of the State in respect of law enforcement affects the objectives of judicial proceedings.[157]

> 'In the United States, the civil justice system frequently performs functions that are discharged in other modern jurisdictions by other governmental institutions'.[158]

The United States is a country in which public policy is privately implemented to a great extent. Issues of political and economic importance are subjected to private litigation. As a result, the United States has a so-called 'compensation culture'.[159] For example, in cases of accidentally caused personal injury Americans primarily rely on tort law to obtain compensation of medical expenses.[160] In other countries, such as the Netherlands

153 *Ibid.*, p. 121.
154 Carrington 2004, p. 1413.
155 *Ibid.*, p. 1413. The French political scientist Alexis de Tocqueville noticed the American habit to litigate and wrote about it in his famous work 'de la Démocratie en Amérique' of 1835. Also: Centner 2008.
156 Magnus 2010, p. 123.
157 Verkerk 2010, pp. 303–305.
158 Von Mehren & Murray 2007, p. 163.
159 Deakin, Johnston & Markesinis 2008, p. 7.
160 Von Mehren & Murray 2007, p. 163.

and Sweden, victims of similar accidents are not so much relying on court proceedings but rather on the well-established system of health insurance.

Civil litigation started to play a role in American policy making in the eighteenth century, when popular democracy received considerable attention. Today, the American legal system is still highly democratic, at least when compared to other legal systems. In controversial issues such as abortion, wrongful birth and wrongful life, same sex marriage and death sentence, politicization of the law is deeply rooted.[161] The same applies to punitive damages, which are considered a charged political question.

> 'Punitive damages has become an issue like gun control or abortion, generating heated rhetoric and an unwillingness to undertake sustained and dispassionate analysis'.[162]

The transfer of public policy powers from the government to private litigation, as well as decision making by juries is considered an aspect of adversarial legalism that characterises the American legal system and civil justice in particular. The extensive use of punitive damages in the United States in comparison to other countries may well be explained by the modest role of the American State as well as the position of civil litigation in American society. In essence, the punitive damages remedy is a procedural mechanism that serves as an incentive for potential plaintiffs to initiate civil litigation as 'private attorneys general'.[163] Punitive damages ought to contribute to the enforcement of public norms and the deterrence of wrongful behaviour. The notion that punitive damages are considered a useful complement to other forms of enforcement is for example shown by the inclusion of a punitive damages remedy in the 1991 amendments to the Civil Rights Act.[164] To conclude, it follows from the above that private litigants in the United States for example stay motivated because potential punitive damages awards function as a 'vehicle by which private individuals enforce public values'.[165] European countries hardly know the concept of the citizen as a private prosecutor,[166] for the reasons that law enforcement is an issue that is primarily dealt with by governmental authorities.

The other characteristics that distinguish Europe from the United States and which can all be explained from the value attached to private enforcement will be described below.

3.4.2. The Influence of Safety Regulation on Tort Litigation

There is also a difference between the United States and Europe as regards the influence of safety regulation on tort litigation. Americans seem to have developed a litigation strategy, whereas within the European Union the focus as regards the assurance of safety

161 Deakin, Johnston & Markesinis 2008, p. 7.
162 Galanter 1998, p. 14.
163 Mallor & Roberts 1999, p. 1003; Redish & Mathews 2004, p. 2.
164 42 U.S.C. § 1981(a)-(b) (1994); Mallor & Roberts 1999, p. 1003.
165 Redish & Mathews 2004, p. 38.
166 Kagan 2007, p. 57.

in society is on regulation by governmental authorities. American tort litigation, especially punitive damages, has an important regulatory function, perhaps even as a surrogate for governmental regulation.[167] The difference between Europe and the United States in respect of safety regulation will be illustrated with an example from product liability law. Product liability law regulates the legal responsibility of, among others, producers for damage caused by a product. The victim of a product related accident should be able to obtain compensation for damages. American courts were the first to recognise this and to anticipate the consequences of the industrial revolution. In 1944, the California Supreme Court acknowledged that consumers need to be protected against business, and that business should bear the costs of harm inflicted on consumers.[168] In 1963, the same court imposed strict liability, also known as liability without fault, on the manufacturer of a defective product.[169] For this reason, the United States is known as birthplace of product liability law. Nowadays, American product liability law is a highly developed legal field. No other country in the world has or probably ever will have a similar method of product liability legislation and practice.[170] In the United States, it is very common for victims of product related accidents to start civil proceedings and to obtain compensation – often by joining a class action – for damages suffered. An important reason for the attractiveness of product liability law is the underdevelopment of other compensation schemes.[171] In the United States, product liability litigation is originally perceived as a surrogate for other compensation mechanisms. As a result, claimants in the United States have more actual interest in a claim than claimants in Europe. The product liability system is more extensively used in the United States, at least when compared to the European Union where product liability law is a 'minority area of practice'.[172]

In 1985, the European legislator issued a product liability Directive in which 'the model of extended liability was borrowed largely from the law of the United States'.[173] From the 1960s onward, consumers were increasingly injured by unsafe products. Europe was however confronted with 'the inadequacy of traditional legal principles to deal with the modern phenomenon of product liability'.[174] The real catalyst for the development of European product liability legislation was the Thalidomide disaster. In the 1950s and 1960s, thousands of pregnant women around the world used the pharmaceutical drug Thalidomide to prevent morning sickness. As a result of using the medicine, they gave birth to severely deformed children. Another example is the DES case. DES (diethylstilbestrol) was prescribed to pregnant women to prevent miscarriage. Today, the devastating effects of exposure to the drug are still noticeable: so called 'DES daughters' suffer from various forms of rare cancer. Society has learned a hard lesson from these

167 Magnus 2010, p. 121.
168 *Escola v. Coca Cola Bottling Co.*, 150 P.2d 436 (Cal. 1944).
169 *Greenman v. Yuba Power Products, Inc.*, 377 P.2d 897 (Cal. 1963).
170 Product liability occupies a central role in American law: thousands of product liability suits are filed each year. Owen 2005, p. 24.
171 Howells & Wilhelmsson 1997, p. 211.
172 Howells 2000, p. 306.
173 Deakin, Johnston & Markesinis 2008, p. 703.
174 Howells & Mildred 1998, p. 990.

awkward experiences: a high level of consumer protection is needed in order to prevent consumers from suffering damage relating to defective products. Consumers have certain expectations with regard to the products they use. First and foremost, consumers expect products to be safe. The safety of products must therefore be ensured in the best possible way. If the prevention of unsafe products has failed, there should at least be compensation for damage. Thus, consumer protection can be achieved in two ways. *First*, damage resulting from defective products should be prevented by way of product safety regulation. Product safety regulation encourages producers to create safe products. *Second*, consumers must be compensated if damages occur despite the existence of preventative measures. Product liability law is the instrument by which injured persons can obtain compensation.

It seems that Europeans deal with safety in a different way than Americans. An American author who has lived with his family in Germany for a while explains it in this way that Europeans seem to take more responsibility for their own actions, whereas Americans feel that others have responsibilities as to their safety.[175] Europeans may therefore not rely on tort litigation to the same extent as Americans do. The author gives an unambiguous suggestion to the Americans.

> 'How simple to fix the American litigation system: require people to pay attention to take charge of their lives. If you keep yourself safe, you don't need a lawyer to sue for your injuries. My experiences keeping my young kids safe in Europe allowed me to discover that one culprit of some of our litigation woes is responsibility. Americans decline to act responsibly when they fail to use care to avoid accidents. As a result, they are more likely to be injured. Furthermore, rather than accepting responsibility for their mistakes, they commence lawsuits. Europeans forgo blaming others because they approach responsibility differently'.[176]

The different ways of dealing with safety can be illustrated by the approach to product liability. The idea of maintaining public safety is not the primary incentive of product liability claims within the European Union. In the European Union, product safety law is primarily left to public regulation.[177] Numerous product safety laws together form a strong regulatory regime. An important aspect of product safety law is product recall. This mechanism is often used in situations where unsafe products have already reached the market and/or the consumer.[178] Industries that are frequently affected by product recall are for instance the automotive industry, the pharmaceutical industry and the food industry.[179] Product liability litigation is only necessary to serve a supplementary preventive role and as a method of redress or compensation in rare situations where a defective product did cause damage. In contrast, product liability law is the main

175 Centner 2008, p. 6.

176 *Ibid.*, p. 7.

177 Reimann 2003, p. 251; Howells & Wilhelmsson 1997, p. 265.

178 Freshfields Bruckhaus Deringer Report 2007, Getting it right: product recall in the EU, available at www.freshfields.com/publications/pdfs/2008/mar10/21238.pdf (last visited August 2011). For example: Directives 96/79/EC and 96/27/EC.

179 *Ibid.*

regulatory tool to monitor, or even enhance, product safety in the United States. This is also reflected by the imposition of punitive damages in this legal field.

To conclude, the United States developed a litigation strategy whereas the European Union developed a regulation strategy to ensure the safety of products. This way of dealing with safety regulation is in fact not exclusively applicable to product liability law, but can be seen as an important characteristic of the American and European legal culture.

3.4.3. The Influence of Other Compensation Mechanisms on Tort Litigation

Another characteristic can be derived from the influence of other compensation mechanisms on tort litigation. Tort law is not the only possible compensation mechanism. Other important mechanisms are first-party insurance and social security. In contrast to the American legal system, where other compensation schemes are less relied upon, these two systems are well developed in Europe. In the United States, victim protection through tort law is for a large part based on the strong feeling to protect victims for the shortcomings of social security.[180] In contrast, compensation via tort law is considered a marginal phenomenon in Europe, as the greater part of losses that fall in society are compensated via social security and first-party insurance.

> 'If there is no defendant whose liability can be established according to the principles of the law, then the claimant is left without redress so far as private law is concerned. He may, of course, look to the Welfare State or to a private loss insurance contract he may have made'.[181]

The availability of first-party insurance and social security is first and foremost a policy choice made by the government. Such policy choices influence the intensity of tort litigation.

First-party insurance is a system whereby a person buys, by means of paying a premium, a type of insurance coverage such as health insurance, accident insurance and travel insurance.[182] The first-party insurance policy is concluded for possible future harm and corresponding damage.[183] If damage occurs and the damage is covered by the insurance policy, the insurer directly pays compensation to the victim. Compensation via first-party insurance is somewhat different than compensation via tort law, as payment by the insurance occurs irrespective of liability or the cause of the damage. Furthermore, in case of first-party insurance the insured is usually entitled to a fixed amount of compensation instead of full compensation of the damage. First-party insurance is an established compensation mechanism in both Europe and the United States.

The victim of an accident with consequential loss could perhaps also rely upon social security and social insurance laws, which is a system of public compensation. Social

180 Magnus 2010, p. 121.
181 Rogers 2006, p. 4.
182 Hartlief 1997, p. 28.
183 Bruggeman 2010, p. 83.

security is normally funded via general means, *i.e.* the national government, and via premiums of insured and their employers.[184] Europe knows an extensive apparatus of social security, which forms a reflection of the Welfare State in which the State is responsible for social welfare.[185] In contrast, the reliance on social security in the Unites States is by far not as high as in Europe:

> 'Rather than adopt social insurance programs [...], Americans remain obsessed with litigation'.[186]

The American approach can be illustrated by the status of health insurance prior to the health care measures that were recently taken by President Obama. In the United States, in principle only the old, disabled and poor people were covered by social security in case of health risks.[187] The alternative for those who did not fall into this category was private health insurance; yet approximately fifteen per cent of the American population did not have any health insurance.[188] This all changed when the Affordable Care Act was signed into law in March 2010.[189] However, even with the new law the differences between the United States and Europe as regards social security are significant. Since World War II, the United States has spent considerably less on social benefits than Western European Countries.[190] In 1995, public social welfare expenditures in the United States equalled 17.1 per cent of GDP as compared to 35–37 per cent in Scandinavian countries and 25–30 per cent in Germany, the Netherlands, Italy and the UK.[191]

The most important function of social security is to provide income security to persons who are unable to earn their own money, for example because of their disability, age or unemployment.[192] Furthermore, social security supplements incomes if the income is below the social minimum and provides for partial support in the costs of medical care, housing and raising children. Examples of existing social security laws in the Netherland are the Sickness Act (in Dutch: *Ziektewet*) and the Unemployment Insurance Act (*Werkloosheidswet*).[193] Social security is an accessible system for compensation. Just as with first-party insurance, the insured has a right to receive a social security benefit no matter what the cause of the situation leading to his damage is.[194] Moreover, social security benefits are fixed amounts that are often only temporarily rewarded. Victims will for that reason keep looking for other compensation systems, *i.e.* tort law and first-party insurance. In contrast to social security, which has certain limits

184 *Ibid.*, p. 352.
185 Magnus 2010, p. 118.
186 Centner 2008, p. 11; Magnus 2010, p. 118.
187 Magnus 2010, p. 119.
188 *Ibid.*, referring to US Census Bureau, Income, Poverty, and Health Insurance Coverage in the United States: 2007 (2008), p 19 ff., available at www.census.gov/prod/2008pubs/p60-235.pdf (last visited June 2011).
189 See www.whitehouse.gov/healthreform/ (last visited June 2011).
190 Kagan 2007, p. 44.
191 *Ibid.*
192 *Ibid.*, p. 654.
193 Bruggeman 2010, p. 352.
194 Hartlief 1997, p 29.

on compensation like first-party insurance, due to the principle of full compensation tort law is especially interesting for victims who have suffered personal injury to receive compensation for the top of their income and for immaterial damage.[195]

In conclusion, it follows from the above that in addition to tort law there are other possible compensation systems for victims who have suffered personal injury, which all influence each other. The compensation mechanisms of first-party insurance and social security have been developed to a wider extent in Europe than in the United States. In Europe, situations involving personal injury are often dealt with by social security or first-party insurance.[196] Tort law has therefore become a rather marginal phenomenon. This provides a plausible explanation for the underdevelopment of tort litigation in Europe when compared to the United States. However, we have to keep in mind that there is a 'retreat of the European Welfare State' development going on.[197] Also due to the financial crises that has captivated the world in the past years, there is a policy of retrenchment which also means that social security benefits have been reduced. This makes tort law a more appealing compensation mechanism for Europeans.[198]

3.4.4. The Influence of Procedural Aspects on Tort Litigation

Lastly, in comparison to the United States European countries do not have a developed system of procedural aspects that create a tort litigation climate.[199] Examples from the American legal system are the jury system, the possibility of contingency fee or 'no cure no pay' arrangements and the possibility of class actions; these kinds of substantive and procedural law mechanisms facilitate victim protection. It is especially interesting to see how such features contribute to civil litigation, as they simplify access to court.

As mentioned above, a fundamental characteristic of the American legal system is adversarial legalism.[200] The outcome of a legal procedure is to a large extent influenced by the parties' lawyers who have to reveal the truth, in contrast to Continental European legal systems where the judge has a more inquisitorial role to actively reveal the truth.

Another feature of the American legal system unknown to Continental European legal systems is the use of juries that are composed of laymen. As a passive decision maker, the jury fits well in an adversary system.[201] The jury has substantial influence in tort litigation as it may decide on issues of fact and is able to influence the amount of damages awards without having to motivate its decision. Opponents of punitive damages are concerned about the competences of juries, as they fear that juries are more easily persuaded by victims asking for compassion and award outrageous amounts of (punitive) damages as a result. However, empirical studies that investigate decision-making of

195 *Ibid.*
196 Magnus 2010, p. 118; Also: U. Magnus (ed.), *The Impact of Social Security on Tort Law*, Vienna: Springer, 2003.
197 *Cf.* Howells & Mildred 1998, p. 988.
198 Magnus 2010, p. 118.
199 The article of professor Magnus (Magnus 2010) gives an extensive overview of among others the procedural aspects of American tort law and has been used as the main source for this subparagraph.
200 Burnham 2006, p. 41.
201 *Ibid.*, p. 85.

judges and juries show that this assertion is incorrect.[202] The difference between judge and jury awards is not as striking as often thought.[203]

Furthermore, the sometimes difficult decision for a victim whether or not to start expensive proceedings may become easier due to the American rule on litigation costs in connection with the system of contingency fees or remuneration of lawyers on the basis of 'no cure, no pay'. The American rule implies that the parties in a civil lawsuit have to pay for their own legal representation costs, no matter what the outcome of the lawsuit is.[204] The effect of the American rule is that it most likely influences the amount of damages awards, as juries will usually take litigation costs into account. Punitive damages are indeed used in the United States to evade the American rule of adjudicating costs:[205] it is considered appropriate to award something more than pure compensatory damages. Furthermore, the risk of having to pay a considerable amount of litigation costs is taken away by the possibility of a contingency fee or 'no cure no pay' arrangement, which obliges the client to pay the lawyer only if the case has been won. In that way even people who cannot normally afford a lawsuit are able to find a lawyer, simply because:

> 'There is no deterrent to trying one's luck in an American court'.[206]

Thus, the American rule combined with contingency fees facilitates access to court for everyone and gives an incentive for claimants to initiate civil proceedings. A drawback of the contingency fee system is that it allows lawyers, who will have an economic incentive in each case, to refuse to take up doubtful claims.[207] In contrast, Continental European legal systems apply the European rule which means that the losing party also has to pay – in line with a fixed list of amounts – for the litigation costs of the winning party. This will prevent most claimants from bringing doubtful or risky cases before the court.[208] Claimants are not able to exclude the risks of having to pay litigation costs in the same way as Americans can, as contingency fees arrangements are illegal in most European countries where lawyers should stick to fixed hourly rates in order to uphold their independence, incorruptibility and integrity.[209] The American rule in connection with contingency fees stimulates the claim culture in the United States:

> 'The attractions of suing in tort are thus much greater in the US than in Europe. Unlike in Europe, litigation costs in the US do not serve as a natural barrier to the pursuit of hopeless or undeserving claims'.[210]

202 § 2.5 above.
203 Burnham 2006, p 123.
204 Centner 2008, pp. 34–35; Magnus 2010, p. 112; Burnham 2006, p. 143.
205 Behr 2003, p. 122.
206 Howells 2000, p. 307.
207 Magnus 2010, p. 114.
208 *Ibid.*, p. 112.
209 *Cf.* Beer 2008, pp. 136–139; Magnus 2010, pp. 113–114.
210 Magnus 2010, p. 113.

A characteristic of the American legal system that is closely attached to the American rule is the absence of legal aid from public funds.[211] Legal aid is considered unnecessary exactly because of the American rule and contingency fees which enable even the poorer people to start a civil procedure. On the other hand, the already explained European rule has made legal aid from public funds necessary. In Europe, a poorer person is usually only entitled to financial support if his claim has reasonable prospects of success.[212] Thus, legal aid is used to filter out claims of little value or importance.[213]

The last feature of American law worth mentioning here that facilitates tort litigation is the class action or collective civil litigation. Under both Federal and State law, a group of plaintiffs may bring a common civil action that is based on common questions of fact and law, and in so doing each individual plaintiff avoids the high costs of legal proceedings.[214] The class action fits into the role that is assigned to American private civil justice, as it contributes to law enforcement. The possibility to join a class forms an incentive for individual victims who would otherwise refrain from initiating a civil claim because of rational lack of interest, *i.e.* when the damage is too small.[215] Most European civil law systems do not know a mechanism that is similar to the American class action, although in recent years the European interest in class actions has increased.[216] However, in tort law class actions still play a small role.[217]

To conclude, the procedural law mechanisms that are available in American law create a legal climate in which tort litigation can flourish. Although the procedural aspects barely have direct effect on the application of punitive damages awards, it is safe to state that their indirect influence cannot be neglected. In other words, the procedural law mechanisms set up conditions and thereby indirectly facilitate the imposition of punitive damages awards.

The next paragraphs will go into the European punitive damages debate, especially the reasons for the growing European interest in this legal remedy. This is also the topic of the second part of this book.

4. Opposition from Private International Law Perspective Slowly Loses Ground

Before going into the reasons for the increased European attention for punitive damages, it is interesting to see how punitive damages awards are dealt with in Continental Europe from a private international law ('PIL') perspective, especially now that certain developments favouring the recognition of punitive damages have taken place there. For

211 Centner 2008, p. 22.
212 For Dutch law: Article 12 *Wet op de Rechtsbijstand.*
213 Magnus 2010, p. 114.
214 Von Mehren & Murray 2007, p. 182.
215 Magnus 2010, p. 116.
216 *Cf.* Cauffman 2009, nr. 17, pp. 690–708.
217 Magnus 2010, p. 116.

example, recent court decisions show that France and Spain seem to have taken a more favourable approach in that matter.

The focus in this paragraph will be on American punitive damages awards, as PIL decisions in Europe usually deal with these awards. Most European courts are hostile against American punitive damages judgments, and refuse to recognise and enforce them because they are considered contrary to public policy (*ordre public*).[218] American courts are also aware of this:

> 'Some legal systems not only decline to recognize punitive damages themselves but refuse to enforce foreign punitive judgments as contrary to public policy'.[219]

In fact, all European decisions relating to the recognition of punitive damages – whether with a negative or a positive outcome – have been made with reference to the public policy exception.[220] The public policy exception can be explained in two ways: punitive damages are considered anomalous due to their criminal law function and the amount of the award is usually considered excessive or disproportionate.[221]

The attitude, from a PIL perspective, towards punitive damages differs per Member States. The French legal system increasingly shows less opposition. The French Supreme Court recently overruled the decision[222] of a lower court holding that punitive damages are incompatible with French public policy.[223] The Court ruled that 'the principles underlying an award of punitive damages are not in themselves contrary to public policy', but that 'incompatibility may result from the awarded sum if it is disproportionate in relation with the injury suffered and the breach of the contractual obligations of the debtor'.[224] Thus, foreign punitive damages awards can in principle be recognised in France except if they are not proportionate to the harm sustained and the contractual breach. The judgment for which recognition was asked was an American judgment in which US$ 1.39 million in compensatory damages and US$ 1.46 million in punitive damages had been awarded. This was considered to be clearly disproportionate by the French court.

Other Member States in which the recognition question has been raised are Germany, Italy and Spain. The German[225] and Italian[226] Supreme Courts have both denied the recognition of a punitive damages award on public policy grounds. However, it should be

218 Requejo Isidro 2009, p. 243; Gotanda 2007, p. 508; Berch 2010, p. 77; Rouhette 2007, p. 328.

219 *Exxon Shipping Co. v. Baker*, 128 S. Ct. 2605 (2008), § 2623; Berch 2010, p. 77.

220 Requejo Isidro 2009, p. 245.

221 In this book: Marta Requejo Isidro, *Punitive Damages: How do they look like when seen from abroad.*

222 Cour d'Appel de Poitiers, 26 February 2009.

223 Arrêt nº 1090 du 1 décembre 2010 (09–13.303) – Cour de cassation – Première chamber civile.

224 Translation from Marta Requejo Isidro, *Punitive Damages: How do they look like when seen from abroad.*

225 BGH, IXth Civil Senate, 4.6.1992, Docket No. IX ZR 149/91 [1992]; *Cf.* Hay 1992.

226 Corte di Cassazione, 19.1.2007, n. 1183. *Cf.* Barzaghi 2005; Ostoni 2005; Quarta 2008.

noted that the Italian refusal is at odds with two domestic decisions in which *danni punitive*, the Italian translation of punitive damages, have explicitly been awarded.[227]

Contrary to the German and Italian decisions, the enforcement of punitive damages has been allowed in a Spanish[228] decision. The Spanish Supreme Court enforced an American treble damages award imposed on a Spanish company for the unauthorised use of intellectual property, violation of a registered trademark, and unfair competition.[229] According to the company, enforcement of the damages award should be refused because it was penal in nature and therefore contrary to Spanish public policy. However, the public policy exception was not accepted by the Court. According to the Court, the damages award did not only have a compensatory but also a punitive and preventive function.[230] Furthermore, the Court stated that Spanish law does not know a strict separation between civil and criminal compensation systems.[231] The Court also made explicit reference to the international character of the case and its relationship with Spain, and clarified that the interest pursued by the damages award is the protection of intellectual property rights which is a commonly accepted desire.[232] The Court, obviously in favour of punitive damages, concluded that punitive damages can be used to compensate the inadequacies of criminal law.[233]

As stated above, the refusal or approval of punitive damages awards on PIL grounds illustrates the general view on such awards in Continental Europe. Although the public policy exception is a high hurdle to be taken when it comes to the recognition of punitive damages, the decisions of the French and Spanish courts do show that opposition is – slowly – fading. The contribution of Marta Requejo Isidro in this book gives an interesting insight in developments from a private international law perspective.[234]

5. The Growing European Attention for Punitive Damages

There appears to be growing 'European' attention for punitive damages, despite the opposition towards punitive damages in civil law systems caused by certain obstacles that are intrinsic to the civil law tradition. The developments are visible enough to form the reason for this book. It is important to find out which developments have led to the idea that punitive damages may form a useful addition to the array of private law remedies that already exist in Europe and how to explain these developments. This will be done by taking a closer look into these developments, which eventually give rise to the question whether it is possible and desirable to introduce punitive damages into European civil

227 Requejo Isidro 2009, p. 248, referring to Tribunale di Torre Annunziate, Sez. Stralcio, 24 February 2000 and Tribunale di Torre Annunziata, Sez. Stralcio, 14 March 2000.

228 Requejo Isidro 2009, p. 247, referring to *Miller Import Corp. v. Alabastres Alfredo, S.L.*, Sentencia del Tribunal Supremo, 13 November 2001 (Exequátur No. 2039/1999).

229 Gotanda 2007, p. 521.

230 *Miller Import Corp. v. Alabastres Alfredo, S.L.*, at § 241.

231 *Ibid.*, at § 242.

232 *Ibid.*, at § 242; Requejo Isidro 2009, p. 247.

233 Requejo Isidro 2009, p. 248.

234 Marta Requejo Isidro, *Punitive Damages: How do they look like when seen from abroad.*

law systems.[235] Therefore, both an immediate and a contributory cause for the increased attention will be introduced in the following subparagraph and further explained in paragraphs 6 and 7.

5.1. An Immediate and a Contributory Cause

An immediate cause for the growing interest in punitive damages may be referred to as *private enforcement,* a rather contemporary – at least for Continental Europe – concept that finds its origins in the field of competition law (in the United States known as antitrust law), whereas an important contributory cause may be found in perspectives on the functions of tort law which are increasingly subject to change. Both causes will be described at this point.

First, tort law has been discovered as a potential instrument to enforce various legal standards on both EU and national level, for example in the field of environmental law, consumer law and competition law.[236] Law enforcement through private law mechanisms, such as tort law, is known as private enforcement. The concept of private enforcement will be explained in detail below.

Second, there is growing attention for the need to improve tort law remedies so as to enable enforcement of *tort law* standards. Take the infringement of personality rights due to wrongful publications by the tabloid press.[237] In most instances, the victim saves himself the trouble of bringing a civil action for damages, even if he has the right to do so. If the victim does decide to file a claim, the tabloid usually seems quite willing to rectify and pay damages. However, the damages awarded are as a rule not in proportion to the profits made by the tabloid, which enables tabloids to infringe personality rights without having to suffer substantial consequences. This has been illustrated by a German case concerning Princess Caroline von Monaco.[238] The *Bundesgerichtshof* ('BGH') decided that the gains incurred at the expense of Caroline's rights – a tabloid illegitimately placed pictures and a false interview with incorrect details about her personal life – were to be returned. The reasoning of the BGH that compensation is not an effective method to deal with infringements of personality rights is quite interesting. According to the Court, using the method of compensation would not lead to effective prevention of such infringements, as the compensation awarded is usually far below the profits resulting from the infringement.[239]

The immediate cause will be further explained in §6, whereas §7 concerns the contributory cause.

235 This is essentially the subject of the PhD research that I am doing at Maastricht University.
236 Cauffman & Weyts 2009, p. 4.
237 E.g. in Dutch literature: Hartlief 2005; Boukema 2008.
238 BGH 15 November 1994, BGHZ 128, 1 = NJW 1995, 861.
239 Koziol 2009, p. 286.

6. Private Enforcement: How It All Started

Every legal system has to deal with the (lack of) enforcement of legal norms, *i.e.* norms to protect public and individual interests. A wide range of public law mechanisms, such as criminal law and administrative law, has been created in order to detect and deter wrongful conduct in society. However, the traditional reliance on such mechanisms logically does not produce satisfactory results in all situations relating to the prevention of damage or sufferance of damage as a result of wrongful conduct of others. The insufficiency may be caused by various reasons, such as the lack of capacity of governmental supervisors, police forces and public prosecutors to respond to each (minor) offence. Moreover, instituting criminal proceedings is generally seen as the ultimate resort (*ultimum remedium*).[240]

European policy makers, legislators and legal scholars keep searching for useful instruments to deal with different forms of wrongful conduct, and pay increased attention to tort law and punitive damages as a potential law enforcement instrument.[241] In recent years, private enforcement has become a re-emerging term in the European juridical debate. Tort law in particular has been put forward as a law enforcement instrument. At this point, it is important to first explain the origin and meaning of the term law enforcement. Law enforcement, which means both *ex ante* prevention of objective law infringements and *ex post* action-taking against such infringements by the use of legal sanctions or remedies,[242] is usually divided into public enforcement and private enforcement.[243] Public enforcement refers to the use of governmental authorities to detect and to sanction violators of public law norms. In that sense, law enforcement is seen as a traditional task of the government. Public enforcement action taking is authorised by criminal law, administrative law, tax law, constitutional law and other parts of the law that deal with the organization of the State and aspects of it that are of direct concern to the State.[244] We speak of private enforcement when a private person (for example a consumer, an entrepreneur or a governmental entity acting as a private person) uses a private law mechanism in order to obtain justice. He may for example file a civil suit, which could result in a damages award or an injunction. Law enforcement has then become a matter of private initiative, and not a matter of the government.[245]

Where does the phenomenon of private enforcement actually come from? Whereas private enforcement is a rather unknown concept in Europe, quite the opposite is true for the United States, where private enforcement is the primary method of enforcing numerous laws, such as securities laws, consumer protection laws, civil rights laws, antitrust laws and environmental laws.[246] For example, more than 90 per cent of

240 Bolt & Lensing 1993, p. 80.
241 *Cf.* Van Boom 2006.
242 Van Boom 2007a.
243 *Cf.* Holmes 2004.
244 Polinsky & Shavell 2005, p. 3.
245 Zippro 2009, pp. 2–3; Polinsky & Shavell 2005, p. 4.
246 Landes & Posner 1975, p. 2; Carrington 2004, pp. 1413–1414.

antitrust laws[247] are privately enforced in the United States.[248] Research shows that between 1941 and 1985 a total of 29 588 antitrust claims have been filed in American courts. Since 1985, 600 to 1000 antitrust claims per year are being filed.[249]

The Americans started to rely on private regulation, especially the regulation of business, during the period of industrialization in the 19th century.[250] A good example stemming from this time is the Federal antitrust law. The Sherman Antitrust Act of 1890,[251] the first Federal law to prohibit trusts and monopolies, was created to protect smaller businesses from anticompetitive behaviour and still forms an important basis for American antitrust litigation. Congress designed the act with the idea that private enforcement would be the best method to enforce it, as 'the big commercial trust were politically powerful institutions that were able to intimidate and subvert public enforcement'[252] by the United States Department of Justice that was responsible for law enforcement. Under the original version of the Sherman Act, private claimants were able to recover double damages for any harm resulting from infringements of antitrust law. This was later increased into treble damages, plus the award of attorney's fees to prevailing claimants.[253] Such damages were then made applicable to all actions in which private parties sought recovery under the antitrust laws.[254]

Direct compensation of private parties has always been an important goal of private enforcement. But private enforcement also plays a role in the 'self-policing capacity of business', so to pursue public enforcement goals.[255] The federal legislator is said to have created private enforcement rights to complement public enforcement of antitrust laws,[256] for fear that 'the government would not have the necessary resources to uncover, investigate and prosecute all violations of the antitrust laws'.[257] However, the 'core' rationale for private enforcement is deterrence.[258] The possibility for private parties and their lawyers to be rewarded works not only as an incentive for claimants but also has deterrent effect on defendants. In the law and economics theory, the goal of antitrust

247 For an overview of federal antitrust laws, see Cavanagh 1987, p. 779, footnote 5.

248 Zippro 2009, p. 15; Adriaanse 2007, p. 314.

249 Zippro 2009, p. 165, referring to: C.A. Jones, *Private enforcement of Antitrust Law in the EU, UK and USA*, Oxford University Press 1999, p. 79 and the Annual Report of the Director for the years 1941–1985 of the Administrative Office of the United States Court.

250 Carrington 2004, p. 1414.

251 Act of July 2, 1890, 26 Stat. 209, codified at 15 U.S.C. §§ 1–7.

252 Carrington 2004, p. 1414.

253 The treble damages provision was originally embodied in Section 7 of the Sherman Act and later incorporated into Section 4 of the Clayton Act (Act of October 15, 1914, 38 Stat. 730, 731, codified at 15 U.S.C. §§ 12–27).

254 15 U.S.C. § 15(a).

255 Buxbaum 2007, p. 43.

256 The United States has a tripartite system to enforce federal antitrust laws: public enforcement is in the hands of the Antitrust Division – which has both criminal and civil powers – on the one hand, and the Federal Trade Commission on the other, whereas private enforcement is in the hands of private parties. *Cf.* Cavanagh 2005, p. 148.

257 Cavanagh 2005, pp. 152–153; Buxbaum 2007, p. 43.

258 Baker 2004, p. 382; Buxbaum 2007, p. 44.

damages is to achieve optimal deterrence, whereas the goal of antitrust law is to enhance economic efficiency.[259]

American business is not the only area that is largely normalised through private enforcement. Also standards of professional conduct (think of lawyers, doctors, accountants) are often privately enforced; doctors, for example, regularly face damages actions.[260]

The fact that there is extensive use of private enforcement in the United States whereas private enforcement is rather unfamiliar in Continental Europe may be explained by the different approaches towards the division between public law and private law in the two areas, as will be described in the next subparagraph.

6.1. *Private Enforcement in Europe*

The previous paragraph explains the concept of private enforcement in general, taking into consideration the traditional reliance on private enforcement in the United States. This traditional reliance can be contrasted to a more limited reliance in Europe. However, despite their unfamiliarity with the concept, European policy makers have shown more interest in private enforcement. This has even been noticed in the United States.[261] This paragraph describes the reasons for the increased attention for private enforcement in Continental Europe and the important role of tort law and claims for damages and injunctions in that matter.

The several privately enforced American laws mentioned above are laws that in a civil law country would be denoted as public law, while the distinction between public and private law is hardly ever noticed in American law.[262] In contrast, as already mentioned in paragraph 3.3 above, civil law countries differentiate public law norms from private law norms.[263] Private law norms regulate legal relationships between individuals, and therefore focus on the individual.[264] Because private law rules – such as tort law, contract law and property law – are of no direct concern to the State, they are as a rule privately enforced. Conversely, public law norms are in principle still designed to protect public interest goals and controlled by governmental organs through public enforcement. This

259 Buxhaum 2007, p. 45, see also footnote 17 on the same page for an overview of literature concerning the development of the law and economics theory in the field of antitrust law.

260 Carrington 2004, p. 1415.

261 E.g. Baker 2004, p. 380: 'With private enforcement of competition law having suddenly arrived as a policy goal in the U.K., the European Union, and elsewhere ...'.

262 Carrington 2004, p. 1413.

263 The public-private distinction goes back to Roman law, and civil law countries have stuck to it until now. Ulp. D. 1,1,1,2 = Inst. 1,1,4. Huius studii duae sunt positiones, publicum et privatum. Publicum ius est quod ad statum rei Romanae spectat, privatum quod ad singulorum utilitatem: sunt enim quaedam publice utilia, quaedam privatim. See Spruit 2001, p. 22; Dubber 2009, p. 3.

264 *Cf.* Kortmann & Sieburgh 2009, p. 255, referring to Opzoomer (Het Burgerlijk Wetboek verklaard door C.W. Opzoomer, deel 1, 3e druk, p. 7).

is reflected in the monopoly position of the government to prosecute and punish citizens, and to control safety regulation through regulators.[265]

It must be noted that the distinction between private law and public law in civil law countries is not as strict anymore as it used to be.[266] There is more and more overlap between the two, which could be an explanation for changing policy views resulting in the increased interest of European policymakers in the concept of private enforcement and the current tendency to look at the instrumental function of tort law in order to reach public interest goals.

Mechanisms from tort law, contract law, property law, family law and other parts of the law that regulate legal relationships between individuals may be used to enforce public law norms. Contract law may for example be used for private enforcement of anti-discrimination law or competition law, respectively. Firstly, in case a landlord relies on a term from the tenancy agreement to dissolve the agreement for discriminatory reasons, such as disliking the tenants religion, the tenant can fight the unjustified dissolution in court on the basis of contractual principles such as *pacta sunt servanda*.[267] Secondly, the consumer who suffers damage due to anti-competitive behaviour may request the court to declare agreements that are in breach of competition law void. In this context of the growing European interest in punitive damages, private enforcement is seen from a narrow perspective, namely private enforcement via tort law, more specific damages actions in tort. The following explains how private enforcement in general and punitive damages in particular have become part of the European agenda, by which I primarily mean the EC agenda.

6.2. *The European Court of Justice Takes the Lead...*

As in the United States, the debate on private enforcement in Europe started in the field of competition law. These developments are extensively dealt with in this book by Angela Ortega González.[268] At this point, some remarks will do.

In 2000, the European Union openly declared that it wants to become 'the most competitive and dynamic knowledge-based economy in the world'.[269] The special action plan that has been developed to this end is known as the 'Lisbon strategy'. Part of the strategy is an optimal functioning competition law, seeing that anticompetitive behaviour is harmful to the economy as a whole.[270] The core of EC competition law are Articles 81 and 82 of the EC Treaty (new Articles 101 and 102 TFEU) regarding the prohibition of anticompetitive agreements, decisions or concerted practices, as well as the prohibition

265 Kortmann & Sieburgh 2009, p. 255, referring to the framer of the new Dutch civil code Meijers (Ontwerp voor een Nieuw Burgerlijk Wetboek, Toelichting, Eerste gedeelte (Boek 1–4), Den Haag 1954, pp. 12–13).

266 Slok & Van 1990, p. 1828.

267 Cauffman & Weyts 2009, p. 309.

268 Angela Ortega González, *Punitive Damages for Cartel Infringements: Why didn't the Commission Grasp the Opportunity?*.

269 Lisbon Strategy, Presidency Conclusions of Lisbon European Council 23 and 24 March 2000, SN 100/00, at 5.

270 Basedow 2007, p. 1; Boot 2008, p. 200 ff.

to abuse a dominant position, respectively. These provisions have been formally worked out in Regulation 1/2003.[271] According to Articles 4 to 6 of this Regulation, the Commission, national competition authorities (NCAs) *and* national courts are empowered to apply Articles 81 and 82 EC (new Articles 101 and 102 TFEU). This means that the Regulation leaves room for private enforcement.[272] Private enforcement does not necessarily have to substitute public enforcement of EC competition law, but should merely act as a complement to it.[273] Under Regulation 1/2003, the Commission and NCAs constitute a network of competition authorities responsible for public enforcement of the applicable Community antitrust rules. As part of their enforcement activities, these authorities adopt, among other things, decisions finding that an undertaking has infringed antitrust law as well as decisions imposing fines. Public enforcement is indispensable for effective protection of the rights conferred and effective enforcement of the obligations imposed by the Treaty.[274]

The complementary nature of public and private enforcement of rights deriving from EC law was already recognised by the European Court of Justice ('ECJ') in the case *Van Gend & Loos* of 1963:

> 'The vigilance of individuals concerned to protect their rights amounts to an effective supervision in addition to the supervision entrusted by Articles 169 [new 226] and 170 [new 227] to the diligence of the Commission and of the Member States'.[275]

Private enforcement was also the central theme in a Court ruling of 1984, namely *Von Colson and Kamann v. Land Nordrhein-Westfalen*.[276] In this case, which is outside the ambit of competition law, the Court had to rule on the compatibility of national sanctions for breach of the Equal Treatment Directive.[277] Without giving solid reasons, an employer had rejected a female applicant for a job. Although this was held to be discriminatory according to the German court deciding the case, only the travel expenses incurred by the claimant were compensated (on the basis of §611a(2) BGB), whereas other claims were dismissed.[278] The ECJ decided that this was unacceptable and required 'effective, proportionate and dissuasive sanctions' for unequal treatment of men and women in work related circumstances.[279] This requirement has been laid down in Directive 2002/73,[280] which amends the earlier Directive.

271 Council Regulation (EC) No 1/2003 of 16 December 2002 on the implementation of the rules on competition laid down in Articles 81 and 82 of the Treaty (new Articles 101 and 102 TFEU).

272 *Cf.* Boot 2008, p. 201.

273 Paulis 2007, p. 9; Green Paper, par. 1.1; Annex to Green paper, par. 13.

274 Green Paper, par. 1.1.

275 Case 26/62, *Van Gend en Loos NV Algemene Transport- en Expeditie Onderneming v. Nederlandse Administratie der Belastingen* [1963] ECR 1, at IIb.

276 Case 14/83, *Von Colson and Kamann v. Land Nordrhein-Westfalen* [1984] ECR 1891.

277 Directive 76/207/EEC on the implementation of the principle of equal treatment for men and women as regards access to employment, vocational training and promotion, and working conditions, OJ 1976 L 039.

278 *Ibid.*, at § 5.

279 *Ibid.*, at § 23.

280 Directive 2002/73/EC amending Directive 76/207/EEC, Article 8d.

Despite these early observations by the ECJ, enforcement in the field of competition law is still mainly controlled by the Commission in conjunction with NCAs. The enforcement of competition law has been a matter of public enforcement for half a decade – fines that have been imposed by the Commission and the NCAs are deposited with the European and national treasuries[281] – whereas the situation of individual victims has not really been cared about for quite some time.[282] A turning point came in 2001, when the ECJ acknowledged in *Courage Ltd. v. Crehan*[283] the right of any individual, that includes contracting parties,[284] to claim damages before national courts for loss caused by anticompetitive behaviour (the case concerned Article 81 EC). Individuals are hence entitled to compensation, a development that 'can make a significant contribution to the maintenance of effective competition in the Community'.[285] The ECJ further decided that if effective European procedural rules are lacking every Member State needs to create an operative procedure for individuals enabling them to privately enforce competition law.[286]

Courage Ltd. v. Crehan was later confirmed and elaborated on by the ECJ in the *Manfredi* case.[287] According to the Court, it is for the national courts to set the criteria for determining an appropriate award of damages for harm caused by anticompetitive behaviour, provided that the principles of equivalence and effectiveness are observed.[288] Thus, national courts play an essential role in applying EC law.[289] The Court pointedly mentioned the possibility to award punitive damages founded on EC competition law, if such damages may be awarded pursuant to similar actions based on national law.[290] Furthermore, it was stated by the Court that 'injured persons must be able to seek compensation not only for actual loss (*damnum emergens*) but also for loss of profits (*lucrum cessans*) plus interest'.[291]

Nowadays, the right to damages for breach of EC law is an established right which goes hand in hand with the principle that national remedies must secure the effectiveness of EC law. The principle of effectiveness (*effet utile*) of EC law has been developed by the ECJ from the 1990s onwards into a requirement for national courts to give adequate effect to directly applicable Community rights in cases arising before them.[292] Equally

281 Boot 2008, p. 200.

282 Paulis 2007, p. 8.

283 Case C-453/99, *Courage Ltd. v. Crehan* [2001] ECR I-6297.

284 *Courage Ltd. v. Crehan*, at 27; Cauffman & Weyts 2009, p. 321.

285 *Ibid.*, at. 26–27.

286 *Cf.* Boot 2008, p. 201.

287 Joined cases C-295/04 to C-298/04, *Manfredi v. Lloyd Adriatico* [2006].

288 *Manfredi*, at 92, 98.

289 *Cf.* Regulation 1/2003, paragraph 7.

290 *Manfredi*, at 93, 99.

291 *Ibid.*, at 95.

292 E.g. Case 14/83, *Von Colson and Kamann v. Land Nordrhein-Westfalen* [1984] ECR 1891; Case C-213/89, *R. v. Secretary of State for Transport ex parte Factortame Ltd. and Others* [1990] ECR I-2433; Case C-177/88, *Dekker v. Stichting voor Jong Volwassenen (VJV) Plus* [1990] I-ECR 3941; Case C-377/89, *Cotter and McDermott v. Minister for Social Welfare and Attorney General* [1991] ECR I-1155; Case C-208/90, *Emmott v. Minister for Social Welfare* [1991] ECR I-4269; Case C-271/91, *Marshall v. Southampton and South West Area Health Authority II* [1993] ECR I-4367; Case C-410/98, *Metallgesellschaft & Hoechst v. Inland Revenue* [2001] ECR I-1727; Case C-453/99, *Courage Ltd. v.*

important for the correct observance of EC law by the Member States are the established principles of practical possibility (national conditions and procedures should not make the exercise of Community rights impossible in practice), equivalence (the remedies and forms of action available to ensure the observance of national law must be made available in the same way to ensure the observance of Community law), as well as the requirement of proportionality of penalties.[293] Furthermore, as was established by the ECJ in the *Francovich* case[294] and further developed in *Brasserie du Pêcheur* and *Factortame III*,[295] a State may be held liable in damages under the principle of (State) liability for breach of EC law.[296]

6.3. ... And the European Commission Carries the Work Forward

The elaboration of the principle of effectiveness by the ECJ has given extra impulse to the European debate on private enforcement.[297] After *Courage Ltd. v. Crehan*, the Commission conceived the idea to stimulate natural and legal persons – this may be consumers or competitors – who are harmed as a result of anticompetitive behaviour, to obtain justice by asking for compliance of EC competition law in civil disputes before national courts.

Private enforcement of EC competition law can take different forms: private persons can for example claim nullity of an unlawful agreement, file an action for injunctive relief in order to stop the anticompetitive behaviour, or file an action for enforcement of a contract.[298] Most importantly however, especially in the context of the punitive damages debate, a private person may claim compensation for damages suffered.[299] The sanction of nullity is explicitly provided for by Article 81(2) EC itself.[300] Damages actions and actions for injunctive relief may either be based on Article 10 EC, or national conditions and procedures (following the ECJ case law on the effectiveness of directly applicable Community law mentioned above).[301] Furthermore, one must keep in mind that damages claims for anticompetitive behaviour can not only be based on EC competition law, but also on national competition law regimes.

In most Member States, claims for damages resulting from competition law infringements will be based on tort law. For example, the legal basis for bringing an action for damages in the Netherlands is the general tort provision, Article 6:162 BW.

Crehan [2001] ECR I-6297. See Craig & De Búrca 2003, pp. 239–253; Annex to Green Paper, at § 19–22.

293 Craig & De Búrca 2003, p. 232.

294 Cases C-6 & 9/90, *Francovich and Bonifaci v. Italy* [1991] ECR I-5357.

295 Cases C-46/93 & C-48/93 *Brasserie du Pêcheur SA v. Germany* and *R. v. Secretary of State for Transport ex parte Factortame Ltd. and others* [1996] ECR I-1029.

296 Craig & De Búrca 2003, pp. 257–267.

297 *Cf.* Kortmann & Sieburgh 2009, p. 249.

298 Annex to Green Paper, at § 16.

299 Cauffman & Weyts 2009, p. 303.

300 Article 81(2) EC: 'Any agreements or decisions prohibited pursuant to this Article shall be automatically void'.

301 Annex to Green Paper, at § 17.

Tort law has not (yet) been harmonised at European level. This means that there are to date 27 different legal systems for the private enforcement of EC competition law.[302]

From 2004, the Commission has taken three initiatives – which are all described in the contribution of Angela Ortega González – to identify the obstacles to private enforcement in the Member States and to find a way forward. First, the Ashurst report gives recommendations to facilitate private enforcement of Articles 81 and 82 EC (new Articles 101 and 102 TFEU), as the level of damages in competition law cases is too low and constitutes a disincentive to claimants.[303] An option to increase the level of damages is by introducing a form of punitive damages. Second, it appears from the Green Paper that the Commission seeks a more effective system of law enforcement – the national competition authorities and the Commission simply lack capacity to deal with all competition law infringements – which she believes can be achieved by means of civil actions for damages brought by private persons.[304]

Third, in the White Paper of 2008, which forms a reaction to the Green Paper, deliberations on punitive damages have not returned and the Commission has taken a more reserved position.[305] The Commission does not repeat its point of view with regard to double damages and the possible deterrent effect such damages may have. Instead, the focus of the White Paper is on *full compensation* of victims of anticompetitive behaviour. However, one must not forget that the suggestions done by the Commission in the White Paper should be seen as the 'minimum necessary' to achieve the objective of effective enforcement of competition law to ensure full compensation of victims.[306] With regard to damages actions, this means that 'the *acquis communautaire* on the definition of damages should be codified as a minimum standard'.[307] Similar to the ECJ, the Commission leaves the choice for the introduction of a form of punitive damages in order to ensure this objective to the Member States.[308] Nonetheless, the Commission has pointed out already that the appropriateness of the current definition of damages must be reconsidered, in particular if the current situation in Europe does not change in the (near) future; it should then be considered what further incentives can be developed in order to ensure that victims of anticompetitive behaviour file their antitrust damages claim.[309]

The discussion on private enforcement of competition law has raised dust throughout Europe. More importantly, in the context of this book, it has stirred up the interest in punitive damages. Consequently, the private enforcement debate is seen as the immediate cause for the current attention for punitive damages. Private enforcement of public norms is thought about as a complement to public enforcement. Hence, we speak of a complementary form of law enforcement using private law mechanisms, which according to contemporary ideas could perhaps even work better if one has access to strong and

302 Boot 2008, p. 201.

303 Ashurst report 2004, p. 118 ff.

304 Green Paper, p. 1.

305 White Paper on Damages Actions for Breach of EC Antitrust Rules, COM (2008) 165.

306 *Ibid.*, at § 316.

307 *Ibid.*, at § 194.

308 *Ibid.*

309 *Ibid.*, at § 195.

effective remedies such as punitive damages. The next paragraph concerns the contributory cause, which has to do with the functions of tort law.

7. Changing Perspectives on the Functions of Tort Law

The contributory cause of increased European interest in punitive damages is closely related to the immediate cause: a similarity lies in the instrumental view on tort law. As stated above, there is growing attention for the need to improve tort law remedies so as to enable enforcement of *tort law* standards. From this perspective, tort law and the way in which tort law could be improved are considered as such. This entails that the primary focus is no longer on tort damages actions to fulfil a certain higher goal, *i.e.* private enforcement in general. Rather, the focus is on law enforcement *in* tort law.[310] In civil law countries, private law has its traditional remedies such as the action for damages, nullity, and termination of contract. The main remedy available in tort law is the action for damages to compensate the victim for harm suffered. Furthermore, where damage is impending the claimant may ask for the other important remedy to prevent future harm, namely injunctive relief.[311] However, the question has come to mind whether compensation of the victim, which is the traditional function of tort law in civil law countries, is still the most important function today. This paragraph will explain the contributory cause by looking into the changing perspectives, primarily in legal doctrine, on the functions of tort law in present day society. To start with, some tortuous situations for which punitive damages could especially be appropriate will be described.

7.1. Punitive Damages in Specific Tort Situations: Pressurize Wrongdoers?

While at European level the debate seems to be concentrated on law enforcement, at national level punitive damages are considered as potential mechanism for the enforcement of *tort law* standards. The debate concentrates on certain specific torts, such as the infringement of personality rights. A good example is that of illegitimate publications by the tabloid press as referred to above. The risk of high damages being imputed might urge tabloids to reconsider the contents of their publications. The example of the tabloid press has often been discussed in Dutch literature.[312] In the Netherlands, the debate on punitive damages is quite alive. There is on-going discussion whether the incorporation of the remedy into Dutch tort law is possible and desirable. In 1993, the Netherlands Comparative Law Association issued a consultative report on punitive damages.[313] The report has an optimistic outcome regarding the introduction of punitive damages.[314] The government however expressed doubts on punitive damages, due to fear for the rise of a so called claim culture.[315] Nonetheless, in political as well as academic

310 *Cf.* Van Boom 2006; Van Boom 2007b.
311 Von Bar 1998, p. 2.
312 E.g. Hartlief 2008, p. 776; Hartlief 2009a, p. 65; Giesen 2009, p. 310; Boukema 2008; Van Schaik 1999.
313 Bolt & Lensing 1993.
314 *Ibid.*, p. 84.
315 Kamerstukken II, 1998–1999, 26 630, nr. 1.

circles one is increasingly interested in the instrumental use of tort law.[316] Punitive damages may be useful, but more research into the subject is considered necessary.[317]

Other situations in which the tortfeasor is accused of calculated conduct (in Dutch: *lucratieve fouten*) to make profits in excess of compensation payable to the claimant are imaginable.[318] In England, such calculative conduct is a form of conduct that may give rise to punitive damages.[319]

Equally problematic are situations in which there is small chance that the tortfeasor will be sued (*lage veroordelingskans*).[320] A small chance of being sued exists, for instance, if the damage caused by a single tortfeasor is vast and widespread, whereas the harm to each individual victim is very small (*strooischade*).[321] None of the victims is likely to bring a civil action for damages because of apathy or lack of interest. The risk of punitive damages being imposed, in all likelihood through a collective action, may then serve as a deterrent for potential tortfeasors.

To conclude, one might also think of other situations in which a stronger incentive such as punitive damages might be appropriate. What to do for example with failing governmental supervisors resulting in (economic) disasters, or insurers who fail to give their clients what they are entitled to?[322] In these situations, questions relating to law enforcement and punitive damages arise. Furthermore, as mentioned in paragraph 2, in American tort law punitive damages are not available for each tort. On the contrary, a certain conduct and state of mind of the defendant is needed, such as outrageous conduct, evil motive, reckless indifference of the rights of others etc. It may be justified, both for deterrence reasons and to take account of the victim's needs, to award punitive damages if the nature of the infringement (*aard van de normschending*) is clearly inadmissible, *i.e.* when the legal norm has been breached in a very serious or grave manner. An example is the Dutch case of a father who claimed damages for the nervous shock that he suffered as a result of the horrifying murder of his daughter by her husband; it has been suggested that also private law should respond firmly to such grave infringements.[323] A recent Dutch example where punitive damages could be appropriate is that of a women whose healthy leg has been amputated due to grave mistakes by the doctor in attendance as well as the hospital.[324] The woman, who emphasises that she wants to prevent hospitals from making similar mistakes again, claims civil damages of € 1.5 million, of which € 1 million in immaterial damages. She is however confronted with the limits of the Dutch tort and

316 Not everyone agrees, for example Kortmann 2009, p. 19 *et seq.*

317 *Cf.* Bolt & Lensing 1993; Hartlief 1997; Van Boom 2006; Barendrecht 2002.

318 *Cf.* Van der Heijden 2001; Cauffman 2007, p. 785.

319 *Rookes v. Barnard* [1964] 1 All England Law Reports (All ER) 367. The House of Lords has identified three categories in which punitive damages can be awarded: (1) oppressive, arbitrary or unconstitutional action by government servants, (2) conduct calculated by the defendant to make a profit in excess of compensation payable to the plaintiff; and (3) express statutory authorization.

320 Kerkmeester 1998; Barendrecht 2002, p. 607.

321 *Cf.* Tzankova 2005.

322 *Cf.* Smeehuijzen 2008.

323 Hartlief 2009b, p. 1710.

324 Tonia Wolters told her story in the Dutch current affairs programma Knevel & Van den Brink on Friday June 3, 2011. See www.eo.nl/programma/knevelenvandenbrink/2010-2011/page/programarchivepage.esp?programarchivepage=11858802 (last visited June 2011).

compensation system, as the maximum immaterial damages sum ever awarded in the Netherlands is €150,000.[325] Indeed, the Dutch judge has a restraint approach when it comes to awarding immaterial damages, also – and this is interesting – when compared to surrounding European countries. In Germany for example, relatively high immaterial damages awards have been granted to civil claimants.

Thus, several tort situations in which stronger enforcement mechanisms could be necessary are imaginable. However, the next paragraphs explain why punitive damages are not an option in this regard.

7.2. Compensation is Still the Primary Function

With reference to paragraph 3.2 on the traditional function of tort law, it is generally agreed that the primary function of tort law in European civil law systems is to compensate the injured person for the actual loss he has suffered and especially to point out in which situations there exists a right to such compensation.[326] If the injured person brings an action for damages and the court rules in his favour, the person held liable must restore him fully to the status that obtained prior to the injury (*restitutio in integrum).* In most European countries, the principle of *restitutio in integrum* is adopted as the starting point, although there are exceptions. In Austria for example, the extent of compensation is determined in general by the degree of fault (according to §1324 ABGB).[327] Furthermore, international conventions (for example in the field of transport law, such as the Warsaw Convention) and national (strict liability) rules sometimes impose caps on damages awards.[328]

Under the classical theory, tort law has certain positive side effects such as loss spreading and loss allocation, restitution (an example of restitutionary damages in Dutch law is Article 6:104 BW, providing that the profits made by the tortfeasor may influence the extent of compensation), satisfaction, declaration of right, prevention, law enforcement, retribution and even punishment. Although these are *additional* side effects that cannot exclusively form the basis of a damages award, it seems unwise to neglect such contributory functions and to focus merely on the compensatory function of tort law.[329] An important reason for this is that victims may have needs that go beyond mere compensation. Research shows that satisfaction and retribution play an important role for victims of a tort to come to terms with a bad experience.[330] One also has to keep in mind that there is increased attention for private enforcement to complement other enforcement mechanisms, and that the tort system interacts and competes with other compensation schemes (social security and insurance, private first party insurance). There are doubts as to whether tort law is useful when compensation is regarded as its

325 Rb. 's Hertogenbosch 11 April 2007, JA 2007, 99 (man becomes gravely handicapped due to attempted murder); Lindenbergh 2008, p. 77.

326 Van Gerven, Lever & Larouche 2000, p. 740; Magnus 2001b, p. 185; Koziol *et al.* 2005, p. 152.

327 Koziol 2001, p. 8; Koziol *et al.* 2005, p. 153.

328 Magnus 2001b, p. 188; Koziol *et al.* 2005, p. 153.

329 Hartlief 1997, p. 16 ff.; Hartlief 2009a, p. 117; Magnus 2001b, p. 185.

330 See, for the Netherlands, e.g.: Chao-Duivis 1990; Huver *et al.* 2007; Akkermans *et al.* 2008; Mulder 2009; Mulder 2010.

primary and only aim, for the reason that social security law or private insurance may be better tools to achieve this goal. However, the mere reliance on social security or private insurance to obtain compensation would lead to undesirable situations and abuse of the system, as the occurrence of damage would then be the only decisive factor for compensation, no matter who caused the damage and under what circumstances.[331] Yes, compensation is an important function of tort law, but its utility goes further: some value must also be attached to the preventive function.

Most modern legal systems offer protection to victims of accidents on the basis of social security combined with tort law – if there has been involvement of a liable tortfeasor – and private insurance. The role of tort law in this respect should certainly not be underestimated and perhaps even strengthened, keeping in mind the retreat of the Welfare State that has started in recent years due to financial crises and overspending of governments.[332] The next paragraph will go further into the preventive function of tort law.

7.3. But… the Economic Analysis of Tort Law Steps In

Under the influence of law and economics scholars, especially the preventive function of tort law has become increasingly important over the past decennia. Because of the economic implications of damages in tort, (micro) economics models can be applied to tort law so to explain tort rules in terms of economic efficiency.[333] Economic analyses of tort law were developed more than half a century ago in the United States. That is obviously no accident, as damages in tort have always played a central role in American society. According to Calabresi (senior judge of the U.S. Court of Appeals for the 2nd Circuit and one of the founders of the law and economics theory), the central objective of tort law is minimization of the social costs of a tort, *i.e.* the total accident costs, administration costs, costs of properly allocating accident losses by way of insurance, and accident prevention costs of the tortfeasor and the victim.[334] The idea behind the traditional law and economics approach to tort law is to strive for maximum utility, with the intention of achieving social welfare (welfare economics). Later, the influence of behavioural economics became apparent. It is nowadays believed that tort law may influence the conduct of rational and reasonable individuals like tortfeasors and victims (also known as the neo-classical model of tort law).[335] By giving economic incentives to potential tortfeasors to avoid damage, tort law has an economic function in contributing

331 Magnus 2006, p. 722, referring to Faure M.G. & Hartlief T., 'Social Security versus Tort Law as Instruments to Compensate Personal Injuries: A Dutch Law and Economics Perspective', in: U. Magnus (ed.), *The Impact of Social Security Law on Tort Law*, Vienna: Springer, 2003.

332 Magnus 2006, p. 722.

333 Among the founders of the tort law and economics movement are Ronald H. Coase, Guido Calabresi and Richard A. Posner. *Cf.* Faure 2009, p. xxiv. The contribution in this book of Louis Visscher gives a profound analysis of the law and economics of punitive damages: Louis Visscher, *The Law and Economics of Punitive Damages*.

334 Schäfer & Müller-Langer 2009, p. 4.

335 Faure 2009, p. xxv; Magnus 2006, p. 721.

to public welfare. According to Magnus: 'in the interest of preventing damage, it should not be cheaper to cause damage than to avoid it'.[336]

Although the economic analysis of tort law is often criticised by lawyers, it has been argued that relating theories were created by them.[337] An example is the Learned Hand formula, designed by the American judge Hand in 1947 to determine the optimal standard of care in the tort of negligence.[338] According to judge Hand, a tortfeasor should be held liable if the burden (B) to take adequate precautionary measures is less than the probability (P) that an accident occurs, multiplied by the gravity of the injury (L) (thus: $B < PL$). The required level of care is that of a reasonable person under the given circumstances.[339] Also within tort law systems in Europe, instruments to assess the sufficiency of preventive measures have been developed.[340] At the very least, also for jurists prevention thus plays a role as (subsidiary) function of tort law.

7.4. *Prevention in 'European' Tort Law*

Most European countries indeed accept prevention or deterrence as a desirable side effect of tort law.[341] Liability to pay damages may lead to special prevention of a particular tortfeasor and to general prevention of the public at large.[342] The preventive function – at least to some extent – of damages in tort is explicitly recognised in, for example, Austria, France, England, Belgium, Germany, and the Netherlands.[343] However, in none of the European countries, damages may be awarded for a preventive purpose only.[344] In other words, the damages award should in any case have a compensatory objective.

It follows also from the existence of the injunctive relief remedy that 'preventive legal protection' is an established element of tort law.[345] The idea behind injunctions is that it

336 Magnus 2001b, p. 186.

337 Schäfer & Müller-Langer 2009, p. 6.

338 *United States v. Carroll Towing Co.*, 159 F.2d 169 (2d Cir. 1947), at § 173.

339 *Ibid.*, at § 174.

340 Van Maanen, Townend & Teffera make a comparison to the formula that was developed by the Dutch Supreme Court in 1965 (*Kelderluik*, HR 5 november 1965, NJ 1966, 136). In this case, the court developed certain factors, *i.e.* relevant viewpoints to determine if an individual has created certain endangered circumstances (in Dutch: *gevaarzettende situaties*) for which adequate precautionary measures are required. Similar factors to determine the standard of care in situations of increased risk have been created in England, France and Germany. Even the 'European standard of care', as recommended in the *Principles of European Tort Law* that were developed for the purpose of harmonizing tort law, is composed in a similar way: PETL, Article 4:102 ('The required standard of conduct is that of the reasonable person in the circumstances, and depends, in particular, on the nature and value of the protected interest involved, the dangerousness of the activity, the expertise to be expected of a person carrying it on, the foreseeability of the damage, the relationship of proximity or special reliance between those involved, as well as the availability and the costs of precautionary or alternative methods'). Van Maanen, Townend & Teffera 2008, pp. 871–888.

341 Koziol *et al.* 2005, p. 153.

342 Magnus 2006, p. 720; Koziol 2001, p. 7.

343 Koziol 2001, p. 5; Galand-Carval 2001, p. 78; Rogers 2001, p. 53; Cousy & Vanderspikken 2001, p. 27; Wissink & Van Boom 2001, p. 144; Magnus 2001a, p. 89.

344 Magnus 2001b, p. 186.

345 Von Bar 1998, p. 2, fn. 3; Von Bar 2000, p. 141 ff.

is better to prevent damage than to compensate it. Injunctions are available in European countries for different interests protected by tort law standards, but are most often used to protect land, business interests, and personality rights.[346] Especially in the latter situation, think of libel and infringements of the private sphere, where money can sometimes not compensate the injustice done to a victim, injunctive relief may be an effective remedy.[347]

The preventive goal of damages in tort has not remained unnoticed in European harmonizing efforts. Article 10:101 Principles of European Tort Law ('PETL') emphasises that damages aim at compensation as well as prevention of harm.[348]

According to the PETL commentary, preventing harm means that 'by the prospect of the imposition of damages a potential tortfeasor is forced or at least encouraged to avoid harm to others'.[349] Not only does the liability of the tortfeasors to pay damages result in compensation of the victim for his loss, it also serves – or in any case should serve – as a deterrent.[350] The principles prepared by the study group on a European Civil Code (DCFR) also pay attention to the preventive function of tort law, but focus more on the right to prevention of damage as such.[351]

While the preventive function of tort law, including damages in tort, has been accepted in European legal systems, a punitive purpose of tort law is refused in most European countries.[352] Punitive damages that are disproportionate to the actual loss and only aim at punishment of the tortfeasor are clearly not allowed by the PETL. To support the argument against punitive damages, a reference is made to the preamble of Regulation 864/2007 on the law applicable to non-contractual obligations (Rome II), which reads as follows:

> '... In particular, the application of a provision of the law designated by this Regulation which would have the effect of causing noncompensatory exemplary or punitive damages of an excessive nature to be awarded may, depending on the circumstances of the case and the legal order of the Member State of the court seised, be regarded as being contrary to the public policy (*ordre public*) of the forum'.[353]

The Commentary to Article 10:101 PETL concludes however that 'the borderline between the aim of prevention and the aim of punishment may be sometimes difficult to draw'.[354] The preventive effect of mere compensation is open to discussion (*cf. Von Colson and Kamann v. Land Nordrhein-Westfalen* as referred to above), which leads to increased

346 Von Bar 2000, p. 143.
347 *Ibid.*, p. 144.
348 PETL, Article 10:101.
349 Koziol *et al.* 2005, p. 150.
350 Law and economics theories do not refer to prevention as a side effect of tort law: the economic analysis of tort law pays considerable attention to prevention as main function.
351 Von Bar, *Principles of European Law – Non-Contractual Liability Arising out of Damage Caused to Another*, Munich: Sellier, 2009, Articles 1:101, 1:102, 1:103, 2:101, 6:101, 6:301.
352 Koziol *et al.* 2005, p. 150.
353 Regulation (EC) No 864/2007, 11 July 2007, at § 32.
354 Koziol *et al.* 2005, p. 150.

attention for the additional functions of tort law, especially deterrence and punishment, in Continental Europe. It is noteworthy, at least, that these additional functions are in American tort law to a large extent performed by the punitive damages remedy. This could be a plausible explanation for the growing interest in punitive damages in European legal systems.

8. The *Status Quo* and the Road Ahead

This final paragraph will briefly reflect on the *status quo* of the European punitive damages debate, and also on questions and possibilities that could arise in the road ahead.

Punitive damages are a point of debate in Europe, both at EC and at national level. The increased European interest in punitive damages can be partly explained by the attention paid to private enforcement of competition law. As competition law forms only a part of EC law (albeit a fundamental part that concerns the European economy as a whole) the question is whether the implications of the above mentioned competition law cases extend to breaches of other directly effective EC law. The ECJ already made reference to the development of a broader principle for the future in *Brasserie du Pêcheur.*[355] And not only the ECJ, but also the Commission has referred to the development of a broader principle:

> 'The Commission acknowledges that some of the problems identified in the Green Paper also occur in other areas of civil/tort litigation and that some of the suggestions of the White Paper might thus also be appropriate beyond the boundaries of antitrust damages actions. Where there is a need, a technical feasibility and a clear political will to adopt measures with a more horizontal scope, that route should therefore seriously be considered'.[356]

Indeed, the debate on private enforcement is no longer merely concentrated in the field of (EC) competition law. On both European and national level, one speaks already of private enforcement of antidiscrimination law, intellectual property law, environmental law, personality rights and consumer law.[357] The third part of this book contains contributions relating to punitive damages and special themes.

The question if compensation of the victim is still the most important function of tort law today forms the contributory cause for the current debate. If the functions of tort law change, the available remedies should perhaps change accordingly. The *status quo* of tort law in Continental European systems is that compensation is indeed the main function of tort law. However, there seems to be more demand and calls from society to strengthen law enforcement remedies and to react firmly to grave misconduct, also in civil cases. For that reason, thoughts of a strong civil sanction in the form of punitive damages should be kept in mind.

[355] Craig & De Búrca 2003, p. 263, referring to paragraph 22 of Brasserie du Pêcheur.
[356] Annex to White Paper, at § 312.
[357] Cauffman & Weyts 2009, pp. 308–359.

This contribution has also examined possible reasons for the absence of punitive damages in Continental Europe. As regards the first explanation, *i.e.* the traditional functions of tort law, it can be said that Continental European legal systems primarily accept a compensatory function of tort law. Furthermore, a punitive function of tort law is explicitly *not* accepted. Thus, the punitive damages remedy seems to be incompatible with the current functions of tort law in Continental Europe. However, one should keep in mind that this forms first and foremost a dogmatic and theoretical obstacle to punitive damages which does not necessarily need to have much practical effect. This is especially so as history tells us that the functions of tort law have always been subject to change and are dependable on social and political desires. Punitive damages would perhaps have existed in Continental Europe if the social and political desires would have been different there. In other words, despite their incompatibility with the functions of tort law, punitive damages could perhaps become part of private law in Continental Europe if this is considered a proper policy decision like in the American legal system. Moreover, the fact that punitive elements in private law already exist in Europe also does not correspond fully to the alleged functions of tort law.

A similar finding can be made with regard to the second explanation, namely the strict division between private and criminal law, which is another reason for the non-existence of punitive damages in Continental Europe. The private-criminal law distinction is in fact a dogmatic solution to deal with the organization of a certain legal system. Common lawyers who also know this distinction do not let it stand in their way when taking certain policy decisions. In other words: the availability of punitive damages in the American legal system is a matter of policy that is not hindered by the mere existence of important theoretical objections such as the private criminal division.

Likewise, other dogmatic arguments against punitive damages as well as the refusal of punitive damages on private international law grounds are, although justifiably given as reasons for the non-existence of punitive damages in Continental Europe, also merely theoretical obstacles which have been created by the legislator and could be overcome in practice if necessary.

However, the cause relating to the role of government does not only express a way of thinking but forms an actual barrier. Whereas the other explanations are primarily theoretical, the third reason is not theoretical but rather a matter of practice. There are several political, cultural and societal differences between the American legal system and European legal systems that explain the non-existence of punitive damages in the latter area and that may also form a serious impediment to incorporation of punitive damages there.

There seem to be no definite answers as to what exact role punitive damages should and could play in Continental Europe. This is of course connected to the 'system strangeness' (in Dutch: *systeemvreemdheid*) of the remedy and resulting difficulties surrounding the possible introduction of punitive damages in civil law countries.[358] However, with continuous debate going on for over ten years now, it is certainly time to do more research into the subject. The current state of affairs with regard to punitive

358 Hartlief 2009a, p. 67.

damages continues to raise questions. For example, the divergences between the Member States as regards 'compensation in excess of actual damage sustained' – with special reference made to punitive and exemplary damages – is even considered as one of the obstacles to the functioning of the internal market.[359]

But when it comes down to it the European legislator refers to the national legislator, whereas the latter also does not seem to know how to proceed. What can be said is that the phenomenon of punitive damages continuously crops up, in both European – particularly efforts to enforce and harmonise laws – and national debates. Several arguments to be receptive to an instrument such as punitive damages can be put forward, such as strengthening law enforcement, giving a clear signal via tort law for reasons of deterrence and compensation, and stimulating the functioning of the internal market. In 2008, the Institute for European Tort Law declared the following:

> 'With the growing discourse on the subject on the Continent, it seems worthwhile and even an urgency to discuss, thoroughly and on a comparative basis, the nature, role and suitability of punitive damages in tort law and private law in general'.[360]

As stated in the introduction, this book comes at the right time. In the following twenty inspiring contributions in which answers are given and questions are posed, the authors of this book give helpful views and insights that contribute to the current debate. To start with, seven common law jurists will share their punitive damages experience and practical knowledge with us in part one. These authors know the ins and outs of the legal remedy and are therefore best able to show the difficulties and pitfalls, but also the advantages and positivity that surround it. Then, in the second part of this book European authors critically describe the punitive damages debate from a national law point of view (*i.e.* Belgium, France, Germany and Spain). Furthermore, the punitive damages debate will be seen from a European law perspective, as well as from a private international law perspective. Part three of this book builds on the second part, and consists of several contributions describing punitive damages in relation to a special, contemporary theme.

In conclusion, this book will certainly give food for thought. Furthermore, it improves perception of the punitive damages debate and directs those who are looking for answers to the question whether 'Europe is missing out' towards a more substantiated solution, instead of the often heard scepticism based on simple lack of information and fear for the unknown.

359 This was a point of discussion in the Proposal for a Regulation of the European Parliament and the Council on the Law Applicable to Non-Contractual Obligations ('Rome II'), COM(2003) 427 final, p. 5.

360 ETL Conference on Punitive Damages held in Vienna on 17 November 2008; Koziol & Wilcox 2009, Preface.

Bibliography

Adriaanse 2007
Adriaanse, P.C., 'Private handhaving (van het mededingingsrecht) in opmars. Bespreking van het preadvies 'Privaatrechtelijke aspecten van het mededingingsrecht' van mr. W.A.J. van Lierop en mr. H.E. Pijnacker Hordijk voor de Vereniging voor Burgerlijk Recht', *NTBR*, 2007, pp. 314–320.

Adriaanse *et al.* 2008
Adriaanse, P.C., *et al.*, 'Het EVRM-kader voor invoering van punitive damages in mededingingszaken. Europese toestanden in het schadevergoedingsrecht?', *NTBR*, 2008, pp. 274–286.

Akkermans *et al.* 2008
Akkermans A.J. *et al.*, *Slachtoffers en aansprakelijkheid. Een onderzoek naar behoeften, verwachtingen en ervaringen van slachtoffers en hun naasten met betrekking tot het civiele aansprakelijkheidsrecht. Deel II, Affectieschade*, Den Haag: WODC, 2008.

American Jurisprudence 2d
Westlaw Online Database 2009.

Ashworth 2003
Ashworth, A., *Principles of Criminal Law*, Oxford: Oxford University Press, 2003.

Baker 2004
Baker, D.I., 'Revisiting History – What Have We Learned About Private Antitrust Enforcement That We Would Recommend To Others?', *Loy Consumer L Rev*, pp. 379–408.

Barendrecht 2002
Barendrecht, J.M., 'Aansprakelijkheid en welzijn', *NJB*, 2002, pp. 605–617.

Barzaghi 2005
Barzaghi, A., 'Recognition and Enforcement of United States Judgments in Italy', *N Y Int'l L Rev*, 2005, pp. 61–122.

Basedow 2007
Basedow, J., 'Introduction', in: J. Basedow (ed.), *Private enforcement of EC Competition Law*, Alphen aan de Rijn: Kluwer Law International, 2007.

Beer 2008
Beer, J.M., 'No win no fee, of waarom een Engels plantje in Nederlandse bodem niet gedijt', *TvVP*, 2008, pp. 136–139.

Behr 2003
Behr, V., 'Punitive Damages in American and German Law, Tendencies towards approximation of apparently irreconcilable concepts', *Chi – Kent L Rev*, 2003, pp. 105–161.

Berch 2010
Berch, J.J., 'The Need for Enforcement of U.S. Punitive Damages Awards by the European Union', *Minn J Int'l L*, 2010, pp. 55–106.

Blatt, Hammesfahr & Nugent 2008
Blatt, R.L., Hammesfahr, R.W., Nugent, L.S., *Punitive Damages, A State-By-State Guide to Law and Practice*, Eagan, MN: Thomson Reuters/West, 2008.

Bolt & Lensing 1993
Bolt, A.T. & Lensing, J.A.W., *Privaatrechtelijke boete*, Preadvies voor de Nederlandse Vereniging voor Rechtsvergelijking, Deventer: Kluwer, 1993.

Boot 2008
Boot, J., 'Privaatrecht & boete. Over double damages bij privaatrechtelijke handhaving van mededinging', *Ars Aequi*, 2008, pp. 200–208.

Bornstein *et al.* 2008
Bornstein, B.H. *et al.* (eds.), *Civil Juries and Civil Justice – Psychological & Legal Perspectives*, New York: Springer, 2008.

Boukema 2008
Boukema, 'Roddel, Schuld & Boete – Een pleidooi voor stevige schadevergoeding', *NJB* 2008, pp. 1464–1470.

Bruggeman 2010,
Bruggeman, V., *Compensating catastrophe victims – A comparative law and economics approach*, Alphen aan de Rijn: Kluwer Law International, 2010.

Burnham 2006
Burnham, W., *Introduction to the law and legal system of the United States*, St. Paul, MN: Thomson/West, 2006.

Buxbaum 2007
Buxbaum, H.L., 'Private Enforcement of Competition Law in the United States – of Optimal Deterrence and Social Costs', in: J. Basedow (ed.), *Private enforcement of EC Competition Law*, Alphen aan de Rijn: Kluwer Law International, 2007.

Carrington 2004
Carrington, P.D., 'The American Tradition of Private Law Enforcement', *German Law Journal*, 2004, pp. 1413–1429.

Cauffman 2007
Cauffman, C., 'Naar een punitief Europees verbintenissenrecht? Een rechtsvergelijkende studie naar de draagwijdte, de (grond)wettigheid en de wenselijkheid van het bestraffend karakter van het verbintenissenrecht'. *TPR*, 2007, pp. 799–873.

Cauffman 2009
Cauffman, C., 'Een model voor een Belgische class action? De advocatuur neemt het voortouw', *RW*, 2009, pp. 690–708.

Cauffman & Weyts 2009
Cauffman, C. & Weyts, B., 'Privaatrecht en rechtshandhaving', in: A. Scheltema *et al.*, *Preadviezen voor de Vereniging voor de Vergelijkende Studie van het Recht van België en Nederland 2009*, Den Haag: Boom Juridische Uitgevers, 2009.

Cavanagh 1987
Cavanagh, E.D., 'Detrebling Antitrust Damages: An Idea Whose Time Has Come?', *Tulane L Rev*, 1987, pp. 777–848.

Cavanagh 2005
Cavanagh, E.D., 'Antitrust Remedies Revisited', *Or L Rev*, 2005, pp. 147–226.

Centner 2008
Centner, T.J., *America's Blame Culture. Pointing Fingers and Shunning Restitution*, Durham, NC: Carolina Academic Press, 2008.

Chao-Duivis 1990
Chao-Duivis, M.A.B., 'Vergelding als schadevergoeding', *NJB*, 1990, pp. 513–520.

Clerk *et al.* 2006
Clerk, J.F. *et al.*, *Clerk and Lindsell on Torts*, London: Sweet & Maxwell, 2006.

Clermont & Eisenberg 1992
Clermont, K.M. & Eisenberg, T., 'Trial by Jury of Judge: Transcending Empiricism', *Cornell L Rev*, 1992, pp. 1124–1177.

Cooter 1989
Cooter, R.D., 'Punitive Damages for Deterrence: When and How Much?', *Ala L Rev*, 1989, pp. 1143–1196.

Corpus Juris Secundum
Westlaw Online Database 2009.

Corstens 2002
Corstens, G.J.M., *Het Nederlands strafprocesrecht*, Deventer: Kluwer, 2002.

Cousy & Vanderspikken 2001
Cousy, H.A. & Vanderspikken A., 'Damages under Belgian Law', in: U. Magnus (ed.), *Unification of Tort Law: Damages*, The Hague: Kluwer Law International, 2001.

Craig & De Búrca 2003
Craig, p. & De Búrca, G., *EU Law - Text, cases and materials*, Oxford: University Press, 2003.

Daniels & Martin 1990
Daniels, S. & Martin, J., 'Myth and Reality in Punitive Damages', *Minn L Rev*, 1990, pp. 1–64.

Deakin, Johnston & Markesinis 2008
Deakin, S., Johnston, A., Markesinis, B., *Markesinis and Deakin's Tort Law*, Oxford: Clarendon Press, 2008.

De Haan 1999
De Haan, P., *Recente ontwikkelingen in de verhouding publiek-/privaatrecht*, Amsterdam: Koninklijke Nederlandse Academie van Wetenschappen, 1999.

Dubber 2009
Dubber, M.D., 'Criminal law between Public and Private Law', available at SSRN: http://ssrn.com/abstract=1499538 (last visited July 2011), 2009, pp. 1–18.

Eisenberg *et al.* 1997
Eisenberg, T. *et al.*, 'The Predictability of Punitive Damages', *J Legal Stud*, 1997, pp. 623–661.

Eisenberg *et al.* 2002
Eisenberg, T. *et al.*, 'Juries, Judges, and Punitive Damages: An Empirical Study', *Cornell L Rev*, 2002, pp. 743–782.

Eisenberg *et al.* 2006
Eisenberg, T. *et al.*, 'Juries, Judges and Punitive Damages: Empirical Analyses Using the Civil Justice Survey of State Courts 1992, 1996 and 2001 Data', *J Empirical Legal Stud*, 2006, pp. 263–295.

Ellis 1982
Ellis, D.D., 'Fairness and Efficiency in the Law of Punitive Damages', *S Cal L Rev,* 1982 pp. 1–78.

Faure 2009
Faure, M.G. (ed.), *Tort Law and Economics*, Cheltenham: Edward Elgar Publishing, 2009.

Galand-Carval 2001
Galand-Carval, S., 'Damages under French Law', in: U. Magnus (ed.), *Unification of Tort Law: Damages*, The Hague: Kluwer Law International, 2001.

Galanter 1998
Galanter, M., 'Shadow Play: The Fabled Menace of Punitive Damages', *Wis L Rev*, 1998, pp. 1–14.

Giesen 2009
Giesen, I., 'Handhaving in, via, door en met het privaatrecht: waar staan we nu?', in: E.F.D. Engelhard *et al.* (eds.), *Handhaving van en door het privaatrecht, Vijftien bijdragen over handhaving van het privaatrecht en privaatrechtelijke handhaving*, Den Haag: Boom Juridische Uitgevers, 2009.

Gotanda 2007
Gotanda, J.Y., 'Charting Developments Concerning Punitive Damages: Is The Tide Changing?', *Colum J Transnat'l L*, 2007, pp. 507–528.

Green Paper
European Commission's Green Paper on Damages Actions for Breach of EC Antitrust Rules, COM (2005) 672; Commission Staff Working Paper Annex to the Green Paper SEC (2005) 1732.

Harris 1989
Harris, A.P., 'Rereading Punitive Damages: Beyond the Public/Private Distinction', *Ala L Rev*, 1989, pp. 1079–1116.

Hartlief 1997
Hartlief, T., *Ieder draagt zijn eigen schade*, Deventer: Kluwer 1997.

Hartlief 2005
Hartlief, T., 'Leven in een claimcultuur: wie is er bang voor Amerikaanse toestanden?', *NJB*, 2005, pp. 830–834.

Hartlief 2008
Hartlief, T., 'Handhaving in het aansprakelijkheidsrecht. Op weg naar een betere samenleving?', *WPNR*, 2008, pp. 769–777.

Hartlief 2009a
Hartlief, T., *Anno 2010*, Amsterdam: Uitgeverij deLex, 2009.

Hartlief 2009b
Hartlief, T., 'De schrik van het burgerlijk recht', *NJB*, 2009, p. 1710.

Hay 1992
Hay, P., 'The Recognition and Enforcement of American Money-Judgments in Germany – The 1992 Decision of the German Supreme Court', *Am J Comp L*, 1992, pp. 729–750.

Holmes 2004
Holmes, K., 'Public enforcement or private enforcement? Enforcement of competition law in the EC and UK', *ECLR*, 2004, pp. 25–36.

Howells 2000
Howells, G.G., 'The Relationship Between Product Liability and Product Safety – Understanding a Necessary Element in European Product Liability Through a Comparison with the U.S. position', *Washburn L J*, 2000, pp. 305–346.

Howells & Mildred 1998
Howells G.G. & Mildred M., 'Is European Products Liability more protective than the Restatement (third) of Torts: Products Liability?', *Tenn L Rev*, 1998, pp. 985–1030.

Howells & Wilhelmsson 1997
Howells G.G. & Wilhelmsson T., 'EC & US approaches to consumer protection – should the gap be bridged?', *Yearbook of European Law*, 1997, pp. 207–268.

Hubbard 2008
Hubbard, F.P., 'Substantive Due Process Limits on Punitive Damages Awards: "Morals Without Technique"', *Fla L Rev*, 2008, pp. 349–399.

Huver *et al.* 2007
Huver, R.M.E. *et al.*, Slachtoffers en aansprakelijkheid. Een onderzoek naar behoeften, verwachtingen en ervaringen van slachtoffers en hun naasten met betrekking tot het civiele aansprakelijkheidsrecht. Deel I, Terreinverkenning, Den Haag: WODC, 2007.

Jurgens & Van Ommeren 2009
Jurgens, G.T.J.M. & Van Ommeren, F.J., *De opmars van het onderscheid tussen publiekrecht en privaatrecht in het Engelse recht – Vanuit rechtsvergelijkend perspectief*, Den Haag: Boom Juridische uitgevers, 2009.

Kagan 2007
Kagan, R.A., 'American and European Ways of Law: Six Entrenched Differences', in: V. Gessner & D. Nelken (eds.), *European Ways of Law – Towards a European Sociology of Law*, Oxford: Hart Publishing, 2007.

Kerkmeester 1998
Kerkmeester, H.O., 'Punitive damages ter veroordeling van een lage veroordelingskans', *NJB*, 1998, pp. 1807–1813.

Kircher & Wiseman 2000a
Kircher, J.J. & Wiseman, C.M., *Punitive Damages Law and Practice, part 1*, Eagan, MN: Thomson/West, 2000.

Kircher & Wiseman 2000b
Kircher, J.J. & Wiseman, C.M., *Punitive Damages Law and Practice, part 2*, Eagan, MN: Thomson/West, 2000.

Klein 1999
Klein, S.R., 'Redrawing the Criminal-Civil Boundary', *Buff Crim L Rev*, 1999, pp. 679–721.

Koenig & Rustad 2001
Koenig, T.H. & Rustad, M.L., *In Defense of Tort Law*, New York: New York University Press, 2001.

Kortmann 2009
Kortmann, J., *The Tort Law Industry*, Amsterdam: Vossiuspers UvA, 2009.

Kortmann & Sieburgh 2009
Kortmann, J. & Sieburgh, C., 'Handhaving door Nederlands privaatrecht', in: A. Scheltema *et al.*, *Preadviezen voor de Vereniging voor de Vergelijkende Studie van het Recht van België en Nederland 2009*, Den Haag: Boom Juridische Uitgevers, 2009.

Koziol 2001
Koziol, H., 'Damages under Austrian Law', in: U. Magnus (ed.), *Unification of Tort Law: Damages*, The Hague: Kluwer Law International, 2001.

Koziol *et al.* 2005
Koziol, H. *et al.*, *European Group on Tort Law 2005, Principles of European Tort Law, Text and Commentary*, Vienna: Springer-Verlag, 2005.

Koziol 2008
Koziol, H., 'Punitive Damages – A European Perspective', *La L Rev*, 2008, pp. 741–764.

Koziol 2009
Koziol, H., 'Punitive Damages: Admission into the Seventh Legal Heaven or Eternal Damnation? Comparative Report and Conclusions', in: H. Koziol & V. Wilcox (eds.), *Punitive Damages: Common Law and Civil Law Perspectives*, Vienna: Springer, 2009.

Koziol & Wilcox 2009
Koziol, H. & Wilcox, V., *Punitive Damages: Common Law and Civil Law Perspectives*, Vienna: Springer, 2009.

Kuklin 1989
Kuklin, B., 'Punishment: the civil perspective of punitive damages', *Clev St L Rev*, 1989, pp. 1–118.

Landes & Posner 1975
Landes, W.M., & Posner, R.A., 'The Private Enforcement of Law', *J Legal Stud*, pp. 1–46.

Lindenbergh 2008
Lindenbergh, S.D., *Smartengeld, tien jaar later*, Deventer: Kluwer, 2008.

Magnus 2001a
Magnus, U., 'Damages under German Law', in: U. Magnus (ed.), *Unification of Tort Law: Damages*, The Hague: Kluwer Law International, 2001.

Magnus 2001b
Magnus, U., 'Comparative Report on the Law of Damages', in: U. Magnus (ed.), *Unification of Tort Law: Damages*, The Hague: Kluwer Law International, 2001.

Magnus 2006
Magnus, U., 'Tort Law in General', in: J.M. Smits (ed.), *Elgar Encyclopedia of Comparative Law*, Cheltenham: Edward Elgar Publishing, 2006.

Magnus 2010
Magnus, U., 'Why is US Tort Law so Different?', *JETL*, 2010, pp. 102–124.

Mallor & Roberts 1999
Mallor, J., & Roberts, B.S., 'Punitive Damages: On the Path to A Principled Approach?', *Hastings L J* 1999, pp. 1001–1014.

Mann 1992
Mann, 'Punitive Civil Sanctions: The Middleground between Criminal and Civil Law', *Yale L J*, 1992, pp. 1795–1873.

Morris 1931
Morris, C., 'Punitive Damages in Tort Cases', *Harv L Rev*, 1931, pp. 1173–1209.

Mulder 2009
Mulder, J.D.W.E., *Compensatie na geweld. Wie krijgen er een vergoeding van het Schadefonds Geweldsmisdrijven en wat zijn de effecten van zo'n financiële vergoeding*, Tilburg: Intervict/PrismaPrint, 2009.

Mulder 2010
Mulder, J.D.W.E., 'Hoe schadevergoeding kan leiden tot gevoelens van erkenning en gerechtigheid. Lessen uit de praktijk van het Schadefonds Geweldsmisdrijven', *NJB*, 2010, pp. 293–296.

Ostoni 2005
Ostoni, L., 'Italian Rejection of Punitive Damages in a U.S. Judgment', *J L & Com*, 2005, pp. 245–262.

Owen 1976
Owen, D.G., 'Punitive Damages in Products Liability Litigation', *Mich L Rev*, 1976, pp. 1257–1371.

Owen 1989
Owen, D.G., 'The Moral Foundations of Punitive Damages', *Ala L Rev*, 1989, pp. 705–739.

Owen 1994
Owen, D.G., 'A Punitive Damages Overview: Functions, Problems and Reform', *Vill L Rev*, 1994, pp. 363–413.

Owen 1997
Owen, D.G., *Philosophical Foundations of Tort Law*, New York: Oxford University Press, 1997.

Owen 2005
Owen, D.G., *Products Liability Law*, St. Paul, MN: Thomson/West, 2005.

Paulis 2007
Paulis, E.P., 'Policy Issues in the Private Enforcement of EC Competition Law', in: J. Basedow (ed.), *Private enforcement of EC Competition Law*, Alphen aan de Rijn: Kluwer Law International, 2007.

Polinsky & Shavell 2005
Polinsky, A.M., & Shavell, S., 'The Theory of Public Enforcement of Law', Harvard Law School John M. Olin Center for Law, Economics and Business Discussion Paper Series, Paper 529, 2005.
Available at http://lsr.nellco.org/harvard_olin/529 (last visited July 2011).

Quarta 2008
Quarta, F., 'Recognition and Enforcement of U.S. Punitive Damages Awards in Continental Europe: The Italian Supreme Court's Veto', *Hastings Int'l & Comp L R*, 2008, pp. 753–782.

Redish & Mathews 2004
Redish, M.H. & Mathews, A.L., 'Why Punitive Damages are Unconstitutional', *Emory L J*, 2004, pp. 1–54.

Reed & Fitzpatrick 2006
Reed, A. & Fitzpatrick, B., *Criminal Law*, London: Sweet & Maxwell, 2006.

Reimann 2003
Reimann, M., 'Product Liability in a Global Context: the Hollow Victory of the European Model', *ERPL*, 2003, pp. 128–154.

Requejo Isidro 2009
Requejo Isidro, M., 'Punitive Damages From a Private International Law Perspective', in: H. Koziol & V. Wilcox (eds.), *Punitive Damages: Common Law and Civil Law Perspectives*, Vienna: Springer, 2009.

Restatement of Torts
Restatement (Second) of Torts 1979.

Robbennolt 2002
Robbennolt, J.K., 'Determining Punitive Damages: Empirical Insights and Implications for Reform', *Buff L Rev*, 2002, pp. 103–203.

Rogers 2001
Rogers, W.V.H., 'Damages under English Law', in: U. Magnus (ed.), *Unification of Tort Law: Damages*, The Hague: Kluwer Law International, 2001.

Rogers 2006
Rogers, W.V.H., *Winfield and Jolowicz on Tort,* London: Sweet & Maxwell, 2006.

Rouhette 2007
Rouhette, T., 'The Availability of Punitive Damages in Europe: Growing Trend or Nonexistent concept?', *Defense Counsel Journal*, 2007, pp. 320–342.

Rustad & Koenig 1993
Rustad, M. & Koenig, T., 'The Historical Continuity of Punitive Damages Awards: Reforming the Tort Reformers', *Am U L Rev*, 1993, pp. 1269–1333.

Ryan 2003
Ryan, P.S., 'Revisiting the United States Application of Punitive Damages: Separating Myth from Reality', *ILSA J Int'l & Comp L*, 2003, pp. 69–93.

Schäfer & Müller-Langer 2009
Schäfer, H-B. & Müller-Langer, F., 'Strict Liability versus Negligence', in: M.G. Faure (ed.), *Tort Law and Economics*, Cheltenham: Edward Elgar Publishing, 2009.

Schlueter 2005a
Schlueter, L.L., *Punitive Damages – Volume 1*, LexisNexis 2005.

Schlueter 2005b
Schlueter, L.L., *Punitive Damages – Volume 2*, LexisNexis 2005.

Sebok 2007
Sebok, A.J., 'Punitive Damages: From Myth to Theory', *Iowa L Rev*, 2007, pp. 957–1036.

Sebok 2009
Sebok, A.J., 'Punitive Damages in the United States', in: H. Koziol & V. Wilcox (eds.), *Punitive Damages: Common Law and Civil Law Perspectives*, Vienna: Springer, 2009.

Slok & Van 1990
Slok, W.M.K. & Van, A.J., 'De Privaatrechtelijke boete en artikel 6:106 Nieuw BW', *NJB*, 1990, pp. 1823–1829.

Smeehuijzen 2008
Smeehuijzen, J.L., 'Schadevergoeding wegens onzorgvuldige afwikkeling van letselschadevorderingen', *NTBR*, 2009, pp. 328–340.

Spruit 2001
Spruit, J.E., *Cunabula iuris - Elementen van het Romeinse privaatrecht*, Deventer: Kluwer, 2001.

Sunstein *et al.* 2003
Sunstein, C.R. *et al.*, *Punitive Damages - How Juries Decide*, Chicago: The University of Chicago Press, 2003.

Tzankova 2005
Tzankova, I.N., *Strooischade: Een verkennend onderzoek naar een nieuw rechtsfenomeen* (Allen Overy Onderzoeksreeks), Den Haag: SDU, 2005.

Van Boom 2006
Van Boom, W.H., *Efficacious Enforcement in Contract and Tort*, Den Haag: Boom Juridische Uitgevers, 2006.

Van Boom 2007a
Van Boom, W.H., 'On the Intersection between Tort Law and Regulatory Law - A Comparative Analysis', in: W.H. Van Boom, M. Lukas, & C. Kissling (eds.), *Tort and Regulatory Law*, Vienna: Springer-Verlag, 2007.

Van Boom 2007b
Van Boom, W.H., 'Effectuerend Handhaven in het Privaatrecht', *NJB*, 2007, pp. 982–991.

Van Dam 2006
Van Dam, C., *European Tort Law*, Oxford: Oxford University Press, 2006.

Van der Heijden 2001
Van der Heijden, E.M., 'Punitive damages en de calculerende schadeveroorzaker', *NJB*, 2001, pp. 1749–1756.

Van Gerven, Lever & Larouche 2000
Van Gerven, W. Lever J. & Larouche, P., *Tort Law*, Oxford: Hart Publishing, 2000.

Van Maanen, Townend & Teffera 2008
Van Maanen, G.E., Townend, D., Teffera, A., 'The Dutch 'Cellar Hatch' Judgment as a Landmark Case fort Tort Law in Europe: A Brief Comparison with English, French and German Law with a Law and Economics Flavour', *ERPL*, 2008, pp. 871–889.

Van Schaik 1999
Van Schaik, R., 'De calculerende pers. Smartengeld bij onrechtmatige perspublicaties', *Mediaforum* 1999, pp. 169–173.

Von Bar 1998
Von Bar, C., *The Common European Law of Torts, Vol. 1: The core areas of tort law, its approximation in Europe, and its accommodation in the legal system*, Oxford: Oxford Clarendon Press, 1998.

Von Bar 2000
Von Bar, C., *The Common European Law of Torts, Vol. 2: Damage and damages, liability for and without personal misconduct, causality, and defences*, Oxford: Oxford University Press, 2000.

Von Mehren & Murray 2007
Von Mehren, A.T., Murray, P.L., *Law in the United States*, Cambridge: Cambridge University Press, 2007.

Verkerk 2010
Verkerk, R.R., *Fact-Finding in Civil Litigation, A Comparative Perspective*, Antwerp: Intersentia, 2010.

Wells 2010
Wells, M.L., 'A Common Lawyer's Perspective on the European Perspective on Punitive Damages', *La L Rev*, 2010, pp. 557–578.

White 2003
White, G.E., *Tort Law in America*, Oxford: Oxford University Press, 2003.

White Paper
European Commission's White Paper on Damages Actions for Breach of EC Antitrust Rules, COM (2008) 165.

Wilcox 2009
Wilcox, V., 'Punitive Damages in England', in: H. Koziol & V. Wilcox (eds.), *Punitive Damages: Common Law and Civil Law Perspectives*, Vienna: Springer, 2009.

Wissink & Van Boom 2001
Wissink, M.H. & Van Boom, W.H., 'Damages under Dutch Law', in: U. Magnus (ed.), *Unification of Tort Law: Damages*, The Hague: Kluwer Law International, 2001.

Yeazell 2008
Yeazell, S.C., *Civil Procedure*, New York: Aspen Law & Business, 2008.

Zimmermann 1992
Zimmermann, R., *The Law of Obligations, Roman Foundations of the Civilian Tradition*, Deventer: Kluwer, 1992.

Zippro 2009
Zippro, E.-J., *Privaatrechtelijke Handhaving van Mededingingsrecht*, Deventer: Kluwer, 2009.

PART I

PUNITIVE DAMAGES FROM A COMMON LAWYER'S PERSPECTIVE

Jim Gash*

UNDERSTANDING AND SOLVING THE MULTIPLE PUNISHMENTS PROBLEM

1. Introduction

The American tort system has a major and unresolved problem. State and federal courts, state and federal legislators, a wide array of commentators, and lawyers from both sides of the litigation table all agree that there is a problem. All also agree that there is currently no satisfactory solution, though as discussed herein, the United States Supreme Court has recently endeavoured to minimise this problem, but with only limited success. Briefly stated, this problem is how to handle situations where a defendant, who has injured multiple potential plaintiffs by a single act or course of conduct, faces multiple punitive damages awards for that conduct.[1] The so-called 'Multiple Punishments Problem'[2] (sometimes called 'Multiple Punitive Damages Problem')[3] has spawned (i) numerous majority and dissenting opinions in both state[4] and federal[5] courts, (ii) a variety of law

* Associate Professor, Pepperdine University School of Law, Malibu, California.

1 Unlike criminal law in the United States, civil defendants do not have the protection of the double jeopardy clause preventing multiple punishment for the same conduct. See *United States v. Halper*, 490 U.S. 435, 451 (1989) (declaring that the 'protections of the Double Jeopardy Clause are not triggered by litigation between private parties'). But see Schwarzer 1991, p. 116 ('Surely allowing successive awards of punitive damages for the same conduct is offensive to the most basic notions of due process and to the spirit underlying the constitutional bar against double jeopardy'.).

2 See, e.g., Colby 2003, p. 594.

3 See, e.g., Schwartz *et al.* 1999, p. 1032, n. 123.

4 See, e.g., *Ex parte* Holland, 696 So.2d 811, 816–19 (Ala. 1997) (pointing out the potential for the first plaintiff in a multiple-claimant tort case to impair the ability of the remaining members to protect their interests but refusing to use mandatory class actions to deal with the problem); *Ferguson v. Lieff, Cabraser, Heimann & Bernstein*, 69 P.3d 965, 1049–51 (Cal. 2003) (recognizing the unfairness of multiple punishment and suggesting a 'non-opt out' class action solution); *Spaur v. Owens-Corning Fiberglass Corp.*, 510 N.W.2d 854, 865 (Iowa 1994) (recognizing the seriousness of multiple punitive damages and calling for a national solution); *Loitz v. Renington Arms Co.*, 563 N.E.2d 397, 417 (Ill. 1990) (expressing concern for the imposition of multiple punitive damages and its effect on manufacturers and their economic contributions to society).

5 See, e.g., *Dunn v. Hovic*, 1 F.3d 1371, 1398 (3d Cir.) (Weis, J., dissenting) (noting that 'both state and federal courts have recognised that no single court can fashion an effective response to the national problem flowing from mass exposure to asbestos products'.), modified in part, 13 F.3d 58 (3d Cir. 1993); *Racich v. Celotex Corp.*, 887 F.2d 393, 396–99 (2d Cir. 1989) (declaring that a national rule on the issue of multiple punitive damages is necessary); *Roginsky v. Richardson-Merrell, Inc.*, 378 F.2d 832, 841–42 (2d Cir. 1967) (explaining the problem of multiple punitive damages and recognizing courts' limits in

review articles from leading commentators,[6] (iii) numerous state statutes,[7] (iv) multiple failed attempts at federal legislation,[8] and (v) a largely ineffective attempt at a remedy to this problem by the United States Supreme Court in its most recent punitive damages decisions.[9]

The multiple punishments problem was first identified in the 1960s by federal appellate judge Henry Friendly: 'The legal difficulties engendered by claims for punitive damages on the part of hundreds of plaintiffs are staggering'.[10] Nearly a half century later, the problem remains as 'staggering' in breadth, and the question of whether due process (or anything else) imposes any restraints on multiple punitive damages awards has been aptly characterised by Professor David Owen, a leading commentator on

solving the problem); *In re* N. Dist. of Cal. 'Dalkon Shield' IUD Prod. Liab. Litig., 526 F. Supp. 887, 895, 899–900 (N.D. Cal. 1981), vacated on other grounds, 694 F.2d 847 (9th Cir. 1982) (pointing out the potential abuse 'implicit in repeated awards of punitive damages'); *McBride v. Gen. Motors Corp.*, 737 F. Supp. 1563, 1569–70 (M.D. Ga. 1990) (struggling with a resolution to multiple punitive damages against the same defendant); *Campbell v. ACands, Inc.*, 704 F. Supp. 1020, 1022–23 (D. Mont. 1989) (declaring that the 'continued imposition of punitive damages serves no purpose within the contemplation of the statutory or common law of Montana authorizing punitive damages'); *Juzwin v. Amtorg Trading Corp.*, 718 F. Supp. 1233, 1234–35 (D.N.J. 1989) (holding that multiple punitive damages violate due process in certain circumstances).

6 See, e.g., Prosser 1971, p. 13 (warning that the multiple punitive damages problem 'might well lead to a re-examination of the whole basis and policy of awarding punitive damages'.); Colby 2003, *supra* note 2, p. 594 ('Numerous commentators have bemoaned this risk of unfair piling on, dubbing it the 'multiple punishment' problem'); Denemark 2002, pp. 932–34 (describing the multiple punitive damages problem and pointing out the inadequacy of any single court or state legislature to combat it); Jeffries 1986, p. 142 (recognizing the threat multiple punitive damage awards pose on the viability of business entities); Owen 1982a, pp. 44–47, 50 (explaining the problems of measurement and control of punitive damages especially in products liability litigation); Seltzer 1983, pp. 51–52 (discussing the emergence and existing problem of multiple punitive damages).

7 See, e.g., Fla. Stat. § 768.73(2)(a)-(b) (2011) (disallowing punitive damages in situations where the defendant has previously been assessed punitive damages for the same act or single course of conduct); Ga. Code Ann. § 51-12-5.1(e)(1) (2011) (allowing only one award of punitive damages for any act or omission arising from product liability); Minn. Stat. § 549.20(3) (2011) (using other punitive and compensatory awards against a defendant as a factor in determining a punitive damage award); Mo. Ann. Stat. § 510.263(4) (West 2011) (requiring that defendant be credited with a prior punitive damage award by the amount previously paid for the same conduct).

8 An early attempt to introduce punitive damages reform occurred in 1984. See S. 44, 98th Cong., 2d Sess. § 12 (1984). Members of the American Bar Association rejected this proposal declaring, '[W]e have rejected much more radical suggestions that have been made, such as allowing only one punitive damages award & then deeming the company sufficiently punished. Such a provision was at one time part of proposed federal product legislation but eventually dropped as patently unfair, since the first verdict might be a small one or one maneuvered by the defendant'. A.B.A. Report of the Special Comm. on Punitive Damages, *Punitive Damages: A Constructive Examination* 78–81 (1986) (citing the 1984 proposal) [hereinafter A.B.A. Report]. Still later attempts were made. See The Multiple Punitive Damages Fairness Act, S. 5148–49, 104th Cong. (1995); see also The Multiple Punitive Damages Fairness Act of 1997, S. 454–55, 105th Cong. (1997).

9 See *State Farm Mut. Auto. Ins. Co. v. Campbell*, 538 U.S. 408, 423 (2003) (strongly implying that due process imposes limits on multiple punitive damages awards); *Philip Morris USA v. Williams*, 549 U.S. 346 (2007) (attempting to curb the impact of the multiple punishments problem).

10 *Roginsky v. Richardson-Merrell, Inc.*, 378 F.2d 832, 839 (2d Cir. 1967).

punitive damages, as 'the most momentous question as yet unresolved by the Court'.[11] Senator Orrin Hatch of Utah, a staunch supporter of tort reform, has declared the multiple punishments problem 'one of the most egregious and unconscionable... abuses and excesses in our civil justice system'.[12] Even well-known Harvard Law School Professor Laurence Tribe, a long and fervent supporter of punitive damages,[13] concedes that due process ought to limit in some way the recovery of multiple punitive damages awards for the same conduct through 'some double jeopardy-like doctrine'.[14] Adding their voices to the chorus are the highly respected American Law Institute,[15] the American Bar Association,[16] and the American College of Trial Lawyers.[17] Yet the solution to this ongoing problem has proven elusive.[18] All quarters involved in attempting to solve the problem agree, however, that a comprehensive solution can only be accomplished on a national, rather than state, level.[19] A potential solution to this problem previously advocated by the author of this chapter involves passing federal legislation that, *inter alia*, creates a National Punitive Damages Registry (hereinafter 'Registry').[20] This solution can, and perhaps should, be adapted for use by European countries.

Under such a proposal, a defendant who causes injury to multiple plaintiffs through a single act or course of conduct would be eligible to file a Prior Punitive Damages Statement (hereinafter 'Statement') with the Registry after either (i) a punitive damages verdict is entered against the defendant, or (ii) a settlement that includes a punitive

11 Owen 1994, p. 406. See also Colby 2003, *supra* note 2, p. 587 (characterizing the multiple punishments problem as 'the single most discussed and debated issue in the law of punitive damages'); Sharkey 2003, p. 432 ('The multiple punishments problem has confounded jurists and scholars for the better part of the past three decades'.); Schwartz 2003, pp. 8–9 ('A major problem in our liability system is the multiple imposition of punitive damages'.).

12 143 Cong. Rec. S454 (1997) (statement of Sen. Hatch).

13 Professor Tribe has argued numerous cases in support of punitive damages awards. See, e.g., *State Farm*, 538 U.S. 408 (2003) (arguing for respondent that punitive damages were not excessive); *Honda Motor Co., Ltd. v. Oberg*, 512 U.S. 415 (1994) (arguing for respondents seeking to uphold the punitive damages award); *TXO Prod. Corp. v. Alliance Res. Corp.*, 509 U.S. 443 (1993) (arguing for respondents seeking to uphold the punitive damages award).

14 See Transcript of Oral Argument, *State Farm Mut. Auto. Ins. Co. v. Campbell*, No. 01-1289, at *35 (U.S. Dec. 11, 2002) (colloquy between Justice Stevens and Professor Tribe).

15 2 A.L.I., *Reporters' Study, Enterprise Responsibility for Personal Injury* 260–65, 412–39 (1991) [hereinafter A.L.I. Report].

16 A.B.A. Report, *supra* note 8, pp. 78–81.

17 American College of Trial Lawyers 1989, pp. 20–26.

18 Accord Owen 1994, *supra* note 11, p. 383 (lamenting that 'this very serious problem of repetitive punitive damages awards remains to date a problem without a satisfactory judicial or legislative resolution'.).

19 See, e.g., The Multiple Punitive Damages Fairness Act of 1997, *supra* note 8, S. 454 ('The only effective means of addressing these problems is through a nationwide solution, which the legislation I introduce today would provide'.) (Statement of Sen. Hatch); *Dunn v. Hovic*, 1 F.3d 1371, 1398 (3d Cir.) (noting that 'both state and federal courts have recognised that no single court can fashion an effective response to the national problem flowing from mass exposure to asbestos products'), modified in part, 13 F.3d 58 (3d Cir. 1993).

20 See Gash 2005. The proposal outlined in this chapter was first published in the Northwestern Law Review, and portions of this chapter rely heavily upon the research and analysis reflected in that article.

damages component is reached between the defendant and one or more of the plaintiffs. Following such a verdict or settlement, the defendant would prepare the Statement, which would include a detailed description of the conduct for which the defendant was being punished and the amount of such punishment, and then would move the trial court for an order certifying the Statement. The trial court would then certify the Statement after ensuring that it fairly and accurately describes the conduct at issue and accurately reflects the amount of punitive damages being paid. The defendant would then file the certified Statement with the Registry, which would then immediately post the Statement on a publically accessible web site for all to see. Once the Statement was posted on the Registry, the defendant would be entitled to a dollar-for-dollar credit against any future punitive damages verdicts entered against that defendant based upon the conduct described in the Statement listed on the Registry. To receive this credit, the defendant would have to prove by clear and convincing evidence (i) that it had been punished for the same conduct at issue, and (ii) the amount of such punishment. Participation in the Registry would be entirely voluntary at the option of the defendant. Failure to file a Statement with the Registry after a punitive damages verdict or settlement, however, would waive a defendant's entitlement to a credit against future punitive damages awards. A variety of procedural mechanisms would ensure the effective and efficient application of this proposal by both state and federal courts.

Not only would this proposal fully resolve the multiple punishments problem because it would be national in scope, but it would also advance each of the public policies underlying punitive damages theory. This proposal has the added benefit of preempting any further action by a United States Supreme Court that has repeatedly (if not clumsily) attempted to alter the punitive damages landscape in recent years[21] and has strongly implied that it considers multiple punitive damages awards to violate due process, at least in some (as yet undefined) circumstances.[22]

Part 2 of this chapter traces the history of the multiple punishments problem, explaining why this problem is of relatively recent origin and outlining the responses and various failed attempts to resolve this problem offered by courts,[23] legislatures,[24] and commentators.[25] Part 3 outlines a proposal to solve this problem, which includes the creation of a National Punitive Damages Registry and the procedural mechanisms necessary to make the proposal a workable solution.[26]

21 See Gash 2004, p. 1191 (chronicling the Supreme Court's modifications of punitive damages jurisprudence over the past fifteen years).

22 *State Farm*, 538 U.S. at 423. See also *infra* notes 129–43 and accompanying text.

23 See *infra* Part 2.3.

24 See *infra* Part 2.4 & 2.5.

25 See *infra* Part 2.6.

26 See *infra* Part 3.

2. The Multiple Punishments Problem

Punitive damages have a long and well-chronicled history.[27] Their origins trace back to the Code of Hammurabi of 2000 B.C.,[28] and have been part of our common law fabric for nearly two centuries.[29] Punitive damages are currently authorised and awarded in all but five American states.[30] While the particular standard varies slightly from state to state, it is generally sufficient to prove that the defendant's conduct was 'reckless' or 'willful and wanton'.[31] For the sake of consistency and clarity, this chapter will generally refer to the conduct necessary to warrant punitive damages as 'reprehensible'. The United States Supreme Court has repeatedly ratified the constitutional validity of punitive damage awards, even while steadily imposing new restraints.[32] Yet the multiple punishments problem only emerged in the latter half of the twentieth century.[33] This is true primarily because legal and technological changes combined to give birth to the modern mass tort claim during that time.

By definition, the multiple punishments problem can only arise when there exists the possibility of multiple punitive damages awards against a defendant for a single act or course of conduct. In the vast majority of cases filed in the United States and around the world, a single plaintiff sues a single defendant for injuries or damages arising out of the defendant's conduct, e.g., a car accident.[34] Even if the defendant's conduct rises to the level of reprehensibility required to trigger punitive damages, once that case is resolved

27 See generally *Wangen v. Ford Motor Co.*, 294 N.W.2d 437, 448 (Wis. 1980) (tracing punitive damages back to eighteenth-century England and pointing out that punitive damages have a century-old foundation in America); Ellis 1982, p. 2 (describing punitive damages emerging as a 'borderland that both bridges and separates criminal law and torts' and stating that England's common law courts 'first confirmed their authority to award punitive damages in the eighteenth century); Owen 1982b, p. 103 (pointing out that damages for antisocial behavior have been around for thousands of years and that punitive damages awards have been very well established in the United States).

28 See Owen 1994, *supra* note 11, p. 368 (tracing the history of punitive damages from the Code of Hammurabi and including the Hittite Laws, the Hebrew Covenant Code of Mosaic law, the Hindu Code of Manu, early Roman civil law, and English law).

29 See *Day v. Woodworth*, 54 U.S. 363, 371 (1851) (reporting that at that time punitive damages had been accepted for 'more than a century').

30 See Owen 1994, *supra* note 11, p. 368 & n.30 (listing Louisiana, Massachusetts, Nebraska, New Hampshire, and Washington as the five states generally prohibiting punitive damages awards).

31 See generally Blatt *et al.* 2004, p. 235 (illustrating the conduct required for punitive damages in each state); Voigt 2003, p. 5 ('Today, courts state the standard for punitive damages as follows: 'Punitive damages must be based on conduct which is malicious, wanton, reckless, willful, or oppressive'.') (quoting *Feld v. Merriam*, 485 A.2d 742, 747–48 (Pa. 1984)).

32 See *Browning-Ferris Indus. of Vt., Inc. v. Kelco Disposal, Inc.*, 492 U.S. 257 (1989); *Pacific Mut. Life Ins. Co. v. Haslip*, 499 U.S. 1 (1991); *TXO Prod. Corp. v. Alliance Res. Corp.*, 509 U.S. 443 (1993); *Honda Motor Co. v. Oberg*, 512 U.S. 415 (1994); *BMW of N. Am., Inc. v. Gore*, 517 U.S. 559 (1996); *Cooper Indus., Inc. v. Leatherman Tool Group, Inc.*, 532 U.S. 424 (2001); *State Farm*, 538 U.S. 408 (2003); *Philip Morris USA v. Williams*, 549 U.S. 346 (2007).

33 See *infra* notes 38–48 and accompanying text.

34 See generally Seltzer 1983, *supra* note 6, p. 40 ('Typically, punitive damages claims arose from a single incident involving only two parties, making it possible for a jury to determine an appropriate award without considering the possibility of additional awards by other juries'.). Accord Owen 1982a, *supra* note 6, p. 15 ('Punitive damages were developed largely as a punishment and deterrent for trespassers,

there is no risk that the defendant will be punished (or even sued) again for that same conduct. It is only when the defendant's act or course of conduct injures multiple plaintiffs that the defendant is exposed to the risk of multiple lawsuits and multiple punitive damages awards. While it is certainly true that there were at least some cases involving multiple punitive damages awards prior to the latter half of the twentieth century, those cases were few and far between and did not pose the wide-scale threat that such awards now pose. Primarily responsible for the dramatic rise in the number of cases implicating the problem was the birth of products liability and other mass tort claims.[35]

2.1. *The Birth of Products Liability and Mass Torts*

Until nearly fifty years ago, products liability as it is now known did not exist.[36] Through the combined efforts of California Supreme Court Justice Roger Traynor and University of California at Berkeley Law School Dean William Prosser, a new species of tort was born in the early 1960s.[37] Traynor authored the first case to recognise strict products liability,[38] and Prosser incorporated the new tort into his contemporaneous draft of the Restatement (Second) of Torts.[39] Once evolved, strict products liability ushered in a new era of mass torts, allowing a virtually unlimited number of lawsuits to be brought against a defendant for a single design or warning decision; anyone injured by a product with a design or warning defect could now sue.[40] To the extent that a jury could find that the design or warning decision was sufficiently reprehensible to warrant the imposition of punitive damages, the risk of multiple punitive damages awards for a single act or course of conduct was squarely presented.

Within a few years after strict products liability was born, courts began allowing punitive damages in such cases. The first such case was *Toole v. Richardson-Merrell, Inc.*,[41] in which a California appellate court ruled that a plaintiff did not have to show deliberate intent to injure, but instead could prevail on a lesser showing of recklessness.[42] At approximately the same time, awareness of environmental contamination and the

oxen thieves and other such human malefactors. When the device is transferred to the complex bureaucracy of a modern manufacturing concern, the fit is awkward in many respects'.).

35 A second development – the shift in focus from viewing punitive damages as redressing private wrongs, to viewing them as redressing public wrongs – also played a contributing role. See *infra* Parts 2.6.4 & 2.6.5.

36 See generally Keeton *et al.* 1984, p. 692–93; Shapo 1994, § 1.01[1].

37 See generally Gash 2002, pp. 85–88 (tracing history of the birth and rise of strict products liability).

38 *Greenman v. Yuba Power Prods.*, 377 P.2d 897 (Cal. 1963).

39 Restatement (Second) of Torts § 402(A) (1964). See also Madden & Owen 2000, p. 252 ('Justice Traynor in 1963 constructed the new tort law doctrine in *Greenman v. Yuba Power Prods., Inc.*, Dean Prosser, Reporter for the Second Restatement, in 1964 incorporated the principle into Restatement Second, Torts § 402A, published by the American Law Institute the following year; and, thereafter, a flood of jurisdictions rapidly adopted the new strict tort doctrine'.).

40 See Jeffries 1986, *supra* note 6, p. 142 ('In the mid-1970's, unprecedented numbers of punitive awards in product liability and other mass tort situations began to surface. Many of these awards were also unprecedented in amount. And these trends continued and accelerated into the 1980's'.).

41 *Toole v. Richardson-Merrell, Inc.*, 251 Cal. App. 2d 689, 714 (1967).

42 *Ibid.*, at 714.

potential adverse health effects of such contamination was being discovered.[43] As with products liability claims, environmental injury claims hold the potential for numerous plaintiffs to allege individual injuries arising out of a single act or course of conduct on behalf of a single defendant.[44] The convergence of products liability and environmental torts in the middle part of the latter half of the twentieth century led to an explosion of litigation in these areas.[45] And because punitive damages were available in these cases, the number and size of punitive damages awards experienced a corresponding dramatic increase.

As previously mentioned, the danger of multiple punitive damages awards presented by mass tort claims was first recognised and articulated by the Second Circuit in Judge Friendly's *Roginsky v. Richardson-Merrell, Inc.* opinion.[46] The plaintiff in *Roginsky* alleged that his ingestion of an anti-cholesterol drug called MER/29 caused, *inter alia*, cataracts in his eyes.[47] At trial, Roginsky was awarded both compensatory and punitive damages against Richardson-Merrell.[48] Roginsky's lawsuit, however, was not the only one alleging personal injuries caused by MER/29. While his was the first to be tried of seventy-five such cases then pending in the Southern District of New York, several hundred more claims were pending elsewhere, and three such cases had resulted in verdicts against the defendant in which punitive damages had been awarded.[49] Though the court ultimately vacated Roginsky's punitive damages award for insufficient evidence,[50] it did so only after expressing serious concerns about the potentially devastating consequences of allowing multiple punitive awards for the same conduct: 'We have the gravest difficulty in perceiving how claims for punitive damages in such a multiplicity of actions throughout

43 See, e.g., Geiser 1988, p. 643 (reporting that the threat of environmental pollution was thrust into the national spotlight when President Carter had to declare a state emergency at Love Canal in New York in 1978 and the acute awareness of health and safety risks posed by environmental contamination continued throughout the decade); A.L.I. Report, *supra* note 15, ch.13, p. 384 (explaining that 'the mass marketing of a variety of chemical and pharmaceutical products has exposed individuals to risks that could not have been anticipated a generation ago').

44 See generally Greenberg 2004, pp. 209–10 (using environmental contamination cases as examples of mass tort scenarios with 'hundreds or thousands of individual claims that may be spread across the nation, or even the world'); Rabin 1987, p. 30 (pointing out the problems created by toxic tort scenarios where 'claims are potentially unbounded').

45 See generally *In re* N. Dist. of Cal. 'Dalkon Shield' IUD Prod. Liab. Litig., 526 F. Supp. 887, 895, 899–900 (N.D. Cal. 1981) ('[T]he latter half of the twentieth century has witnessed a virtual explosion in the frequency and number of lawsuits filed to redress injuries caused by a single product manufactured for use on a national level'.), vacated on other grounds, 694 F.2d 847 (9th Cir. 1982); Ellis 1982, *supra* note 27, pp. 2–3; Hensler & Peterson 1993, p. 961 & n.2 (stating that '[i]n some parts of the country, mass tort claims threaten[ ] to overwhelm the civil justice system'); Hondorf 1989, pp. 541–43 (describing the 'big case phenomenon' born out of mass exposure to toxic agents that created 'chaos in the judicial system' in recent times).

46 *Roginsky v. Richardson-Merrell, Inc.*, 378 F.2d 832 (2d Cir. 1967).

47 *Ibid.*, at 834.

48 *Ibid.*, at 834. Roginsky was awarded US$ 17,500 in compensatory damages and US$ 100,000 in punitive damages.

49 *Ibid.*, at 834. MER/29 was used by approximately 400,000 people before it was removed from the market, and more than 1,500 lawsuits alleging personal injury were filed between 1961 and 1967. See Seltzer 1983, *supra* note 6, pp. 51–52.

50 *Ibid.*, at 851.

the nation can be administered to avoid overkill'.[51] Though Judge Friendly had no occasion to decide the matter, he openly questioned whether multiple punitive damages awards could eventually rise to the level of a due process violation.[52]

Since *Roginsky*, many other courts have criticised multiple punitive damages awards and have questioned their constitutional validity.[53] To date, however, it does not appear that any court has yet overturned a punitive damages award on this basis.[54] In contrast, a number of dissenting judges and commentators have strenuously argued that such awards do violate due process, at least in some situations.[55]

2.2. *The Breadth of the Problem*

It is difficult to underestimate or understate the potential breadth of the multiple punishments problem. The problem can arise in any scenario where multiple people are injured (physically or financially) by a single act or course of conduct that a rational jury concludes was sufficiently reprehensible to warrant the imposition of punitive damages. This, of course, means that any tangible item that is mass-produced and marketed can potentially invoke the problem if the item proves to be defective. Likewise, any chemical or other toxin produced, distributed, sold, used, handled, or disposed of can potentially invoke the problem if such production, distribution, sale, use, handling, or disposal is done in such a way as to cause injury to multiple people. Additionally, any form of mass transportation (*i.e.*, planes, trains, or automobiles) can invoke the problem because of the potential to injure multiple people through a single act. Furthermore, other forms of mass disaster can invoke the problem, such as a fire or a structural collapse of part or all of a building.

While the theoretical scope of this problem is virtually limitless, the problem is much more than just theoretical. To date, the multiple punishments problem has arisen in

51 *Ibid.*, at 839.

52 *Ibid.*, at 840.

53 See e.g., *Racich v. Celotex Corp.*, 887 F.2d 393, 396–99 (2d Cir. 1989) (cautioning that public policy counsels against the legitimacy of awarding multiple punitive damages in mass tort litigation and also that these awards may violate due process); *McBride v. Gen. Motors Corp.*, 737 F. Supp. 1563, 1577 (M.D. Ga. 1990) (acknowledging that due process may limit multiple punishments of defendants).

54 See generally Nadel 1982, p. 1261 (observing that courts 'have generally held that no principle exists which prohibits a plaintiff from recovering punitive damages against a defendant or defendants simply because punitive damages have previously been awarded against the same defendant or defendants for the same conduct').

55 See e.g., *Dunn v. Hovic*, 1 F.3d 1371, 1398 (3d Cir.) (Weis, J., dissenting) (arguing that limited funds should play into a court's review of jury verdicts), modified in part, 13 F.3d 58 (3d Cir. 1993); Colby 2003, *supra* note 2, p. 603 ('There must, therefore, be some limit, either as a matter of policy or as a matter of due process, to the amount of times defendants may be punished for a single transaction'.) (quoting Judge Weinstein in *In re* 'Agent Orange' Prod. Liab. Litig., 100 F.R.D. 718, 728 (E.D.N.Y. 1983)). See *also* The Multiple Punitive Damages Fairness Act of 1997, S. 454–55, 105th Cong. §§ 3, 4, 6 (1997).

cases involving Agent Orange,[56] DES,[57] formaldehyde,[58] automobiles,[59] tampons,[60] IUD's,[61] hotel fires,[62] walkway collapses,[63] and, of course, asbestos.[64]

Likewise, the negative effects of the multiple punitive damages awards are very real and practical in nature.[65] Defendants who are repeatedly punished in the form of punitive damages face very real threats of bankruptcy.[66] The ripple effect caused by such bankruptcies is felt by numerous constituencies. Plaintiffs who have yet to be compensated for their injuries may be deprived of any recovery at all.[67] Employees of the defendant can and do lose their jobs.[68] Employees of enterprises that are dependant on the defendant for supplies or income may also lose their jobs.[69] Stockholders of the defendant and other dependent companies lose their investments.[70] And consumers and the

56 See, e.g., *In re 'Agent Orange'*, 100 F.R.D. at 728.

57 See, e.g., *Payton v. Abbott Labs.*, 83 F.R.D. 382 (D. Mass. 1979); *Bichler v. Eli Lilly & Co.*, 436 N.E.2d 182 (N.Y. 1982).

58 See, e.g., *Louderback v. Orkin Exterminating Co.*, 26 F. Supp. 2d 1298 (D. Kan. 1998).

59 See, e.g., *Clarys v. Ford Motor Co.*, 592 N.W.2d 573 (N.D. 1999).

60 See, e.g., *Graham v. Playtex Prods., Inc.*, 993 F. Supp. 127 (N.D.N.Y. 1998).

61 See, e.g., *In re* N. Dist. of Cal. 'Dalkon Shield' IUD Prods. Liab. Litig., 526 F. Supp. 887 (N.D. Cal. 1981), vacated, 693 F. 2d 847 (9th Cir. 1982).

62 See, e.g., *In re* MGM Grand Hotel Fire Litig., 570 F. Supp. 913 (D. Nev. 1983).

63 See, e.g., *In re* Federal Skywalk Cases, 93 F.R.D. 415 (W.D. Mo. 1982).

64 See, e.g., *Jackson v. Johns-Manville*, 750 F.2d 1314 (5th Cir. 1985), aff'd on reh'g, 781 F.2d 394 (5th Cir. 1986).

65 See, e.g., Dobbs 1993, p. 501 (observing that multiple punitive damages can both bankrupt a defendant and preclude recovery by late-coming plaintiffs).

66 See, e.g., Statement of Hon. William W. Schwarzer, Asbestos Litig. Crisis in Fed. and State Cts.: Hearings Before the Subcomm. on Intellectual Prop. and Judicial Admin. of the House Comm. on the Judiciary, 102 Cong., 2d Sess. 132–33 (1992) ('Punitive damages compete with compensatory damages for the increasingly scarce resources of asbestos defendants and their insurers. Until the claims of future claimants become liquidated, distribution of punitive damages to current claimants creates a risk of exhausting funds before potential claimants discover their injuries'.).

67 See, e.g., *Edwards v. Armstrong World Indus.*, 911 F.2d 1151, 1155 (5th Cir. 1990) ('If no change occurs in our tort law or constitutional law the time will arrive when Celotex's [asbestos] liability for punitive damages imperils its ability to pay compensatory claims and its corporate existence'.); *Fisher v. Johns-Manville Corp.*, 512 A.2d 466, 478 (N.J. 1986) (cautioning that depletion of defendants' funds by early plaintiffs often leave no monetary compensation for later plaintiffs).

68 See, e.g., *Juzwin v. Amtorg Trading Corp.*, 705 F. Supp. 1053, 1055 (D.N.J.) (stating that 'if the successive fines serve to render companies insolvent, innocent employees and trade creditors are injured as well'), vacated on other grounds, 718 F. Supp. 1233 (D.N.J. 1989); *Wangen v. Ford Motor Co.*, 294 N.W.2d 437, 470–71 (Wis. 1980) (Coffey, J., dissenting) ('If the manufacturer is not in a strong financial position so as to be able to bear these added costs, he will be faced with the threat of being forced out of business or into bankruptcy, thus resulting in a loss of jobs'); Slaughter & Vinson 1998, p. 299 (noting that multiple punitive damages awards may increase unemployment due to the threat of financial disaster from the increased litigation and products).

69 See, e.g., *Wangen*, 294 N.W.2d at 470–71 ('Moreover, imposition of multiple punitive damage awards could have an adverse impact not only on the manufacturer but also on those commercial businesses that supply materials for use in construction of [other products]'.).

70 See Pace 1997, p. 1628 ('Proponents of limiting a defendant's liability for intentional misconduct also argue that large punitive damage awards actually harm consumers, employees, and shareholders of the corporation, because the corporation ultimately must pass these expenses on to them'.); Schwartz *et*

economy lose a once-valuable contributor to the country's economic health.[71] These effects have been well summarized by a Wisconsin Court:

> 'If the manufacturer is not in a strong financial position so as to be able to bear these added costs, he will be faced with the threat of being forced out of business or into bankruptcy, thus resulting in a loss of jobs (unemployment) and the curtailment of competition, to the detriment of the consumer. If bankruptcy or the loss of business and jobs is to be avoided, it is the consumer who will ultimately bear the burden of punitive damage awards through the payment of higher prices for goods in the market place... Moreover, imposition of multiple punitive damage awards could have an adverse impact not only on the manufacturer... but also on those commercial businesses that supply materials for use in construction of [other products]'.[72]

The experience of the United States with asbestos provides a compelling example of the multiple punitive damages award problem and why this problem needs to be fixed immediately. Over the past 45 years, asbestos litigation has inundated the country's civil courts and is predicted to be 'one of the most costly litigated issues, if not the most, in the history of American jurisprudence'.[73] While the first modern asbestos lawsuit was filed in 1966,[74] asbestos litigation exploded in the 1970s and 80s; by 1982, 21,000 claims had been filed against 300 companies with tens of thousands of new claims being filed each successive year.[75] In the midst of the asbestos crisis from 1979–81, average total compensation per claim paid by all defendants and their insurers equated US$ 60,000, while average amount of punitive damages awarded per case from January 1982-July 1982 was about US$ 600,000.[76] Projected to end up costing US$ 200 to US$ 275 billion,[77] this so-called 'asbestos-litigation crisis,'[78] has forced at least eighty companies to file for

al. 1999, *supra* note 3, p. 1030 ('Economic harm to the company also affects shareholders, such as pension funds and ordinary citizens, and other investors who face the loss of their savings'.).

71 See, e.g., *Browning-Ferris Indus. of Vt., Inc.*, 492 U.S. at 297 (O'Connor, J., concurring in part and dissenting in part) (cautioning that fear of large punitive damages awards 'product manufacturers may curtail their research and development of new and beneficial products'); Pace 1997, *supra* note 70, p. 1622 (warning that potentially unlimited liability might cause 'the cautious manufacturers [to] be over-deterred and unwilling to invest in research and development for potentially valuable products,' resulting in valuable products being taken off the market leaving consumers with depleted product options).

72 *Wangen v. Ford Motor Co.*, 294 N.W.2d 437, 470–71 (Wis. 1980) (Coffey, J., dissenting).

73 Christian & Craymer 2003, p. 998.

74 Perillo 2004, p. 1052.

75 See Christian & Craymer 2003, *supra* note 73, p. 992. See also Charles W. Schwartz & Lewis C. Sutherland, ALI/ABA Course of Study, *Class Certification for Environmental and Toxic Tort Claims* 310 (1996).

76 See Stacy Molton, Commercial Law and Practice Course Handbook Series, *Asbestos: Alternatives Where No Insurance is Available* 55 (1986).

77 See Stacy Molton, Commercial Law and Practice Course Handbook Series, *Asbestos: Alternatives Where No Insurance is Available* 55 (1986); see also American Academy of Actuaries' Mass Tort Subcommittee 2007, p. 3.

78 See, e.g., *Amchem Prods. Inc. v. Windsor*, 521 U.S. 591, 597 (1997) (addressing the certification of a class of asbestos related claims that evolved 'in response to an asbestos-litigation crisis'.).

Chapter 11 bankruptcy protection.[79] To date, there have been more than 700,000 asbestos claims by workers against more than 6,000 different companies.[80] This litigation is predicted to continue through 2040, resulting in a predicted US$ 33 billion dollar loss in capital investment alone.[81]

The multiple punishments problem is not limited to the ill effects of multiple jury verdicts imposing punitive damages against the defendant. The mere threat of multiple punitive damages awards causes defendants to factor such a possibility into the settlement process.[82] This, in turn, unnecessarily escalates the settlement amount, thereby triggering some or all of the parade of horribles discussed above.[83]

2.3. *Courts' Response to the Problem*

While *Roginsky* was the first case to raise and discuss the multiple punishments problem, it was certainly not the last. Since *Roginsky*, numerous state and federal courts have faced the problem and attempted to address it in a variety of ways. Some courts have ignored the problem or dismissed it as unproblematic. For example, in *Wangen v. Ford Motor Co.*,[84] a Wisconsin state court case involving a defectively designed fuel tank in Ford Mustang automobiles,[85] the court acknowledged that there was a real risk that multiple punitive damages awards could be 'catastrophic'.[86] Nevertheless, the court concluded that the problem could be effectively managed through the use of 'judicial controls'.[87]

Other courts have questioned the wisdom of allowing multiple awards. For example, in *Maxey v. Freightliner Corp.*,[88] a diversity case involving a defectively designed fuel system that caused diesel trucks to erupt in flames, the jury awarded US$ 150,000 in compensatory damages and US$ 10 million in punitive damages.[89] After acknowledging the potentially 'devastating' effects of multiple punitive damage awards were 'real and apparent,'[90] the court vacated the punitive damage award on other grounds.[91] The court

79 See Behrens & Tedesco 2003, p. 1; see also Carroll *et al.* 2002; see also American Academy of Actuaries' Mass Tort Subcommittee 2007, p. 14, 32.

80 See Carroll *et al.* 2002, *supra* note 79, p. 996–97; *Asbestos Litigation Reform*, NAMIC.ORG, (June 12, 2006, 3:41:32 PM), www.namic.org/fedkey/06Asbestos.asp.

81 See Behrens & Tedesco 2003, *supra* note 79, pp. 73–74.

82 See, e.g., *Dunn v. Hovic*, 1 F.3d 1371, 1398 (3d Cir.) (Weis, J., dissenting) ('[T]he potential for punitive awards is a weighty factor in settlement negotiations and inevitably results in a larger settlement agreement than would ordinarily be obtained. To the extent this premium exceeds what would otherwise be a fair and reasonable settlement for compensatory damages, assets that could be available for satisfaction of future compensatory claims are dissipated'.), modified in part, 13 F.3d 58 (3d Cir. 1993).

83 *Dunn*, 1 F.3d at 1398.

84 *Wangen v. Ford Motor Co.*, 294 N.W.2d 437 (Wis. 1980).

85 *Ibid.*, at 263.

86 *Ibid.*, at 294.

87 *Ibid.*, at 297.

88 *Maxey v. Freightliner Corp.*, 450 F. Supp. 955 (N.D. Tex. 1978).

89 *Ibid.*, at 957.

90 *Ibid.*, at 962 ('Each jury has before it only one case[;] it is the aggregate effect of several juries' faithful adherence to the law that poses risk of ultimate destruction'.).

91 *Ibid.*, at 964.

went on to question the wisdom of multiple punitive damages awards, noting that after the first punitive damages award, the public interest has been vindicated.[92]

Still other courts, including the United States Supreme Court,[93] have openly questioned the constitutionality of allowing multiple awards.[94] One court went so far as to declare multiple awards, at least as applied to the case before it, an unconstitutional denial of due process rights.[95] That court, however, ultimately reversed itself and upheld the award's constitutionality.[96]

In *Juzwin I*, the court rejected defendants' contentions that multiple punitive damage awards violated both the Double Jeopardy Clause of the Fifth Amendment,[97] and the Excessive Fines Clause of the Eighth Amendment.[98] The court did find, however, that the Due Process Clause of the Fourteenth Amendment places constitutional limits on the imposition of multiple punitive damages awards.[99] Rejecting the notion that due process requires 'simply the provision of a judicial proceeding'[100] and recognizing that a class action was not a possible solution,[101] the court pronounced that 'subjecting defendants to the possibility of multiple awards of punitive damages for the single course of conduct alleged in this action would deprive defendants of the fundamental fairness required by the Due Process Clause'.[102]

Shortly thereafter, however, the court vacated its opinion and reinstated the punitive damages award.[103] The court in *Juzwin II* did adhere, however, to its prior ruling that 'repetitive awards of punitive damages for the same conduct violate a defendant's due process rights'.[104] In order to prevail on a due process challenge to multiple punitive damages awards, however, the court declared that several conditions first had to be met. First, there must have been a full and fair hearing to develop the total scope of the conduct of the defendant when the prior punitive damages verdict was entered.[105] Second, there

92 *Ibid.*, at 962.

93 *State Farm*, 538 U.S. at 423. See also Gash 2004, p. 1191 (analyzing the Supreme Court's allusion to the unconstitutionality of multiple punitive damages awards).

94 See, e.g., *Simpson v. Pittsburgh Corning Corp.*, 901 F.2d 277, 280–81 (2d Cir. 1990) (implying that if the defendant had presented a sufficient record, court may have stricken later punitive damages award as unconstitutional); *In re* Federal Skywalk Cases, 680 F.2d 1175, 1188 (8th Cir. 1982) ('Unlimited multiple punishment for the same act determined in a succession of individual lawsuits and bearing no relation to the defendants' culpability or the actual injuries suffered by victims, would violate the sense of 'fundamental fairness' that is essential to constitutional due process'.).

95 *Juzwin v. Amtorg Trading Corp.*, 705 F. Supp. 1053, vacated, 718 F. Supp. 1233 (D.N.J. 1989).

96 *Juzwin I*, 705 F. Supp. at 1053.

97 *Ibid.*, at 1058–59.

98 *Ibid.*, at 1059–60.

99 *Ibid.*, at 1063. Accord *In re* N. Dist. of Cal. 'Dalkon Shield' IUD Prods. Liab. Litig., 526 F.Supp. 887, 899 (N.D. Cal. 1981), vacated, 693 F.2d 847 (9th Cir. 1982) ('A defendant has a due process right to be protected against unlimited multiple punishment for the same act... not because they violate 'double jeopardy' but simply because overlapping damage awards violate that sense of 'fundamental fairness' which lies at the heart of constitutional due process'.).

100 *Juzwin I*, 705 F. Supp. at 1064.

101 *Ibid.*, at 1064.

102 *Ibid.*, at 1064.

103 *Juzwin v. Amtorg Trading Corp.*, 718 F. Supp. 1233 (D.N.J. 1989) ('*Juzwin II*').

104 *Ibid.*, at 1234.

105 *Ibid.*, at 1235.

must have been adequate representation at the prior trial.[106] Third, there must have been an instruction to the jury that it would be the one and only punitive damages verdict entered against the defendant.[107] Fourth, other conditions of the prior trial must have been fair.[108] Because these conditions had not been met in any prior trial, the court reinstated the punitive damages award entered by the jury.[109]

In *Dunn v. Hovic*, another case that wrestled with the due process limitations on multiple punitive damages awards, the United States Court of Appeals for the Third Circuit reviewed a punitive damages award in a Virgin Islands products liability case involving asbestos to determine whether due process limits multiple punitive damages awards.[110] Noting that it was aware of no federal or state court that had ever struck down a punitive damages award on the basis that multiple punitive awards violate either common law tort principles or federal due process,[111] and recognizing that it was constrained by its role as the *de facto* Supreme Court of the Virgin Islands to follow common law principles as set forth in the Restatements,[112] (which allow for consideration of the potential for multiple punitive damages awards as a factor in setting the amount of the award, but does not preclude multiple awards),[113] the court declined to strike the punitive damages award as unconstitutional, even while acknowledging and sympathizing with those who have expressed concern about multiple punitive damages awards.[114] The court characterised the problem as 'essentially a policy matter' that is 'best left to the United States Congress or the legislature of the Virgin Islands'.[115] The court did not, however, rule out the possibility that a defendant in another case (who had been subject to multiple punitive damages awards) could demonstrate that a particular punitive award violated due process, but concluded that the defendant in the case before it failed to make such a showing.[116] In light of its holding, the court instructed district courts in the Third Circuit to 'determine whether a punitive award to a plaintiff in a particular case should be struck by carefully scrutinizing the 'punitive damages overkill' evidence submitted to them, both with respect to past awards actually paid by the defendant and the defendant's ability to satisfy future punitive damages awards'.[117] The court then proceeded to consider

106 *Ibid.*, at 1235.

107 *Ibid.*, at 1235.

108 *Ibid.*, at 1235.

109 *Ibid.*, at 1235.

110 *Dunn v. Hovic*, 1 F.3d 1371, 1385 (3d Cir.) (Weis, J., dissenting) ('The principal issue impelling us to take this otherwise routine product liability case in banc is the effect of successive punitive damages awards in mass tort cases arising from the same course of conduct'.), modified in part, 13 F.3d 58 (3d Cir. 1993).

111 *Dunn*, 1 F.3d at 1386 (stating that 'OCF [the defendant] has brought no majority opinion from any court to our attention (and our research has not disclosed such a case) which holds that multiple punitive damages claims must be struck on either basis' of due process or common law tort grounds).

112 *Ibid.*, at 1387.

113 *Ibid.*, at 1387 (citing RESTATEMENT (SECOND) OF TORTS § 908 cmt. e (1977)).

114 *Ibid.*, at 1387.

115 *Ibid.*, at 1387.

116 *Ibid.*, at 1389–90.

117 *Ibid.*, at 1391.

the multiple punitive awards as a factor in affirming the panel's remittitur of the punitive damages verdict from two million to one million dollars.[118]

Despite the variance in the courts' approach and to the multiple punishments problem, virtually all courts have agreed that the only way to fully and finally resolve the problem is through a nationwide solution.[119] Absent congressional action, the only other hope for a national solution is for the United States Supreme Court to intervene.

To the dismay and disappointment of many Court observers,[120] the United States Supreme Court has yet to squarely address the multiple punitive damages problem. This does not mean, however, that the Court is not aware of the problem or that it has not taken steps to limit the scope of the problem. To the contrary, the Court has alluded to the problem three times, but will very likely not revisit this matter in the foreseeable future.[121]

The Court's first reference to the multiple punishments problem came in Justice Ginsburg's dissent in *BMW of North America, Inc. v. Gore*.[122] In *Gore*, the plaintiff sued BMW for repainting his car prior to his purchase in order to conceal damage caused by acid rain.[123] The jury awarded Gore US$ 4,000 in compensatory damages and US$ 4 million in punitive damages.[124] In reducing the punitive award to US$ 2 million, the Alabama Supreme Court presumed that the jury had improperly reached its verdict by multiplying the number of times BMW had sold refinished cars as new nationwide (983) by the reduced value to such cars as a consequence (US$ 4,000).[125] Concluding that even the reduced punitive damages award operated to punish BMW excessively for its conduct,[126] the United States Supreme Court struck down the award as a violation of due process.[127] In her dissent, Justice Ginsburg made clear that the Court was aware of the multiple punishments problem, but that this case was not the proper vehicle for addressing that issue:

> 'Petitioner invites the Court to address the question of multiple punitive damages awards stemming from the same alleged misconduct. The Court does not take up the invitation, and rightly so, in my judgment, for this case does not present the issue'.[128]

118 *Ibid.*, at 1391.

119 See, e.g., *Dunn*, 1 F.3d at 1386 (reporting that 'both state and federal courts have recognised that no single court can fashion an effective response to the national problem flowing from mass exposure to asbestos products'.). See also *supra* note 19.

120 See, e.g., Owen 1994, *supra* note 11, p. 406 & 413, n.152 (complaining that the Court should have taken a recent case [*Dunn*] when presented with the opportunity).

121 See Gash 2011, p. 525.

122 *BMW of N. Am., Inc. v. Gore*, 517 U.S. 559 (1996).

123 *Ibid.*, at 563 & n.1.

124 *Ibid.*, at 565.

125 *Ibid.*, at 567.

126 Importantly, the conduct at issue was legal in most states. *Ibid.*, at 573 & n.13.

127 *Ibid.*, at 585–86.

128 *Ibid.*, at 612, n.4 (Ginsburg, J., dissenting). Justice Ginsburg went on to explain that the question in this case was 'hypothetical' because (i) this was the first punitive damages award entered against BMW for this conduct, (ii) BMW failed to raise the multiple punitive damages issue below, and (iii) Alabama's common law allows prior punitive awards to be considered as a factor in considering whether an award is excessive. *BMW*, 517 U.S. at 612, n.4. In his concurrence, Justice Breyer also obliquely alludes to

The multiple punishments problem again came up in *State Farm Mutual Automobile Insurance Co. v. Campbell*,[129] the Court's second most recent punitive damages case. In *State Farm*, the jury awarded Campbell US$ 2 million in compensatory damages and US$ 145 million in punitive damages in an action alleging that State Farm had acted in bad faith in refusing to settle an earlier case against Campbell.[130] At trial, Campbell was permitted to introduce into evidence other acts by State Farm that Campbell argued demonstrated State Farm's reprehensible motives and intent in its dealings with Campbell.[131] After the jury's verdict, the trial court reduced the compensatory award to US$ 1 million and the punitive award to US$ 25 million, but the Utah Supreme Court reinstated the US$ 145 million punitive award.[132]

In an opinion written by Justice Kennedy, the Court overturned the US$ 145 million award, concluding that because the other acts evidence introduced by Campbell lacked a sufficient 'nexus' to the conduct that harmed Campbell,[133] it could not be considered in measuring the level of State Farm's reprehensibility.[134] And when evaluated with reference only to the conduct that harmed Campbell, the US$ 145 million award was grossly excessive in violation of State Farm's due process rights.[135]

Previously, during the course of the oral argument in *State Farm*, Justice Stevens had asked Campbell's counsel, Professor Laurence Tribe, whether another plaintiff could introduce the same evidence as Campbell and then also receive US$ 145 million punitive damages award.[136] Professor Tribe responded:

> 'No. I think that it's a penalty that is like – there ought to be some double jeopardy like doctrine that if they can show that they've already been punished for this course of conduct, they ought not to have to pay the penalty a second time'.[137]

When pressed for his authority for his proposition, Professor Tribe retorted that he 'just made it up'.[138] While the official transcript reports that laughter ensued,[139] Justice Kennedy was apparently not amused. Accordingly, in his majority opinion, Justice Kennedy included a passage that strongly suggests that he and at least five other members

multiple punitive damages in hypothesizing about which economic theory the Alabama Supreme Court may or may not have relied upon in reducing the jury's punitive award: 'Larger damages might also 'double count' by including in the punitive damages award some of the compensatory, or punitive, damages that subsequent plaintiffs would also recover'. *BMW*, 517 U.S. at 593 (Breyer, J., concurring).

129 *State Farm Mut. Auto. Ins. Co. v. Campbell*, 538 U.S. 408 (2003).

130 *Ibid.*, at 415. The compensatory award was reduced by the trial judge to US$ 1 million.

131 *Ibid.*, at 414–15. See also Gash 2004, p. 1191 (extensively analyzing the *State Farm* opinion and its likely impact on future punitive damages cases).

132 *State Farm*, 538 U.S. at 415.

133 *Ibid.*, at 422.

134 *Ibid.*, at 424.

135 *Ibid.*, at 429.

136 Transcript of Oral Argument, *State Farm Mut. Auto. Ins. Co. v. Campbell*, No. 01–1289, at *35 (U.S. Dec. 11, 2002) (colloquy between Justice Stevens and Laurence Tribe).

137 *Ibid.*, at *35.

138 *Ibid.*, at *35.

139 *Ibid.*, at *35.

of the Court at that time[140] agreed with Professor Tribe that the Constitution limits the imposition of multiple punitive damages awards, albeit through due process rather than double jeopardy.[141]

Just after declaring that the other acts evidence admitted against State Farm could not be considered in calculating the proper amount of punitive damages to be awarded,[142] Justice Kennedy declared:

> 'Punishment on these bases creates the possibility of multiple punitive damages awards for the same conduct; for in the usual case nonparties are not bound by the judgment some other plaintiff obtains'.[143]

While the most logical reading of this passage is that a majority of the United States Supreme Court at that time considered the imposition of multiple punitive damages to be constitutionally suspect, the Court stopped short of declaring this in its most recent opinion, *Philip Morris USA v. Williams*,[144] which is discussed and analyzed later in this chapter.[145]

Because neither Congress nor the United States Supreme Court has yet fixed the problem, a number of state legislatures have attempted to provide their own solutions. As demonstrated below, however, while admirable, these state statutes are destined for failure because they have no extra-territorial effect.

2.4. *State Legislative Response to the Problem*

Several state legislatures have taken a proactive role in attempting to reduce or eliminate multiple punitive damages awards. The legislative solutions vary from state to state, but they all have one thing in common – they are utterly ineffective in their goal of eliminating multiple awards because the legislation has no effect outside the state's own borders. What follows is a sampling of six state statutes that attempt, directly or indirectly, to address the multiple punishments problem.

2.4.1. Georgia

Georgia's statute, enacted in 1987, provides in relevant part:

> 'In a tort case in which the cause of action arises from product liability, there shall be no limitation regarding the amount which may be awarded as punitive damages. Only one award

140 Joining Justice Kennedy in his majority opinion in *State Farm* were Chief Justice Rehnquist and Associate Justices Stevens, O'Connor, Souter, and Breyer.

141 *State Farm*, 538 U.S. at 423.

142 *Ibid.*, at 423.

143 *Ibid.*, at 423. For this proposition, Justice Kennedy cites only to Justice Breyer's oblique allusion to multiple punitive damages in his concurrence in *Gore. Ibid.*, at 423.

144 *Philip Morris USA v. Williams*, 549 U.S. 346 (2007).

145 See *infra* at Part 2.6.5.

> of punitive damages may be recovered in a court in this state from a defendant for any act or omission if the cause of action arises from product liability, regardless of the number of causes of action which may arise from such act or omission'.[146]

Accordingly, Georgia's statute limits the recovery of multiple punitive damages awards to the field of products liability (as opposed to all mass torts) and to only one award. Such an approach is unsatisfactory for several reasons. First, due to federalism principles in the United States, the statute has no force and effect outside of Georgia and thus cannot limit multiple awards arising out of the same 'act or omission' entered in other jurisdictions. Second, the statute fails to take into account any settlements reached that include a punitive damages component.[147] Third, products liability cases represent only a portion of the cases that present the multiple punishments problem, and there does not seem to be any compelling reason to distinguish such cases from the others. Fourth, the statute does not take into account the size of the first punitive award, leaving open the very real possibility that the punishment and deterrence from the award will be inadequate. For example, if the first of many potential plaintiffs to go to trial has suffered only minor harm, then the punitive award is likely to be relatively small because, *inter alia*, the punitive damages award must bear a reasonable relationship to the size of the compensatory award under settled United States law.[148] In contrast, if a more seriously injured plaintiff were to go to trial first, the punitive award would likely be much greater. This leaves open the very real possibility that a defendant could manipulate the trial process to ensure that a lesser-injured party's case is tried first.[149] For the latter two and other reasons, the Georgia statute was struck down as unconstitutional.[150]

2.4.2. Missouri

Missouri's statute, enacted in 1992, provides perhaps the most comprehensive attempt at a solution to the problem of any state statute. It provides in pertinent part:

> 'Within the time for filing a motion for a new trial, a defendant may file a post-trial motion requesting the amount awarded by the jury as punitive damages be credited by the court with amounts previously paid by the defendant for punitive damages arising out of the same conduct on which the imposition of punitive damages is based… If the trial court sustains

146 Ga. Code Ann. § 51-12-5.1 (2011).

147 For example, if a defendant settles a case for an amount that factors in the very real risk of punitive damages, that defendant can still be found liable for, and have to pay, a later large punitive damages verdict.

148 See *BMW of N. Am., Inc. v. Gore*, 517 U.S. 559, 580–83 (1996) (declaring that punitive damages should bear a reasonable relationship to the harm inflicted); *Reid v. Lockheed Martin Aeronautics Co.*, 205 F.R.D. 655, 681 (N.D. Ga. 2001) (reiterating that 'any punitive damages awarded to Plaintiffs must bear a reasonable relationship to their compensatory damages') (citing *Gore*, 517 U.S. at 580–83.)).

149 Accord Denemark 2002, *supra* note 6, p. 962 (pointing out the possibility of defendant's manipulating the 'first-comer' rule to minimise punitive damages).

150 *McBride v. Gen. Motors Corp.*, 737 F. Supp. 1563 (M.D. Ga. 1990) (declaring Ga. Code Ann. § 51-12-5.1 (e)(1) unconstitutional).

> such a motion the trial court shall credit the jury award of punitive damages by the amount found by the trial court to have been previously paid by the defendant arising out of the same conduct and enter judgment accordingly... '.[151]

Accordingly, Missouri's statute provides that once a punitive award has been entered against a defendant, that defendant may later move a court in which a subsequent punitive award has been entered for the same conduct for an order reducing the latter award by the amount paid as a result of the prior award.[152] While certainly a step in the right direction, this statute is only effective if the later trials take place in Missouri, and it fails to take into account prior settlements that include a punitive damages component. It also fails to provide later trial courts with the necessary tools for comparing the conduct in the prior case(s) with the conduct presently before the court.

2.4.3. Florida

Florida's statute, enacted in 1986, provides in pertinent part:

> 'Except as provided in paragraph (b), punitive damages may not be awarded against a defendant in a civil action if that defendant establishes, before trial, that punitive damages have previously been awarded against that defendant in any state or federal court in any action alleging harm from the same act or single course of conduct for which the claimant seeks compensatory damages. For purposes of a civil action, the term 'the same act or single course of conduct' includes acts resulting in the same manufacturing defects, acts resulting from the same defects in design, or failure to warn of the same hazards, with respect to similar units of a product'.[153]

The exception referenced in the above-quoted language removes the bar to multiple punitive awards 'if the court determines by clear and convincing evidence that the amount of prior punitive damages awarded was insufficient to punish that defendant's behavior'.[154] In such a case, the trial court must make specific findings of fact justifying this conclusion, and even if the trial court does so conclude, the defendant is entitled to a credit in the amount of any prior punitive damages award.[155] Once again, this statute represents a good first step, but it is necessarily inadequate because it only limits punitive awards in Florida and fails to account for prior settlements that include a punitive damages component. It also inexplicably requires trial courts to determine before trial whether the prior punitive damages award was based upon the same conduct as that

151 Mo. Ann. Stat. § 510.263(4) (2011).

152 The statute also provides an escape clause, allowing the court to refuse to allow the credit if the trial court finds that (i) the defendant failed to prove the conduct out of which the prior award arose was the same, (ii) the defendant persisted in the wrongful conduct after learning of its dangerousness, or (iii) the punitive damages laws in the state from which the prior award came materially differ from Missouri's laws. Mo. Ann. Stat. § 510.263(4) (2011).

153 Fla. Stat. § 768.73(2)(a)-(b) (2011).

154 *Ibid.*, at § 768.73(2)(b).

155 *Ibid.*, at § 768.73(2)(b).

involved in a case that has yet to be tried. Requiring a trial court to compare the evidence admitted in a trial over which it did not preside with evidence that has not yet been admitted in a case over which the court has not yet presided seems to ask the impossible.

2.4.4. Connecticut

While Connecticut has not adopted a statute limiting multiple punitive damage awards *per se*, its statute does have the incidental effect of limiting the potential harm caused by such awards in products liability cases:

> 'Punitive damages may be awarded if the claimant proves that the harm suffered was the result of the product seller's reckless disregard for the safety of product users, consumers or others who were injured by the product. If the trier of fact determines that punitive damages should be awarded, the court shall determine the amount of such damages not to exceed an amount equal to twice the damages awarded to the plaintiff'.[156]

While this statute does not eliminate multiple punitive damage awards, it does do two things that minimise the harm potentially caused by such awards. First, it removes the power to set the amount of the award from the jury and gives it to the trial court, coinciding with proposals made by some commentators.[157] Second, it sets a cap on the amount of the punitive damages award of twice the compensatory award, again mirroring proposals by some commentators.[158] Once again, while this statute mutes some of the negative effects of multiple punitive damages awards, it does so only in Connecticut and it fails to provide any credit for prior punitive damages verdicts or prior settlements that include a punitive damages component.

2.4.5. Minnesota

Minnesota's statute, enacted in 1992, uses the existence or prospect of multiple punitive damages awards as a factor to be considered when determining the appropriate amount of punitive damages to be awarded in any given case:

> 'Any award of punitive damages shall be measured by those factors which justly bear upon the purpose of punitive damages, including the seriousness of hazard to the public arising from the defendant's misconduct, the duration of the misconduct and any concealment of it, the degree of the defendant's awareness of the hazard and of its excessiveness, the attitude and conduct of the defendant upon discovery of the misconduct, the financial condition of the defendant, and the total effect of other punishment likely to be imposed upon the defendant

156 Conn. Gen. Stat. Ann. § 52–240b (2011).

157 See, e.g., Owen 1994, *supra* note 11, pp. 411–12 (discussing reform proposals to strip juries of their right to determine punitive damages).

158 Owen 1994, *supra* note 11, pp. 409–10 (describing the use of caps and multipliers of punitive damages to mitigate excessive punitive damages awards, but also recognizing the inflexibility of these proposals).

> as a result of the misconduct, including compensatory and punitive damage awards to the plaintiff and other similarly situated persons, and the severity of any criminal penalty to which the defendant may be subject'.[159]

As with all other state statutes, this approach applies only inside Minnesota and does not account for prior settlements that include a punitive damages component. Additionally, this approach carries with it only the potential for minimising or eliminating multiple punitive damages awards because prior awards are only a factor to be considered. In fact, allowing consideration of prior punitive damages as a factor could actually prove to be counterproductive because it involves notifying the jury that another jury has already found the defendant worthy of punishment.[160] Moreover, the statute requires trial courts to speculate on how many individuals might later file suit and on what future juries in other jurisdictions might or might not do.

2.4.6. Oregon

Oregon's statute, enacted in 1989, allows the trial court to reduce the punitive damages award after taking into account prior awards based upon the same conduct:

> '[U]pon the motion of a defendant the court may reduce the amount of any judgment requiring the payment of punitive damages entered against the defendant if the defendant establishes that the defendant has taken remedial measures that are reasonable under the circumstances to prevent reoccurrence of the conduct that gave rise to the claim for punitive damages. In reducing the awards of punitive damages under the provisions of this subsection, the court shall consider the amount of any previous judgment for punitive damages entered against the same defendant for the same conduct giving rise to a claim for punitive damages'.[161]

Accordingly, under this statute the trial judge must consider the existence of prior punitive damages awards in deciding whether or not to reduce the size of the jury verdict against the defendant. Once again, while this gives trial judges some discretion to minimise the effects of multiple punitive damages awards, it does not require them to do so. More importantly, this statute only applies to cases brought in Oregon and does not account for prior settlements that include a punitive damages component. It also fails to provide trial courts with the tools necessary to make these determinations.

While the attempts by these states to alleviate some of the unfairness caused by multiple punitive awards are laudable, they all suffer from the same shortcoming – they have no force and effect outside their own borders.[162] This self-evident truth is uniformly

159 Minn. Stat. § 549.20(3) (2011).

160 See Jeffries 1986, *supra* note 6, pp. 146–47 (stating that introducing prior punitive damage evidence to the jury could work against the defendant 'if, as seems inevitable, the jury takes a history of prior awards as evidence of liability in the instant case'.); Seltzer 1983, *supra* note 6, pp. 59–60 (warning that introducing prior punitive damage evidence can 'backfire against the defendant').

161 Or. Rev. Stat. § 31.730(3) (2011).

162 See e.g., *Fischer v. Johns-Manville Corp.*, 512 A.2d 466, 480 (N.J. 1986) ('At the state court level we are powerless to implement solutions to the nationwide problems created by asbestos exposure and litigation arising from that exposure'.).

recognised.[163] Indeed, the powerful and influential American Law Institute concluded in a 1991 report that a piecemeal approach might actually be counterproductive:

> 'This kind of single-state action, however, is an ineffectual response to the problem, because one state cannot control what happens in other jurisdictions. In fact, the state that acts alone may simply provide some relief to out-of-state manufacturers at the expense of its own citizen-victims, a situation that hardly provides much law reform incentive for state legislators'.[164]

Because none of the proposed solutions have gained sufficient support or approval from courts, only the United States Congress can fully solve this problem. Moreover, it is in the best interest of all concerned for Congress to pass legislation that not only solves the multiple punitive damages problem in a way that is fair to both plaintiffs and defendants, but that also equips trial courts to substantively and procedurally manage the solution when it is applied to a variety of factual scenarios. What follows is a discussion and critique of federal legislation sponsored by Senator Hatch, and then a proposal that more effectively solves the multiple punishments problem.

2.5. *Failed Federal Legislation*

Recognising the need for a federal legislative solution to this persistent problem, current Senators Orinn Hatch and Joseph Lieberman, and former Senator John Danforth have proposed 'The Federal Multiple Punitive Damages Act (hereinafter 'Act').[165] The Act was first proposed in 1995 but was not passed.[166] The Act was then reintroduced in 1997 but again failed to pass.[167]

While the Act would accomplish its goal of severely limiting the instances in which multiple punitive damage awards could be entered against a defendant based upon a single act or course of conduct, it still fails to deal with critical aspects of the problem and thus can be vastly improved both in its effectiveness and in its marketability. The proposal urged in this chapter fills the gaps left by the Act, materially improves the ability of judges to eradicate the multiple punishments problem, minimises the anticipated

163 See, e.g., *Leonen v. Johns-Manville Corp.*, 717 F. Supp. 272, 284–85 & n.7 (D.N.J. 1989) ('The problems associated with awarding exemplary damages in successive... litigations are... nationwide problems and call for a uniform solution'.); *W.R. Grace & Co. v. Waters*, 638 So. 2d 502, 505 (Fla. 1994) ('[L]ike the many other courts which have addressed the problem, we are unable to devise a fair and effective solution. Were we to adopt the position advocated by [defendant and limit multiple punitive awards], our holding would not be binding on other state courts or federal courts'.).

164 A.L.I. Report, *supra* note 15, p. 261 (1991). As discussed *infra*, the A.L.I. Report came out in support of a national class action solution to the multiple punitive damages problem. See *infra* note 178–184 and accompanying text.

165 See Schwartz 2003, *supra* note 11, p. 17; See The Multiple Punitive Damages Fairness Act, S. 5148–49, 104th Cong. (1995); see also The Multiple Punitive Damages Fairness Act of 1997, S. 454–55, 105th Cong. (1997).

166 The Multiple Punitive Damages Fairness Act, S. 5148–49, 104th Cong. (1995). Different legislation that would have had a similar effect was unsuccessfully introduced in the 1980s. See *supra* note 8.

167 The Multiple Punitive Damages Fairness Act of 1997, S. 454–55, 105th Cong. (1997).

objections to eliminating the problem, and better fulfills the policy concerns animating punitive damages jurisprudence. Before turning to the proposal, however, the Act in its most recent form will be briefly analysed and critiqued.

The most recent version of the Act contains the following Congressional findings, none of which are particularly controversial:

> (1) Multiple or repetitive imposition of punitive damages for harms arising out of a single act or course of conduct may deprive a defendant of all the assets or insurance coverage of the defendant, and may endanger the ability of claimants to receive compensation for basic out-of-pocket expenses and damages for pain and suffering.
> (2) The detrimental impact of multiple punitive damages exists even in cases that are settled, rather than tried, because the threat of punitive damages being awarded results in a settlement that provides for a higher award amount than would ordinarily be obtained. To the extent this premium exceeds what would otherwise be a fair and reasonable settlement for compensatory damages, assets that could be available for satisfaction of future compensatory claims are dissipated.
> (3) Fundamental unfairness results when anyone is punished repeatedly for what is essentially the same conduct.
> (4) Federal and State appellate and trial judges, and well-respected commentators, have expressed concern that multiple imposition of punitive damages may violate constitutionally protected rights.
> (5) Multiple imposition of punitive damages may be a significant obstacle to global settlement negotiations in repetitive litigation.
> (6) Limiting the imposition of multiple punitive damages awards would facilitate the resolution of mass tort claims involving thousands of injured claimants.
> (7) Federal and State trial courts cannot provide solutions to problems caused by the imposition of multiple punitive damages because they lack the power or authority to prohibit subsequent awards in other courts.
> (8) Individual State legislatures can create only a partial remedy to address problems caused by the multiple imposition of punitive damages, because each State lacks the power to control the imposition of punitive damages in other States.[168]

In light of these findings, the Act provides the following general rule:

> Except as provided in subsection (b), punitive damages shall be prohibited in any civil action in Federal or State court in which such damages are sought against a defendant based on the same act or course of conduct for which punitive damages have already been awarded against such defendant.[169]

Therefore, the general rule expressly prohibits the imposition of multiple punitive damages awards based upon the same act or course of conduct. The Act does, however, contain two limited exceptions to this prohibition. The first exception applies when the

168 The Multiple Punitive Damages Fairness Act of 1997, S. 454–55, 105th Cong. § 3 (1997).
169 *Ibid.*, at § 6(a).

trial court determines 'in a pre-trial hearing that the claimant will offer new and substantial evidence of previously undiscovered, additional wrongful behavior on the part of the defendant'.[170] The second exception applies when the trial court 'determines in a pre-trial hearing that the amount of punitive damages previously imposed [was] insufficient to either punish the defendant's wrongful conduct or deter the defendant and others from similar behavior in the future'.[171]

The Act further provides that if the trial court invokes either exception to the general rule, it must (i) make specific factual findings justifying the departure,[172] (ii) reduce the punitive award in the amount(s) the defendant previously paid in punitive damages based upon the same instance or course of conduct,[173] and (iii) prevent the jury from learning of the court's pre-trial determination.[174]

While a good start, the Act leaves numerous questions unanswered and fails to address important substantive and procedural areas that must be addressed if multiple punitive damages are to be effectively managed or eliminated. For example, why is the trial court making such determinations before the trial? More specifically, how is the trial court supposed to ascertain before the evidence is presented whether the plaintiff is offering or will offer 'new and substantial evidence of previously undiscovered, additional wrongful behavior on the part of the defendant'?[175] Likewise, unless the trial court personally presided over the previous trial at which punitive damages were awarded (highly unlikely), how is the trial court supposed to determine whether the evidence offered by the plaintiff in this trial is 'new and substantial' or 'previously undiscovered'?

Another related set of questions the Act raises is how the trial court is supposed to determine before the evidence is presented whether the prior punitive damages award was 'insufficient to either punish the defendant's wrongful conduct or deter the defendant and others from similar behavior in the future'.[176] It seems self-evident that the trial court could only make such a determination after evaluating the witnesses and other evidence offered by both the plaintiff and the defendant over the course of the trial.

Yet another critically important substantive question is not even raised by the Act – a question that must be answered if a federal legislative solution is to be workable. That question is how to handle settlements that include a punitive damages component. It is uncontroversial to say that one of the primary goals of the judicial system is to encourage parties to resolve their disputes outside of court. By allowing defendants to receive a credit for prior punitive damages paid as a result of the same act or course of conduct only after going to trial, the goal of encouraging settlements is severely undermined.

170 *Ibid.*, at § 6(b)(1).
171 *Ibid.*, at § 6(b).
172 *Ibid.*, at § 6(c)(1).
173 *Ibid.*, at § 6(c)(2).
174 *Ibid.*, at § 6(c)(3).
175 Taken at face value, this seems to direct the trial court to conduct a lengthy pre-trial hearing that could involve the introduction of much, if not most, of the plaintiff's case-in-chief. It would also require the plaintiff to offer at least some (if not all) the evidence relating specifically to punitive damages – evidence that would never even be offered unless the jury first determined that punitive damages were appropriate at all. It would also give the defendant a 'free look' at the plaintiff's punitive damages evidence before trial started, enabling the defendant to better prepare to counter this evidence at the actual trial.
176 *Ibid.*, at § 6(b).

What follows below is a proposal that comprehensively resolves the multiple punishments problem. This proposal attempts to address and answer all of the questions lingering in the Act and provides substantive fairness for both plaintiffs and defendants, making the proposal a materially more politically viable solution than the Act. But prior to examining the proposal, the other proposals put forth by commentators over the past twenty years will be briefly discussed.

2.6. *Commentators' Response to the Problem*

Over the past two decades, several proposed solutions to the multiple punishments problem have been offered by legal commentators. For a variety of reasons, none has yet been adopted (at least nationally) and none is likely to be adopted in the foreseeable future. What follows is a brief description and critique of these suggested solutions.

2.6.1. Class Actions

A number of prominent legal organizations and commentators have argued that the best solution to the multiple punitive damages problem is to utilise class actions.[177] For example, both the American Law Institute (hereinafter 'ALI') and the American Bar Association (hereinafter 'ABA') have advanced essentially the same proposed class action solution.[178] Both organizations agree that because existing class action rules are not sufficiently flexible to allow for effective use in mass tort cases, new federal legislation would be necessary.[179] The ALI and ABA solutions 'encourage the use of court-ordered class actions for trial as well as pre-trial preparation of any common question of law or fact in mass tort cases'.[180] This proposed solution would authorise mandatory class actions for all state and federal cases arising out of a mass tort claim.[181] There are numerous recognised problems with instituting such mandatory class actions for mass tort cases, including how to deal with conflicting state laws that would otherwise govern the members' claims,[182] how to deal with claims that have not yet accrued at the time of class certification,[183] federalism concerns about the propriety of federal court determination of state law,[184] lack of personal jurisdiction over one or more of the

177 See, e.g., American College of Trial Lawyers 1989, *supra* note 17, pp. 25–26 (proposing class actions as the remedy to multiple punitive damages awards); Denemark 2002, *supra* note 6, p. 967 (stating the problem of multiple awards 'simply disappears if all plaintiffs are joined into one class action'.).

178 See Revised Final Report and Recommendations of the A.B.A. Commission on Mass Torts (1989); A.L.I., Complex Litigation Project, Tentative Draft No. 2 (1990); and A.L.I. Report, *supra* note 15, ch.13.

179 See A.B.A. Report, *supra* note 8, ch.7, p. 72; A.L.I. Report, *supra* note 15, ch. 13, p. 409–10.

180 A.L.I. Report, *supra* note 15, ch.13, p. 413.

181 A.L.I. Report, *supra* note 15, ch.13, p. 414.

182 A.L.I. Report, *supra* note 15, ch.13, p. 419.

183 See *In re* Sch. Asbestos Litig., 789 F.2d 996, 1006 (3d Cir. 1986) (explaining that under-inclusiveness in a mandatory class action lawsuit would defeat its purpose); Crowley 2001, pp. 1528–29 (pointing out that class actions would adversely affect the compensation of plaintiffs not included in the class).

184 A.L.I. Report, *supra* note 15, ch.13, p. 419.

parties,[185] violation of the Anti-Injunction Statute,[186] and depriving litigants of the individualised choices and autonomy that otherwise accompany tort litigation. For these reasons and others, as both the ALI and the ABA concede, courts have consistently been hostile to using class action procedures in mass tort cases.[187] There is also little indication that Congress has any interest in modifying the class action rules to implement the proposed solutions.

2.6.2. Judicial Reformation of Common Law

One author has argued that the problem is one of common law origin and thus can be solved by judicial reformation of the common law.[188] Therefore, it is argued, a national legislative solution is unnecessary to solve the multiple punitive damages problem. After outlining the problem in some detail, Professor Denemark urges courts to take matters into their own hands and unilaterally grant defendants a credit for punitive damages that had previously been paid.[189] While Professor Denemark's judicial solution does take into account both verdicts and settlements,[190] it does not provide trial judges the necessary tools to make the determinations suggested in the proposal below.[191] More importantly, Professor Denemark's solution depends upon trial judges across the country voluntarily adopting the same approach to the problem,[192] an eventuality that most certainly will not happen because numerous courts have already disclaimed the authority to make such changes to the common law.[193]

185 A.B.A. Report, *supra* note 8, ch.7, p. 74.

186 A.B.A. Report, *supra* note 8, ch.7, p. 74.

187 A.B.A. Report, *supra* note 8, ch.7, p. 74; A.L.I. Report, *supra* note 15, ch.13, p. 409 (citing *In re* 'Agent Orange' Prods. Liab. Litig., 818 F.2d 145, 164 (2d Cir. 1987) aff'd 818 F.2d 145 (2d Cir. 1987)); Patton 1986, p. 560–61 (1986) (stating that although numerous judges, lawyers, and scholars think class actions are the solution to mass torts 'in actual practice, the class action device has proved generally unavailing as the mechanism to deal with thousands of separate lawsuits arising out of a common tort'.).

188 Denemark 2002, *supra* note 6, p. 931.

189 *Ibid.*, pp. 971–77.

190 *Ibid.*, pp. 972–74.

191 For example, while Professor Denemark declares that 'Plaintiffs' lawyers would presumably be able to learn in discovery what awards have been paid and will thus be better to advise clients than they can today,' Denemark 2002, *supra* note 6, p. 976, he neither elaborates on how they would learn of these awards nor proposes a mechanism for discovering them. In contrast, the proposal's creation of a National Punitive Damages Registry and its mandatory notification procedures ensure that the plaintiffs and their counsel will be notified of the prior punitive damages payments.

192 See Denemark 2002, *supra* note 6, p. 977 ('Judges in other jurisdictions that have not yet reached the question will not be bound to follow the setoff approach, but as more precedent accrues, a consensus may take shape that a setoff should be the law'.).

193 See, e.g., *Jackson v. Johns-Manville Sales Corp*, 781 F.2d 394, 415 (Miss. 1986) ('Congress' silence in the face of a desperate need for federal legislation in the field of asbestos litigation does not authorise the federal judiciary to assume for itself the responsibility for formulating what essentially are legislative solutions'.); *Spaur v. Owens-Corning Fiberglass Corp.*, 510 N.W.2d 854, 866 (Iowa 1994) (pointing out that 'both state and federal courts have recognised that no single court can fashion an effective response to the national problem flowing from mass exposure to asbestos products'.).

2.6.3. Other Proposals

A handful of other solutions to the multiple punitive damages problem have been proffered over the years, including abolishing punitive damages completely,[194] limiting recovery to the first plaintiff to receive a punitive damages verdict,[195] placing an aggregate ceiling on punitive damages for a single act or course of conduct,[196] creating a products liability insurance pool out of which the defendant's rival's premiums would be paid,[197] simply allowing the defendants to introduce evidence of prior awards to juries in later cases,[198] and entirely eliminating the jury from the determination of punitive damages awards.[199]

2.6.4. Limit Punitive Awards to only Private Wrongs

In a fairly recent article, a compelling argument was made that the historical practice of awarding punitive damages was limited to redressing private wrongs, hence the defendant could only be punished for harm caused to the individual plaintiff before the court.[200] In this article, Colby argues: 'Historically, then, punitive damages, even when regarded as punishment, were consciously limited to the amount necessary to punish the defendant for the wrong done, and the harm caused, to the individual plaintiff only'.[201] Accordingly, under this approach, the multiple punishments problem would be reduced as long as the jury followed the court's admonition to consider only the harm to the plaintiff when determining the appropriate level of punishment. But even Colby acknowledges that it is now generally accepted that punitive damages are modernly awarded to vindicate the public's interest in punishing the defendant for the harm (or threatened harm) to the public at large.[202] For example, the United States Supreme Court, in striking down the punitive damages award in *Gore*, evaluated whether the full scope of defendant's conduct was sufficiently reprehensible to justify the punitive damages award, rather than

194 See, e.g., Cole & Sales 1984, p. 1117.
195 This is the approach essentially utilised by the proposed federal legislation supported by Schwartz 2003, *supra* note 11, p. 9. There are numerous problems with such an approach, including encouraging manipulation of the trial schedule by defendants, see A.B.A. Report, *supra* note 8, ch.7, p. 73.
196 See, e.g., Owen 1982a, *supra* note 6, p. 48 (proposing an aggregate cap of the lesser of either five million dollars or five percent of the defendant's net worth).
197 See, e.g., Arnold 1983, p. 370.
198 See, e.g., Restatement (Second) of Torts § 908 cmt. e; *Fischer v. Johns-Manville Corp.*, 512 A.2d 466, 480 (N.J. 1986); Morris 1931, p. 1173.
199 See, e.g., Mallor & Roberts 1980, pp. 963–66.
200 See generally Colby 2003, *supra* note 2, pp. 613–28.
201 Colby 2003, *supra* note 2, p. 628.
202 See Colby 2003, *supra* note 2, pp. 603–07 (citing, *inter alia*, *In re* 'Agent Orange' Prod. Liab. Litig., 100 F.R.D. 718, 728 (E.D.N.Y. 1983). See also Cabraser 2001, p. 981 ('Punitive damages are not an entitlement of the victims, but of society: a punitive damages award is a civil punishment visited upon defendants to vindicate the public interest in deterrence, and to penalise conduct that violates the social contract and injures society'.); Boutrous & Olson 1990, p. 918 ('[P]unitive damages are imposed for purposes of retribution and deterrence by a system which simultaneously compensates the victim for his injury, and punishes the defendant for the wrong done to society by his conduct'.).

considering only the harm to the individual plaintiff in that case.[203] Nevertheless, this seems to be the type of approach the Supreme Court favoured in *Philip Morris*.

2.6.5. The Supreme Court's Final (Partial) Solution to the Multiple Punishments Problem

In 2008, the Supreme Court of the United States ventured into punitive damages for what is very likely the last time for the foreseeable future. *Philip Morris USA v. Williams* arose when the widow and personal representative of Jesse Williams' (Williams) estate brought an action against cigarette manufacturer Philip Morris, Inc., seeking compensatory and punitive damages for the death of her husband.[204] Williams began smoking Philip Morris cigarettes in the 1950s and continued until his death in 1997.[205] Williams died of lung cancer, which a jury found was primarily caused by his years of smoking.[206] Despite his family's efforts to the contrary, Williams continued to smoke defendant's cigarettes.[207] Upon learning he had cancer, Williams said, 'those darn cigarette people finally did it. They were lying all the time'.[208]

Despite a Surgeon General's report in 1964 which highlighted the connection between smoking and lung cancer, Philip Morris continued to 'encourage the impression that there was a genuine and continuing controversy' that the dangers of smoking were not clear.[209] Williams asserted that this type of publicity was fraudulent because Philip Morris 'knew that there was no legitimate controversy about the health effects of smoking and that defendant itself had no doubt that cigarette smoking carried serious health risks, including the risk of lung cancer'.[210]

After a full trial, the jury found in favour of Williams on both negligence and fraud grounds,[211] awarding US$ 21,485.80 in economic damages and US$ 800,000 in non-economic damages.[212] With respect to the negligence claim, the jury found Williams to be fifty percent at fault, and no punitive damages were awarded for this claim.[213] As for the fraud claim, the jury awarded US$ 79.5 million in punitive damages.[214] The trial court reduced that amount to US$ 32 million, finding the amount to be 'excessive under the United States Constitution'.[215] The trial court also reduced the non-economic damages to US$ 500,000 pursuant to Oregon state law.[216]

203 See *BMW of N. Am., Inc. v. Gore*, 517 U.S. 559, 572–74 (1996).
204 *Philip Morris USA v. Williams*, 48 P.3d 824, 828 (Or. Ct. App. 2002).
205 *Ibid.*, at 829.
206 *Ibid.*, at 829.
207 *Ibid.*, at 829. Williams' wife and children repeatedly told him that cigarettes were bad for his health, and his son attempted to give him articles that highlighted the dangers of smoking. *Ibid.*, at 829.
208 *Ibid.*, at 829.
209 *Ibid.*, at 833.
210 *Ibid.*, at 831.
211 *Ibid.*, at 828.
212 *Ibid.*, at 828.
213 *Ibid.*, at 828.
214 *Ibid.*, at 828.
215 *Ibid.*, at 828.
216 *Ibid.*, at 828.

Both parties appealed.[217] The Oregon Court of Appeals reversed the trial court's remittitur, reinstating the original amount of punitive damages.[218] In its decision to reinstate the US$ 79.5 million punitive damages award, the Court of Appeals evaluated Oregon's statutory 'criteria for an award of punitive damages' to determine whether a punitive damages award of any size was justified under the facts of the case,[219] finding that each of them supported a punitive damages award.

Next, the Court of Appeals considered the Oregon Supreme Court's decision in *Parrott*[220] as well as the *Gore* guideposts.[221] In light of all of the evidence, the court concluded that a punitive damages award of US$ 79.5 million was not unconstitutionally excessive and therefore should not have been reduced by the trial court.[222]

Philip Morris then sought review from the Oregon Supreme Court, which was denied.[223] The United States Supreme Court granted review, vacated, and remanded the case 'in light of *State Farm Mutual Automobile Insurance Co. v. Campbell*,'[224] a case it had decided while *Philip Morris* was on appeal.

On remand, the Oregon Court of Appeals re-examined the case in light of *State Farm*, but ultimately concluded that it was correct when it had previously reinstated the jury's original US$ 79.5 million punitive damages award.[225] The court concluded that 'an award of punitive damages in the amount of US$ 79.5 million does not violate the Due Process Clause under the guidelines provided by *State Farm* because the amount of the award is reasonable and proportionate to the wrong inflicted on decedent and the [citizens]' of the state of Oregon.[226]

After the Oregon Supreme Court affirmed the decision of the court of appeals,[227] the United States Supreme Court granted certiorari limited to the following issues as presented by Philip Morris: (1) their 'claim that Oregon had unconstitutionally permitted it to be punished for harming nonparty victims; and (2) whether Oregon had in effect disregarded the constitutional requirement that punitive damages be reasonably related to the plaintiff's harm'.[228]

2.6.5.1. *Before the United States Supreme Court*

Those who follow the Supreme Court's punitive damages jurisprudence carefully would have expected this case to provide the Court with the vehicle to clarify some of the

217 *Ibid.*, at 828.
218 *Ibid.*, at 843.
219 *Ibid.*, at 843.
220 *Ibid.*, at 840. In *Parrott*, the Court affirmed a verdict with a ratio of 87:1 for punitive and compensatory damages because the defendant's acts were 'particularly egregious'. *Ibid.*, at 841.
221 *Ibid.*, at 840–842.
222 *Ibid.*, at 842.
223 *Ibid.*, at 842.
224 *Ibid.*, at 842.
225 *Ibid.*, at 842 ('On remand, we reach the same result that we reached in our previous decision'.).
226 *Ibid.*, at 145.
227 *Ibid.*, at 1182.
228 *Philip Morris USA v. Williams*, 127 S. Ct. 1057, 1062 (2007).

uncertainty and ambiguity lingering in the wake of *State Farm*.[229] Court watchers were also anxious to see where newly appointed Chief Justice Roberts and Associate Justice Alito would come out on punitive damages, and how their addition to the Court since the last punitive damages case might tip the balance one way or the other.[230]

From all outward appearances, *Philip Morris* did not seem to be much more than a stripped down version of the prior *State Farm* case – a deep-pocketed member of an unpopular industry seeking to overturn a very large punitive damages award that followed a trial exposing its misdeeds. Indeed, many of the problems with the evidence in *State Farm* that could otherwise distract from the core substantive due process issue, *i.e.*, whether the punitive damages award was 'grossly excessive,' were not present in *Philip Morris*. For example, the trial court in *Philip Morris* did not admit evidence of individuals in other states who were harmed by the defendant, as had been done in *State Farm*.[231] Moreover, the evidence admitted at trial in *Philip Morris* did not concern other acts, whether similar or dissimilar, committed by Philip Morris, as had been the case in *State Farm*.[232] Accordingly, conventional wisdom suggested that the Supreme Court's opinion would focus on the *Gore* guideposts, with particular attention paid to the nearly 100:1 ratio of punitive damages to compensatory damages.[233] But lurking just beneath the surface was the real issue driving this case – the multiple punishments problem.

229 See Carol J. Gatewood, *Philip Morris Gives Justices a Chance to 'Exorcise' Phantom Plaintiffs*, LAW.COM, Oct. 31, 2006, www.law.com/jsp/llf/PubArticleLLF.jsp?id=1162375513739 ('The U.S. Supreme Court is presented today with the opportunity to untangle the web of confusion concerning punitive damages'.); Anthony J. Sebok, *The Upcoming Supreme Court Argument Involving Punitive Damages Awards and Big Tobacco: Can These Awards Be Based on Injury to Persons Other than the Plaintiff? Part Two in a Two-Part Series*, FINDLAW.COM, Oct. 24, 2006, http://writ.lp.findlaw.com/sebok/20061024.html (stating as one of the issues left unresolved by *Gore* and *State Farm*: 'Can punitive damages be used to punish a defendant for conduct that harms anyone other than the plaintiff (or plaintiffs, if there is more than one)?').

230 See Greg Stohr, *Roberts, Alito Will Decide Punitive Damages Caps at High Court*, BLOOMBERG.COM, October 30, 2006, www.bloomberg.com/apps/news?pid=20601070&sid=a1lNoJr8Oq2w&refer=politics (stating that Roberts and Alito are the 'wild cards in the case' and must decide whether to side with the conservatives, Scalia and Thomas, or the more centrist justices: Breyer, Kennedy, Souter, and Stevens); Joan Biskupic, *US$ 79.5M in Punitive Damages at Core of Supreme Court Case*, USA TODAY, Oct. 27, 2006, *available at* www.usatoday.com/news/washington/judicial/2006-10-26-damages_x.htm (quoting Mark Levy, a lawyer who closely monitors punitive damages jurisprudence: "The court is on the knife edge,' Levy says. If Roberts and Alito join the justices who dissented in the State Farm case and want to leave the matter to the states, Levy says, there would be 'a sudden and radical change in this area of the law'.').

231 *State Farm Mut. Auto. Ins. Co. v. Campbell*, 538 U.S. 408, 420–21 (2003) (stating that the trial court was convinced that there was no limit to the geographic scope of evidence that could be admitted under Court precedent); *Philip Morris*, 127 S. Ct. at 1061 (explaining that the plaintiff's attorney in *Philip Morris* had asked the jury to "think about how many other Jesse Williams' in the last 40 years in the State of Oregon there have been").

232 *State Farm*, 538 U.S. at 420–21.

233 See, e.g., CNNMoney.com, *Supreme Court to Hear Philip Morris Appeal*, May 30, 2006, http://money.cnn.com/2006/05/30/news/companies/scotus_philipmorris/index.htm ('The high court set no [sic] precise ratio between punitive and actual damages for determining what would be 'excessive' in violation of the Constitution's due process clause. But exceptions could be made, said [Justice] Kennedy, 'if a particularly egregious act has resulted in only a small amount of economic damages'. That legal standard will now be tested in this latest appeal'.).

While Justice Kennedy's majority opinion in *State Farm* purported to rely on principles of federalism in deciding that a jury is not permitted to punish a defendant for lawful, out-of-state conduct,[234] he also characterised the potential for multiple punishments as 'a more fundamental reason' for disallowing the other acts evidence.[235]

2.6.5.2. The Majority Opinion

Those who hoped the Court would provide additional clarification on the ratio guidepost were sorely disappointed – the Court declined to reach the *Gore* factors at all.[236] Writing for a bare five-member majority, Justice Breyer reversed the decision of the Oregon Supreme Court and vacated the US$ 79.5 million verdict.[237] From the very beginning of the opinion, Justice Breyer made it clear that the Court's eye was on the multiple punishments problem rather than on the *Gore* factors: 'The question we address today concerns… whether the Constitution's Due Process Clause permits a jury to base [a punitive damages] award in part upon its desire to punish the defendant for harming persons who are not before the court'.[238] The 'persons who are not before the court' are, of course, others who have been harmed by the defendant's same conduct who could later bring their own claims for punitive (and compensatory) damages. This opening statement in the opinion foreshadowed later pronouncements that make clear that the lurking and unresolved multiple punishments problem is heavily influencing the Court's punitive damages jurisprudence.

After summarizing the material facts and the procedural history of the case, Justice Breyer briefly traced the evolution of the Supreme Court's incursion into punitive damages.[239] He then declared that due process 'forbids a State to use a punitive damages award to punish a defendant for injury that it inflicts upon nonparties or those whom they directly represent, *i.e.*, injury that it inflicts upon those who are, essentially, strangers to the litigation'.[240] He then went on to explain that this was true for at least two reasons. First, punishing a defendant for harm to a nonparty would deprive the defendant of an opportunity to present all available defenses.[241] Second, punishing a defendant for harm to a nonparty 'would add a near standardless dimension to the punitive damages equation,' leaving open such questions as the number of victims and the circumstances and seriousness of their injuries.[242] But the more important, yet here not explicitly stated, reason is the multiple punishments problem. As Justice Kennedy (joined by, *inter alia*,

234 *State Farm*, 538 U.S. at 422.
235 *Ibid.*, at 422–23.
236 *Philip Morris*, 127 S. Ct. at 1062.
237 *Ibid.*, at 1062. Joining Justices Breyer were Chief Justice Roberts and Associate Justices Kennedy, Souter, and Alito.
238 *Ibid.*, at 1060.
239 *Ibid.*, at 1062–63.
240 *Ibid.*, at 1063.
241 *Ibid.*, at 1063.
242 *Ibid.*, at 1063.

Justice Breyer) noted in *State Farm*, punishing a defendant for harm caused to nonparties 'creates the possibility of multiple punitive damages awards for the same conduct'.[243]

Justice Breyer then clarified language from earlier opinions that had suggested that punishing a defendant for harm to others was permissible. First, he explained that while the Court had previously stated that it would be permissible to consider 'the potential harm defendant's conduct could have caused' when assessing punitive damages, only the potential harm to the plaintiff was appropriately considered.[244] Second, Justice Breyer corrected a misimpression left by the Court's suggestion in *Gore* that the Alabama Supreme Court's punitive damages calculation that likely included a consideration of harm to nonparties was 'error-free'.[245]

Justice Breyer then turned to the difficult task of distinguishing between the proper use of evidence of harm to nonparties and the improper and unconstitutional use of such evidence. Williams argued, and Philip Morris conceded, that harm to nonparties caused by the conduct that harmed the plaintiff was admissible and highly relevant to show the extent of the reprehensibility of the defendant's conduct.[246] Justice Breyer readily agreed: 'Evidence of actual harm to nonparties can help to show that the conduct that harmed the plaintiff also posed a substantial risk of harm to the general public, and so was particularly reprehensible'.[247] And while it may consider such evidence when evaluating defendant's reprehensibility, 'a jury may not go further than this and use a punitive damages verdict to punish a defendant directly on account of harms it is alleged to have visited on nonparties'.[248] Accordingly, Justice Breyer declared that due process required that juries be properly instructed on the permissible uses of evidence of harm to nonparties.[249]

Turning to the facts of this case, Justice Breyer agreed with Philip Morris that the Oregon Supreme Court upheld the jury's punitive damages award pursuant to a mistaken premise that it was permissible for the jury to punish Philip Morris for the harm it caused to nonparties.[250] The Oregon Supreme Court, Justice Breyer determined, had failed to grasp the difference between allowing a jury to consider harm to others when evaluating reprehensibility on the one hand and actually punishing Philip Morris for such harm on the other hand.[251] That the Oregon Supreme Court failed to appreciate this distinction was betrayed by its declaration that '[i]f a jury cannot punish for the conduct, then it is difficult to see why it may consider it at all'.[252] As Justice Kennedy had done in *State*

243 *State Farm Mut. Auto. Ins. Co. v. Campbell*, 538 U.S. 408, 423 (2003) (citing *BMW of N. Am., Inc. v. Gore*, 517 U.S. 559, 593 (1996) (Breyer, J., concurring)).

244 *Philip Morris*, 127 S. Ct. at 1063.

245 *Ibid.*, at 1063.

246 *Ibid.*, at 1064.

247 *Ibid.*, at 1064.

248 *Ibid.*, at 1064.

249 *Ibid.*, at 1064 ('We therefore conclude that the Due Process Clause requires States to provide assurance that juries are not asking the wrong question, *i.e.*, seeking, not simply to determine reprehensibility, but also to punish for harm caused to strangers'.).

250 *Ibid.*, at 1064–65.

251 *Ibid.*, at 1064–65.

252 *Ibid.*, at 1064–65.

Farm,[253] Justice Breyer analogised to recidivism statutes that permit taking into account a criminal defendant's other misconduct in determining the appropriate punishment for the offense before the court.[254]

In an attempt to provide practical guidance to lower courts called upon to apply this case, Justice Breyer explained that courts must take care not to 'authorize procedures that create an unreasonable and unnecessary risk of any such confusion occurring'.[255] Consequently, when there is a significant risk that the jury will misunderstand the distinction between using evidence of harm to nonparties in evaluating the defendant's level of reprehensibility and directly punishing the defendant for such harm, a court must put in place procedures (presumably jury instructions) that protect against such a risk, if requested by the defendant to do so.[256] While constitutionally mandated to take some precautions, states are afforded some flexibility in determining what those precautions will look like.[257] Concluding that the Oregon Supreme Court misunderstood and misapplied the constitutional standard, the Court remanded the case to the Oregon Supreme Court to apply the correct standard.[258]

While the Court's declaration that a jury may only punish a defendant for the harm caused to the plaintiff then before the court should serve to reduce the multiple punishments problem, this solution is far from perfect and leaves much of the problem still intact. First, the Court's solution rests on the illusion that juries will be able to follow its proposed limiting instructions. Justice Stevens, in his dissent in *Philip Morris*, states that the distinction the Court draws between considering harm to nonparties in the reprehensibility analysis and not considering it when computing damages to directly punish the defendant is a 'nuance [that] eludes me'.[259] Practically speaking, if the nuance eludes a Supreme Court Justice, it can be expected to elude the vast majority of jurors as well. This is not a minor point. Before the Court can rest easy knowing its conceptual understanding of how to solve the multiple punishments problem is being implemented, it must necessarily develop a framework 'so that courts can reach consistent and predictable results'.[260] Accordingly, while the Court's final word in *Philip Morris* purports to be a solution, it is not a particularly good or comprehensive one.

Second, limiting the scope to the recovery of private wrongs runs counter to other competing theories of punitive damages. As a result, there may be other state interests in allowing punitive damages that the Court's framework does not take into account. For example, 'punitive damages have been used to pursue not only the goals of retribution and deterrence, but also to accomplish, however crudely, a societal compensation goal: the redress of harms caused by defendants who injure persons beyond the individual

253 *State Farm Mut. Auto. Ins. Co. v. Campbell*, 538 U.S. 408, 423 (2003).

254 *Philip Morris*, 127 S. Ct. at 1065 (citing *Witte v. United States*, 515 U.S. 389, 400 (1995)).

255 *Ibid.*, at 1065.

256 *Ibid.*, at 1065.

257 *Ibid.*, at 1065 ('Although the States have some flexibility to determine what *kind* of procedures they will implement, federal constitutional law obligates them to provide *some* form of protection in appropriate cases'.).

258 See *Ibid.*, at 1065.

259 *Philip Morris USA v. Williams*, 127 S. Ct. 1057, 1066–67 (2007) (Stevens, J., dissenting).

260 Gash 2005, *supra* note 20.

plaintiffs in a particular case'.[261] The Court's solution does not consider that states may have an interest in assessing punitive damages to vindicate public interests. Conversely, the polar opposite theory – that punitive damages should only consider harm to the individual plaintiff[262] – argues against the Court's idea of allowing the jury to consider harm to nonparties under the *Gore* 'reprehensibility' guidepost. Thus, on both ends of a theoretical spectrum that may periodically describe a particular state's interest in assessing punitive damages, the Court's solution is inadequate.

3. A Proposal to Fully Solve the Multiple Punishments Problem

The proposal offered by the author of this chapter was first published in 2005 in the Northwestern Law Review, and contained an Appendix with proposed statutory language for national legislation.[263] What follows is a brief overview of the highlights of the proposal, which could be readily adapted to the tort system and structure of any European country.

3.1. Post-Judgment Certification

The first aspect of the proposal addresses the mechanism for allowing a trial judge to determine whether a punitive damages award has previously been entered against a defendant for the same act or course of conduct as that currently before the court. Under the proposal, when a defendant facing the possibility of multiple punitive damages based upon a single act or course of conduct wants to receive a credit for a payment of punitive damages, it must obtain an order from the trial court assigned to the case pursuant to which the punitive damages were paid certifying a Prior Punitive Damages Statement (the 'Statement'). As part of the request for certification, the defendant would be required to provide a detailed description in the Statement of the act or course of conduct for which the defendant was being punished. The defendant could seek this certification after either a punitive damages verdict or a settlement that expressly delineates the amount being allocated to punitive damages. In the case of a settlement, the settling parties would then have to jointly move the trial court for an order certifying the settlement, similar to good faith settlement motions routinely filed in jurisdictions that retain joint and several liability.[264]

261 Sharkey 2003, *supra* note 11, pp. 351–52.

262 See Colby 2003, *supra* note 200, pp. 613–28; see also Brief for the Petitioner, *Philip Morris USA v. Williams*, 127 S. Ct. 1057 (2007) (No. 05-1256), 2006 WL 2190746, at *17–21.

263 See Gash 2005.

264 See Moore & Thomas 2004, § 27.43 (explaining that when parties agree to settle and move the court to approve the settlement as made in good faith, the good faith settlement frees the settling defendant from further liability).

3.2. *National Punitive Damages Registry*

The second aspect of the Proposal for solving the multiple punishments problem is the creation of a National Punitive Damages Registry (the 'Registry') created and funded by federal legislation. The purpose and function of the Registry would be to serve as the central data center for the registration and posting of all Statements certified by trial courts and filed with the Registry. When a certified Statement arrived at the Registry, it would be catalogued and scanned onto the Registry's web site, which would be designed to facilitate easily cross-referenced access by any internet user. To effectively register a punitive damage payment with the Registry, the defendant would need to file with the Registry a duly authorised certification order from a state or federal trial court. This certification order would contain the Statement that details the act or course of conduct that led to the punitive damages payment by the defendant. The Statement would also need to state the exact amount of punitive damages paid.[265] Once a defendant has properly registered a Statement with the Registry, it would be immediately accessible on the internet.

Registration of the duly-certified Prior Punitive Damages Statement would entitle the registering defendant to a dollar-for-dollar credit against future punitive damages in the amount reflected in the Statement, but only for the same act or course of conduct detailed in the Statement, and the defendant would bear the burden of proving by clear and convincing evidence that this award is based upon the same act or course of conduct as that described in a duly registered Statement.

If the punitive damages award in the subsequent case exceeded the amount reflected in the Statement contained in the Registry, the defendant would be required to pay as punitive damages the greater of either (i) the difference between the actual punitive damages award and the amount reflected in the Statement,[266] or (ii) the lesser of the actual punitive damages awarded by the jury or an additional fifty percent of the compensatory damages awarded.[267] If, however, the punitive damages award is equal to

265 Such a requirement would fill a gap left by current law in helping defendants prove prior punitive damages payments. See *Dunn v. Hovic*, 1 F.3d 1371, 1389 (3d Cir.) ('[T]he factual record made by the defendant must, as a prerequisite to relief on due process grounds, include evidence demonstrating the amount of punitive damages it has actually paid in the past'.), *modified in part*, 13 F.3d 58 (3d Cir. 1993).

266 This is calculated by subtracting the amount reflected in the Prior Punitive Damages Statement from the punitive damages amount awarded by the jury in the instant case. Therefore, if the Prior Punitive Damages Statement reflected an earlier payment of US$ 10,000 and the current punitive award is in the amount of US$ 15,000, then the defendant will be required to pay US$ 5,000 as punitive damages, having received a US$ 10,000 credit for the earlier payment.

267 This is calculated by comparing the punitive damages award in the instant case with the compensatory damages award in the instant case. If the punitive damages award does not exceed one-half of the compensatory award, then the plaintiff receives an amount equal to the punitive damages award. If, however, the punitive damages award does exceed one-half of the compensatory damages award, then the plaintiff will receive one-half of the compensatory damages award. Therefore, if the punitive and compensatory damages awarded by the jury are US$ 10,000 and US$ 20,000 respectively, then the plaintiff will receive US$ 10,000. If, however, the punitive damage award is less than US$ 10,000, then the plaintiff will receive only the amount of such punitive award. If, on the other hand, the punitive award is greater than US$ 10,000, then the plaintiff will still only receive US$ 10,000, as that amount

or less than the amount reflected in the Statement, the plaintiff would receive as punitive damages the lesser of (i) the actual punitive damages award, or (ii) an additional fifty percent of the compensatory damages awarded by the jury to the plaintiff.

The proposal's conditional inclusion of an award equal to fifty percent of the plaintiff's compensatory damages differs from the approach taken in the Act or in any state statute. The basis for this inclusion is a consideration of one of the justifications for punitive damages – offsetting the plaintiff's attorneys' fees. Many courts and commentators argue that punitive damages are justified at least in part because they help pay the plaintiff's attorneys' fees incurred in bringing the case to trial and in bringing the defendant's reprehensible conduct to light.[268] Assuming this to be both true and sufficiently compelling, a persuasive case could be made for including within the proposal a provision that expressly grants to plaintiffs who prevail on claims for punitive damages their reasonable attorneys' fees, at least when such fees are greater than the amount the plaintiffs would otherwise collect in attorneys' fees under the proposal after accounting for the defendant's credit.[269] Such a provision was considered, but ultimately rejected in favour of using a figure of fifty percent of the compensatory damages as a benchmark for a variety of reasons more fully discussed in the Northwestern Law Review article where this proposal was first published.[270]

After a defendant who has previously registered a Statement is required to pay an additional amount following a later punitive damages verdict or settlement, that defendant would be entitled to move the trial court presiding over the subsequent case for an order certifying a Modified Prior Punitive Damages Statement (hereinafter 'Modified Statement'), which would add any additional details not contained in the original Statement and would add to the amount contained in the original Statement the amount of the subsequent payment made in conjunction with the case before the court. The Modified Statement would have to include, of course, a description of both cases for which punitive damages were paid.[271] The trial court would then evaluate the defendant's motion and, once approved, would enter an order certifying the Modified Statement. Consequently, the defendant would thereafter, where appropriate, be entitled to a credit in the amount contained in the Modified Statement.

4. Conclusion

Despite considerable scholarly debate and frequently expressed judicial concern, the multiple punishments problem continues to plague our tort system. While several state legislatures have attempted to mitigate the effects of this problem, such attempts are

represents the lesser of either the punitive damages award or one-half of the compensatory damages award.

268 See *supra* note 267.

269 *Cf.* Murphy 1998, p. 463 (arguing that plaintiffs who prove liability for punitive damages should be allowed to recover reasonable attorney's fees, but nothing else).

270 See Gash 2005, *supra* note 20.

271 In the event the defendant duly filed multiple Modified Statements as the result of a series of punitive damages awards or settlements, each subsequent Modified Statement would need to describe all prior cases in which punitive damages had been paid for which defendant was seeking a credit.

doomed to fail because they have no extraterritorial effect. Accordingly, this problem cries out for a national solution. While the United States Supreme Court's most recent pronouncement in *Philip Morris v. Williams* has ameliorated some of the impact of the multiple punishments problem, a comprehensive national solution is still needed. To date, the United States Congress has failed to rise to the occasion and pass meaningful legislation on this issue. Moreover, the Act it considered adopting does not adequately address all of the issues presented by the problem and would not provide courts with the appropriate tools for dealing with the problem even if the Act were passed.

In contrast, the proposal set forth in this chapter fully addresses the multiple punishments problem in a manner that is easily understood and applied by courts. Moreover, the proposal resolves the problem in a way that materially advances the objectives of punitive damages better than does either the Act or the status quo.

Bibliography

American Academy of Actuaries' Mass Tort Subcommittee 2007
American Academy of Actuaries' Mass Torts Subcommittee, 'Overview of Asbestos Claims Issues and Trends', American Academy of Actuaries, 2007, pp. 3–32.

American College of Trial Lawyers 1989
American College of Trial Lawyers, *Report on Punitive Damages of the Committee on Special Problems in the Administration of Justice*, Irvine, California: American College of Trial Lawyers, 1989, pp. 20–26.

Arnold 1983
Arnold, R.H., 'Punitive Damages in Products Liability Litigation: Redirecting the Windfall', *J of Products Liability*, 1983.

Behrens & Tedesco 2003
Behrens, M.A. & Tedesco, R.M., 'Two Forks in the Road of Asbestos Litigation', Mealey's Litigation Report: Asbestos, 2003.

Blatt *et al.* 2004
Blatt, R.L. *et al.*, *Punitive Damages A State-By-State Guide to Law & Practice*, Eagan, Minnesota: West Publishing Company, 2004.

Boutrous & Olson 1990
Boutrous, T.J. & Olson, T.B., 'Constitutional Restraints on the Doctrine of Punitive Damages', *Pepperdine L Rev*, 1990, pp. 907–930.

Cabraser 2001
Cabraser, E.J., 'Unfinished Business: Reaching the Due Process Limits of Punitive Damages in Tobacco Litigation Through Unitary Classwide Adjudication', *Wake Forest L Rev*, 2001, pp. 979–1041.

Carroll *et al.* 2002
Carroll, S.J. *et al.*, *Asbestos Litigation Costs and Compensation: An Interim Report*, San Diego, California: Rand Publishing, 2002.

Colby 2003
Colby, T.B., 'Beyond the Multiple Punishment Problem: Punitive Damages as Punishment for Individual, Private Wrongs', *Minn L Rev*, 2003, pp. 583–678.

Cole & Sales 1984
Cole, K.B. & Sales, J.B., 'Punitive Damages: A Relic That Has Outlived Its Origins', *Vand L Rev*, 1984, pp. 1117–1172.

Christian & Craymer 2003
Christian, G.S. & Craymer, D., 'Texas Asbestos Litigation Reform: A Model for the States', *S Texas L Rev*, 2003, pp. 981–1011.

Crowley 2001
Crowley, M.A., 'From Punishment to Annihilation: Engle v. R.J. Reynolds Tobacco Co.–No More Butts–Punitive Damages Have Gone Too Far', *Loy L A L Rev*, 2001, pp. 1513–1538.

Denemark 2002
Denemark, H.A., 'Seeking Greater Fairness When Awarding Multiple Plaintiffs Punitive Damages For a Single Act by a Defendant', *Ohio St L J*, 2002, pp. 931–978.

Dobbs 1993
Dobbs, D.B., *Law of Remedies*, Eagan, Minnesota: West Publishing Company, 1993.

Ellis 1982
Ellis, D.D., 'Fairness and Efficiency in the Law of Punitive Damages', *S Cal L Rev*, 1982, pp. 1–77.

Gash 2002
Gash, J., 'Beyond Erin Brockovich and A Civil Action: Should Strict Products Liability Be the Next Frontier for Water Contamination Lawsuits?', *Wash U L Q*, 2002, pp. 51–125.

Gash 2004
Gash, J., 'Punitive Damages, Other Acts Evidence, and the Constitution', *Utah L Rev*, 2004, pp. 1191–1277.

Gash 2005
Gash, J., 'Solving the Multiple Punishments Problem: A Call for a National Punitive Damages Registry', *Nw U L Rev*, 2005.

Gash 2011
Gash, J., 'The End of an Era: The Supreme Court (Finally) Butts Out of Punitive Damages for Good', *Fla L Rev*, 2011, pp. 525–563.

Geiser 1988
Gieser, S.C., 'Federal and State Environmental Law: A Trap for the Unwary Lender', *BYU L Rev*, 1988, pp. 643–703.

Greenberg 2004
Greenberg, M.S., 'What Mediators Need to Know about Class Actions: A Basic Primer', *Hamline L Rev*, 2004, pp. 191–224.

Hensler & Peterson 1993
Hensler, D.R. & Peterson, M.A., 'Understanding Mass Personal Injury Litigation: A Socio-Legal Analysis', *Brook L Rev*, 1993, pp. 961–1061.

Hondorf 1989
Hondorf, S.P., 'A Mandate for the Procedural Management of Mass Exposure Litigation', *N Ky L Rev*, 1989, pp. 541–591.

Jeffries 1986
Jeffries, J.C., 'A Comment on the Constitutionality of Punitive Damages', *Va L Rev*, 1986, pp. 139–158.

Keeton *et al.* 1984
Keeton, W.P. *et al.*, *Prosser and Keeton on the Law of Torts*, Eagan, Minnesota: West Publishing Company, 1984.

Madden & Owen 2000
Madden, M.S. & Owen, D.G., *Products Liability*, St. Paul, Minnesota: West Group, 2000.

Mallor & Roberts 1980
Mallor & Roberts, 'Punitive Damages: Toward a Principled Approach', *Hastings L J*, 1980, pp. 969–699.

Moore & Thomas 2004
Moore, E.C. & Thomas, M.P., *California Civil Practice*, San Francisco, California: Bancroft Whitney, 2004.

Morris 1931
Morris, C., 'Punitive Damages in Tort Cases', *Harv L Rev*, 1931, pp. 1173–1209.

Murphy 1998
Murphy, R.W., 'Superbifurcation: Making Rook for State Prosecution in the Punitive Damages Process', *N C L Rev*, 1998, pp. 463–556.

Nadel 1982
Nadel, A.G., 'Annotation, Propriety of Awarding Punitive Damages to Separate Plaintiffs Bringing Successive Actions Arising Out of Common Incident or Circumstances Against Common Defendant or Defendants ('One Bite' or 'First Comer' Doctrine)', *A L R*, 1982.

Owen 1982a
Owen, D.G., 'Problems in Assessing Punitive Damages against Manufacturers of Defective Products', *U Chi L Rev*, 1982, pp. 1–60.

Owen 1982b
Owen, D.G., 'Punitive Damages: Comment: Civil Punishment and the Public Good', *S Cal L Rev*, 1982, pp. 103–120.

Owen 1994
Owen, D.G., 'A Punitive Damages Overview: Functions, Problems and Reform', *Vill L Rev*, 1994, pp. 363–413.

Pace 1997
Pace, K.A., 'Recalibrating the Scales of Justice through National Punitive Damage Reform', *Am U L Rev*, 1997, pp. 1573–1638.

Patton 1986
Patton, T.E., 'Utilizing the Class Action Device in Mass Tort Litigation', *Tort Ins L J*, 1986, pp. 560–571.

Perillo 2004
Perillo, L.A., 'Scraping Beneath the Surface: Finally Holding Lead Based Paint Manufacturers Liable by Applying Public Nuisance and Market-Share Liability Theories', *Hofstra L Rev*, 2004, pp. 1039–1093.

Prosser 1971
Prosser, W.L., *The Law of Torts*, Eagan, Minnesota: West Publishing Company, 1971.

Rabin 1987
Rabin, R.L., 'Rethinking Tort and Environmental Liability Laws: Needs and Objectives of the Late 20th Century and Beyond', *Hous L Rev*, 1987, pp. 27–52.

Schwartz *et al.* 1999
Schwartz, V.E. *et al.*, 'Reining in Punitive Damages 'Run Wild': Proposals for Reform by Courts and Legislatures', *Brook L Rev*, 1999, pp. 1003–1034.

Schwartz 2003
Schwartz, V.E., *Death by a Thousand Cuts: How to Stop Multiple Imposition of Punitive Damages*, Washington, D.C.: National Legal Center for the Public Interest, 2003, pp. 8–17.

Schwarzer 1991
Schwarzer, W.W., 'Punishment Ad Absurdum', *Cal Law*, 1991.

Seltzer 1983
Seltzer, R.A., 'Punitive Damages in Mass Tort Litigation: Addressing the Problems of Fairness, Efficiency, and Control', *Fordham L Rev*, 1983, pp. 37–92.

Shapo 1994
Shapo, M.S., *The Law of Products Liability*, Salem, New Hampshire: Butterworth Legal Publishers, 1994.

Sharkey 2003
Sharkey, C.M., 'Punitive Damages as Societal Damages', *Yale L J*, 2003, pp. 347–453.

Slaughter & Vinson 1998
Slaughter, A. & Vinson, D., *Products Liability: Pharmaceutical Drug Cases*, Columbus, Ohio: Shepards/McGraw-Hill, 1998.

Voigt 2003
Voigt, S.T., 'Changing Standard of Punitive Damages Indicates Need for Legislative Reform', *Lawyers J*, 2003, p. 5.

Mark A. Geistfeld*

DUE PROCESS AND THE DETERRENCE RATIONALE FOR PUNITIVE DAMAGES

1. Introduction

Courts in the U.S. have widely recognized that punitive damages 'are aimed at deterrence and retribution'.[1] As conventionally justified, however, the deterrence rationale for punitive damages apparently violates the federal constitutional requirement of due process for reasons that are likely to be of concern for any jurisdiction that justifies punitive damages in this manner.

In a line of relatively recent cases, the U.S. Supreme Court has held that the Due Process Clause of the U.S. Constitution imposes procedural and substantive limitations upon tort awards of punitive damages.[2] The Court most recently addressed this constitutional inquiry in *Philip Morris USA v. Williams*.[3] The jury awarded US$ 821,485 in compensatory damages and US$ 79.5 million in punitive damages to the plaintiff due to the fraudulent manner in which the defendant tobacco company had induced her husband to smoke its cigarettes, ultimately causing his premature death. The defendant Philip Morris had engaged in a long-running scheme designed to dupe the general public into smoking cigarettes, leading the Oregon Supreme Court to conclude that this reprehensible conduct justified the US$ 79.5 million award.[4] In doing so, the court concluded that due process does not prohibit the jury 'from using punitive damages to punish a defendant for harms to nonparties'.[5] Following an appeal by the defendant, the U.S. Supreme Court reached the contrary conclusion and held that 'the Constitution's Due Process Clause forbids a State to use a punitive damages award to punish a defendant

* Sheila Lubetsky Birnbaum Professor of Civil Litigation, New York University School of Law.

1 *State Farm Mut. Auto. Ins. Co. v. Campbell*, 538 U.S. 408, 416 (2003).

2 In 1989, the Court left open the question 'whether due process acts as a check on undue jury discretion to award punitive damages in the absence of any express statutory limit'. *Browning-Ferris Indus. v. Kelco Disposal, Inc.*, 492 U.S. 257, 277 (1989). A decisive, affirmative answer to that question was provided by the Court a few years later in *BMW of N. Am., Inc. v. Gore*, 517 U.S. 559 (1996).

3 *Philip Morris USA v. Williams*, 549 U.S. 346 (2007). Hereinafter: '*Williams*'.

4 *Williams v. Philip Morris Inc.*, 127 P.3d 1165, 1175 (Or. 2006), cert. granted in part, 126 S.Ct. 2329 (2006).

5 *Ibid.* at 1181–82.

for injury that it inflicts upon nonparties or those whom they directly represent, *i.e.*, injury that it inflicts on those who are, essentially, strangers to the litigation'.[6]

By holding that the punitive award cannot punish the defendant for having caused harms to nonparties, *Williams* essentially limits punitive damages to the amount justified solely by the violation of the plaintiff's individual tort right. Unlike the criminal law, tort law is based upon individual rights and a corresponding set of individual duties.[7] Due to this individual right-duty nexus, tort law can tailor punitive damages to punish the defendant dutyholder for the way in which she violated the plaintiff's right, while also deterring the defendant from violating the plaintiff's right in the future – a purpose commonly called 'individual or specific deterrence'.

The limitation of punitive damages to individual deterrence could rule out punitive damage awards that are formulated to ensure that dutyholders will adequately consider the total social costs of their conduct, not merely the costs faced by an individual rightholder. To promote this objective of general deterrence, tort law must subject risky actors to liability for the full cost of the injuries that they have tortiously inflicted on others. Liability for compensatory damages can achieve this outcome, but in many cases the tortious actor is not sued by the full set of victims. The ensuing liability shortfall can be offset by the award of punitive damages to those victims who successfully sue and recover compensatory damages. These punitive awards, however, are based on nonparty harms for which the defendant has otherwise avoided liability. Consequently, if harms to nonparties are excluded from the damages calculation as a matter of due process, then it would seem to follow that courts are prevented from formulating punitive damages to further the social interest in general deterrence.

Of the two types of deterrence, general deterrence is of much greater practical importance. After all, how many cases are there in which an individual dutyholder threatens repeated violations of the tort right held by the same individual? The deterrence rationale for punitive damages instead has substantially greater practical import insofar as these damages deter both the defendant and similarly situated actors from breaching their tort duties owed to others in the community.

The issue is highlighted in a recent case involving a sports utility vehicle manufactured by Ford Motor Company with a design that allegedly had a higher incidence of rollover causing thirty more deaths per year as compared to another design on the market, thereby constituting a defect according to the plaintiff. Based on this evidence of defect, the plaintiff's attorney made the following closing arguments to the jury with respect to the claim for punitive damages:

1. 'This is how Ford looks at this. That little bit of thirty people being killed every year didn't matter. Those thirty people, those thirty extra people getting killed in a year didn't matter to them because it was just a little bitty number'.

6 *Williams*, at 353.

7 See, e.g., *Palsgraf v. Long Island R.R.*, 162 N.E. 99, 100 (N.Y. 1928) (holding that a tort plaintiff can recover only by showing that the defendant's breach of duty constitutes a "wrong' to herself, *i.e.*, a violation of her own right, and not merely a wrong to someone else, nor conduct 'wrongful' because unsocial').

2. 'It does matter about those people getting killed. Those thirty people do count. Those thirty people – that's thirty more people that got killed that year. If you expect these vehicles to last about twenty years, that's six hundred more people getting killed using this vehicle as opposed to [the alternative design that was available on the market]. That's serious'.
3. 'And that doesn't count the paralyzed people, the quadriplegics, the people with serious injuries, the thousands of people that have been in these events because of this rollover propensity of this vehicle that they knew about, and they knew it since day one but they chose profit over safety every time because they looked at it as numbers. They didn't look at it as lives, as people'.
4. 'I submit to you that the evidence is that they did it because they thought it was a little, small number… [T]hey did not look at it as thirty lives a year[ ], they didn't look at it as six hundred lives. That's how they should have looked at it, but that was not how they did it'.
5. 'They got together at the highest levels of Ford Motor Company and they made a judgment that rather than delaying and improving the [SUV in question], they were going to sell the vehicle as it was and that they were going to risk people's lives and they were going to risk serious injuries like we have here today. They were going to risk people's brains'.
6. '[Plaintiff] is here today with a brain injury and six hundred other people, or however many it is, lost their lives, and numerous others have brain injuries or are paralyzed, quadriplegic, have extremely serious injuries. We believe that you should tell Ford Motor Company what you think about this kind of thing'.[8]

The jury awarded the plaintiff US$ 15,000,000 in punitive damages. On appeal, the Supreme Court of South Carolina overturned the punitive damages award because it was based on nonparty harms in violation of *Williams*. 'It is unmistakable that the closing argument relied heavily on inadmissible evidence'.[9] In light of this type of ruling, *Williams* would seem to foreclose an award of punitive damages that is justified by the social concern for general deterrence.

In this chapter, I will show that punitive damages can still further the social interest in general deterrence, at least for what is arguably the most important class of cases. As explained more fully in section 2 below, the individual tort right is now routinely situated in mass markets, a social circumstance that is far different from the type of rights-violations redressed by the early common law.[10] These changed circumstances explain why tort liability in the twentieth century started to be justified in terms of social interests such as the promotion of general deterrence. For reasons given in section 3, this type of rationale for punitive damages is now ruled out by *Williams*, which held that the punitive award must be limited to the violation of the plaintiff's tort right in order to satisfy the federal constitutional requirement of due process. The punitive award, in other words, must vindicate the plaintiff's tort right and nothing more. Nevertheless, section 4 explains why a punitive award that fully vindicates the individual tort right will also further the social interest in general deterrence when the individual tort right is situated

8 *Branham v. Ford Motor Co.*, 701 S.E.2d 5, 21–22 (S.C. 2010).

9 *Ibid.* at 22.

10 This portion of the argument is largely based on Geistfeld 2011a.

in a mass market, the circumstances present in products liability and numerous other tort cases. A punitive award that vindicates the individual right will necessarily supply the requisite protection for all similarly situated rightholders in the market. In these cases, a constitutional requirement of due process does not foreclose an award of punitive damages that promotes general deterrence, but the rationale for these awards must nevertheless be framed in terms of the individual tort right in order to pass constitutional muster.

2. Individual Rights and Mass Markets

As Justice Oliver Wendell Holmes famously observed, 'Our law of torts comes from the old days of isolated, ungeneralized wrongs, assaults, slanders, and the like, where the damages might be taken to lie where they fell by legal judgment'.[11] Justice Holmes made this observation at the end of the nineteenth century when courts in the U.S. were consolidating the highly individuated liability rules under the writ system into a general principle of negligence liability. Having recognized that tort law originated with 'isolated, ungeneralized wrongs,' Justice Holmes then observed that 'the torts with which our courts are kept busy today are mainly the incidents of certain well known businesses. They are injuries to person or property by railroads, factories, and the like'.[12] As the economy expanded throughout the twentieth century, individuals became increasingly situated in a mass market of some sort. In this context, the nature of an individual-rights violation is often quite different from the isolated, ungeneralized wrongs that were redressed by the early common law. Today, tort liability routinely involves the individual redress of widespread wrongs in mass markets, the consequences of which are fully illustrated by the modern regime of strict products liability.

Under the early common law, the duty of product sellers was largely limited by the contractual relationship. This limitation of duty was finally demolished by Judge Benjamin Cardozo in the 1916 landmark opinion *MacPherson v. Buick Motor Co.*[13] In the following years this decision was widely adopted, subjecting product sellers to a general rule of negligence liability for defective products. The widespread adoption of negligence liability then created a rationale for strict liability. In the highly influential case *Escola v. Coca Cola Bottling Co.*, Justice Roger Traynor of the California Supreme Court argued in a concurring opinion that the negligence rule, if properly applied, would involve insurmountable problems of proof: 'An injured person... is not ordinarily in a position to refute [the manufacturer's evidence of reasonable care] or identify the cause of the defect, for he can hardly be familiar with the manufacturing process as the manufacturer himself is'.[14] This evidentiary problem does not exist under a rule of strict liability, and so the adoption of that rule would give product sellers the financial incentive to distribute nondefective products. Traynor found further support for the rule of strict liability in the implied warranty of merchantability and the related ancient rule that

11 Holmes 1897, p. 467.
12 *Ibid.* at 467.
13 *MacPherson v. Buick Motor Co.*, 111 N.E. 1050, 1053 (N.Y. 1916).
14 *Escola v. Coca Cola Bottling Co.*, 150 P.2d 436, 441 (Cal. 1944) (Traynor, J., concurring).

imposed strict liability on the sellers of contaminated food.[15] The doctrinal and policy arguments for strict liability were compelling. In 1963, the California Supreme Court accepted Traynor's argument for strict products liability.[16] The rule of strict products liability was then adopted in section 402A of the *Restatement (Second) of Torts* in 1965. By 1971, twenty-eight states had adopted the *Restatement (Second)* rule of strict liability for product defects; by 1976, forty-one states had adopted it. Today, only a few states have formally rejected the rule of strict products liability, although each nevertheless largely applies the liability rules adopted by the other states.

The growth of products liability has been astounding, with much of it attributable to issues that had not been extensively considered when the *Restatement (Second)* rule of strict products liability was promulgated in the 1960s. This liability rule was formulated to deal with cases in which a defect caused the product to malfunction and injure the user, such as an exploding bottle of soda.[17] By the 1970s, the allegations of defect moved beyond malfunctioning products. Even if the product functioned according to design, plaintiffs began claiming that the design itself was defective for not containing a particular safety feature, like a guard on a machine. Plaintiffs also claimed that properly designed and manufactured products were defective for not adequately warning consumers about product risks. The claims of design and warning defects now constitute the bulk of products liability suits. Allegations of warning defects, for example, are involved in the massive number of suits involving asbestos liability.[18] 'From an inauspicious beginning in the late 1960s, asbestos litigation has generated over 730,000 claims, at an overall cost of at least US$ 70 billion'.[19] The asbestos cases are an extreme example, but they illustrate how the scope of tort liability far exceeds that which was contemplated when courts first adopted the rule of strict products liability.

This extension placed tort law in the center of disputes involving widespread harms. Whereas product cases initially involved singular accidents caused by an isolated product malfunction (like the exploding bottle of soda), the extension of products liability to encompass product designs and warnings implicates *all* consumers of the product because each one is exposed to the risks of the defective design or warning. Like tort law more generally, products liability no longer is limited to isolated, ungeneralized wrongs but now often redresses the widespread accidental harms that can occur in mass markets.

In a mass market, the individual tort right of each consumer is necessarily interrelated. Individual consumers have different preferences for product safety and other aspects of quality, making it ordinarily infeasible for product sellers in a mass market to completely satisfy the preferences of everyone. Product sellers in mass markets respond to aggregate consumer demand, and so product liability rules are formulated by reference to the safety

15 See *ibid.* at 441–42.

16 See *Greenman v. Yuba Power Prods., Inc.*, 377 P.2d 897, 900–01 (Cal. 1963).

17 See generally Green 2009 (showing that the rule of strict products liability was initially formulated to deal with the problem of malfunctioning products).

18 E.g., *Borel v. Fibreboard Paper Prods. Corp.*, 493 F.2d 1076 (5th Cir. 1973).

19 Hanlon & Smetak 2007, p. 526.

expectations of the ordinary or average consumer, not the particular plaintiff.[20] Because a manufacturer's safety decision depends on the safety needs of the average or ordinary consumer, any particular rights-violation can have categorical effects for similarly situated rightholders. A single claim seeking recovery for injuries caused by a defectively designed product, for example, implicates all other identically designed products in the entire market. One claim can also influence the litigation decisions of similarly situated consumers, further influencing the manufacturer's safety decisions with respect to the entire market.[21] Litigation of the individual tort case does not involve an isolated instance of wrongdoing that was characteristic of the claims adjudicated by the early common law, but can now affect other rightholders (consumers) in the mass market. The imposition of liability in a single case involves conduct directed towards the market as a whole, creating categorical effects that are not present in the traditional torts context.

3. The Deterrence Rationale for Punitive Damages and the Constitutional Problem of Due Process

The growth of mass markets throughout the twentieth century coincides with the increased prominence of punitive damages practice in the U.S., including the constitutional regulation of this practice by the U.S. Supreme Court. Though awarded infrequently, punitive damages have been a focal point in the debate over tort reform. Public scrutiny is invited by the enormous punitive awards in some product cases, like the US$ 28 billion punitive damages award one jury levied against a tobacco company.[22] The reasons for these developments, once again, are most easily illustrated by product cases.

The plaintiff can receive punitive damages in a 'great majority' of states, but 'only when the tortfeasor has committed quite serious misconduct with a bad intent or bad state of mind such as malice'.[23] Most courts in the U.S. have recognized that product cases 'require a unique description of what specific conduct will render [the manufacturer] liable for punitive damages'.[24]

20 See, e.g., *Campbell v. General Motors Corp.*, 649 P.2d 224, 233 n.6 (Cal. 1982) (holding that under the consumer-expectations test, 'the jury considers the expectations of a hypothetical reasonable consumer, rather than those of the particular plaintiff in the case').

21 Mass torts routinely involve defective products. The litigation dynamic for a mass tort involves a movement from the immature to mature stages. See Nagareda 2007, p. 11–28.
The transition to the mature stage of litigation comes only when the threat to prevail is such that defendants face a substantial probability of loss in the event of trial. The usual way to establish the credibility of this threat, not surprisingly, is through actual plaintiff victories in some early cases.
Ibid. at 15.

22 These awards are often substantially reduced by judicial review. See, e.g., *Bullock v. Philip Morris USA*, 138 Cal. App. 4th 1029, 174–80 (2006) (affirming remittitur that reduced punitive damages award of US$ 28 billion to US$ 28 million).

23 Dobbs 2000, p. 1062.

24 *Owens-Illinois, Inc. v. Zenobia*, 601 A.2d 633, 653 (Md. 1992) (quoting 2 J. Ghiardi and J. Kircher, Punitive Damages Law and Practice § 21.01, at 2 (1985)).

> 'In summary, case law establishes that a defendant must have specific knowledge of a product's defect and its potential for harm before an exemplary award is appropriate. This knowledge is usually gained through defendant's testing procedures before marketing or through postmarketing consumer accident reports and complaints received by the defendant'.[25]

As one court described this inquiry, 'the plaintiff must prove (1) actual knowledge [or a willful refusal to know] of the defect on the part of the defendant, and (2) the defendant's conscious or deliberate disregard of the foreseeable harm resulting from the defect'.[26]

To understand why this standard requires actual knowledge of defect, we need to understand why a manufacturer would sell a product that it knows to be defective. Under the risk-utility test adopted by the majority of U.S. jurisdictions, a product design or warning is defective only if the burden or cost of the safety precaution (denoted B) is less than the expected injury costs that would be avoided by the precaution (the probability of accident P multiplied by the amount of loss L), or $B < PL$.[27] When the risk-utility test is adequately enforced, it would be less costly for the manufacturer to make the safety investment (and pay the cost B) than to incur liability for the associated injury costs (with expected liability costs of PL). This financial calculus changes, however, if the manufacturer does not expect to incur liability for every case in which a defect causes physical harm.

Suppose the manufacturer expects that only one out of ten consumers with meritorious claims will actually sue and recover, perhaps because they are unable to identify the defect (like the failure to warn of a risk of cancer) as the cause of their injuries (cancer). To maximize profits, the manufacturer would make the safety decision by comparing the cost of the precaution (B) with these expected liability costs ($1/10 \cdot PL$). The cost of the safety precaution could exceed the manufacturer's expected liability costs, creating an incentive to sell the defective product:

$$\textit{Expected Liability} = 1/10 \cdot PL < B < PL = \textit{Expected Injury Costs}$$

This deterrence problem can be solved by punitive damages. If each plaintiff who recovers compensatory damages were to receive a total damages award ten times greater than the actual loss, the manufacturer's expected liability costs would equal the expected injury costs ($1/10 \cdot PL \cdot 10 = PL$). When punitive damages are formulated in this manner, the manufacturer has a sufficient financial incentive to comply with the tort duty:

$$B < 1/10 \cdot PL \cdot 10 = PL$$

The deterrence rationale explains why punitive damages should be awarded only when the manufacturer has actual knowledge of the defect, but these extracompensatory damages 'are aimed at deterrence *and* retribution'.[28] As in the case of deterrence, the retributive rationale for punitive damages also requires actual knowledge of the defect.

25 *Ibid.*
26 *Ibid.*
27 See Geistfeld 2011b.
28 *State Farm Mut. Auto. Ins. Co. v. Campbell*, 538 U.S. 408, 416 (U.S. 2003) (emphasis added).

When used for retributive purposes, punitive damages are supposed to punish a defendant in order to vindicate the plaintiff's tort right. The premise of these awards is that the plaintiff's tort right is not adequately protected by the compensatory damages remedy, thereby justifying extracompensatory damages in certain cases. The prior analysis assumed that the amount of the defendant's liability or damages (D) equals the legal valuation of the loss (L). This assumption is unrealistic because in the event of a fatal accident, the defendant dutyholder does not have to pay damages for the decedent rightholder's loss of life's pleasures.[29] Liability in a case of wrongful death is governed by a *wrongful death statute* that gives specified beneficiaries, typically immediate family members, a right to recover for their own injuries stemming from the decedent's loss of life. Wrongful death statutes do not provide recovery for the decedent's loss of life's pleasures, however, because tort damages cannot compensate a dead person. Consequently, a defendant can incur less tort liability by killing the plaintiff rather than injuring him. For example, the average jury verdict in New York City from 1984–1993 in a case of wrongful death was over US$ 1 million, whereas the average verdict in a case of brain damage was over US$ 3 million.[30] As illustrated by the problem of wrongful death, the compensatory damages remedy does not fully protect the rightholder's interest in bodily integrity, and so the tort right is not wholly defined by an entitlement to compensatory damages. The tort right instead is primarily concerned about the prevention of injury, obligating sellers to provide reasonably safe or nondefective products. By selling a product it knows to be defective, a manufacturer has acted in conscious disregard of the plaintiff's right, even if the manufacturer fully expects to pay compensatory damages. The defendant's payment of compensatory damages in such a case would not fully vindicate the rights-violation, explaining why the defendant can be subject to extracompensatory liability as punishment or retribution.[31]

These attributes of punitive damages have created significant practical problems. Punitive damage awards are not coordinated across cases and jurisdictions. For deterrence purposes, only one or a few plaintiffs has to receive a particularly large punitive award to restore the seller's financial incentive for complying with the tort duty (US$ 28 billion?). However, plaintiffs who subsequently sue could still seek punitive damages as retribution or punishment for the way in which the defendant knowingly violated their individual tort right. What ensures that a defendant manufacturer does not incur an excessive amount of punitive damages across the full spectrum of cases?

To address this problem, the U.S. Supreme Court has held that defendants are protected against excessively high punitive damage awards by the Due Process Clause of the U.S. Constitution. To determine whether a punitive damages award satisfies due

29 McClurg 2005, p. 18–33.

30 Geistfeld 2008, p. 358 (citing Edward A. Adams, *Venue Crucial to Tort Awards: City Verdicts Depend on Counties*, N.Y.L.J., April 4, 1994, at 1, 5).

31 Although premature death is the most extreme example, any physical harm ordinarily is an irreparable injury that cannot be adequately restored by an award of compensatory damages, explaining why a defendant's willingness to pay compensatory damages does not bar an award of punitive damages. See Geistfeld 2011c (explaining why the valuation of injury within the tort duty exceeds the valuation of injury within the compensatory damages remedy, a 'misalignment' that is then enforced by awards of punitive damages in the appropriate cases).

process, judges must evaluate the award in terms of three factors: '(1) the degree of reprehensibility of the defendant's misconduct; (2) the disparity between the actual or potential harm suffered by the plaintiff and the punitive damages award; and (3) the difference between the punitive damages awarded by the jury and the civil penalties authorized or imposed in comparable cases'.[32]

In elaborating upon this inquiry, the Court has held 'that, in practice, few awards exceeding a single-digit ratio between punitive and compensatory damages, to a significant degree, will satisfy due process'. The Court partially justified the single-digit ratio with the 'long legislative history, dating back over 700 years and going forward to today, providing for sanctions of double, treble, or quadruple damages to deter and punish'.[33] Historical practice is a defensible way to address the intractable problem of telling the jury how it can appropriately translate reprehensibility into a dollar damages award. Yet reprehensibility involves many factors, and so the Court recognizes that even higher awards can be justified, making the single-digit ratio only a presumptive requirement.

The Court has identified the reprehensibility factor as '[t]he most important indicium of the reasonableness of a punitive damages award'.[34] All else being equal, greater reprehensibility merits more punishment and justifies a greater quantum of punitive damages. The constitutionality of virtually any punitive damages award, therefore, depends on whether the size of the award is an excessive retributive sanction for the defendant's reprehensible misconduct, and yet the Court has offered little guidance on the matter. Outside of the historical practice that can justify punitive awards up to four times greater than the compensatory damages, what enables a court to translate reprehensibility into an even greater amount of damages?

The Court's due process jurisprudence has also created considerable uncertainty over the deterrence rationale for punitive damages. In *Philip Morris USA v. Williams*, the Court recently held that 'the Constitution's Due Process Clause forbids a State to use a punitive damages award to punish a defendant for injury that it inflicts on nonparties or those whom they directly represent, *i.e.*, injury that it inflicts on those who are, essentially, strangers to the litigation'.[35] By holding that the punitive award cannot punish the defendant for having caused harms to nonparties, *Williams* essentially limits punitive damages to the amount justified solely by the violation of the plaintiff's individual tort right. This constitutional limitation would seem to rule out the deterrence rationale for punitive damages, at least as conventionally formulated. If, for example, the manufacturer expects to be sued by only one out of ten injured consumers and accordingly decides to sell a defective product, then the deterrence-based total damages award must be ten times greater than the compensatory damages recovered by the plaintiff. The plaintiff would receive damages based on the tortious harms allegedly suffered by nine other consumers who are not pursuing their claims, yielding a punitive award that is based on nonparty harms in violation of *Williams*.

32 *State Farm Mut. Auto. Ins. Co. v. Campbell*, 538 U.S. 408, 418 (2003).
33 *Ibid.* at 425.
34 *Ibid.* at 419 (quotation omitted).
35 *Williams*, at 353.

Lacking a deterrence rationale, the punitive award must be justified solely in the retributive terms of punishing the defendant for having consciously violated the plaintiff's right to physical security. Is retribution inherently subjective and arbitrary, violating due process unless constrained by some objective measure such as the single-digit ratio? Or is there a way to conceptualize the appropriate amount of damages for retributive purposes?

4. The Vindication of Individual Rights in Mass Markets

To punish the defendant and vindicate the plaintiff's tort right, the punitive award must first disgorge any wrongful gains the defendant expected to derive by violating the right. The mere elimination of the expected wrongful gains is not enough, however, because the award would not punish the defendant for having adopted this wrongful perspective in the first instance. The punitive award must be increased further to reject altogether the wrongful perspective, thereby vindicating the right in its entirety.[36]

To illustrate, suppose the defendant manufacturer estimated that it faced only a ten percent chance of incurring liability for the defective product. For every tortiously caused harm (L), the defendant expected to pay damages (D) in only one out of ten cases. For the tortious risk faced by each one of these individual rightholders, including the plaintiff, the defendant ignored the legally required valuation ($P \bullet L$) and instead considered only its expected liability costs, $(P \bullet D) \bullet (1/10)$. To eliminate this aspect of the expected wrongful gain, vindication of an individual tort right requires the defendant to incur total damages D that would equate its wrongful perspective $(P \bullet D) \bullet (1/10)$ with the perspective required by the tort right ($P \bullet L$):

$$\text{Solve for } D, \text{ where } (P \bullet D) \bullet (1/10) = (P \bullet L).$$

The solution is $D = 10L$, and so the total amount of damages D must be ten times greater than the measure of full compensation L in order to eliminate the expected wrongful gains. To punish the defendant for having adopted this wrongful perspective, the damages must then be increased to fully vindicate the individual tort right. The historical practice of double or treble damages serves as a presumptive guideline according to the U.S. Supreme Court, yielding a total award in this particular case that is 20 to 30 times greater than the compensatory damages.

Vindicating the individual tort right only requires the jury to consider the defendant manufacturer's misconduct toward the plaintiff, thereby satisfying the important due process requirement that the punitive award cannot be based on harms suffered by nonparties to the litigation. Vindictive damages are based on the defendant's *expected* wrongful gain vis-à-vis the individual rightholder, an amount that does not require the court to determine the tortious harms *actually* suffered by nonparties. To be sure, that same misconduct also applies to a much larger group of similarly situated rightholders

36 See generally Geistfeld 2008b, pp. 272–73 (developing this conception of punitive damages and applying it to the facts and constitutional concerns of *Williams*). The ensuing analysis is an elaboration of an argument from this article. See *ibid.* at 297–301.

(consumers), but the punitive awards is formulated solely by reference to the individual tort right. In mass markets, an award that vindicates the individual right necessarily accounts for the dutyholder's misconduct toward similarly situated rightholders, increasing the award in the prior example by a factor of ten – the equivalent of ten fully compensatory awards to ten different victims. In mass product markets, vindication of the individual tort right necessarily accounts for harms to nonparties as required by the social objective of deterrence.

5. Conclusion/Recommendations

Any evaluation of punitive damages must consider whether it is appropriate to pursue the objectives of punishment and deterrence within the tort system. Tort cases now frequently involve widespread wrongs in mass markets, as when a corporation distributes a defectively designed product to large numbers of consumers. Behavior causing widespread social harms ought to be punished and deterred in many cases, but liability for social wrongdoing is ordinarily a matter of criminal law. Punishing such behavior with punitive damages suffers from the obvious problem that tort law does not provide defendants with the procedural safeguards of the criminal law. Consequently, the requirements of due process limit the defendant's liability to the violation of plaintiff's individual tort right, the only legal claim that can be fairly defended by the defendant in a tort suit. The limitation of punitive damages to the amount required to vindicate the plaintiff's tort right, however, does not prevent these awards from furthering the social interest in general deterrence. In a mass market, the rights violation suffered by the plaintiff/consumer (physical harm caused by the defective product design or warning) is no different from the violations faced by a large number of similarly situated rightholders (other consumers in the market exposed to the defective product). Due to the interdependence of rights-violations in mass markets, a punitive award that fully vindicates the plaintiff's tort right will necessarily account for the manner in which the defendant failed to adequately account for the interests of similarly situated rightholders. Punitive damages can further the social interest in general deterrence, even though the fundamental requirement of due process limits a defendant's tort liability to the amount of damages that vindicate the plaintiff's individual tort right.

Bibliography

Dobbs 2000
Dobbs, D., *The Law of Torts*, St. Paul: The West Group, 2000.

Geistfeld 2011a
Geistfeld, M., 'Legal Ambiguity, Liability Insurance, and Tort Reform', *DePaul L Rev*, 2011, pp. 539–571.

Geistfeld 2011b
Geistfeld, M., *Principles of Products Liability 2nd*, New York: Foundation Press, 2011.

Geistfeld 2011c
Geistfeld, M., 'The Principle of Misalignment: Duty, Damages, and the Nature of Tort Liability', *Yale L J*, 2011, pp. 142–193.

Geistfeld 2008a
Geistfeld, M., *Tort Law: The Essentials*, New York: Aspen Publishers, 2008.

Geistfeld 2008b
Geistfeld, M., 'Punitive Damages, Retribution, and Due Process', *S Cal L Rev*, 2008. pp. 263–309.

Green 2009
Green, M., 'The Unappreciated Congruity of the Second and Third Torts Restatements on Design Defects', *Brooklyn L Rev*, 2009, pp. 807–837.

Hanlon & Smetak 2007
Hanlon, P., & Smetak, A., 'Asbestos Changes', New York University Annual Survey of American Law, 2007, pp. 525–606.

Holmes 1897
Holmes, O. W., 'The Path of the Law', *Harv L Rev*, 1897, pp. 457–478.

McClurg 2005
McClurg, A., 'Dead Sorrow: A Story About Loss and a New Theory of Wrongful Death Damages', *Boston U L Rev*, 2005, pp. 1–51.

Nagareda 2007
Nagareda, R., *Mass Torts in a World of Settlement*, Chicago: University of Chicago Press, 2007.

David G. Owen*

PUNITIVE DAMAGES AS RESTITUTION

1. Introduction

Punitive damages, it seems, cause more consternation than any other aspect of private law. Straddling the civil and criminal law, they are assessed as 'damages' to a plaintiff against a defendant in a private lawsuit, though they are widely said to be non-compensatory and in the nature of a penal fine. Yet, because punitive damages are a remedy at private law, criminal law safeguards – such as the beyond-a-reasonable-doubt burden of proof, the privilege against self-incrimination, and prohibitions against double jeopardy – do not apply. Thus mixing features of tort and criminal law, punitive damages are either 'highly praised [or] roundly denounced depending on who is paying the piper'.[1]

Why this odd amalgamation of principles from disparate legal realms should be allowed at all in modern law, which normally is divided neatly into private remedial law on the one side, and public criminal law on the other, has long vexed courts and commentators who have debated the purposes and legitimacy of such damages for many years.[2] The clash of views on this topic is colorfully portrayed by early supreme court decisions of different American states, one remarking: 'The idea is wrong. It is a monstrous heresy. It is an unsightly and unhealthy excrescence, deforming the symmetry of the body of law'.[3] By contrast, another characterized punitive damages law as 'an outgrowth of the English love of liberty regulated by law' that 'restrains the strong, influential, and unscrupulous, vindicates the right of the weak, and encourages recourse to, and confidence in, the courts of law by those wronged or oppressed by acts or practices not

* Carolina Distinguished Professor of Law, University of South Carolina. Thanks to Karen Miller, Douglas Rushton, and Brooks Miller for editorial assistance.

1 *In re Paris Air Crash*, 427 F. Supp. 701 (C.D. Cal. 1977), p. 705 (allowing punitive damages in wrongful death actions). See Zipursky 2005, p. 107 ('Punitive damages are a tricky subject because they have this double aspect, both civil and criminal').

2 Two prominent American scholars, Sedgwick and Greenleaf, engaged in a heated debate over the doctrine's legitimacy in the 1800s. See Owen 1976, p. 1263, n. 22. Despite this scholarly disagreement, American courts continued to allow punitive damages, and the remedy subsequently provoked serious study in America by Professor Clarence Morris in 1931. See Morris 1931.

3 *Fay v. Parker*, 53 N.H. 342 (1872), p. 382.

cognizable in, or not sufficiently punished, by the criminal law'.[4] Its grounding in essential justice with deep roots in early English law, drawing from diverse traditions of ancient legal cultures,[5] suggests that the punitive damages remedy is strong enough to endure the onslaught of recurring due process assaults in the United States Supreme Court[6] and other challenges to this hybrid creation of the law.[7]

For the last couple of decades, spurred by a decision of the United States Supreme Court,[8] followed by a spate of others,[9] punitive damages jurisprudence and commentary have focused increasingly on the goals of punitive damages law and how those goals should control the legal standards governing when and in what amounts punitive damages should be assessed.[10] Among the various functions of punitive damages identified by courts and commentators over the years are: retribution, deterrence, education of the offender, compensation of the victim, and law enforcement.[11] From this list of functions, the two most prominent, recurring goals of punitive damages are widely thought to be retribution and deterrence. While economic theorists view deterrence and cost-internalization as the proper engines of this form of legal remedy, other scholars, drawing from the retributive role of tort law, stress the importance of punitive damages in vindicating the rights of victims.[12] As the remainder of this essay will develop, I believe that punitive damages law most securely rests on the vindication of victims' rights.[13]

2. 'Compensation' and 'Restitution'

While American courts typically refer only to 'punishment' (meaning retribution) and 'deterrence' as the purposes of punitive damages,[14] such damages have a third important

4 *Luther v. Shaw*, 147 N.W. 18 (Wis. 1914), p. 20.

5 See Owen 1976, pp. 1262–1263, n. 17.

6 Beginning, essentially, with *Browning-Ferris Indus. of Vt., Inc. v. Kelco Disposal, Inc.*, 492 U.S. 257 (1989), through *Philip Morris USA v. Williams*, 549 U.S. 346 (2007). For constructions of various models around this due process jurisprudence, see, e.g., Markel 2009; Colby 2008, p. 433; Sebok 2007, p. 1031; Geistfeld 2008, p. 284. For an argument that the Supreme Court's meddling with punitive damages may be over, see Gash 2011.

7 Much of this essay draws from Owen 2010.

8 See *Pacific Mut. Life Ins. Co. v. Haslip*, 499 U.S. 1 (1991), p. 19 (holding that due process of law requires that punitive damages law be tethered to the purposes for such awards).

9 Most notably, *BMW of N. Am., Inc. v. Gore*, 517 U.S. 559 (1996), and *State Farm Mut. Ins. Co. v. Campbell*, 538 U.S. 408 (2003).

10 Indeed, the Supreme Court now ties the constitutionality of punitive damages to their being assessed according to their various functions. See *Pacific Mut. Life Ins. Co. v. Haslip*, 499 U.S. 1 (1991), p. 19.

11 See, e.g., Owen 1994 (examining these functions); see also Ellis 1982, p. 3 (specifying punishment, deterrence of plaintiff and others, 'preserving the peace,' 'private law enforcement,' and compensation for 'otherwise uncompensable losses' and attorney's fees).

12 See Markel 2009, pp. 1387–1388, n. 5; pp. 1393–1394, n. 31, 32 & 35 (listing Guido Calabresi, Bruce Chapman & Michael Trebilcock, Thomas Galligan, Keith Hylton & Thomas Miceli, Mitchell Polinsky & Steven Shavell, and Catherine Sharkey as examples of the 'cost-internalization' or 'deterrence' school, and Mark Geistfeld, Thomas Colby, Mark Galanter & David Luban, John Goldberg, Anthony Sebok, and Benjamin Zipursky as examples of the 'victim vindication' school).

13 See Owen 2010.

14 See, e.g., *State Farm Mut. Ins. Co. v. Campbell*, 538 U.S. 408, p. 416 (noting that the purposes of punitive damages are retribution and deterrence); *Cooper Indus. v. Leatherman Tool Group, Inc.*, 532 U.S. 424

function – providing victims with added *compensation*, sometimes called 'aggravated damages,' for the purpose of victim vindication and redress[15] – despite the almost universal proclamation in American law that punitive damages are 'non-compensatory'. Recently, scholars have begun to rediscover the value of punitive damages in forcing flagrant wrongdoers to fully restore the aggravated losses suffered by their victims.[16]

Through the offices of tort damages and restitution, tort law seeks justice between private parties in private disputes by requiring that wrongdoers pay money damages to victims whom they have wronged. Victims of civil wrongs thus have a right to receive such compensation from the wrongdoers who have a corresponding duty to make such payments.[17] Punitive damages may be viewed as a tag-along form of compensatory damages available in special situations where a victim's injury is attributable to some egregious act of misconduct by a defendant. Thus, punitive damages serve to provide robust redress to victims of aggravated wrongdoings, as a form of private retribution, for their panoply of losses aggravated by the flagrancy of the wrong.

While tort law broadly rests on the blameworthiness of an actor whose conduct causes a victim's harm,[18] the kind of wrongdoing prevalent in most accident cases is devoid of the kind of malice, hostility, or conscious denial of another's rights of personhood that often animate intentionally inflicted harm. When an actor's careless, inadvertent conduct results in accidental loss, normal rules of tort law damages well delimit the kind of compensatory repair demanded of the tortfeasor. These damages are incomplete in American law, in that they exclude large categories of important losses that accident victims may endure – such as a reduction in life expectancy and intangible losses of many kinds (such as most forms of lost opportunities) – and they conspicuously exclude payment of the victim's litigation expenses necessary for the collection of damages for the losses. Yet, as discussed below, fairness to injurers, practicality, and an American tradition of open access to courts all support limiting damages in this respect in ordinary accident cases.

(2001), p. 432 (stating that punitive damages 'operate as 'private fines' intended to punish the defendant and to deter future wrongdoing'); *Owens-Corning Fiberglas Corp. v. Malone*, 972 S.W.2d 35 (Tex. 1998), p. 40 (asserting that 'the purpose of punitive damages is to punish a party'); *Mississippi Code Ann.*, St. Paul, MN: West Group, 2004, § 11-1-65(1)(f)(i) (stating that their purpose is 'to punish what occurred giving rise to the award and to deter its repetition by the defendant and others'); *Restatement (Second) of Torts*, Philadelphia, PA: American Law Institute, 1965, § 908(1).

15 Various legal systems allow 'aggravated damages,' 'moral damages,' or some other form of relief to augment a victim's award in cases of serious wrongdoing. See Owen 1976, p. 1264, n. 23 (noting that England's use of 'aggravated damages' serves much the same function as punitive damages, and that Switzerland, Turkey, Norway, and Mexico provide for damages that are 'punitive' in nature). The essays in this very volume point to a growing interest in punitive damages in Europe and around the world despite traditional skepticism of such relief outside the United States. See also Koziol & Wilcox 2009 (collecting essays by various authors on the role of punitive damages in various jurisdictions, including Anthony J. Sebok and Vanessa Wilcox).

16 See Owen 2010. John Goldberg should be credited with revealing that punitive damages were embedded in the very idea of legal injury in eighteenth century English law, as chronicled by Blackstone, and that the idea appears to have migrated to America. See Goldberg 2006; note 34.

17 See, e.g., Goldberg 2005; Zipursky 2003; Zipursky 1998.

18 See Holmes, Jr., 1881. I explain my views on the central role of fault in tort law in Owen 1992; Owen 1995a.

In cases of flagrant wrongdoing, on the other hand, fairness to injurers falls away as a major consideration, suggesting that more than the traditionally restrictive kinds of damages available in ordinary tort cases may be appropriate.[19] Thus, when an actor deliberately, willfully, wantonly, or recklessly causes harm to another person, punitive damages traditionally have been allowed in American law. In injury situations involving such egregious misconduct – where normal, narrowly tailored principles of compensatory damages insufficiently address the full, restorative needs of victims – notions of retributive justice and deterrence emerge from the shadows of tort law and take center stage in the law's efforts to determine an adequate response. In cases of flagrantly inflicted harm, the public surely has an interest in seeing that the rules of law are enforced robustly, to discourage flagrant wrongdoers and others from so misbehaving in the future. Yet, in such cases, the law has an even more profound interest in forcing wrongdoers to restore *in full* the wellbeing of those harmed by such aggravated misconduct. Punitive damages thus might be justified as a kind of 'private revenge'[20] or 'private retributive justice';[21] yet it is, at bottom, compensatory in extracting money from a flagrant wrongdoer and using it to repair resulting damage to a victim's broad basket of goods.[22]

Rarely is 'restitution' mentioned as an explicit goal of punitive damages, but it is a better term than 'compensation' for such robust damages in private law. While restitution often is viewed as lying outside the law of torts in a nether land of law and equity,[23] it more broadly is conceived as part of the broader remedial realm of tort.[24] Yet, even in this misty land where scholars disagree on the nature and borders of the domain,[25] '[w]hen the defendant has acted in conscious disregard of the claimant's rights,'[26] principles of restitution and unjust enrichment, broadening as they do the remedial strength of tort, require a wrongdoer to restore to the victim *more* than simply the victim's 'measureable injury'.[27] Over and above the obligation to provide victims with compensation for wrongfully inflicted loss, the law of restitution and unjust enrichment demands that flagrant wrongdoers disgorge to victims any benefits obtained from the wrongdoing.[28] The term 'compensation' fairly may be used to describe the process of

19 My general views in this regard are outlined in Owen 1982a; Owen 1994; Owen 2010.

20 See, e.g., Colby 2008, p. 433; Sebok 2007, p. 1031.

21 See Owen 2010.

22 For a brief discussion of how the freedom ideal protects individual choices on what goods to hold, see Owen 2008b, pp. 569, 571–572.

23 The new *Restatement of the Law, Third: Restitution and Unjust Enrichment*, 2011, § 1 cmt. *d*, in fact purports to distinguish restitution from tort: 'Restitution is the law of nonconsensual and nonbargained benefits in the same way that torts is the law of nonconsensual and nonlicensed harms'.

24 This was the view of one of the world's great scholars of restitution, the late Peter Birks, Regius Professor of Civil Law and Fellow of All Souls College, University of Oxford. See Birks 1995, p. 31; see also Owen 1995b, p. 7 ('Birks proposes that tort law be viewed broadly to include all appropriate responses to tortious behavior, including the restitution of wrongful gains'.).

25 See comments and reporter's notes to *Restatement of the Law, Third: Restitution and Unjust Enrichment* 2011, § 1; see also Rendleman 2011.

26 *Restatement of the Law, Third: Restitution and Unjust Enrichment* 2011, § 3 cmt. *c*.

27 *Restatement of the Law, Third: Restitution and Unjust Enrichment* 2011, § 3. Section 3 provides: 'A person is not permitted to profit by his own wrong'. See comment *c* thereto, entitled 'Recovery exceeding the claimant's loss'.

28 *Restatement of the Law, Third: Restitution and Unjust Enrichment* 2011, § 3 cmt. *c*.

forcing flagrant wrongdoers to disgorge all funds illicitly gained at the expense of victims (including funds dubbed '*extra*-compensatory'), yet 'compensation' more naturally suggests the narrower concept of providing money for a victim's wrongfully damaged goods recognized by the formal law of 'compensatory' damages – distinguished, as they are of course, from the 'punitive' kind. Hence, the flexibility and robust nature of the notion of 'restitution,' better than 'compensation,' describes the work of punitive damages as a remedial device for flagrant wrongs.

3. Restitution for 'Theft'

How private retributive justice accomplishes the restitutionary needs of victims may be illustrated by a metaphor based on theft.[29] A person who deliberately steals something of value from another person ordinarily is a flagrant wrongdoer (a 'thief') who deserves, retributively, to pay the victim a punitive form of *aggravated* damages because he or she has 'stolen' a bundle of goods from the victim that need fully to be returned in order to prevent the unjust impoverishment of the victim and the unjust enrichment of the thief. The scales of justice, thrown out of balance by the offense, can only be restored by corresponding restitution for the theft.[30]

Punitive damage awards serve this remedial purpose by rectifying the consequences of a theft or other flagrant wrong. Such damages provide at least three forms of 'extra-compensatory' relief for losses suffered by victims of thefts and other forms of aggravated wrongs, losses for which the normal rules of tort-law damages fail to provide full compensation. First, while modern rules of compensatory damages provide victims substantial redress, conventional tort damages fail to restore many of an injury victim's actual losses, particularly those involving intangible harm, as previously discussed. For example, a severely injured person who is rendered immobile for many months may lose a number of important interpersonal relationships and will surely suffer a large variety of missed (often unknown) opportunities, including the opportunity to live out his or her pre-accident life expectancy. There is no practical way for the law to ascertain such amorphous losses, as real as they may be. Ordinarily, therefore, in fairness to injurers, American law excludes such losses from its basket of compensatory relief, leaving them to victims as a risk of life. Yet, when actors inflict injury intentionally or pursue their private interests in a manner they know exposes others to substantial undue risks, the equities of the situation change considerably, and responsibility for ordinarily nonrecoverable intangible losses in justice should be shifted from victims to those whose flagrant misconduct caused their suffering.[31]

29 The discussion of this metaphor draws substantially from Owen 2010, which developed the metaphor first discussed in Owen 1989, pp. 708–713.

30 'A person who is unjustly enriched at the expense of another is subject to liability in restitution'. *Restatement of the Law, Third: Restitution and Unjust Enrichment* 2011, § 1.

31 See, e.g., *Stuart v. W. Union Tel. Co.*, 18 S.W. 351 (Tex. 1885), p. 353 (observing that the punitive damages doctrine probably 'has its foundation in a failure to recognize as elements upon which compensation may be given many things which ought to be classed as injuries entitling the injured person to compensation'); see also Eliot 1881, p. 572 (asserting that punitive damages ameliorated '[t]he difficulty of estimating compensation for intangible injuries'); see generally Colby 2003, p. 615 (noting that early

Another, more esoteric (yet very real) kind of loss suffered by victims of theft and other flagrant wrongdoing springs from the very reprehensibility of the wrong. When an actor flagrantly violates the rights of another person, the actor 'steals' the victim's autonomy and thereby asserts that the thief is of greater worth than the victim.[32] If such autonomy thefts are not subject to penalties in addition to requiring the thief to restore the stolen goods (compensatory damages), the rectification of the transaction is woefully incomplete. This is because such theft transactions contain two distinct components: (1) the transfer of goods from the victim to the thief, and (2) the deliberately wrongful nature of the transfer in violation of the plaintiff's vested rights – the illicit transfer of *freedom* from the victim to the thief. While compensatory damages explicitly redress the first component, at least to some extent, punitive ('extra-compensatory' or 'aggravated') damages importantly redress both aspects of the theft. That is, in addition to more robustly restoring the victim's tangible stolen goods, punitive damages serve to restore the equality of the victim to the thief by removing the extra worth and freedom held unjustly by the thief and returning them to the victim.[33] By vindicating a person's right to remain free from flagrantly inflicted harm, through restitution for the aggravated nature of the victim's injuries attributable to the aggravated nature of the wrong,[34] the law reaffirms and restores the equal freedom and worth of the victim in relation to the perpetrator of the flagrant wrong.

Finally, although the payment of attorneys' fees and other costs of litigation ordinarily is not articulated as an explicit purpose for punitive damages, it sometimes is,[35] and the American system requiring plaintiffs to incur these substantial costs to rectify a theft or other aggravated wrong appears fundamentally unfair. Because at least one-third of an American plaintiff's recovery ordinarily is expended on legal fees, a verdict that does not include a sum for these and other litigation expenses almost always leaves the plaintiff substantially worse off than he or she was before the injury. And whether or not requiring an injured plaintiff to suffer this significant detriment makes sense in an ordinary case, it plainly is illogical and unjust when victims use private law to seek redress from thieves.

American courts recognized that punitive damages served 'not only as punishment, but also as compensation for otherwise non-compensable harms'); Ellis 1982, p. 12–20 (tracing historical origins of punitive damages to difficulty in proving intangible injuries).

32 See Owen 1995a, pp. 220–221.

33 'When the defendant has acted in conscious disregard of the claimant's rights, the whole of the resulting gain is treated as unjust enrichment, even though the defendant's gain may exceed… the measureable injury to the claimant'. *Restatement of Law, Third: Restitution and Unjust Enrichment*, 2011, § 3 cmt. *c.*

34 See, e.g., *Clark v. Cantrell*, 529 S.E.2d 528 (S.C. 2000), p. 533 (Waller, J.) ('[P]unitive damages [provide] vindication… and compensate or satisfy for the willfulness with which the private right was invaded'.); see generally Goldberg 2006, p. 442 (explaining Blackstone's conception that 'money awarded should suffice to provide satisfaction for the victimization, including not only the harm caused to the victim, but also the objective fact of having been mistreated by another' and noting 'Blackstone's observation that claims for particularly heinous or willful wrongs may subject the tortfeasor to a statutory multiplier or 'very large and exemplary damages' [as] part of the redress to which the victim is entitled because of the nature of the tortfeasor's mistreatment of the victim'); Sebok 2007 (arguing that punitive damages provide redress by allowing private revenge for abusive, harmful behavior).

35 See, e.g., *St. Luke Evangelical Lutheran Church, Inc. v. Smith*, 568 A.2d 35 (Md. 1990); *Triangle Sheet Metal Works, Inc. v. Silver*, 222 A.2d 220 (Conn. 1966), p. 225.

In such cases, surely it is the thieves – not the victims – who should pay the costs of driving the legal system to restore *all* the stolen goods to their rightful owners.

The theft metaphor reveals the elementally restorative purpose served by punitive damages. As a matter of desert, of retribution, but most fundamentally restitution, it seems self-evident that thieves should fairly be required to disgorge all benefits from their aggravated wrongdoing and commensurately to erase from their victims' lives all traces of such wrongs.[36] Punitive damages are thus a particularly appropriate remedy for assuring that flagrant wrongdoers are held to answer fully for their victims' many losses.

4. Restitution and Oversized Awards

One of the most controversial aspects of punitive damages in the United States is the sometimes enormous size of such awards. From the first punitive damages case that caught the attention of the United States Supreme Court in 1989,[37] that court has been troubled by the growing size of such awards (albeit in a very small number of cases), worried that the absolute magnitude of such punitive assessments is somehow out of fairness bounds. But the sheer size of jury awards of punitive damages in some prominent cases – such as the McDonald's hot coffee spill case (US$ 2.3 million),[38] the Exxon Valdiz oil spill case (US$ 5 billion),[39] *Philip Morris v. Williams* (US$ 79.5 million)[40] and other tobacco cancer cases, and, now quite long ago, the Ford Pinto subcompact fuel system fire case (US$ 125 million)[41] – may simply be a symptom of the problem, which is that juries in some cases put punitive damages to the uses the law long stated them to be: 'punishment' and 'deterrence'. The problem in these cases was that the punishment and deterrence assessed by the juries were largely of the *public* form, meaning that plaintiffs' lawyers invited juries to teach corporate offenders a lesson that would punish such defendants in a magnitude that, by a single verdict, would at once award retributive relief to *all* such victims and would deter *all* large companies from the kind of flagrant misbehavior alleged in those cases.

This 'enormous verdict' problem eventually spurred the United States Supreme Court to rule that individual plaintiffs could not try to serve as private attorneys general

36 See, e.g., Geistfeld 2008, p. 284 (explaining that 'the inadequacy of compensatory damages continues to supply a defensible rationale for punitive damages – the type of explanation required by any retributive rationale for these awards').

37 See, e.g., *Browning-Ferris Indus. v. Kelco Disposal, Inc.*, 492 U.S. 257 (1989), p. 282 (O'Connor, J., concurring in part and dissenting in part, asserting that punitive damage awards were then 'skyrocketing').

38 *Liebeck v. McDondald's [sic] Rests., P.T.S., Inc.*, No. 93-02419, 1994 WL 16777706 (D.N.M. Sept. 16, 1994) (conditionally remitting the US$ 2.7 million verdict to US$ 480,000); see also Owen 2008a (2d ed.), § 18.1, p. 1180 (discussing *Liebeck*).

39 *Exxon Shipping Co. v. Baker*, 554 U.S. 471 (2008), pp. 480–481, 514 (reducing the US$ 5 billion jury verdict, already remitted by the Court of Appeals to US$ 2.5 billion, to US$ 507.5 million).

40 *Philip Morris USA v. Williams*, 549 U.S. 346 (2007), pp. 350–352 (vacating the US$ 79.5 million verdict); see also Owen 2008a (2d ed.), § 18.7, p. 1280 (discussing *Philip Morris USA*).

41 *Grimshaw v. Ford Motor Co.*, 174 Cal. Rptr. 348 (Ct. App. 1981) (affirming the trial court's remittitur of the punitive award to US$ 3.5 million), examined in Schwartz 1990–1991; Owen 1982b.

seeking *public* retribution for all such victims across America.[42] These rulings have had their intended effect of forcing judges across the nation to cut down large awards of punitive damages more so than they did before.[43] It should be noted, however, that the very high awards in the celebrated cases above are exceedingly rare in the United States. Rather, what juries and courts *normally* do with punitive damages is to provide relatively small amounts of extra compensation – call it *restitution* – for theft victims, to return to this metaphor, to provide them with some amount of 'aggravated' damages naturally flowing from aggravated wrongs. This truly reparative function of punitive damages is revealed empirically by how modest most punitive damage awards truly are – on average, less than their compatriot compensatory awards.[44]

At least as significant as the recent Supreme Court rulings on punitive damages in curtailing the threat of runaway punitive damages awards is the long tradition of trial and appellate courts striking or remitting high punitive awards,[45] as occurred in each of the celebrated verdicts previously discussed.[46] Moreover, reform legislation in a large number of American states has adopted various arbitrary measurement approaches that reduce or remove discretion from the trier of fact.[47] The most common form of limitation, drawing on millennia of legal systems across many civilizations,[48] is to cap punitive

42 See cases cited in notes 9 & 40, above.

43 See Owen 2008a (2d ed.), § 18.7, p. 1287.

44 See *Bureau of Justice Statistics, United States Department of Justice, Civil Justice Survey of State Courts, 2001 – Civil Jury Cases and Verdicts in Large Counties*, 2004, NCJ-202803; see generally Sebok 2007, pp. 969–973 (examining data that punitive damages awards average slightly less than compatriot compensatory awards).

45 See Owen 1982b, pp. 50–59.

46 Note, however, that after the United States Supreme Court vacated the US$ 79.5 million verdict in *Philip Morris USA v. Williams*, 540 U.S. 801 (2003), the verdict was reinstated on remand. See Williams v. Philip Morris, Inc., 92 P.3d 126 (Or. Ct. App. 2004), pp. 145–46, *aff'd*, 127 P.3d 1165 (Or. 2006). On appeal, the United States Supreme Court vacated the verdict a second time in *Phillip Morris USA v. Williams*, 549 U.S. 346 (2007), pp. 350–52, and the Oregon Supreme Court thereafter upheld the verdict once again, in *Williams v. Philip Morris Inc.*, 176 P.3d 1255 (Or. 2008), the appeal of which the United States Supreme Court this time refused to hear. See *Philip Morris USA Inc. v. Williams*, 129 S. Ct. 1436 (2009).

47 See, e.g., *Alabama Code*, St. Paul, MN: West Group, 1999, § 6–11–21 (greater of US$ 1.5 million or 3 times compensatory damages in actions for physical injury); *Colorado Rev. Stat. Ann.*, St. Paul, MN: West Group, 2003, § 13–21–102(1)(a) (punitive damages may not exceed compensatory damages); *Ford Motor Co. v. Cammack*, 999 S.W.2d 1 (Tex. App. 1998) (US$ 22.5 million award reduced to US$ 4 million, pursuant to statutory cap of 4 times actual damages); see generally *BMW of N. Am., Inc. v. Gore*, 517 U.S. 559, 615 (1996) (describing punitive damages cap statutes in Colo., Conn., Fla., Ga., Kan., Nev., N.D., and Va., and bills (some enacted) in Del., Ill., Ind., Md., Minn., N.J., and Tex.); Owen 2008a (2d ed.), § 18.6, pp. 1261–1263; Sunstein, Kahneman & Schkade 1998, pp. 2126–2127; Hawkins 1998; *Development in the Law – The Civil Jury* 1997, p. 1533.

48 See Owen 1976, pp. 1262–1263, n. 17 & 18.

damages at some multiple of the plaintiff's compensatory award – at one,[49] two,[50] three,[51] four,[52] or five[53] times provable compensatory damages – an approach that has the virtue of tying total damages to a victim's actual, provable losses under traditional rules of compensatory damages. Some jurisdictions use other forms of limits on punitive awards, such as absolute dollar amounts,[54] a percentage of the defendant's net worth,[55] or the amount (or some multiple thereof) by which the defendant profited from the misconduct.[56]

The multiple damages approach (possibly together with some other form of arbitrary limitations, and perhaps a floor of litigation expenses) appears to be a good (if imperfect) solution to the risk of over-punishment.[57] While such arbitrary limits on punitive damages reduce a court's flexibility in tailoring a punitive assessment to a wrongdoer's particular misconduct, such multiples have the virtue of respecting the prominence of a victim's actual damages in fashioning restitutionary limits for a punitive award.[58]

5. Conclusion

When courts and commentators debate the role of punitive damages, they usually focus on two functions – punishment (retribution) and deterrence – goals long recognized as central pillars of private law.[59] More sensitively, however, scholars long have teased out

49 As in Colorado. See *BMW of N. Am., Inc. v. Gore*, 517 U.S. 559, 615 (1996). Compare *Exxon Shipping Co. v. Baker*, 554 U.S. 471 (2008), p. 514 (adopting a punitive damages limit of one times compensatory damages for maritime cases).

50 As in Conn., N.D., Ohio, Okla. (in certain instances), and Tex. See *BMW of N. Am., Inc. v. Gore*, 517 U.S. 559, 615 (1996).

51 As in Fla. and Nev., and in bills in Del., Ill., and Ind. (enacted). See *BMW of N. Am., Inc. v. Gore*, 517 U.S. 559, 615 (1996).

52 As in a Maryland bill. See *BMW of N. Am., Inc. v. Gore*, 517 U.S. 559, 615 (1996).

53 As in New Jersey. See *New Jersey Stat. Ann.*, St. Paul, MN: West Group, 2006, § 2A:15–5.14(b) (greater of 5 times compensatory damages or US$ 350,000).

54 Such as US$ 350,000, in Virginia. See *Virginia Code Ann.*, St. Paul, MN: West Group, 1987, § 8.01–38.1; or US$ 5 million, in certain cases, in Kansas. See *Kansas Stat. Ann.*, St. Paul, MN: West Group, 1992, § 60–3702(e)(2).

55 See *Mississippi Code Ann.* 2004, § 11–1–65 (providing distinct caps on punitive damages for various brackets of net worth); *Kansas Stat. Ann.* 1992, § 60–3702(e) (lesser of 50% of defendant's net worth, if necessary to penalize defendant, otherwise highest annual gross income over five years preceding punishable act, or US$ 5 million).

56 See *Oklahoma Stat. Ann.*, St. Paul, MN: West Group, 2002, tit. 23, § 9.1(C); *Kansas Stat. Ann.* 1992, § 60–3702(f) (1½ times amount of profit defendant gained or is expected to gain). For a considered proposal to tailor punitive damages assessments to the profitability of the misconduct, see Dobbs 1989.

57 See Owen 1982a, p. 119.

58 See *Alabama Code* 1999, § 6–11–21 (greater of US$ 1.5 million or 3 times compensatory damages in actions for physical injury); *Colorado Rev. Stat. Ann.* 2003, § 13–21–102(1)(a) (punitive damages may not exceed compensatory damages).

59 '[P]reventing future harm has been quite important in the field of torts. The courts are concerned not only with compensation of the victim, but with admonition of the wrongdoer'. Keeton, Dobbs, Keeton & Owen 1984 (5th ed.), § 4, p. 25; see also Keeton, Dobbs, Keeton & Owen 1984 (5th ed.), p. 26 ('This idea of prevention shades into that of punishment of the offender for what the offender has already

several others: compensation of the victim, law enforcement, and education of the offender.[60] Although it is rarely expressed explicitly, another fundamental function of punitive damages is *restitution* – embedded in deterrence and the other functions, yet grounded most importantly in compensation – whereby a flagrant wrongdoer is required fully to restore everything stolen from the victim. In my judgment, restitution may be viewed as the central pillar of punitive damages law. While it usually resides quietly and out of sight, restitutionary justice lies naturally beside and draws succor from compensatory and retributive justice in the private law regime. What has troubled the United States Supreme Court, as it has reviewed multi-million dollar punitive damage judgments in recent decades, is how inflated the public retribution side of this remedy has become, on occasion, in relation to the principal enterprise of private law – returning goods wrongfully taken by an actor from a victim. When punitive damage verdicts rely too heavily on the public's interest in large-scale retribution and deterrence, and focus too little on victim compensation and restitution, then the Court quite understandably has become uncomfortable with results that look suspiciously like they sprang from a public-law scheme for inflicting punishment that has masked itself in a regime marked 'private'.

When American courts assert categorically that a plaintiff is not 'entitled' to punitive damages,[61] and that the purpose of punitive damages is to punish and deter, not to compensate the plaintiff, I believe that their emphasis is wrong. What I think courts have *meant* by such assertions is that punitive damages are distinct from the developed, narrow law of limited 'compensatory' relief ordinarily available in tort, and that punitive damages are assessed in addition thereto to fully restore the rights of victims of aggravated wrongdoing by providing additional relief. Such damages are 'aggravated' beyond normal 'compensatory' amounts in order to restore all stolen freedoms and equality of worth to theft victims by removing all booty held illicitly by the thief. This is what I think the law principally and properly means by the punitive damages goals of 'punishment and deterrence' – *private* retribution and *private* deterrence in pursuit of restorative goals. For these thefts, private law principles of restitutionary justice in fact demand that a thief return full payment, in money damages, for a victim's stolen freedoms as well as stolen goods.

done, since one admitted purpose of punishment is to prevent repetition of the offense'.); Morris 1930, p. 733 (explaining that tort judgments serve two quite different functions, compensation and punishment, resulting in 'a rough and ready sort of justice').

60 See Owen 1994; Ellis 1982.

61 While most states hold that punitive damages are awardable only in a jury's discretion, a legislature might beneficially provide plaintiffs with a *right* to their award, in cases of flagrantly harmful misconduct, to advance this remedy's restitutionary goal. Such an *entitlement* to punitive damages draws from Blackstone, see note 34, and early case decisions in American law. See note 31. Hence, I am attracted to the sentiment that '[a] plaintiff is entitled to recover punitive damages if the act complained of is determined to be willful, wanton or reckless'. *Camp v. Components, Inc.*, 330 S.E.2d 315 (S.C. Ct. App. 1985), p. 316.

Bibliography

American Law Institute 2011
American Law Institute, Restatement of the Law, Third: Restitution and Unjust Enrichment, Philadelphia, PA: American Law Institute, 2011.

Birks 1995
Birks, P., 'The Concept of a Civil Wrong', in: D.G. Owen (ed.), *Philosophical Foundations of Tort Law*, Clarendon: Oxford, 1995, pp. 31–51.

Colby 2003
Colby, T.B., 'Beyond the Multiple Punishment Problem: Punitive Damages as Punishment for Individual, Private Wrongs', *Minn L Rev*, 2003, pp. 583–678.

Colby 2008
Colby, T.B., 'Clearing the Smoke from *Philip Morris v. Williams*: The Past, Present, and Future of Punitive Damages', *Yale L J*, 2008, pp. 392–479.

Developments 1997
'Developments in the Law – The Civil Jury', *Harv L Rev*, 1997, pp. 1408–1536.

Dobbs 1989
Dobbs, D.B., 'Ending Punishment in 'Punitive' Damages: Deterrence – Measured Remedies', *Ala L Rev*, 1989, pp. 831–918.

Eliot 1881
Eliot, E.C., 'Exemplary Damages', *Am L Reg*, 1881, pp. 570–577.

Ellis 1982
Ellis, D.D., 'Fairness and Efficiency in the Law of Punitive Damages', *S Cal L Rev*, 1982, pp. 1–78.

Gash 2011
Gash, J., 'The End of an Era: The Supreme Court (Finally) Butts Out of Punitive Damages for Good', *Fla L Rev*, 2011, pp. 525–597.

Geistfeld 2008
Geistfeld, M.A. 'Punitive Damages, Retribution, and Due Process', *S Cal L Rev*, 2008, pp. 263–310.

Goldberg 2005
Goldberg, J.C.P., 'The Constitutional Status of Tort Law: Due Process and the Right to a Law for the Redress of Wrongs', *Yale L J*, 2005, pp. 524–627.

Goldberg 2006
Goldberg, J.C.P., 'Two Conceptions of Tort Damages: Fair v. Full Compensation', *DePaul L Rev*, 2006, pp. 435–468.

Hawkins 1998
Hawkins, A.M., Note 'Balancing Act: Public Policy and Punitive Damages Caps', *S C L Rev*, 1998, pp. 293–310.

Holmes, Jr. 1881
Holmes, O.W., Jr., *The Common Law*, Boston, MA: Little, Brown, and Company, 1881.

Keeton 1984
Keeton, W.P., Dobbs, D.B., Keeton R.E. & Owen D.G., *Prosser and Keeton on the Law of Torts*, St. Paul, MN: West Group, 1984 (5th ed.).

Koziol 2009
Koziol, H. & Wilcox, V. (eds.), *Punitive Damages: Common Law and Civil Law Perspectives*, Vienna: Springer, 2009.

Markel 2009
Markel, D., 'How Should Punitive Damages Work?', *U Pa L Rev*, 2009, pp. 1383–1484.

Morris 1930
Morris, C., 'Rough Justice and Some Utopian Ideas', *Ill L Rev*, 1930, pp. 730–736.

Morris 1931
Morris, C., 'Punitive Damages in Tort Cases', *Harv L Rev*, 1931, pp. 1173–1209.

Owen 1976
Owen, D.G., 'Punitive Damages in Products Liability Litigation', *Mich L Rev*, 1976, pp. 1257–1371.

Owen 1982a
Owen, D.G., 'Civil Punishment and the Public Good', *S Cal L Rev*, 1982, pp. 103–122.

Owen 1982b
Owen, D.G.(b), 'Problems in Assessing Punitive Damages Against Manufacturers of Defective Products', *U Chi L Rev*, 1982, pp. 1–60.

Owen 1989
Owen, D.G., 'The Moral Foundations of Punitive Damages', *Ala L Rev*, 1989, pp. 705–740.

Owen 1992
Owen, D.G., 'The Fault Pit', *Ga L Rev*, 1992, pp. 703–724.

Owen 1994
Owen, D.G., 'A Punitive Damages Overview: Functions, Problems & Reform', *Vill L Rev*, 1994, pp. 363–414.

Owen 1995a
Owen, D.G., 'Philosophical Foundations of Fault in Tort Law', in: D.G. Owen (ed.), *Philosophical Foundations of Tort Law*, Oxford: Clarendon, 1995, pp. 201–228.

Owen 1995b
Owen, D.G., 'Why Philosophy Matters to Tort Law', in: D.G. Owen, *Philosophical Foundations of Tort Law*, Clarendon: Oxford, 1995, pp. 1–28.

Owen 2008a
Owen, D.G., *Products Liability Law*, St. Paul, MN: Thomson-West, 2008 (2d ed.).

Owen 2008b
Owen, D.G., 'Against Priority', *Sw U L Rev*, 2008, pp. 557–574.

Owen 2010
Owen, D.G., 'Aggravating Punitive Damages', *U Pa L Rev PENNumbra*, 2010, pp. 181–194.

Rendleman 2011
Rendleman, D., 'Measurement of Restitution: Coordinating Restitution with Compensatory Damages and Punitive Damages', *Wash & Lee L Rev*, 2011, forthcoming.

Schwartz 1991
Schwartz, G.T., 'The Myth of the Ford Pinto Case', *Rutgers L Rev*, 1991, pp. 1013–1068.

Sebok 2007
Sebok, A.J., 'Punitive Damages: From Myth to Theory', *Iowa L Rev*, 2007, pp. 957–1036.

Sunstein, Kahneman & Schkade 1998
Sunstein, C.R., Kahneman, D. & Schkade, D., 'Assessing Punitive Damages (with Notes on Cognition and Valuation in Law)', *Yale L J*, 1998, pp. 2071–2154.

Zipursky 1998
Zipursky, B.C., 'Rights, Wrongs, and Recourse in the Law of Torts', *Vand L Rev*, 1998, pp. 1–100.

Zipursky 2003
Zipursky, B.C., 'Civil Recourse, Not Corrective Justice', *Geo L J*, 2003, pp. 695–756.

Zipursky 2005
Zipursky, B.C., 'A Theory of Punitive Damages', *Tex L Rev*, 2005, pp. 105–171.

Anthony J. Sebok*

THE U.S. SUPREME COURT'S THEORY OF COMMON LAW PUNITIVE DAMAGES: AN INAUSPICIOUS START

1. Introduction

Until 2008, the U.S. Supreme Court's views about punitive damages were limited to testing state common law punitive damages verdicts against the limits set out by the U.S. Constitution. The U.S. Supreme Court was not required, and it did not provide, a theory about the proper purpose and method for ascertainment of punitive damages as a matter of common law or private law theory. In *Exxon Shipping Co. v. Baker*,[1] the U.S. Supreme Court did in fact venture beyond the outer limits permitted by the U.S. Constitution and set out a theory about the proper content of common law punitive damages. In this essay I examine the U.S. Supreme Court's constitutional limitations on common law theory of punitive damages before 2008 and compare them to the limitations entailed by the common law theory adopted in *Exxon Shipping*. I conclude by suggesting that the theory of punitive damages adopted by the Court in *Exxon Shipping* is narrow and in tension with leading theories of punitive damages, including the leading theories of law and economics. I further conclude that the theory is unlikely to have influence outside the narrow legal sphere in which it was adopted, maritime law.

2. The Different Kinds of Judicial Theories about Punitive Damages in the United States

Punitive damages have been, by necessity, the subject of judicial review in the United States for many centuries. This is, of course, because the United States applied English common law before the Revolution and then it continued to use the common law (with some exceptions) after the United States gained independence from Great Britain. The vast majority of judicial opinions about punitive damages have been issued by state courts reviewing state court judgments; this phenomenon is easily explained by the fact that punitive damages arise, for the most part, under state tort law and the vast majority of state tort suits are brought in state court.

* Professor, Benjamin N. Cardozo School of Law, Yeshiva University, New York, NY, U.S.A., J.D., Yale Law School, 1991, Ph.D. Princeton University, 1993.

1 *Exxon Shipping Co. v. Baker*, 554 U.S. 471 (2008).

When state courts – especially state supreme courts – have reviewed punitive damages they have, for the most part, reviewed them from the perspective of their state's law of damages. That is to say, the questions presented to these state courts typically went to the question of whether the court articulated the correct standard to the fact finder for allowing punitive damages to be awarded (this typically referred to the mental state of the defendant) and whether the damages, if properly awarded, were excessive. And, with the exception of a handful of states that passed legislation specifically addressing punitive damages, the problem posed to state courts considering punitive damages was a problem of *common law*.

In contrast, the federal courts of the United States, and especially the Supreme Court of the United States, were historically unconcerned about punitive damages, except where their availability might have arisen as a matter of federal common law or diversity jurisdiction.[2] This changed, of course, beginning in the late 1980's in the United States when there was a series of cases reviewing the constitutional permissibility of punitive damages. Beginning with *Browning-Ferris Indus. of Vt., Inc. v. Kelco Disposal, Inc.*,[3] and ending with *Philip Morris USA v. Williams*,[4] the United States Supreme Court embarked on an effort to provide constitutional boundaries for the state's common law of punitive damages.

Before going on to examine the content of the arguments contained in the U.S. Supreme Court's first major discussion of the *common law* theory of punitive damages, it is important to understand the relationship between the U.S. Supreme Court's putative *constitutional* theory of punitive damages and the various common law theories that the states have always been using to set out the grounds and limits of punitive damages in their own jurisdictions.

A punitive damages rule – whether it be the product of common law or a statute – must, analytically, possess a certain structure (much like any other liability rule).[5] A punitive damages rule must describe *when* the court will allow punitive damages to be awarded; *why* a court will allow punitive damages to be awarded; and *how* punitive damages will be awarded.

The *when* question refers to two things: (i) case type and (ii) defendant's culpability. For example, as a result of so-called tort reform, a jurisdiction may have chosen to prohibit punitive damages in products liability cases or medical malpractice cases. Or a jurisdiction may have developed as a matter of common law, or as a result of 'tort reform', a view about the degree of culpability that deserves punitive damages; for example,

2 *See*, e.g. *The Amiable Nancy*, 16 U.S. 546 (U.S. 1818) (admiralty law) and *Day v. Woodworth*, 54 U.S. 363 (U.S. 1852) (diversity).

3 *Browning-Ferris Indus. of Vt., Inc. v. Kelco Disposal, Inc.*, 492 U.S. 257 (1989).

4 *Philip Morris USA v. Williams*, 549 U.S. 346 (2007).

5 This assumes that a jurisdiction permits punitive damages at all. Five states prohibit common law punitive damages as a matter of statute or common law: Louisiana, Massachusetts, Nebraska, New Hampshire, and Washington. Louisiana is a civil code jurisdiction that refused to recognize punitive damages, except as statutorily authorized. Nebraska and New Hampshire are common law jurisdictions that refused to adopt the remedy of punitive damages entirely. Massachusetts and Washington are common law jurisdictions that do not recognize punitive damages except as may be recovered under specific statutory authorization.

instead of permitting punitive damages in cases where the defendant has acted recklessly, a jurisdiction might permit punitive damages only where the defendant has acted intentionally.

The *why* question can be broad or narrow – it refers to the rationales that lay behind the award of punitive damages. Reference to a rationale may help inform both the fact finder's decision whether to award punitive damages at all and, if the decision to award is positive, how large to make the award. For example, the decision to award might be different, depending on the facts of a case, if the rationale for punitive damages is to secure 'satisfaction' for the injured dignity of the plaintiff as opposed to providing general deterrence to prevent actors similarly situated from engaging in the same antisocial conduct. In the United States common law theory of punitive damages, virtually all jurisdictions have adopted a pluralistic rationale for punitive damages that allows fact finders to invoke a set of overlapping rationales.[6]

The *how* question refers to the evidence and tools that the fact finder is supposed to use in deciding whether to award punitive damages and, if the decision is positive, the amount of those damages. Inevitably the 'how' question is intertwined with the 'when' and 'why' questions. If a jurisdiction takes the position that a defendant may properly be asked to pay punitive damages if they acted 'wantonly,' then the fact finder will have to access evidence that either supports or rebuts the claim that the defendant acted wantonly. If a jurisdiction takes the position that one purpose of punitive damages is to punish a defendant for the injuries that he caused to non-parties in addition to the injuries that he was proven to have caused the plaintiff, then the fact finder will have to access evidence that either supports or rebuts the claim that the defendant's acts injured non-parties. But the 'how' question might be informed by reasons that are independent of the 'when' and 'why' question. For example, a jurisdiction might adopt a rule – either as a matter of legislation or as a product of common law precedent – that punitive damages must be two times the amount of compensatory damages awarded by the fact finder. Such a rule would be perfectly coherent and easy to implement, and might exist without regard to the particular types of cases or types of mental states associated with punitive damages in that jurisdiction, or the rationale or rationales adopted by that jurisdiction to explain to fact finders why punitive damages are awarded.

To its credit, the U.S. Supreme Court, in its attempt to set out a constitutional theory of punitive damages, attempted to remain neutral with regard to how the states could answer the 'when, why and how' questions that comprise the heart of any common law theory. The Court insisted that it would not impose its own particular common law theory of punitive damages on the states, but would set out the outer boundaries beyond which no common law theory could go. The Court's assumption has always been, therefore, that within the outer limits of the Constitution, the states are free to adopt a wide range of legal principles relating to punitive damages. Of course, this formal respect for state common law – which the U.S. Supreme Court was bound to observe given the federalist structure of the U.S. Constitution, was hard to maintain in practice. This is for the simple reason that it is not clear how the U.S. Supreme Court could identify unconstitutional reasons for awarding punitive damages without evaluating the *content*

6 Sebok 2009, pp. 29–58; Sebok 2002, pp. 131–132.

of the reason proffered by any state's common law theory of punitive damages. As the review of the case law below will show, the U.S. Supreme Court has dealt with this challenge on two levels. First, it has set out the minimum set of reasons which, from a constitutional point of view, no state can be permitted to adopt as part of its common law theory of punitive damages, and second, in its most recent case, concerning federal maritime law, it has set out a theory about the content of federal common law theory of punitive damages. The gap between these two levels, and the significance of this gap, will be discussed at the conclusion of this essay.

3. The U.S. Supreme Court's Constitutional Theory of Punitive Damages

The difficulty faced by the U.S. Supreme Court can be seen over the course of eight cases. In the first, *Browning Ferris*,[7] the U.S. Supreme Court rejected the claim that a defendant could challenge a state common punitive damages award under the Eighth Amendment's Excessive Fines Clause. The U.S. Supreme Court was asked a very specific 'how' question that was clearly motivated by a 'why' question: Could a state's common law permit the award of punitive damages without the full range of protections provided by a constitutionally minimally adequate system of state-sanctioned punishment (whether criminal or civil)? The affirmative answer to this question in *Browning Ferris* logically entailed the conclusion that the rationale that lay behind the states' common law of punitive damages was that they were something other than state-sanctioned punishments, which made a certain degree of sense since punitive damages are, as literal matter, entirely within the control of a private party and not a state actor (it must be kept in mind that the judge in a punitive damages case does not have the power to impose punitive damages *sua sponte*). The U.S. Supreme Court closed the door to an Excessive Fines Challenge but left open the possibility that it might entertain other constitutional grounds for appeal.

In the second case, *Pac. Mut. Life Ins. Co. v. Haslip*,[8] the U.S. Supreme Court rejected the defendant corporation's argument that it had been denied due process when an Alabama jury determined a punitive-damages award that was 'more than 4 times the [plaintiff's] amount of compensatory damages [and] more than 200 times [her] out-of-pocket expenses'.[9] Justice Blackmun, writing for the majority, applied the Due Process Clause to what he called the 'common-law method' of determining punitive damages. In Justice Blackmun's eyes, the common-law method consisted of a jury determining the sum of money the defendant ought to pay, based on 'the gravity of the wrong and the need to deter similar wrongful conduct,' and then both the trial court and appellate courts review the award.[10] Justice Blackmun conceded that, given the diversity of state common law approaches to punitive damages, there could be no guarantee that its results would always be compatible with the Due Process Clause. Nevertheless, he held that the methods used to determine the award in *Haslip* satisfied the Due Process Clause because

7 See above, fn. 3.

8 *Pac. Mut. Life Ins. Co. v. Haslip*, 499 U.S. 1 (1991).

9 *Ibid.*, at 23.

10 *Ibid.*, at 15.

it 'did not lack objective criteria'.[11] As the dissenters in this case noted, the U.S. Supreme Court's pluralism with regard to the 'how' and 'why' questions were breathtaking in its permissiveness. As Justice O'Connor pointed out, it is not clear what 'objective criteria' Blackmun found in Alabama's procedures other than the jury receiving general instructions that they should base the award on the 'character and degree of the wrong... and [the] necessity of preventing similar wrong'.[12] What Justice O'Connor objected to, in reality, was that the permissible common law theory of punitive damages under the U.S. Constitution could include any set of reasons other than those prohibited in *Browning Ferris* and any type of method of determining how much to award those damages as long as they were based on some set of 'objective criteria,' without regard to the content of those criteria.

In the third case, *TXO Production Corp. v. Alliance Resources Corp.*,[13] the defendant, hoping to exploit the U.S. Supreme Court's invocation of 'objective criteria' in *Haslip*, suggested a set of 'objective criteria' under which the Court ought to review the plaintiff's award. The test proposed by TXO would have examined '(1) awards of punitive damages upheld against other defendants in the same jurisdiction, (2) awards upheld for similar conduct in other jurisdictions, (3) legislative penalty decisions with respect to similar conduct, and (4) the relationship of prior punitive awards to the associated compensatory awards'.[14] The U.S. Supreme Court rejected TXO's suggestion. Instead, the Court held that, after a review of the common-law method used by West Virginia, that the process contained some 'objective criteria' and therefore met the *Haslip* test, and upheld a US$ 10 million punitive-damages award arising from a suit in which only US$ 19,000 in actual damages were awarded. Again, the 'why' and 'how' questions were given the greatest degree of latitude by the U.S. Supreme Court.

In the fourth case, *Honda Motor Co. v. Oberg*,[15] the U.S. Supreme Court held that states must allow for judicial review of the size of punitive damages awards, and Oregon's failure to do so violated due process. Although the Court's decision centered on procedural issues, the Court took the opportunity to reiterate that punitive damages awards that are so large as to be 'grossly excessive' are unconstitutional. But this case too reflected the most minimal restriction on a state's common law answer to the 'how' question: A state can do what it wants, but it must provide an opportunity for review under the U.S. Constitution – a review, which, as of 1994, seemed to permit any mechanism for the awarding of damages as long as they relied upon 'objective criteria'.

The fifth case, *BMW of N. Am., Inc. v. Gore*,[16] the U.S. Supreme Court retreated from the permissive and pluralistic position it had adopted in the first three cases. In *BMW*, the Court adopted a version of the petitioner's proposal in *TXO* that appellate courts

11 *Ibid.*, at 17–18, 23.
12 *Ibid.*, at 48. Justice O'Connor noted that the jury received no guidance as to what 'relation, if any, should exist between the harm caused and the size of the award, nor how to measure the deterrent effect of a particular award... [nor] information... about criminal fines for comparable conduct or the range of punitive-damages awards in similar cases.
13 *TXO Production Corp. v. Alliance Resources Corp.*, 509 U.S. 443 (1993).
14 *Ibid.*, at 455–456.
15 *Honda Motor Co. v. Oberg*, 512 U.S. 415 (1994).
16 *BMW of N. Am., Inc. v. Gore*, 517 U.S. 559, 575 (1996.

scrutinize jury verdicts under an 'objective test' that had some minimum content. The three 'guideposts' developed by Justice Stevens eschewed historical comparisons between compensatory and punitive awards and instead called on courts to review punitive damages verdicts produced by fact finders according to three criteria: (a) the 'reprehensibility' of the defendant's conduct, (b) the ratio between punitive and non-punitive damages, and (c) comparable civil penalties in the jurisdiction. The U.S. Supreme Court refused to say that Alabama had to inform its juries of certain criteria in order to insure that the 'how' question, as answered by its common law, met constitutional standards, but it did say that, after the 'how' question was answered by a jury, any judicial review would have to test the result against the three criteria now set out in *BMW*, suggesting that unless a trial judge guided the discretion of the jury with an eye to meeting the three criteria, there would be a risk that the jury's answer to the question 'how large should the punitive damages in this case be?' would violate the U.S. Constitution.

In the sixth case, *Cooper Industries, Inc. v. Leatherman Tool Group Inc.*,[17] the Supreme Court stated that courts must consider all three *Gore* factors when reviewing a punitive damages award for excessiveness and do so through de novo review. The latter point may not seem significant, but it reflected yet another small step towards the U.S. Supreme Court narrowing the range of acceptable common law theories of punitive damages. The reason for adopting a *de novo* review, which is much more permissive than review under an 'abuse of discretion' standard was that a 'jury's award of punitive damages does not constitute a finding of 'fact'.'[18] The U.S. Supreme Court supported this surprising conclusion by arguing that, although at one time in the Eighteenth and Nineteenth Centuries punitive damages may have been awarded as a functional substitute for certain non-economic damages, such as emotional distress resulting from insult and humiliation, that theory of punitive damages was no longer valid as a matter of common law theory.[19] Punitive damages now, as a matter of state common law, do not serve a compensatory function (at least for noneconomic damages) but serve to punish and deter. While the historical premises that lay behind *Cooper Industries* conclusion are controversial, the implication of its analysis is clear – the U.S. Supreme Court was stating that at least one answer to the 'why' question was now taken off the table – no state could claim that punitive damages served the compensatory function they allegedly once served in the past.[20]

In the seventh case, In *State Farm Mutual Automobile Insurance Co. v. Campbell*,[21] the U.S. Supreme Court made further progress towards establishing federal constitutional limitations to both how a state could answer the 'how' and 'why' questions in its common law. In *State Farm*, a Utah jury awarded a US$ 145 million punitive damage award stemming from bad faith, fraud, and intentional infliction of emotional distress claims based on State Farm's initial refusal to settle a case, in which the compensatory damages,

17 *Cooper Industries, Inc. v. Leatherman Tool Group Inc.*, 532 U.S. 424 (2001).
18 *Ibid.*, at 687.
19 *Ibid.*
20 Sebok 2003.
21 In *State Farm Mutual Automobile Insurance Co. v. Campbell*, 538 U.S. 408, 425 (2003).

which related to emotional distress, were less than US$ 1 million. The Court said that, in order to guarantee that a punitive damages award would meet the reprehensibility criterion in *BMW*, a trial court must instruct juries that they 'may not use evidence of out-of-state conduct to punish a defendant for action that was lawful in the jurisdiction where it occurred'.[22] The U.S. Supreme Court also stated that, in order to ascertain reprehensibility, juries may not calculate punitive damages based upon the hypothetical claims involving potentially illegal acts that were not related to the harm caused by the defendant to the plaintiff: 'A defendant should be punished for the conduct that harmed the plaintiff, not for being an unsavory individual or business'.[23] Finally, while the U.S. Supreme Court declined once again to create a bright-line ratio which a punitive damages award cannot exceed, it came very close to endorsing some such rule: 'few awards exceeding a single-digit ratio between punitive and compensatory damages, to a significant degree, will satisfy due process'.[24]

Thus, the U.S. Supreme Court narrowed the range of permissible answers to the 'how' question yet again: Common law punitive damages theory in the states cannot permit punishment for out of state conduct, or conduct that is 'unrelated' to the harm caused by defendant to the plaintiff; and it indicated that perhaps a mathematical device, such as a ratio, might be required in any common law approach to punitive damages. The first two limitations on the 'how' question said a lot about what the U.S. Supreme Court thought had to be the correct answer to the 'why' question; that is, it became clear that a state could not allow private litigants to punish defendants through punitive damages for having a 'bad character' unless that bad character somehow contributed to the specific act that harmed the plaintiff. An adequate theory of punitive damages had to eschew some of the goals of public law, which were to punish an actor for risks and harms they imposed on the public in general. The third limitation on the 'how' question – the suggestion that a fixed ratio might be necessary to conform to the constitution – did not provide any clear explanation to the 'why' question that might inform it. The answer to this question would have to wait for the *Exxon Shipping* decision.

In the eighth case, *Philip Morris USA v. Williams*,[25] the U.S. Supreme Court refined its holding in *State Farm* and held that that juries can consider harm to others in assessing the *reprehensibility* of the defendant's conduct, but courts must adequately instruct the jury that it cannot *punish* the defendant specifically for harm done to others. In *Philip Morris*, the plaintiff's estate sued for the wrongful death of a smoker and won an US$ 821,000 compensatory damages award and a US$ 79.5 million punitive damages award. The U.S. Supreme Court held that the trial judge's instructions impermissibly allowed the jury to punish the defendant tobacco company for having caused death and injury to smokers in the state where the plaintiff lived. *Philip Morris* illustrates problems which the U.S. Supreme Court faces when it tries to pick and choose among various answers to the 'why' question in the course of applying to constitutional limits to the state's common law of punitive damages. A theory of punitive damages which was

22 *Ibid.*, at 422.
23 *Ibid.*, at 423.
24 *Ibid.*, at 425.
25 See above, fn. 4.

explicitly committed to *public retribution* would not find any reason to forbid a jury to punish a defendant for similar conduct which harmed non-parties identically situated to the plaintiff.[26] Nor would a theory that viewed punitive damages as a mechanism for optimal deterrence.[27] A theory that viewed punitive damages as a theory of private retribution might be more sympathetic to the position adopted by the U.S. Supreme Court in *Philip Morris*, although even those inclined to support the decision must admit that it was very poorly articulated.[28] As Justice Stevens commented in dissent that, 'this nuance eludes me. When a jury increases a punitive damages award because injuries to third parties enhanced the reprehensibility of the defendant's conduct, the jury is by definition punishing the defendant – directly – for third-party harm'.[29]

As the review above demonstrates, the effort by the U.S. Supreme Court to set out limits under the federal constitution to state's common law theories of punitive damages has brought it, inevitably, into the knotty and treacherous realm of theory. It may be impossible to discuss the Due Process Clause's limits on the punitive damages produced by the states without having a theory of what punitive damages ought to do. The results from the Supreme Court so far are not very satisfying. According to the U.S. Supreme Court's eight modern constitutional decisions, punitive damages are not like criminal or civil fines in that they do not qualify for review under the Eighth Amendment, but they are not compensatory damages either, in that their 'function' is to punish and deter private wrongs. Punitive damages may not be awarded without objective criteria known to defendants before they act, and those objective criteria much take into account the reprehensibility of the defendant's conduct, the relationship between the size of the punitive damages award and the injury caused by the defendant, and comparable civil and criminal penalties for similar acts by the defendant (if any). In measuring the reprehensibility of the defendant's act, the risk of harm or harm imposed by the defendant on others may be taken into account, but the harms caused to others may not be taken into account when ascertaining the ratio between the punitive damages and the injury caused by the defendant. Finally, as a 'rule of thumb' an adequate ratio between the punitive damages and the injury caused by the defendant should remain in the 'single digits' absent certain special circumstances. This is a somewhat a theoretical collection of principles, and one that does not conform at all to leading academic theories of punitive damages, especially those based on optimal deterrence. The question that remains is, can the U.S. Supreme Court do better?

26 Markel 2009.

27 Polinsky & Shavell 1998.

28 Sebok 2007.

29 *Philip Morris USA v. Williams*, at 360. As Erwin Chemerinsky observed: 'Trial judges are likely to struggle for years with formulating jury instructions that simultaneously tell the jury to consider and not consider harm to people other than the plaintiffs. Appellate courts are left with little guidance on when the size of a punitive damages award is appropriate and when it is unconstitutional. Juries can consider harm to others in determining reprehensibility, but they cannot base punitive damages on harm to others. How can an appeals court possibly determine whether a punitive damages award violates this command?'. See Chemerinsky 2007, p. 72.

4. The U.S. Supreme Court's Common Law Theory of Punitive Damages

The *Exxon Shipping* case arose after more than a decade of litigation following the catastrophic oil spill caused by the drunkenness of the captain of a supertanker owned and operated by Exxon, the multinational oil company. After settling with a variety of parties who sued it, including the United States Government, to whom it paid significant restitution, Exxon ultimately faced a class action of approximately 32,000 fishermen, property owners, and other private parties who sought punitive damages, leading to a US$ 5 billion punitive damage award against Exxon in addition to a total of US$ 507.5 million in compensatory damages. Among the questions on appeal was whether the US$ 5 billion punitive damages award was excessive.[30]

The case did not arise through any state's domestic law. The accident occurred in navigable waters and was, therefore, governed by federal maritime law. Maritime law is predominantly judge-made law. The federal courts were given jurisdiction over maritime law in Article III of the Constitution.

As Justice Souter noted in his opinion overturning the punitive damages award:

> 'Today's enquiry differs from due process review because the case arises under federal maritime jurisdiction, and we are reviewing a jury award for conformity with maritime law, rather than the outer limit allowed by due process; we are examining the verdict in the exercise of federal maritime common law authority, which precedes and should obviate any application of the constitutional standard...'
>
> 'Our review of punitive damages today, then, considers not their intersection with the Constitution, but the desirability of regulating them as a common law remedy for which responsibility lies with this Court as a source of judge-made law in the absence of statute'.[31]

It is striking that Justice Souter's opinion did not limit itself to the role of punitive damages in federal maritime law, or even federal common law. Instead he launched into a general theoretical discussion of the place of punitive damages *in law* – allowing, for example, the U.S. Supreme Court to indulge in a practice which for which it has been criticized in the past, which is comparing domestic practice in the United States with the views about punitive damages in other countries, including the views of other countries concerning American punitive damages.[32]

Having set for himself the task of ascertaining 'the place of punishment in modern civil law,' Justice Souter began by framing his inquiry in broad terms, asking whether the US$ 2.5 billion punitive award against Exxon exceeded the bounds justified by the punitive damages goal of deterrence.[33]

30 Another major question was whether Exxon could be held vicariously liable for the recklessness of its employee, the captain.

31 *Exxon Shipping Co. v. Baker*, at 501–502.

32 *Ibid.*, at 496–497.

33 *Ibid.*, at 490.

After examining how the common-law rationale for punitive damages evolved, Justice Souter emphasized the modern consensus that 'punitives are aimed not at compensation but principally at retribution and deterring harmful conduct'.[34] Under this theory, judges and juries should refine their judgments not only to reach an optimal level of penalty and deterrence, but also to ensure consistent results in like cases. Based on its review of the punitive damages scholarly literature, Justice Souter concluded that these goals were not being met, and that the variability of individual awards of awards indicated that punitive damages were starkly unpredictable, even if the mean ratio for punitive damages awarded was roughly 1:1 compared to the underlying compensatory damages awarded in the same case.

Thus, while *Exxon Shipping* specifically concerned punitive damages in a maritime case, the U.S. Supreme Court clearly intended it to be an instance of a larger program of insuring consistency across punitive damage awards in cases involving similar claims and circumstances. According to Justice Souter, the key to any adequate common law theory of punitive damages was the proposition that 'a penalty should be reasonably predictable in its severity, so that even the [theoretical bad actor][35] can look ahead with some ability to know what the stakes are in choosing one course of action over another'.[36] For Justice Souter, the problem that a common law theory of punitive damages had to solve was how to deal with 'outlier' awards. The fact that each defendant might face a 'fair' *ex ante* risk of punishment, given the equal probability of outliers on both sides of the mean does not take the problem away: Exxon could take little comfort in knowing that for every US$ 5 billion punitive damages award, there had to be equally culpable defendants who were being asked to pay almost nothing. So the problem Souter faced was how to insure that the *ex ante* awards produced by the common law of punitive damages were regular and consistent. He doubted the effectiveness of verbal thresholds – the practice of trial courts avoiding unpredictable outliers by instructing the jury that punitive damages are to deter, but not bankrupt or destroy, a defendant and should be proportionate to the wrongfulness of the conduct. Justice Souter observed that 'instructions can go just so far in promoting systemic consistency when awards are not tied to specifically proven items of damage'.[37] Likewise, Justice Souter found that traditional post verdict and appellate standards, such as the 'shocks the conscience' standard or 'passion and prejudice' test, even with the enumeration of more specific factors, would not yielded consistent awards.

In a search for a better way, Justice Souter looked to its experience in the realm of criminal sentencing, which also, over the previous thirty years employed various devices rein in the 'relatively unguided discretion' of sentencing judges.[38] Justice Souter rejected a universal hard cap, like the maximum term of imprisonment in a criminal case, because there is no standard universal tort injury. On the other hand, he found a ratio based on the median of punitive damage awards much more promising and opted for a 1:1 ratio as

34 *Ibid.*, at 494–495.

35 The reference to 'the bad man' comes from Oliver Wendell Holmes: Holmes 1897, p. 459.

36 *Exxon Shipping Co. v. Baker*, at 502.

37 *Ibid.*, at 504.

38 *Ibid.*, at 505.

an upper limit for punitive damages in ordinary cases falling under maritime law and, by extension, all of common law. Justice Souter made clear that the common law opens the door to higher awards in some circumstances, such as when the defendant's conduct is intentional or malicious, driven by a desire for gain, or unlikely to be discovered. Likewise, a higher award may be permissible when a plaintiff experiences only modest economic harm.

The U.S. Supreme Court's first foray in developing its own theory of the common law of punitive damages leaves many questions unanswered. The first is why it emphasized predictability to the extent that it did, given that the common law of damages is rife with unpredictability. Anyone who practices or teaches private law in the United States knows that fact finders can be highly unpredictable in their judgments relating to compensatory damages, especially pain and suffering damages. While this fact had drawn some attention from legislative tort reformers in the form of caps on damages in some areas of tort law (especially medical malpractice law), the mere fact that damages are highly unpredictable in the American common law has not been raised as a reason to doubt the whole foundation of the common law's approach to compensatory damages.

But of course one can say that punitive damages are different. While they are not, as the U.S. Supreme Court held in *Browning Ferris*, exactly like criminal or civil fines (and thus not subject to the Eighth Amendment's scrutiny), their rationale – the answer to the 'why' question – is not identical to the answer given for the rationale for compensatory damages under the common law. As Justice Souter noted, their main rationale is 'retribution and deterrence'. But even taking this difference into account, it is not clear why predictability – achieved by making punitive damages a function of compensatory damages – is the most important value. If one were to take seriously the goal of private retribution, it is not clear why the verbal formulas dismissed by Justice Souter do not provide juries with a more precise and textured means of ascertaining the degree to which the defendant's conduct expressed contempt and indifference to the plaintiff's rights in private law.[39] And if one were to take seriously the idea that punitive damages are a form of social retribution, then it is not clear why the degree of punishment should be tethered to the actual amount of damages awarded at trial.[40] The *Exxon Shipping* case is a good example: although the punitive damages were measured against the actual damages awarded to the plaintiffs who took the oil company to a final judgment, the jury may have also been thinking about the social damage caused by the oil spill for which no punitive damages would be awarded, either because no suits were brought on behalf of the 'public' or because where there had been suits (such as the U.S Government's suit and suits brought by other private parties) they had been settled, thus removing any opportunity for a jury to impose punitive damages based on the actual losses suffered by those non-parties.

The most important rationale that the U.S. Supreme Court excludes under its common law theory of punitive damages is the influential law and economics view that punitive damages should be designed to promote optimal deterrence.[41] As first set out by Polinsky

39 Sebok 2007, pp. 1029–1031.
40 Markel 2009.
41 Sharkey 2010, p. 41.

and Shavell, punitive damages perfect the cost-internalization strategy undertaken by common law courts that have embraced the Hand Test.[42] Perfection of the Hand Test is needed because of the problem of underenforcement: not all inefficient acts result in liability equal to the social loss they cause. This is for multiple reasons, although Polinsky and Shavell emphasize just two, underdetection and undercompensation. It might be the case that underenforcement is the result of other imperfections as well, such as false negatives in adjudication and the cost of adjudication. In any event, as illustrated by Judge Posner in *Mathias v. Accor Economy Lodging Inc.*, the theory of optimal deterrence may, on occasion demand a ratio much higher than 1:1 even absent any extraordinary conditions, such as malice or very minor compensatory damages. In *Mathias*, 347 F.3d 672 (7th Cir. 2003), Judge Posner justified a 37:1 ratio in a case involving hotel patrons who suffered thousands of dollars of injuries due to the presence of vermin in their room because, as Judge Posner reasoned, unless the gain obtained by the hotel from having rented all the rooms in their hotel (which, presumably had the same vermin) was taken from them, they would not be deterred by the threat of tort damages.

5. Conclusion

In the face of these various powerful theoretical rationales for punitive damages which might regularly exceed a 1:1 ratio, the U.S. Supreme Court's decision to adopt the 1:1 ratio is odd, and its heavy emphasis on predictability as a guiding feature for any theory of punitive damages within the common law is especially odd. Some experts have hailed the *Exxon Shipping* decision for its potential to spill over into state common law theories of punitive damages as well – and thus have a salutary effect on state law similar to the effect that *Daubert v. Merrell Dow Pharm., Inc.*,[43] had on state evidence law.[44] The early results seem to suggest that the U.S. Supreme Court's foray into theorizing about the common law of punitive damages has not had a significant impact on ether the lower federal court's application of the Due Process Clause to state common law punitive damages decision or the states' own evolving interpretation of their own common law of punitive damages. This may be for a number of reasons, but one reason might be that the theory of punitive damages articulated in *Exxon Shipping* is not one which many other courts find attractive, persuasive, or applicable to the common law punitive damages of their own jurisdictions.

6. Recommendations for Europe

What lessons, if any, can be drawn from the United States' Supreme Court's attempt at defining the common law theory of punitive damages? The argument of this essay is not that the U.S. Supreme Court's current 'theory' – such as it is – is demonstrably worse than the theories that were otherwise adopted or assumed by the individual states. This essay does not compare the theory put forward in *Exxon Shipping* with other judicially-

42 Polinsky & Shavell 1998.

43 *Daubert v. Merrell Dow Pharm., Inc.*, 509 U.S. 579 (1993).

44 Schwartz, Silverman & Appel 2009, pp. 901–906.

generated theories, such as those that might be gleaned from reading the few state supreme court decisions that attempt to offer such a theory. One reason this essay has not done so is that supreme courts in the states have been very wary of imposing a single theory on their own common law doctrine of punitive damages, preferring instead to give juries and judges in the lower courts a variety of rationales under which verdicts could be crafted. *All* American judicial theories of punitive damages are relatively under-theorized – not only the theory recently offered by the U.S. Supreme Court.

The lesson, if any, that this essay offers the European reader is: Before adopting punitive damages, get the theory right. The collision between the United States Supreme Court and the states was produced, to a great degree, by the frustration experienced by litigants that the verdicts received in cases like *BMW of N. Am., Inc. v. Gore* were based on dubious (and not merely unconstitutional) theories of punishment and retribution. One suspects that had the verdicts been based on a robust theory of law – even one that the justices of the U.S. Supreme Court would not have personally adopted – the state court verdicts might have survived. Continental Europe has an advantage over the United States in that if punitive damages were to be adopted in its private law, it would only occur after serious debate and negotiation by the legislator. If European legislators heed the cautionary tale described in this essay, and prepare a robust theory of punitive damages to support the legal doctrine of punitive damages, then they may be able to produce decisions with greater durability and persuasiveness than *Exxon Shipping*.

Bibliography

Chemerinsky 2007
Chemerinsky, E., 'More Questions about Punitive Damages,' *Trial*, 2007, p. 72.

Holmes 1897
Holmes, O.W., 'The Path of the Law', *Harv L Rev*, 1897, pp. 457–498.

Markel 2009
Markel, D., 'Retributive Damages: A Theory of Punitive Damages as Intermediate Sanction', *Cornell L Rev*, 2009, pp. 239–340.

Polinsky & Shavell 1998
Polinsky, A.M. & Shavell, S., 'Punitive Damages: An Economic Analysis', *Harv L Rev*, 1998, pp. 869–962.

Sebok 2007
Sebok, A.J., 'Punitive Damages: From Myth to Theory', *Iowa L Rev*, 2007, pp. 957–1036.

Sebok 2003
Sebok, A.J., 'What Did Punitive Damages Do? Why Misunderstanding the History of Punitive Damages Matters Today', *Chi-Kent L Rev*, 2003, pp. 163–206.

Sebok 2009
Sebok, A.J., 'United States', in: H. Koziol & V. Wilcox (eds.), *Punitive Damages: Common Law and Civil Law Perspectives*, Vienna: Springer, 2009, pp. 155–196.

Sharkey 2004
Sharkey, C.M., 'Punitive Damages as Societal Damages', *Yale L J*, 2004, pp. 347–453.

Sharkey 2009
Sharkey, C.M., 'The Exxon Valdez Litigation Marathon: A Window On Punitive Damages', *U St Thomas L J*, 2009, pp. 25–54.

Schwartz, Silverman & Appel 2009
Schwartz, V. E., Silverman, C., and Appel, C. E., 'The Supreme Court's Common Law Approach to Excessive Punitive Damage Awards: A Guide for the Development of State Law', *S C L Rev*, pp. 881–914.

Danuta Mendelson*

PUNITIVE DAMAGES *SENSU STRICTO* IN AUSTRALIA

1. Introduction[1]

Punitive damages *sensu stricto* (also known as 'exemplary' and 'vindictive')[2] are awarded as part of a civil claim for damages in tort.[3] This chapter outlines the position of common law punitive damages in the context of civil punishments as they exist in the present-day Australia. The Commonwealth of Australia is a Federation comprising of six States (New South Wales, Victoria, Tasmania, South Australia, Western Australia and Queensland) and two Territories (the Australian Capital Territory and the Northern Territory). In general, the *Commonwealth of Australia Constitution Act 1900* (UK),[4] vests the Federal Parliament with an exclusive Commonwealth power to make laws with respect to powers specified under the *Constitution*[5] as well as enumerated concurrent federal and State powers;[6] States are also vested with exclusive State power to enact laws within the fields of their legislative competence.[7] These fields include the law of torts, which until 2002 was mainly governed by case law.

* Danuta Mendelson holds a Chair in Law (Research) at Deakin University School of Law, Australia.

1 This chapter is based on a paper presented at the 15th Congress of the Ius Commune on 26 November 2010. I am very grateful to Prof. Dr. Van Dam, Mrs. Lotte Meurkens and the organizers of the Workshop on Liability and Insurance for inviting me to the Catholic University of Leuven, Belgium.

2 *Whitfeld v. De Lauret* (1920) 29 CLR 71, per Isaac J. at p. 81.

3 The Australian law of contract does not recognise punitive damages; however, punitive damages for a breach of contract may be awarded under the law of torts if the defendant's conduct also amounts to a tort which sounds in such damages.

4 As well as subsequent enabling statutes.

5 Under the *Commonwealth of Australia Constitution Act*, s. 122, the Federal Parliament may make laws for the government of any territory.

6 Concurrent powers of the Commonwealth Government are enumerated in s. 51 of the *Commonwealth of Australia Constitution.*

7 *Commonwealth of Australia Constitution*, s. 107, 108 and 109'. While the Commonwealth and the States have the power to make laws within their respective fields of exclusive power; States are precluded from enacting valid legislation where the Commonwealth has 'covered the field': *Victoria v. The Commonwealth* ('the *Payroll Tax Case*') [1971] HCA 16; (1971) 122 CLR 353; *New South Wales v. Commonwealth* (2006) 229 CLR 1.

Punitive damages were developed by the English common law judiciary in the 18th century. The High Court of Australia has affirmed the institution of punitive damages.[8] However, some judicial decisions relating to punitive damages have been overcome by statutory provisions, though the process of legislative intervention is still continuing. In order to elucidate the uneasy relationship between the common law approach to punitive damages and legislative responses to this institution within modern Australian torts jurisprudence, I shall briefly examine:

(a) Conceptual and taxonomic differences between compensatory and punitive damages (§2);
(b) The most notable English historical precedents (§3);
(c) Common law punitive damages within the modern Australian legal framework (§4);
(d) Statutory compensation and restitution orders under criminal law (§5);
(e) Distinction between punitive and aggravated damages (§6);
(f) The place of common law Punitive Damages in contemporary Australian jurisprudence (§7).

The sole purpose of punitive damages is punishment and deterrence.[9] Yet, they are awarded within the context of the law of torts – a civil jurisdiction, the primary aim of which is compensation.

2. Difference in the Law of Torts between Compensatory & Punitive Damages

As a general rule, Australian courts award two categories of damages for tortiously inflicted harm[10]: compensatory and punitive.[11] Each category reflects a different conception of the law of torts: (1) as the quintessentially private law of compensation through monetary redress and (2) as a judicial mechanism for setting normative standards within society by way of deterrence through monetary punishment.[12]

8 In *Garcia v. National Australia Bank Ltd* (1998) 194 CLR 395 Gaudron, McHugh, Gummow and Hayne J.J. stated at p. 403 [at 17]: 'It should be emphasised that it is for this Court alone to determine whether one of its previous decisions is to be departed from or overruled'.

9 I shall refer to this head of damages as 'punitive damages'.

10 In certain actions, for example nuisance, the equitable remedy of injunction may be granted.

11 *Whitfeld v. De Lauret* (1920) 29 CLR 71, Knox C.J. at p. 77: 'Damages may be either compensatory or exemplary. Compensatory damages are awarded as compensation for and are measured by the material loss suffered by the plaintiffs. Exemplary damages are given only in cases of conscious wrongdoing in contumelious disregard of another's rights'.

12 For a general discussion see: Goldberg, 2004. See also, e.g.: *Aristocrat Technologies Australia Pty Ltd and Another v. DAP Services (Kempsey) Pty* (2007) 157 FCR 564, per Black C.J. and Jacobson J. at p 570 [43]: 'The objectives of an award of additional damages include deterrence: *Copyright Act 1968* (Cth), s 115(4)(b)(ia). An element of penalty is an accepted factor in the remedy: *Autodesk v. Yee* (1996) 68 FCR 391 at p. 384'.

Compensatory damages are based on the principle of *restitutio in integrum* as articulated by Lord Blackburn in *Livingstone v. Rawyards Coal Co.*:[13]

> 'where any injury is to be compensated by damages, in settling the sum of money to be given for reparation of damages you should as nearly as possible get at that sum of money which will put the party who has been injured, or who has suffered, in the same position as he would have been in if he had not sustained the wrong'.[14]

These damages include fair compensation[15] for past and future economic loss; any needs created by the wrongful conduct that would not otherwise have existed;[16] and non-economic or non-pecuniary loss such as pain and suffering.[17] However, where the plaintiff's harm involves 'injury to the plaintiff's feelings caused by insult, humiliation and the like'[18] the court, particularly in actions for intentional torts, may also award aggravated damages, which form part of compensatory system. The High Court of Australia in *New South Wales v. Ibbett*[19] emphasized that:

> 'Aggravated damages are a form of general damages, given by way of compensation for injury to the plaintiff, which may be intangible, resulting from the circumstances and manner of the wrongdoing.[20]'

When awarding aggravated damages, the court assesses monetary value of the 'intangible' emotional harm (shame, degradation, dishonour, etc) sustained by the plaintiff, while treating it as compensable loss.

Punitive damages are different – the Australian High Court in *XL Petroleum (NSW) Pty. Ltd v. Caltex Oil (Australia) Pty Ltd*,[21], a case involving trespass to land, emphasised the acceptability of punishment[22] and deterrence as legitimate goals of civil actions:

13 *Livingstone v. Rawyards Coal Co* [1880] 5 AC 25 at p. 39.

14 See also: *Brighty v. Norton* (1862) 75 Eng. Rep. 1256 at p. 1258, per Blackburn J.

15 *Teubner v. Humble* (1963) 108 CLR 491, per Windeyer J. at p. 505.

16 In *Griffiths v. Kerkemeyer* (1977) 139 CLR 161, the High Court of Australia followed the English Court of Appeal decision in *Donnelly v. Joyce* (1974) QB 454. For further discussion see: Mendelson, 2005.

17 Trespassory torts are actionable per se: damages are awarded for infringement of the claimant's dignitary interests (sense of dignity, honour and decorum) through battery, assault, false imprisonment, and trespass to land.

18 *Lamb v. Cotogno* (1987) 164 CLR 1 at 8, adopting Lord Devlin's definition in *Rookes v. Barnard* (No.1) [1964] AC 1129.

19 *New South Wales v. Ibbett* [2006] HCA 57; (2006) 229 CLR 638.

20 *Ibid.*, at 646–7[§ 31]. Their Honours referred to *Uren v. John Fairfax & Sons Pty. Ltd* (1966) 117 CLR 118 at p. 129–130.

21 *XL Petroleum (NSW) Pty Ltd v. Caltex Oil (Australia) Pty Ltd* (1985) 155 CLR 448, at p. 471.

22 In *Australian Consolidated Press Ltd v. Uren* (1967) 117 CLR 118; affirmed by the Privy Council in *Australian Consolidated Press Ltd v. Uren* (1967) 117 CLR 221, the Australian High Court rejected the restrictive approach adopted by the House of Lords in *Rookes v. Barnard* (1964) AC 1129.

> 'an award of exemplary damages is intended to punish the defendant for conduct showing a conscious and contumelious disregard for the plaintiff's rights and to deter him from committing like conduct again ...'

Consequently, these damages are aimed at the defendant, and the court does not determine their quantum by reference to the plaintiff's injury,[23] but on the basis of whether the defendant's conduct calls for a *judicial* retribution in the name of deterrence.[24]

The dichotomy between punishment and compensation goes back to the distinction drawn by Aristotle in his *Nicomachean Ethics*. Aristotle distinguished rules and forms governing distributive justice, from the principles of 'corrective' justice.[25] The position of punishment within this paradigm has been a matter of controversy ever since the time of rediscovery of Aristotelian works in the 12th century, and is still unsettled. Lee[26] argued that criminal law is not part of corrective justice, even though it 'might seem at first sight its most natural interpretation'.[27] This is because 'a crime is usually committed on the person or property of an individual'; however, 'criminal law is not concerned with the offence as an offence against the individual or with the adjustment of individual rights; it is concerned with the offence ... against public order, against the regulations laid down to ensure an orderly social life'.[28]

Offences against public order attract punishment, and as such, they are the bailiwick of public, not private, law. This is particularly true of common law, which since the 14th century has developed two independent jurisdictional streams – criminal and civil – to adjudicate wrongful conduct. According to Sir William Blackstone's *Commentaries on the Laws of England*,[29] private wrongs involve 'an infringement or privation of the private or civil rights belonging to individuals, considered as individuals', whereas public wrongs are based on 'a breach and violation of public rights and duties, which affect the whole community'. Civil proceedings for damages in tort focus on determining defendant's liability and assessment of compensation for the harm sustained by the individual claimant. In criminal proceedings, however, the Crown in the right of State takes over from the victim of the crime, focusing on the question whether the defendant has committed an offence against public law and the appropriate punishment for this transgression. Consequently, criminal and civil proceedings differ markedly in aims, rules and procedures. For example, the standard of proof beyond reasonable doubt governs criminal prosecutions, whereas outcomes in civil litigation are determined on

23 *Gray v. Motor Accident Commission* (1998) 196 CLR 1 at p. 7[15].
24 *Whitfeld v. De Lauret* (1920) 29 CLR 71, Isaacs J. at p. 81: 'From a very early period exemplary damages have been considered by very eminent Judges to be punitive for reprehensible conduct and as a deterrent'.
25 Aristotle 1934, ch ii, p. 1131b. Corrective justice has also been referred to as 'rectificatory' or 'commutative' justice'.
26 Lee, 1937.
27 *Ibid.*, at p. 130.
28 *Ibid.*
29 Blackstone 1768,p. 2. Blackstone's definition reflected the Roman law's approach to the division of unlawful conduct.

the basis of the civil standard of proof (the balance of probabilities);[30] limitation of actions periods are quite different, as is the admissibility of evidence,[31] etc.

However, the line separating private from public wrongs is not always clear; contingent as it is on the hierarchy of moral values and socio-political preferences of a society at a given time: under common law, the same incident can give raise to criminal prosecution and civil litigation. In his *Commentaries*, Blackstone provided an example of criminal conversation with a man's wife (adultery), which at the time was both, a public crime enforced in ecclesiastical courts and a tort, 'wherein the damages recovered [from the adulterer] are usually very large and exemplary'.[32]

3. *Wilkes v. Wood* – The English Precedent

Blackstone referred to 'exemplary' damages twice (in relation to the now obsolete wrong of criminal conversation, and in cases where creators of nuisance do not remove or abate nuisance after the initial verdict against them).[33] However, he avoided any discussion of their nature, and did not comment on the case of *Wilkes v. Wood*,[34] with which, given its importance and fame,[35] he would have been familiar. In *Wilkes v. Wood* Richard Pratt, the Chief Justice of the Court of Common Pleas thus distinguished compensatory from punitive damages:

> 'A jury have it in their power to give damages for more than the injury received. Damages are designed not only as a satisfaction to the injured person, but likewise as a punishment to the guilty, to deter from any such proceeding for the future, and as a proof of the detestation of the jury to the action itself'.

In *Wilkes v. Wood,* John Wilkes, controversial Member of Parliament and a political journalist, successfully claimed damages for trespass to land. He was charged with seditious libel over the Editorial in the (1763) 45 *The North Briton* (his weekly publication devoted to political polemics and satire), which attacked George III's speech to the Parliament on the Paris Peace Treaty of 1763. Mr. Wood, as the King's messenger (he was accompanied by a constable and four other messengers), acting under a general warrant issued by Lord Halifax, the Secretary of State, entered Wilkes' house, 'breaking his locks,

30 See for example: *Evidence Act 1995* (Cth), s. 140 Civil proceedings: standard of proof: '(1) In a civil proceeding, the court must find the case of a party proved if it is satisfied that the case has been proved on the balance of probabilities. (2) Without limiting the matters that the court may take into account in deciding whether it is so satisfied, it is to take into account: (a) the nature of the cause of action or defence; and (b) the nature of the subject-matter of the proceeding; and (c) the gravity of the matters alleged'. Reproduced in s 140 of *Evidence Act 1995* (NSW), *Evidence Act 2001* (Tas) and *Evidence Act 2008* (Vic) respectively.

31 *Hollington v. F. Hewthorn and Company, Ltd, and Another* [1943] KB 587.

32 Blackstone 1768, p. 139.

33 Blackstone 1768,p. 220.

34 *Wilkes v. Wood* (1763) 98 Eng Rep 489.

35 Between 1763 and 1769 approximately 40 cases, known as the Wilkes Cases came before the courts on the issue of general warrants.

and seizing his papers, &c'. Pratt C.J. found the general warrant to be invalid (it did not include inventory 'of the things thus taken away' and no offenders names were specified in the warrant);[36] jury awarded Wilkes £1000 (a very considerable sum at the time).

While historically, juries were known to award damages that were sufficiently large to suggest an element of punishment,[37] *Wilkes v. Wood* was the first case in which the court adopted punitive (exemplary) awards as a separate head of damages. Though the doctrine was formulated by the Court of Common Pleas rather than the Court of King's Bench, by the end of the 18th century, punitive damages came to be frequently awarded in actions for intentional torts (assault, battery,[38] false imprisonment),[39] as well as torts (for example, libel) in which malice had to be established.[40]

Punitive damages formed part of the English law, and were received into the Colony of New South Wales in 1828. Until the enactment of the *Privy Council (Limitation of Appeals) Act 1968* (Cth); the *Privy Council (Appeals from the High Court) Act 1975* (Cth) and the decision in *Kirmani v. Captain Cook Cruises Pty Ltd [No. 2]*,[41] it was a judicial practice in Australia to follow precedents from the English appellate courts. It is not surprising therefore that according to Isaacs J. of the High Court of Australia, in *The Herald and Weekly Times Ltd v. McGregor*[42] (a defamation case), punitive damages were 'a special doctrine of substantive law which was gradually evolved',[43] allowing:

> 'damages by way of retribution as contrasted with compensation, representing what Pollock calls 'indignation at the defendant's wrong rather than a value set upon the plaintiff's loss' (*Torts*, 12th ed., p. 189)'.

Isaacs J. cited the statement of Heath J. in the English case of *Merest v Harvey*[44] that juries were 'permitted to punish insult by exemplary damages'.[45]'

36 In *Huckle v. Money* (1763) 95 Eng. Rep. 768 (CP 1763); 2 Wils KB 205 Pratt C.J. found general warrants to be invalid; on appeal Lord Mansfield determined that only general warrants not authorised by statute should declared invalid.

37 See: *Huckle v. Money* (1763) 95 Eng. Rep. 768 (CP 1763); *Fabrigas v. Mostyn* (1774) 2 Black, W. 929 at p. 929; 96 Eng. Rep. 549 at p. 549, per De Grey C.J.

38 *Grey v. Grant* (1764) 2 Wils 251; 95 English Reports 794; *Merest, Esq v. Harvey* (1814) 128 English Reports 761; 5 Taunton 442.

39 *Beardmore v. Nathan Carrington* (1764) 2 Wils 244 95 English Reports 791; *Edgell v. Francis* (1840) 133 English Reports 315.

40 *Bramley v. Chesterton* (1857) 2 C B (N S) 592; 140 English Reports 548.

41 *Kirmani v. Captain Cook Cruises Pty. Ltd. [No. 2]* (1985) 159 CLR 461.

42 *The Herald and Weekly Times Ltd v. McGregor* (1929) 41 CLR 254 at p. 266.

43 *Ibid.*, at p. 266.

44 *Merest v. Harvey* (1814) 5 Taunton 442 at p. 444.

45 *The Herald and Weekly Times Ltd v. McGregor* (1929) 41 CLR 254 at p. 266. Isaacs J. also referred to Wilmot L.C.J. in *Tullidge v. Wade* (1769) 3 Wils 18 (action in trespass for loss of services by a father against a man who seduced his daughter was described by Wilmot L.C.J.at p. 19 as 'brought for example's sake'; with the jury having the right to give 'liberal damages').

4. Common Law Punitive Damages within the Modern Australian Legal Framework

One of the most important cases discussing punitive damages is *Gray v. Motor Accident Commission.*[46] In *Gray*, the defendant Bransden deliberately drove his motor car into a group of people, injuring the plaintiff, Mr. Gray. Bransden was convicted of intentionally causing grievous bodily harm, and sentenced to seven years' imprisonment. Gray successfully sued in negligence for damages for personal injury, but the trial judge dismissed his claim for exemplary damages on the basis that Bransden had already been punished by the criminal court. The High Court of Australia affirmed this decision. Gleeson C.J., McHugh, Gummow and Hayne J.J. observed that:

> 'The increasing frequency with which civil penalty provisions are enacted,[47] the provisions made for criminal injuries compensation,[48] the provisions now made in some jurisdictions for the judge at a criminal trial to order restitution[49] or compensation to a person suffering loss or damage (including pain and suffering) as a result of an offence[50] all deny the existence of any 'sharp cleavage' between the criminal and the civil law'.[51]

Their Honours' statement needs further elucidation. Penalties, whether physical or economic, are at the core of every criminal law system; however, it was only in the final three decades of the 20th century, that Australian legislatures begun to routinely insert civil penalties (whether expressed in terms of penalty units or penalties specified in monetary amounts) into civil statutes. These civil penalties may be relatively minor or run into hundreds of thousands of dollars. For example, *Medical Treatment Act 1988* (Vic), s. 5 allows adults with full mental capacity ('sound mind') to execute a 'refusal of treatment certificate' relating to medical treatment generally or of a particular kind for the patient's current condition. The legislation has also created an offence of medical trespass to punish registered medical practitioners who 'knowing that a refusal of treatment certificate applies to a person, undertake or continue to undertake any medical treatment to which the certificate applies'. The punishment is 5 penalty units (US$ 597.25).

At the other end of penal monetary spectrum, *Corporations Act 2001* (Cth), s. 1317G provides for civil pecuniary penalties of US$ 200,000 for an individual; or US$ 1 million for a body corporate for contraventions of its provisions listed in s. 1317E. Pecuniary penalties are defined under s. 1317G as 'a civil debt payable to ASIC [Australian Securities and Investments Commission] on the Commonwealth's behalf'. The legislation specifies in s. 1317H (2) that 'ASIC or the Commonwealth may enforce the order as if it were an

46 *Gray v. Motor Accident Commission* (1998) 196 CLR 1.
47 See e.g. *Corporations Law Act 1989* (Cth), Pt 9.4B; since replaced by *Corporations Act 2001* (Cth).
48 See e.g. *Criminal Injuries Compensation Act 1978* (SA).
49 See e.g. *Criminal Law (Sentencing) Act 1988* (SA), s. 52; *Sentencing Act 1991* (Vic), Pt 4, D 1.
50 See, e.g., *Criminal Law (Sentencing) Act 1988* (SA), s. 53; *Sentencing Act 1991* (Vic), Pt 4, D 2.
51 *Ibid.*, at pp. 7–8 [16].

order made in civil proceedings against the person to recover a debt due by the person. The debt arising from the order is taken to be a judgment debt'.

Just like criminal fines, civil penalties are meted out as punishment for the defendant's breach of a statutory prohibition (rather than the damage suffered by the plaintiff); and, just like fines; they are collected by the Crown (Federal, State or Territory treasury). Yet, unlike criminal fines, civil penalties are imposed on defendants whose liability is determined on the balance of probabilities. The proof on the balance of probabilities is also a feature of common law punitive damages, though they are awarded for the benefit of the individual plaintiff, not the State.

Defendants who are tried, convicted and punished in a criminal court, as well as being found liable in civil proceedings on facts arising from the same incident, have to pay compensatory, and if applicable, aggravated, but not exemplary damages. In *Gray* the High Court of Australia observed that that since the object of awarding exemplary damages is to punish the wrongdoer in 'an emphatic and a public way', the court should take into consideration the fact that this was already achieved by criminal conviction, or that conviction is likely to follow. Though the issue was not discussed at the time, it is arguable that compensatory,[52] but not punitive damages should be awarded where the court orders the defendant to pay a civil penalty.

5. Statutory Compensation and Restitution Orders under Criminal Law

Though it did not pertain to *Gray*, in tandem with legislation vesting civil courts with power to impose civil penalties in certain cases, in some States, criminal courts' jurisdiction has been extended to include (in addition to imposition of prison sentences, community orders, and fines), the power to make orders requiring the offender to make restitution[53] or pay compensation to the injured victim of the offence.[54] For example, in Victoria, by virtue of the *Sentencing Act 1991*, s. 85B, persons who had suffered an injury as a direct result of the offence of which the offender has been found guilty or convicted, may ask the sentencing court to order:

> 'the offender to pay compensation of such amount as the court thinks fit for ...(a) pain and suffering experienced by the victim as a direct result of the offence; (b) ... any expenses actually incurred, or reasonably likely to be incurred, by the victim for reasonable counselling services as a direct result of the offence; (c) ... any medical expenses actually and reasonably incurred, or reasonably likely to be incurred, by the victim as a direct result of the offence; (d) any other expenses actually and reasonably incurred, or reasonably likely to be incurred, by the victim as a direct result of the offence, not including any expense arising from loss of or damage to property'.[55]

52 See e.g., compensation orders under *Corporations Act 2001* (Cth), s. 1317H; s. 1317HA and s. 1317HB.

53 For example in cases of theft, see *Sentencing Act 1991* (Vic), s. 84.

54 *Sentencing Act 1991* (Vic), s. 50(3)(b); s. 74; s. 77; and s. 83F(2)(ii).

55 *Sentencing Act 1991* (Vic), s. 86 sets out a statutory regime of compensation by offenders found guilty of causing for property losses to the victim.

In cases where the victim has suffered loss, destruction, or damage to property as a result of the offence, under s. 86(1), the court may order that the offender 'pay any compensation ... that the court thinks fit'. Where a person has been found 'guilty or convicted of an offence connected with the theft', s. 84 of *Sentencing Act 1991* (Vic) enables the court to make restitution orders.[56] These curial powers are not new. Provisions of *Lex Ribuaria*, a 7th century collection of the laws of the Ripuarian Franks from Colonge in Germany, mandated that the fine imposed on the wrongdoer should not be collected 'until compensation was paid to the private victim of the injury.[57] This ancient principle is preserved in the *Sentencing Act*, which provides that where the offender pleads insufficient means to pay both, a fine and restitution or compensation, 'the court must give preference to restitution or compensation, though it may impose a fine as well'.[58]

Section 85L of the *Sentencing Act 1991* (Vic) vests in the victims of an offence the right 'to recover damages for any expense or other matter so far as it is not satisfied by payment or recovery of compensation under' the provisions of the *Sentencing Act*. However, given the expense of civil litigation and the impecunious state of most offenders, for the vast majority of victims this option is theoretical rather than practical. Statutory language of the *Sentencing Act* refers to compensatory and restitutionary 'orders' with the implication that the orders form part of the punishment. In substance, however, these orders cross the boundary from criminal law to private law, and indeed, under *Sentencing Act 1991* (Vic), s. 85M 'a compensation order, including costs ordered to be paid by the offender on the proceeding for that order, must be taken to be a judgment *debt* due by the offender to the person in whose favour the order is made and payment of any amount remaining unpaid under the order may be enforced in the court by which it was made'.[59] The writ of debt is one of the oldest common law Forms of Action, and the notion of debt as civil institution goes back to Aristotle.[60] However, offender-debtors can only repay a debt if they are capable and/or have the means of doing so. In the great majority of cases, imposition of restitutionary and compensatory orders as part of sentencing process is not realistic. In these cases, to alleviate financial hardships suffered by victims of crime, since the 1970s,

56 Under s. 84(1), the court may, inter alia, order that: (a) 'the person who has possession or control of the stolen goods restore them to the person entitled to them; and/or (b) 'the offender deliver or transfer to another person goods that directly or indirectly represent the stolen goods (that is, goods that are the proceeds of any disposal or realisation of the whole or part of the stolen goods or of goods so representing them)'; and/or (c) 'a sum not exceeding the value of the stolen goods be paid to another person out of money taken from the offender's possession on his or her arrest'.

57 Harding 2002 at p. 27. The author adds that is such cases, however, 'a third of the sum was to be pledged before witnesses to the king's fisc (not given to the judge), 'so that firm peace shall endure forever' (*ut pax perpetua stabilis permaneat*)'.

58 *Sentencing Act 1991* (Vic), s. 50(4)(b). The priority of payment of restitution or compensation to the victim over penalties to be paid by the offender to the State is reinforced by *Confiscation Act 1997* (Vic), s. 30, which mandates that where the offender's property is restrained (confiscated and sold by the State), the State must ensure that any order for restitution, compensation or damages made under the *Sentencing Act 1991* 'is satisfied, to the value of the restrained property', before the proceeds from the restrained property can be used for any other purpose. See also *Confiscation Act 1997* (Vic), s. 31.

59 Likewise, s. 85(1) of *Sentencing Act 1991* specifies that restitutionary orders involving payments of money (rather than specific restitution of stolen goods under s. 84(1)(c) of the *Sentencing Act 1991* (Vic)), 'must be taken to be a judgment debt due by the offender to the person in whose favour the order is made ....'

60 Aristotle 1934, p. 1132a.

all Australian States and Territories have enacted statutory schemes which enable victims and their close relatives to obtain capped statutory compensation for personal injury.[61] The availability of statutory compensation does not affect a person's right to commence or maintain common law proceedings;[62] though again, the award of punitive damages would be contingent on whether the defendant has been or is likely to be sentenced.

The expanded the power of the civil courts to impose civil penalties and the criminal courts to make compensatory and restitutionary orders has meant that in the 21st century, punitive damages are no longer the sole institution through which judges in civil proceeding can express their condemnation of the particular defendant's egregious conduct. The question then arises, what is the place and function of punitive damages in modern Australian law?

6. Distinction between Punitive and Aggravated Damages

In their reluctance to draw a firm and principled line between aggravated and punitive damages, the courts have not made the answer to this question easy.

Historically, until mid-18th century, heads of damages for personal injury were generally undifferentiated. Plaintiffs suing in tort would claim (lay) a single sum in damages with the determination of the final amount left to the court's discretion. For example, in *Fabrigas v. Mostyn*,[63] Mr. Fabrigas, a native Minorquin, sued General Mostyn, the Governor of Minorca, for trespass and false imprisonment. In 1771, while in Minorca, Mostyn without a legal cause, but on suspicion that Fabrigas may be fomenting unrest, having seized and imprisoned the plaintiff for six days, banished him for 12 months to Carthagena (which was under Spanish rule). The plaintiff claimed £10,000 in damages. On the facts in *Fabrigas*, though unarticulated, the jury's award of £3000 and £90 in costs was punitive. However, De Grey C.J. observed that it was:

> 'very difficult [for the court] to interpose with respect to the quantum of damages [awarded by juries] in actions for any personal wrong. Not that it can be laid down, that in no case of personal injury the damages can be excessive. Some may be so monstrous and excessive, as to be in themselves an evidence of passion or partiality in the jury'.[64]

Even after punitive damages were doctrinally distinguished from aggravated, the judiciary did not insist that the distinction be observed. The difficulty of observing the

61 *Victims Support and Rehabilitation Act 1996* (NSW), s. 18, 19; *Crimes (Victims Assistance) Act 1989* (NT), s. 13; *Victims of Crime Act 2001* (SA), s. 20; *Criminal Injuries Compensation Act 1976* (Tas), s. 6; *Victims of Crime Assistance Act 1996* (Vic), s. 8, 8A, 10, 10A, 12, and 13; *Criminal Injuries Compensation Act 2003* (WA), s. 31–34; *Victims of Crime (Financial Assistance) Act 1983* (ACT), s. 10 and 19; *Criminal Offence Victims Act 1995* (Qld), s. 25. See also: *In the matter of an application under the Criminal Injuries Compensation Act 1983* [2004] ACTSC 60. For a discussion see Mendelson 2010, p. 89–93.

62 *Victims Support and Rehabilitation Act 1996* (NSW), s. 43; *Criminal Offence Victims Act 1995* (Qld), s. 22; *Criminal Injuries Compensation Act 1976* (Tas), s. 9.

63 *Fabrigas v. Mostyn* (1774) 2 Black, W. 929; 96 Eng. Rep. 549.

64 *Fabrigas v. Mostyn* (1774) 2 Black, W. 929; 96 Eng. Rep. 549, at p. 929.

distinction was noted by Windeyer J. of the High Court of Australia in *Uren v. John Fairfax Ltd. & Sons*,[65] a defamation case, his Honour noted that:

> 'in truth a punitive or vindictive element does lurk in many cases in which the damages were aggravated by the defendant's conduct… Limiting the scope of terms that often were not distinguished in application makes possible an apparently firm distinction between aggravated compensatory damages and exemplary or punitive damages. How far the different labels denote concepts really different in effect may be debatable. I suspect that in seeking to preserve the distinction we shall sometimes find ourselves dealing more in words than ideas'.[66]

Justice Windeyer's concerns over the failure to clearly conceptualise aggravated damages were exemplified in *Carson v. John Fairfax & Sons Ltd*,[67] another defamation case determined by the High Court. In *Carson*, McHugh J. observed that common law juries can award aggravated damages when they consider it 'necessary to provide a proper consolation for the plaintiff'.[68] He cited with approval Lord Hailsham L.C., who in *Broome v. Cassell & Co*[69] said that juries can 'inflict an added burden on the defendant proportionate to his conduct', if 'the injury to the plaintiff is actually greater and, as the result of the conduct exciting the indignation, demands a more generous solatium'.[70] McHugh J. added that 'in awarding aggravated damages, the anger or indignation which the jury feels at the way the defendant has treated the plaintiff is a proper reason for making a large rather than a small award to compensate the plaintiff'.[71]Lord Hailsham L.C. and McHugh J. conflated the notion of aggravated damages with extra financial burden as punishment imposed on the defendant (quintessence of the punitive damages doctrine). The reference to aggravated damages as providing 'consolation' is baffling, for this is the function of damages for pain and suffering.[72] The institution of 'solatium' was rejected in *Blake v. Midland Rly. Co.*[73] and does not form part of the English and Australian common law. Urging juries to express their 'anger or indignation' at the defendant's conduct by compensating the plaintiff for a 'greater injury' through 'large' rather than 'small' awards erases the line between aggravated and punitive damages.

Judicial failure to provide clear distinction between the two, may explain why several legislatures have responded by abolishing outright or placing limitations upon both, exemplary and aggravated damages.

65 *Uren v John Fairfax Ltd. & Sons* (1966) 117 CLR 118.
66 *Ibid.*, at p. 151–152.
67 *Carson v. John Fairfax & Sons Ltd* (1993) 178 CLR 44.
68 *Ibid.*, at p 109.
69 *Broome v. Cassell & Co.*, [1972] AC 1027, at p. 1071.
70 *Ibid.*, at p. 1073.
71 *Carson v. John Fairfax & Sons Ltd* (1993) 178 CLR 44, at p. 109.
72 *Thatcher v. Charles* (1961) *104 CLR 57*, per Windeyer J. at pp. 71–72.
73 *Blake v. Midland Rly. Co.* (1852) 21 L.J. Q.B. 233 at p. 237.

7. The Place of Common Law Punitive Damages in Contemporary Australian Jurisprudence

In *Lamb v. Cotogno*,[74] a case involving an award of punitive damages for trespass to the person, Mason C.J., Brennan, Deane, Dawson and Gaudron J.J. in a joint judgment, proclaimed that 'exemplary damages may be awarded in Australia for a wide range of torts'.

Indeed, by the late 1990s some State and Territory courts began awarding punitive damages for negligence[75] in addition to battery,[76] assault,[77] false imprisonment,[78] tort of interfering with contractual relations,[79] trespass to land,[80] trespass to goods, misfeasance in public office,[81] malicious prosecution,[82] conversion and trespass to goods,[83] deceit, defamation, libel and slander.[84] At this point the High Court decided to rein in the judicial enthusiasm for this head of damages, and in *Gray v. Motor Accident Commission*,[85] the majority observed that:

> 'exemplary damages could not properly be awarded in a case of alleged negligence in which there was no conscious wrongdoing by the defendant. Ordinarily, then, questions of exemplary damages will not arise in most negligence cases be they motor accident or other kinds of case'.[86]

The High Court in *Gray* provided for an exception involving cases where employees can establish that they suffered harm because the employer-defendant recklessly failed to protect their safety.[87] Such awards of punitive damages could be awarded only if the defendant has not been already punished. For example, punitive damages would be precluded in the case of successful prosecution under the *Occupational Health and Safety Act 2004* (Vic), s. 32, which provides that a 'person who, without lawful excuse, recklessly engages in conduct that places or may place another person who is at a workplace in

[74] *Lamb v. Cotogno* (1987) 164 CLR 1.
[75] *Backwell v. AAA* (1997) 1 VR 182; *Hart v. Herron* (1996) Aust Torts Reports 81–395; *Gray v. Motor Accident Commission* (1998) 196 CLR 1; *B and C and D Pty Ltd v. Leonard M Marinovich* [1999] NTSC 127.
[76] *Fontin v. Katapodis* (1962) 108 CLR 177; *Lamb v. Cotogno* (1987) 164 CLR 1.
[77] *New South Wales v. Ibbett* (2006) 229 CLR 638.
[78] *Trobridge v. Hardy* (1956) 94 CLR 147;*Watson v. Marshall and Cade* (1971) 124 CLR 621; *ZHU v. Treasurer of NSW* (2004) 218 CLR 530.
[79] *ZHU v. Treasurer of NSW* (2004) 218 CLR 530.
[80] *XL Petroleum (NSW) Pty Ltd v. Caltex Oil (Australia) Pty Ltd* (1985) 155 CLR 448; *New South Wales v. Ibbett* (2006) 229 CLR 638.
[81] *Farrington v. Thomson & Bridgland* [1959] VR 286.
[82] *Commonwealth Life Assurance Society Ltd. v. Smith* (1938) 59 CLR 527; *A v. New South Wales* (2007) 230 CLR 500.
[83] *Healing (Sales) Pty Ltd. v. Inglis Electrix Pty Ltd* (1969) 121 CLR 584; 42 ALJR 280.
[84] *The Herald and Weekly Times Ltd v. McGregor* (1929) 41 CLR 254.
[85] *Gray v. Motor Accident Commission* (1998) 196 CLR 1.
[86] *Ibid.*, at 9 [22].
[87] *Coloca v. BP Australia Limited; Thompson v. James Hardie & Co Pty Ltd* [1992] 2 VR 441.

danger of serious injury' commits an indictable offence'. The penalty under s. 32(a) and (b) is 'a term of imprisonment not exceeding 5 years, or a fine not exceeding 1800 penalty units, or both' for a natural person; and 'a fine not exceeding 9000 penalty units' for a body corporate.

The case of *Lamb v. Cotogno* is both an authority for the modern doctrine of punitive damages at common law, and an example of its jurisprudential and practical shortcomings. In *Lamb*, Garry James Lamb, the defendant, drove into the driveway of Giuseppe Cotogno's property and served him with summons. Cotogno refused to accept the service of summons, threatened to kill Lamb; and when Lamb got into his car and began to drive away, Cotogno 'threw himself across the bonnet of the car and held on to the guttering at the sides of the windscreen'.[88] While driving at speed of 35 to 40 kilometers per hour along the road, Lamb tried to dislodge him; eventually he braked so sharply that Cotogno was thrown from the bonnet onto the road, fracturing bones in both feet. Lamb drove off.[89] The trial judge determined that while Lamb acted without malice, exemplary damages should be awarded against him because he 'callously abandon[ed] the plaintiff on the road and sped off in the night leaving him lying on a darkened road'.[90]

The High Court acknowledged that under the then relevant legislation any damages, including punitive damages, awarded against Lamb would be paid by his motor vehicle insurer. However, according to their Honours:

> 'Whilst an award of exemplary damages against a compulsorily insured motorist may have a limited deterrent effect upon him or upon other motorists also compulsorily insured, the deterrent effect is undiminished for those minded to engage in conduct of a similar nature which does not involve the use of a motor vehicle'.[91]

Their Honours added:

> 'Moreover, whilst the smart or sting will obviously not be the same if the defendant does not have to pay an award of exemplary damages, it does serve to mark the court's condemnation of the defendant's behaviour and its effect is not entirely to be discounted by the existence of compulsory insurance'.[92]

Presumably, their Honours meant that the case would deter bicycle riders from speeding off in the night leaving their victims unattended. If so, the *Cotogno* deterrent was ineffective. For example in *Hollis v. Vabu*,[93] a cyclist collided with a pedestrian, Mr. Hollis, causing the latter to fall and badly injure his knee. The cyclist said 'sorry mate'

88 *Lamb v. Cotogno* (1987) 164 CLR 1 at 5.
89 *Ibid.*, at 5.
90 *Ibid.*, at 6.
91 *Ibid.*, at 10.
92 *Ibid.*, at 10. This approach was affirmed in *Gray v. Motor Accident Commission* (1998) 196 CLR 1at 13 [34]: 'the fact that the tortfeasor was insured under a compulsory scheme of insurance against any liability for exemplary damages would not bar the award of such damages'.
93 *Hollis v. Vabu* (2001) 207 CLR 21.

and left the scene, pushing his bicycle. Mr. Hollis, obtained compensatory (but not punitive) damages from the cyclist's employer.

However, the High Court's approach raises more serious questions. Namely, why should public policy considerations, which are extraneous to the case at the bar, govern recovery of civil damages? Why should Mr. Cotogno get a windfall that is paid for by all compulsorily insured innocent motorists through increased premiums?

It is arguable that if Mr. Lamb's conduct of driving away from Mr. Cotogno was punishable, he should have been tried for it under criminal law.[94] Under criminal law, however, the prosecution would have had difficulty establishing *mens rea* (the judge found that he acted without malice), and Mr. Lamb would have been able to raise defence of provocation (not available in civil actions except in Queensland).

The *Cotongo* case was overcome by the Parliaments of New South Wales and Victoria, which prohibited outright any awards of punitive damages under their respective compulsory motor vehicle accident regimes.[95] Legislation in Queensland, Tasmania,[96] and South Australia ensured that such damages are personally payable by the tortfeasor, and cannot be claimed against motor vehicle insurers.[97]

The power of courts to award punitive damages was further constrained in 2002 and 2003. During that period all Australian Parliaments enacted Torts Reform legislation, which, *inter alia*, codified principles of the cause of action in negligence for personal injury (breach of duty of care, causation and defences), imposed tests on availability of damages and caps on quantum.[98] The Northern Territory Parliament prohibited outright 'awards of aggravated damages or exemplary damages in respect of a personal injury'.[99] Likewise, the Commonwealth legislation prohibits courts from awarding exemplary and/or aggravated damages in respect of product liability[100] and unconscionable conduct[101] relating to claims for death or personal injury under the *Trade Practices Act 1974* (Cth).[102] The prohibition applies to both intentionally and negligently occasioned personal injury.

In New South Wales, *Civil Liability Act 2002* (NSW), s. 21, which limits 'exemplary, punitive and aggravated damages', provides that: 'In an action for the award of personal injury damages where the act or omission that caused the injury or death was negligence, a court cannot award exemplary or punitive damages or damages in the nature of aggravated damages'. In Queensland, a court cannot award punitive or aggravated damages

94 See e.g., *Road Safety Act 1986* (Vic), s. 61 at www.austlii.edu.au/au/legis/vic/consol_act/rsa1986125/s61.html.

95 *Motor Accidents Compensation Act 1999* (NSW), s. 144; *Motor Accidents Act 1988* (NSW), s. 81A; *Transport Accident Act 1986* (Vic), s. 93; *Accident Compensation Act 1985* (Vic), s. 135A(7)(c) and for post 20 October 1999, s. 134AA, s. 134AB(22)(c), s. 134A.

96 *Motor Accidents (Liability and Compensation) Act* 1973 (Tas), s. 14(6)(b).

97 *Motor Accidents Insurance Act 1994* (Qld), s. 55 as amended; *WorkCover Queensland Act 1996* (Qld), s. 319; *Motor Vehicles Act 1959* (SA), s. 113A.

98 The analysis in this part is mostly based on Chapter 2 in Mendelson 2010 at p. 41–7.

99 *Personal Injuries (Liabilities and Damages) Act 2003* (NT), s. 19.

100 *Trade Practices Act 1974* (Cth), Div 2A of Part V and Part VA (consumer protection and liability of manufacturers and importers for defective goods).

101 *Trade Practices Act 1974* (Cth), Pt IVA.

102 *Trade Practices Act 1974* (Cth) s. 87ZB(1). See also: *Musca v. Astle Corp Pty Ltd* (1988) 80 ALR 251.

for personal injury, *unless* 'the act that caused the personal injury was (a) an unlawful intentional act *done with intent to cause personal injury*; or (b) an unlawful sexual assault or other unlawful sexual misconduct'.[103] This means that in these jurisdictions while punitive and aggravated damages would be available for some, but not all intentional torts; by definition they cannot be awarded for unintentional torts, such as negligence.

Legislation in Victoria,[104] South Australia,[105] Tasmania,[106] Western Australia[107] and the Australian Capital Territory[108] does not refer to punitive damages in relation to either intentionally or negligently inflicted personal injuries, which means that they are governed by common law. In most jurisdictions, punitive damages remain available for injuries and death resulting from smoking or other use of tobacco products. Australian Capital Territory, Northern Territory Queensland, and Tasmania prohibit recovery of aggravated or punitive damages in personal injury proceedings against a deceased estate.[109] Under the Commonwealth, Queensland, Tasmania, the Northern Territory, and the Australian Capital Territory legislation, the Crown (the government) is not liable to pay punitive damages for the conduct of police officers, though the officers found liable can be personally punished in this manner.[110] In contrast, New South Wales has preserved the plaintiff's right to an award of punitive damages from the Crown for torts committed by police officers (*New South Wales v. Ibbett*[111]).[112]

Punitive damages are not available for breach of contract; and, importantly, in 2005 all Australian jurisdictions legislatively abolished punitive damages for defamation.[113] However, with notable exception of defamation, the legislative provisions have been uncoordinated, and usually enacted on *ad hoc* basis. Thus in some jurisdictions, some torts still sound in punitive damages while others do not; a negligently injured person may claim punitive damages in Victoria but not in New South Wales, Queensland, or the

103 *Civil Liability Act 2003* (Qld), s. 52.

104 In Victoria, punitive damages are specifically available under proportionate liability rule, however, proportionate liability does not apply to personal injury cases; see *Wrongs Act 1958* (Vic), s. 24AF(1).

105 *Civil Liability Act 1936* (SA). Under *Civil Liability Act* 1936 (SA), s. 70 (2),.

106 *Civil Liability Act 2002* (Tas). See however, *Administration and Probate Act* 1935 (Tas), s. 27(3)(a). See also: *Motor Accidents (Liability and Compensation) Act* 1973 (Tas), s. 14(6)(b).

107 *Civil Liability Act 2002* (WA), s. 6(1); *Civil Liability Act 2002* (WA), s. 3A(1)(a) and (b).

108 *Civil Law (Wrongs) Act 2002* (ACT). But see: *Civil Law (Wrongs) Act 2002* (ACT), s. 16(2), which provides that exemplary damages are not available for a surviving cause of action once a person has died. But see: *Public Interest Disclosure Act* 1994 (ACT), s. 29(1).

109 *Law Reform (Miscellaneous Provisions) Act 1955* (ACT), s. 5; *Administration and Probate Act 1935* (Tas), s 27(3); *Law Reform (Miscellaneous Provisions) Act 1956* (NT), s. 6; *Succession Act 1981* (Qld), s. 66 (2)(b).

110 *Australian Federal Police Act 1979* (Cth), s. 64B(3); *Police Service Administration Act 1990* (Qld), s. 10.5(2); *Police Administration Act 1978* (NT), s. 163(3); *Law Reform (Miscellaneous Provisions) Act 1955* (ACT), s. 5; *Administration and Probate Act 1935* (Tas), s. 27(3); *Law Reform (Miscellaneous Provisions) Act 1956* (NT), s. 6.

111 *New South Wales v Ibbett* [2006] HCA 57.

112 *Police Legislation Amendment (Civil Liability) Act 2003* (NSW).

113 *Defamation Act 2005* (NSW), s. 37; see also: *Civil Law (Wrongs) Act* 2006 (ACT) Ch. 9; *Defamation Act* 2006 (NT); *Defamation Act* 2005 (Qld); *Defamation Act* 2005 (SA); *Defamation Act* 2005 (Tas); *Defamation Act* 2005 (Vic); *Defamation Act* 2005 (WA). The legislation was enacted partly in response to the High Court's decision in *Carson v. John Fairfax & Sons Ltd* [1993] 178 CLR 44.

Northern Territory. As a result, the law of punitive damages in Australia is a highly unsatisfactory farrago of provisions, rules and case law.

8. Conclusion

If the trend towards legislative abolition of common law punitive damages in torts continues unabated, they are likely to become virtually extinct. Is this trend regrettable? Possibly not, for punitive damages are not a remedy; yet, unlike compensatory damages, the court (judge or jury) is vested with unrestricted discretion in determining their quantum. In Australia, statutory law has developed jurisprudentially more apposite ways of deterring wrongdoers and punishing contumelious conduct through the system of civil penalties. Europe would be wise to give punitive damages a wide berth and explore the notion of civil fines instead.

Bibliography

Anonymous 1889
Anonymous, *The Criminal Code of the Anglo-Saxons*, Green Bag, 1889, pp. 186–187.

Aristotle 1934
Aristotle, *Nicomachean Ethics* V, ch ii, translated by H. Rackham, Cambridge Massachusetts: Harvard University Press, 1934.

Beever 2008
Beever, A., 'Corrective Justice and Personal Responsibility in Tort Law', *OJLS*, 2008, pp. 475–500.

Blackstone 1768
Blackstone, W., *Commentaries on the Laws of England*, Oxford: Printed at the Clarendon Press, 1765–1768 facsimile of the first edition.

Goldberg 2004
Goldberg, J.C.P., 'Tort Law for Federalists (and the Rest of Us): Private Law in Disguise', *Harv J L & Pub Pol'y*, 2004, pp. 3–16.

Harding 2002
Harding, A., *Medieval Law and the Foundations of the State,* Oxford: Oxford University Press, 2002.

Lee 1937
Lee, H.D.P., 'The Legal Background of Two Passages in the *Nichomachean Ethics*', *CQ*, 1937, pp. 129–140.

Mendelson 2005
Mendelson, D., 'Jurisprudential Legerdemain: Damages for Gratuitous Services and Attendant Care', *JL M,* 2005, pp. 402–412.

Mendelson 2010
Mendelson, D., *The New Law of Torts*, Melbourne: Oxford University Press 2010.

Pollock 1885
Pollock, F., 'King's Peace', *LQR*, 1885, pp. 37–50.

Raymond 1936
Raymond, P.E., 'Origin and Rise of Moral Liability in Anglo-Saxon Criminal Law', *Or L Rev*, 1936, pp. 93–117.

Sofia Michaelides-
Mateou*

PUNITIVE DAMAGES IN CYPRIOT LAW

1. Introduction to the Cyprus Legal System

Since its independence in 1960, the Republic of Cyprus has its own legal system. Prior to this, as a British colony for over eighty years (1878–1960), the legal system was founded on the English legal system and as a result, Cypriot law is still largely based on English common law with some exceptions where the legal system has followed civil law.

Cyprus has a written Constitution, which is the supreme law, and the Cyprus Courts apply the following laws:

a) the Constitution of the Republic;
b) the laws which have been retained in force by virtue of Article 188 of the Constitution;
c) the English Laws which were applicable in Cyprus before 1960;
d) the principles of Common Law and Equity, and;
e) the Laws enacted by the House of Representatives.[1]

Additionally, the common law doctrine of *stare decisis* applies and Supreme Courts' judicial precedents are binding on lower courts. In 2004, the Republic of Cyprus became a member of the European Union and the Constitution was amended to the effect that European law has supremacy over the Constitution and national legislation.

Civil proceedings are generally filed in one of the six District Courts which have jurisdiction to hear and determine at first instance all civil actions except matters for the Rent Control Tribunal, Industrial Tribunal and the Family Court. The District Courts have jurisdiction over actions that have arisen wholly or partly within their geographic territories of their respective districts or where the defendant resides or carries out his business within the district at the time the action is filed.

The aggrieved party may ask the court to grant most of the remedies available under common law namely damages as well as equitable remedies, such as, *inter alia*, injunctions, specific performance and *quantum meruit* which are granted in accordance with the

* Dr. Sofia Michaelides-Mateou is Assistant Professor of Contract Law, The Law of Torts and Air Law, University of Nicosia, Cyprus.

1 In accordance with the provisions of s. 29(l)(b) of the Courts of Justice Law (14/60).

court's discretion. However, the most commonly sought and granted remedy is that of damages providing compensation for losses suffered.

1.1. The National Court System

The judicial system of the Republic of Cyprus is, since its inception, structured by the Cypriot Constitution as a two-tier system. The Supreme Court has both original and appellate civil and criminal jurisdiction and has the function of Supreme Constitutional Court, administrative court, admiralty court, appellate court and court with exclusive jurisdiction to issue prerogative writs.

There are six subordinate courts, which are under the supervision of the Supreme Court, namely: (i) the five District Courts, which exercise civil and criminal jurisdiction. The Civil Division can hear all civil issues as well as matters relating to discrimination in all other fields beyond the scope of work and employment, as provided by the Race Directive 43/2000 such as social security and healthcare, education, access to and supply of goods, and services; (ii) three Assize Courts which have unlimited jurisdiction to adjudicate over criminal matters; (iii) the five District Family courts, which have jurisdiction to hear all family matters; (iv) the Labour Disputes Courts, often referred to as 'the Labour Courts', which have jurisdiction to hear employment issues and matters relating to discrimination in employment and occupation; (v) the Rent control courts; and (vi) the Military court.

With regard to awarding damages and in particular punitive damages, the Cyprus District Courts having civil jurisdiction at first instance have the discretion to grant punitive damages as deemed fit in the circumstances of each case.

This paper examines how the Cypriot courts deal with the awarding of punitive damages by providing a brief overview of basic legal principles in a number of areas of law and an analysis of case law where appropriate.

Paragraph 2 analyses the general approach of Cypriot courts to punitive damages. Paragraph 3 looks at the law relating to trespass to land as laid down in case law, which states that punitive damages may be granted where the behaviour of the defendant deserves punishment in order to set an example. Paragraph 4 deals with punitive damages in relation to actions for defamation by discussing two cases, one of which appealed to the European Court of Human Rights challenging, inter alia, the compatibility of Cypriot defamation law with the right to freedom of speech. In paragraph 5, punitive damages for breach of contract is examined by looking particularly at a case in relation to a rent agreement and in paragraph 6 claims for damages arising from defective products are examined. Paragraph 7 provides a synopsis of claims for punitive damages for competition law infringements through an analysis of the relevant legal principles applicable in Cyprus as well as an example of how the UK courts approach this area. Paragraphs 8 and 9 consider punitive damages in patent cases and employment infringement cases respectively. The final paragraph offers brief concluding remarks.

2. Punitive Damages in Cypriot Law

Exemplary damages, or 'punitive' damages as they are sometimes referred to, are mainly awarded in tortious actions. The court may grant such a remedy when it deems that such a penalty is appropriate in the specific circumstances of a case as an additional 'punishment' for the wrongdoer or to set an example such as in cases where the wrong was committed with malice, or when the defendants conduct was wanton or capricious.

Exemplary or punitive damages are only granted in certain circumstances by the courts in Cyprus, especially when it wants to punish the defendant, act as a deterrent and set an example for the wrongdoer. In assessing the amount of exemplary damages to be awarded, the courts in Cyprus hold the view that such damages must not only be reasonable but also effective.

Punitive damages have been awarded mainly in tort cases. In order for the claimant to succeed in an action for punitive damages, he or she must successfully show that the defendant's behaviour has been particularly repulsive and/or repeated. The courts decided in the 1982 case of *Papakokkinou & others v. Kanther*[2] (hereafter *Papakokkinou* case) that such behaviour was one of arrogance, immoral motive or tendency to humiliate the other party.

The readiness (or lack) of the Cypriot courts to grant punitive damages will be illustrated by providing an overview of various legal actions and a brief consideration of relevant case law in the following areas: trespass to land, defamation, breach of contract, products liability, competition law, patents law, employment and labour law.

3. Punitive Damages for Trespass to Land

In the *Papakokkinou* case, the respondent trespassed upon a significant part of the nearby property owned by the appellant and in the process of improving access to her house by constructing a wider road she blotted out the pathway that was separating the two properties, thus entailing a defacement of the property and an alteration of its character. Prior to litigation, the appellant asked the respondent to remedy the situation and to repair the damage done to her property. The respondent failed to reply and the appellant brought an action in court claiming damages exceeding £18,000 as well as a mandatory and prohibitory injunction.

The trial court found in favour of the appellant, held the respondents liable for damages for trespass and awarded £750 in damages and an injunction to the respondent not to interfere with the property of the appellant in the future. The court only awarded partial costs as the applicant had inflated her claim and the plaintiff had made no effort to calculate the loss in value of the land before and after trespassing.

The £750 damages award comprised two heads of damages: £50 for damage caused to the trees, an amount which was derived from the timber value of 20 pine trees, and £700 for damage to the property – which was calculated on the basis of the costs of re-instating

2 *Berengeria Papakokkinou and Others v. Princess Zena De Tyra Kanther* [1982] 1 CLR 65.

the property to the condition it had prior to the trespass by conveying a quantity of soil equal to that removed by the respondent.

The plaintiffs appealed. The Appeal Court considered the principles of law relating to punitive and exemplary damages. Exemplary damages, which are an extraordinary species of damage, have the purpose to punish and not to compensate which is the normal measure for assessing damages in the law of torts. The Court stated that until the decision of *Rookes v. Barnard,*[3] it was accepted that an award of exemplary damages was permissible when the defendants behaviour deserved punishment in order to set an example and that therefore an award could be granted which was out of range with the loss actually suffered by the plaintiff in order to punish the defendant's conduct and to proclaim efficacy of the law. However, in *Rookes v. Barnard*, Lord Devlin held that exemplary damages are an anomaly which should not be extended. The House of Lords held that the exemplary damages award should be limited to three cases, namely: (i) civil wrongs which resulted from the use of oppressive and unconstitutional conduct, (ii) civil wrongs committed in gross disregard to the rights of the injured party in circumstances aimed to make a profit, and (iii) where statute expressly permits an award of exemplary damages. The decision was disapproved of in other countries such as Australia, Canada and New Zealand and in the case of *Australian Consolidated Press v. Uren*[4] the Privy Council examined the freedom of courts in other Commonwealth jurisdictions not to follow the decision of *Rookes*. The Council held that the precise rules governing the award of exemplary damages are a matter of policy of national courts, and that courts of different commonwealth jurisdictions may therefore have different rules regarding this point.

The Appeal court in the *Papakokkinou* case went on to state that in Cyprus, there is no authoritative pronouncement on the applicability of the principles laid out in *Rookes*, but the case of *Savvas Paraskevas v. Despina Mouzour*[5] of 1973 suggests that exemplary damages need not be confined within the limits set out in *Rookes*. In fact, the cases *Cyprus Ltd. v. Times Newspapers Ltd. and Others*[6] of 1972 and *Toumba v. Loutsios*[7] of 1975 followed the principle that exemplary damages may be awarded where the conduct of the defendant is deserving of punishment. In *Papakokkinou*, the Court of Appeal held that:[8]

(1) the underlying principle in assessing the damage should be the amount of money that should put the plaintiff in the position he would be in if he had not suffered the wrong. The Court of Appeal held that it would uphold this amount if the award was designed to restore the injured party to the position he would enjoy but for the civil wrong and provided the outcome was one that was considered as fair between the parties as this was the second basic rule that governed the determination of damages in any case, namely, that having duly reflected on the assessment of compensatory damages, the Court remains unpersuaded that the award should be set aside for any reason;

3 *Rookes v. Barnard* [1964] 1 All ER 367.
4 *Australian Consolidated Press v. Uren* [1967] 3 All ER 523.
5 *Savvas Paraskevas v. Despina Mouzour* [1973] 1 CLR 78.
6 *Cyprus Ltd. v. Times Newspapers Ltd. and Others* [1972] 4 JSC 455.
7 *Toumba v. Loutsios* [1975] 1 JSC 115.
8 *Papakokkinou*, at 67–70.

(2) the court cannot participate in the elucidation of issues relating to damage because this is the parties' responsibilities;
(3) conduct accompanied by a marked element of arrogance, insolence, or malice may justify an award of exemplary damages, especially if it tends to humiliate the victim of the tort; the respondent acted in gross disregard to the appellant's rights and that her wanton and capricious conduct was grossly negligent and blameworthy. The Court of Appeal went on to state that the trial Court wrongly deprived the appellant of an award of exemplary damages, an award to which they were plainly entitled;
(4) in assessing the quantum of exemplary damages the gravity of the behaviour of the defendant as well as her means are considerations to which the Court should have regard. The case must be considered in its entirety and it is wrong to separate exemplary and compensatory damages. The Court awarded 1500 pounds to the appellant;
(5) it was unnecessary to conclude on the precise limits to an award of exemplary damages and whether the rule in *Rookes v Barnard* [1964] 1 All E.R. 367 as, based on any view of the law, the defendant was liable to exemplary damages. (The court went on to state that if it had to choose between the two streams of authority, it would follow the wider approach which would allow an award of exemplary damages for tortuous conduct when such conduct is intrinsically blameworthy and deserving of punishments from a civil court);
(6) there were no reasons for suspending the injunction initially granted by the Court of First Instance. Where the rights of the citizens are grossly violated an injunction should be made even if the other remedies were not exhausted.

The Court of Appeal in the *Papakokkinou* case held that exemplary damage aim to punish rather than to compensate and that punitive damages are allowed where the behaviour of the defendant deserves punishment in order to set an example. In the *Papakokkinou* case, the respondent absolutely disregarded the rights of the victim – she was seeking only to make further profit and never consulted her neighbour – and that conduct deserved to be punished. It was held that the Trial Court wrongly deprived the plaintiffs of an award of exemplary damages, an award they were entitled to.

The Court of Appeal further held that the underlying principle in assessing the damage should be the amount of money which would put the plaintiff in the position he would be in if he had not suffered the wrong and in assessing the quantum of exemplary damages, the Appeal Court awarded £1,500 to the appellant.

4. Punitive Damages for Defamation

4.1. *General Press Agency 'Poullias & Coniaris Ltd'. v. Christoforos Christofides*

The case of *General Press Agency 'Poullias & Coniaris Ltd. v. Christoforos Christofides*[9] of 1981 concerns an appeal against a £2,500 damages award in a libel case.

9 *General Press Agency 'Poullias & Coniaris LTD'. v. Christoforos Christofides* [1981] 1 CLR 190.

Legal action was brought against the appellants for libel, consisting of a publication in the newspaper 'ETHNIKI'. The facts of this case are as follows. On 19 January 1975, the respondent – a member of the House of Representatives – delivered a speech during the memorial service for those who had died during the coup d'état of 15 July 1974 and the Turkish invasion. After the memorial service, on 22 January a publication appeared on page two of the daily newspaper 'ETHNIKI'. The plaintiff alleged that the publication as a whole was defamatory of him and claimed damages.

The Trial Court reached the conclusion that it was a gravely defamatory publication because it portrayed the plaintiff as being politically unscrupulous, afflicted by the malaise of fascism and a person with no loyalty to his fatherland, and in fact, an enemy and traitor of its national roots.[10]

The Court stated that it is clear that in actions such as this one, where there are several defendants who have all committed the same tort, there can be only one damages award against all of them.[11] However, the issue that had to be decided was whether the damages should be fixed at a high sum which the more blameworthy party ought to pay or at a low sum for the least blameworthy party. The Court was asked to interfere with the award of damages imposed by the trial court because:[12]

> (a) [the trial Court] erred in law in that, though it accepted the legal principles that form the facts and circumstances of the present case, and that the liability of appellant-defendant 3 did not warrant the award of exemplary or aggravated damages, it nevertheless decided that the proper amount of damages to the plaintiff was the sum of £2,500, which were, in effect tantamount to exemplary or aggravated damages and/or that the amount of the said damages was too excessive;
> (b) that the [trial] Court erred in law once it reached the conclusion that there was no malice by the appellant regarding the publication and proceeded to award such a large amount of damages, which in effect, amounts to a miscarriage of justice; and
> (c) that because the [trial] Court had accepted that ETHNIKI at the material time had the smallest circulation in Cyprus, it wrongly reached the conclusion that because of the position of the plaintiff (being a member of Parliament) it was of no consequence.

The Court stated that, in assessing the damages, it is entitled to take into consideration the conduct of the plaintiff, his position and standing, the nature of the libel, the mode and extent of the publication, the absence or refusal of any retraction or apology, and the whole conduct of the defendant from the time when the libel was published until the very moment of judgment.[13] The Court should also take into consideration the conduct of the defendant before action, after action, and at the trial of the action as well as the evidence led in aggravation or mitigation of damages.[14]

10 *Ibid*, at 195.
11 *Ibid*, at 197.
12 *Ibid*, at 197.3.
13 *Ibid*, at 191.
14 *Ibid*.

However, the Court re-iterated that there is a great difference between aggravated damages and truly punitive or exemplary damages. It went on to say that the purpose of awarding damages in tort nowadays is not to punish the wrongdoer, but to compensate the person to whom the wrong has been done and that it would not be right to allow punitive or exemplary damages to creep back into the assessment in some other guise:

> 'For instance, it might be said: 'You must consider not only what the plaintiff ought to receive, but what the defendant ought to pay'. There are many other phrases which could be used, such as those used in the extracts which I have cited from some of the decided cases. In my view, that distinction between compensatory and punitive damages has now been laid down quite clearly by the House of Lords in *Rookes v. Bernard*, and ought to be permitted to have its full effect in the sphere of libel actions as well as in other branches of tort'.[15]

Considering that the action against defendant two was withdrawn and dismissed with no order as to the costs, the Court, bearing in mind that the extent of the publication of the libel against the appellant was limited in view of the smaller circulation of ETHNIKI (which finally had ceased being published), had to decide whether in this case the trial court tried to protect the more innocent party to a joint publication.

Concluding, the Court, by referring to *Heydon's* case,[16] held that if the plaintiff sues all three defendants jointly, then, in accordance with a settled rule of law which goes back to 1611, there can be only one judgment and one assessment of damages, even though one of them is malicious and the others are not and that it would, therefore not be right to allow punitive or exemplary damages to creep back into the assessment in some other guise.[17] In spite of the fact that the trial court held that the three defendants were liable only to pay compensatory damages, the Court ruled that, in awarding the sum of £2,500 the trial court erred in law as that sum awarded was, in effect, punitive or exemplary damages and crept back into the assessment in some other guise and that the proper amount of damages to be awarded to the respondent, having regard to the nature of the libel in question, was £1 500.

4.2. *Alithia Publishing Ltd. & Constantinides v. Cyprus*

In a more recent case, that of *Alithia Publishing Ltd. & Constantinides v. Cyprus*,[18] the editor of the newspaper "ΑΛΗΘΕΙΑ" published and signed twelve articles, one in December 1992 and eleven in January 1993 at a time which coincided with the pre-election period of the presidential elections of February 1993. In these articles, the respondent and some of his friends who were tradesmen, were accused of fraud and 'damage to the Republic'. The respondent and another both sued the appellant for libel,

15 *Ibid*, at 199.

16 *Heydon's Case* [1584] 3 Co. Rep. 7a.

17 *General Press Agency 'Poullias & Coniaris LTD'. v. Christoforos Christofides*, at par 200.

18 *Alithia Publishing Ltd. & Constantinides v. Cyprus* [2002] 1Γ ΑΑΔ 1863 (Civil action, Volume 1 Part 3 Cyprus Supreme Court Decision), ECtHR Application (no. 17550/03).

seeking compensation. During the trial the plaintiffs recognized that the articles were defamatory to a large extent.

The Court of First Instance found bad faith on the part of plaintiffs and an intent to defame the respondent in any possible way and ordered the plaintiff to pay the respondent £30,000.00 in damages and £5,000.00 in exemplary damages.[19]

The plaintiffs appealed and challenged (a) the findings and conclusions of the Court of First Instance regarding the critical aspects of the case, (b) the accuracy of the interim decision of the Court not to introduce any witness and other written evidence, (c) whether the provisions of the Civil Wrongs Act also referred to as Cap. 148 (Cypriot Legislation), which refer to defamation, and the provisions of Article 19 of the Constitution, establishing the freedom of speech, were complied with and (d) the amount of compensation.

Dismissing the appeal with costs, the court held, regarding the amount of compensation awarded, that the amount granted could not, in any measure, be considered excessive. The allegation that the amount of damages was excessive and the product of an incorrect guidance was rejected.[20] By referring to *Ed. Et. Ltd. Nicholas L.*,[21] the court stated that the intervention of the Court of Appeal on damages awarded is justified only if the amount is clearly excessive and that such a conclusion is justified only where it is shown that such an amount of damages could not be awarded by the first instance court. It was clear, by reference to relevant case law, that the measure of damages depends on the nature, character and extent of damage to the individual's reputation as shown in the conclusive part of the decision of the Court of Appeal.[22]

The Court concluded that by any measure, the amount of £30,000.00 which was awarded, and the added sum of £ 5,000.00 which was awarded in the form of exemplary damages, could not be regarded as excessive. It is important to note that there was no suggestion that the Court's guidance on this aspect of the case (*i.e.* the exemplary damages award) was in any way incorrect.

It is interesting to note that the applicants in the *Alithia Publishing* case appealed to the European Court of Human Rights (ECtHR), challenging, *inter alia*, the compatibility of Cypriot defamation law as set out in the Civil Wrongs Act, Cap. 148, with the right to freedom of speech as guaranteed in the Constitution of the Republic of Cyprus and the European Convention on Human Rights (paragraphs 3, 34–41 ECtHR). On 29 November 2002, the Supreme Court by a majority judgment upheld the district court's judgment and the corresponding award of damages.[23] In its judgment delivered on 22 May 2008, the ECtHR found that the Cypriot courts had carefully examined the case against the applicants and had concluded that the applicants had not sufficiently proven their primarily factual allegations (paragraphs 50–52 ECtHR). The applicants showed malice and had deliberately disregarded the principles of responsible journalism and the Court

19 *Ibid*, at 1864.
20 *Ibid*, at 1893.
21 *Ed. Et. Ltd. Nicholas L.* [1993] 1 AAD 285.
22 *Ibid.*, at 291.
23 *Alithia Publishing Ltd. & Constantinides v. Cyprus*, at 1869.

therefore unanimously held that there had been no violation of Article 10 (paragraphs 71–72 ECtHR).

It should be stressed that regarding punitive damages, the Cypriot Appeal Court upheld the award granted by the Court of First Instance which granted an award of exemplary damages in addition to the ordinary compensatory damages awarded.[24]

5. Punitive Damages for Breach of Contract (Rent Agreement)

In the case of *Chloe Larkou v. Anthou Kleanthous & Kyriakou Chatzikyriakou*[25] of 1999, involving breach of contract, *i.e.* a rent agreement, the court did not grant an award of punitive damages. The appellant owned a building in Nicosia, Cyprus consisting of 14 apartments which were rented. The respondent was interested in renting apartment 203 that was owned by the appellant, which appeared to be available for rent. After signing the contract, the husband of the appellant – who was acting on behalf of his wife – revealed to the respondent that the previous rent agreement was still running for a period of approximately 2 months and stated that in the meantime the defendant could use another apartment (apartment 102) in the same building. A handwritten clause to this effect was added to the signed contract. The respondent who had not noticed this amendment, refused to pay the guarantee and the first monthly rent as provided in the contract. The appellant filed an action claiming damages including the amount of the guarantee and a sum of money representing the entire contract period which amounted to £2,450.

The Court of First Instance held that the respondent violated the lease agreement but dismissed the action – despite a finding of breach of contract – because it provided no basis to award the applicant any amount of money.[26] It also rejected the appellant's claim for exemplary damages. The appellant argued on appeal that the Court of First Instance failed to properly assess the evidence and also erred in not awarding the appellant exemplary damages.[27]

The Court of Appeal held *inter alia* that: the applicant could not prove beyond reasonable doubt that the parties made any effort to let this specific apartment after the last tenant had vacated it (the applicant published some advertisements to let apartments in this building but without referring to apartment 203 in particular); there was no clear and specific evidence of the date on which, after signing the contract, apartment 203 would remain vacant; and that the applicant could not prove that her loss was caused by the behaviour of the respondent and that the non-rent of apartment 203 was related to breach of contract by the respondent.[28]

The Court, stating that exemplary damages may be awarded even if they are not specifically included in the pleadings of the parties, so long as the facts of the case justify

24 *Ibid*, at 1893.
25 *Chloe Larkou v. Anthou Kleanthous & Kyriakou Chatzikyriakou* [1999] 1Γ AAΔ 1792 (Civil action, Volume 1 Part 3 Cyprus Supreme Court Decision).
26 *Ibid*, at 1793.
27 *Ibid*.
28 *Ibid*, at 1796.

such an award and that damages can only be awarded in relation to civil offences and not in cases of breach of contract, held that:

> 'the amount of £350 as a guarantee was not a separate debt or damage because, under the terms of the contract it would be returned to respondent at the end of the rental contract; and that damages could not be claimed for the rent period between 01/16/1995 and 3/31/1995 in respect of flat 203 as, during this period, the apartment was still leased to a third party and thus the claim should have been made in respect of flat 102'.[29]

The appellant's argument that the court should have awarded her punitive damages as the Court found that the contract was terminated by the fault of the defendant, was unsuccessful and the appeal was dismissed with costs.

6. Punitive Damages in Products Liability Cases

The Faulty Products (Civil Liability) Laws[30] of 1995 to 2002 govern liability in respect of damage to persons or property resulting from defective or faulty products.[31] Claims for products liability in Cyprus may be brought under the Defective Products (Civil Liability) Laws of 1995 to 2002,[32] the Sale of Goods Law 1994,[33] the Contract Act[34] and the General Safety of Products Law 2004.[35] Generally the Defective Products (Civil Liability) Laws of 1995 to 2002 Act provides that if a claimant can successfully prove that any damage, defined as resulting from death or personal harm or any loss or damage of property which at the time was intended for private use or consumption, and used as such, was wholly or partly caused by a defective product, the producer is liable for such damage. Liability for such damage may not be excluded or limited as an exemption or limitation clause purporting to limit liability will be ineffective (sections 5 and 7).

A producer includes any person manufacturing the product or any component part thereof, including the production of any raw material, or a person who appears to be the producer by placing his name or trade mark or other logo on the product and the manufacturing of the product is defined as the design or manufacture of the product or any industrial processing of the product or component part thereof, including any raw material (section 5).

29 *Ibid.*
30 Faulty Products (Civil Liability) Laws 1995 to 2002 (105(I)/95 Implementing the Product Liability Directive 85/374 EEC.
31 Damage defined as damage caused due to death or personal harm, or any loss or damage of property which at the time was intended for private use or consumption.
32 Defective Products (Civil Liability) Laws of 1995 to 2002: Law No. 105(I)/95 (as amended).
33 Sale of Goods Law of 1994: Law No. 10(I)/94.
34 Contract Law Act, Cap 149.
35 General Safety of Products Law of 2004: Law No. 41(I)/2004.

Without prejudice to the liability of the producer, the following are liable as if they were the producer:

(a) any person importing the product in his ordinary course of business, with intent to supply it to another; and;
(b) any person that supplied the product to another and (i) who is requested in writing by the other person or any person suffering damage allegedly caused by the product, to reveal the identity of the producer or the person that supplied him with the product; (ii) the above request is made within reasonable time from the cause of damage; and (iii) fails to comply with the above request within reasonable time.

If the claimant can successfully show that the damage suffered was caused wholly or partly due to a defective product he will have satisfied the causation aspect and will not have to prove fault or defect on behalf of the producer. The producer shall then be liable and the aggrieved party may claim damages.

The purpose of awarding damages is to place the claimant in the position he would have been in had he not have suffered the injury. Generally, there is no limit placed on the type or quantum of damages awarded in a tortious action, as this is assessed on a case by case basis according to the causation, *i.e.* that the claimant has successfully proven the damages were caused by the defective product and on the general principles of remoteness.[36]

To sum up, in Cyprus the court has the discretion to decide whether it would be appropriate to award punitive damages on the facts of each particular case concerning product liability.

7. Punitive Damages for Competition Law Infringements

7.1. The Legal Basis for Competition Law Infringement Actions in Cyprus

In Cyprus, the legal basis for instigating a legal action for claims in competition law is national law as well as EC law.[37]

The Protection of Competition Law of 2008[38] (which was enacted to provide for the control and suppression of restrictive competition collusions and practices, the protection of competition, the function of the commission for the protection of competition as well as the application of the Council Regulation (EC) No. 1/2003),[39] together with the Control of Concentrations of Enterprises Laws of 1999 and 2000,[40] lay down the framework of

36 Damage will be recovered if not too remote, in other words, only damage that is proximate and immediate can be recovered.

37 Council Regulation (EC) No. 1/2003 of 16 December 2002 on the implementation of the rules on competition laid down in Articles 81 and 82 of the Treaty.

38 Protection of Competition Law, No. 13(1)/2008 available at www.wipo.int/wipolex/en/text.jsp?file_id=190042.

39 Council Regulation (EC) No. 1/2003 of 16 December 2002 on the implementation of the rules on competition laid down in Articles 81 and 82 of the Treaty.

40 The Control of Concentrations Between Enterprises Law (The "Merger Law"), Law No. 22(I)/1999.

rules and regulations aiming to maintain effective competition within the Cypriot market.

The Commission for Protection of Competition[41] ('CPC') was established to ensure the smooth operation of the economy within the rules of fair competition and to decide whether to initiate proceedings for the investigation of an infringement.

A claimant has a statutory right to file a civil action for breach of the law and to ask for remedies which are in the form of damages for loss or damage suffered as a result of anti-competitive practices which constitute a violation of the law as well as an interim injunction preventing the breach from continuing. Specifically, a person who has suffered any damage as a result of a breach of competition law can apply to the relevant District Court to claim damages for loss, and/or financial injury from any act or omission of an undertaking or association of undertakings done in contravention of sections 3 and/or 6 of this Law and/or Articles 81 and/or 82 EC, a final decision of the Commission or of other Competition Authority or of the European Commission, ascertaining the said infringement shall constitute a rebuttable presumption about the truth of its context and an interim injunction to prevent the contravention from continuing.[42]

The final remedies that are available in such action are a *mandamus* or injunction, compensation, a court order for the execution of a transfer, contract or other document to be carried out by a person nominated by the Court, in the case where a judgment or order to execute any transfer, contract or other document is not carried out, payments of costs or any other declaratory judgments.

The provisions in the law regarding damages are not defined but as a general rule, the claimant can recover any loss or damage suffered as a direct result of a breach of the law. The basis is the actual loss or damage suffered by the defendant but may also include loss of profit which passes the test of reasonable foreseeability. Specific damages which have been proved may therefore be claimed to compensate the aggrieved party and normally take the form of monetary compensation. General damages such as loss of goodwill and loss of a business opportunity and other such damages which cannot be determined in a fixed amount may be claimed but will be difficult to prove.

As follows from the above, exemplary damages as such, are available under Cyprus law but are rarely awarded. They are not recognized in the law *per se*, however the courts may decide to set a high amount of damages in order to set an example or to deter similar behaviour.[43]

The recent changes in Cyprus Competition Law are an attempt to more effectively deal with perhaps the most serious form of competition law violation, namely that of cartels. Cartels, which are not illegal as such, will be when they have as their object or effect the prevention, restriction or distortion of competition. The Competition Law also

41 The Commission for Protection of Competition was established in 1990 with the enactment of the Protection of Competition Law 207/89. The law in question was abolished with the enactment of the Protection of Competition Law 2008 (Law no. 13 (I) /2008). The Protection of Competition Law 13 (I) /2008, *inter alia*, determines the Commission as the competition authority of the Cyprus Republic, responsible for the application of Regulation 1/2003, and of Articles 101 and 102 TFEU, where necessary.

42 S. 40 (1) & (2) Protection of Competition Law.

43 Georgiades 2011, pp. 39–40.

applies to actions outside Cyprus relating to a cartel as described above. If the CPC is to consider a cartel that may affect trade between member states it must, in accordance with Council Regulation 1/2003, apply the provisions of Article 81 of the EC Treaty.[44]

If the Commission for Protection of Competition, subsequent to a complaint or acting on its own accord, considers that there is a *prima facie* case, an investigation will follow and it may obtain necessary information from the undertakings under investigation by proving a written request outlining the legal basis for the investigation as well as what information is requested to enable the investigation to take place. A reasonable time limit must be set and the penalties for non-compliance must also be stated. The undertaking under investigation has the right to secrecy and confidentiality and the information provided must be used solely for the purposes of the investigation. Once the preliminary investigation has been concluded and in the event of a *prima facie* infringement, a statement of objection is issued to the undertaking concerned. After a formal hearing, by means of written addresses and a formal oral hearing, and on conclusion of the case, a fully reasoned decision is issued by the CPC which may be appealed in the Supreme Court which then renders a final decision.

The Competition Laws provide for both civil and criminal sanctions. A criminal offense is committed by any person who continues to apply a prohibited agreement or abuses its dominant position in contravention of a CPC decision ordering the cessation of the agreement or abuse, and is punishable with imprisonment of up to one year and/or a pecuniary penalty.[45] The same punishment is set for a person who knowingly provides false, inaccurate information or withholds true information in order to mislead the CPC.[46] Civil sanction include an order or recommendation to cease the infringement within a specified time and avoid repetition, a fine for continued infringement of a specific amount for every day of the continued infringement, a fine of up to 10 per cent of the undertakings turnover in the year in which the infringement took place or the year preceding the infringement, and other interim measures that the CPC deems fit.[47]

Pecuniary penalties may be imposed by the CPC only within five years from the date of the infringement or, in the event that the infringement continued or was repeated, from the date the infringement ended.[48]

A claimant who has suffered loss as a result of the conduct of a cartel can claim damages for the proven losses suffered and additionally, may seek an injunction to prevent the continuance of the cartel. Although it is possible to award punitive damages, the Cyprus courts do not readily do so. However, they do seem to more readily impose deterrent fines and not merely nominal fines as the CPC may impose a fine of up to 10 per cent of the undertakings turnover.[49]

44 Keane & Demetriades 2009, pp. 1–3.
45 *Ibid.*
46 *Ibid.*
47 *Ibid.*
48 *Ibid.*
49 *Ibid.*

7.2. *Competition Law Infringements: a UK perspective*

In the United Kingdom, in 2007 the High Court had to consider which different types of remedies are available in a civil action for damages by claimants who suffered losses as a result of competition law. An infringement of competition law is a tort for which the main remedy is that of damages.[50] The case of *Devenish Nutrition & Others v. Sanofi-Aventis (SA) France & Others*[51] was a result of actions which followed the decision of the European Commission that found that a number of firms had infringed EU competition law by participating in a cartel with regards to the sale of vitamins used in chicken food.[52] The EC court clarified that in the absence of specific Community rules, it is national law which will determine the conditions for claiming damages.[53]

In the litigation proceedings brought by the claimants who had all bought, directly or indirectly, vitamins from one or more of the defendant cartels, the court had to consider whether the claimants were entitled to compensatory damages, exemplary damages, restitutionary damage and an account of profits.[54] It was not disputed that the compensatory damages could have been awarded by the court. The court had to determine whether, as a result of the difficulty in quantifying compensatory damages arising from problems relating to obtaining adequate evidence, exemplary and restitutionary damages should be available. In English law, exemplary damages which are available in addition to compensatory damages are discretionary and granted only in exceptionally cases with the intention to punish and deter.[55] Such a remedy is available in the antitrust context where 'the defendant's conduct has been calculated by him to make a profit for himself which may well exceed the compensation payable to the plaintiff,'[56] which was what had occurred in the vitamin cartel.

The UK court outlined that the European Community courts have held that in principle, exemplary damages are not precluded by European law, but that within the EU, only England and Wales, Cyprus and Ireland provide for exemplary damages and that this award is unknown in other jurisdictions.[57] In fact, in some countries such as Germany an award of punitive or exemplary damages is deemed to be contrary to public policy.[58] The court went on to further state that where the discretionary remedy of exemplary damages is related to the enforcement of rights pertaining to the EC Treaty, it would not readily grant a remedy which is generally unavailable in most member states and that in any event, in cartel cases the manner in which the UK courts award damages are adequate.[59]

50 *Courage Ltd v. Crehan* (C-453/99) [2002] Q.B. 507; [2001] E.C.R. I-6297.

51 High Court of Justice Chancery Division, 19 October 2007 [2007] EWHC 2394 (Ch).

52 Commission Decision of 21 November 2001 relating to a proceeding pursuant to Article 81 of the EC Treaty and Article 53 of the EAA Agreement (Case COMP/E-1/37–512 – Vitamins [2003] OJ L6/I.

53 High Court of Justice Chancery Division, 19 October 2007 [2007] EWHC 2394 (Ch).

54 *Ibid.*

55 *Kuddus v. Chief Constable of Leicestershire* [2001] UKHL 29; [2002] A.C.

56 *Rookes v. Barnard* [1964] 1 AC 1129, at 37 per Lord Devlin.

57 *Devensih Nutrition Ltd. & Others v. SanofiAventis SA (France) & Others.* [2007] EWCH 2394 (Ch.), at 33.

58 Brown 2007, pp. 1–3.

59 *Devensih Nutrition Ltd. & Others v. SanofiAventis SA (France) & Others.* [2007] EWCH 2394 (Ch.).

The Court held that in the antitrust context, imposing a fine and exemplary damages serve the same purpose of punishing and deterring anti-competitive behaviour. The principle of Community law against double jeopardy, that of *ne bis in idem*, precludes an award of exemplary damages where the defendant has already been fined or has had a fine imposed, reduced or commuted by the European Commission. This was in line with the courts philosophy towards awarding exemplary damage, in general, namely that 'the fact that a defendant has been fined for his conduct is a powerful factor against the award of exemplary damages, although it may not be conclusive in itself'.[60]

Considering the principle that a person should not be punished twice for the same wrong, it held that exemplary damages could not be awarded in cases where the CPC had already imposed a punitive fine as it stated that the fines imposed by the CPC have the same function as exemplary damages and that to award exemplary damages would run counter to the CPC's decision to fine the defendant. In accordance with Article 16(1) of Regulation 1/2003/EC, national courts are precluded from taking decisions which run counter to a Community decision and therefore the court could not hold that a fine imposed by the CPC was insufficient.[61]

The Court therefore did not grant exemplary damages on the basis of double jeopardy, the difficulties in assessing damages and the fact the claimants were only part of an affected class and the difficulty in apportioning the award between the many claimants. Restitutionary damages, which are not an available remedy in competition cases, as well as an account for profits were denied but compensatory damages were awarded.

In this important decision the court therefore confirmed that in cases of infringement of competition law, compensatory damages are an adequate remedy in the UK and that alternative remedies will not be available simply because it will be difficult to quantify compensatory damages.

With respect to private enforcement of civil remedies for infringements of competition law: this is a relatively new area of the law of torts and one that is not consistently dealt with within the EU. Even though the European courts have held that, in principle, an award for exemplary damages is not precluded by EU law, the High Court in the *Devenish* case makes clear that following public enforcement of antitrust laws and the imposition of a fine, compensatory damage will be the adequate remedy.

The decision that exemplary damages, restitutionary damages and loss of profits should not be awarded by the English courts when the wrongdoer has already been fined is an important one regarding future cases where claimants seek civil remedies for violations of competition laws in the UK as well as in Cyprus. It seems unlikely that the Cyprus court (which is influenced by the UK common law) will award exemplary damages in such case and even improbable that they would grant such a remedy in new areas of law.

8. Punitive Damages in Patent Cases

Cyprus joined the European Patent Organization in December 1997 and became a member of the Patent Cooperation Treaty and in April 1998 the new Cyprus Patent

60 *Devensih Nutrition Ltd. & Others v. SanofiAventis SA (France) & Others* [2007] EWCH 2394 (Ch.).
61 *Ibid.*

Law[62] was enacted in order to more effectively deal with current legal issues arising in this area.

There are only a few patent cases which were heard in the relevant District Courts or the Supreme Court as there are no specialized courts to hear IP cases.[63] Few cases are heard by the courts as most are settled when the claimant applies for the interim order of an injunction. In the event that a case does proceed to trial, experts are called in the specific area of the patent.[64] When an application has been filed, the District Court can invalidate the patent wholly or partially only in certain circumstances, when the object of the invention does not fall under the definition of the term; the patents invention is not revealed in a satisfactory manner and the right to the patent did not belong to the person to whom the patent was granted. All necessary documentation and other information needed to proceed with the case is requested from the patent owner. Invalid patents will be invalidated from the date on which the patent was granted. Proceedings for infringement must be filed within five years after the infringing act.

The claimant will be awarded remedies according to the facts of each case and dependant on the damages suffered, which include special damages, general damages, nominal damages, punitive damages, preliminary injunctions, final injunctions, permanent injunctions and court orders. The court's decision will be based on previous judicial precedent and the remedies granted in similar or identical cases.[65] It is, however, in the courts discretion to award damages which are different to similar previous cases. Damages are normally awarded to compensate for the loss suffered which must be proven and it is possible to award punitive or exemplary damages in copyright infringement cases as they are available in Cyprus law of torts, even though they are rarely granted.

9. Punitive Damages for Employment and Labour Law Infringements

In two employment cases, *Koulla Charalambous v. LSG Handling Ltd.*[66] and *Janet Panayides v. The Junior School*,[67] the courts did grant an award of exemplary damages to the claimants. These cases are very recent and have not been officially cited yet.[68]

The courts considered that the following factors should be granted before granting damages over the minimum standard: the daily wages and the general income of the employee, the duration of employment, the employee's age, any continuance loss of his or her future career prospects, any material damage suffered by the employee, the general behaviour and conduct of the parties and the real circumstances under which the

62 Cyprus Patent Law 16(I)/1998.

63 See cases of *Nicos Christodoulides v. The Republic of Cyprus through the Registrar of Patents* [1972] 3 CLR 71, *F. Hofmann-La Roche and Company v. The Attorney-General of The Republic* (1983) 1B C.L.R. 994, *Codal Synto Ltd. v. Bayer Aktiengesellshaft* [1996] 1A AAΔ 197 (Civil action, Volume 1 Part 1 Cyprus Supreme Court Decision).

64 Tramountanelli 2010, p 9.

65 *Ibid.*

66 *Koulla Charalambous v. LSG Handling Ltd.* [2011] Employment Court.

67 *Janet Panayides v. The Junior School* [2011] Employment Court.

68 Available at www.internationallawoffice.com/newsletters/detail.aspx?g=a61cbb33 Accessed: 16 April 2011.

employment was terminated. In addition, the courts considered the circumstances under which the dismissal took place and specifically that no notice or warning was given to either claimant regarding any inappropriate fulfilment of their duties. Taking both considerations into account and on the basis that the dismissal were considered to be illegal, the Employment Court awarded exemplary damages to both claimants.[69]

With regard to exemplary damages, the courts stated that the employee has the burden of proof to show that he or she is entitled to be awarded higher damages.

10. Conclusion

In Cyprus, the award of punitive damages which is aimed at making an example to the defendant and to punish him for his conduct, as explained in the *Papakokkinou* case, may be granted by the courts, particularly in the law of torts. However, as is illustrated by the above overview of the courts' approach to awarding such damages in the various areas of the law discussed, it is clear that the Cypriot courts do not readily award punitive or exemplary damages to the injured party and that the courts would probably be even more reluctant to grant such damages in fairly new areas of law such as competition law and patent law.

69 *Ibid.*

Bibliography

Argyrides & Chrysistomides 2006
Argyrides, I. & Chrysistomides G., 'Product Liability in Cyprus', in: Global Legal Group (ed.), *The International Comparative Legal Guide to Product Liability*, London: Global Legal Group, 2006, pp. 102, 106.

Brown 2007
Brown, M., 'Vitamins Cartel – Action for Damages', *EU & UK Antitrust/Competition Legal Alert*, 2007, pp. 1–3. Available at: www.mayerbrown.com.

Georgiades 2011
Georgiades, O., 'A practical cross-border insight into competition litigation work', *The International Comparative Legal Guide to competition Litigation*, London: Global Legal Group 2011, pp. 39–40.

Keane, Demetriades & Co LLC 2009
Keane, T.M., Demetriades C. & Co LLC, 'Cartel Regulation in Cyprus', in: W. Rowley & M. Low (eds.), *Cartel Regulation, Getting the fine down in 38 jurisdictions worldwide*, London: Law Business Research Ltd, 2009, pp. 1–3. Available at: www.mcmillan.ca/Files/ARTICLE_GTDT_Cartel_Regulation_2009.pdf.

Kyriakides & Kyriakides 2009
Kyriakides, M. & Kyriakides, H., 'Insurance & Reinsurance in Cyprus', in: Kanefsky, p. (ed.), *Insurance and Reinsurance in 33 jurisdictions worldwide*, London: Law Business Research Ltd, 2009, p. 85. Available at: www.blaney.com/sites/default/files/Canada.pdf.

Tramountanelli 2010
Tramountanelli, P., 'Patents in Europe 2010', *Intellectual asset Management*, London: IAM Ltd 2010. Available at: www.iam-magazine.com/issues/complete.ashx?g=19469c10-7c1d-4a93-becd-6fa4789b4a1e.

Jonathan Morgan*

REFLECTIONS ON REFORMING PUNITIVE DAMAGES IN ENGLISH LAW

1. Introduction

English law has displayed considerable ambivalence about punitive damages since the landmark 1964 decision in *Rookes v. Barnard*.[1] In *Rookes*, the House of Lords attempted to rationalise and confine this head of damages (traditionally known in England as 'exemplary damages'); but in two subsequent leading cases, some decades apart, the judges have showed differing degrees of enthusiasm for punishment through tort.[2] In the face of such disagreement, it may be that legislative intervention is necessary – indeed in *Rookes v. Barnard* the House of Lords implied that while total abolition of punitive damages was the rational course for the law to take, only Parliament could take such a drastic step. The Law Commission for England and Wales has considered punitive damages, resulting in formal proposals for their reform in 1997.[3] However, the Government announced that it did not intend to implement those proposed reforms.[4] We are left with the common law cultivated by the hands of the judges – and in this area, in rather an uncertain state.

This paper will discuss the basis for the judicial disagreement over punitive damages before turning to the Law Commission's project. First, it argues that reform of the law in this area is undermined by an absence of hard data about the effects of punitive damages upon those whom they are supposed to deter. This is a serious indictment of the Law Commission's method. It then turns to two particularly problematic issues: vicarious liability and the insurability of punitive damages. Finally, although not strictly a matter of punitive damages at all, the paper briefly examines the costs of litigation – which certainly do have a deterrent and arguably punitive effect, a problem that has led to insistent calls for reform of the English libel laws. Here at least, it seems, the political will currently exists for legislative reform.

* Fellow and Tutor in Law, St. Catherine's College, Oxford, and Lecturer, Faculty of Law, University of Oxford.

1 *Rookes v. Barnard* [1964] AC 1129.

2 *Broome v. Cassell & Co Ltd.* [1972] AC 1027 ('*Broome v. Cassell*'); *Kuddus v. Chief Constable of Leicestershire* [2002] 2 AC 122 ('*Kuddus*').

3 Law Commission 1997 ('Law Com Rep').

4 Written Answer, Hansard (House of Commons), vol. 337, col. 502W (9 November 1999).

2. The Common Law: Judicial Disagreement

In the leading case of *Rookes v. Barnard*,[5] Lord Devlin spoke for all of their Lordships on the subject of punitive damages. He commented that being designed to punish and deter rather than to compensate, they 'may well be thought [to confuse] the civil and criminal functions of the law'. The question was 'whether it is open to the House to remove an anomaly from the law of England'.[6] In Lord Devlin's view, it was not – 'your Lordships could not, without a complete disregard of precedent, and indeed of statute, now arrive at a determination that refused altogether to recognise the exemplary principle'.[7] Thus far, Lord Devlin's endorsement of punitive damages looks grudging indeed. But he went on to hold that in two exceptional categories, punitive damages could 'serve a useful purpose in vindicating the strength of the law and thus affording a practical justification for admitting into the civil law a principle which ought logically to belong to the criminal'. These exceptional categories were: first, 'oppressive, arbitrary or unconstitutional action by the servants of the government'; and secondly, cases in which 'the defendant's conduct has been calculated by him to make a profit for himself which may well exceed the compensation payable to the plaintiff'. The second category was necessary to show that the law 'cannot be broken with impunity', to 'teach a wrongdoer that tort does not pay'.

Lord Devlin was conscious that confining punitive damages to these categories was novel, and that there was 'powerful, although not compelling' authority for wider availability. Nevertheless, he decided that only in the two exceptional categories could punitive damages be awarded (plus also, of course, where there was explicit statutory authority). Perhaps the most important aspect of his speech was to clarify the distinction between punitive damages in the strict sense and 'aggravated damages', awarded where the claimant is upset, outraged or humiliated by the arrogant way in which the tort has been committed.[8] Such damages are compensatory, pure and simple – the defendant has 'aggravated the injury', *i.e.* by increasing the claimant's distress.[9] Non-pecuniary losses are axiomatically compensable in tort, and 'aggravated damages' would better be subsumed under that general heading, rather than seen as a special category.[10]

Lord Devlin's restatement – and confinement – of punitive damages proved highly unpopular in the wider common law world. It was not followed in Australia,[11] or

5 *Rookes v. Barnard* [1964] AC 1129.

6 Lord Devlin commented that 'so far as I know, the idea of exemplary damages is peculiar to English law' (by which he must be taken to mean 'the (English) common law' worldwide).

7 *Rookes v. Barnard* [1964] AC 1129, 1226.

8 'There may be malevolence or spite or the manner of committing the wrong may be such as to injure the plaintiff's proper feelings of dignity and pride. These are matters which the jury can take into account in assessing the appropriate compensation'.

9 *Cf. Thompson v. Commissioner of Police* [1997] 2 All ER 762, 771: aggravated damages 'are primarily to be awarded to *compensate* the claimant for *injury* to his proper pride and dignity and the consequences of his being humiliated' (emphasis added). A corporation, which has no feelings to be hurt, cannot recover aggravated damages: *Collins Stewart Ltd v. Financial Times Ltd* [2005] EWHC 262 (QB).

10 The Law Commission similarly holds that aggravated damages are 'purely compensatory', a view supported by a majority of its consultees: Law Com Rep, par. 2.40.

11 *Uren v. John Fairfax & Sons Pty. Ltd.* [1967] ALR 25.

Canada,[12] or New Zealand,[13] at a time when decisions of the House of Lords were still generally treated as authoritative in those countries. This 'wholesale condemnation' of *Rookes v. Barnard* emboldened even the English Court of Appeal in *Broome v. Cassell & Co Ltd* not to follow it,[14] the Master of the Rolls, Lord Denning going so far as to say that *Rookes v. Barnard* was '*per incuriam*' (*i.e.* decided in ignorance of the relevant law; the 'categories' had not been canvassed in argument before the House of Lords). *Rookes* was said to be open to 'devastating criticism',[15] primarily that 'the new doctrine is hopelessly illogical and inconsistent'.[16] Instead of Lord Devlin's categories, Lord Denning MR preferred to follow the pre-existing law: punitive damages would be available wherever the defendant's conduct was 'wanton, as where it discloses fraud, malice, violence, cruelty, insolence or the like, or, as it is sometimes put, where he acts in contumelious disregard of the plaintiff's rights'.[17]

Not surprisingly, the House of Lords reacted with displeasure to this insubordination from the Court of Appeal, and the Lord Chancellor, Lord Hailsham of St Marylebone, rebuked Lord Denning MR with a lecture on the doctrine of precedent.[18] But the House of Lords had by the time of *Broome v. Cassell* discarded the rule that it was bound by its own decisions,[19] and so *Rookes v. Barnard* was in principle amenable to reconsideration. However, the House chose to reaffirm *Rookes*, holding that the jury had been entitled to discern an intention to profit by the defendant on the facts of the case (through a grave libel upon the plaintiff), and upholding the award of punitive damages. Although apparently it was 'not the place to argue out the general case for or against punitive damages in English law,'[20] several of the Law Lords did comment upon the principle of the matter.

Most sternly opposed was Lord Reid. He considered 'pure punishment', resulting in an 'undeserved windfall' for claimants, to be an undesirable anomaly in tort law. The objections to punitive damages assessed by lay juries were so serious as to be 'overwhelming': uncontrolled, potentially emotional or irrational decision-making which 'contravenes almost every principle which has been evolved for the protection of offenders' in the criminal law. Lord Reid, a party to *Rookes v. Barnard* revealed that he did not agree with Lord Devlin's opinion that in the 'exceptional categories', punitive damages had a valuable role to play.[21] Lord Reid regarded the categories as essentially arbitrary – the concession that had to be made to authority when, in an ideal world, punitive damages would have been abolished altogether. There was no logical reason not to extend 'category 1' from agents of the state to other (private) powerful bodies. Equally, there was no logical reason why punitive damages could be awarded against a tortfeasor actuated by the profit motive ('category 2') but not one inspired by malice, spite or the

12 *McElroy v. Cowper-Smith and Woodman* (1967) 62 DLR (2d) 65.
13 *Fogg v. McKnight* [1968] NZLR 330.
14 *Broome v. Cassell & Co Ltd* [1971] 2 QB 354, 380.
15 *Ibid.*, at 385 (Salmon LJ).
16 *Ibid.*, at 381 (Lord Denning MR).
17 *Ibid.*, at 379 (quoting with approval *Mayne & McGregor on Damages*, 12th ed. (1961), par. 207).
18 *Broome v. Cassell*, 1053–5.
19 *Practice Statement (Judicial Precedent)* [1966] 1 WLR 1234.
20 *Broome v. Cassell*, 1114 per Lord Wilberforce.
21 'I did not regard disagreement on this side issue as preventing me from giving my concurrence'.

desire to harm – as indeed Lord Denning MR had thought in the Court of Appeal. But for Lord Reid, punitive damages had to be strictly confined and 'it is better in such cases to be content with an illogical result than to allow any extension'.

Lord Diplock similarly viewed punitive damages as an anomaly not to be extended,[22] accordingly opposing any extension to the 'third – and rejected – category' of punitive damages, 'numerically by far the largest', *i.e.* cases 'in which the manner in which the tort has been committed has attracted a whole gamut of dyslogistic judicial epithets such as wilful, wanton, high-handed, oppressive, malicious, outrageous; particularly those where the defendant's manner of doing the tortious act has been characterised by arrogance or insolence'. Damages to soothe the claimant's feelings (*i.e.* 'aggravated damages') would be sufficient redress here, where appropriate. Punishment, however, was certainly not appropriate. Lord Diplock accepted that where the defendant has calculated that committing a tort would bring him financial benefit, punitive damages ought to be available to teach him that tort does not pay. However, Lord Diplock thought that there was no need to retain a special category of punitive damages against public bodies when public law remedies ('the prerogative writs') had been so much developed in recent years. For Lord Diplock the public law route was a preferable way to control abuse of power than the 'blunt instrument' of punitive damages.[23]

A markedly different approach was taken by Lord Wilberforce.[24] His Lordship declared:

> 'It cannot lightly be taken for granted, even as a matter of theory, that the purpose of the law of tort is compensation, still less that it ought to be, an issue of large social import, or that there is something inappropriate or illogical or anomalous (a question-begging word) in including a punitive element in civil damages, or, conversely, that the criminal law, rather than the civil law, is in these cases the better instrument for conveying social disapproval, or for redressing a wrong to the social fabric, or that damages in any case can be broken down into the two separate elements. As a matter of practice English law has not committed itself to any of these theories: it may have been wiser than it knew'.

Lord Wilberforce went on to explain by way of example that a rigid distinction between punitive and compensatory damages does not 'greatly correspond to what happens in reality'. In an ordinary case of malicious assault, libel etc:

> 'Is [the claimant] suing for compensation, for injury to his feelings, to teach his opponent a lesson, to vindicate his rights, or 'the strength of the law,' or for a mixture of these things?

22 But *cf.* Viscount Dilhorne in *Broome v. Cassell*, 1108: 'Power to award exemplary damages may be an anomaly, but I doubt whether it is beneficial to the law to seek to reduce the area of that anomaly at the price of creating other anomalies and illogicalities'.

23 See further Lord Scott in *Kuddus*, at par. 107: 'The developments since Lord Diplock's remarks in *Broome v. Cassell & Co Ltd* have transformed the ability of the ordinary citizen to obtain redress [against the state]. The continuing need in the year 2001 for exemplary damages as a civil remedy in order to control, deter and punish acts falling within Lord Devlin's first category is not in the least obvious'.

24 *Broome v. Cassell*, 1114–6.

> Most men would not ask themselves such questions, many men could not answer them. If they could answer them, they might give different answers'.

Noting the arguments against punitive damages Lord Wilberforce commented that: 'Perhaps the opponents have, marginally, the best of it in logic, but logic in excess has never been the vice of English law[25] and I am impressed, as I think was Lord Devlin, with the fact that the principle has shown, and continues to show, its vitality not only in England but in Australia, Canada and New Zealand'.[26] Thus Lord Wilberforce would not have confined punitive damages in libel cases (at least) to publications calculated to make a profit: he argued that it was irrational to have profit as the condition for their award when the assessment of punitive damages (as in *Broome* itself) proceeded without reference to the profits actually made, no evidence of this having been placed before the trial court.

By the 1970s therefore, the redefinition of punitive damages wrought by Lord Devlin in *Rookes v. Barnard* was firmly cemented into place by a second decision of the House of Lords, despite the criticism in the wider common law world. But it could hardly be said that the senior English judiciary were of one mind. Some, like Lord Wilberforce and Lord Denning MR, envisaged a much wider role for the punitive principle in tort. Others, especially Lord Reid, believed that punitive damages ought really to be abolished altogether or, if that were impossible, they insisted that the exceptional categories must be construed strictly, even at the expense of logic. The latter approach had enduring influence. In *AB v. South West Water* in 1992, the Court of Appeal held that punitive damages could only be awarded in torts where a precedent for punitive damages existed before the 1964 decision in *Rookes v. Barnard*.[27] Applying this test it was held impossible to award such damages in the torts of negligence and public nuisance. An express statement to this effect by Lord Diplock in *Broome v. Cassell* had apparently 'put the matter beyond doubt'.[28]

The illogicality of such an antiquarian approach hardly needs to be stressed; but it cannot stand as a condemnation of the Court of Appeal's reasoning when the House of Lords had been so determined to confine punitive damages in *Broome v. Cassell*. Nevertheless when the issue came before the House in *Kuddus v. Chief Constable of Leicestershire* in 2001, the decision in *AB v. South West Water* was overruled. The question in *Kuddus* was whether punitive damages were available in an action for misfeasance in public office, a tort 'discovered, or rediscovered, relatively recently', *i.e.* since *Rookes v.*

25 *Cf.* also Lord Morris in *Broome v. Cassell*: 'If therefore the working of the law before *Rookes v. Barnard* is exposed to a relentless logical examination it has to be conceded that some features of it were not in principle acceptable. Yet it may be that no serious injustice resulted. And indeed as we have been told the life of the law often lies not in logic but in experience'. (*Cf.* O.W. Holmes, *The Common Law* (1881) p.1).

26 Against this, 'The existence of the principle has its convinced opponents, particularly, I understand, in Scotland'. NB Lord Reid was a highly distinguished Scottish judge!

27 *AB v. South West Water* [1993] QB 507.

28 *Ibid.* at 520 (Stuart-Smith LJ) citing *Broome*, at 1130–1131. *Cf.* Bingham MR at 530: 'I cannot pretend to find the answer at all clear, … but I think it is the basis upon which the Court of Appeal should, until corrected, proceed'.

Barnard.[29] The House of Lords held that punitive damages were recoverable in principle in that tort.[30] The parties' submissions focussed on this narrow point, with no attempt by the defendant to argue that punitive damages should now be removed from English law altogether.[31] Lord Scott of Foscote expressed 'dismay' with the lack of assistance provided by counsel to the court on the wider issue.[32] Nevertheless, some of their Lordships stated their opinions on the matter of principle.[33]

Lord Hutton reserved his opinion over the continued availability of punitive damages in England, but his experience as Lord Chief Justice of Northern Ireland confirmed Lord Devlin's view that punitive damages serve 'a valuable purpose in restraining the arbitrary and outrageous use of executive power and in vindicating the strength of the law'.[34] Lord Nicholls of Birkenhead was even more enthusiastic about punitive damages. His Lordship found their continuing vitality in England and other jurisdictions 'striking'; they played 'a significant role in buttressing civil liberties, in claims for false imprisonment and wrongful arrest'.[35] Lord Nicholls even questioned whether confining punitive damage to the *Rookes v. Barnard* categories remained defensible. Why should powerful companies and individuals not be open to the same discipline as the power of the state?[36] Why should the profit motive suffice but a malicious motive not?[37] Lord Nicholls's remarks are clearly *obiter dicta*; however, they have been relied upon by counsel to argue that the categories are 'on the verge of being abandoned'.[38] Lord Nicholls also stated that the demise of the cause of action test means that punitive damages should no longer be seen as an 'undesirable anomaly whose use is to be restricted' but rather 'a convenient tool which the law should seize and be able to use more widely'.[39]

The contrary stance was taken by Lord Scott. Stating at the outset of his speech that punitive remedies in tort are an anomaly,[40] his Lordship indicated that he would have

29 *Ibid.*, at par. 118 (Lord Scott).

30 *Ibid.*, Lord Slynn, at par. 22, founded his decision upon the 'irrational' nature of the cause of action test, but *cf.* Lord Mackay at [34] ('criticism of *AB v. South West Water Services Ltd* [1993] QB 507 on the basis that it is illogical is not well founded'), Lord Scott at par. [117]-[122].

31 See *Kuddus*, at par. 26 per Lord Slynn, par. 31, 36 per Lord Mackay, par. 68 per Lord Nicholls, par. 72 per Lord Hutton.

32 'My Lords, this is not, in my view, an appropriate manner in which to bring before your Lordships an important issue of principle'. *Kuddus*, at par. 106.

33 *Kuddus*, Lord Scott, at par. 107, and Lord Nicholls, e.g. at par. 60, thought that the narrow 'cause of action' question could not be decided without considering the 'role and propriety' of punitive damages generally (Lord Scott). *Cf.* at par. 25 per Lord Slynn, at par. 36 per Lord Mackay.

34 *Kuddus*, at 75.

35 *Ibid.*, at par. 63. See for a striking example since *Kuddus*, *Muuse v. Home Secretary* [2010] EWCA Civ 453.

36 *Kuddus*, at par. 65. It should be noted that the defendants in *Rookes v. Barnard* [1964] AC 1129 itself were members of a powerful private body (trade union operating closed shop); *cf.* Lord Devlin's comment: 'I should not extend this category – I say this with particular reference to the facts of this case – to oppressive action by private corporations or individuals'.

37 *Kuddus*, at par. 66.

38 *Moseley v. News Group Newspapers* [2008] EWHC 1777 (QB) at par. [180]. Eady J was unconvinced, and held that punitive damages are anyway not available in the ECHR-inspired action for invasion of privacy: at par. 196.

39 *Kuddus*, at par. 60.

40 *Ibid.*, at par. 95.

been 'receptive to a submission that exemplary damages awards should no longer be available'.[41] 'Victims of tortious conduct should receive due compensation for their injuries, not windfalls at public expense'.[42] Given the development and expansion of administrative law in England, it was 'not in the least obvious' that the first *Rookes v. Barnard* category was still needed to curb abuse of power by public authorities.[43] It was 'fanciful' to suggest, in any event, that damages paid by a police force or government department (rather than from the pocket of the wrongdoer himself) would have any deterrent effect.[44] Lord Scott also doubted the continued need for the second category, when the common law had now recognised 'restitutionary damages'.[45] Finally his Lordship referred to Article 6 of the European Convention on Human Rights, as given effect in England by the Human Rights Act 1998, adding further weight to the criticism (voiced, for example, by Lord Reid in *Broome v. Cassell*) that punitive damages lack the procedural safeguards vouchsafed by the criminal law.[46]

Since *Kuddus* there has been little discussion of punitive damages *per se* at the highest level, but there have been interesting developments along parallel lines. The law lords, sitting in the Privy Council as final court of appeal for a number of British Commonwealth Caribbean states, have developed a novel category of 'vindicatory damages' to redress violations of constitutional rights. According to Lord Nicholls, for example, it might be appropriate to award a sum in excess of that necessary for compensation, 'to reflect the sense of public outrage, emphasise the importance of the constitutional right and the gravity of the breach, and deter further breaches'.[47] Recently, however, the Supreme Court has (by a majority) refused to admit 'vindicatory damages' into domestic English tort law, in an action for false imprisonment against the state: *Regina (on the application of Lumba) v. Home Secretary*.[48] Lord Dyson could see no reason to let such a far-reaching principle ('unruly horse') loose in English law when common law rights were adequately vindicated by the award of compensation and, where appropriate, exemplary damages.[49] There was simply no need to recognise a new head of damages that were: 'In truth… akin to punitive or exemplary damages'.[50] The interesting point for present purpose is that the Supreme Court tacitly approved the continued award of punitive damages – at least in actions against public authorities.[51] Thus, the compromise position of Lord Devlin's categories in *Rookes v. Barnard* still holds sway – probably to the satisfaction of neither side in the punitive damages debate.

41 *Ibid.*, at par. 111.
42 *Ibid.*, at par. 121.
43 *Ibid.*, at par. 107.
44 *Ibid.*, at par. 108.
45 *Ibid.*, at par. 109. *Cf. Attorney General v. Blake* [2001] 1 AC 268.
46 *Kuddus*, at par. 110.
47 *Attorney General of Trinidad and Tobago v. Ramanoop* [2006] 1 AC 328 at par. 19.
48 [2011] UKSC 12.
49 *Ibid.*, at par. 101.
50 *Ibid.*, at par. 233 per Lord Collins of Mapesbury. See further Burrows 2011.
51 The minority judges in Lumba argued that 'vindicatory damages' would play a role distinct from punitive damages: *cf. ibid.*, at par. 178 per Lord Hope of Craighead.

3. The Law Commission's Report

Speaking in 1986, Stephenson LJ said that the punitive damages question 'cries aloud... for Parliamentary attention'.[52] The Law Commission became seized of the issue in the 1990s, noting its 'unique opportunity' to clarify the aims and purposes of tort damages in English law.[53] The Commission first issued a consultation paper in 1993,[54] arguing that the limits on recovery flowing from *Rookes v. Barnard* and *AB v. South West Water* were 'unprincipled', and therefore it was necessary to consider the fundamental question – should punitive damages ever be recoverable?[55] The division of opinion on this question was attributable to 'radically different perceptions of the role of the law of civil wrongs' epitomized in the speeches of Lords Reid and Wilberforce in *Broome v. Cassell*.[56] Essentially, whether it is proper for tort law to punish. The chain of deductive reasoning from the proposition that punishment is for the criminal law, to punitive damages being anomalous, may be 'short and straightforward'.[57] But any such arguments, starting from the proposition that the *exclusive* role of tort is to compensate losses, surely beg the question – 'assume what is at issue and fail to address the question of policy involved'.[58] The popularity of the assumption (the dominant one among English judges and commentators) is probably due to an excessive focus upon that branch of tort law which compensates accident victims; but this is an incomplete account since there are torts like libel and trespass which have historically been concerned with protecting rights, over and above compensating loss.[59] Thus, the Law Commission did not accept the *a priori* argument that punitive damages are an 'anomaly' that *must* be abolished. However, total abolition was one of the options for reform they asked consultees to comment upon,[60] along with limited abolition (e.g. removing punitive damages from libel cases),[61] or, conversely, retention of punitive damages on a 'principled basis'.[62]

The Law Commission found the responses so varied that it issued a supplementary consultation paper, primarily to those who had replied to the first consultation.[63] Here, the options were 'expansion', 'abolition' and 'hybrid' models.[64] The first proposal was to expand punitive damages to all wrongs (except breach of contract) 'committed with, or accompanied or followed by conduct which evinces, a deliberate and outrageous disregard of the plaintiff's rights'. The hybrid model was to abolish punitive damages save in the situation of 'a deliberate and outrageous disregard of the plaintiff's rights by servants of

52 *Riches v. News Group Newspapers Ltd* [1986] 1 QB 256, 269C.
53 Law Com Rep, par. 1.5.
54 Law Commission 1993.
55 Law Com Rep, par. 5.1.
56 Law Com Rep, par. 5.28.
57 Wells 2010, p. 567.
58 Law Com Rep, par. 5.29.
59 Law Com Rep, par. 5.30–5.31.
60 Law Commission 1993, par. 6.6.
61 Law Commission 1993, par. 6.7.
62 Law Commission 1993, par. 6.8–6.12. The *status quo* could not be defended 'on any basis of principle' and it was assumed that neither abolitionists nor retentionists would support it: par. 6.5.
63 Law Com Rep, par. 5.10.
64 Law Com Rep, par. 5.14.

the government in the purported exercise of powers entrusted to them by the state'. Of 146 responses, consultees divided 49% in favour of expansion, 28% in favour of total abolition, and 23% in favour of the so-called 'hybrid' approach.[65] The Law Commission spun the results as showing 72% in favour of retention.[66] But one could just as easily say that a (bare) majority (51%) favoured abolition in cases not involving the state. It is, moreover, not clear that a simple head-count of self-selecting respondents should be given any weight in the law reform process.

The main issue of principle facing the case for retention (indeed expansion) was whether punishment through civil proceedings could be sufficiently distinguished from criminal prosecution. If it could not be distinguished then it was open to the criticisms made by Lord Reid (and Lord Morris) in *Broome v. Cassell* (and subsequently by Lord Scott in *Kuddus*), namely that the defendant is deprived of the procedural protection that the criminal law usually affords.[67] The retentionists' case for the distinctiveness of tort relies upon the remedy being in the hands of the individual victim (rather than the state), and upon the lesser social stigma of tort liability compared to criminal convictions. In its final report the Law Commission preferred this latter view, although stating that the issue was difficult and finely balanced.[68] More interestingly perhaps, the Commission suggested that the disagreement here reflected deeper 'differences in the precision with which one wishes to divide different branches and functions of the law'.[69] Those arguing to abolish punitive damages wanted a clear and bright line between crime and tort; those arguing for their retention were 'content rather with a "fuzzy" line' between those branches of the law.[70] As seen, Lord Wilberforce was very much of the second school of thought. More recently, Lord Hoffmann has cited this 'practical wisdom' with approval, remarking that 'Oil and vinegar may not mix in solution but they combine to make an acceptable salad dressing'![71] Perhaps such thinking – woolly or pragmatic, depending on one's allegiance – is characteristic of the common law mind-set.[72] The Law Commission refers dismissively to a '"compensation-only" dogma'.[73]

The Commission decided that the pragmatic arguments in favour of retention were convincing. There were gaps in enforcement of the criminal law that punitive damages

65 Law Com Rep, par. 5.15.

66 *Ibid.*

67 Law Com Rep, par. 5.20–5.21.

68 Law Com Rep, par. 5.26.

69 Law Com Rep, par. 5.25.

70 *Ibid. Cf.* par. 5.11: 'Many consultees were not prepared to accept that any sharp distinction exists between the goals that may legitimately be pursued by the criminal law and the civil law: punishment, deterrence and the marking out of conduct for disapproval *are* legitimate functions of the civil law'.

71 *The Gleaner Co Ltd v. Abrahams* [2004] 1 AC 628, at par. 54.

72 *Cf.* Law Com Rep, par. 5.27(4) – abolition would 'fly in the face of the traditions of the common law'. *Cf.* Wells 2010, 560 (and passim) – in the 'endless innovation' of the common law, formal rules often give way to policy arguments for exceptions; whereas civilian lawyers 'learn that law is a body of rules and are thereby better equipped to maintain the formal distinction' between public and private law.

73 Law Com Rep, par. 5.143. This occurs in the context of considering whether punitive damages should be paid (in whole or in part) to a public fund, to meet the objection that they are a 'windfall' for the claimant. The Law Commission recognised that at least partial retention is necessary or no claimant would ever seek punitive damages, and ultimately recommended that partial recovery by a public fund would be too complex: par. 1.142–1.158.

can fill – 'Civil punishment may therefore be particularly useful, *even if merely to ensure that justice is seen to be done*, in respect of wrongs by police and other officers of the state'.[74] Many consultees had also expressed concern about powerful private defendants who would not be deterred by ordinary damages, in particular media libels published for reasons of profit or spite, where self-regulation has proved ineffective.[75] Moreover, although in general the rational response to deficiencies in the criminal law would be to address them directly as, for example, by increasing the maximum penalty on conviction,[76] it is far from clear that criminal prosecutions for libel would be desirable,[77] or that this would solve the problem of (the perception of) the police 'closing ranks'. The Commission dismissed the policy arguments against retention of punitive damages. Given the cost of litigation,[78] it was unlikely that they would greatly increase spurious claims.[79] Some degree of uncertainty was inevitable when applying concepts such as 'outrageous behaviour',[80] but making the level of punitive awards consistent and predictable (out of fairness to defendants and respect for the Rule of Law) would not undermine their deterrent effect any more than consistency of sentencing in the criminal law.[81]

Having thus weighed the practical arguments in favour of retention, the Commission commented that the case for abolition seemed to be essentially theoretical – again, the concern from 'neatness' for a sharp line between civil and criminal law.[82] As seen above, this argument cannot bear the weight placed upon it. Accordingly, the Law Commission's central recommendation was that punitive damages should be available for any civil wrong (except breach of contract) committed with deliberate and outrageous disregard of a claimant's rights.[83]

These recommendations seem to enjoy the support of strong arguments. However, something important is missing from the Law Commission's reasoning. The centre of the case for retaining, and expanding, punitive damages is their *effect on behaviour* – the supposed deterrence of serious and deliberate wrongs. The Commission spends remarkably little time considering this vital point. The way in which it is glossed over is revealed thus:

74 Law Com Rep, par. 5.27(3) (emphasis added). *Cf. Reg v. Sussex Justices, ex parte McCarthy* [1924] 1 KB 256, 259 per Lord Hewart CJ: it 'is of fundamental importance that justice should not only be done, but should manifestly and undoubtedly be seen to be done'.

75 Law Com Rep, par. 5.12. The Consultation Paper referred to 'Rachman-type landlords' as the classic example: Law Commission 1993, par. 5.20, *cf.* 5.16.

76 Law Commission 1993, par. 5.33; Law Com Rep, par. 5.8.

77 This was the occasion for Lord Hoffmann's comments in *The Gleaner Co Ltd v. Abrahams* [2004] 1 AC 628, [54]; compare *Kiam v. MGN* [2003] QB 281, [76] per Sedley LJ. The common law offence of defamatory libel has since been abolished: Coroners and Justice Act 2009, s. 73.

78 *Cf.* Section 6, below.

79 Law Com Rep, par. 5.30.

80 Law Com Rep, par. 5.31.

81 Law Com Rep, par. 5.36.

82 Law Com Rep, par. 5.37.

83 Law Com Rep, par. 5.42, 5.78–5.80.

> '*If* civil punishment has *some* deterrent effect, *and we consider that it must have*, the abolition of exemplary damages would remove one means of protecting potential victims of wrongdoing'.[84]

No evidence is provided for this claim; perhaps none is needed if one finds 'some deterrent effect' satisfied should one potential tortfeasor on one occasion experience some degree of deterrence (however small) against a contemplated tortious act. But such trivial effects on behaviour would render the game barely worth the candle. A more interesting question, indeed a vital one for a law reform body, would be the precise *extent* of the deterrent effect – perhaps comparing the limited availability of punitive damages in England and their wider role in other common law jurisdictions, including the United States. Then the benefits of punitive damages could be weighed against their cost.

As seen above, the Law Lords in *Kuddus v. Chief Constable of Leicestershire* (subsequent to the Law Commission's Report) disagreed over this matter – Lord Scott deriding as 'fanciful' Lord Hutton's view that punitive awards against chief constables or government departments have a deterrent effect on policemen or other public servants.[85] The disagreement here is slightly unedifying, perhaps futile, because the judiciary have no reliable way of testing (or making or rebutting) such claims. Certainly not if no evidence has been placed before the court. It behoves courts to show caution under such conditions, as Buxton LJ recognised in a case where certain policy arguments against liability in negligence had been made without any data to support them.[86] Buxton LJ declined counsel's express invitation to 'speculate' that liability might cause 'defensive' behaviour by the defendant body, or even its total withdrawal from the field of aviation regulation.[87] Such wide claims about the effect of liability on industry or insurance practice were commonly made in argument; however:

> 'In my respectful view, the Court should be very cautious before reaching or acting on any conclusions that are not argued before it in the way in which technical issues are usually approached, with the assistance of expert evidence'.[88]

But the warning has rarely been heeded. The courts have a very chequered history with the 'over-defensiveness' argument, which has on some occasions been used to deny liability but in other cases, robustly rejected.[89] In none of the decisions, however, has any empirical evidence about the effect of liability on that category of defendant been cited by the judges – no doubt because none is available. It seems, then, that most judges (with Buxton LJ an honourable exception) are quite happy to speculate about the effect of liability on behaviour without the benefit of any evidence beyond their intuitions and

84 Law Com Rep, par. 5.27(1) (emphasis added).

85 *Kuddus*, at 108, *cf.* par. 79 (Lord Hutton). Lord Scott allowed that it might be different with damages enforced 'against the actual wrongdoers which they would have to meet out of their own pockets'. For vicarious liability *cf.* Section 4, below.

86 *Perrett v. Collins* [1998] 2 Lloyd's Rep 255.

87 *Ibid.*, at 276–277.

88 *Ibid.*,at 277.

89 *Cf.* Morgan 2009.

life experience (including that on the bench).[90] The dispute between Lords Hutton and Scott in *Kuddus* should also be seen in such terms. It is intractable because each of their Lordships makes a plausible claim – but a fundamentally *empirical* claim, with no empirical evidence by which to substantiate it.

But the courts are prisoners of the evidence, and arguments, placed before them by the parties (as *Kuddus* again illustrates well), and criticism of judicial policy reasoning must be tempered accordingly.[91] The judges simply cannot rely on evidence that is not cited, and cannot commission research where the data have never been collected. The same excuse does not however exist for legislators and policy-makers, and particularly not for the Law Commission whose *raison d'être* is to advise government on reform of the law of England and Wales. The Law Commission's failure to take seriously empirical studies in its report on punitive damages is a serious embarrassment for which no excuse can be made. It is true that very little empirical research has been done, or is being done, into the effect of private law on real-world behaviour, for a complex of reasons pertaining to the structure and funding of the academic legal profession.[92] But that should not prove an obstacle to a body with the resources of the Law Commission, which could commission such research – if only it recognised the importance of it. It is worth noting that torts scholars of an empirical bent are still relying on figures about the levels of accident compensation in the mid-1970s, from the last major public investigation into the subject – the Royal Commission on Civil Liability and Compensation for Personal Injury ('Pearson Commission' after its chairman) which reported in 1978.[93] This illustrates both the infrequency of public inquiries into these matters, and their enduring value.

Lord Mackay of Clashfern (a former Lord Chancellor – *i.e.* Cabinet Minister, 1987–1997) saw these points clearly in *Kuddus*.[94] Lord Mackay cited a passage from Professor Street's *Principles of the Law of Damages* (1962):

> 'It is believed that in the present state of knowledge, one cannot say whether exemplary damages are desirable. That study of the law in action which would show how efficiently they contribute to the attainment of the several purposes examined above remains to be done. And the practical usefulness of exemplary damages is the basic question, and one to which no amount of theorising can provide an answer'.[95]

Despite the Law Commission's 'very full and careful consultation' it may be, commented Lord Mackay, 'that the study which Professor Street desiderated remains to be done'.

90 Another recent example is the decision to abolish expert witnesses' immunity from actions in negligence: *Jones v. Kaney* [2011] UKSC 13. *Cf.* in particular par. 129 per Lord Hope (dissenting).

91 Buxton 2009, p. 60: 'There is no place in the English forensic process for the sort of review of opinion, practicalities and collateral damage that is undertaken by the Law Commission before it sets about changing the law'.

92 *Cf.* report by Genn, Partington & Wheeler 2006.

93 *Cf.* Cane 2006, passim.

94 *Kuddus*, at par. 37.

95 London, Sweet and Maxwell, 1962, p. 36.

Quite so. After fifty years we are still waiting, and any hopes that Lord Mackay's words might prompt such a study are surely fading.[96]

The Law Commission's failure to carry out that study is the major disappointment in its report on punitive damages. It did not even cite the contemporary U.S. empirical research into punitive damages – a major bone of contention in the American 'Tort Wars'.[97] It is true that this research mostly looks at the incidence, quantum and geographical distribution of punitive damages verdicts,[98] and that American scholars routinely call for further research into the effect of such damages on behaviour.[99] One systematic consideration of product liability's impact on manufacturers' decision-making gloomily asserts that 'many potential effects on business decisions and economic outcomes of central concern cannot be observed or measured'.[100] Few would deny that the collection of such data is, at the very least, challenging. There are pitfalls with both quantitative approaches, and the case-study.[101] But such difficulties might, with sufficient effort and resources, be ameliorated and perhaps even surmounted. The right response is not that which the Law Commission shares with the ostrich.

In more recent projects the Commission has begun to realize the importance of an empirical approach. It acknowledged the need to discern the effect of (ordinary compensatory) liability upon public authority behaviour in its Consultation Paper on that subject – although the state of its knowledge of this vital matter was sketchy indeed at that stage.[102] The Commission's final Report on the subject was a rather muted affair since the Government had firmly opposed its proposals, through fear that they would spell increased public expenditure on compensation.[103] The Commission accepted the Government's 'very real concern about the potential cost of the proposals',[104] but complained that it had not been able to assemble data even about the existing government compensation bill, since the relevant figures are not collected by government departments![105] This made it 'extremely difficult to rebut the concerns of certain consultees – particularly Government – relating to the presumed effect of our proposals'.[106] The Commission accordingly recommended that data on compensation payments should in future be systematically collected, to 'allow for a structured and rational debate'.[107]

These are welcome moves. The Law Commission's thwarted attempt to assemble basic statistical information for the administrative redress project reveals a more general failing of British government to take evidence-based policymaking seriously. Even the Government's formal 'Impact Assessments' have been criticised for the quality of the

96 It was suggested in 2002 that Lord Mackay's citation of Street 'gives one a little, no doubt naïve, hope that the necessary work might now be undertaken': Harris, Campbell & Halson 2002, p. 594.

97 For a summary see e.g. Rustad 1998. *Cf.* more generally Levin 2008, pp. 42–43.

98 See e.g. Daniels & Martin 1990.

99 E.g. Rustad (1998) at p. 69 (conclusion).

100 Garber 1998, p. 238.

101 For one heroic failure *cf.* Kritzler & Kahn Zemans.

102 Law Commission 2008, especially Appendix B. For criticism see Morgan 2009.

103 Law Commission 2010, at 1.3.

104 *Ibid.* at 4.35.

105 *Ibid.* at 1.5.

106 *Ibid.*

107 *Ibid.*, at 4.70; 4.71–4.81 (the only formal recommendation made in the Report).

data used in their cost-benefit analyses.[108] Hopefully the Commission's new sensitivity to empirical evidence will be a lasting change in its *modus operandi*. It does show up the weakness at the heart of the earlier punitive damages report, however.

The end of the affair is also unsatisfactory. Answering a question in the House of Commons about the Government's response to the Law Commission report the minister said:

> 'The contending arguments for a complete legislative overhaul of exemplary damages, as recommended by the Law Commission, or abolition as preferred by many commentators, are finely balanced. In the absence of a clear consensus on the issue the Government have decided not to take forward the Law Commission's proposals for legislation on exemplary damages. It may be that some further judicial development of the law in this area might help clarify the issues'.[109]

Essentially the Government seemed to think that the issue was too controversial to waste precious legislative time upon. But this was a failure of leadership when the Commission had proposed a rationalisation preferable, surely, to the prevailing law in *Rookes v. Barnard* (and at the time of the minister's answer, *AB v. South West Water* too). The final sentence is laughable, and it comes as no surprise that when the issue returned to the House of Lords, as it soon did in *Kuddus*, whatever 'further judicial development' there was scarcely 'help[ed] clarify the issues'. Partly, as seen, this is because the parties chose not to put the issue of fundamental principle before the court (no doubt for good tactical reasons). But a majority of the House did not seem keen to embark upon fundamental review of punitive damages – indeed Lord Slynn of Hadley made direct reference to the minister's statement, cautioning that it should not 'inspire your Lordships to the view that the whole matter should be reopened and the Law Commission's Report revisited'.[110] The judges who were nonetheless tempted to express such views were in sharp disagreement. The saga is a paradigm of the 'judges who can't and the legislators who won't' – an all-too-familiar tale of abortive law reform.[111]

4. Vicarious Liability

One specific controversy is whether an employer should be vicariously liable for punitive damages awarded against an employee for a tort committed in the course of employment. As well as being inherently interesting, the vicarious liability question reveals the courts and the Law Commission failing to get to the heart of the matter so as to produce a coherent legal position. As Chapman and Trebilcock have argued, whether we view punitive damages primarily through the prism of moral desert (retribution) or of creating

108 British Chambers of Commerce 2004, pp. 11 to 13; Comptroller and Auditor General 2004, par. 2.39 to 2.56. *Cf.* Department for Business, Innovation and Skills 2009.

109 Written Answer, Hansard (House of Commons) vol 337, col 502W (9 November 1999).

110 *Kuddus*, at par. 24. As Lord Devlin himself once lamented, 'The work done by the Judges of England is not now as glorious as it was': Devlin 1962, p. 6.

111 Friendly 1963.

optimal incentives for efficient behaviour (deterrence) makes a considerable difference to the answer.[112] The failure to make this meta-choice has meant confused law on punitive damages across the Anglo-American common law.[113] Chapman and Trebilcock's thesis is well borne out through and examination of the English approach.

It was as late as 2006 that a final decision was made about vicarious liability (in favour),[114] although it had been discussed earlier by the Law Commission and by Lord Scott (in particular) in *Kuddus v. Chief Constable*. Lord Scott articulated with clarity the basic point that 'vicarious punishment ... is contrary to principle and should be rejected'.[115] Over two hundred years ago, Story J similarly considered that defendant employers should not be liable for punitive damages when they were 'innocent of the demerit of this transaction, having neither directed it, nor countenanced it, nor participated in it in the slightest degree'.[116] This view makes clear sense if we adopt the retributive perspective: only the wrongdoer should be punished (and that punishment should be his 'just deserts', ruling out a surcharge for deterrence of future possible tortfeasors). As in crime, there can be no room for vicarious punishment.[117]

Since the retributive perspective is a peremptory argument against vicarious liability for punitive damages it must be rejected by those who favour such liability. Yet there has been little direct engagement with it, no acknowledgment even that an issue is there to be faced. Lord Hutton in *Kuddus* sought to defend the useful deterrent effect of punitive damages but made no attempt to rebut Lord Scott's central and formidable point about vicarious punishment.[118] In fairness to Lord Hutton, Lord Scott also engaged in the deterrence debate,[119] a characteristic example of how these different perspectives, with their very different implications for the vicarious liability debate, are nevertheless used interchangeably. This casualness also appears in the Law Commission's comment that at first blush, vicarious liability means that 'the direct punitive, deterrent or symbolic efficacy of the punitive award is at best substantially diluted'.[120] In the case which finally decided the vicarious liability point, Moore-Bick LJ held that Lord Scott's position of 'strict principle' gave way to 'considerations of policy'.[121] However, the 'policy' in question seemed to be ensuring that an 'award of an adequate amount' can be made against

112 Chapman & Trebilcock 1989.

113 *Ibid.*, p. 827.

114 *Rowlands v. Chief Constable of Merseyside Police* [2006] EWCA Civ 1773.

115 *Kuddus* at par. 137; *cf.* par. 131. However the point was not at stake and so the comments are all obiter: par. 138.

116 *The Amiable Nancy* (1818) 16 US (3 Wheat) 546, p. 558–559. US law today displays a considerably more diverse set of views overall: see e.g. Sturley 2010.

117 Also as in crime, the liability of corporate defendants would present difficulties since in one sense, all corporate liability is 'vicarious' and yet attempts are made to distinguish 'mere' vicarious liability from 'direct' corporate criminal liability. See e.g. *Tesco Stores Ltd v. Nattrass* [1972] AC 153 (*cf.* now Corporate Manslaughter and Corporate Homicide Act 2008). *Cf.* more generally Chapman & Trebilcock 1989, pp. 799–801 (making the point that the regime in criminal law should on grounds of consistency apply to punitive damages also).

118 *Kuddus*, par. 79.

119 *Kuddus*, at par. 108, 129.

120 Law Com Rep, at par. 5.211.

121 *Rowlands v. Chief Constable of Merseyside Police*, at par. 47.

employers, 'without being constrained by the financial means of those who committed the wrongful acts in question'. However, such a search for a deep pocket,[122] common enough as a justification for vicarious liability for ordinary compensatory damages, is highly dubious when applied to the punitive damages situation.[123] So with respect, the leading case fails to deal adequately with the retributive perspective either.

As stated, there is an alternative view, emphasizing the deterrent effect of punitive damages. The meta-choice between deterrence and retribution is by no means easy. But it is quite literally fundamental. It reflects well-known (and intractable) debates in penology, and indeed the division in moral philosophy generally between deontic and consequentialist reasoning. That English tort lawyers stride, or slide, untroubled across such epistemological chasms may be productive of derision or awe, according to taste. Again one might note that it seems characteristic of the common lawyer to 'reason' in such a fashion.[124]

Defenders of vicarious liability for punitive damages must, then, eschew any discussion of retribution and concentrate instead upon the possible deterrent effects. (Most would agree that in the situations where such damages are available, defendants' conduct is unquestionably deserving of discouragement.[125]) At first sight this looks surprising. It may be 'possible that exemplary damages awards against the actual wrongdoers which they would have to meet out of their own pockets would have a deterrent effect upon them,' but it is far from obvious that making their *employers* liable will have that effect.[126] Indeed, vicarious liability will, *de facto*, relieve the employee, the primary wrongdoer, of his punitive damages liability. As a matter of law the employer and employee are both liable (jointly and severally), and the employer can recover a complete indemnity from the employee for the vicarious liability generated by the employee's tort.[127] But in practice, this is rarely if ever enforced.[128] The Law Commission's observation that the employee's incentives are 'at best substantially diluted' looks if

122 See Giliker 2010, pp. 41–42 (commenting on *Rowlands*).

123 The usual rationales offered for vicarious liability are 'inapplicable or lamentably weak' in this context: Ellis 1982, pp. 65–66.

124 *Cf.* Milsom 1981, p. 6: 'The life of the common law has been in the unceasing abuse of its elementary ideas. If the rules of property give what now seems an unjust result, try obligation; and equity has proved that from the materials of obligation you can counterfeit almost all the phenomena of property. If the rules of contract give what now seems an unjust answer, try tort. Your counterfeit will look odd to one brought up on categories of Roman origin, but it will work'.

125 See Ogus 1997. With intentional torts the chance of causing harm is very high, almost certainly (therefore) exceeding the *ex ante* chances of being sued. Thus, a purely compensatory damages regime will likely lead to underdeterrence. (Ogus also discusses the notion of 'illicit profits', but these can be defined only morally, not by economics.).

126 *Kuddus*, at 108 (Lord Scott).

127 *Lister v. Romford Ice and Cold Storage Co Ltd* [1956] AC 555.

128 *Cf. Morris v. Ford Motor Co Ltd* [1973] QB 792. In economic terms, the employee is likely to be considerably more risk averse and would therefore require much higher payment (wages) to bear the risk: Sykes 1984.

anything to be an understatement.[129] The employer's vicarious liability operates in practice to the exclusion of the employee's personal liability.[130]

Nevertheless, the Law Commission argued that vicarious liability offers a 'wider, if indirect' way of promoting the deterrent effect of punitive damages.[131] Employers could curb the behaviour that might otherwise lead to punitive awards, by controlling and educating their workforces.[132] Lord Hutton similarly supported punitive awards against chief constables vicariously, rather than against individual constables, arguing that 'such awards will bring home to officers in command of individual units that discipline must be maintained at all times'.[133] However, some commentators doubt the plausibility of these 'control' arguments. Professor Ellis suggests that employers might be cautious about disciplining employees 'whose evidence might directly affect the probability and amount of any assessment' of punitive damages.[134] More broadly, he points out that there are other ways of limiting vicarious liability – employing fewer workers, using independent contractors, ceasing trading altogether – and it is 'indeterminate' which combination of measures a given employer will adopt.[135] Ellis concludes that it would be better to leave the threat of sanctions directly upon the potential wrongdoer: 'Almost invariably, employers are in a worse position to anticipate which employee will commit an act for which punitive damages may be assessed and to prevent its occurrence'.[136] Similarly, Professor Giliker doubts the deterrence rationale for vicarious liability generally, stressing the point that it may remove the employee's incentives.[137]

Again, these are ultimately *empirical* claims that ought to be tested in this way, if the debate about the deterrent efficacy of vicarious punitive liability is to be settled. Again, however, there is no acknowledgment of this point in the judicial discourse in England – nor, more worryingly, in the Report of the Law Commission. A further concern is that the important choice between deterrent and retributive rationales for punitive damages is made tacitly, if at all – with some statements subscribing to both positions, although they are incompatible.

5. Liability Insurance

Another particularly troublesome issue is whether it should be legally permissible to insure against liability to pay punitive damages. The starting point for analysis is the sanctity of insurance contracts – should an insurer agree to insure such a risk, he must

129 Law Com Rep, at 5.211.

130 *Cf.* Law Com Rep, at 5.219: 'The immediate impact of vicarious liability is clearly that the primary wrongdoer escapes punishment by the law'. This point seems to be overlooked by Chapman & Trebilcock 1989, who support vicarious liability but on the basis that the employer's liability is *additional* to that of the employee: p. 820 (citing Coffee 1981, pp. 393–400).

131 Law Com Rep, at 5.219.

132 Law Com Rep, at 5.220.

133 *Kuddus*, at 79.

134 Ellis 1982, p. 69.

135 Ellis 1982, p. 70.

136 *Ibid.*

137 Giliker 2010, pp. 242–243.

indemnify the insured when it occurs. Of course this cannot be an absolute consideration, as we see in the rule that insurance against *criminal* penalties is invalid.[138] However, if public policy is to prevail it must be cogent and strong, for upholding the sanctity of contracts is itself a 'paramount' public policy.[139]

Only one English decision has directly confronted the question, which is perforce the leading case – *Lancashire County Council v. Municipal Mutual Insurance Ltd.*[140] Punitive damages had been awarded against police officers and council employees for whom the chief constable and the local authority were, respectively, vicariously liable. The Court of Appeal held that the employers' liability insurance coverage extended to these punitive damages. Simon Brown LJ said that it would be 'wholly inappropriate' for the court 'for the first time [to] create and impose a rule of public policy' that such damages were uninsurable.[141] Only in a very clear case could public policy be relied upon by an insurer to defeat its liability to the insured. Yet here, there were a number of policy concerns 'not by any means all pointing in the same direction'.[142] Moreover, the courts 'should be wary of minting new rules of public policy when the legislature has not done so', and a 'sudden burst of common law creativity' was particularly inappropriate when the whole issue was under consideration by the Law Commission.[143] The Court of Appeal essentially declined to recognise the rule of public policy for constitutional reasons – this was better done (if at all) by Parliament and the Law Commission – and so the default position of upholding the insurance remained in place.

Finally, Simon Brown LJ said that it would be particularly inappropriate to hold the insurance inapplicable when the liability was vicarious rather than personal – 'the most extreme position of all'.[144] It is certainly the case that concerns regarding liability insurance and punitive awards are considerably weaker in such situations – although as Ellis notes, arguments in favour of allowing the insurability of vicarious punitive liability are really arguments against punitive vicarious liability per se.[145] There is therefore no positive authority on insurability of *personal* liability for punitive damages in English law. For this reason, and given the enthusiasm of the Court of Appeal to divest themselves of responsibility for the public policy question, the Law Commission's Report assumes central importance. Again, however, it seems that the Commission failed properly to distinguish between retributive and deterrent conceptions of punitive damages, leaving its arguments incomplete.

Like the Court of Appeal, the Law Commission was keen to stress the difficulty of the policy question – as revealed in the diversity in its consultees' responses[146] – but unlike

138 Generally accepted in civil law as well as common law jurisdictions: see in this book Nordin, E. & Wuyts, D., *The Insurability of Punitive Damages under Belgian Law.*

139 *Printing and Numerical Registering Co v. Sampson* (1875) LR 19 Eq 462, 465 per Jessel MR. *Cf.* Law Com Rep, 5.242.

140 [1997] QB 897.

141 *Ibid.*, at 909.

142 *Ibid.*

143 *Ibid.* Judgment was given between the Commission's Consultation Paper and final Report.

144 *Ibid.*

145 Ellis (1982), p. 75.

146 A 'very wide range of opinions' Law Com Rep 5.235.

the court the Commission did not simply revert to sanctity of contract as the default option.[147] The case against insurability seems to be a simple and powerful one, and runs in parallel to that against vicarious liability. If the insurer pays the punitive damages, rather than the defendant, it seems obvious that the punitive effect is seriously undermined.[148] It is for precisely this reason that insurance against criminal penalties is disallowed.[149]

The Law Commission was unconvinced by this argument, dismissing it with surprising celerity. Although allowing that 'any retributive and deterrent purposes of this category of damages may be diluted by our proposed approach to insurance', the Commission nevertheless recommended that insurability should be possible.[150] The objectives would not be 'wholly frustrated' because 'the insurance industry, in controlling the availability and cost of such insurance, is in a position to exert significant pressure on present or potential insured parties'.[151]

Two things should be noted about this crucial stage in the Law Commission's reasoning. First, that no evidence was cited for this view, beyond two judicial dicta which themselves offer no more than assertion.[152] Secondly, the Commission again runs together retribution and deterrence as the purpose of punitive damages.

There is in fact a strong argument to suppose that the *deterrent* function may in large part be preserved, notwithstanding liability insurance. Learned commentators such as Priest and Baker discuss the incentives that insurers themselves have to deter policy-holders from incurring liability – to curb such well known problems as moral hazard (whereby insuring a certain event means it is more likely to come about) and adverse selection (those with a propensity to cause particular harms are disproportionately likely to purchase insurance against it).[153] As Baker puts it, 'insurance companies have a strong financial incentive to construct the insurance relationship' so as to curb these problems, and have the 'ability to do so through the use of underwriting and insurance contract provisions'.[154] Baker therefore sees no need for the courts to intervene to uphold the deterrent value of punitive damages – insurers are, he concludes, 'in a better position' to do so.[155]

The argument is powerful, but not entirely convincing. If insurers were really concerned with deterring the conduct that leads to punitive damages, which in English law at least will mean intentional wrongdoing, they would exclude it from coverage altogether (and the insurability debate would become a wholly academic one).[156]

147 Although the sanctity of contract argument was relied upon in part: Law Com Rep, at 5.242–5.244.

148 Or indeed 'annihilated': *cf.* Nordin, E. & Wuyts, D., *The Insurability of Punitive Damages under Belgian Law.*

149 *Cf. Askey v. Golden Wine Co Ltd* [1948] 2 All ER 35, 38 per Denning J, cited Law Com Rep, at 5.257.

150 Law Com Rep, at 5.238.

151 *Ibid.*

152 Law Com Rep, at 5.239–5.240 citing *Lamb v. Cotogno* (1987) 164 CLR 1, 9 and *Lancashire CC v. Municipal Mutual* [1997] QB 897, 909.

153 Priest 1989; Baker 1998.

154 Baker 1998, p. 126–127. On underwriting, Chapman & Trebilcock 1989, p. 822: 'question how easy it is to monitor *ex ante* for many forms of conduct that have traditionally attracted punitive damages, such as malicious or wilful wrongdoing'.

155 Baker 1998, p. 101.

156 *Cf.* Ellis 1982, p. 72: punitive damages are inconsistent with basic tenets of insurability.

However, even in the United States, where this has been a much-litigated question,[157] 'insurers have not modified policies to exclude coverage of punitive liability despite invitations to do so by the courts'.[158] This presents, as Priest says, a 'puzzle'.[159] It seems that there is continuing consumer demand for coverage, and insurer willingness to provide it, in America at least: a proposal to eliminate punitive damages coverage from the US industry standard form was dropped after 'extraordinary debate' when it was 'vehemently attacked by some segments [of the insurance industry] ... particularly sales representatives'.[160]

The current practice of English liability insurers is not entirely clear. The Law Commission stated in 1997 that 'most' defamation insurance excludes malicious libels,[161] and that the police were 'finding it difficult' to obtain coverage for punitive damages.[162] On the other hand, Simon Brown LJ had said the previous year that 'newspapers, we are told, regularly insure against exemplary damages for defamation'.[163] It may be that insurance practice is simply inconsistent – Priest blames insurers' failure to makes their minds up about coverage of punitive damages for the 'judicial schizophrenia on the issue'.[164] At any rate, the very existence of insurance coverage for punitive damages shows an incomplete concern with deterrence on the part of insurers.[165] The 'preservation of deterrence' argument – which is only a rebuttal of the argument against insurability, rather than a positive argument in favour of insurability – succeeds only in part. The Law Commission's treatment of this important issue is cursory, and does not engage with the scholarly literature.

Furthermore, even were insurance compatible with the *deterrence* rationale for punitive damages, it is quite inconsistent with a *retributive* rationale, for the same reasons that insurance against criminal sanctions is invalid.[166] Insurance reduces the punishment of the wrongdoer, while making others in the same risk pool who are innocent of wrongful behaviour liable for higher premiums.[167] Baker admits that: 'The incentives of insurance companies do not mesh as neatly with the retributive objectives of tort law. Accordingly, retribution provides a somewhat stronger case for judicial regulation [of

157 Presumably because punitive awards are much more common.

158 Priest 1989, p. 1033.

159 *Ibid.*

160 Widiss 1994, p. 488.

161 Indeed, note that the Defamation Act 1952, s.11, makes it unlawful to indemnify another against civil liability in libel where the person knows that the matter is defamatory and that there is no good defence to publication. Moreover, the publisher is obliged to use 'diligence, care and restraint' to avoid legal complaints in the specimen libel insurance policy reproduced in Matthews, Morgan & O'Cinneide 2008, p. 983.

162 Law Com Rep, at 5.269, n. 820.

163 *Lancashire CC v. Municipal Mutual* [1997] QB 897, 908.

164 Priest 1989, p. 1010.

165 This is not the only concern of insurance, of course – insurance always intends to undermine incentives to take care. The primary function of insurance is to spread losses. Some degree of moral hazard and adverse selection is tolerable (it is anyway inevitable) in insurance, provided it does not reach the point at which the pool of premium-payers unravels.

166 Chapman & Trebilcock 1989, p. 801.

167 *Ibid.*

liability insurance]'.[168] 'Indeed, provided that the problems of moral hazard and adverse selection can be addressed, softening the retributive punch of the common law would seem to be good business [for insurers]. Thus, the more importance courts give to notions of retribution in developing their approach to punitive damages, the stronger the objection to insurance for punitive damages'.[169] As Baker says, with insurance in place the retributive function of a punitive award will be 'muted' at best, although he does point to the likely social stigma of a punitive award notwithstanding insurance coverage.[170] Yet the Law Commission completely elides the important difference between deterrence and retribution as the basis for punitive damages, once again.

The Commission also advances some questionable arguments in favour of insurability. They point out that where defendants lack means they are not worth suing unless they carry insurance; thus, the argument runs, it would be 'futile' to discuss advancing aims of punitive damages unless defendants are given the capacity to pay them.[171] The suggestion here is the very odd one that if we are to punish a defendant, we need to make sure that someone else will bear the penalties to be imposed upon him. Equally dubious is the Commission's argument that insurance, by guaranteeing a solvent defendant, will promote 'satisfaction' of claimants, of importance where 'a significant number of cases in this area could involve the violation of important rights of plaintiffs, yet no or very little compensatable loss'.[172] This argument seems to envisage yet another purpose for punitive damages – not a punitive one focused on the defendant's conduct at all, but rather a claimant-oriented goal, the vindication of rights. However in English law this is traditionally done by the award of nominal damages, or a simple declaration by the court, where the defendant is found to have infringed the claimant's rights in a tort actionable per se, without causing loss.[173] The House of Lords has disapproved the enlargement of actionability per se as a 'peg' on which to hang claims for punitive damages.[174] Punitive damages are not available under the Human Rights Act 1998 to remedy violations of Convention rights.[175] On the other hand, as discussed above, the Supreme Court has recently rejected a new category of 'vindicatory damages', partly on the ground that their function would overlap with punitive damages.[176]

Baker argues that in one respect, the deterrent or (as he prefers) 'preventive' function of punitive damages might be advanced by insurance. Insurability means that punitive damages are more likely to be paid, and therefore claimed, and this enhances the 'norm projection' function of such awards.[177] However, Baker admits that the 'outrageous wrongdoer' is likely to be well aware of the relevant legal standards; it is the prospect of paying a large punitive award that will alter his behaviour and yet this, as seen above, is

168 Baker 1998, p. 101.
169 *Ibid.*, at p. 128.
170 *Ibid.*, at p. 112.
171 Law Com Rep, at 5.237.
172 Law Com Rep, at 5.241.
173 See e.g. *Constantine v. Imperial Hotels* [1944] KB 693.
174 *Watkins v. Home Office* [2006] UKHL 17.
175 *Anufrijeva v. Southwark LBC* [2004] QB 1124, [55].
176 See p. 187 above.
177 Baker 1998, p. 109.

undercut by the same presence of insurance. Thus any educative advantages of insurability would appear to be outweighed by the negative consequences for deterrence. The overall case for insurability of punitive damages, as advanced by the Law Commission, appears weak.

6. Costs

The award of costs (which 'follow the event' in the English, loser-pays system) is not strictly an issue of punitive damages at all. But it deserves brief mention, since current concern about over-deterrence in defamation suits has centred on the cost of litigation, rather than the level of damages (punitive or compensatory). The point is not new, however. In *Broome v. Cassell*, Lord Wilberforce (as seen, a supporter of punitive damages) said that:

> 'the strongest argument against [punitive damages] is that English law already contains a heavy, indeed exorbitant, punitive element in its costs system; contrast the United States where it is the absence of this (advocate's costs not being normally recoverable) which is invoked as a justification for punitive damages. One or other must clearly be reformed, and it is Parliament alone that can do it'.[178]

For freedom of speech pressure groups, denouncing the 'chilling effect' of the English libel laws,[179] it is the cost of litigation that has been at the forefront of their campaign. It is costs rather than punitive damages that need reform, in their view. In its recent report on 'Press Standards, Privacy and Libel'[180] the House of Commons Culture, Media and Sport Committee devoted considerable space (paragraphs 237–309) discussing the costs of litigation, whereas only three paragraphs were necessary for damages in libel cases ('much lower than in the past').[181] Of punitive damages in this area it was sufficient to note in passing that they were 'rarely awarded' because of the need to prove deliberate wrongdoing and the profit motive.[182] Punitive damages are evidently not a major concern for parliamentarians, nor the journalists that gave evidence to them.

The costs of libel litigation in England are said to be high compared to other European jurisdictions,[183] a problem which has been exacerbated by the recovery of higher 'success fees' (and 'After the Event Insurance' premiums) under the 'no-win, no-fee' funding system for litigation contained in the Access to Justice Act 1999. As the Committee commented, 'these measures, whatever their virtues, have not slowed the rise in litigation

178 *Broome v. Cassell*, 1114–5.

179 See e.g. www.libelreform.org.

180 House of Commons Culture, Media and Sport Committee 2010.

181 *Ibid.*, par. 122.

182 *Ibid.*, par. 124.

183 *Cf.* Oxford Centre for Socio-Legal Studies 2008. Cited by House of Commons Culture, Media and Sport Committee 2010, par. 247–248. But Howarth 2011, pp. 403–404, describes the figures as 'highly implausible', the study's conclusions as 'unwarranted' and its method 'extremely weak'. The researchers simply asked two lawyers from an English law firm, and from various other countries, to estimate the cost for litigating two anonymised cases.

costs and may have accelerated it, raising at the same time new problems in relation to press freedom'.[184] The editor of the Guardian newspaper testified that the 'staggeringly expensive' defence costs in libel actions were 'a great discouragement to the forms of investigative journalism about things that I think everybody would agree are public interest'.[185] The European Court of Human Rights has recently held that success fees in an action against a newspaper for invasion of privacy had a disproportionate impact upon freedom of speech under Article 10 ECHR.[186]

It may be that these concerns are misplaced or exaggerated. David Howarth has recently argued that there are no reliable empirical data upon which to base the current 'moral panic' about libel costs.[187] Whether or not the perception is correct, however, it exists – and is 'so firmly established in the political debate that those concerned with libel reform usually take it for granted and move immediately to a discussion of what should be done'.[188] Perhaps not surprisingly, the Government has accepted these criticisms of the libel costs regime that are so widely felt, whatever their evidential status. An initial attempt to curb libel fees foundered in the run-up to the General Election of 2010.[189] However, the new Coalition Government has promised to act as part of a more general review of the cost of civil litigation.[190] It has also issued a Draft Bill and Consultation on reform of the substance of libel law.[191] Notably for our purposes, there has been no discussion about punitive damages in all of the concern about the 'chilling effect' of libel law on freedom of speech.

7. Conclusion

Punitive damages linger on in English law, in something of a vestigial state. Perhaps the 'confinement' strategy of Lord Devlin has in the end proved successful, notwithstanding the demise of the 'cause of action test' in *Kuddus*. The separation of compensation from punishment in tort remedies remains a question of great academic interest, but apparently little practical significance. The recent debates over libel and freedom of speech demonstrate this. Libel law strongly influences the behaviour of journalists and other publishers, not necessarily for the good. But it is the impact of costs that it is the major concern, with the incidence of liability (and the substantive defences to it) of secondary concern – and the much-debated topic of punitive damages apparently no concern at all.

Nobody could pretend that the English law on punitive damages is in a rational or satisfactory state. None of the judges who have contributed to that jurisprudence seems to approve of the rules that have, somehow, emerged from the process. It bears all the

184 House of Commons Culture, Media and Sport Committee 2010, par. 253.
185 *Ibid.*, par. 243.
186 *MGN Ltd v. United Kingdom*, 18 January 2011. *Cf. Campbell v. MGN Ltd (no 2)* [2005] UKHL 61.
187 Howarth 2011, p. 419 (and passim).
188 Howarth 2011, p. 398.
189 Ministry of Justice 2010a. *Cf.* 'Overhaul of libel laws "will have to wait"', *The Independent* (London), 8 April 2010.
190 Ministry of Justice 2010b, especially par. 157.
191 Ministry of Justice 2011.

scars of a messy compromise. Abolitionists such as Lord Reid, thwarted by precedent, have grudgingly confined punitive damages as much as they can, whatever the cost in rationality. Expansionists such as Lord Wilberforce, Lord Denning or Lord Nicholls have not been able to attract majority support so as to break free of 'the categories'. The Law Commission's major report on the subject is marred by the complete absence of empirical research into the effect of punitive damages on real world behaviour, and thus efficacy for their stated goal of deterrence. The British Government has been content to leave that report on the dusty shelf marked 'too difficult for legislation'. None of this shows English law, and its mechanisms for reform, in a very good light. This rather dispiriting tale of 'tasks declined' and 'footpaths untrod'[192] at least provides food for thought for the torts scholar – and a cautionary lesson for putative reformers of the law: both the judges who can't, and the legislators who won't.

8. Epilogue: Is Europe Missing Out?

Nothing as strong as a positive recommendation for the European lawyer or policy-maker can be drawn from the foregoing, concerning the substantive question: is Europe missing out by not recognising punitive damages?[193] Largely the concern of this paper has been with the mechanisms of legal change in English law. What the story shows is that, perhaps unsurprisingly, leaving legal reform of a highly controversial matter for judicial elaboration through the common law may not work well. Individual judges will harbour differing views of the proper direction of the law, leading to continuing uncertainty. This does seem to be a subject where legislation is necessary to bring the debate to an end: we will soon 'celebrate' the demi-centenary of *Rookes v Barnard*, with little sign of consensus emerging. How should the legislator proceed? The plea for rigorous empirical research into the impact of (potential) liability on defendants must be reiterated – in both the straightforward situation and problematic variants such as insurability and vicarious liability. The Law Commission for England and Wales does not set a happy example here, either. Finally, on the issue of substance, note that some judges and commentators have cheerfully accepted the 'illogicality' of awarding punitive damages in tort claims – but defended the practice nonetheless, as a pragmatic and sensible addition to the law's armoury.[194] It would be an exercise in legal chauvinism to suggest that English lawyers have any kind of monopoly on common sense; nevertheless, for those who are attracted by the Law Commission's conclusion that punitive damages retain their value in some situations, the relatively fluid and un-theorized common law readily allows them their space where the more thoroughly worked-out character of a Civilian system, perhaps, might not.

192 Browning, *The Lost Leader* (1845).

193 *Cf.* Edelman 2008.

194 *Cf.* text to n. 24 (Lord Wilberforce); Law Com Rep (especially *cf.* text at nn. 65–69); Wells 2010.

Bibliography

Baker 1998
Baker, T., 'Reconsidering insurance for punitive damages', *Wis L Rev*, 1998, pp. 101–131.

British Chambers of Commerce 2004
British Chambers of Commerce, *Are Regulators Raising Their Game? UK Regulatory Impact Assessments in 2002/3*, London: British Chambers of Commerce, 2004.

Burrows 2011
Burrows, A., 'Damages and rights' in: D. Nolan & A. Robertson (eds.), *Rights and Private Law*, Oxford: Hart, 2011.

Buxton 2009
Buxton, R., 'How the common law gets made: *Hedley Byrne* and other cautionary tales', *Law Q Rev*, 2009, pp. 60–78.

Cane 2006
Cane, P.F., *Atiyah's Accidents, Compensation and the Law*, Cambridge: CUP, 2006.

Chapman & Trebilcock 1989
Chapman, B. & Trebilcock, M.J., 'Punitive damages: Divergence in search of a rationale', *Ala L Rev*, 1989, pp. 741–831.

Coffee 1981
Coffee, J.C., 'No Soul To Damn. No Body To Kick: An Unscandalized Inquiry into the Problem of Corporate Punishment', *Mich L Rev*, 1981, pp. 386–460.

Comptroller and Auditor General 2004
Comptroller and Auditor General, *Evaluation of Regulatory Impact Assessments: Compendium Report 2003–04*, London: HMSO, 1994.

Daniels & Martin 1990
Daniels, S. & Martin, J., 'Myth and reality in punitive damages', *Minn L Rev,* 1990, pp. 1–65.

Department for Business, Innovation and Skills 2009
Department for Business, Innovation and Skills, *Better Regulation, Better Benefits: Getting the Balance Right*, London: HMSO, 2009.

Devlin 1962
Devlin, *Samples of Lawmaking*, Oxford: OUP, 1962.

Edelman 2008
Edelman, J., 'In defence of exemplary damages' in: C.E.F. Rickett (ed.), *Justifying Private Law Remedies*, Oxford: Hart, 2008.

Ellis 1982
Ellis, D.D., 'Fairness and efficiency in the law of punitive damages', *S Cal L Rev*, 1982, pp. 1–79.

Friendly 1963
Friendly, H.J., 'The Gap in Lawmaking – Judges Who Can't and Legislators Who Won't', *Colum L Rev*, 1963, pp. 787–808.

Garber 1998
Garber, S., 'Product liability punitive damages, business decisions and economic outcomes', *Wis L Rev*, 1998, pp. 237–297.

Genn, Partington & Wheeler 2006
Genn, H., Partington, M. & Wheeler, S., *Law in the real world: Improving our understanding of how law works*, London: Nuffield Foundation, 2006.

Giliker 2010
Giliker, P., *Vicarious Liability in Tort: A Comparative Perspective*, Cambridge: CUP, 2010.

Harris, Campbell & Halson 2002
Harris, D., Campbell, D. & Halson, R., *Remedies in Contract and Tort*, London: Butterworths, 2002.

House of Commons Culture, Media and Sport Committee 2010
House of Commons Culture, Media and Sport Committee, *Press Standards, Privacy and Libel, 2nd Report of Parliamentary Session 2009–10*, London: HMSO, 2010.

Howarth 2011
Howarth, D., 'The cost of libel actions: A sceptical note', *Cambridge L J*, 2011, pp. 397–419.

Kritzler & Kahn Zemans 1998
Kritzler, H.M. & Kahn Zemans, F., 'Measuring the shadow of punitive damages: Their effect on bargaining, litigation and corporate behavior', *Wis L Rev*, 1998, pp. 157–169.

Law Commission 1993
Law Commission for England and Wales, *Consultation Paper No 132, Aggravated, Exemplary and Restitutionary Damages*, London: HMSO, 1993.

Law Commission 1997 ('Law Com Rep')
Law Commission for England and Wales, *Report No 247, Aggravated, Exemplary and Restitutionary Damages*, London: HMSO, 1997.

Law Commission 2008
Law Commission for England and Wales, *Consultation Paper No 187, Administrative Redress: Public Bodies and the Citizen*, London: HMSO, 2008.

Law Commission 2010
Law Commission for England and Wales, *Report No 322, Administrative Redress: Public Bodies and the Citizen*, London: HMSO, 2010.

Levin 2008
Levin, J., *Tort Wars*, Cambridge: CUP, 2008.

Matthews, Morgan & O'Cinneide 2008
Matthews, M.H., Morgan, J.E. & O'Cinneide, C., *Hepple and Matthews' Tort Cases and Materials*, Oxford: OUP, 2008.

Milsom 1981
Milsom, S.F.C., *Historical Foundations of the Common Law*, London: Butterworths, 1981.

Ministry of Justice 2010a
Ministry of Justice, *Controlling Costs in Defamation Proceedings: Reducing Conditional Fee Agreement Success Fees (Response to Consultation)*, London: HMSO, 2010.

Ministry of Justice 2010b
Ministry of Justice, *Proposals for Reform of Civil Litigation Funding and Costs in England and Wales: Implementation of Lord Justice Jackson's Recommendations*, London: HMSO, 2010.

Ministry of Justice 2011
Ministry of Justice, *Draft Defamation Bill: Consultation Paper CP3/11*, London: HMSO, 2011.

Morgan 2009
Morgan, J.E., 'Policy reasoning in tort law: The courts, the Law Commission and the critics', *Law Q Rev*, 2009, pp. 215–222.

Ogus 1997
Ogus, A., 'Exemplary damages and economic analysis' in: K. Hawkins (ed.), *The Human Face of Law: Essays in Honour of Donald Harris*, Oxford: OUP, 1997.

Oxford Centre for Socio-Legal Studies 2008
Oxford Centre for Socio-Legal Studies, *A comparative study of costs of defamation proceedings across Europe*, Oxford: University of Oxford, 2008.

Priest 1989
Priest, G.L., 'Insurability and punitive damages', *Ala L Rev*, 1989, pp. 1009–1037.

Rustad 1998
Rustad, M.L., 'The incidence, scope and purpose of punitive damages: Unravelling punitive damages: Current data and Further inquiry', *Wis L Rev*, 1998, pp. 15–71.

Sturley 2010
Sturley, M.F., 'Vicarious liability for punitive damages', *La L Rev*, 2010, pp. 501–529.

Sykes 1984
Sykes, A.O., 'The economics of vicarious liability', *Yale L J*, 1984, pp. 1231–1283.

Wells 2010
Wells, M.L., 'A common lawyer's perspective on the European perspective on punitive damages', *La L Rev*, 2010, pp. 557–579.

Widiss 1994
Widiss, A.I., 'Liability insurance coverage for punitive damages? Discerning answers to the conundrum created by disputes involving conflicting public policies, pragmatic considerations and political actions', *Vill L Rev*, 1994, pp. 455–505.

PART II

PUNITIVE DAMAGES IN EUROPE

Evelien de Kezel*

THE PROTECTION AND ENFORCEMENT OF PRIVATE INTERESTS BY (THE RECOGNITION OF US) PUNITIVE DAMAGES IN BELGIUM: LIMITS AND OPPORTUNITIES

1. Introductory Remarks

Without any doubt, there exists a growing tendency in Belgium, as in other European countries, to consider tort law as a policy tool to address social needs.[1] This development is fuelled by a popular desire to strengthen the capacity of private law and to give private law enforcement more teeth and tools. Tort law, for instance, would not only serve the purpose of compensating for loss caused, but would also act as a means to punish irresponsible and reprehensible behaviour, leaving aside the possibilities made available by criminal law, especially in cases where such behaviour cannot (also) be criminally sanctioned.[2]

Illustrative of this view are the comments made by Lindenbergh with respect to a decision of the Supreme Court of the Netherlands of 9 September 2009.[3] The decision dealt with the compensation of survivors who lost a family member as a result of a deliberately caused accident:[4]

> For the legal community, it seems obvious that criminal law is meant to punish and civil law intends to repair by awarding damages. But the question is whether this view is today still acceptable for a plaintiff. As far as I am concerned, the law should show a bit more teeth because I believe this will do more justice to the survivors' feeling that justice has been done.

Both the legislature and the courts have prepared the ground for such use in certain areas of private law in Continental Europe.[5]

* Assistant Professor at the Molengraaff Institute for Private Law, Utrecht, and Attorney at Law at Stibbe, Brussels Bar. The author would like to thank Jachin Van Doninck for his comments on an earlier draft.

1 A so called "instrumentalist view on tort law". See on the issue Kortmann 2009 at p. 6.

2 *Ibid.*

3 Supreme Court, 9 September 2009, LJN BI8583, see www.rechtspraak.nl.

4 See http://weblogs.nrc.nl/rechtenbestuur/2009/11/24/uitspraak-42-smartengeld-alleen-bij-directe-confrontatie-met-het-drama/ (free translation by the author).

5 The author refers to Borghetti's contribution on French law in that regard (Borghetti 2009).

However, this contribution will not focus on the punitive elements which have already been introduced by Belgian legislation or jurisprudence in the area of private law. Instead, the focus will be on considering the role of punitive damages from a Belgian legal perspective. Despite the overall tendency to introduce punitive elements in the private law system, it cannot be denied that the focus of the Belgian tort law system remains unchanged to date, just as it is the case in the other countries in continental Europe. Tort law is still primarily and essentially aimed at compensating for actual loss suffered. That does not mean, however, that it is not worthwhile examining whether the use of private law in protecting citizens' private interests can be strengthened through the use of punitive damages.

Punitive damages are damages awarded to an injured party that exceed the amount necessary to compensate the victim for the actual loss suffered, and act as a reprimand. The rationale behind them is that the interests of both society and the individual plaintiff can be met by imposing additional damages on the defendant. In this contribution, the restraints and possibilities in using punitive damages in protecting and enforcing private interests in Belgium will be explored.

In considering the issue, the author will focus on two key questions. First, the Belgian way of addressing issues of physical loss or harm and how it differs from the US approach will be reviewed. Secondly, the issue whether the Belgian practice leaves room for awarding punitive damages, above or next to damages that are meant to repair actual loss, will be examined. Whether US judgments awarding punitive damages are open for enforcement under Belgian law will also be considered. Finally, EU initiatives which envision the development of new enforcement mechanisms in areas such as competition, environment, consumer protection, and health will be briefly considered. Their ability to bridge "the Atlantic divide" will be assessed.

2. Restraints in Awarding Punitive Damages under Belgian Law: a Different Approach with Respect to Handling Damage Claims

2.1. Awarding Damages under Belgian Law

There are several legal sources for injury compensation under Belgian law.[6] First and foremost, the general rules of tort law offer victims the opportunity to obtain compensation when the damaging act is attributable to a third party "tortfeasor". The Civil Code ("C.C.") also contains liability provisions based on a no-fault behaviour (e.g., nuisance – Article 544 C.C.)[7] on a presumption of fault (e.g., liability of the parents) as well as strict liability (including, for example, liability of the house owner or principal or the

6 Bocken 2001 at pp. 244–273; pp. 270–271.

7 Article 544 C.C. states that ownership is the right to absolute use and enjoyment of goods as long as this use does not breach any law or regulations. If landowners unreasonably disturb the 'relationship' between their property and the neighbouring properties, they must – even when they acted lawfully – compensate the victims and thus restore the balance. Fault is no longer required. The judge examines the conditions prevailing in a certain neighbourhood and then decides whether an unreasonable disturbance has taken place.

keeper of an animal[8] or liability for defective products).[9] When the tortious act also qualifies as a breach of contract, contract law prevails. As a result of an important decision of Belgian's highest appellate court, the Court of Cassation, in 1973,[10] the victim can no longer choose between whether to take an action based on tort or an action based on contract in such cases. Contractual claims are based on Article 1142 C.C. (compensation for injury) and Article 1184 C.C. (forced execution of the contract, with a possible penalty).[11]

When one is a victim of an accident which has caused physical damage to that person, liability can be asserted under both criminal law and tort law. According to Article 4 of the Preliminary Title of the Belgian Criminal Procedure Code, victims of a criminal offence have the option of bringing their case either before a criminal court or a civil (non-criminal) court.

It is upon the victim to decide which type of action should be taken against the tortfeasor: a criminal action (most probably by way of a 'constitution as a civil party'),[12] a tort action, or an action based on strict liability such as one that is available under the Product Liability Act.[13]

The advantage of a criminal action is that the investigating judge will have to gather all the evidence. Belgian criminal courts would assert jurisdiction over the case if one of the constituting elements of the criminal offence were to be situated in Belgium (for instance, in the case of a personal injury claim, such elements would be the actual injury, the appearance of the injuries, the death of the victim).

The causing of death or bodily injury falls under the general provisions sanctioning manslaughter (involuntary homicide) or involuntary bodily injuries (Articles 418–420 of the Belgian Penal Code). The basic elements that make up this type of criminal offences are (i) negligence, (ii) the death or personal injury of a person, and (iii) a causal relationship between the negligence and the death or personal injury. The criminal offence is deemed to exist when these elements are established.

As the term "involuntary bodily injuries or homicide" implies, no specific intent is required for one to be punished under the said provisions of the Penal Code. Unlike US Law, criminal liability in Belgium resulting from negligence is not limited to gross negligence. Negligence or the "lack of prudence or care" is sufficient. The notion of

8 Articles 1384 to 1386 C.C.

9 Article 1384, para. 1 C.C. attributes liability to the custodian of a defective item for damage caused by the defect.

10 Cour de Cassation/Hof van Cassatie, hereafter referred to as "Supreme Court (Belgium)" 7 December 1973, *A.C.* 1974, 395.

11 For more details, see Bocken 2001, pp. 244–273; pp. 270–271.

12 A criminal process can not only be initiated by the Public Prosecutor, but also by the victim of the criminal offence. The first possibility is to summon the suspect of the offence directly before the criminal court. The second possibility is the constitution of a civil party. This means that an investigating judge is automatically entrusted with the case. The judge is obliged to conduct a judicial inquiry against all possible suspects. At the stage of the judicial inquiry, the civil party does not, however, have the right to affect the course of the inquiry. The advantage of a criminal action, by means of a "constitution as a civil party" is that the investigating judge gathers the necessary evidence (whereas in a purely 'civil' suit, the plaintiff-private person is to gather the evidence).

13 See hereafter.

negligence under criminal law is identical to that of fault under tort law.[14] It includes all forms of faults, even the slightest. Consequently, as soon as a fault is established in the sense of Article 1382 of the C.C. (see below), the first elements of Articles 418–420 of the Penal Code would be established.[15]

The victim can also opt for a tort action by bringing the case before a civil (*i.e.*, non-criminal) court, which would necessarily mean that someone's fault must be established.

A pure civil action can also be pursued under the Product Liability Act. Damage claims stemming from defective products do not necessarily lead to a criminal or tort-based action. Victims of damage caused by defective products often seek compensation by way of civil (non-criminal) claims, which can be based on the Product Liability Act of 25 February 1991 (entered into force on 1 April 1991), providing for a strict liability of the producer (the manufacturer). Under this Act, victims are only required to prove the defect in causal connection with the damage, without having to establish negligence. The burden of proof required by this Act is less stringent, since no fault has to be established by the victim, who can actually limit the pieces of evidence to be produced to those relating to the defect of the product, the damage, and the causal relationship between the defect and the damage.[16] As far as damages caused by defective product are concerned, the Act itself contains no limitations for damages caused to the victim, which means that compensation can be claimed for both material (physical) and moral damages. To date, no major product liability cases (such as the tobacco and asbestos litigations in the United States) have ever arisen in Belgium.

Ultimately, the legislator has created a number of special legal regimes which apply to specific areas in order to ameliorate the situation of victims by providing them with quasi-automatic indemnification.[17] The Belgian health insurance system (part of the social security system) provides (albeit limited) financial assistance to the victim.[18] The liability and social security system is supplemented and sometimes substituted by alternative compensation schemes with the focus being shifted towards the needs of the victim. The development of alternative compensation schemes in Belgium started with

14 The requirements for criminal liability under Articles 418–420 of the Criminal Code, are – in general – identical to those for personal tort liability covered by Articles 1382–1383 of the C.C. Belgian law accepts that an offence committed under criminal law necessarily constitutes a fault in the sense of Articles 1382–1383 C.C. Hence, fulfilment of the conditions for liability under Articles 418–420 Criminal Code automatically implies liability under Articles 1382–1383 C.C. See, for example, Supreme Court (Belgium) 19 February 1988, *R.W.* 1988–1989, 159.

15 *Ibid.*

16 For an overview of possible actions under tort law, see Bocken & Boone 2011; see also Vansweevelt & Weyts 2009.

17 With regard to damages for personal injury, it is significant that the Belgian legislator has elaborated a social security system that covers a large part of the economic losses sustained in accidents resulting in personal injury, particularly medical expenses and loss of income. It covers the wide range of medical care and the payment of disability benefits. The beneficiary of the social insurance must pay a share of the cost in order to reduce the medical costs. The right to social security stems, in principle, from employment and is not based on citizenship. For a recent overview, see also Bocken & Boone 2011.

18 Social security is not examined in this article, except as a point of reference.

the introduction of the industrial compensation regulation [1971],[19] followed by the introduction of third-party motor insurance [1995].[20] The recent introduction of a compensation scheme for asbestos victims and for medical injury victims can also be considered part of this development.[21] These compensation schemes were not developed on the basis of an overall plan, but resulted from some fundamental viewpoints on the design of the compensation system, particularly within the area of personal injuries. The main viewpoint was that the general law of torts and social security was an inexpedient compensation mechanism, and that the aim should instead be to develop schemes that were better designed to meet personal injury victims' needs in some appealing areas.

Unless expressed in the contrary, the victim is free to choose from which source(s) compensation may be obtained.[22] However, the social security legislation contains rules regulating the co-ordination between social security benefits and damages, which generally means that, as a main rule, the relevant public authority has a right of recourse against the tortfeasor. Once a social security organisation or liability insurer has compensated the victim, it generally takes over the victim's rights against liable parties (by means of subrogation). However, collateral benefits which do not constitute compensation for damage sustained may be added to any compensation awarded under tort law. This is the case, for example, with sums due under a life insurance policy (*i.e.*, first party insurance). Hence, at least as far as personal injury is concerned, the role of tort law is largely concerned with the final allocation of losses by means of recourse actions brought by social institutions and private insurers. The main function of the system of damages in Belgium is to provide supplementary cover in order to fill the various "gaps" and limitations in the social security system, in particular to compensate the loss of income over and above the limits set by the social security system as well as the so-called non-pecuniary consequences of an injury.

Hereafter, the following will be explored in detail: the characteristics of the fault and no-fault compensation systems in Belgium; how they complement and interact with one another; and the room they leave with respect to awarding punitive damages as an enforcement mechanism.

2.2. *Characteristics of the Fault Liability System in Belgium*

As stated above, within the framework of general civil law, the Belgian Civil Code, which is based on the French Napoleonic Code of 1804, contains the basic provisions governing

19 Act 3 July 1967, *Moniteur Belge* (hereafter "*M.B.*") 13 April 1967.

20 Act 1 July 1956, substituted by Act 21 November 1989, *M.B.* 8 December 1989.
Act 30 March 1994, *M.B.* 31 March 1994, substituted by Act 13 April 1995, *M.B.* 27 June 1995, and by Act 19 January 2001, *M.B.* 21 February 2001.

21 See de Kezel 2009, pp. 191–220.

22 The social security organisations are under an obligation to pay any award due within a certain time period without waiting for the outcome of a civil litigation. As for the victim, the social benefits received from a public body are deducted from the amount of damages, which thus cover 'net losses' only. Any action in tort brought by the victim against the tortfeasor, or any claim under the private insurance policy, can only concern unrecovered losses. In any event, the total amount of compensation awarded to the victim should not exceed the actual damage suffered.

the law of damages in Belgium. Articles 1382 and 1383 of the C.C.,[23] require anyone who, because of his conduct (act or omittance) or negligence, is culpable for having caused harm to another person, to compensate that person for all the damage caused.

Under the fault liability system, the victim must prove the following in order to obtain compensation for the losses suffered: (1) the defendant acted with fault or negligence; (2) the existence of a causal link between this damage and an act or an omission of the defendant; and (3) the damage.[24]

2.2.1. First Condition: the Existence of a Tortious Act[25]

The notion of fault is the main requirement for personal tort liability under Belgian law with the other requirements being a certain and foreseeable damage and a causal relationship between the fault (even a slightest fault) and the damage. Hence, these three basic elements constitute the notion of fault under Belgian law:

1) the accountability of the defendant, which is left to the judge's discretion;
2) the existence of a tortious act;
3) the "foreseeability" of (some) damage.

Under Belgian law there are two types of acts within the concept of "tortious act". The first type is a breach of a statutory provision (an Act or a governmental regulation) containing a specific rule of conduct (an order or a ban) whereby the mere infringement of it automatically constitutes a tortious act for which the infringer can be held liable (if the claimant has suffered a damage or loss as a result of this tortious act).

The concept of a statutory provision is construed extensively by Belgian case law. Even disciplinary rules containing a specific rule of conduct can constitute statutory provisions so that any breach of them can give rise to liability in tort. Still, this concept seems to be limited to (i) the disciplinary rules adopted by professional institutions and which have been subsequently ratified by a statute or by a governmental regulation and (ii) the binding disciplinary rules enacted by professional institutions themselves, provided that those institutions have been empowered by statute to enact these binding rules without ratification by the government.[26]

The second type is the violation of the standard of due care. To determine whether a person has violated this standard, the court must examine whether that person has behaved as a normally prudent and reasonable person, when put in the same circumstances, would have done. It is noteworthy that the Belgian Supreme Court ruled several times that a person who has abided by all the statutory rules of conduct which apply to his/her

23 Which state the following, respectively: "Any act of man which causes damage to another, obliges the one by whose fault the damage occurred to compensate for this"; "A person is not only liable for the damage which he caused by its deed, but also for the damage he caused by its negligence or imprudence".

24 For a recent overview, see Bocken & Boone 2011; see also Vansweevelt & Weyts 2009.

25 Cornelis 1989, no. 13.

26 Cornelis 1989, no. 154; Hannequart & Henry 1999, pp. 52–54.

situation, does not automatically mean that this person has also observed the (general) standard of due care.[27]

2.2.2. Second Condition: the Existence of a Causal Link between the Tortious Act and the Damage

With regard to the establishment of a causal link, Belgian law applies the theory of the "equivalence of conditions". An event is to be considered as the cause of the damage if it has contributed to the occurrence of that damage. A is a cause of B if, when taking into account the concrete circumstances, B would not have occurred without A. All possible causes are judged on an equal basis. Indeed, Belgian law adopts an extremely broad concept of causality and does not distinguish between the tortious acts that have directly caused the damage and those that have done so indirectly.

The burden of proof is placed on the plaintiff (Article 870 Code of Procedural Law and Article 1315 C.C.). The standard of proof required is the "judiciary certitude", which means that the judge must be convinced by a high degree of probability. Hence, Belgian law does not provide for a presumption of causation or a reversal of the burden of proof. In reality, due to technical difficulties, the causal link is sometimes an insurmountable obstacle for the victim, for example, in medical negligence cases. In assessing the evidence, the courts can take into account the difficulty in establishing a negative fact such as absence of information (use of presumptions, etc.).[28]

Belgian law imposes "joint and several" liability when actions of several operators have given rise to the same inseparable damage.

2.2.3. Third Condition: the Existence of Loss Suffered as a Consequence of the Tortious Act

It has to be emphasised that a person who has committed a tortious act cannot be held liable to another person unless this act has inflicted damage to that injured person. According to Article 17 of the Belgian Code of Procedure, no action is admissible unless the claimant has a specific, personal, and direct interest in obtaining a judgment.

Thus, a Belgian court is only to administer justice when a specific, personal interest of a party is harmed or is seriously threatened (Article 18, para. 2 of the Belgian Code of Procedure). In this last situation the court can pronounce a declaratory judgment provided that – and the case-law is very strict on the subject – the claimant establishes that his/her interests are seriously threatened and that a declaratory judgment will be useful in this situation.[29] In that respect, legal scholars underline that litigating parties can never go before a Belgian court for the sole purpose of obtaining legal advice or to perform a test trial.[30]

27 Supreme Court (Belgium) 7 January 1999, *A.C.* 1999, 8; Supreme Court (Belgium), 23 June 1980, *R.W.* 1980–1981, 2324; Supreme Court (Belgium) 27 November 1974, *A.C.*1975, 370.

28 Supreme Court (Belgium) 16 December 2004, *A.C.* 2004, 2081.

29 Fettweis 1987, p. 39, no. 28.

30 Fettweis *1987*, no. 33.

The concept of damage is rather broad under Belgian law. As far as personal injury is concerned compensation may in principle be granted for death, impairment of the victim's health, damage to moveable and immovable goods, and for economic and immaterial losses resulting from the damage. As a rule, damage has to be actual and has to stand firm. Only persons who are directly and personally affected are granted with a right of action. A party to proceedings in Belgium must demonstrate that it has a personal interest; therefore, claims introduced by associations with the aim of protecting the general interest would lack standing under Belgian law.

It must be noted that if the conditions of a tort claim were met, the victim would have the right to claim full compensation for all its losses (see hereafter under section 3.1.1).

Awards available through tort liability law are generally higher than those available through no-fault compensation schemes (described in the following sections).

2.3. *Characteristics of the No-Fault Compensation Schemes in Belgium*

The main alternative compensation schemes for personal injury damages that are in force or are being developed in Belgium are described in this section. They are: (1) the compensation scheme for road traffic injuries; (2) the compensation scheme for victims of industrial injuries; (3) the compensation scheme for asbestos injuries; and (4) the compensation scheme for medical injuries.[31]

2.3.1. The Compensation Scheme for Road Traffic Injuries[32]

In 1956 the legislator introduced compulsory liability insurance for car owners, providing unlimited cover for liability for traffic accidents, in addition to the existing fault liability system.[33] In 1994 a bill inspired by the French *Loi Badinter* was adopted by the Belgian Parliament. This introduced a system of compulsory third party insurance with the aim of improving the legal position of victims of traffic accidents (pedestrians, cyclists, and passengers).[34] According to Article 29 bis of this Act, the liability insurer of the motor vehicle owner is obliged to compensate all bodily injuries resulting from an accident in which this vehicle was involved, regardless of any fault, unless he or she is able to prove that the victim consented to the accident and its consequences (and providing that the victim is not under the age of 14).

The injured party's entitlement to compensation under the scheme is not determined by means of a traditional description based on liability (whether fault or strict liability), but rather is based on a description of the type of accident (road traffic accident) and injuries covered by the scheme (personal injury of a pedestrian, cyclist or passenger). The insurance is compulsory and the injured party is entitled to bring a claim directly against the insurance company; any personal liability incurred by the tortfeasor does not have

[31] The existence of a special compensation scheme for the benefit of victims of crimes is common to all EU countries. Intentional criminal injuries are not considered in this study.

[32] For more details see Bocken 2001, pp. 244–273; pp. 270–271; see also Bocken & Boone 2011.

[33] Act 1 July 1956, substituted by Act 21 November 1989, *M.B.* 8 December 1989.

[34] Act 30 March 1994, *M.B.* 31 March 1994, substituted by Act 13 April 1995, *M.B.* 27 June 1995, and by Act 19 January 2001, *M.B.* 21 February 2001.

any actual practical importance.[35] The compensation scheme is financed on a collective basis by the parties that carry on the activity to which the relevant accidents/injuries can be attributed (drivers of motor vehicles) via the automobile insurance premiums. The insurance scheme for road traffic accidents is designed in such a way that it also covers the instances whereby liability in damages is incurred according to the general law of torts. This does not exclude the possibility of someone who may have incurred liability according to the general law of torts for damage or injury covered by the special scheme in question, so that the issue concerning the co-ordination between the cover under the scheme and the tortfeasor's liability arises.[36]

2.3.2. The Compensation Scheme for Victims of Industrial Injuries

In relation to victims of industrial accidents, the legislature introduced a system of strict liability in 1903, according to which the employer must (regardless of any fault) compensate any losses suffered by its employees for personal injury as a result of an industrial accident. Since the Act of 10 April 1971, however, the legislature has changed this liability system into an insurance system and obliges the employer to take out personal insurance for the benefit of its employees, providing coverage to them in the event of an industrial accident or an accident on the way to or from the workplace.[37] This insurance covers all the medical costs and costs of equipment and provides a fixed level of compensation for economic loss resulting from the disability (set generally at 90% of the employee's earnings). Non-pecuniary damages have been excluded from this scheme.

Compensation is payable irrespective of the existence of liability on the part of the employer. However, the right of the injured employee to bring a claim for compensation against his or her employer or co-workers on the basis of common law has been excluded, except in cases of property damage, accidents which occur on the way to and from the workplace, and where the accident was caused deliberately.[38] For the compensation of victims of occupational diseases, a compensation fund was set up in 1967.[39] The headlines

35 The same applies to any personal liability that is limited to, for example, certain instances of gross negligence where it may also be a formality whether the tortfeasor has incurred liability towards the injured party or only towards the insurance company, based on a right of recourse.

36 The compensation system for road traffic accidents is further complemented by the intervention of the Motor Accident Compensation Fund, which was set up in 1975 by liability insurers pursuant to a legislative mandate. Bodily injury is compensated by this Fund when the compensation system does not apply, for example, when the car that caused the accident cannot be identified or when the liability of the driver is not covered by liability insurance. The damages payable under the scheme are basically on a par with the damages payable according to the general law of torts. In this way, the compensation scheme is distinct from the ordinary social security system.

37 Accidents at work: Act 10 April 1971, *M.B.* 24 April 1971; For the compensation of occupational diseases a compensation fund was set up already in 1967 by the Occupational Diseases Act 3 July 1967, *M.B.* 13 April 1967.

38 As of today, the system still only exists for employees and public servants, the self-employed must claim from the public health insurance in relation to work-related personal injury losses. The claims handling process is special in the sense that a special body is set up to handle the administration of the compensation scheme, including in particular the receipt of claims forms, the investigation into the claims, and the authority to decide on the cases.

39 Act 3 July 1967, *M.B.* 13 April 1967.

of the compensation system are the same from the injured party's point of view. Since it is not always easy to identify at which employer the cause of a disease arose, a fund was established to compensate all employees suffering from occupational diseases whereby all employers contribute to the Fund.

2.3.3. The Compensation Scheme for Asbestos-Related Diseases[40]

The Belgian asbestos fund provides compensation for damages caused by asbestos exposure. The fund provides compensation to asbestos victims on the grounds that in asbestos cases, often no liability arises because of the limitation period or because the enterprise which caused the damage or the causal link has not been or cannot be identified.

The fund became operational on 1 April 2007. Only those affected by either mesothelioma or asbestosis qualify for compensation.[41] Both the victim or, in case of decease, his or her relatives are entitled to compensation. The entitlement for mesothelioma victims has been set at €1,500 per month. In the event of death, the spouse, legal partner or former partner or spouse receive a lump sum of €30,000. Their children are each entitled to €25,000. Asbestosis victims receive a monthly allowance calculated on the basis of €15 per percentage of physical impairment. In the event of death, €15,000 will be given to the spouse, legal partner or former partner or spouse and €12,500 to each of their children. The compensation scheme applies to those exposed to asbestos in Belgium, either in a professional setting or elsewhere. Having compensated the victims, the asbestos fund can exercise recourse against those responsible for the exposure. However, it is limited to cases of wilful misconduct, which makes the option rather theoretical. The fund is financed by contributions from the government, employers, and the self-employed. No distinction is made between those active in the asbestos industry and elsewhere. Therefore, the "polluter pays" principle does not apply.

2.3.4. The Compensation Scheme for Medical Injuries[42]

Another compensation scheme came into existence with the Law of 31 March 2010. The scheme is not operational yet, which means that the general rules for medical negligence claims still apply. The new system is governed by the principle that the patient and his or her next of kin are entitled to compensation for damage caused by a therapeutic event for which the medical practitioner cannot be held responsible, *i.e.*, the so-called "unavoidable damage". If the practitioner is responsible, the system of liability for medical negligence remains in force. Here, the law refers to "avoidable damage". Avoidable damage is damage which a careful medical practitioner acting under similar circumstances would have avoided, taking into account the patient's history and medical condition as well as the scientific knowledge available at the time, or secondly, it is damage within the scope of the rules on faultless liability.

40 See de Kezel 2008, pp. 17–28.
41 Lung cancer victims cannot claim compensation under this scheme.
42 See de Kezel 2009, pp. 191–220.

Through the newly established fund for medical accidents, patients will be able to seek compensation through a mere administrative filing. If the damage is qualified as avoidable, the fund will try to mediate and invite the medical practitioner and/or his or her insurance company to pay compensation (it should be noted that the new legislation did not install mandatory insurance for medical negligence claims). If no or insufficient insurance coverage is provided, the fund will provide compensation. The same applies when the fund considers the proposed compensation to be inadequate. If the practitioner or the insurer denies any wrongdoing, the fund will provide compensation if it finds the damage to be of a "serious" nature. For unavoidable damage, compensation will be provided if the damage is qualified as "serious", which means that the patient is affected by a permanent disability exceeding 25%, a temporary incapacity during six consecutive months or six months within one year, when the damage has a profound effect on the patient's living conditions (a criterion which offers room for discretion), or in case of death. The fund will be government financed. The compensation aims to cover all damages. Once the fund has compensated the victim, it will be able to exercise recourse against the practitioner or his or her insurer, a possibility that supposes a medical accident entailing avoidable damage.

2.3.5. Overview of Alternative Compensation Schemes in Belgium

	Automobile Accident Injuries	Industrial Injuries	Asbestos Injuries	Injuries to Patients
Statutory Basis	Act of 13 April 1995, *M.B.* 27 June 1995 / Act of 19 January 2001, *M.B.* 21 February 2001	Accidents at work: Act of 10 April 1971, *M.B.* 24 April 1971/ Occupational diseases: Act of 3 July 1967, *M.B.* 13 April 1967	Act of 27 December 2006, *M.B.* 28 December 2006/ Royal Decree of 11 May 2007, *M.B.* 29 May 2007	Act of 31 March 2010, *M.B.* 2 April 2010/ Act of 2 June 2010, *M.B.* 1 July 2010
Objective (Goal of the Compensation Mechanism)	To guarantee compensation independently from fault liability and other conditions for tort liability.	To combine accident and liability insurance – to avoid actions for damages.	To guarantee compensation to asbestos victims independently from fault liability and other conditions for tort liability– to simplify causation and evidence issues.	To improve compensation payments and avoid actions for damages based on fault liability.
Applicable areas of the Compensation Scheme (type of operation covered; type of damage covered; which victims can obtain compensation)	Pedestrians, cyclists and passengers.	Any employment relationship. Covers transport between home and the workplace. Accidents, occupational diseases.	All influences from asbestos exposure that result in mesothelioma or asbestosis.	Abnormal medical injuries that are not the result of a medical act or omission.

	Automobile Accident Injuries	Industrial Injuries	Asbestos Injuries	Injuries to Patients
Subject of Compensation	Permanent injury, loss of earning capacity, loss of support, pain and suffering at the same level as stipulated under the general law of torts. No cover for temporary loss of income, pain and suffering.	Permanent injury, loss of earning capacity, loss of support, no non-pecuniary loss, and only up to certain limits (e.g., one's maximum income).	Both pecuniary and non-pecuniary loss for the primary victim and his or her close relatives (if deceased) but only up to fixed amounts.	Same level as stipulated under the general law of torts.
Obligation to Invoke General Law of Tort First?	No	No	No	Yes
Right to Invoke General Law of Tort First?	Yes	No	Yes (but of no practical importance)	Yes
Supplementary Cover Provided by General Law of Torts?	Yes	Only to a limited extent	No	Yes
Action Against Contributor to the Scheme?	Yes	No	No	/
Recourse Against Third Party Tortfeasor?	Yes, if it is other than the contributor to the scheme.	Yes, if it is other than the contributor to the scheme.	Yes, if it is other than the contributor to the scheme.	Yes
Compensation Scheme Operator	No particular operator: Insurance company. Ordinary court of law.	Insurance for accidents at work; Fund for Occupational Diseases Injuries Board; Appeal: social courts	Public Body AFA; Appeal: social courts	Public Body; Appeal: social courts
Financing	Ordinary insurance premiums.	Ordinary insurance premiums (subject to some regulation). Contributions in the event of occupational disease.	Contributions by employers, state funding, and independent workers	State funded.

2.4. *Concluding Remarks*

Contrary to the US approach to damage claims (referred to as the "litigation explosion" or the "tort law industry"),[43] the Belgian approach to health impairment issues is a sort of "administrative approach" of the problem with a view of achieving fair and equal justice for all victims in the same position. The main function of the system of tort law in Belgium with respect to personal injury cases is to provide supplementary cover in order to fill the various "gaps" and limitations in its social security system, in particular to compensate the loss of income over and above the limits set by the social security system as well as the so-called non-pecuniary consequences of an injury. As a result of this system, the tort law system (including the possibility of awarding large sums of punitive damages) plays a fairly moderate role from the injured party's point of view.

Mainly in the field of personal injury compensation, victims are offered access to no-fault compensation schemes where the reimbursement conditions are much simpler than under the tort litigation system. The risk carriers have to contribute to the (public) insurance systems in proportion to the risk of damage generated by them. The idea is that these contribution requirements add to the deterrent and preventive effects of the system, and hence, effectuate the enforcement of private interests. Public agencies or public insurers are charged with managing these no-fault compensation systems.

The counterpart is that an appeal to the tort law system is often made impossible or is considered unnecessary to a (personal injury) victim in Belgium. Hence, the possibility for the tort law system to work as an enforcement mechanism – as is the case in the United States with its litigious culture jury trials, consolidated trials, forum shopping, union involvement (see hereafter) – is often neglected.

2.5. *Public Interest Litigation as a Means to Protect and Enforce Private Rights and Interests in the United States*

Different from the situation in Europe, the idea of social justice in the United States is closely connected with the idea of individuals acting as a "private prosecutor / private attorney general". The US Congress has passed laws authorising an individual or group to act in the public interest.[44] This system is deeply rooted in the American legal tradition. Instruments such as punitive damages are thereby meant to broaden the range of actions to those taking the law into their own hands, be it the environmental or civil rights activist, the deceived consumer or the plaintiff lawyer (in some states punitive damages can even be insured).

"Public interest litigation" in the United States is deemed to be a necessary counter-balance against economic power in a liberal society. In the American legal culture, "public interest litigation" means the use of litigation by private or public parties to achieve policy goals that could not be achieved through the legislative or regulatory processes.[45] Generally, lawsuits are fuelled by a desire to change the defendant's behavior, rather than the hope of collecting a monetary award to redress injuries sustained by the

43 Olson 2009, p. 6.
44 For references, see Kortmann 2009.
45 *Ibid.*

plaintiff. Companies must be held responsible for the victims who have been affected by the damage caused by these companies' actions.

Public interest litigation originated in the United States in the 1960s, when, amid challenges to many social systems such as the Civil Rights Movement and the Vietnam War, many public interest groups were formed with a view to protecting the environment and health, and consumers rights, as well as many other public interests.

Hence, litigation in the United States is used as a means to protect and enforce private rights and interests by setting aside illegal practices and behaviour, and by achieving directly or provoking indirectly the adoption of new standards or rules. Clearly, damages (and public interest litigation) serve a regulatory function in the United States. One can perceive the US model as one in which the judicial system serves as a counterpart to regulatory agencies. In the same way that governments in Europe find it efficient to establish broadly-based compensation mechanisms based on both fault and no-fault standards that are largely funded by tax incomes, it is deemed more efficient in the United States for the legal system to allow individual claimants to address (often product-related) concerns in a single suit with the aim of claiming a large amount of punitive damages from a potential tortfeasor. It is estimated that this also enables the legal system to take more of a market-based approach.[46]

The asbestos litigation in the United States provides the clearest example of the role of private prosecutors in exposing corporate wrongdoing through tort litigation there. In the past decades, asbestos companies and asbestos mining companies concealed the dangers of unprotected asbestos exposure from their workers and consumers for decades in a cold-blooded business decision.[47] Thus, starting from the mid-seventies, the asbestos firms were punished severely in the United States by being held liable for by large punitive damages awards.[48] The asbestos litigation issue also illustrates the significant difference between the United States and Europe. Asbestos (product liability) litigation in the United States is largely covered by private insurers and driven by claim mobilisers such as union workers and lawyers. Health screenings, sponsored by unions and/or lawyers tend to increase the number of plaintiffs. Thus, the US system is regarded by some as a litigation industry.

Asbestos litigation in Europe is on the whole less litigious. From a regulatory point of view, litigation in the field of asbestos injuries in Europe has often led to the creation of public funds as a means to compensate damage in a swift manner.[49] In France and Belgium such a special asbestos fund, the *Fonds d'indemnisation de l'amiante* or FIVA (in France)[50] and the *Fonds amiante* or AFA (in Belgium),[51] was established to indemnify all citizens for damage arising out of occupational or environmental (non-occupational) asbestos-related disease.[52] As for the employee, he may either select this compensation by the fund

46 Polinsky & Shavell 1998, p. 869 *et seq.*

47 See, e.g., Spender 2003.

48 *Ibid.*

49 See above for Belgium. In order to cope with the hundreds to thousands of asbestos cases, agencies or other public institutions are given the tasks of managing these cases.

50 See www.fiva.fr/.

51 See www.afa.fgov.be/.

52 This is, for example, also the case in the Netherlands, the United Kingdom, and Italy. In some countries where no fund has been set up by the legislature, the former asbestos companies have provided a

or bring a claim under the compensation scheme for victims of industrial injuries. Principally, the injured employee cannot file a claim under tort law against the employer.

Judicial systems within Europe are quite similar. Most European lawyers tend to criticize the potential of regulation by private litigation to generate suits against entire industries, resulting in large amounts of (punitive) damages.

In most European countries some portion of the financial consequences of asbestos is borne by the national health systems (rather than private industry (and their insurers), so there is no similar "appeal" to victims for them to show up (see above). Moreover, in Europe asbestos claims tend to be related to the employer rather than the manufacturer, and hence, are being sought under employment liability (or occupational diseases compensation systems) as opposed to product liability. For instance, in Belgium (see above under "no-fault compensation schemes") and France, compensation for occupational asbestos-related diseases is sought generally under the social security system. Compensation in these countries is provided in general without regard to whether the employer is at fault. In France, a higher compensation is possible via a claim under tort law against the employer, but only on the condition that the employee can prove that there was an "intentional fault" or "inexcusable fault" by the employer.[53] In Belgium, a higher compensation is only possible if the employee can prove that there was an "intentional fault" by the employer.

It must be noted that damages awards available through (ordinary) lawsuit are still higher than those available through public funds. Hence, although compensation awards under no-fault compensation schemes are available in a much easier way, the amount of compensation will generally be far lower than will be the case following a lawsuit, with the amount of full compensation of the damage as the absolute limit in Europe.

As a result of all this, the amount of victims compensated and the amount of damages awarded to (e.g. asbestos) victims is proportionally less in most European countries than in the United States.

3. Enforcing US Punitive Damages Awards in Belgium and Other European Countries: a Different Approach with respect to Protecting and Enforcing Private Interests

3.1. Compensation of Damage under Belgian Law: How Do Judges Exercise their Discretionary Power?[54]

3.1.1. The Concept of Damage under Belgian Law: Merely a Matter of Fact

In cases where a tort claim is available under Belgian law, damages awarded by the court are only meant to compensate the actual loss suffered by the victim of the tortious act. A

settlement payment arrangement (a private asbestos fund) as is the case in Switzerland, and was too in the Netherlands and Belgium before the entry into force of the public asbestos fund.

53 A 2002 court ruling expanded the definition of "inexcusable fault", thereby making it easier for an employee to claim against the employer in a liability action. See Court of Cassation (France) 28 February 2002, available at: www.courdecassation.fr/jurisprudence_2/chambre_sociale_576/arret_n_1158.html.

54 See also Cousy & Droshout 2001 pp. 28–53.

victim of a criminal offence or a tort (including damages covered by the Product Liability Act) may claim for all kinds of losses, either material or moral losses. The damage claimed must have occurred or there is certainty that the damage will occur. Hypothetical damage is no ground for an action. Damage occurring in the future can be recovered (only) if its realisation is beyond doubt.[55]

The provisions of the C.C. on the duty to compensate generally apply to all types of losses, including personal injury. Theoretically, the remedy must cover the entire damage suffered by the victim, although Belgian courts usually allow very limited damages as compensation for pain and suffering. Material damage concerns injury or harm caused to private assets belonging to the victim or to his/her business. It also pertains to personal injuries such as physical harm, loss of income, and loss of ability or capacity to earn. The capacity to earn and injuries will normally be evaluated on the basis of an expert's opinion. Intangible losses which extend to pure economic losses such as loss of profit, trade, clientele or business interruption can also be recovered under Belgian law.

The expression "moral damage" (*morele schade, dommage moral*) refers to possible pain and suffering of the victim (and/or the relatives). Compensation could, for example, be claimed by the victim for pain and suffering caused by the negligence (e.g. pain caused by the defective valves, the operation which had to be undergone, the stay of the victim in a hospital...). As has been noted above, Belgian courts are usually reluctant in granting extended compensation for such types of moral damage.

The amount of damages awarded will be determined by different criteria. The courts must take into account all circumstances of the case and evaluate the amount of the damage at the time the judgment is to be pronounced. If the exact amount of damages cannot be assessed on the basis of the precise and objective elements of the case, the court will proceed to an evaluation *ex aequo et bono*, *i.e.*, to an equitable assessment, which will also be rather limited.

Finally, and in light of what has been explained above, it must be emphasised that in Belgium, unlike the situation which exists under US law, the court cannot condemn the offender or wrongdoer to pay punitive damages. The aim of an award of damages under Belgian law is to place the injured person in the same position as he/she would have been in had the incident not occurred. Belgian law provides for the full compensation of the damages unlawfully caused to a third person, without consideration of the severity of the tortfeasor's fault or the economic position of the parties. All civil law claims (whether based on contract or tort) generally stem from the principle of full compensation, (whatever the type of accident or cause of action), the degree of fault, or the economic position of the parties.

It should be noted that in Belgium, there are no statutory limitations on compensation as to the type of recoverable losses or to the amount of damages. Since a landmark ruling of the Supreme Court [1881],[56] compensation for non-pecuniary losses has to be paid on the same basis as that for pecuniary losses.

As a main rule, the tort law regulation system merely sets up a general framework for the assessment of damages (the principle that full compensation should be paid for the

55 Supreme Court (Belgium) 8 January 1974, *Pas.* 1974, 474.
56 Supreme Court (Belgium) 17 March 1881, *Pas.* 1881, I, 163.

individual loss) so that the details are left to the courts. As stated, the tort law principles concerning the right to full compensation of pecuniary and non-pecuniary losses are equally applicable to contractual liability. However, for breach of contract, compensation can only be claimed for damage that was foreseen or foreseeable at the time the contract was concluded. It is sufficient that the occurrence of damage was foreseeable, even if the extent of the damage was not foreseeable (Article 1150 C.C.).

Since legislation only lays down some general principles, large parts of the law of torts in Belgium are developed through jurisprudence (judicial precedent). Thus, what is considered to be legally relevant damage under Belgian civil law rests largely on factual assessment.

3.1.2. Restraints to Punitive Damages under Belgian Law

As stated, the idea of punishment is not considered an aim of the law of tort in Belgium. Punitive damages (that is, damages which punish the defendant for his/her actions as opposed to damages which compensate the victim) are therefore not allowed under Belgian law. However, there is no unanimity as to whether compensation (albeit symbolic, for example, in the case of non-pecuniary loss) is the only aim of damages or whether tort law should serve further aims, such as prevention and deterrence.

It is generally acknowledged that the possibility of being held liable to pay damages may have a deterrent effect on a particular offender and also lead to a general preventive effect in certain cases, such as in cases of defamation and invasion of privacy. But in most other cases (such as personal injury cases), it can be doubted whether the risk of being held liable is likely to influence the conduct of a potential tortfeasor.

The Supreme Court has clearly stated that compensation should not amount to punishment of the tortfeasor [1972].[57] According to the Supreme Court, the aim of compensation for non-pecuniary loss is not to restore damage but to console the victim. By doing so, the judge attempts to compensate the victim for the loss he/she has suffered.[58]

Clearly, Belgian law is not acquainted with the system of punitive damages. Hence, the desire to uphold tort liability for preventive purposes has not played any role of importance in the implementation and financing of alternative compensation schemes such as the asbestos compensation scheme (see above). The emphasis of the Belgian legal system lies on the socialisation of the risk and the acceptance by public bodies and market players of an overriding obligation to provide a timely reparation of the injuries suffered.

3.1.3. Discretionary Powers of the Judge on the Amount of the Damages Award

Once the existence of the damage has been established, the victim has a right to compensation. Judges must award compensation for the losses which are established, but they can determine the amount of the award at their discretion.

57 Supreme Court (Belgium) 10 October 1972, *A.C.* 1973, 146.

58 *Ibid.*

The Supreme Court has always left the determination of the existence of damage and calculation of the amount of damages at the discretion of the trial judge, the judgment to be based on the evidence adduced by the plaintiff and the defendant. The Court has been very reluctant to intervene in any review of an assessment of damage(s), considering this is merely a "question of fact". This is the reason why the Belgian compensation system is still based on what the trial judges traditionally recognised as legally relevant damage. Academics have seldom tried to explore new methods in obtaining compensation by establishing (other) heads of damages. Academic writings have predominantly concentrated on the mere clarification of, and comments concerning, the awards and judgments of the Supreme Court and the lower courts.

When assessing the amount of non-pecuniary damages, the courts have always attached great importance to previous awards so as to introduce an element of consistency in the assessment of damages. However, the amount of damages for non-pecuniary losses has differed in the past – sometimes to a surprising extent – from one court to another.

To eliminate these undesired consequences of judges exercising their discretionary powers, and in order to avoid forum shopping, the two main associations of judges have drawn up a list of nomenclature of indicative amounts (the National Indicative Table) for quantifying damages for personal injury, coupled with the help of academics, practising lawyers, and insurers, in order to provide the judges and practitioners with a guideline when they quantify damages of personal injury cases.

This Table indicates the average amount of damages awarded for different types of injury, and includes information on the percentage of the victim's disability, age, etc.,[59] and was adopted for the first time in 1997. It is reviewed every two years in order to take into account the inflation rate and revise the actual compensation levels. The latest version dates from 2008.[60] The nomenclature is an indicative list and is therefore not binding on trial judges. Nevertheless, it is considered to provide a persuasive overview of the present categories and heads of damage and is commonly used by local courts.[61] Nowadays, the Table is of great importance. Lawyers, in formulating their claims, do so in accordance with the guidelines indicated in the Table, and judges openly use it for awarding damages. The Supreme Court recently indicated that such a judicial method for determining damages is neither contrary to the principles governing the sovereign power of appreciation of trial courts nor to that of total reparation in a specific case.[62] The Table must be considered a tool for awarding damages. The amounts therein mentioned may be adjusted to reflect the personal, individual circumstances of the victim. Thus, judges using their discretionary power may increase or decrease the amounts suggested in the Table. The nomenclature was originally intended to be used for the assessment of damages in traffic accidents, but its use has been extended to apply to all types of accidents that cause physical injury.

59 See Van Den Bossche 2001.

60 Indicative Table 2008, available at: www.fcga-gmwf.be/documents/AN_INDEMNISATION.pdf.

61 See De Temmerman & de Kezel 2002, pp. 103–114; see for an overview of decisions that implemented the guidelines see: Van Oevelen, Persyn, Jocqué & De Temmerman 2007, pp. 933–1529.

62 Supreme Court (Belgium) 11 September 2009, *NjW* 2010, note G. Jocqué.

There are some examples found in cases regarding personal injury losses – though very few – where judges have tended to award higher amounts than they would have when strictly compensating for the actual loss.[63]

However, in cases of IP infringement, Belgian courts have been willing to award so-called double damages for the full compensation of the IP rights holder's damages.[64]

If a victim is not able to provide the necessary evidence of the extent of its damage in such cases, compensation may be limited to the so-called symbolic franc. How does the case law deal with this dilemma? Some decisions strictly adhere to the principle of equivalence of the damage and reparation so that compensation is refused if the victim is unable to prove its loss or will be limited to the symbolic franc if the victim fails to put forward the necessary evidence of the extent of the damage suffered. Several decisions seem to admit, however, that monetary damages can also serve a purpose as a private penalty discouraging offenders of intellectual property rights.[65] Besides taking into account lost profits and other material losses and the administration costs associated with detection and investigation, courts seem to favour adopting a multiplier and deciding that the heads of damage as calculated can be awarded times two *ex aequo et bono* for the loss as a whole. As long as the courts take proper care in establishing that the awarding of such damages serves the purpose of repairing the actual harm and loss suffered and does not envision anything other than reparation, the courts' discretionary power in doing so will not be sanctioned by the Supreme Court.[66] Should it appear that the multiplier is only used to add damages on top of what constitutes actual loss, such a decision will be the subject of Supreme Court review.[67]

It should be noted also that European supreme courts have already begun experimenting with other purposes than merely remedying the damage/harm done through injunctive and compensatory relief (cf. the German *Caroline of Monaco* case[68]), that is, under the condition that there is no huge disproportion between the actual losses and the damages awarded.

Rounding up, it can be said that the Belgian law on damages will not easily lend itself to awarding "punitive damages" exceeding the actual loss suffered as a means of vindicating private interests. The judge's discretionary power to decide on the amount of the award will, however, sometimes obscure the issue.

63 De Kezel 1999.

64 Keustermans & De Maere 2009.

65 Buydens 1995.

66 See, e.g., Supreme Court (Belgium) 22 December 1975, *A.C.* 1975, 498.

67 Supreme Court (Belgium) 13 May 2009, *A.C.* 2009, 1254.

68 In a case involving a fake interview with Princess Caroline of Monaco that was published on the front page and inside of two widely distributed magazines, the *Bundesgerichtshof* recognized the goal of prevention for the first time. The court awarded damages that seemed to intend on punishing as well as compensating. It stated clearly that the assessment of damages in the case of the infringement of the personality right of the plaintiff must take into account the profit underlying the tort, so that the award may have a '*Hemmungseffekt*' (inhibitive effect). Thus, when it comes to recognising monetary damages awards, instruments that are not merely compensatory (but also see to prevention and deterrence) are not per se contrary to public policy, as long as there is no huge disproportion between the actual losses and the damages award.

In all likelihood, the Belgian legal practise will however be confronted with the issue when asked to recognise and enforce punitive damages awarded by tribunals abroad.

How these issues will be addressed essentially boils down to confronting different ideas and legal frameworks on protecting and enforcing private interests. This question will be further investigated below in section 3.2.

3.2. *Enforcement of US Judgments in Belgium: General Guidelines*

There exists no treaty between Belgium or any other European country and the United States on the enforcement of foreign judgments. The explanation for this discrepancy[69] is that the EU governments are hesitant in subjecting their citizens – even in cases where there may be a clear choice of court provisions in business agreements – to the US court system and particularly in paying the awards determined by a US jury. Such enforcement of US judgments occurs almost entirely on an *ad hoc* rather than a rules-based basis. It is a matter left to the discretion of the enforcing court, which can proceed largely unchecked and unguided by any recognised principles or restrictions, either derived from a treaty or other source.[70]

Since no civil court judgment enforcement treaty exists between the United States and Belgium, the recognition and enforcement of US judgments in Belgium is governed by statute.

Before the entry into force of the Belgian Code of Private International Law (in 2004), Article 570 of the Belgian Judicial Code was applicable to the enforcement of US judgments in Belgium.[71] It also served as a model for the new provisions.

69 The aim of the Lugano Convention of 16 September 1988 on jurisdiction and the enforcement of judgments in civil and commercial matters (involving the Member States and Iceland, Norway, Switzerland, and Poland) is to extend the rules of the Brussels Convention of 27 September 1968, which apply between the Member States to relations between the Member States and the EFTA States plus Poland. A judgment obtained by parties in one country from other European countries will be enforced in the courts of the other as a result of the Brussels and Lugano Conventions, which extend across the European Community and thus provide (with the exception of limited instances) that a judgment rendered in Belgium will be enforced in France or the Netherlands, for example, and vice versa. There is a draft for a new convention to extend the Brussels I Regulation which replaced the Brussels Convention to relations between the Member States and the Lugano States. Worldwide international conventions prepared in this context have not come into force. Such is the case of the Hague Convention concluded on 1 February 1971 on Jurisdiction and Recognition and Enforcement of Foreign Judgments in Civil and Commercial Matters, which has not been ratified by a sufficient number of States. In 2005 a new Convention on the Choice of Court Agreements was adopted by the Hague Conference on Private International Law. This convention is not in force yet.

70 However, since the US Supreme Court's late 19th century decision in *Hilton v. Guyot*, 159 US 13 [1895] (a case involving US and French nationals), US courts have been instructed to enforce judgments rendered abroad. The Supreme Court in this case was explicit on this instruction not being dependent upon reciprocity and is (what the Court called) a matter of international "comity".

71 Supreme Court (Belgium) 22 September 2005, Role nr. C030021N, see www.juridat.be.

Besides formal requirements (relating to the existence of an authentic copy of the foreign judgment[72] and the fact that the judgment is final),[73] Articles 22 to 25 of the Belgian Code of Private International law examine whether the recognition would lead to a result that is obviously incompatible with basic principles of Belgian law, especially when there is a violation of Belgian public policy: whether the rights of the defendant are violated; whether the judgment is consistent with an earlier foreign Belgian judgment or with a foreign judgment that can be enforced in Belgium; whether the foreign judgment contradicts Belgian public policy; whether the procedure before the US court has been properly conducted according to due process requirements; and whether the US court took jurisdiction solely on the basis of the nationality of the plaintiff.

Remarkably, Article 570 of the Belgian Judicial Code directed the enforcement court in the past to also review the merits of the case (*revision au fond*). A review of the merits can be defined as an overall control exercised by the enforcement court on the foreign judgment. It encompasses the form as well as the substance of the case and can cover both the factual and the legal findings made by the foreign court. The only practical difference between the review of the merits of the case and an entirely new procedure on the original cause of action is the fact that the burden of proof rests on the defendant in the enforcement proceedings to show that the enforcement cannot be granted.

In a judgment issued in 1981,[74] the Supreme Court held that pursuant to Article 570 of the Judicial Code:

> the Belgian judge is obliged to examine the substance of the dispute (['le fond du litige'], ..., and to verify whether the decision fulfills the conditions mentioned in 1° to 5° of the 2nd paragraph of said article.

Thus, both the text of Article 570 and of the case-law from the highest appellate court relating thereto seem to direct the enforcement court to review the merits of the foreign judgment.

However, the scope of the review of the foreign judgment was far from clear. A few, mostly older writings, advocate that the whole matter should be tried again as if the foreign judgment did not exist, except that the burden of proof is on the defendant. Yet in practice, the review was often limited to a negative and marginal control on the dispute. Some courts have even refused, albeit not explicitly, to review the merits of the foreign judgment. In any event, even without review of the merits, the public policy exception would have already allowed the court to check whether the general outcome of the foreign proceedings was acceptable. It is important to note that the new Belgian Code abolished this requirement of a *revision au fond*.

Hereafter, these questions that play an important role in practice are briefly expounded: (1) Does the foreign judgment contradict Belgian public policy? (2) Has the

72 The Belgian court must verify whether the copy of the foreign judgment meets with all the authenticity requirements set by the law of the country where the judgment is rendered. This is a formal requirement that entails, amongst other things, a sworn translation of the foreign judgment and a duly sealed and signed copy thereof.

73 In order to be enforceable in Belgium, the foreign judgment must be *res judicata* in the country where it was rendered, and all remedies must have been exhausted or the time thereof must have lapsed.

74 Supreme Court (Belgium), 23 January 1981, *Pas.* 1981, I, 547.

procedure before the US court been properly conducted according to due process requirements? (3) Has the US court taken jurisdiction solely on the basis of the nationality of the plaintiff?

3.2.1. Does the Foreign Judgment Contradict Belgian Public Policy?

In the context of the enforcement of foreign judgments, public policy is limited to "international" public policy[75] and consists of these provisions of internal public policy that are so essential to the moral, political or economic order that they necessarily exclude the application in Belgium of any contrary or different foreign law provision, even if the latter would be applicable by virtue of private international law.[76] This definition, repeated in several Supreme Court decisions,[77] is well established where a Belgian court is called upon to directly apply a rule of foreign law. However, in enforcement proceedings, the Belgian court needs to only examine "whether the decision does not contain anything that is contrary to Belgian public policy", *i.e.*, whether the (concrete) effect of the foreign decision is contrary to Belgian international public policy. The enforcement court will therefore not examine the foreign decision as such, but only the practical consequences that its enforcement in Belgium would entail.[78]

It follows that international public policy is in principle less far-reaching in enforcement proceedings than when it comes to applying foreign law, something generally expressed as "the weakened effect of public policy" (*l'effet attenué de l'ordre public*).[79]

3.2.2. Has the Procedure before the US Court Been Properly Conducted According to Due Process Requirements?

This procedural test does not imply that the Belgian court should investigate whether the foreign proceedings duly complied with all the procedural rules of the country where the judgment was rendered. Enforcement will be granted if the Belgian court is satisfied that the defendant was duly served, had a reasonable opportunity to be heard, and was allocated a fair and serene trial.

3.2.3. Has the US Court taken Jurisdiction Solely on the Basis of the Nationality of the Plaintiff?

The foreign judgment's enforcement will only be refused when the foreign court's jurisdiction was based solely on the plaintiff's nationality. It has, however, been argued

75 International public policy is said to represent only a (small) part of the (internal) public policy, which in turn contains all laws relating to the state's essential interests or the legal foundations of the economic or moral order of the community (Supreme Court, 9 December 1948, *Pas.* 1948, I, 699).

76 Supreme Court (Belgium) 4 May 1950, *Pas.* 1950, I, 624.

77 Supreme Court (Belgium), 27 February 1986, *R.C.J.B.* 1989, 56; Supreme Court (Belgium), 2 April 1981, *R.W.* 1982–83, 922; Supreme Court (Belgium), 24 March 1960, *Pas.* 1960, I, 860.

78 Watté 1989, p. 66, § 55.

79 Van Hecke & Lenaerts 1989, p.135; Van Houtte 1973, p. 749.

that Article 570 allows the court to refuse enforcement in other circumstances when the jurisdiction exercised by the foreign court was truly exorbitant, e.g., when the dispute is so closely connected to Belgium that Belgian courts (could) claim exclusive jurisdiction.[80]

Some aspects of the US judgment are likely to surprise a Belgian court, when in enforcement proceedings. Although no guarantee can be given that these features may be sufficient to block enforcement of a future judgment, care should be taken to emphasise the US decision's less "common" aspects – at least to a Belgian court – under both the review of the merits and the public policy exceptions, such as the jury verdicts. If the dispute were to be submitted to a jury, the judgment would face closer scrutiny by the enforcement court. The court would particularly scrutinise the reasoning underpinning the ruling. A judgment rendered without any reasoning would likely have its enforcement refused.

3.3. *Enforcement of US Punitive Damages Awards*[81]*: View of the Supreme Court in France*

3.3.1. A Different Approach with respect to Protecting and Enforcing Private Rights and Interests

Punitive damages have deep roots in American and English common law. Punitive damages under US law are deemed to have four main purposes: (1) to punish the offender for "uncivilised conduct", (2) to deter the offender and others from doing similar things, (3) to reward the plaintiff for enforcing the law and so improve "general law and order", and (4) to supplement inadequate compensatory damages.[82]

These days, punitive damages are mainly used to send messages to large corporations, to fill gaps in regulation, and to reward successful plaintiffs with multiples of what they have lost (public interest litigation), see above.

However, with respect to the punishment objective, it is said that the imposition of punitive damages on corporations may fail to serve its purpose. Punitive damages against corporations may be ineffective because the payment of punitive damages awards by corporations does not often lead to a greater punishment of culpable employees, but instead, punishes the corporation's shareholders and customers.[83]

As demonstrated above for Belgium, most European countries share a different approach with respect to handling damage claims. They also share a different approach as to enforcing private interests. European legal systems often consider US judgments that award punitive damages as being contrary to public policy. In Europe, punitive damages are often considered an (undesired) peculiarity of US law. The European view

80 Vanaroye 1997, p. 51. Other authors come to the same conclusion by applying public policy or fraud, e.g., Hans Van Houtte, 1973.

81 See more in general, Brand 1996.

82 Polinsky en Shavell 1998, p. 869 *et seq.*

83 *Ibid.*

on punitive damages can therefore act as a severe limit on the recognition of a US judgment.

Damages in the EU Member States are traditionally compensatory. In the Rome II Regulation on the law applicable to non-contractual obligations,[84] the European Commission has even suggested that punitive damages are contrary to European public policy.[85] Also, the idea of "double damages" for culpable IP infringement in the draft EU Directive 2004/48/EC on the enforcement of intellectual property rights was finally rejected. Recital 26 rejects punitive damages but calls for the full compensation of all aspects of the patentee's damages (including lost profits, unfair profit of the infringer, moral prejudice).

The French Supreme Court has recently refused recognition of US punitive damages awards on the grounds of contrariety to public policy. This decision will be used in the section below to analyse the issue of recognition of US judgments.

3.3.2. Enforcing US Punitive Damages in France[86]

Since the decision of the French Supreme Court in the *Cornelissen* case on 20 February 2007, the following requirements must be met in order for a French court to recognise and enforce a US judgment: (1) the competence of the rendering court based on the significant connection between the dispute and the jurisdiction to which the case has been referred; (2) compliance with substantive and procedural French public policy; and (3) absence of breach of the law.

Of all European countries, France is probably the country where the recognition of a US punitive damages award will be most easily admitted. Recently, it has even been proposed that the possibility for the judge to award punitive damages in the event of wilful tort or breach of contract be introduced in French civil law. Article 1371, proposal of reform of the law of obligations (the so-called *projet Catala*), reads in French as follows:

> *L'auteur d'une faute manifestement délibérée, et notamment d'une faute lucrative, peut être condamné, outre les dommages-intérêts compensatoires, à des dommages-intérêts punitifs dont le juge a la faculté de faire bénéficier pour une part le Trésor public.*

84 Regulation (EC) No 864/2007 of the European Parliament and of the Council of 11 July 2007 on the law applicable to non-contractual obligations (Rome II). This Regulation defines the law applicable to non-contractual obligations in situations involving a conflict of laws. It covers civil and commercial matters with certain exceptions, such as family relationships and the liability of the State, and applies in all EU Member States, except Denmark, from 2009.

85 Article 24 of the Rome II Regulation explicitly excludes the application of foreign laws insofar as they award damages which go beyond compensation for damage, such as exemplary or punitive damages, as being contrary to Community public policy (*ordre public*). However, the fact that the Regulation can be binding only for courts in the Community means that the clause cannot preclude, for example, a US Court from awarding punitive damages against a European media company (provided that it has jurisdiction).

86 See Boskovic 2006.

However, this proposal has not entered into force (yet). Nevertheless, a recent decision of the French Supreme Court (1 December 2010) may be an indication that the European and US judicial systems are becoming increasingly harmonised. This was the case of *X. v. Fountaine Pajot*, in which the Supreme Court was not only receptive in enforcing a large US judgment, but was also specifically receptive in enforcing a part of that judgment in an area that – as previously indicated – brought out the most antipathy in the other European supreme courts: punitive damages.

Fountaine Pajot involved a contract case in which the plaintiffs added a tort claim to increase its damages. The plaintiffs in this case bought an expensive catamaran from a French manufacturer. They alleged that the ship was defective and sued for breach of warranty as well as for fraud. The US court (California Supreme Court) awarded the plaintiffs US$ 1,393,650 in direct damages (for the repair of the boat) and an even larger amount (US$ 1,460,000) in punitive damages (and US$ 402,084.33 for lawyers' expenses). The plaintiffs then wished to have the decision of the California Supreme Court recognised and enforced in France.

In its holding in the *Fountaine Pajot* case, the Supreme Court held that an award of punitive damages is not, per se, contrary to public policy, insofar as the awarded amount is not disproportionate to the harm sustained as a result of the (in this case) contractual breach[87]

> *attendu que si le principe d'une condamnation à des dommages intérêts punitifs, n'est pas, en soi, contraire à l'ordre public, il en est autrement lorsque le montant alloué est disproportionné au regard du préjudice subi et des manquements aux obligations contractuelles du débiteur; qu'en l'espèce, l'arrêt relève que la décision étrangère a accordé à l'acquéreur, en plus du remboursement du prix du bateau et du montant des réparations, une indemnité qui dépasse très largement cette somme; que la cour d'appel a pu en déduire que le montant des dommages intérêts était manifestement disproportionné au regard du préjudice subi et du manquement aux obligations contractuelles de sorte que le jugement étranger ne pouvait être reconnu en France.*

The German *Bundesgerichtshof* has ruled in a similar manner, but on 4 June 1992 in a leading decision,[88] the *Bundesgerichtshof* refused to enforce a US court judgment that awarded punitive damages in part due to its incompatibility with the state's monopoly on punishment. However, the German court acknowledged that the award could be recognised to the extent that it did not violate German public policy.[89] It pointed out that

87 Supreme Court (France) December 2010, no. 1090.

88 Bundesgerichtshof, 4 June 1992, *Neue Juristische Wocherschrift* 1992, p. 3096 *et seq.*

89 The German law on private international law on extra-contractual obligations of 1999 contains a provision that seems to exclude the recognition of foreign judgments in which a provision has been applied causing a different outcome on the issue of damages than under German domestic law. Article 40(3) of the introductory law to the German Civil Code (BGB) currently states: 'Claims governed by foreign law cannot be relied on if: 1) They go considerably beyond what a reasonable compensation of the injured party requires, and 2) They serve objectives that are manifestly different from a reasonable compensation of the injured party'. This provision leads to a refusal of recognition when either the function or the amount of damages differs from what is accepted under German law.

German public policy would allow for the enforcement of any portion of the punitive award that was in reality purely compensatory. The German court therefore enforced (only) the US$ 350,000 compensatory award. This was a significant improvement on the approach suggested by the defendant and a lower court, according to which a public policy violation would vitiate the entire judgment.

Despite its indication that it would be receptive in enforcing an award of punitive damages, the French Supreme Court actually refused to enforce such award in the *Fountaine Pajot* case. The Court held that the punitive damages awarded by the US court were disproportionate to the underlying court judgment, and therefore refused to enforce them. While the Court justified its refusal to enforce the punitive damages based on the disproportionate amount of the award in relation to the direct damages, it noted that it would have been open to enforcing a more reasonable punitive award that was closer to the amount of actual damages. Hence, the wording of the judgment leaves room for enforcement of (more proportionate) punitive damages awards.

According to some, the public policy of the forum would not so much interfere with the punitive nature of damages, but with their being excessive.[90] How this should be determined is another question. The US Supreme Court tends to consider that the ratio of punitive damages to compensatory damages should not exceed 1:10.[91] The Californian judgment was quite far from this ratio: mind the gap!

3.3.3. Effective Enforcement of US Punitive Damages in Belgium?

As stated above, the Belgian law on damages will not easily lend itself to awarding "punitive damages" that exceed the actual loss suffered as a means of vindicating private interests. The question whether a US court order on punitive damages can be recognised and thus enforced by the Belgian courts raises complex and unusual questions.

How these questions will be answered essentially boils down to confronting different ideas on protecting and enforcing private interests. It is estimated that a Belgian court, when confronted with a demand to enforce US judgments, will be rather reluctant in enforcing awards of punitive damages. The fact that the United States is not a party to any international agreement regarding the recognition and enforcement of foreign judgment is not very helpful in this respect.[92]

At first sight this leads to the conclusion that – although a final assessment can only be given once the judgment has been issued, depending on the specific circumstances of the case – there is a fair chance that the enforcement of a future US punitive damages judgment will be blocked in Belgium.

A remarkable approach by the French Supreme Court[93] towards US punitive damages awards is to enforce (only) the underlying awards (the "compensatory damages") but not

90 See Boskovic 2006.

91 *State Farm v. Campbell*, 2003; *BMW of North America, Inc v. Gore*, 1996.

92 See Quarta 2008.

93 With regard to this issue, see also the Italian Supreme Court's ruling in the Parrott case. In the late summer of 1985, Kurt Parrott, a 15-year-old American, was thrown from his motorcycle in Alabama. The buckle of his helmet failed, and he died when his bare head hit the pavement. The victim's mother sued the Italian company that made the helmet, and a federal district court in Alabama entered a one

to enforce the punitive elements, which are often viewed as disproportionate, and hence, against public policy (*cf.* the French *Fountaine Pajot* case).

Thus, if a US punitive damages judgment were held to be contrary to (national) public policy in Belgium, this finding would in a similar manner only lead to a partial refusal of enforcement: the court will refuse enforcement only insofar as non-compensatory damages were awarded and would grant enforcement for the remainder of the judgment (in cases where the award can be reduced after judicial scrutiny to a reasonable proportion).

It remains uncertain which other criteria judges will develop to consider when the awarded amount of punitive damages would be manifestly disproportionate to the actual loss sustained: the French *Fountaine Pajot* case was far from the 1:10 ratio of punitive damages to compensatory damages, which was considered reasonable by the US Supreme Court. It is important to keep in mind that Belgian judges have a great liberty in assessing the award for actual losses (*cf.* the double damage awards in copyright infringement cases).

4. Closing Remarks: Towards a Better Protection and Enforcement of Private Interests in Belgium and Europe through a Mix of Public and Private Law Enforcement Procedures?

As is the case with the concept of punitive damages, the US collective actions and their potential transferability to the European legal systems have been heavily debated in the past.

In most European countries, including Belgium, public interest class proceedings are not available. Yet, collective redress actions are no longer unknown in Continental European proceedings.[94] Recent legislation in Belgium, for example, notably in the field of environmental law and consumer protection law, has already allowed individual claims to be brought together for a better enforcement of consumer legislation and environmental legislation. Some European countries have already introduced certain collective redress procedures. Such is the case for the Netherlands, Portugal, England and Wales, and Sweden.[95]

Certain environmental and consumer associations in Belgium are allowed to act before the courts in order to obtain cease and desist orders.[96] However, they are not entitled to bring actions for damages before the courts. Group actions or traditional representative actions by institutionalised representatives cannot be taken in Belgium.

million dollar judgment against the Italian manufacturer accused of producing a defective item that allegedly contributed to the death of the plaintiff's son. The Italian Supreme Court refused in 2007 to enforce any of the US$ 1 million award to a victim's mother of a motorcycle accident as it was a case where no clear distinction between punitive and compensatory damages could be made. (See Quarta 2008).

94 See De Schutter 1999 at p. 907 ss.

95 For more information see the national reports on the EC's site on collective redress, available at: http://ec.europa.eu/consumers/redress_cons/collective_redress_en.htm.

96 E.g., consumer associations with legal personality can request a cease and desist order with respect to unfair trade practices (Article 98 of the Law on Trade Practices).

The introduction of collective actions is currently being debated by the legislature, at both the European level and the national (Belgian) level.[97] It is important to note that class actions are not deemed contrary to public policy. Certain features of the class action system, such as the "opt out" system, will, however, likely surprise a Belgian court. It has even been said that the fact that persons who fall within the class are bound by a court decision even if they did not explicitly agree to be involved in the action, violates their right of access to justice as guaranteed by Article 6(1) of the European Human Rights Convention. The fact that the parties have the possibility to 'opt out' of the class action is deemed insufficient as many parties are not aware that they can 'opt out'. Nevertheless, it must be pointed out that the United States has recently made efforts to restrict its own class action system.[98]

The European legislator has made it clear that Europe is searching for other solutions to better enforce private interests.[99] Significant differences remain between the American and the European legal systems, despite an evolution towards the involving of tortious liability in Europe.

Therefore, the focus is now on the exchange of experiences of the success or shortcomings of the models that have already been introduced in Europe.[100] In most Member States, the balance between public and private enforcement is deeply rooted in their national systems. Any European solution would have to take into account these various legal traditions.

What is tort law for?[101] Broadly construed, both under US law and European law, tort law enforces the responsibilities we owe one another not to harm other people or disregard other people's rights which confer on them authority over their persons and possessions.[102]

Hence, tort law is fundamentally concerned with the question of what behaviour we may reasonably demand from each other with respect to legally protected rights and interests such as life and health, property and personality, liberty and security. In his inaugural lecture on 'The Tort Law Industry', Kortmann asserts that the question we are currently facing is whether we should abandon the compensatory principle of tort law in favour of a more instrumentalist approach. An important aspect of the public versus private enforcement debate and the related issue of introducing punitive damages ties indeed into this question: should the scope of any future EU-wide integrated collective enforcement mechanism be restricted to providing for injunctive and compensatory relief only? Kortmann himself opposes the idea of using tort law as a social

97 See the EC's public consultation paper, available at: http://ec.europa.eu/consumers/redress_cons/collective_redress_en.htm.

98 See, e.g., the "Class actions fairness Act". In 2005 Congress enacted the Class Action Fairness Act (CAFA) in reaction to abuses of the class action device in state courts.

99 See the EC's consultation paper on collective redress, electronic copy available at: http://ec.europa.eu/consumers/redress_cons/collective_redress_en.htm#cr.

100 *Ibid.*

101 The question was raised by Gardner, who explains that that 'corrective justice' cannot be a complete answer to the question of what tort law is for, see Gardner 2010.

102 On the question see Keating 2010.

policy tool.[103] However, the author's view is that private enforcement mechanisms can (and should *cf.* the view already expressed by Lindenbergh)[104] be used also for purposes other than merely remedying damage/harm done,[105] and thus serve as a useful addition to enforcement of private interests.[106] A broader view on redress mechanisms would include not only injunctive and compensatory relief, but also regulatory (aimed at influencing behaviour), restorative (including non-monetary redress), and/or punitive (fines and the expression of rejection or disapproval of certain behaviour) redress.[107]

A number of studies[108] have already demonstrated that a mix of public and private law enforcement provides for the most effective enforcement of legal rules. Moreover, such an approach would do more justice to the fact that the enforcement mechanisms that currently exist within Europe in this context in the Member States (inter alia several administrative compensation schemes), vary widely in set-up and scope as well as to their public or private nature.[109]

To conclude: it is important to keep in mind that – although certain features of the US litigation system do not seem to fit into the European legal tradition – because of the latter's different approach in handling damage claims and enforcing private interests, the goals underlying both systems seem to be the same and, from the European perspective, the different approaches inherent in both systems seem to be converging.

103 Kortmann 2009.

104 See para. 2.

105 Via cooperation and interaction with public enforcement mechanisms such as the criminal law system.

106 Van der Heijden, de Kezel & Enneking 2011.

107 Van der Heijden, de Kezel & Enneking 2011.

108 For references, see Van der Heijden, de Kezel & Enneking 2011.

109 It should also be noted that any attempt to institute an EU-wide collective redress mechanism would be impeded by the fact that in practice, the public/private distinction is vague at best and subject to diverging interpretations in the different Member States. *Cf.* the 2008 Study "Evaluation of the effectiveness and efficiency of collective redress mechanisms in the European Union" commissioned by the European Commission, electronic copy available at: http://ec.europa.eu/consumers/redress_cons/collective_redress_en.htm#Studies.

Bibliography

Bocken 2001
Bocken, H., "Tort law", in H. Bocken & W. De Bondt (eds.), *Introduction to Belgian law*, The Hague: Kluwer Law International, 2001.

Bocken & Boone 2011
Bocken, H., & Boone, I., *Inleiding tot het schadevergoedingsrecht – buitencontractueel aansprakelijkheidsrecht en andere schadevergoedingsstelsels*, Gent: Gandaius, 2011.

Borghetti 2009
Borghetti, J.S., "Punitive damages in France", in H. Koziol & V. Wilcox (eds.), *Punitive Damages: Common Law and Civil Law Perspectives*, Vienna: Springer 2009.

Boskovic 2006
Boskovic, O., "Les dommages et intérêts en droit international privé. Ne pas manquer une occasion de progrès", *La Semaine Juridique*, 2006.

Brand 1996
Brand, R.A., "Punitive Damages and the Recognition of Judgments", *Netherlands International Law Review*, 1996, pp. 143–186.

Buydens 1995
Buydens, M., "La réparation du dommage en droit de la propriété industrielle", *TBH*, 1995, pp. 448–463.

Cornelis 1989
Cornelis, L., *Beginselen van het Belgische buitencontractuele aansprakelijkheidsrecht, De onrechtmatige daad*, Antwerpen: Maklu, 1989.

Cousy & Droshout 2001
Cousy, H., & Droshout, D., "Belgium", in W.V.H. Horton Rogers (ed.), *Damages for non-pecuniary loss in a comparative perspective*, Vienna: Springer, 2001.

de Kezel 1999
de Kezel, E., "De vergoeding voor het verlies van een kind tengevolge van een verkeersongeval", *TPR*, 1999, pp. 579–633.

de Kezel 2008
de Kezel, E., "Een oplossing voor de asbest problematiek via schadevergoedingsfondsen? Het nieuw opgerichte Fonds voor Asbestslachtoffers in België", *TvPP*, 2008, pp. 17–28.

de Kezel 2009
de Kezel, E., "Medische aansprakelijkheid in België: van fault via no fault tot een tweesporensysteem", in T. Hartlief & W.R. Kastelein (eds.), *Medische Aansprakelijkheid: Actuele en Toekomstige Ontwikkelingen*, Den Haag: Sdu Uitgevers, 2009, pp. 191–220.

De Schutter 1999
De Schutter, O., *Fonction de Juger et Droit Fondamentaux. Transformation du Contrôle Juridictionnel dans Les Ordres Juridiques Américain et Européens*, Brussels: Bruylant, 1999.

De Temmerman & de Kezel 2002
De Temmerman, B., and de Kezel, E., "Normering in België: de Indicatieve Tabel", *TvVP*, 2002, pp. 103–114.

Fettweis 1987
Fettweis, A., *Manuel de Procédure Civile*, Liège: Faculté de Droit de Liège, 1987.

Gardner 2010
Gardner, J., "What is Tort Law for? Part 1: The Place of Corrective Justice", 2010, electronic copy available at: http://papers.ssrn.com/sol3/papers.cfm?abstract_id=1538342.

Hannequart & Henry 1999
Hannequart, Y. & Henry, P., "Les rapports entre la déontologie et la responsabilité civile", in *Liber amicorum Jozef Van den Heuvel*, Antwerpen: Kluwer, 1999, pp. 52–54.

Keating 2010
Keating, G.C., "Is Tort a Remedial Institution?", 2010, electronic copy available at: http://papers.ssrn.com/sol3/papers.cfm?abstract_id=1633687.

Keustermans & De Maere 2009
Keustermans, J. & De Maere, T., "Foutbegrip en schadevergoeding in het auteursrecht: *double damage*?", *Auteurs & Media*, 2009, pp. 388–391.

Kortmann 2009
Kortmann, J., *The Tort Law Industry*, Amsterdam: Vossiuspers UvA, 2009.

Olson 1991
Olson, W.K., *The Litigation Explosion*, New York: Dutton, 1991.

Polinsky & Shavell 1998
Polinsky, A.M. & Shavell, S., "Punitive Damages: an Economic Analysis", *Harv L Rev*, 1998, pp. 869–962.

Quarta 2008
Quarta, F., "Recognition and Enforcement of U.S. Punitive damages awards in Continental Europe: The Italian Supreme Court's Veto", *Hastings International and Comparative Law Review*, 2008, p. 735–752, electronic copy available at: http://papers.ssrn.com/sol3/papers.cfm?abstract_id=1182442.

Spender 2003
Spender, P., "Blue Asbestos and Golden Eggs: Evaluating Bankruptcy and Class Actions as Just Responses to Mass Tort Liability", *Sydney Law Review*, 2003, electronic copy available at www.austlii.edu.au/au/journals/SydLRev/2003/11.

Van Den Bossche 2001
Van Den Bossche, M., (ed.), *De nieuwe indicatieve tabel. Een praktisch werkinstrument voor de evaluatie van menselijke schade*, Brussel: Larcier, 2001.

Van der Heijden, de Kezel & Enneking 2011
Van der Heijden, M.-J., de Kezel, E. & Enneking, L., "Formal Reply to the European Commission Staff Working Document Public Consultation: Towards a Coherent European Approach to Collective Redress", 2011, electronic copies available at:
http://ec.europa.eu/competition/consultations/2011_collective_redress/utrecht_university_en.pdf.

Van Hecke & Lenaerts 1989
Van Hecke, G. & Lenaerts, K., *Internationaal Privaatrecht*, Antwerpen: E. Story-Scientia, 1989.

Van Houtte 1973
Van Houtte, H., "De 'openbare orde' als beletsel voor de erkenning of tenuitvoerlegging van buitenlandse vonnissen", *RW, 1973*, pp. 738–749.

Van Oevelen *et al.* 2007
Van Oevelen, A, *et al.*, "Overzicht van rechtspraak. Onrechtmatige daad: schade en schadeloosstelling (1993–2006)", *TPR*, 2007, pp. 933–1529.

Vansweevelt & Weyts 2009
Vansweevelt, T. & Weyts, B. *Handboek buitencontractueel aansprakelijkheidsrecht*, Antwerpen: Intersentia, 2009.

Watté 1989
Watté, N., "Quelques remarques sur la notion de l'ordre public en droit international privé", *RCJB*, 1989, pp. 66–104.

Ulrich Magnus*

PUNITIVE DAMAGES AND GERMAN LAW

1. Introduction

Punitive damages are a legal institute well known in Common Law jurisdictions,[1] much less in Civil Law countries. Yet, the expression has become a global term of art. It is generally understood as a sanction of civil law, namely a money award which does not primarily intend to compensate the victim for a loss but to punish the wrongdoer for a wrong. Nonetheless, the term 'punitive damages' is an ambivalent notion. In a sense, any remedy of damages has the function to punish the liable person by means of money. The liable person must pay for the damage he or she has caused. In fact, it was a great historical step for ancient societies to allow a wrongdoer to give money instead of his or her eye, arm or other limb as retorsion for the wrong inflicted on the victim and to allow the tortfeasor so to speak to buy the penal sanction of suffering the same harm as done to the victim. Since these archaic beginnings the civil law of damages and the criminal law developed in different directions. In civil law the victim's loss and its compensation became the focus of the law of damages whereas in criminal law the conduct of the culprit is the centre of interest.[2]

For the following, punitive damages are understood as damages which primarily or even exclusively pursue the aim of putting a legal sanction on the tortfeasor's conduct irrespective of whether and to which extent that conduct caused a specific loss.

However, it must be stressed that the borderline between a punitive, penal function and the preventive, deterrent effect of compensatory damages is a fine one. Damages which shall compensate the ensued loss certainly have also a certain preventive, deterrent effect. The thread to become liable in civil law may influence the conduct of potential

* Professor (em.) of Civil, Private International and Comparative Law at the University of Hamburg; Judge (ret.) at the Hamburg Court of Appeal.

1 For a survey of English law on punitive damages see Wilcox 2009, pp. 7–53; for a survey of the situation in the United States see Sebok 2009, pp. 155–196 and 311–322.

2 Bydlinski 1996, p. 92 *et seq.* has justified the distinction between civil and criminal law with the general principle that in civil law the interests of both sides – creditor and debtor – have to be taken into account and must justify the respective solution while in criminal law a concentration on one side may be admissible. In civil law the allocation of a right to one specific creditor is necessarily the allocation of an obligation to a specific debtor. Seen from both angles the allocation must be justified. In the same sense with respect to punitive damages Koziol 2010, notes 2/59 – 2/62.

wrongdoers. They may in general try to avoid becoming liable; and even the single person may, in its conduct, pay attention to the compensatory sanction and try to avoid it. Moreover, even potential victims may behave more cautiously being aware that their negligent conduct may qualify as contributory negligence and may reduce their right to damages. The difficulty is that this preventive, deterrent effect of a 'quasi-punitive' nature is hardly precisely to measure. In some situations it is most likely that potential wrongdoers will avoid causing damage because they can and will calculate the costs of becoming liable and the costs of avoiding damage, compare these costs and choose the cheaper way. One could imagine that for instance businesses which are obliged to care for the security of their customers in their shops will, under the thread of possible compensation claims, install such safety measures as are necessary to avoid at least middle and major injuries to their customers. The level of possible claims may steer the businesses' expenditure for preventive measures. The compensatory function of damages can thus influence the behaviour of those persons or entities which plan, and have time to plan, their activity in a rational way. On the other hand, there may be situations where the thread of becoming liable has almost no impact on the conduct of potential wrongdoers. One can imagine that a car-driver when forced to react within less than a second is not, at least not much, influenced by the consideration how to avoid the sanction of compensatory damages but how to avoid the accident.

It is therefore a matter of definition how to distinguish the punitive and preventive functions of the law of damages.[3] Here, punitive damages is a sanction the awarding and extent of which depends mainly if not solely on the extent to which the conduct of the wrongdoer is disapproved. The extent of the loss plays a much less significant role for assessing the extent of this sanction.

2. General Attitude of German Law towards Punitive Damages

2.1. General Concept of the German Law of Damages

The German law of damages is founded on the compensatory function of damages. It is the view clearly prevailing in the courts[4] and in legal doctrine[5] that the remedy of damages does generally not serve penal functions. Instead it serves the aim of compensating the loss which the liable person caused. The central objective of damages is to make the victim whole. In principle, this is achieved by restoring the victim to the position it would have been in had the loss-causing event not happened.[6] By this award the full loss – no less but also nothing more – shall be compensated. The restitution in full (*restitutio in integrum*) is the aim but must not lead to enrichment either.[7] The

3 In the same sense Jansen/Rademacher 2009, p. 77.

4 See for instance BGHZ 7, 223 (224); BGHZ 18, 149 (151); BGHZ 128, 117 (120 *et seq.*); BGH NJW 2004, 2526 (2528).

5 For instance, Ebert 2004, p. 442 *et seq.*; Lange & Schiemann 2003, p. 12 *et seq.*; Magnus 2011, Vor §§ 249–255, note 15; Oetker, 2007, § 249, note 8; Schulze 2009, Vor §§ 249–253, note 2; Thüsing 2001, 18 *et seq.*

6 See § 249 BGB (Civil Code).

7 See, e.g., BGHZ 154, 395.

dogmatic fundament is the idea to give the rights and goods of the victim – even in their concrete form in which they exist in the victim's sphere – the widest possible protection.

For this last-mentioned reason, German law effectuates the compensation principle primarily by awarding the aggrieved party a claim for restitution in kind. In theory, that party can request that the wrongdoer in person makes good the damage, heals the injured or repairs the damaged goods. In practice, restitution in kind is however the great exception. No victim would accept medical treatment by the wrongdoer unless it is an experienced doctor nor would the normal wrongdoer be able and willing to undertake such task. Therefore normally, the victim receives the sum of money necessary for restitution.[8] The restitution costs are the normal measure of damages. Not only do they include the market-value of damaged goods (for instance of a car) but also even higher costs for repair or for providing a comparable good. The courts accept and award here restitutionary costs (for concrete repair) that exceed the market-value of the good up to 30%.[9]

The amount of damages does not depend on the extent of the wrongdoer's fault. Even slightest negligence obliges to compensate the full damage. The loss of the victim is generally the relevant yardstick, not the wrongdoer's conduct.

Besides the main aim of compensation the majority of German legal doctrine attests the law of damages a limited preventive function as a welcome side-effect.[10] The preventive function has the already mentioned effect that the threatened sanction of compensation may deter a potential wrongdoer from causing damage. Normally this function does not affect the amount of damages (for exceptions see below under section 3.). In particular, a victim cannot request damages for preventive measures where thus far no actual loss occurred.

2.2. *Non-Pecuniary Losses*

German law is traditionally reluctant in allowing monetary compensation for non-pecuniary losses. Full recovery is only granted where such losses can be restored in kind. Frequently this is impossible. However, in cases of defamation or similar kinds of violation of personality rights restitution in kind, for instance the publication of an excuse or the like, may be possible and may better restore the injured person's reputation than money can do.

On the other hand, compensation in money of losses of a non-pecuniary or immaterial nature is only available where a statute so provides (§253(1) BGB). There is a limited number of such provisions, the most important being §253(2) BGB which allows for an adequate indemnification of immaterial losses in case of bodily harm, violation of the

8 § 249(2) sent. 1 BGB.

9 With respect to damaged cars: BGHZ 115, 381; BGH NJW 1999, 500; BGH NJW 2005, 1108 (1110).

10 Compare Grünewald 2011, Vor § 249, note 2; Magnus 2011, Vor §§ 249–255, note 11; Oetker 2007, § 249, note 9; Schubert 2011, § 249, note 4; Schulze 2009, Vor §§ 249–253, note 2; but see also Wagner 2009, Vor § 823, note 41, who argues that only the preventive function can explain the present German tort law because this function does not only apply between individuals but also between collectives like insurance companies which often have to bear the damages.

personal freedom and violation of the sexual self-determination.[11] Whether these provisions serve mainly compensatory or other objectives is still disputed (see thereto section 3.2 below).

2.3. *Reasons for the Rejection of Punitive Damages*

German law is rather strict in rejecting punitive damages. Several reasons are advanced for this position:[12]

2.3.1. Different Objectives of Criminal and Civil Law

First, a strict distinction between civil and criminal law sanctions is drawn. Both pursue different objectives; civil law intends to provide just compensation, criminal law to suppress unsocial behaviour. Punitive damages are regarded as sanctions of a criminal law character because they are assessed in relation to the wrongdoer's behaviour.[13]

Under a general perspective the clear distinction between civil law and criminal law is undeniable. However, this distinction does not finally exclude the possibility that civil law may partly support the objectives of criminal law and vice versa.

2.3.2. Different Legal Principles and Methods

Secondly, the methods of both branches of law are different;[14] in criminal law the state – or the society as such – investigates crimes generally ex officio. In all major cases the state as prosecutor is even obliged to investigate crimes and disposes of specific, precisely fixed competences for this purpose. On the other hand criminal law provides for strict safeguards for suspected and accused persons, foremost the principle *in dubio pro reo*, also the right to be silent. In civil law the aggrieved person is not obliged to pursue the wrongdoer's liability and to claim damages; in addition, the parties can widely dispose over the dispute. Furthermore, there is no strong civil law presumption of innocence; although the claimant must generally prove the facts of the claim there are many situations where the burden of proof is reversed or facilitated. Civil law cares much less for specific safeguards for defendants who for instance normally loose the suit when they are silent.

11 For a survey over the other provisions see Oetker 2007, § 253, note 1.

12 See in particular BGHZ 118, 312 (338 *et seq.*). In this leading case the German Supreme Court was concerned with the recognition and enforcement of a US judgment that had awarded substantial punitive damages for sexual abuse (in addition to relatively high compensatory damages). The Court rejected the recognition and enforcement of the US judgment in Germany and exposed extensively the reasons why punitive damages contradict the German legal order and offend the German ordre public. See also Greger 1989, p. 3103. On the other hand, a more recent judgment of the Constitutional Court did not reject the service in Germany of a US statement of claim that requested punitive damages (BVerfGE 91, 335). The court left open whether punitive damages are irreconcilable with fundamental principles of German law. For a broad comparative account see Koziol 2009, pp. 275–308.

13 See BGHZ 118, 312 (338 *et seq.*).

14 *Ibid.*

Again, these differences are undeniable. But again it is questionable whether they are so fundamental and deep-rooted as to exclude the possibility that civil law partially takes over or at least supports functions similar to those of criminal law.

2.3.3. The Argument of Double Punishment

A further argument advanced against punitive damages has greater weight: Punitive damages could be regarded to lead to double punishment where for the same conduct a criminal sanction, in particular a fine, and also punitive damages are imposed.[15] This would offend the general principle of *ne bis in idem* and even violate the German constitution whose Article 103(3) prohibits double punishment.[16] Although being a sanction of civil law, punitive damages expressly qualify as a punishment. There is a double sanction for the same conduct if a civil punitive 'fine' and a criminal fine are imposed for the same behaviour. Although cases are frequent where civil damages and a criminal fine concur without violating the prohibition of double punishment (as in many cases of bodily injury), here for the same crime and with the same purpose of punishment two sanctions are imposed. Seen from the perspective of the wrongdoer it makes also no difference that criminal money fines go to the state while civil damages go to the injured person.[17]

If punitive damages are regarded as equivalent to a criminal sanction the only way to avoid a double punishment is to exclude punitive damages in those cases where, and to the extent that, a criminal sanction has already been imposed. But even this way would not succeed where criminal action is taken only after punitive damages have already been awarded.

2.3.4. Principle of Proportionality

It is further argued that punitive damages violate the principle of proportionality.[18] This principle belongs to the fundamental constitutional principles.[19] Under German law of civil liability, compensation for the caused loss is the adequate aim. Any recovery beyond that limit would enrich the aggrieved person and has to be avoided. The loss is the yardstick for the assessment of civil law compensation. Damages which – like punitive

15 *Ibid.* The court mentions this argument but leaves open whether it finally applies. See to the problem Zekoll 1987, p. 152 *et seq.*

16 See thereto Schmidt-Assmann 2011, Article 103 GG, notes 258 *et seq.*

17 The Federal Supreme Court did not regard the award of preventive damages for the violation of personality rights as a criminal sanction; see BGH NJW 2005, 215 (216); in the same sense already the Constitutional Court (BVerfGE 34, 269 (293)) although to the former case law of the Federal Supreme Court which did less focus on the preventive function of damages for personality infringements. A recent decision of the Constitutional Court (BVerfG NJW 2006, 595) supports the decisions of the Federal Supreme Court, however without detailed discussion.

18 See BGHZ 118, 312 (328 *et seq.*).

19 See with respect to damages BVerfGE 34, 269 (285 *et seq.*); generally Grzeszick 2011, Article 20 GG, notes 107 *et seq.*

damages – have no relation to the actual loss are out of proportion and offend the principle of proportionality.[20]

2.3.5. Windfall Profit

Punitive damages can be regarded as a windfall profit for the injured person. In 'ordinary' cases the victim would receive only compensatory damages. If the behaviour of the wrongdoer is outrageous and constitutes a breach of fundamental social norms as required for punitive damages then much higher sums are awarded. The individual injured would then 'profit' from the fact that in the common interest the behaviour of the wrongdoer should be punished. By contrast, in criminal law the victim of a crime does generally not profit from the money sanctions imposed on the criminal wrongdoer. In civil law the victim would if the threshold for punitive sanctions is passed.

The windfall argument is not conclusive because it gives no clear reason why deeply unsocial, outrageous behaviour should not be banned by specific civil law sanctions. Nonetheless, it adds to the scepticism against punitive damages.

2.3.6. Discrimination of Creditors

A further argument that can also be advanced against punitive damages is the certain discrimination between victims, namely those who are awarded mere compensatory damages and those who in addition receive punitive damages.[21] Even if the losses of both categories of victims are the same, nevertheless the recovery for the loss is different if punitive damages are accepted. The difference is due to a fact which in the German law of damages is to be neglected, namely the malice of the wrongdoer.

2.3.7. Too Great Discretion

It can be, and has been,[22] argued that the extent of punitive damages is too much left to the discretion of the respective court. Indeed, there are only vague parameters for the assessment of punitive damages. Common Law courts regularly take into account the kind of infringement, the impairment of the claimant, and in particular the conduct of the wrongdoer whose financial position is also being given attention. Even a potential gain of the wrongdoer can play a role.

2.3.8. Different Attitudes towards the Role of Private Parties with Respect to the Enforcement of the Law

If one compares Germany with the United States where punitive damages play a greater role than in all other jurisdictions there is also a significant difference in attitude with

20 BVerfGE 34, 269 (285 *et seq.*); BGHZ 118, 312 (328 *et seq.*).
21 BGHZ 118, 312 (328 *et seq.*).
22 *Ibid.*

respect to the enforcement of the law.[23] The United States expressly encourage private persons to act as private attorneys general. Punitive damages and many other means give incentives to private persons to pursue with their own also the common interest and to act indeed like private prosecutors. In German civil law private parties have no authority nor specific incentives to act as private attorneys general.[24] In the United States there is a greater need for activating private persons to enforce the law because of less regulation and state supervision. In Germany the contrary is true. Here, society trusts and expects that in principle the state regulates matters and enforces the law.

In some Common Law jurisdictions, particularly in the United States, punitive damages serve partly also the function of compensating for legal costs which under general law are not recoverable (the so-called American rule). In Germany, there is no need for such a rule because the winning party is reimbursed for all necessary legal costs.

2.3.9. Evaluation

In sum there is a good number of arguments against punitive damages. In Germany the majority view regards them as valid enough to generally reject punitive damages. However, these arguments are not so convincing that they exclude, without exception, damages which come close to punitive damages. In certain situations, a punitive or at least deterrent function is accepted.

3. Exceptions

3.1. General Remark

German law knows of several situations where the yardstick for compensation is not strictly the actual loss. One such situation is the case that it is too difficult and/or too costly to prove the exact loss although it is certain that a loss was caused. Then, the court can estimate the loss.[25] Another situation is the facilitation and simplification of assessment if the loss can be calculated in an abstract way, for instance where an abstract indemnification for the loss of the use of a (necessary) good, in particular of a car, is granted.[26] This kind of assessing the compensation in an abstract way, which does not precisely reflect the ensued loss, does not aim at a punitive or penal function of damages. The examples show however that anyway the actual loss is not always the strict measure for assessing the extent of compensation. Mainly reasons of practicality require a more loosely calculated amount of the recoverable damages. The overall aim of compensation of the ensued loss does not exclude this method of assessing damages.

23 See thereto Magnus 2010, pp. 102–124.

24 BGHZ 118, 312 (328 *et seq.*).

25 § 287 ZPO.

26 See BGHZ 98, 212 (GS); for further examples of abstract assessment of damages s. Magnus 2011, Vor §§ 249–255, note 112.

Under German law it is not inconsistent with the aim of compensation if the calculation of damages does not exactly correspond to the actual loss.

3.2. *Damages for Pain and Suffering*

One situation where a penal element might be present is the assessment of damages for pain and suffering in case of bodily harm (so called *Schmerzensgeld, pretium doloris*). The German Federal Supreme Court accorded the *pretium doloris* two functions:[27] the compensatory function and the function to satisfy the injured person's feelings (so called *Genugtuungsfunktion*). The latter function has been criticised as introducing penal elements into the law of damages because for this function the wrongdoer's conduct and not the loss is the primary yardstick of assessment.[28] On the other hand, this argument has been doubted because the function to grant the victim satisfaction can also be regarded as an extended compensation for the infringement of immaterial rights which otherwise were not protected.[29]

In practice, the satisfaction function plays if at all a minor role where damages for pain and suffering for bodily harm are awarded. The primarily compensatory character of these awards is evident when courts grant substantial damages for pain and suffering even to comatose victims who can no longer feel any satisfaction.[30]

However, a special case is the assessment of damages for an infringement of personality rights. Here, the deterrent function plays an essential role (see below under 3.4).

Under a general perspective, the practice of German courts in assessing the *pretium doloris* for bodily harm can hardly be qualified as punitive. There are tables of amounts for pain and suffering which the courts have granted for certain injuries in the past.[31] The courts follow more or less these standardised amounts when new cases are brought before them and adapt the amounts only slowly to inflation and further developments. In particular, where the wrongdoer is under a strict liability and compulsory insurance (as in most car accidents) the specific conduct and any quasi-punitive or preventive effect of the *pretium doloris* is of little if any weight.[32]

3.3. *Private Penalties*

Punishment and civil law are not separated as far as private penalties are concerned. German law does not ban such penalties:[33] Private parties can include penalty clauses in their contract.[34] In principle, an agreed punitive sanction is accepted here. However, if a

27 BGHZ 18, 149 (154 *et seq.*) (GS); BGHZ 128, 117 (120 *et seq.*).

28 See for instance, Canaris 1999, p. 102 *et seq.*; Huber 2011, § 253, note 26; sceptical also Schiemann 2005, § 253, note 29–32.

29 Oetker 2007, § 253, note 13.

30 BGHZ 120, 1 (4 *et seq.*).

31 See, for instance, Hacks, Ring & Böhm 2011; Slizyk 2011.

32 In this sense also Huber 2011, § 253, note 26; Schiemann 2005, § 253, note 33.

33 §§ 339 – 345 BGB.

34 Within the limits of §§ 307, 309 no. 6 BGB businesses can validly include penalty clauses in their standard terms even in contracts with consumers.

party so requests, the courts are entitled to reduce too extensive penalties which are out of proportion to the possible damage that may result from the event for which the penalty is agreed on.[35] The courts then limit the penalty to an amount that is reasonable taking into account all relevant circumstances. Between businesses generally no such reduction takes place;[36] but in extraordinary cases the penalty can be reduced as well,[37] or the respective clause can be entirely invalid.[38]

Thus, German law permits privately contracted punitive sanctions, however, only to a reasonable extent.

3.4. Violation of the General Personality Right

The case where German law openly accepts a deterrent function of damages awards is the infringement of the general personality right, in particular by press media. The development started already in the 1950s. In 1958 the Federal Supreme Court for the first time awarded money for the invasion of the recently invented[39] general personality right:[40] in that case the picture of a brewery owner riding over a hurdle was used without his consent for advertising potency pills. The court accepted the money sanction because otherwise there would have been no remedy at all against the infringement. Nonetheless, the compensatory character of the damages award remained the primary aim.

In the 1990s the court stressed the preventive character of damages for violated personality rights and extended considerably the sums awarded for such infringements. In the leading case[41] a newspaper had published alleged interviews with Caroline of Monaco which were completely invented. The added pictures were unauthorized and made by paparazzi. The court saw in the publication a grave infringement of the general personality right of Caroline of Monaco for which damages were justified. The court further held that the amount of damages should have a 'real inhibition effect' (*echter Hemmungseffekt*)[42] that deters the unauthorized and ruthless commercialisation of another's person. The amount of damages need not fully correspond to the gain but should be felt by the infringer. Furthermore, the amount is insofar limited as its extent must not unproportionally impair the freedom of the press,[43] for instance by endangering the economic existence of the publishing wrongdoer.[44]

35 § 343 BGB.
36 § 346 HGB (Commercial Code).
37 The basis is § 242 or § 315 BGB.
38 This consequence is based either on § 307 or § 138 BGB; see thereto Grüneberg 2011, § 343, note 8 with references to case law.
39 The Federal Supreme Court recognised a general personality right for the first time in BGHZ 13, 338.
40 BGHZ 26, 349 (so called *Herrenreiterfall*).
41 BGHZ 128, 1 (*Caroline I*).
42 *Ibid.* at [16]; also BGH NJW 2005, 215 (218).
43 BGHZ 128, 1 (16) (Caroline I); BGH NJW 2005, 215 (218).
44 See in particular BGH NJW 2005, 215 (218).

The amounts of damages for the infringement of the general personality right are moderate. Thus far the courts awarded no more than €100,000.[45] However, in many cases the awards were in the range of €10,000.[46]

It can be argued that the German courts accept punitive damages for the protection of personality rights.[47] Yet, compared to the amounts often reached in the United States, it is hard to qualify the German awards as punitive damages awards. Indeed, they pursue openly a preventive and deterrent effect. As already mentioned, there is however a borderline between a clear punitive aim and a mere preventive effect.[48] Though both intend to impress a wrongdoer – and the public – so that the wrong is neither repeated by the wrongdoer nor committed by others for the first time, punitive damages are less related to the actual loss and grant the court (in the United States the judge or the jury) greater discretion with respect to the amount. The aim of preventing losses on the other hand is related to the concrete loss. As used in German law the preventive function supports the compensatory function even in cases of violation of personality rights; prevention as applied by the courts is not imaginable without a strict relation to a concrete loss. The aim to prevent damage alone does not justify the award of damages.

3.5. *GEMA*

A further case often cited for a punitive function in German law is the claim for double licence fees that the courts grant to the GEMA, the association for protecting the rights of composers, text-writers or music publishers. This association is authorised by authors to investigate violations of the intellectual property rights of writers, composers etc. When a defendant has infringed such a right, the GEMA is allowed to recover the double licence fee.[49] These extended damages shall compensate for the organisational efforts and costs of investigation.

Although this special kind of compensation abstracts from the actual loss it is hardly a real punitive sanction but instead a standardised extended amount of compensation. Its justification is much doubted because ordinary victims must always bear their costs for the pursuit of their rights themselves.[50]

3.6. *Infringement of Intellectual Property Rights*

Another group of cases where the actual loss does not always steer the extent of compensation comprises violations of immaterial property rights. Where an intellectual property right has been infringed, German statute law admits three different methods of

45 See Slizyk 2011, under: Persönlichkeitsrechtsverletzung.
46 *Ibid.*
47 See for instance, Körner 2000, p. 241 *et seq.*; Müller 2000, p. 259 *et seq.*
48 See also Wagner 2009, Vor § 823, note 43–44; Wagner 2006, p. A 74 *et seq.*
49 BGHZ 17, 376 (383); BGHZ 59, 286.
50 See Magnus 2011, Vor §§ 249–255, note 115; Oetker 2007, § 249, note 200; Schiemann 2005, § 249, note 118; *contra* for instance Grüneberg 2011, § 249, note 64.

assessing the damages amount between which the injured right owner can freely choose: firstly, to calculate (and prove) the own concrete loss; secondly, to request the gain the infringer has made; thirdly, to claim a normal licence fee.[51] Although neither the infringer's gain nor the licence fee must necessarily equal the injured person's actual loss, there is a certain plausibility that the loss corresponds to these figures.

In particular the possibility of gain-stripping deviates considerably from the regular concept of compensatory damages.[52] Nonetheless, statute law treats the three methods as equivalent ways of assessing damages thus qualifying the claim as a damages claim.[53] In fact, gain-stripping and licence fee can be regarded as mere ways to alleviate the burden of proof; to prove the own loss is particularly difficult in case of infringed intellectual property rights. These two methods of assessment facilitate the injured party's burden to prove his or her loss.[54]

3.7. *Damages for Violation of Antitrust Provisions*

Specific damages rules which partly deviate from the ordinary rules of the assessment of damages apply to losses caused by violations of antitrust provisions. When a recoverable loss is certain but not precisely proved, courts are allowed to estimate the loss by measuring the respective profit which the wrongdoer has gained through the violation.[55] Moreover, the antitrust authority is entitled to strip the full economic benefit the wrongdoer gained from that violation unless the benefit was already stripped off by damages or fines.[56]

4. Conclusions

Some conclusions can be drawn. First, it would be unrealistic to state that German law is on the way to introduce or has already introduced sanctions that equal punitive damages à la United States. In comparison to the concept of punitive damages as used in the United States, German law does not provide a same or similar concept. There is also no need or other justification to introduce punitive damages in the US-sense in Germany. The activation of private parties to act in the interest of the common good and to remunerate them generously if they do so appears unnecessary as long as the state fulfils this task in a sufficient manner.

51 See § 97(1) Urheberrechtsgesetz (Copyright Act); § 139(2) Patentgesetz (Patent Act); § 24(2) Gebrauchsmustergesetz (Utility Model Act); §§ 42(2), 45 Geschmacksmustergesetz (Design Act). These provisions have codified long standing case law.

52 It has therefore been argued that this claim is actually a claim under *negotiorum gestio* (§ 687(2) BGB); see among others Schiemann 2005, § 249, note 201.

53 See the text of the provisions cited in fn. 49.

54 See also Oetker 2007, § 252, note 56.

55 § 33(3) sent. 3 Gesetz gegen Wettbewerbsbeschränkungen (Antitrust Act – GWB).

56 § 34 GWB.

On the other hand, it can be stated that in German law the preventive function of the law of damages has gained momentum since one or two decades.[57] This function supports the general compensatory function of damages. In case of infringements of the general personality right the preventive function may even prevail over the mere compensatory function of damages. The greater importance of prevention as an element of damages assessment is the result of the observation that in certain fields the unauthorised exploitation of essential immaterial rights of other persons promises enormous profit and that these violations of rights can only be stopped if equivalent amounts of damages are awarded. One could argue that the possibility of their exploitation has raised the value of these rights to the present dimensions. Compensation has just to follow suit. Moreover, it is an observation relevant for civil law that the infringement of another's right should not be more profitable than to avoid the infringement. It is the merit of the economic analysis of law to have increased the recognition of this insight.

The distinction between preventive and punitive sanctions may not be always easy. Nonetheless, the preceding considerations show that there is a discernable borderline. Prevention as used in German law does not solely focus on the wrongdoer's conduct but remains strictly and proportionately related to the damage of the claimant. Punishment on the contrary focuses primarily on the wrongdoer's behaviour and does not require a strict proportion to the caused loss. Interests of the general public strongly influence the extent of punitive damages. German law leaves the punishment to the province of criminal law with its specific safeguards for suspected or accused persons.

A last conclusion is concerned with the method of assessing damages. German law has opened to a certain extent the method to prove an actual loss. In general, it is the claimant's burden to adduce precise proof of the own loss. In many situations this is difficult, sometimes impossible, in particular in the field of infringed intellectual property rights or violation of antitrust provisions. Although the German courts have a discretion to estimate the extent of a loss where it is certain that a loss occurred (§287 ZPO), statutory law has introduced, as mentioned, further ways to assess the loss and calculate the amount of damages. In order to facilitate the victim's burden of proof and instead of the courts' discretion it seems preferable to give the victim further specific means of proving the loss like relying on the gain the wrongdoer made or on the fee a (licence) contract would foresee. These additional ways of assessing losses reduce the courts' discretion and increase moderately the protection of victims in critical situations. But it is far from introducing punitive damages into German law.

5. The European Perspective

With a view to Europe's future law of damages, the Proposal for a Common Frame of Reference ('CFR') which the Commission recently published does not provide for punitive damages. On the contrary, it strictly confines damages to the aim of compensation by putting 'the creditor as nearly as possible into the position in which the creditor would have been if the obligation had been duly performed' (Article 164 CFR). The CFR as

57 It is telling that also the Principles of European Tort Law (2005) provide: 'Damages also serve the aim of preventing harm'. (Article 10:101 sent. 2).

proposed in the Feasibility Study would merely cover sales contracts and related service contracts, however, not other contracts or torts. It is therefore a rather limited piece of (intended) legislation.

However, in my view a full-fledged European law of damages should not provide for punitive damages either. The main reason is also here that punishment should be left to criminal law. Civil law has to balance the interests of the wrongdoer and the victim in a reasonable manner. It cannot and should not focus on one aspect alone, namely on the suppression of unwanted behaviour of the wrongdoer. A further reason is that the European political and social environment accords the state a more caring and active role than the United States do. To achieve the common good of a society is in the first line the task of the state. To further the common interest through encouragement of private law enforcement cannot – and certainly not generally – substitute the responsibility of the state and its authorities. Only in certain areas where criminal or administrative measures do not appear to be sufficiently effective may it be possible and even necessary to give incentives for private law enforcement. The German experience shows that this is the case with respect to the violation of personality rights and other immaterial property rights and the infringement of antitrust provisions. But even in these fields civil law damages should not punish instead of compensate. It is the preventive potential of damages that could and should be activated. The assessment of damages should basically remain related to the actual loss also in these mentioned fields. However, the level of damages could be raised until a noticeable deterrent effect is reached.

A future European law of damages should therefore strengthen the preventive function of this area of law but not adopt US-like punitive damages.

Bibliography

Bydlinski 1996
Bydlinski, F., *System und Prinzipien des Privatrechts*, Wien: Springer, 1996.

Canaris 1999
Canaris, C-W., 'Gewinnabschöpfung bei Verletzung des allgemeinen Persönlichkeitsrechts', in: Festschrift für Deutsch, Köln, Berlin, Bonn, München: Heymanns, 1999, pp. 85–110.

Ebert 2004
Ebert, I., *Pönale Elemente im deutschen Privatrecht*, Tübingen: Mohr Siebeck, 2004.

Greger 1989
Greger, R., 'Anmerkung zu OLG München NJW 1989, 3102', *NJW*, 1989, pp. 3103–3104.

Grzeszick 2011
Grzeszick, B., 'Art. 20 GG', in: Th. Maunz, G. Dürig, & R. Herzog (eds.), *Grundgesetz Kommentar*, München: Beck, 2011.

Grüneberg 2011
Grüneberg, Ch., 'Vor §§249–254', in: O. Palandt, *Bürgerliches Gesetzbuch*, München: Beck, 2011.

Hacks, Ring &Böhm 2011
Hacks, S. & Ring, A. & Böhm P., *Schmerzensgeld-Beträge*, München: Beck, 2011.

Huber 2011
Huber, Ch., '§253 BGB', in: *Nomos-Kommentar BGB, Schuldrecht*, Teilbd. 1, Baden-Baden: Nomos, 2011.

Jansen & Rademacher 2009
Jansen, H. & Rademacher, L., 'Punitive Damages in Germany', in: H. Koziol & V. Wilcox (eds.), *Punitive Damages: Common Law and Civil Law Perspectives*, Wien: Springer, 2009, pp. 75–86.

Körner 2000
Körner, M., 'Zur Aufgabe des Haftungsrechts – Bedeutung präventiver und punitiver Elemente', *NJW*, 2000, pp. 241–246.

Koziol 2009
Koziol, H., 'Punitive Damages: Admission into the Seventh Legal Heaven or Eternal Damnation? Comparative Report and Conclusions', in: H. Koziol & V. Wilcox (eds.), *Punitive Damages: Common Law and Civil Law Perspectives*, Wien: Springer, 2009, pp. 275–308.

Koziol 2010
Koziol, H., *Grundfragen des Schadensersatzrechts*, Wien: Jan Sramek, 2010.

Koziol & Wilcox 2009
Koziol, H. & Wilcox, V. (eds.), *Punitive Damages: Common Law and Civil Law Perspectives*, Wien: Springer, 2009.

Lange & Schiemann 2003
Lange, H. & Schiemann, G., *Schadensersatzrecht*, Tübingen: Mohr Siebeck, 2003.

Magnus 2010
Magnus, U., 'Why is US Tort Law so Different?', *JETL*, 2010, pp. 102–124.

Magnus 2011
Magnus, U., 'Vor §§249–255 BGB', in: *Nomos-Kommentar BGB, Schuldrecht*, Teilbd. 1, Baden-Baden: Nomos, 2011.

Müller 2000
Müller, P., *Punitive Damages und deutsches Schadensersatzrecht*, Berlin: De Gruyter, 2000.

Oetker 2007
Oetker, H., '§§249–255 BGB', in: *Münchener Kommentar zum Bürgerlichen Recht*, Bd. 2, München: Beck, 2007.

Principles of European Tort Law 2005
Principles of European Tort Law – Text and Commentary, by the European Group of Tort Law, Wien: Springer, 2005.

Schiemann 2005
Schiemann, G., '§§249–254 BGB', in: *Staudinger Kommentar zum Bürgerlichen Gesetzbuch mit Einführungsgesetz und Nebengesetzen*, Berlin: Sellier & De Gruyter, 2005.

Schmidt-Assmann 2011
Schmidt-Assmann, E., 'Art. 103', in: Th. Maunz, G. Dürig, & R. Herzog (eds.), *Grundgesetz Kommentar*, München: Beck, 2011.

Schubert 2011
Schubert, C., '§§249–255 BGB', in: G. Bamberger & H. Roth (eds.), *Beck'scher Online-Kommentar BGB*, München: Beck, 2011.

Schulze 2009
Schulze, R., '§§249–253 BGB', in: R. Schulze *et al.*, *Bürgerliches Gesetzbuch Handkommentar*, Baden-Baden: Nomos, 2009.

Sebok 2009
Sebok, A.J., 'Punitive Damages in the United States', in: H. Koziol & V. Wilcox (eds.), *Punitive Damages: Common Law and Civil Law Perspectives*, Wien: Springer, 2009, pp. 155–196.

Slizyk 2011
Slizyk, A., *IMM-DAT. Die Schmerzensgeld-Datenbank*, München: Beck, 2011.

Thüsing 2001
Thüsing, G., *Wertende Schadensberechnung*, München: Beck, 2001.

Wagner 2006
Wagner, G., 'Neue Perspektiven im Schadensersatzrecht – Kommerzialisierung, Strafschadensersatz, Kollektivschaden, Gutachten für den 66. Deutschen Juristentag', in: *Verhandlungen des 66. Deutschen Juristentages Stuttgart 2006*, München: Beck, 2006.

Wagner 2009
Wagner, G., 'Vor §823, §823', in: *Münchener Kommentar zum Bürgerlichen Recht*, Bd. 5, München: Beck, 2009.

Wilcox 2009
Wilcox, V., 'Punitive Damages in England', in: H. Koziol & V. Wilcox (eds.), *Punitive Damages: Common Law and Civil Law Perspectives*, Wien: Springer, 2009, pp. 7–53.

Zekoll 1987
Zekoll, J., *US-amerikanisches Produkthaftpflichtrecht vor deutschen Gerichten*, Baden-Baden: Nomos, 1987.

Chantal B.P. Mahé*

PUNITIVE DAMAGES IN THE COMPETING REFORM DRAFTS OF THE FRENCH CIVIL CODE

1. Introduction

'Obviously disproportionate' was the description given by the *Cour de cassation* about a 1,460,000 USD punitive award ordered by the Supreme Court of California (County of Alameda), in addition to 1.8 million USD compensatory damages, against a French manufacturer for non-performance of a 826,000 USD deal concluded with American purchasers.[1] The *Cour de cassation* confirmed the exequatur refusal of the Californian decision on the ground that:

> 'if a condemnation to pay punitive damages is, as such, not contrary to public order, it is otherwise when the amount of damages is obviously disproportionate compared to the harm suffered and the contractual breach' (transl. CM).

The reasoning of the French Supreme Court echoes the cautious admission of punitive damages by three recent competing reform drafts of the *Code civil*.[2] These drafts all contain a punitive damages provision revealing a consensus, among the drafters, about the admissibility of this common law concept within French civil liability. French private law indeed, is not at odds with repressive mechanisms. Several legal scholars even share

* Assistant professor, Faculty of Law, Private Law Department, VU University Amsterdam. I would like to thank the editors and Frances Gilligan for their comments and suggestions on an earlier draft of this paper. The usual disclaimer applies.

1 Cass. 1e civ., 1 December 2010, § 09–13303, available at: www.legifrance.gouv.fr. About the enforcement of US punitive damages awards in Belgium, Germany and Italy, see Evelien de Kezel's contribution in this book.

2 These drafts are, chronologically presented:
(1) The 'Avant-projet de réforme du droit des obligations (Articles 1101 à 1386 du Code civil) et du droit de la prescription (Articles 2234 à 2281 du Code civil), Rapport à Monsieur Pascal Clément, Garde des Sceaux, Ministre de la Justice', from September 2005, supervised by Prof. Catala and Viney and published at www.justice.gouv.fr/Art_pix/RAPPORTCATALASEPTEMBRE2005.pdf;
(2) The '*Proposition de loi § 657 portant réforme de la responsabilité civile*' from July 2010 (www.senat.fr/dossier-legislatif/ppl09-657.html), and;
(3) The Draft published in '*Pour une réforme du droit de la responsabilité*', Paris: Dalloz 2011, under the supervision of Prof. Terré.

the belief that covert punitive damages are ordered in practice.[3] Still, the design of these provisions betrays a reluctance towards the allowance of damages which are out of proportion with the losses caused.

Indeed, punitive damages fundamentally depart from the exclusively compensatory function of French civil liability summed up in its founding principle of '*réparation intégrale*' or full reparation.[4] According to this traditional reparation rule, damages aim at repairing 'all, but no more than, the harm suffered': they must neither lead to losses, nor to profit for the victim ('*ni perte, ni profit pour la victime*') and are not linked to the gravity of the damaging behaviour.[5] But sanctioning the seriousness of certain damaging behaviour is precisely what all three drafting groups are aiming for when adopting a punitive damages provision. No consensus emerges from these drafts, however, as to the damaging behaviour to be sanctioned and the features of the sanction itself (e.g. calculation basis, upper limit, beneficiaries, insurability). This paper offers a comparative analysis of the three competing punitive damages provisions, each establishing a different balance between the call for a punitive mechanism as private enforcement tool and the continued loyalty towards the traditional compensatory function of civil liability. After an overview of the respective fundamentals of the competing reform drafts (par. 2), follows a detailed comparison of their respective punitive damages provision (par. 3).

2. The Competing Reform Drafts – General Highlights

In July 2010, the First Legislative Chamber registered a new bill proposal – hereafter the Béteille Proposal[6] – the purpose of which is to reform and codify present tort law. Its punitive damages provision is to be found in Article 1386–25 Béteille Proposal.[7] This

3 See Borghetti 2009. This author describes a series of punitive mechanisms one encounters in French civil law, among which a contractual mechanism such as penalty clauses (*clauses pénales*) or a more general device like civil fines. Civil fines are defined as 'provided for in a civil statute (…) and to which one can be sentenced by a civil court' (Borghetti 2009, § 18) when the litigious conduct do also not constitute a criminal offence. French law distinguishes civil fines from criminal fines and administrative fines (see Behar-Touchais 2002, § 8–14). They are a serious competitor to punitive damages. However, contrary to punitive damages, their amount often remains low. There is one major exception though: Article L. 442–6-III Commercial Code provides that those who infringes certain prohibited practices in business-to-business relations can be ordered to pay a fine up to € 2 million. He further discusses the 'widely shared belief' in the existence of a judicial practice of covert punitive damages award taking in order to take into account – in violation of the full reparation rule – of the seriousness of the defendant's behaviour and/or the gain he or she thereby achieved, Borghetti 2009, § 22–29.

4 E.g. Cass. 2e civ., 23 janvier 2003, Bull. civ. II § 20.

5 E.g. Fabre-Magnan 2004, § 338, Le Tourneau & Cadiet 2007, § 2523s. An exception to this principle exists, though, in case of fraudulent breach of contract (Article 1150 *Code civil, faute dolosive*) e.g. a deliberate non-performance of a contractual obligation combined with the promisor's intention to harm. In that case, the promisor might be condemned to compensate foreseeable as well as unforeseeable damages suffered by the promisee, see e.g. Fabre-Magnan 2004, § 217, Vignolle 2010, § II.A.

6 The proposal is named after the First Chamber member Laurent Béteille who initiated it. It has not been submitted to voting yet. This proposal expired on October 18th, 2011.

7 Article 1386–25 provides that:
'In cases where the law expressly provides so, when the damage results from a deliberate wrongdoing or a deliberate breach of contract and has lead to an enrichment of the wrongdoer resp. promisor that the

proposal follows up an information report of the First Legislative Chamber Law Commission on the reform of French civil liability – hereafter Béteille & Anziani report.[8] The Béteille Proposal 'translate[s], into legislative form' the recommendations of that prior report.[9] The Béteille & Anziani report and Béteille Proposal both follow in the footsteps of the *Avant-Projet de réforme du droit des obligations* published in 2005 under the leadership of Professor Catala – hereafter Catala Draft – which contains a punitive damages provision at Article 1371 Catala Draft.[10] In 2010, a third reform draft was officially submitted by the so-called Terré drafting group to the Minister of Justice and published in March 2011 – hereafter the Terré Tort Draft. Punitive damages are codified in Article 69 al. 2 Terré Tort Draft.[11] While the Béteille Proposal originates from a

sole compensatory damages cannot eliminate, the judge can condemn, by a motivated decision, the inflictor of the damage to the payment, in addition to compensatory damages for the harm suffered in accordance with Article 1386-22, of punitive damages, the amount of which may not stand out twice the amount of the compensatory damages.
According to shares decided by the judge, the punitive damages are respectively paid to the victim and to a fund which purpose is to compensate harm similar to the one suffered by the victim. When such a fund does not exist, the share of the punitive damages which is not attributed to the victim should be paid to the Treasury'. (Transl. CM).

8 Anziani, A. & Béteille, L., Rapport d'information fait au nom de la commission des lois constitutionnelles par le groupe de travail relative à la responsabilité civile, § 558 (2008–2009), released in July 2009 (www.senat.fr/notice-rapport/2008/r08-558-notice.html). Laurent Béteille and Alain Anziani, both former lawyers, are respectively right-wing and left-wing members of the Working Group on Tort Law, part of the First Chamber law commission, created in November 2008. Among the three most recommended innovations is the allocation of punitive damages in case of lucrative faults, See Anziani & Béteille 2009, Recommendation § 24, p. 7.

9 Béteille Proposal, Exposé des motifs, p. 3. The Béteille Proposal contemplates the replacement of the present Article 1382 up to Article 1386 by no less than 66 new provisions. Revised Chapter II – Fourth Title, Third Book – of the Civil Code, entitled 'De la Responsabilité', clearly indicates that, like the Catala Draft, its scope stretches out beyond tort to contractual liability. This fundamental direction dictates the rephrasing of Article 1382 where the notion of non-performance of a contractual obligation makes its entry. Article 1382 would then sound: 'Tout fait quelconque de l'homme ou toute contravention à une obligation contractuelle, qui cause à autrui un dommage, oblige son auteur à le réparer'. After a first section comprising of general provisions, a second one is dedicated to the conditions for one to be held liable. The third section concentrates on the effects of one's liability and the last section deals with two specific liability regimes: product liability and liability for traffic accidents.

10 Article 1371 Catala Draft provides that:
'One whose fault is manifestly [deliberate], particularly a [lucrative fault], may be ordered to pay punitive damages besides compensatory damages. The judge may direct a part of such damages to the Treasury. The judge must provide specific reasons for ordering such punitive damages and must clearly distinguish their amount from that of other damages awarded to the victim. Punitive damages may not be the subject of a contract of insurance' (Transl. CM).
This translation departs from the official one proposed by Levasseur (Levasseur 2008, p. 86) because it is, in my view, not faithful to the original text on two decisive elements, namely the translation of *délibéré* as premeditated and the replacement of the expression *faute lucrative* by an improper description.
About Article 1371 Catala Draft, see Rowan 2009, p. 325 ff, Rowan 2010, pp. 513–517 and Borghetti 2009, § 34–46.

11 Article 69 Terré Tort Draft reads as follows:
'Subject to any specific provision, the form and amount of the reparation may have a symbolic reach.
When the harm is caused by an intentional fault, the judge may condemn the wrongdoer, by an especially reasoned decision, to exemplary damages' (Transl. CM).

legislative body, the Catala Draft and the Terré Tort Draft are both initiatives of university scholars; the only difference being that the latter group is composed of an equal number of university scholars and legal practitioners. The present paragraph provides for further insights on the respective general background of the competing punitive damages provisions which are examined in paragraph 3.

2.1. *Scope of Application and General Purpose of the Reform*

The Catala Draft considers reforming contract law, tort law and prescription law as well.[12] The drafters' general purpose is not to depart from the positive law derived from Articles 1382–1386 of the *Code civil* but rather to adjust it (*'le changement dans la continuité'*): codification through the consolidation of case law is the motto.[13] This especially reflects the approach followed by the drafters of the 60 tort law provisions, headed by Professor Viney.[14] The Béteille Proposal which comprises of contractual and non-contractual liability rules opts, like the Catala Draft, for the consolidation of judge made tort law.[15] The Terré Tort Draft focuses on non-contractual liability rules but is part of a wider reforming endeavour of the French law of obligation which resulted, in 2009, in a reform draft on contract law – hereafter Terré Contract Draft.[16] In contrast with the Catala Draft and the Béteille Proposal, it seeks to re-codify French tort law by restructuring it rather than by consolidating existing case law.[17]

2.2. *The Drafts' Preparatory Works*

The text of the Catala Draft encloses preliminary comments regarding its major orientations. Unfortunately, the comments on the tort law chapter are silent about the motives leading to the adoption of a punitive damages mechanism,[18] nor do these comments throw light on its specific features such as its scope of application or the beneficiaries of the award.[19] The comments focus instead on the functions of civil

12 About the Catala Draft in general, see Vogenauer 2009, p. 9–14.

13 The drafters seek to modernise the *Code civil* in order for it to recover its lost status of *ius commune* of the French law of obligation. Catala 2005, § 2.

14 Viney 2005b, p. 143.

15 Béteille Proposal, Exposé des motifs, p. 3.

16 See F. Terré (ed.), *Pour une réforme du droit des contrats*, Dalloz: Paris, 2009, 310 p.

17 Terré 2011, § 3–4.

18 The introductory comments provide no inventory of legal deficiencies justifying the introduction into general tort law of a repressive mechanism, neither explanations as to the adequacy of punitive damages to the problems identified, nor about the method(s) according to which the drafting group worked, nor do they refer to relevant publications on this issue.

19 Shortly before the publication of the Catala Draft, Viney pleaded for a combined restitutionary and punitive mechanism conceived to deprive an inflictor from any profit deriving from his or her wrongdoing – a so-called lucrative fault – and to deter subsequent similar wrongdoing. Such a mechanism would stand out, still not abandon, the traditional compensatory vision of civil liability as proclaimed by the *Cour de cassation*. Viney supports that an official recognition of punitive damages, now applied in a disguised way, would lead to the adoption of an adequate regime insofar that its scope of application would be clearly defined, excesses could be sanctioned and insurability against punitive

liability,[20] its primary function being a compensatory one, while Article 1371 Catala Draft forms as a cautious step towards the admissibility of a punitive function of civil liability.[21]

The Béteille & Anziani report upon which the Béteille Proposal directly builds, is far meatier. It exposes along its 110 pages the principles guiding the reform, identifies the priorities of the reform and formulates for each a series of recommendations. These recommendations are based on a study of positive tort law and the consultation of national stakeholders.[22] It holds a comparative law component which, however, remains limited.[23] No justification for inserting punitive damages within civil liability law is, here also, provided for, still it is indirectly broached. The report notices that serious damaging behaviour such as lucrative faults benefit from a gap flowing from civil and criminal law: the gain obtained by the defendant is neither neutralized by civil liability law, nor sanctioned by criminal law.[24]

One of the distinctive features of the Terré Tort Draft is precisely the impact of comparative law,[25] first, on the identification process of the striking features of French tort law and corresponding reform priorities and second, on the proposed solutions.[26] The influence of comparative law on the treatment of lucrative faults and punitive damages is tangible.[27] A justification for the insertion of exemplary damages is to put an end to the judicial practice of covert punitive damages.[28]

The doctrine prior to the Catala Draft had already paved the way for the discussion about the introduction of punitive damages and provided for justifications.[29] The debate closely involved lucrative faults. A common perception is that, in response to lacunas in civil and criminal legislation,[30] lower civil judges have, when assessing the award for non-

awards be excluded. This, as a result, would reinforce the efficacy of such a mechanism as well as legal security in general. A major motive behind the proposed incorporation into the Civil Code of punitive damages is thus to bring the theory of the law in the books in accordance with practice of law in action. The required adequacy between the compensation awarded, on one hand, and the harm suffered, on the other hand, the so-called *réparation intégrale* rule which excludes any influence of the seriousness of the infringement on the amount of damages, has indeed been in practice bypassed either by lower courts judge or the legislator. See Viney 2005a, § I.

20 Viney 2005b, p. 148.

21 Though not recognised as a specific function of tort law, preventive function is indirectly admitted in Article 1369-1 Catala Draft dealing with specific relief (Article 1369-1 Catala Draft).

22 See Anziani & Béteille 2009, p. 129 ff.

23 The Anziani & Béteille report contains a brief description of punitive damages under common law, Anziani & Béteille 2009, p. 29.

24 Anziani & Béteille 2009, p. 80 & 88. The reporters further assert that the claim for the introduction of punitive damages would not be as loud if criminal courts would award higher amount of civil damages to victims of a criminal offence. The reporters observe that criminal judges award far lower amount of damages than their civil counterparts, as a result one of their recommendations is to tackle this 'cultural difference'. Anziani & Béteille 2009, p. 89. Comp. with Law Commission Report § 1.15.

25 The other one being the choice for restructuring of French tort law.

26 See Rémy 2011, p. 43 and Rémy & Borghetti 2011, p. 67.

27 Rémy-Corlay 2011, pp. 200–201 and 222.

28 See below § 3.1.3.

29 See e.g. Carval 1995, Fasquelle 2002, § 21–35, Jourdain 2002, § 7–11, Viney 2002, p. 66.

30 Jourdain 2002, § 8, Viney 2002, § II.A.

pecuniary losses and exercising thereby their sovereign power of appreciation, taken into account the seriousness of the defendant's conduct getting round the full reparation principle.[31] Codifying punitive damages would end the legal uncertainty created by such covert practices[32] and reel off the law in the books and the law in action. Punitive damages are considered an effective legal tool due to their dissuasive effect on potential wrongdoers,[33] and their incentive impact on victims as well.[34] The discussion also points at possible risks linked to punitive damages, such as the possible undue enrichment of the victim and an increase in damages claim which would plagued lower jurisdictions.[35] Though civil fines would avoid such consequences as they are paid to the treasury, this device, due its maximum amount, lacks flexibility.[36]

2.3. *Punitive Damages Provisions: Main Focus and Context*

The draft provisions on punitive damages introduce a significant exception to the *réparation intégrale* principle which all three drafts propose to codify.[37] Though significant, because this exception acknowledges the punitive function of civil liability in addition to its traditional compensatory one, punitive damages are nevertheless meant to apply in limited cases.

Article 1386-25 Béteille Proposal and Article 1371 Catala Draft focus both on so-called lucrative faults. Article 1371 Catala Draft lacks precision as to its exact scope of application and the assessment of the damages award, leaving its further interpretation to the judge.

Article 1386-25 Béteille Proposal is, in contrast, characterised by a clear-cut scope of application and an upper limit for the amount of damages to be allocated. As the principle

31 See e.g. Jourdain 2002, § 7, Fasquelle 2002, § 21-24 (case law analysis), Borghetti 2009, § 22-30 (with case law illustrations). Apparently one also encounters such practices in Italian and German civil case law, see e.g. Anziani & Béteille 2009, p. 84.

32 Fasquelle 2002, § 24.

33 Viney depicts the full reparation principle, which ignores the seriousness of the defendant's conduct and the gains he or she made by his or her wrongdoing, as an incentive to commit an infringement ('*un pousse-au-crime*)', Viney 2002, § 1. She further stresses the shortcoming of that principle as 'it is delusion' when applied to non-pecuniary losses.

34 Fasquelle 2002, § 27.

35 *Ibid.*, § 35.

36 About civil fines see above note 3. Fasquelle 2002, § 31. For a comparison between the device of civil fines and punitive damages see Behar-Touchais 2002, esp. § 15-23.

37 The *réparation intégrale* rule, a founding principle placed ahead of the reparation chapter of each drafts, is stated at:
Article 1370 in the Catala Draft, which purpose is 'to place the victim as far as possible in the position he would have been in had the act created liability not occurred' whereby the damages awarded 'should produce neither profit nor loss for the victim', Transl. Levasseur 2008 p. 86;
Article 1386-24 in the Béteille Proposal, which reads: 'L'allocation de dommages et intérêts a pour objet de replacer la victime dans la situation où elle se serait trouvée si le fait dommageable n'avait pas eu lieu, de sorte qu'il n'en résulte pour elle ni perte ni profit. (...)';
Article 49 in the Terré Tort Draft, whereby 'La victime d'un dommage peut *en général* demander réparation de son entier préjudice (...). La réparation tend à placer le demandeur dans la situation où il se trouverait si le dommage ne lui avait pas été causé; il ne peut *en principe* en résulter pour lui ni perte, ni profit' (ital. CM).

of full reparation (*réparation intégrale*) dictates, the seriousness of the damaging behaviour is, in principle, not taken into account when determining the amount of damages to be awarded, thereby excluding its punitive character. Repressive trends in French case law and legislation, however, tempers the unqualified character of this founding principle, as the Béteille & Anziani report observes. While the consultation conducted by the First Chamber Working Group on Tort Law does not reveal any consensus,[38] the reporters see punitive damages as an 'interesting innovation' whose introduction into French private law ought to be 'moderate'.[39] The key issue to them is not whether a repressive mechanism like punitive damages has a place within French civil liability, but rather whether such a legal mechanism ought to be generalised. Despite the reporters' efforts to meet the criticism expressed against Article 1371 Catala Draft, reluctance to this innovation remains.[40]

In the Terré Tort Draft, punitive damages (Article 69) are directed against intentional violation of one's moral integrity. The Terré drafting group indeed views the restitution of profits as an adequate sanction against lucrative faults of non-contractual (Article 54 Terré Tort Draft) and contractual basis (Article 120 Terré Contract Draft dealing with *dol*).[41] Though Article 69 al. 2 uses the expression 'réparation exemplaire', which rather evokes a compensatory mechanism, the drafters' comments make it clear that it is meant as a punitive damages mechanism.[42]

3. Detailed Comparative Analysis of Competing Provisions

In the following paragraphs the distinctive features of the three competing punitive damages provisions will be compared. Attention will be paid especially to the damaging behaviour they aim at sanctioning, the setting off of the damages award, its beneficiaries and insurability.

38 Interviews were conducted with economic actors representing the business sector as well as consumers' interests, and also with legal practitioners, magistrates and representatives of judges' organisations. Academics were also interviewed among which drafters of the Catala Draft. These interviews reveal a total absence of consensus about punitive damages and an opposition between, on the one hand, academics which are rather favourable towards the introduction of punitive damages in French law and, on the other hand, economic actors and legal practitioners which are globally reluctant to it. Though the necessity of legislative action against certain damaging behaviours such as lucrative faults is widely shared, doubts rise about punitive damages as being the appropriate legal tool to combat these. Anziani & Béteille 2009, pp. 79–100.

39 Anziani & Béteille 2009, p. 88, § 4.

40 See Vignolle 2010, § II.B, who strongly opposes the vision that civil liability might endorse a punitive function.

41 See above note 5.

42 Rémy-Corlay 2011, p. 222.

3.1. *Damaging Behaviour: Lucrative Faults versus Infringement of One's Moral Integrity*

3.1.1. The Imprecision of Article 1371 Catala Draft

Article 1371 Catala Draft formulates a *general rule* that applies to 'manifestly deliberate [faults], particularly (...)' – thus not exclusively – to *lucrative faults*.[43] For punitive damages to be awarded is further required that the damaging behaviour opens a right to compensatory damages. Furthermore, Article 1371 Catala Draft is non-sector specific and applies to contractual breach as well as to non-contractual wrong (Article 1340 Catala Draft). It clearly breaks away from the *réparation intégrale* principle as it associates the damages award with the seriousness of the behaviour of the inflictor.[44]

Article 1371 Catala Draft introduces two new types of '*faute*', that are the '*faute manisfestement délibérée*' and the '*faute lucrative*', the latter being a species of the former. The *faute lucrative* is described as 'a wrongdoing, the beneficial consequences of which – for the wrongdoer – are not neutralised by the sole compensation of the harm caused' (transl. CM).[45] The general category of 'manifestly deliberate fault' is a notion which does not originate from the Civil Code, nor case law. Although new, this category is characterised neither by a Draft provision, nor by the preliminary comments and remains therefore imprecise.[46] One could associate this category with – but not assimilate it to – already existing concepts, such as the notion of *faute volontaire*, a *deliberate* wrongful *act*, or *faute intentionnelle*, whereby the inflictor intentionally sought the harmful consequences of his wrongful behaviour.[47]

This lack of precision led to heavy criticism from e.g. the *Cour de cassation*.[48] What is here at stake is obviously, from the perspective of the inflictor, the exact determination

43 Levasseur translated the expression *faute lucrative* by 'fault whose purpose is monetary gain' which is an incorrect translation because it departs from the definition given to this notion by the Catala Draft. This translation unduly suggests that the application of Article 1371 supposes that the wrongdoer not only wittingly committed a damaging act but also intended the resulting financial profit. Article 1371 Catala Draft remains unclear on that point.

44 Chagny 2006, § 8, Méadel 2007, § 5.

45 The concept is – only – defined in the preliminary comments, Viney 2005b, p. 148. The characterisation of a fault as lucrative thus does not include the *intention* of the wrongdoer to financially profit from his or her behaviour. A distinctive characteristic of this provision lies in its non-sector specific scope of application.

46 The picture becomes even more blurred when looking at Viney's position expressed prior to publication of the Catala Draft. Indeed, according to her, punitive damages should *not* sanction *fautes intentionnelles* from which the wrongdoer did *not* obtain any *profit*, because these faults are already sanctioned by their non-insurability (Article L. 113-1 Insurance Code). Viney 2005a, § I. Given its formulation, Article 1371 primarily aims at 'manifestly deliberate fault' and possibly applies to *faute intentionnelle* which would then fall within this general category. Méadel 2007, § 5.

47 See e.g. Fabre-Magnan 2004, § 279. The concept of *faute volontaire* had lost material relevancy in present civil liability, see e.g. Fabre-Magnan 2004, pp. 758–761.

48 For this very reason, this concept as well as the concept of *fautes lucratives* is not only labelled as imprecise but firstly as improper by the *Cour de cassation*. Rapport Cour de cassation 2007, pp. 68–69. According to the Supreme Court, drafters should avoid departing from existing concepts of fault, a quite conservative approach as it implicitly excludes innovations on that matter.

of the behaviour falling into the grip of punitive damages, thus legal security. Those who point out the imprecision of Article 1371's scope of application, fear that its interpretation, *de facto* imposed on the judge, would pave the way to inconsistencies and even, arbitrary punitive damages awards.[49] The deterrent impact of this mechanism would be sensibly limited if the victim is required to prove the *intention* of the wrongdoer to profit from his damaging behaviour, as proving such intention is difficult. Such requirement would subsequently restrict the availability of punitive damages and thereby the protection of victims.

In a similar vein, Pierre highlights the twofold requirement of a manifestly *and* deliberate fault, which, he views, limits the application of Article 1371 to 'intelligent faults' and faults 'nurtured by the inflictor'.[50] A more general issue is also the difficulty in establishing the lucrative character of a fault and the causality between the harmful act or contractual breach, on one hand, and the exact resulting profit for the wrongdoer, on the other hand.[51]

More fundamental criticism relates to the rupture with civil liability founding principles operated by Article 1371: sanctioning the seriousness of the behaviour of the inflictor conflicts with the neutrality of the damages towards the gravity of the wrongdoing. This approach is considered as contrary to the ethic of civil liability because it would turn civil liability into 'para-criminal' liability.[52]

The drafters of Article 1386-25 Béteille Proposal took account of the criticism, but headed, nevertheless, into the same direction.

3.1.2. Article 1386-25 Béteille Proposal: a Clear Response to Article 1371's Shortcomings

Article 1386-25 Béteille Proposal applies (1) when the law expressly provides so, (2) the prejudice results from a deliberate wrong (*faute délictuelle volontaire*) or a deliberate breach of contract (3) opening right to compensatory award for the victim and (4) leading to profit for the responsible wrongdoer respectively the promisor. Contrary to the Catala Draft, the Béteille Proposal favours a sector-specific approach as punitive damages only apply 'in cases where, the law expressly states so'. Article 1386-25 characterises in general terms the damaging behaviour to be punished, thereby justifying its incorporation into the *Code civil*.

An obvious consequence of Article 1386-25's formulation is that the effective introduction of punitive damages into French civil liability requires further legislative action. Given the reluctance towards this alien legal concept,[53] such a requirement paves the way for postponement.

49 Rapport Cour de cassation 2007, p. 68-69, Méadel 2007, § 10, Dreyer 2008, § 7, Pierre 2010, § I. The latter also pinpoints the twofold requirement of a manifestly and deliberate fault, which excessively narrows the application scope of Article 1371 Catala Draft to 'intelligent faults' and faults 'nurtured by the wrongdoer'.

50 Pierre 2010, § I.

51 Dreyer 2008, § 8.

52 Mésa 2009, § I-A.

53 See e.g. the reluctance expressed by several consultees in Anziani & Béteille 2009, pp. 86-88.

In contrast with Article 1371 Catala Draft, punitive damages under Article 1386–25 do not sanction all lucrative faults. Taking over a fundamental criticism against Article 1371, the Béteille & Anziani report excludes a *general* punitive damages provision on the ground that it would seriously undermine the fundamental distinction between civil and criminal liability.[54] The reporters also question that punitive damages have, in essence, a general preventive function against all lucrative faults and thereby oppose the necessity of a *general* punitive damages provisions.[55] Instead, they identify specific legal fields where punitive damages could apply as in those fields, the reporters view,[56] neither civil nor criminal law insure a just compensation for the harm suffered and an efficient sanction of the inflictor. Thanks to its general characterisation of deliberate and lucrative faults, this provision is meant to set out a framework for further legislation and judicial action and to ensure the internal coherence of the legal policy against such behaviour. Two of the scarce commentators of the Béteille & Anziani report challenge the sector-based approach. One commentator fears that contract and consumer law will not benefit from this innovation.[57] The other pleads that the general application of punitive damages would free the judge from any reluctance to allocate such awards which he considers desirable.[58] If, as Article 1386–25 states, further sector-specific legislation is required, its major impact is therefore beyond all the official recognition, in line with the Catala Draft, and also, therefore, of the repressive function of civil liability beside its traditional compensatory role.[59]

Article 1386–25 targets deliberate *acts* (wrongdoing resp. breach).[60] It does not require that the inflictor intended to make profit out of the wrongdoing respectively

54 Such general provision would also re-introduce the concept of private penalty (peine privée) which French law has continuously combated. The Report further construes the call for a general punitive damages provision as a supposed answer to the unjustified differences between damages awarded by criminal judges compared to their civil counterparts. The reporters recommend – as better solution – that damages awards allocated by criminal judges – when also deciding a civil claim – at least equal those of their civil counterparts. See Anziani & Béteille 2009, pp. 89–90, Recommandation § 22.

55 The reporters consider punitive damages as ineffective in cases where victims, especially in consumer conflicts, have no economic interest to act in justice due to the low damages award expected compared to the high costs of a lawsuit. The introduction of class actions instead would tackle these situations. Anziani & Béteille 2009, p. 91–93, Recommandation § 23.

56 First mentioned are personality rights relating e.g. to ones privacy or reputation, secondly competition law and also environmental law, Anziani & Béteille 2009, pp. 93–95.

57 Mésa 2009, § I.B.

58 Pierre 2010, § I.B.1. This author further signals the risk that a cumulating of sector-based provisions might create distortions and incoherence.

59 Outside these fields, it could provide a ground for lawyers to contest the high level of damages allocated to a victim compared to the harm suffered, especially in presence of a lucrative fault and when the judicial decision does not indicate that the damages awarded aim at compensating the material and immaterial harm suffered as well. They could then pretend that, given the substantial amount of damages allocated to a victim, the judge covertly awarded punitive damages contrary to Article 1386–25. Article 1386–25 Béteille Proposal requires indeed the judge awarding punitive damages to motivate its decision.

60 About the concept of *faute volontaire*, see above § 3.1.1. One first notice that the expression *faute lucrative*, present in Article 1371 Catala Draft, has here disappeared from Article 1386–25 Béteille Proposal and has instead been replaced by a description which strongly resembles though the definition the Catala Draft opted for.

breach.[61] By employing an existing and well characterised concept, the drafters avoid the lack of precision that Article 1371 was criticised for.[62] This choice also responds to conservative criticism of the *Cour de cassation*.[63]

The central role of lucrative faults in both Article 1371 Catala Draft and 1386–25 Béteille Proposal reveals a line of continuity but reluctance towards the codification of this concept nevertheless remains. Commenting on the Béteille & Anziani report, Vignolle, a legal practitioner, contests the need for legislative recognition of the concept of lucrative faults. He suggests instead that, when lucrative faults do not qualify as a criminal infraction, which, in his view, they usually do, judges treat these as a fraudulent breach of contract (*faute dolosive, Article 1150 Code civil*). A victim might on this ground claim and obtain compensation for foreseeable and unforeseeable damage as well as for the special and immaterial harm suffered which, according to Vignolle, renders any recourse to punitive damages superfluous.[64]

3.1.3. Articles 68 and 69 Terré Tort Draft: a Total Shift of Focus

Intentional infringement of one's moral integrity and not lucrative faults are at the heart of the punitive damages provision of the Terré Tort Draft.

If this draft also deals with *fautes lucratives* (Article 54 Terré Tort Draft) these are sanctioned by the siphoning-off of the inflictor's profits.[65] The Terré Tort Draft favours restitutionary above punitive damages as an adequate remedy against lucrative faults,[66] on the ground that punitive awards are excluded by the Draft Common Frame of Reference and might be considered as contrary to public order according to the Rome II Regulation.[67]

Article 69 Terré Tort Draft, conditions allocation of punitive damages to a twofold requirement: an *intentional* infringement and an infringement of one's *moral integrity* which comprises of e.g. one's dignity, honour, reputation or privacy. Here again, the seriousness of the damaging behaviour – its intentional character combined to a specific category of infringement – is taken into account for the assessment of the damages award, this being contrary to positive law. To justify the resulting restricted application of punitive damages, the drafters observe that such approach is in line in with English common law where they are awarded in very limited cases.[68]

61 As a result, situations where the author of an unwitting harmful act, profits from it, fall out of Article 1386–25 scope.

62 See above § 3.1.1. The burden of the proof of the *faute volontaire* still implicitly lies on the victim but could be reversed in the sector-specific legislation.

63 See above footnote 47.

64 Vignolle 2010, § II.B.

65 See for general comments Rémy & Borghetti 2011, p. 82.

66 Rémy-Corlay, member of the drafting group, observes that, in France, restitutionary and punitive award tend to be mixed up because they depart from the founding principle of full reparation. Rémy-Corlay 2011, p. 200.

67 See Comment C on Article VI.-6:101 DCFR and cons. 32 of Regulation 864/2007.

68 Rémy-Corlay 2011, p. 200.

The Drafters consider that rights relating to personal integrity deserve, as it is now the case in positive law, a specific and high level of protection (Article 68 Terré Tort Draft),[69] but also, if not most of all, a *declared* judicial policy of protection.[70] According to the traditional full reparation principle, damages ought to compensate no less, but no more than the harm caused. The assessment of damages becomes highly problematic, however, when the infringement leads to non-patrimonial prejudice, as in the case of infringement of one's moral integrity.[71] Lower court judges assess non-patrimonial harm by using their sovereign power of appreciation and are not required to specify or explain their decision as to the amount allocated.[72] Article 69 Terré Tort Draft echoes the perception that lower judges presently use that sovereign power, and subsequent absence of a duty to give reasons, to inflict high amount of damages in case of non-pecuniary damage in order to sanction the seriousness of certain damaging behaviour while, on the face, they are abiding to the mandatory principle of full reparation.[73] By adopting a punitive damages provision, the Terré Tort Draft expressly aims at officially recognising that the reparation of harm caused by an infringement of one's moral integrity falls outside the scope of the full compensation principle.[74] The drafters' purpose here is to end:

> 'l'hypocrisie actuelle, qui se contente d'imposer au juge du fond le respect formel du principe de réparation intégrale et le laisse arbitrer librement la mesure de la réparation, sous couvert du principe d'appréciation souveraine'.[75]

For its drafters, Article 69 Terré Tort Draft is meant to clarify and to consolidate an existing judicial practice.

3.2. *The Assessment of the Punitive Award*

Article 1371 Catala Draft foresees that a wrongdoer respectively promisor who benefits from her manifestly deliberate fault '*may* be ordered to pay *punitive damages* besides compensatory damages'. The proposed sanction is thus additional to compensatory award and not automatic but to be decided by the judge. Here again, Article 1371 as well

69 Article 9 Code civil states that these rights have constitutional value. According to constant case law, the sole proof of the infringement is sufficient to ground a compensation award (e.g. Cass. civ. 1e, 5 novembre 1996, Bull. civ. I, § 38).

70 Rémy & Borghetti 2011, p. 86.

71 Rémy-Corlay 2011, p. 222.

72 See e.g. Fabre-Magnan 2004, § 339, Le Tourneau & Cadiet 2007, at § 2511: 'C'est une vérité incontestable pour la Cour régulatrice que le juge du fond justifie suffisamment l'évaluation d'un préjudice par le seul énoncé du chiffre retenu, sans être tenu d'en préciser les divers éléments (...), chiffre dont l'équivalence avec le préjudice causé est simplement affirmé, même s'il s'agit [de l'euro] dit symbolique'. According to these authors, the Supreme Court even encourages lower judges, by its judicial policy, not to disclose the *underlying assessment of their* awards for non-pecuniary losses. See Le Tourneau & Cadiet 2007, at § 2512.

73 See above § 2.2.

74 Rémy & Borghetti 2011, op.cit.

75 *Ibid.*

as the '*Exposé des motifs*' are silent as to the exact characterisation and calculation of the award.[76] It is, consequently, for the judge to determine 1) whether the award be allocated 2) whether it should be based on e.g. the harm caused to the victim or the subsequent benefit made by the inflictor or promisor and 3) according to which proportion. Article 1371 imposes a duty to justify specifically his or her decision. The punitive character of this award derives from the fact that it is additional to compensatory damages and directed against a specific category of harmful behaviour.

This proposition encountered much critical response, mainly of a fundamental nature, while some comments concentrated on more technical aspects. In general, opponents do not contend the necessity of intervening against lucrative faults but fiercely oppose the introduction of punitive damages into French civil liability where compensation of the harm suffered is central and not punishment of a given behaviour. The adoption of such a punishment mechanism introduces, in their view, a confusion between the respective functions of civil liability law and criminal law.[77] For proper legislative action against lucrative faults, some opponents refer to criminal and administrative law arguing that rather than reforming civil liability law, criminal law ought instead to be reformed in order to tackle the phenomenon of lucrative faults.[78] Alternative solutions within the frame of civil liability, however, have been suggested. Méadel favours a mechanism which would take into account the benefit made by the wrongdoer.[79] Pierre, though not fundamentally opposed to punitive damages, strongly disapproves of Article 1371 for not specifying the mode of calculation of the punitive award.[80] He views the absence of an upper limit as a wide open doorway to the ordering of excessive awards, a threat to 'the economic equilibrium of civil liability'. The specific motivation duty that Article 1371 imposes on judges – and subsequent judicial control – is apparently not considered as a sufficient safeguard against such judicial arbitrariness.

Article 1386-25 Béteille Proposal labels, just like Article 1371 Catala Draft, the remedy to apply in case of lucrative faults as punitive damages. This award is, as in Article 1371, non-automatic, additional to compensatory damages and the decision whether such an award should be allocated is entrusted to the judge who Article 1386-25 expressly requires to render 'a reasoned decision'. The calculation mechanism of punitive awards is a major concern expressed by consultees in the Béteille & Anziani report.[81] The fundamental difference between both draft provisions relates subsequently to the

76 In her comments prior to the publication of the Draft, Viney is supportive of a penalty (*pénalité*) combined with a benefit-based award – she labelled as being punitive – depriving the wrongdoer of all profit gained as a result of his wrongdoing or contractual default. Viney 2005a, § I.

77 Rapport Cour de cassation 2007, § 92, Dreyer 2008, § 13.

78 Rapport Cour de cassation 2007, p. 69 in fine, Dreyer 2008, § 15.

79 Méadel [Méadel 2007, § 26] who is also critical towards sanctioning lucrative faults by the allocation of punitive damages nuances, though, the alleged incompatibility between this punitive mechanism and the primary function of liability as incarnated in the founding principle of *réparation intégrale*. To her, the incompatibility argument is little convincing since the *réparation intégrale* principle is not mandatory (*d'ordre public*), as attested by the many legislative provisions which depart from it. See on that issue e.g. Borghetti 2009, § 3–21.

80 Pierre 2010, § II.B.

81 Anziani & Béteille 2009, p. 95.

assessment of a punitive damages award. Article 1386–25 defines its basis and delimits its amount, thereby strongly restraining the discretionary power ascribed to the judge under Article 1371 Catala Draft.

Article 1386–25's explicit *limitation of the punitive award* to twice the amount of the compensatory damages is inspired by fear of excessive damages awards.[82] Under French law, the assessment of damages is, as earlier mentioned, a matter of discretionary power of lower courts. Given the absence of judicial control by the Supreme Court on that factual aspect, the reporters consider it essential to limit statutorily the amount of punitive damages that a judge may award.[83] Consultees also warned for a possible rebuff of this provision by the Constitutional Council if the amount of punitive damages is not limited in one way or another.[84] Coming to the *basis for assessment of the punitive damages*, the Béteille & Anziani report recommended that it be proportional to the compensatory damages allocated, a recommendation to which Article 1386–25 abides. The purpose of this provision, however, is to sanction and deter deliberate harmful behaviour from which one had financially benefited. One would thus expect that the calculation basis for punitive damages would be the benefit made rather than the compensatory damages.

Several authors question the dissuasive effect of punitive damages as designed in Article 1386–25 Béteille Proposal.[85] Mésa pleads for an alternative solution: the principle of *full restitution*.[86] Restitution is not only faithful to the founding principle of full reparation, but its deterrent impact on lucrative faults is also stronger as it deprives the inflictor of the subsequent profits.[87]

Article 69 Terré Tort Draft provides that in case of an infringement of one's moral integrity, 'the form and amount of the reparation may be symbolic'. It then states that when such infringement is intentional, 'the judge may condemn the inflictor (..) to an exemplary reparation'.[88] It is for the judge to decide whether the award be allocated and what its amount ought to be.

82 *Ibid*, p. 97.

83 *Ibid*, p. 96.

84 *Ibid*, p. 87. Punitive damages might be assimilated to a repressive mechanism, all the more if it is insufficiently delimited. It should thus conform to the required proportionality between penalty and incriminated behaviour (Article 8 of the Déclaration des Droits de l'Homme) to avoid being declared unconstitutional by the Constitutional Council. The reporters took account of this remark, Anziani & Béteille 2009, p. 96.

85 Vignolle 2010, § I.A., Mésa 2009, § II.A.

86 Mésa 2009, § II.A, The latter is indeed the mirror image of the first since it also aims at restoring the *status quo ante* but focuses on the wrongdoer instead of the victim. This change of perspective presents several comparative advantages. Contrary to punitive damages, a restitutionary award contains no repressive component and appears therefore compatible with the traditional compensatory function of civil liability and abides as well to the constitutional principle of *légalité des peines*. The author also sees as a further advantage the fact that the seriousness of the fault has, in line with the full reparation principle, no impact on the assessment of the restitutionary damages, since the focus is on the gain realised by the defendant.

87 Mésa 2009, § II.B.

88 See the recommendation of the British Law Commission report on the issue of terminology, at Law Commission Report, recommendation no. 16, p. 184.

The decision as to the *allocation* of exemplary damages depends on the discretionary power of the judge, a common scheme between all three competing drafts. Furthermore, the Terré Tort Draft does not specify any *calculation basis*, nor provide for an upper *limit* of the punitive award. Despite critical comments on Article 1371 Catala Draft on these two aspects, the Terré drafting group opted for a similar approach. Indeed, in contrast with the Article 1386–25 Béteille Proposal,[89] Article 69 al. 2 Terré Tort Draft fully entrusts the assessment of the amount of exemplary damages to the wisdom of the lower judge. But Article 69 requires an especially reasoned judicial decision, like Article 1371,[90] with a view to enable its judicial control by upper courts.[91] The Terré drafters apparently consider this requirement as a sufficient safeguard against the risk of arbitrary damages award, often associated with punitive damages and feared by many French commentators. Article 1386–25 only imposes a 'reasoned decision', favouring thereby a statutory to procedural protection against such risks.

None of the competing provisions indicate if the victim should claim punitive damages, due to the reparatory function of the award, or whether the initiative belongs to the judge, due to the punitive character of the award.

3.3. *The Beneficiaries of the Award*

When it comes to the designation of the beneficiary of the award to be paid by the inflictor, the French legal community seems even more divided than regarding the previous items.

Once more, Article 1371 Catala Draft stands out by its imprecision. Article 1386–25 Béteille Proposal echoes critical comments toward the latter but heads nevertheless for the same direction: the plurality of beneficiaries. This approach might appear quite peculiar to common law lawyers. The Terré Tort Draft here again differentiates itself by pointing out the victim as the exclusive beneficiary of the punitive award.

Article 1371 Catala Draft states that the judge, when ordering the payment of punitive damages 'may direct *part of* such damages to the Treasury (Ital. CM)', thereby implicitly providing that the – other part of the – award is to be primarily allocated to the victim, as compensatory damages are.[92] This choice of beneficiaries, about which the drafters comments remain silent, unleashed mainly negative reactions. Commentators oppose the allocation of an additional award to the victim and also contest the Treasury being an appropriate beneficiary. To Dreyer, the allotment of a punitive award to the victim potentially leads to his or her unjust enrichment.[93] The *Cour de cassation* further signals its non-conformity with the compensatory purpose of civil liability where neutrality of the

89 The formulation of Article 1386–25 Béteille Proposal reveals the drafters' intention to address the risk of arbitrary judicial decisions.

90 Departing from positive law, all competing drafts enjoin the judge allocating punitive or exemplary damages to motivate his or her decision. Article 1371 Catala Draft ('specific reason') and 69 al. 2 Terré Tort Draft ('*décision spécialement motivée*') even impose a specifically reasoned decision.

91 Rémy & Borghetti 2011, p. 86.

92 Comp. with Méadel 2007, § 23–24. As Article 1371 does not explicitly mention the victim as beneficiary of the punitive award, Méadel sees the Treasury as the sole beneficiary.

93 Dreyer 2008, § 9, contra Pierre 2010, § II.A.2.

award for the victim is central.[94] Following a more pragmatic approach, Chagny positively views the allocation of punitive damages to victims as it constitutes an incentive for the same to intervene against lucrative, wrongful behaviour. Civil liability serves then as a private enforcement tool which directly benefits the victim but indirectly the community as well.[95] As to the allocation of the punitive award to the Treasury, the *Cour de cassation* characterises it as 'weird'.[96] If implemented, it would create a confusion between the concept of punitive damages as understood in common law and the device of civil fines (*amende civile*) with which French private law is familiar.[97] The highest Court thus suggests that the punitive award be instead assigned to a compensation fund (*fonds d'indemnisation*).

Article 1386-25 Béteille Proposal also foresees a plurality of beneficiaries: part of the punitive damages is to be directed to the victim and another part to a fund which purpose is to compensate losses as suffered by the victim. In the absence of such fund, its share should benefit the Treasury. The Béteille & Anziani Report revealed that consultees were strongly divided on the issue of the beneficiaries of the punitive damages.[98] Despite the lack of consensus, the Béteille & Anziani Report recommends that the award be allocated in part to the victim. The reporters deem it to be of the essence of punitive damages that the victim be a beneficiary. Still they partly side with the *Cour de cassation* when proposing that part of the award be allocated to an indemnification fund, prior to treasury. Also contested by the consultees is the choice, in Article 1371 Catala Draft, to charge the judge with the decision whether or not to direct part of the award to another beneficiary than the victim.[99] Article 1386-25 Béteille Proposal diverges slightly from Article 1371 Catala on that point too: the plurality of beneficiaries is codified while the designation of the beneficiary fund and the proportion of the award it is to receive is a matter of sovereign power of the lower judge. Again, the Béteille Proposal builds upon Article 1371 Catala Draft but attempts to avoid its shortcomings.

Neither the text of Article 69 Terré Tort Draft, nor the drafters comments, explicitly designate the beneficiary of the punitive damages. It clearly follows though from the system of Articles 68 and 69 Terré Tort Draft. According to Article 68 Terré Tort Draft, any person can obtain reparation of (non-)patrimonial harm caused by the infringement of his or her moral integrity. The originality of the Terré Tort Draft lies in the fact that the victim can be a private individual as well as a legal entity. Legal entities, Article 68 Terré Tort Draft stipulates, may claim for reparation, provided, however, they are the victim of serious fault (*faute grave*). It then follows from Article 69 Terré Tort Draft that the

94 Rapport Cour de cassation 2007, § 92, p. 69.

95 Chagny 2006, § 14, p. 1226.

96 It furthermore renders obscure the purpose aimed at by this repressive mechanism, Rapport Cour de cassation 2007, § 92, p. 69. See also Méadel 2007, § 24.

97 See supra note 3.

98 A consumer organisation pleads for the exclusive allocation of the punitive award to the victim, see also Pierre 2010, § II.A.2. On the contrary, the *Cour de cassation* and Ministry of Justice exclude the victim as a beneficiary who would then enjoy a double compensation as, in practice, the seriousness of the behaviour often influences the compensation award of non-patrimonial harm. A critic often heard is that allocating punitive damages to the victim constitutes a private penalty. In order to avoid that, many suggested that the punitive damages be instead exclusively directed to a specific indemnification fund. Anziani & Béteille 2009, p. 98.

99 Anziani & Béteille 2009, p. 99.

(victim's) reparation right, based on Article 68 might either be a symbolic award or exemplary damages. Contrary to both the Catala Draft and Béteille Proposal, the victim, according to the Terré group, is thus the sole beneficiary of the exemplary damages. This constitutes a far stronger incentive for the victim whose moral integrity has intentionally been damaged to take legal action; thereby increasing the deterrent impact of this provision.

3.4. *The Insurability Issue*

Before looking at how the competing drafts deal with the insurability of punitive award, attention must be paid to the legal context of that issue. Especially relevant here is Article L.113-1 of the Insurance Code, the second paragraph of which provides that 'the insurer shall not be answerable for losses and damage caused by the insured person's intentional wrongdoing or fraud'. As previously mentioned, the notion of intentional wrongdoing (*faute intentionnelle*) means that not only was the damaging behaviour deliberate (*faute volontaire*) but the wrongdoer also intended the subsequent damaging harm.[100]

Article 1371 Catala Draft clearly settles the issue of insurability by stating that [p]unitive damages may not be the subject of a contract of insurance'. In contrast, Article 69 Terré Tort Draft is silent on that matter. However, since it requires an *intentional* wrongdoing for the allocation of exemplary damages, the non-insurability against such punitive award derives from Article L. 113-1 Insurance Code and does not need to be expressly provided for in the reform draft.

Article 1386-25 Béteille Proposal is also silent on that aspect, although the Béteille & Anziani report pays attention to it.[101] Consequently, one could be insured against punitive award sanctioning his or her deliberate damaging behaviour as long as any intentional wrongdoing cannot be proved.

4. Conclusion

Presently, the introduction into French civil law of punitive or exemplary damages is envisaged by three competing reform drafts of the *Code civil*. The punitive damages provision of the Béteille Proposal could be depicted as an improved version of the

100 See above, footnote 33.

101 The reporters are not opposed to the insurability against punitive damages condemnation, while the consultees are divided on that issue. Arguments against insurability put forward by consultees are many. It first would be contrary to public morals according to Article 6 Civil Code, which stipulates that 'Statutes relating to public policy and morals may not be derogated from by private agreements'. Another argument is that as one cannot insure itself against criminal sanctions, one should neither be allowed to insure itself against punitive damages. The mechanism of punitive damages would lose its deterrent impact if the wrongdoer does not personally take on the sanction told Jourdain to the Law Commission. Conversely the Ministry of Justice considers that the insurance premium against such sanction would be so high that it will itself deter the committing lucrative fault. Furthermore, preventing insurability against punitive damages would leave a heavy financial burden on companies and might on the long term lead to relocation of economic activities, Anziani & Béteille 2009, pp. 97–98, see also Pierre 2010, § II.A.1.

corresponding provision of the Catala Draft. In short, the Béteille Proposal operates a compromise between the call from university scholars for punitive damages and the fear from legal practitioners and the business sector for excessive and arbitrary damages awards. Its punitive damages provision is indeed sector-based and designed to avoid excesses through the limitation of the punitive award and mandatory disclosure of the judge's reasoning, while the award's beneficiaries range from the victim, an indemnification fund to the treasury.

In contrast, the Terré Tort Draft follows a quite different approach. There, exemplary damages would apply against intentional infringements of one's personal integrity as restitutionary damages are considered a more appropriate tool against lucrative faults. Assessment of an exemplary award is left to the discretion of the judge who is nevertheless required to render an especially reasoned decision, while the award only benefits to the victim.

Opponents to punitive damages invoke their incompatibility with the fundamental principle of full reparation and the disruption their introduction would cause to the frontier between civil and criminal law. Those in favour of a – restrictive – punitive damages' codification consider that it would fill in a gap which has led, in the judicial practice, to covert punitive damages award. A declared civil liability policy towards certain serious damaging conducts would enhanced legal security, indeed a punitive damages device would have a dissuasive impact on potential wrongdoers and an incentive effect on victim to claim damages.

Whether a punitive damages provision will end up in the civil code is difficult to say. The phenomenon of lucrative faults, revealing the limits of the full reparation principle, has inspired the incorporation of a punitive damages provision in the two first reform drafts. Discussions prior and following publications of the first drafts focused indeed on lucrative faults. Since the Terré Tort Draft opts for restitutionary damages against lucrative faults, a tool which, in contrast with punitive damages, is compatible with basic reparation principles, the attractiveness of punitive damages might water down.

Bibliography

Anziani & Béteille 2009
Anziani, A. & Béteille, L., *Rapport d'information fait au nom de la commission des lois constitutionnelles par le groupe de travail relative à la responsabilité civile*, § 558 (2008–2009), 15 juillet 2009, available at:
www.senat.fr/notice-rapport/2008/r08-558-notice.html.

Behar-Touchais 2002
Behar-Touchais, M., 'L'amende civile est-elle un substitut satisfaisant à l'absence de dommages et intérêts punitifs?' *LPA*, 2002, no. 232, p. 36s.

Bérard 2011
Bérard, F. de, 'Punitive damages et ordre public international français : de la mesure pour l'arlésienne', *GP*, no. 83, p. 13s.

Borghetti 2009
Borghetti, J.-S., 'Punitive damages in France', in: H. Koziol & V. Wilcox (eds.), *Punitive Damages: Common Law and Civil Law Perspectives*, Vienna: Springer, 2009, pp. 55–73.

Carval 1995
Carval, S., *La responsabilité civile dans sa fonction de peine privée*, Paris: L.G.D.J., 1995.

Catala Draft
Avant-projet de réforme du droit des obligations (Articles 1101 à 1386 du Code civil) et du droit de la prescription (Articles 2234 à 2281 du Code civil), Rapport à Monsieur Pascal Clément, Garde des Sceaux, Ministre de la Justice, 22 septembre 2005, available at: www.justice.gouv.fr/Art_pix/RAPPORTCATALASEPTEMBRE2005.pdf.

Catala 2005
Catala, P., 'Présentation générale de l'avant-projet', in: *Avant-projet de réforme du droit des obligations (Articles 1101 à 1386 du Code civil) et du droit de la prescription (Articles 2234 à 2281 du Code civil), Rapport à Monsieur Pascal Clément, Garde des Sceaux, Ministre de la Justice, 22 septembre 2005*, pp. 2–7.

Chagny 2007
Chagny, M., 'La notion de dommages et intérêts punitifs et ses répercussions sur le droit de la concurrence'. Lectures plurielles de l'article 1371 de l'avant-projet de réforme du droit des obligations, *JCP (G)*, 2006 no. 25, pp. 1223–1227.

Dreyer 2008
Dreyer, E., 'La faute lucrative des médias, prétexte à une réflexion sur la peine privée', *JCP (G)*, no. 43, I 201, pp. 22–26.

Fabre-Magnan 2004
Fabre-Magnan, M., *Les obligations*, PUF: Paris, 2004.

Fasquelle 2002
Fasquelle, D., 'L'existence de fautes lucratives en droit français', *LPA*, 2002, no. 232, p. 27s.

Jourdain 2002
Jourdain, P., 'Rapport introductif', *LPA* 2002, no. 232, p. 3s.

Law Commission Report 1997
'The Law Commission', *Aggravated, Exemplary and Restitutionary Damages*, Report no. 247, 1997.

Le Tourneau & Cadiet 2007
Le Tourneau, P., Cadiet, L., *Droit de la responsabilité et des contrats*, Dalloz: Paris 2007.

Méadel 2007
Méadel, J., 'Faut-il introduire la faute lucrative en droit français?', *LPA*, 2007 no. 77, p. 6s.

Mésa 2009
Mésa, R., 'La consécration des fautes lucratives: une solution au problème d'une responsabilité civile punitive?', *GP*, 2009, no. 325, p. 15s.

Pierre 2010
Pierre, P., 'L'introduction des dommages et intérêts punitifs en droit des contrats – Rapport Français', *RDC*, 2010, no. 3, p. 1117s.

Rapport Cour de cassation 2007
Rapport du groupe de travail de la Cour de cassation sur l'avant-projet de réforme du droit des obligations et de la prescription, 15 juin 2007, available at: www.courdecassation.fr/institution_1/autres_publications_discours_2039/discours_2202/travail_cour_10699.html.

Rémy 2011
Rémy, P., 'Réflexions préliminaires sur le chapitre *Des délits*', in F. Terré *et al.*, *Pour un réforme de la responsabilité civile*, Paris: Dalloz, 2011, pp. 15–59.

Rémy & Borghetti 2011
Rémy, p. & Borghetti J.-B., 'Présentation du projet de réforme de la responsabilité délictuelle', in F. Terré *et al.*, *Pour un réforme de la responsabilité civile*, Paris: Dalloz, 2011, pp. 61–86.

Rémy-Corlay 2011
Rémy-Corlay, P., 'De la réparation', in F. Terré *et al.*, *Pour un réforme de la responsabilité civile*, Paris: Dalloz, 2011, pp. 191–222.

Rowan 2009
Rowan, S., 'Comparative Observations on the Introduction of Punitive Damages in French Law', in: J. Cartwright, S. Vogenauer & S. Whittaker (eds), *Reforming the French Law of Obligations: Comparative Observations on the Avant-projet de réforme du droit des obligations et de la prescription (the 'Avant-projet Catala')*, Oxford: Hart Publishing, 2009, pp. 325–345.

Rowan 2010
Rowan, S., 'Reflections on the Introduction of Punitive Damages for Breach of Contract', *Oxford J Legal Stud*, no. 3 (2010), pp. 495–517.

Terré Tort Draft
Terré, F. *et al.*, *Pour un réforme de la responsabilité civile*, Paris: Dalloz, 2011.

Terré Contract Draft
Terré, F. *et al.*, *Pour un réforme du droit des contrats*, Paris: Dalloz, 2009.

Vignolle 2010
Vignolle, P.-D., 'La consécration des fautes lucratives: une solution au problème d'une responsabilité civile punitive?' (Acte II), *GP*, 2010, no. 4, p. 7s.

Viney 2002
Viney, G., 'Rapport de synthèse – Faut-il moraliser le droit français de la réparation du dommage?', *LPA*, 2002, no. 232, p. 66s.

Viney 2005a
Viney, G., 'L'appréciation du préjudice', *LPA*, no. 99, p. 89s.

Viney 2005b
G. Viney, Sous-titre III – De la responsabilité civile (Articles 1340 à 1386) – Exposé des motifs, in *Avant-projet de réforme du droit des obligations (Articles 1101 à 1386 du Code civil) et du droit de la prescription (Articles 2234 à 2281 du Code civil), Rapport à Monsieur Pascal Clément, Garde des Sceaux, Ministre de la Justice, 22 septembre 2005*, pp. 141–151.

Vogenauer 2009
'The *Avant-projet de réforme*: An Overview', in: J. Cartwright, S. Vogenauer & S. Whittaker (eds), *Reforming the French Law of Obligations. Comparative Observations on the Avant-projet de réforme du droit des obligations et de la prescription (the 'Avant-projet Catala')*, Oxford: Hart Publishing, 2009, pp. 3–31.

Marta Otero Crespo*

PUNITIVE DAMAGES UNDER SPANISH LAW: A SUBTLE RECOGNITION?

1. Introduction

It is absolutely beyond discussion that punitive damages are a Common Law institution, born in England and developed in the United States, but filtering and entering into the continental European legal systems. Expressed in a very simple way, punitive damages are a private penalty imposed in civil procedures in an amount that exceeds the purely compensatory damages, punishing the defendant and deterring him and others from similar outrageous conducts.[1]

Although their natural habitat is the Anglo-American world, the truth is that in recent years their entrance and even their hidden presence in continental Civil Law jurisdictions have been highly debated, in both the Germanic and Latin legal families.[2] Spain is not an exception concerning the punitive damages phenomenon, so in the next few lines we will attempt to sketch how Spanish positive law and legal literature are dealing with this controversial award. But before going further into this crucial problem, it may be useful to offer some general remarks about the Spanish tort law system, especially some related to the functions of the law of torts.

1.1. *Tort Law in Spain: General Remarks*

Tort Law is a branch of law that addresses and provides remedies for civil wrongs. Under certain preconditions a person who has suffered an injury may find satisfaction, usually through the recovery of its monetary equivalent. In Spain the basic provisions of liability are Articles 1902 to 1910 of the Spanish Civil Code (henceforth CC).[3] Among these

* Lecturer in Civil Law, Research Group *De Conflictu Legum*, University of Santiago de Compostela, Spain.

1 Salvador Coderch 2000a, p. 3.

2 Indispensable, Requejo Isidro, M., *Punitive Damages: How Do They Look Like When Seen From Abroad?* (contained in this publication).

3 The basic character of these provisions comes from two diverse tracks. On the one hand, the CC itself contains several articles with implicit remissions to those Articles 1902–1910 CC; on the other hand, outside the CC there are many dispositions of different hierarchical level that, implicitly or explicitly, are spinning around the principles settled by these Articles 1902–1910 CC. See De Ángel Yagüez 2008, p. 13.

articles, our focus of attention must be Article 1902 CC. According to its content, the person who, as a result of an action or omission, causes damage to another by his fault or negligence shall be obliged to repair the damage caused.[4] This article has its roots in Article 1382 of the French Civil Code,[5] and both contain general clauses of liability, in clear contrast to the German BGB[6] or the English torts.[7]

A brief historical review regarding why someone should repair the damage caused shows two different answers, which appeared at separate times but nowadays co-exist in harmony. From one point of view, in the nineteenth century, the liberal bourgeois minds of the drafters of the CC considered that the author of an injury should be accountable for the harm caused when he had behaved negligently. However, if the wrongdoer had acted with due diligence, in a morally irreproachable manner, he had to remain unpunished. Under these ideological premises there arose liability for fault.[8] On the other hand, an individual could also be found liable regardless of fault on his part: the mere creation of a risk by having performed a particular activity was enough to consider him liable for an injury. The rationale for this type of liability, which is called strict liability or liability for risk, is objective. This type of liability was 'reborn'[9] in the industrial development era in the nineteenth century entailing a clear review of the traditional doctrine of fault. Machinery became a continuous source of accidents, generating a new

4 Article 1902 CC 'El que por acción u omisión causa un daño a otro, interviniendo culpa o negligencia, está obligado a reparar el daño causado'.

5 Literally, 'tout fait quelconque de l'homme, qui cause à autrui un dommage, oblige celui par la faute duquel il est arrivé à le réparer'. This provision was passed without any discussion about its background philosophy, precisely based on the searching for a general protective clause of liability. This general clause of liability guarantees to each citizen the recovery of his own loss; each citizen is entitled to claim for the damages suffered. In this sense, Portalis in his Preliminary statement stressed that the Law should establish only general principles ('maximes générales du droit'), not specific rules ('l'office de la loi est de fixer, par de grandes vues, les maximes générales du droit: d'établir des principes féconds en conséquences, et non de descendre dans le détail des questions qui peuvent naître sur chaque matière. C'est au magistrat et au jurisconsulte, pénétrés de l'esprit general des lois, à en diriger l'application', Portalis 1999, p. 19). Not in vain the French Civil Code was the first entirely made by the bourgeoisie and designed as well to satisfy their expectations and needs, both in form as in the content. As noted in García Rubio & Méndez García 2005, p. 58, the form is abstract, following the Montesquieu convictions, and in its content, its key institutions are governed under the logic of individualism and bourgeois liberalism. Specifically, on the nature of general clause in Article 1328 Code civil, see French authors, e.g., Mazeaud & Tunc 1961, p. 62 ss.; Viney & Jourdain 2006, p. 363 ss.; and even Spanish legal writers, Santos Briz 1963, p. 115; De Ángel Yagüez 1993, p. 261; Díez-Picazo 1999, p. 65; Del Olmo García 2001, pp. 276, 282; López Jacoiste 2002, p. 145.

6 Section 823 BGB *Liability in damages* '(1) A person who, intentionally or negligently, unlawfully injures the life, body, health, freedom, property or another right of another person is liable to make compensation to the other party for the damage arising from this. (2) The same duty is held by a person who commits a breach of a statute that is intended to protect another person. If, according to the contents of the statute, it may also be breached without fault, then liability to compensation only exists in the case of fault'.

7 Enneccerus 1950, p. 647; Pérez González & Alguer 1950, pp. 657–658.

8 Liability for fault (*responsabilidad subjetiva*) perfectly fitted the needs of the Industrial Revolution Era. See Jordano Fraga 1987, p. 58; Díez-Picazo 1999, pp. 83–85; Díez-Picazo 2000, pp. 153–156; García Rubio 2002, pp. 26–29.

9 On the origins of strict liability and its development from the Ancient cultures to the present, Fernández Martín-Granizo 1972, pp. 22–23 and 41–71.

mentality that raised the compensation to victims for damage irrespective of the existence or not of the subjective element of fault. Their first legislative highlights were observed in the field of labour law (labour accidents), reaching new heights with liability for Public Administration,[10] traffic accidents, air navigation, hunting, nuclear accidents, damages derived from the use of goods, products or services, among others.

The birth and consolidation of liability for risk have also set the starting point for the shift in the interpretation of traditional legal principles based on fault. This shift aims to obtain the maximum protection standard for the victims. In Spain, that goal has led the doctrine to develop new practical solutions: remaining theoretically loyal to the dogma of fault, negligence is presumed or even, in matters of evidence, the literature and the judiciary support reversing the pre-established burden of proof in order to achieve this protective effect of the victim. Consequently, there has been an evolution in the judicial interpretation of Article 1902 CC by introducing certain corrective criteria, transforming its subjective foundation into a more strict liability one.

1.2. The Functions of Tort Law: Compensation, Prevention and Punishment

As mentioned above, the duty to repair the damage caused can be linked to a subjective or an objective standard. It is unarguable that when the mechanism of tort law comes into play, a clear willingness to restore the victim to the *status quo* at the time immediately prior to the causation of harm may exist. But although reimbursement or compensation is the most obvious function, the law of torts may also be called to perform another role or roles. In that sense, we might wonder whether restoration is the only function or, on the other hand, could coexist with other goals.

If we assume the determinations of the Spanish legal literature and jurisprudence, tort law may be called upon to perform – at least theoretically – three functions: firstly, a compensatory role; secondly, a preventive function; and third and lastly, a punitive purpose.[11] As we have already stated, of those three, the compensatory role is the most classically accepted as orthodox,[12] setting up as it does the primary function of tort law as being to compensate for the damage suffered. The sum awarded becomes the substitute for legal and economic damage, leaving the victim in a patrimonial situation unscathed. The appropriate ethic of liability promotes this role focusing on re-establishing a balance upset by the harm inflicted. As a consequence of this 'ethical' view, under Spanish law it is possible to graduate liability according to the seriousness of the injury, and the

10 Now constitutionally reflected in Article 106.2 Spanish Constitution 1978.

11 Díez-Picazo 1999, pp. 42–48 also mentions a fourth role, a limiting role ('*función de demarcación*'). According to this function, tort law also establishes the frontiers between freedom of action and the protection of some legal interests. From a different perspective, the economic analysis of law raises two functions and purposes of civil liability: justice and reducing the costs of accidents (See in detail, Calabresi 1984, p. 44 ss.).

12 Professor Pantaleón concluded in his unpublished doctoral thesis in 1981 that the function of Spanish tort law is 'exclusively compensatory'. See Pantaleón 1981, p. 820. This idea is constantly repeated in his works. More recently he has held that 'Prevention is not an aim of the law of torts, but a factual and occasional by-product of compensation', Pantaleón 2005, p. 6.

presumption of innocence is not applicable in civil liability cases, as determined by our Constitutional Court in its ruling of 8 April 1991.[13]

However, the above observations do not mean that other roles cannot be attributed to the law of torts, voiding or cancelling the essential restoring task of the tort law system. Following this line of thought, part of the Spanish legal literature acknowledges a secondary role to the other two functions (the preventive and punitive ones),[14] and among the authors some discriminate between these two secondary purposes. This minority doctrinal subsection does support the view that civil liability may be called upon to perform a preventive role, but it is more reluctant to accept the admission of the punitive role, asserting that this punishment function would only be tolerable from an instrumental point of view, directed towards the prevention aim.[15]

It is clear that in order to achieve prevention, the award of damages itself is a disincentive to potentially harmful behaviours.[16] The basis of this function lies in the precautionary principle, allowing the existence of liability in cases of mere threat of harm or injury. The Spanish professor Salvador Coderch, among others, upholds this preventive function, considering this defensive role perfectly compatible with the traditional compensatory function of tort law;[17] and, without doubt, the greatest efforts to defend this conception of liability can be detected in the economic analysis of law.[18] Nonetheless, professor Pantaleón believes that precluding the realization of unreasonably dangerous conducts is not a normative function of tort liability under Spanish law.[19] His proposal is not inconsistent with the deterrent effect, in fact the threat of liability can promote prevention; however, the preventive function would be called upon to play a secondary role, subject to countervailing requirements.

The last of the purposes of civil liability, the so-called punitive function, is the most alien to our legal tradition and may raise objections from academics as well. Those who have not supported the punitive function as a feasible role of tort law, consider that its defence would entail a drastic break with the ancient compensatory function. However, in our opinion it seems worth noting that this punitive function was already present at the origin of the rules which afterwards developed into the present-day tort law system; but the truth is that this punitive role was completely relegated to nil in all the continental legal jurisdictions.[20] So we do not consider its defence as a novelty, but rather as a possible return to the origins, although with nuances. If the compensatory function of liability

13 RTC 1991, 72. See Pantaleón 1996, p. 1691.

14 De Ángel Yagüez 1995, pp. 229–233 admits that nowadays tort law can display these secondary functions due to the complex setting of the institution; there are many factors that contribute to distort the purity of the traditional compensatory role. See also, e.g., Bourié 2007, p. 219.

15 Reglero Campos 2008, p. 64.

16 Article 10:101 PETL *in fine* states that 'damages also serve the aim of preventing harm', without specifying how this goal is going to be reached. We have to mention also Article 2:104 PETL, which deals with preventive expenses, 'expenses incurred to prevent threatened damage amount to recoverable damage in so far as reasonably incurred'. See Magnus 2008, pp. 202–206.

17 Salvador Coderch & Castiñeira Palou 1997, p. 152.

18 Calabresi 1984, p. 79; Salvador Coderch & Castiñeira Palou 1997, p. 133 ss.; Reglero Campos 2008, pp. 64–69.

19 Pantaleón 2000, p. 443; De Ángel Yagüez 1993, p. 60.

20 Díez-Picazo 1999, p. 44.

focuses on the victim, to leave him in the situation that existed prior to the occurrence of the damage, the punitive function departs from the opposite perspective; that is, the prominent role is given to the tortfeasor, to the agent that has caused the injury, imposing on him an appropriate punishment for the harm he has done and also seeking to deter other potential agents by means of the penalty. At the same time the punitive function of civil liability punishes and prevents. Thus, prevention and punishment could be a side effect – a psychological one – of the compensatory function, but could not become the foundation or criterion for determining the extent of compensation.

Nowadays, many factors contribute to distort the purity of the compensatory function, calling into question if there is 'a single function' of tort law.[21] This does not mean that the primarily compensatory function is denied. It is sustained that compensation cannot be defended as the unique function anymore, especially when the protection of some particular rights or interests considered as particularly vulnerable by the legislator is coming into play. In all of these cases the establishment of a system of compensatory awards together with punitive damages is fairly justified.

The defence of this punitive purpose of tort law has been strengthened particularly after the arrival in our system of this punitive damages figure. As is outlined below, there are now a significant number of provisions in Spanish positive law that, although not openly referring to punitive damages, are subtly designing compensation mechanisms that go beyond mere compensation of the victim, either orchestrating dissuasive sanctions, diluting the thin line between civil liability and unjust enrichment, or pre-setting operations for determining the non-economic damages scheming.

2. Punitive Damages in Spain

2.1. General Approach

The Spanish legal literature usually translates 'punitive damages' as 'daños punitivos'. In our view, this is a hasty and incorrect translation that does not satisfactorily reflect the substance of the concept. 'Damages' are a sum of money claimed or awarded in compensation for a loss or an injury, hence the correct equivalence should be 'compensación', never 'daño'. Accordingly, it would be more proper to speak of 'compensaciones punitivas' or 'indemnizaciones sancionatorias'[22], instead of 'daños punitivos'.

Although, as indicated earlier, the notion of 'punitive damages' is associated with the Common law tort system, today they are restricted to American law, after being abandoned in English law.[23] Their rejection in British law occurred in *Rookes v Barnard*,[24]

21 De Ángel Yagüez 1995, pp. 229–233.

22 Salvador Coderch & Castiñeira Palou 1997, p. 163 ss; Salvador Coderch & Azagra Malo 2004, pp. 1–4. The Spanish Supreme Court in its decision STS 12 January 2009 (RJ 2009, 544) uses both 'compensación sancionadora o pena de indemnización' and also the inaccurate 'daños punitivos'.

23 Markesinis & Deakin 2008, pp. 944–951; Lunney & Oliphant 2008, pp. 855–864; Wilcox 2009, pp. 7–53.

24 *Rookes v Barnard*, [1964] AC 1129.

where Lord Devlin considered punitive damages awards as clearly opposed to the compensatory function of Tort Law itself, mainly because of their punitive, criminal character.[25] This resolution supports the idea that tort law should focus on the victim, to compensate the loss suffered; on the other hand, punitive damages focus on the tortfeasor in order to punish him, therefore transcending the orbit of private law. Due to its criminal trace, this kind of punitive award cannot be generally recognized. After *Rookes v Barnard* punitive damages disappeared from the English legal panorama. In present-day English Law, the closest institution to punitive damages are the so-called 'exemplary damages' that may be awarded in England and Wales; but even those are considered an anomalous civil remedy; as a consequence, they must be limited and can only be awarded in cases where two tests – the 'categories test' and the 'cause of action test'- are satisfied.[26] Concerning these 'exemplary damages' the Law Commission Report no. 247 (1997) 'Aggravated, Exemplary and Restitutionary Damages'[27] has made the following recommendations: a judge (never a jury) should award exemplary damages (or as the Law Commission prefer to call them, 'punitive damages') for any tort or equitable wrong, as well as for statutory wrongs if an award would be consistent with the policy of the statute under which the wrong arises; but only if the defendant's conduct showed a deliberate and outrageous disregard of the plaintiff's rights, and the other remedies awarded would be inadequate to punish the defendant for his conduct. Additionally, no award should usually be made where the defendant has already been convicted of an offence involving the conduct in which the claim for punitive damages is based; and the court should take into account any other sanctions which may have been imposed when deciding whether punitive damages are necessary, and therefore available. Besides, the court should retain a 'safety-valve' discretion in order to refuse punitive damages where they would otherwise be available, if an exceptional factor exists which makes such refusal proper. The Law Commission Report also deals with 'aggravated damages', a sum awarded as compensation for the plaintiff's mental distress, where the manner in which the defendant has committed the tort, or his motives in so doing, or his conduct subsequent to the tort, have distressed or outraged the plaintiff. Such behaviour or motive 'aggravates' the harm done to the plaintiff, and entitles him to a larger or additional compensatory amount. Aggravated damages are therefore specially designed to compensate the plaintiff for any injury to his dignity or moral sphere; nonetheless, the Report suggests they be used for purely compensatory -not punitive- purposes.[28]

Far from following the path marked by the House of Lords, punitive damages have reached their peak in the United States of America, achieving the highest levels of

25 Lord Devlin set up a threefold test in order to permit this kind of exemplary awards. There must be a concurrence of (1) oppressive, arbitrary or unconstitutional action by servants of the government; (2) wrongful conduct which has been calculated by the defendant to make a profit for himself which may well exceed the compensation payable to the plaintiff; and (3) where such an award is expressly authorised by statute. See *Rookes v. Barnard* [1964] AC 1129, 1230.

26 See Law Commission Report N° 247 (1997), Part IV, paragraph 1.86, p. 53.

27 Avalaible at: www.lawcom.gov.uk/lc_reports.htm#1997.

28 See Law Commission Report N° 247 (1997), paragraphs 1.39 ss., p. 25 ss.

popularity in product liability cases.[29] With the exception of only five states,[30] this 'smart money' is generally accepted and imposed by a jury (sometimes, a judge) in lawsuits for damages intentionally or wilfully caused. In the words of Prosser 'such damages are given to the plaintiff over and above the full compensation for his injuries, for the purpose of punishing the defendant, of teaching him not to do it again, and of deterring others from following his example'.[31]

In Spain punitive damages were at first rejected, to the point of being considered contrary to the Constitution.[32] By contrast, we can observe today a certain openness towards their recognition. The best example of this trend is the 'Auto' of the Supreme Court 13 November 2001.[33] This resolution of *exequatur* recognizes a US decision that included punitive damages. The amount awarded for the violation of intellectual property rights pursued a compensatory aim, but also purportedly for prevention and punishment – *i.e.*, an evident deterrent effect –. Despite the prudence with which this ruling should be treated, the fact is that the Spanish Supreme Court did not consider punitive damages contrary to *ordre public*: quite the opposite, it literally sustained that 'we can not speak of punitive damages as an entity threatening *ordre public*'.[34]

This openness is also pervading other legal systems. For instance, in France the *Avant-projet de réforme du droit des obligations et de la prescription* sponsored by Pierre Català cautiously opened the door to '*dommage et intérêts punitifs*';[35] in Germany many legal writers and judicial decisions are involved in the punitive damages debate;[36] in the field of private international law Regulation 864/2007 of the European Parliament and of the Council, on the law applicable to non-contractual obligations, 11 July 2007 (Rome II), implicitly recognizes this type of damage (Article 26 and Recital No. 32), relaxing the application of traditional *ordre public* exception.[37] Moreover, the ECJ judgment of 13 July 2006, Case *V. Manfredi and others v Lloyd Adriatico Assicurazioni SpA and Others*[38] tacitly acknowledges the existence in Community law of some provisions including special exemplary awards or punitive damages, in the field of unfair competition.

29 Classical examples are, e.g., *BMW of North America, Inc. v. Gore* [116 S. Ct. 1589 (1996)], *Pacific Mutual Life Insurance co. v. Haslip* [499 US 1 (1991)], punitive damages awarded after the Exxon Valdez oil spill in Alaska or tobacco cases. See Polinsky & Shavell 1998, p. 901 ss; Sebok 2009, p. 155 ss.

30 These are Louisiana (a Civil code jurisdiction), Massachusetts, Nebraska, New Hampshire, and Washington (Sebok 2009, p. 155).

31 Prosser 1971, p. 9.

32 Martín-Casals 1989, p. 1231 ss.

33 'Auto' of the Supreme Court, 13 November 2001, JUR 2002, 608.

34 Requejo Isidro, 1995, pp. 83–112; Requejo Isidro, 1996, pp. 71–97; Salvador Coderch, 2000 b., pp. 139–152; Requejo Isidro, 2009, pp. 237–255; Del Olmo García, 2009, pp. 137–154.

35 See Viney 2006, p. 168. Also, the Groupe de travail sur la Responsabilité Civile is dealing with these 'dommages et intérêts punitifs' or 'fautes lucratives'. See Les 28 Recommendations du Groupe de Travail Sur La Responsabilité Civile, p. 79 ss. See also Mahé, 'Punitive Damages in the Competing Reform Drafts of the French Civil Code' (contained in this publication).

36 About punitive damages and German ordre public, see Brockmeier 1999, passim; from a substantive perspective, Jansen & Rademacher 2009, p. 75 ss.

37 Koch 2009, p. 197 ss.

38 *V. Manfredi and others v. Lloyd Adriatico Assicurazioni SpA and Others,* TJCE 2006, 204.

2.2. *A Subtle Presence in Substantive Law*

There is no express mention of punitive damages in Spanish substantive law. However, by questioning the real nature of some sorts of compensations, academics claim that subspecies of this type of awards can be detected in our system; under very specific factual situations the awards granted play a significant punitive-deterrent role. We believe it is possible to go further and support the idea that there are detailed and well-defined cases in which punitive damages are associated with non-pecuniary losses, unjust enrichment, or a prearranged system for the assessment of damages caused under the application of some laws, in a general way. In this regard Article 1107 CC, included among the general provisions of the law of obligations (in other words, it is not a sectoral rule), deserves special attention.[39]

2.2.1. Article 1107 CC

According to the general non- contractual liability clause contained in Article 1902 CC, whoever causes negligently an injury to another, is accountable for the damage caused and shall answer for it, restoring the defendant to the *status quo* previous to the loss. This duty to compensate in cases of mere negligence covers the entire loss, no matter what the gravity of the act or omission, or the degree of care of the tortfeasor. If the damage is attributable to him, he is obliged to compensate the integrity of the loss. This is the so-called full compensation principle.[40]

Within the rules of Chapter II of Book IV labelled 'Obligations and Contracts' Article 1107 CC provides that in case of non-performance, the good faith debtor -that is, the one who infringes his obligation without intentional fault- is liable for 'the harm foreseeable or foreseen at the time when the obligation was contracted'; whereas the debtor who intentionally failed to perform the obligation is liable for 'all the harm that knowledgeably arises from the failure to comply with the obligation'.[41] In the contractual sphere the Spanish Civil Code follows the French model, when it comes to establishing the amount of the award, making differences depending on whether the debtor has acted negligently or fraudulently. In the first case, the debtor must compensate only the foreseeable damage; in the second case, he must pay for all the damage derived from his non-compliance. In other words, Article 1107 CC expressly takes into account the seriousness of the conduct performed to determine how far the obligation to repair the damage extends. We are therefore facing a distinction that certainly favours the good faith debtor against the intentional one; this feature has led some Spanish legal writers to infer a *punitive attitude.*

39 One can also trace the presence of punitive awards in some other provisions like Article 1478 CC (remedies against the bad faith seller for the hidden defects in the sale of goods), the Annex (point 1.1) of the Ley sobre Responsabilidad civil y seguro en la Circulación de Vehículos a Motor (damages intentionally caused by drivers), or in Article 124 Ley 27/1992 de Puertos del Estado y de la Marina Mercante (the assessment of damages based on the profits obtained by the tortfeasor).

40 Pantaleón 1993, pp. 1998–1999; Miquel González 1993, pp. 67–69.

41 Gómez Pomar 2002, p. 197 ss.; León González 2006, p. 133 ss.; Carrasco Perera 2010, p. 1241 ss.

However, the qualification of Article 1107 CC as a punitive provision is not widely accepted. To start with, from a systematic point of view, it is placed under contractual liability rules, and there is no agreement in our literature and courts about its applicability beyond the contractual sphere. According to some legal authors, the full compensation principle that reigns in tort law makes it utterly impossible to apply the graduation sanctioned by Article 1107 CC.[42] Professor Pantaleón is particularly insistent on the non-extension of Article 1107 CC to non-contractual situations, stressing that the particular distribution of risks between the parties can only take place in the context of liability for breach of contractual obligations.[43]

But for those who believe that general provisions regulating compensation for damages apply not only to contract schemes but also to the non-contractual ones, it is clear that Article 1107 CC paragraph 2 shows a clear punitive nuance; if compensation can be graduated depending on the degree of the agent's fault, even if it results in the victim's over-compensation, aren't we facing real punitive damages under Spanish general rules of liability?[44]

2.2.2. Patent Law, Trademark Law, Intellectual Property Law and Law on Legal Protection of Industrial Design

Several special rules have also been discussed in the field of Commercial law in order to decide whether they embrace punitive damages. We will see that a positive answer remains doubtful, and that in our view, what the academics have considered as 'punitive' are in fact lost profits (*lucrum cessans*), or losses coming from an unjust enrichment scenario.[45]

The so-called 'triple method for the assessment of damages', of German origin,[46] referred to in the former Article 66.2 Act 11/1986, of 20 March, on Patents (LP), 43 of Act 17/2001, of 7 December, on Trademarks (LM) and Article 140 of Royal Legislative Decree 1/1996, of 12 April, on Intellectual Property (LPI), and joined years later by Article 55 of Act 20/2003, of 7 July, on Legal Protection of Industrial Design (LPJDI), has been a focus of strong debate.[47] Since the reform by the Act 19/2006, of 5 June,[48] the triple method has disappeared from the current wording of these rules, but a retrospective analysis is nevertheless worth doing.

42 This academic confrontation can be found in Carrasco Perera 1989, p. 725; De Ángel Yagüez 1993, pp. 45–45; García Rubio 1991, p. 248; Díez-Picazo 2000, p. 346; Albaladejo 2003, p. 1253; Reglero Campos 2008, p. 535.

43 Pantaleón 1991, pp. 1020, 1031–1032 and 1042.

44 Del Olmo 2009, p. 140.

45 About this *condictio* and its main features, see Basozábal Arrúe 1998, p. 104; García Rubio 2009, p. 125.

46 Basozábal Arrúe 1997, p. 1263 ss.

47 Article 32 of the Unfair Competition Act (Ley 3/1991, de Competencia Desleal) perfectly distinguishes between action for damages and unjust enrichment, without including any reference to this triple method for the assessment of damages.

48 This Act implemented the Directive 2004/48/EC of the European Parliament and of the Council of 29 April 2004 on the enforcement of Intellectual Property Rights.

Until 2006 – prior to the transposition into Spanish law of Directive 2004/48/EC-, the Spanish legislature offered three possibilities for the assessment of damages in actions covered by the above-mentioned special Acts, protecting intangible property. First, Article 66 LP, explicitly recognized that compensation for damages caused by violation of patent rights gave rise to the compensation of *damnum emergens* and *lucrum cessans*, paragraph 2 of the provision determining how this *lucrum cessans* or lost profits could be assessed. In this regard, the plaintiff was entitled to use one of the following three criteria: a) the benefits that the patent owner would have obtained if there were no competition from the infringer; b) the benefits that the wrongdoer actually obtained through the use of the patented invention; c) the price the infringer would have to pay to the patentee had he (the infringer) been granted a license allowing him to lawfully carry out his commerce. Criteria *b* and c were completely foreign to the Spanish law of torts, whilst *a* was simply the usual definition of *lucrum cessans*.

Article 43 LM picked up the same basis for calculating the lost profits, including in its third paragraph that 'the fixing of compensation would take into account, among other circumstances, notoriety, reputation and prestige of the trademark and the number and type of licenses granted at the time the violation was started. In the case of damage to the reputation of the trademark, severity of injury and degree of diffusion in the market would be considered, in addition to the circumstances of the offence'. Paragraph 5 stated that 'The right holder of a trademark which the court consider has been infringed has, without providing any proof of harm, the right to claim damages of up to 1% of the profits made by the infringer through the use of the illegally marked goods. Additionally, the above mentioned right holder can also claim a greater award for damages if he proves that the trademark infringement caused him greater harm'. This wording was justified by the need to ease the right holder's burden of proving *lucrum cessans*.[49] Along the same lines, in cases where a Court prohibited a trademark infringement, Article 44 LM established a system of fines for each day of delay in the cessation of the infringement, with a minimum amount of 600 euro per day (the so-called 'coercive damages').[50]

The LPI reduced the possibilities of choice: Article 140 LPI said that the aggrieved party might choose, as compensation, between the benefits that he himself could have obtained if the defendant had not infringed his right, and the price that he would have received had he authorized exploitation to the latter. Non- pecuniary loss award did not require the proof of patrimonial damage; the circumstances of the offence, gravity of harm and extent of unlawful dissemination of the work should be taken into account for its assessment.

In 2003, the triple method of assessment of damages was re-established in Article 55.2 LPJDI, which reproduces the LM fines system under identical preconditions, as well as the minimum daily amount of 600 euro.

49 Del Olmo 2009, p. 148 and authors there considered.

50 Initially they were called 'coercive fines' but after Parliamentary discussions it was changed to 'coercive damages', especially after considering that the money is paid to an individual and not the state. Fernández-Novoa 2004, p. 510; Naveira Zarra 2003, p. 19.

In our view, none of the provisions (or methods of assessment of damages) described enclose punitive damages: they are just operations to calculate the *lucrum cessans* or even the unjust enrichment. The only punitive 'shadow' that can be detected in the domain of intellectual property is to be found in the assessment of non- pecuniary damages or loss of prestige of the design as it expressly refers to the 'gravity of the injury' as an indicator; moreover, non-patrimonial losses could be awarded without proving any economic harm.[51] The truth is that the diction is poor, because the items of patrimonial and non-patrimonial damages are independent, so that makes absurd the clarification that the second compensation ('daño moral') would be granted independently of economic losses.[52]

Since the 2006 reform, implementing Directive 2004/48/EC, the texts have changed their wording to introduce new features for the quantification of damages. On the one hand, 'research costs' (the expenses incurred to obtain reasonable evidence of the commission of the infringement) are expressly included as a heading of compensation. Moreover, the Act no longer provides criteria for determining lost profits as a subheading for damages: now these parameters will be used to determine the compensation in a global sense. The victim is now granted the choice between, additionally, the negative economic consequences (among which are included cumulatively now, the criteria of a) and b) of the former writing); and then, the price the offender should have paid the right holder to avoid the infringement of intangible property. As we argued above, remnants of punitive damages might be found here: the punitive dye is seen in non-pecuniary damage compensation (*per se* awardable even if no financial loss is proved), because, the following sentence is still preserved: 'for its assessment shall be taken into account the circumstances of the offence, the gravity of harm and the extent of unlawful dissemination of the work'.

2.2.3. Article 123 LGSS: the Surcharge of Benefits

One of the most exotic cases, and, in our view, one providing a clear case of punitive damages, is Article of the General Act on Social Security (Ley General de la Seguridad Social – LGSS), Royal Decree 1/1994, of 20 June, particularly in the above-mentioned Article 123 LGSS. In accordance with this article, '1. All benefits paid out following a labour accident or professional illness will be increased by 30–50%, depending on the seriousness of the wrongdoer's fault, whenever the said harm was caused by engines, machines and pieces of equipment; in centres and workplaces that do not have obligatory safety devices; or where these devices are in an unusable condition; or when safety and hygiene measures are not observed or the basic aspects of salubrity or appropriateness for the employee in his work have been ignored, given their characteristics and the age, sex and other conditions of the worker. 2. The employer is directly accountable for the liability arising under the previous paragraph and this shall not be subject to any insurance, being void any agreement or contract made to cover, compensate, or transmit

[51] García Martín 2008, p. 711.
[52] Carrasco Perera 2007, p. 1798.

his liability. 3. The liability provided for in this provision is independent from and may be compatible with any other liability, even criminal, arising from the same conduct'.

This provision contains the so-called 'surcharge of benefits', that is, a surcharge that an employer has to pay and which increases the financial benefits that the employee (or their heirs, if any) is entitled to receive because of a labour accident. This duty to pay the sanction arises when the employer has failed at work (*i.e.*, lack of safety and hygiene practices) and only because the worker has suffered an accident or work-related illness. However, the lawmaker inserted in Article 123 LGSS a series of specific rules: first, the accurate assessment for the surcharge is set depending on the gravity of the misconduct of the employer; second, the surcharge is not insurable; third, the payment of the surcharge is perfectly compatible with and independent from other responsibilities that may derive from the same factual situation.[53] The rules are easy to understand: otherwise the surcharge would be completely meaningless, since its purpose is to prevent accidents caused by corporate violations, therefore attributable to the employer. Had the employer previously adopted the necessary measures, the damaging event would have been avoided; the surcharge is an indirect means of favouring the compliance of the employer's duties.

Article 123 LGSS has already been dissected in detail by the literature; it has also been subject to a vast case law application. Of particular interest is an excerpt from the Foundation of Law no. 2 of the Spanish Supreme Court decision (Civil Chamber, Plenary Section), of 23 April 2009[54], as it summarizes the position of our Courts in both civil and labour law enforcement. 'The payment of surcharges for breach of safety measures can not be offset or deducted from the compensation under tort liability (…) the deduction of that surcharge for the loss or damage suffered as a result of an accident at work 'would deprive [the surcharge] of its purpose, and that the surcharge, in a society with high accident rates, is intended to avoid accidents caused by corporate violations of the rules (…)' After presenting several arguments and positions held in relation to the compatibility or incompatibility between labour compensation and the surcharge of benefits by social security, it is been concluded, as relevant here, that (…) the law indicates that the surcharge of benefits is (…) not intended to repair the damage, but to punish those who have caused it'.

The Article 123 LGSS qualification as a sanction is almost unanimous. Still, some authors defend the mixed nature of the surcharge. According to this opinion, the surcharge would not only have a public nature (coercive or punishing condition), but would also display a partially compensatory role. Considering the impossibility of insurance, and the fact that the labour authorities through administrative procedure impose the surcharge, we cannot agree with such a position.[55]

In conclusion, the surcharge may and should be considered as a particular case of punitive damages, imposed as an objective consequence in response to a entrepreneur's

53 Salvador Coderch 2000 b., pp. 140–141; Roca Trías 2004, p. 923; Fernández Gregoraci 2008, p. 117; Carrancho Herrero 2010, p. 279 ss.

54 Spanish Supreme Court decision (Civil Chamber, Plenary Section) of 23 April 2009, RJ 2009, 4140.

55 Luque Parra 1999, pp. 541–546; Gómez & Luque & Ruiz 2001, pp. 1–16; García Rubio, Lete, Gómez Abelleira & Regueiro Ferreiro 2003, p. 165.

failure that causes an infringement of the measures of safety and health at work. Its main features are the impossibility of insurance, its assessment according to the gravity of the fault (30–50%, hence there is no discretion in setting the surcharge), and pre-litigation or administrative procedure for its imposition.[56]

2.2.4. Article 10 LOIMH and Other Provisions for Compensation for Discrimination in Contract law

A more recent and less often treated topic in Spanish private legal writing is the nature of potential claims arising from discriminatory conducts within the private Contract Law.[57] The study of the issue is linked to the EU Directives governing the implementation of the principle of equal treatment in Contract Law, related case law, and transpositions into national laws. These instruments have led to a set of laws in which the use of preventive and punitive language has become common when it comes to establishing compensation for violation of the principle of non- discrimination. Although there are several European Union tools that manifest themselves in similar terms, we will go in depth into just two of them. First, the Directive 2000/43/EC – of 29 June 2000 – on the principle of equal treatment between persons irrespective of racial or ethnic origin; second, the Directive 2004/113/EC – of 13 December 2004 – implementing the principle of equal treatment between men and women in access to and supply of goods and services.[58] Both texts contain identical provisions establishing the applicable sanctions in case of a breach of the principle of equal treatment. Article 15 of Directive 2000/43/EC provides that 'Member States shall lay down the rules on sanctions applicable to infringements of the national provisions adopted pursuant to this Directive and shall take all measures necessary to ensure that they are applied. The sanctions, which may comprise the payment of compensation to the victim, must be effective, proportionate and dissuasive'. Article 8.2 Directive 2004/113/EC provides that 'Member States shall introduce into their national legal systems such measures as are necessary to ensure real and effective compensation or reparation, as the Member States so determine, for the loss and damage sustained by a person injured as a result of discrimination within the meaning of this Directive, in a way which is dissuasive and proportionate to the damage suffered.[59] The fixing of a prior upper limit shall not restrict such compensation or reparation'[60], while

56 Again, Fernández Gregoraci 2008, p. 122 ss.

57 Some doctrinal exceptions are García Rubio 2006, p. 1657 ss.; García Rubio 2007, p. 131 ss.; García Rubio 2008, p. 176 ss; García Rubio 2011, 1073 ss.; Navas Navarro 2007, p. 1619 ss; Navas Navarro 2008, p. 1475 ss.; Navas Navarro 2009, p. 1467 ss. and Mesa Marrero 2011, p. 1195 ss.

58 In recent times, Directive 2010/41/EU of the European Parliament and of the Council of 7 July 2010, on the application of the principle of equal treatment between men and women engaged in an activity in a self-employed capacity and repealing Council Directive 86/613/EEC.

59 The DCFR has included also a regulation about non-discrimination and once more the preventive-punitive aim is explicitly formulated. Article II.-2:104 Remedies '(2) Any remedy granted must be proportionate to the injury or anticipated injury; the dissuasive effect of remedies may be taken into account'. See Thüsin & Horler 2009, p. 207 ss.

60 Identical wording is used by Article 10 Directive 2010/41/EU of the European Parliament and of the Council, of 7 July 2010, on the application of the principle of equal treatment between men and women engaged in an activity in a self-employed capacity and repealing Council Directive 86/613/EEC. Under

Article 14 reiterates that 'Member States shall lay down the rules on penalties applicable to infringements of the national provisions adopted pursuant to this Directive and shall take all measures necessary to ensure that they are applied. The penalties, which may comprise the payment of compensation to the victim, shall be effective, proportionate and dissuasive (...)'. Therefore, the Community lawgiver has chosen to deal separately with the system of compensation to the victim and the system of penalties applicable to infringements of national provisions adopted pursuant to this Directive (although it is acknowledged that they also can include compensation to the victim). In Spain these Directives have been implemented into national law through the Act 62/2003 of 30 December on fiscal, administrative and social order and the Organic Act 3/2007 of 22 March for the effective equality between women and men (henceforth LOIMH).[61]

The statutory provision that aspires to collect all penalties linked to discriminatory acts and behaviours is Article 10 LOIMH, located in Title I ('Legal Consequences of anti-discrimination conducts'), and therefore a rule of general application. It states that 'the acts (...) which constitute or cause discrimination on grounds of sex, shall be deemed null and void and shall be subject to liability through a system of redress or compensation that should be real, effective and proportionate to the injury suffered, and, where appropriate, through an effective and dissuasive system of penalties to prevent the implementation of discriminatory conduct'.[62] We will focus on Article 10 LOIMH. The provision includes two systems with different mechanisms as a response to the causation of damage: a system of redress or compensation firstly (private law, *ex post*), and a system of sanctions, secondly (criminal and / or administrative, *ex ante*). While the compensation system shall be real, effective and proportionate, the sanctions scheme shall be effective and deterrent, preventing the implementation of discriminatory conducts. Thus, formally at least, the first system matches the traditional regulatory role of liability in private law, while the second system possesses preventive and punitive features. So interpreted, Article 10 LOIMH is consistent with the basic principles of the Spanish legal system because the sanctions scheme is fixed by law and pre-established, and respects the traditional compensatory role attributed to the rules of civil liability.

However, although this interpretation pleases the few writers on Spanish doctrine that have directly addressed the issue, we cannot agree with it. Article 10 LOIMH has its immediate predecessor in Article 10 of the Draft for the equality of women and men in the light of Directive 2004/113/EC, which determined that 'the acts and clauses of legal transactions that constitute or cause discrimination on grounds of sex shall be deemed null and void and shall be subject to liability through a system of redress or compensation that shall be real, effective and proportionate to the injury suffered, and, where

the heading 'Compensation or reparation' it is stated: 'The Member States shall introduce such measures into their national legal systems as are necessary to ensure real and effective compensation or reparation, as Member States so determine, for the loss or damage sustained by a person as a result of discrimination on grounds of sex, such compensation or reparation being dissuasive and proportionate to the loss or damage suffered. Such compensation or reparation shall not be limited by the fixing of a prior upper limit'.

61 In Spanish, *Ley Orgánica para la igualdad efectiva de mujeres y hombres*.

62 This provision should be linked to Article 72 LOIMH, where there are established the legal consequences arising from the breach of non-discrimination principle.

appropriate, through an effective and dissuasive system of penalties to prevent the implementation of discriminatory conduct'. This wording was not approved by the authors, mainly because of the technical deficiencies that hindered its implementation and scope.[63] The truth is that this drafting complied with Article 8.2 Directive 2004/113/EC only poorly, if at all, as it stipulates that 'Member States shall introduce into their national legal systems such measures as are necessary to ensure real and effective compensation or reparation, as the Member States so determine, for the loss and damage sustained by a person injured as a result of discrimination within the meaning of this Directive, in a way which is dissuasive and proportionate to the damage suffered.[64] The fixing of a prior upper limit shall not restrict such compensation or reparation'. The Directive considers that individuals harmed by discrimination should receive a 'dissuasive'[65] compensation; this means the recognition of a punitive effect, contrary to the traditional functions of tort law in continental legal systems.

According to the literal interpretation of the above considered provisions, it is clear that the scope of the Directive is broader than the Spanish transposition, and therefore both the Draft and the text as finally approved are not a perfect implementation of the Community rule. For that reason, we conclude that very probably the Spanish lawgiver has failed to respect the spirit of Community law.

Apart from the LOIMH, Article 18.2 of Act 51/2003, of 2 December, on equal opportunities, non-discrimination and universal accessibility for disabled people, may also be considered an optimal channel for the entrance of punitive damages in our law. In cases of discrimination causing damage that affect a victim's dignity, 'the compensation for moral damage proceeds even in the absence of economic harm and shall be assessed according to the circumstances of the violation and the gravity of the injury'. Again, the lawmaker refers to the gravity of the injury as a guideline for the assessment of non-pecuniary damages. The Spanish legislator clearly chooses (consciously or unconsciously) a criterion in which the punishment component is present. The drafting of another anti-discrimination rule is more appropriate. In this sense, Article 18 paragraph 1 of Act 51/2003 on equal opportunities, non-discrimination and universal accessibility for disabled people provides that 'the judicial protection of the right to equal opportunities for persons with disabilities includes the adoption of all necessary measures to stop the violation and prevent further violations and to restore the injured party in the exercise of his right'. It expressly includes the preventive function (inhibitory action) and does not fix the range of measures to be taken (compensatory or punitive?).

63 García Rubio 2006, pp. 2–4.

64 This proportionality requirement means that the award granted must be adequate; in the same sense the European Court of Justice has emphasized the need for adequate compensation. See *Von Colson and Kamann v. Land Nordhein- Westfalen* (Case 14/83); *Marshall v. Southampton and South West Hampshire Area Health Authority* (Case 271/91).

65 This dissuasive effect was guaranteed by the European Court of Justice (Cases *Von Colson*, *Marshall* and *Draehmpaehl*). However, some authors have expressed the view that the bottom line of this jurisprudence is not that the ECJ wants to promote punitive damages and to impose them upon jurisdictions against their will; in fact, the ECJ is not even concerned with national categories of tort law, so its ultimate aim is to enforce community law and to sanction deviations from the boundaries the latter imposes upon Member States. See for further details Koch 2009, p. 205.

2.2.5. Article 9 LOPHIPI

Article 9 *Organic Act 1/1982, of 5 May, for the civil protection of honour, personal and family privacy and image* (henceforth LOPHIPI) regulates legal guardianship in cases of illegal intromissions that cause a violation of any of these rights. Since the Act reform in 2010, Article 9 in its second paragraph 2 includes the measures to be taken to impede the trespass,[66] and also those necessary for 'the restoration of the injured party on the full enjoyment of his rights, with the declaration of intrusion suffered, the immediate cessation thereof and the replacement of the previous state', 'preventing imminent or further intrusions', 'compensation for damage' and finally 'the appropriation of profit obtained through the illegitimate intrusion by the injured party'. This provision aims not only to achieve full compensation for the victim: it also highlights the need to deploy preventive and deterrent measures of immediate or deferred effect. The special characteristics of the rights at stake (honour, personal and family privacy and image) account for a lawmaker's option that goes beyond the traditional restorative function of tort law for the damages suffered, introducing some kind of civil sanction or even punitive damages. The lawgiver expressly separates all these measures into different sub-paragraphs. But, as this writing comes from 2010, we should study its content previous to the reform by the Organic Act 5/2010, 22 June,[67] in order to understand the intense academic debate around the former Article 9.3 LOPHIPI.

Prior to its amendment in 2010, Article 9.3 LOHIPI provided that 'compensation will extend to non-pecuniary losses and these will be assessed with regard to the circumstances of each case and the gravity of the harm caused, for which purpose account will be taken, where appropriate, of the extent to which the harm has been made known through the mass media. The profit that the person who caused the damage has obtained will also be taken into account'. This cryptic wording did not clarify whether the benefit of the injured party should be considered only for the non-pecuniary damage assessment or to estimate all the damage caused. Besides, it did not state whether the benefit ought to be materially restored, or simply taken into account when determining compensation.[68]

This provision raised two problematic questions. We shall deal first with the fact that non-pecuniary damages were assessed 'according to the circumstances of the case[69] and the gravity of the actual injury caused'. The allusion to the 'gravity' as a guideline for the determination of damages led to doubts concerning their qualification as punitive damages. The truth was that the lawgiver favoured for a severe liability that went beyond mere compensation for the injured party. Such liability had not only a clear, predominant punitive intention, but also a secondary deterrent effect at the moment of granting a *quantum* for non- pecuniary losses: a type of losses with no market value because it cannot be equated with a patrimonial asset.[70]

66 López Jacoiste 1988, p. 540; Martín-Casals 1990, p. 384 ss.

67 Ley Orgánica 5/2010, 22 June.

68 Díez-Picazo 2008, p. 246.

69 The judge must find the most suitable solution to the specific case, and the resolution must also be motivated (not arbitrary), Martín-Casals 1990, p. 388 ss.

70 Non-pecuniary damages or 'daño moral' have been awarded in Spain since 1912. In its decision of 6 December 1912 the Supreme Court (JC 1912, 95) considered that this type of damage could be

We turn now to the words 'The profit that the person who caused the damage has obtained will also be taken into account'.[71] Some legal writers lean on this final sentence as a second argument to assert the presence of punitive awards or civil penalties in Spanish substantive law. However, we believe that far from being understood as a case of punitive damages, this is an explicit case of *conditio* for invasion of personality rights.[72] The real rationale of the rule was to restore the benefits obtained by the wrongdoer to the victim, refunding any profits the agent could have gained from his wrongful behaviour. The legal literature had indicated – prior to the reform in 2010- that this refunding operation would take place only in case of illegitimate invasion of image rights, but never with the right to honour, where interference would only generate a compensation for the damage and not one of unjust enrichment.[73] The rationale for this assertion was the idea that nobody could put on the market his own honour: therefore it would not be possible to sue for compensation or even for unjust enrichment on the grounds of the violation of the right to honour.[74] However, this restriction is no longer valid. The action for unjust enrichment is feasible, as stated by the Preamble of Organic Act of 2010:

> 'in recent times criminal offenders have gained access to mass media (...), disseminating false information (...) and obtaining an unjust economic gain violating the dignity of those who have suffered the consequences of those actions (...) and their relatives, who are subjected to a new traumatic experience resulting from this public invasion of their honour and privacy. Given the limitations of Criminal law, it was considered that the appropriate way to respond adequately to this phenomenon is to articulate an effective civil action, under the Organic Act 1/1982, allowing victims to act against this type of conduct by urging its dismissal, the compensation for the non- pecuniary damages caused, and the avoidance of any unjust enrichment resulting from the trespass'.

Turning back to Article 9.2 LOPHIPI, to be honest we have to admit that our previous characterization as a case of unjust enrichment is not a general opinion. Thus, Bercovitz Rodríguez-Cano has recently sustained a 'punitive damages' nature.[75] We still affirm that we are dealing with the simple restitution of the profit derived from unjust enrichment: the Act seeks to undo the improper transfer of wealth, specifically giving the action of unjust enrichment a total independence from recovery of damages. There are two different causes of action, and the first could never be subsumed in the second.

Despite the efforts of the legislature in 2010 to orchestrate a strengthened and clearer scheme in order to protect the dignity of victims of crimes and their relatives, the fact is that the system still suffers from systematic deficiencies. An example is the disorder in

compensated. See Díez-Picazo 2008, pp. 66–68. Nowadays it is no longer a point of discussion and there are several provisions containing its express compensability.

71 This is now in Article 9.2 LOPHIPI.

72 Del Olmo 2009, pp. 141–144, and its further references.

73 Díez-Picazo 2007, p. 1610, where the author raises the complex relationship between this two actions (action for damages and unjust enrichment); also García Rubio 2009, pp. 129–130.

74 This right of personality had not been settled in order to achieve a monopoly of exploitation. See Díez-Picazo 2008, p. 252.

75 Bercovitz Rodríguez-Cano 2010, p. 2.

the listing of the actions available to the victims (cessation and withdrawal,[76] action for damages and unjust enrichment), and the precision of awarded damages in paragraphs 2 and 3 of Article 9 LOPHIPI.

Although in our view Article 9.2 LOPHIPI is not a clear case of punitive damages, it is obvious that the Spanish lawgiver has not been indifferent to the special nature of the rights at stake. Both in 1982 and in 2010, the lawmaker introduced (first), and maintains (after), this aggravated *ex lege* criterion for the assessment and quantification of non-pecuniary damages binding our Courts in that sense.

3. Conclusion

What can be concluded about the presence and suitability of punitive damages under Spanish law? As it was mentioned earlier, any research work on punitive damages is intimately connected to the functions fulfilled by the tort liability institution. In this regard we have defended the multi-functionality of the law of torts, going beyond the traditional role of compensation. Apart from purely theoretical disquisitions which may engage the legal doctrine, it seems undeniable that in the 21st Century, the law of damages is surely called to play, at least a function of general deterrence as well as a function of punishment -although with less intensity-. It is clear that punishment is not the leading role of civil liability, and that this function is better performed by Criminal law and also Administrative law. However, the imposition of 'sanctions' or 'penalties' is not really alien to the Civil law tradition: to prove it, we do not need to undertake legal archaeological work (*i.e.*, *Lex Aquilia de damno*). It suffices to consider others figures like the deprivation of parental rights,[77] the indignity to inherit,[78] or the existence of criminal clauses in private contract law ('cláusula penal': a provision with a clear coercive-punitive function, to the extent that the penalty stipulated exceeds the quantum required under the rules of contractual liability, punishing the debtor for breach of contract).[79]

As we have seen above, legal authors have mistakenly considered some provisions as examples of punitive damages. Due to certain wordings, methods for the assessment of lost profits or unjust enrichment are confused with punitive damages; in other cases, the punishment intention is clearly seen, as happens with the surcharge of social security benefits, the coercive fines contemplated under trademark and industrial design Acts (600 euros per day), or the more recent cases of quantification of damages resulting from discriminatory conducts.

Be it as it may, it is undeniable that punitive damages do really breathe in our system, more or less camouflaged under certain compensatory clothes. Perhaps private law rules are not the most technically correct venue for this institution, but if they are real, we cannot ignore them.

76 Martín Casals 1990, p. 383.

77 A judge can adopt the deprivation of parental rights (*patria potestas*) in the terms of Article 156 CC. Since the 2010 Criminal Code reform this deprivation of *patria potestas* has also been considered a criminal sanction under certain circumstances.

78 García Rubio & Otero Crespo 2011, p. 286.

79 Marín García 2008, p. 4.

In 1997 Professors Salvador Coderch and Castiñeira Palou wisely suggested a cautionary reluctance to the reception of punitive damages in Spain.[80] More than a decade later, and again appealing for prudence, the existence in our law of specific cases opening the doorway to punitive damages can be affirmed: but they are still far from being considered as a general concept of tort law, existing as an individual head of damage. The admission of punitive damages under Spanish law is no longer a matter of 'all or nothing'. We may be able to declare that our tort law system is not immune to the gradual access of punitive damages, and that some provisions do appreciate this logic disguised as punitive. Another different issue is, that punitive damages could be considered as conflicting with the traditional pillars of continental tort law and thus, a great and not insignificant part of the legal literature is reluctant to accept their transplanting into our legal system.

80 Salvador Coderch & Castiñeira Palou 1997, pp. 172–173.

Bibliography

Albaladejo García 2002
Albaladejo García, M., 'Los daños indemnizables en la responsabilidad contractual y en la extracontractual o aquiliana', in: A. Cabanillas Sánchez, *Estudios jurídicos en homenaje al profesor Luis Díez-Picazo*, Vol. 2, Derecho civil, Derecho de obligaciones, Madrid: Civitas, 2002, pp. 1251–1274.

Barros Bourié 2007
Barros Bourié, E., *Tratado de responsabilidad extracontractual,* Santiago de Chile: Jurídica de Chile, 2007.

Basozábal Arrúe 1997
Basozábal Arrúe, X., 'Método triple de cómputo del daño: la indemnización del lucro cesante en las leyes de protección industrial e intelectual', Vol. L, Fasc. III, *Anuario de Derecho Civil,* 1997, pp. 1263–1300.

Basozábal Arrúe 1998
Basozábal Arrúe, X., *Enriquecimiento injustificado por intromisión en derecho ajeno,* Madrid: Civitas, 1998.

Bercovitz Rodríguez-Cano 2010
Bercovitz Rodríguez-Cano, R. 'La dignidad de las víctimas de los delitos', *Aranzadi Civil,* 2010, pp. 1–3 (BIB 2010, 1814).

Brockmeier 1999
Brockmeier, D., *Punitive damages, multiple damages und deutscher ordre public.* Tübingen: Mohr Siebeck, 1999.

Calabresi 1984
Calabresi, G., *El coste de los accidentes. Análisis económico y jurídico de la responsabilidad civil,* Barcelona: Ariel, 1984.

Carrancho Herrero 2010
Carrancho Herrero, M.T., *Responsabilidad civil del empresario en el ámbito de los riesgos laborales,* Madrid: La Ley, 2010.

Carrasco Perera 1989
Carrasco Perera, A., 'Comentario al art. 1101 Cc', in: M. Albaladejo (dir.), *Comentarios al Código civil y compilaciones forales,* Tomo XV, vol. 1º, Madrid: Edersa, 1989, pp. 377–444.

Carrasco Perera 2007
Carrasco Perera, A., 'Comentario al art. 135 LPI', in: R. Bercovitz Rodríguez-Cano (coord.), *Comentarios a la Ley de Propiedad Intelectual,* 2ª ed., Madrid: Tecnos, 2007, pp. 1789–1801.

Carrasco Perera 2010
Carrasco Perera, A., *Derecho de contratos,* Pamplona: Thomson Reuters-Aranzadi, 2010.

Deakin, Johnston & Markesinis 2008
Markesinis, B. S. & Deakin, S. F., *Tort Law,* Oxford: Clarendon Press, 2008.

De Ángel Yagüez 1993
De Ángel Yagüez, R., *Tratado de Responsabilidad Civil,* Madrid: Civitas, 1993.

De Ángel Yagüez 1995
De Ángel Yagüez, R., *Algunas previsiones sobre el futuro de la responsabilidad civil (con especial atención a la reparación del daño),* Madrid: Cuadernos Civitas, 1995.

De Ángel Yagüez 2008
De Ángel Yagüez, R., 'La responsabilidad civil. Cuestiones previas de delimitación', in: I. Sierra Gil de la Cuesta (coord.), *Tratado de Responsabilidad Civil,* T. I, Barcelona: Bosch, 2008, pp. 3–124.

Del Olmo García 2001
Del Olmo García, P., 'Responsabilidad por daño puramente económico causado al usuario de informaciones falsas', Vol. LIV, fasc. I, *Anuario de Derecho Civil,* 2001, pp. 257–368.

Del Olmo 2009
Del Olmo, P., 'Punitive damages in Spain', in: H. Koziol & V. Wilcox (eds.), *Punitive Damages: Common Law and Civil Law Perspectives,* Vienna: Springer, 2009, pp. 137–154.

Díez-Picazo 1999
Díez-Picazo, L., *Derecho de daños,* Madrid: Civitas, 1999.

Díez-Picazo 2000
Díez-Picazo, L., 'Culpa y riesgo en la responsabilidad civil extracontractual', in F. Pantaleón (ed.), *La responsabilidad en el Derecho, AFDUAM,* 2000, pp. 153–166.

Díez-Picazo 2007
Díez-Picazo, L., '*Commodum ex negotiatione*', LX fasc. IV, *Anuario de Derecho Civil,* 2007, pp. 1601–1618.

Díez-Picazo 2008
Díez-Picazo, L., 'Indemnización de daños y restitución de enriquecimientos', in: J.A. Moreno Martínez, *La responsabilidad civil y su problemática actual,* Madrid: Dykinson, 2008, pp. 237–254.

Enneccerus 1950
Enneccerus, L., *Derecho de Obligaciones,* in: B. Pérez González & J. Alguer, *Derecho de Obligaciones,* 11ª revisión por H. Lehmann, traducción de la 35ª edición alemana con estudios de comparación y adaptación a la legislación y jurisprudencia españolas, Vol. I, doctrinal especial, 2ª ed. al cuidado de J. Puig Brutau, Barcelona: Bosch, 1950.

Fernández Gregoraci 2008
Fernández Gregoraci, B., 'Recargo de las prestaciones de la Seguridad Social: un supuesto específico de 'punitive damages'', *Anuario de Derecho Civil,* 2008, pp. 113–146.

Fernández Martín-Granizo 1972
Fernández Martín-Granizo, M., *Los daños y la responsabilidad objetiva en el Derecho positivo español,* Pamplona: Aranzadi, 1972.

Fernández-Novoa 2004
Fernández-Novoa, C., *Tratado sobre Derecho de marcas,* 2ª ed., Madrid: Marcial Pons, 2004.

García Martín 2008
García Martín, I., 'Cálculo de la indemnización de daños y perjuicios', in: A. Bercovitz Rodríguez- Cano (dir.), *Comentarios a la Ley de Marcas,* T. I, Navarra: Aranzadi, 2008, pp. 699–720.

García Rubio 1991
García Rubio, M.P., *La responsabilidad precontractual en el Derecho español,* Madrid: Tecnos, 1991.

García Rubio 2002
García Rubio, M.P., *Introducción al Derecho civil,* Barcelona: Cálamo, 2002.

García Rubio *et al.* 2003
García Rubio, M.P. *et al.*, 'The impact of Social Security Law on Tort Law in Spain', in: U. Magnus (ed.), *The Impact of Social Security Law on Tort Law,* Vienna: Springer, 2003, pp. 165–175.

García Rubio & Méndez García 2005
García Rubio, M.P. & Méndez García, J.F. (coords.), *Douscentos anos do Code civil des Français na USC (1804–2004),* Santiago de Compostela: Universidade de Santiago de Compostela, 2005.

García Rubio 2006
García Rubio, M.P., 'La igualdad de trato entre hombres y mujeres y su repercusión en el Derecho de contratos (Análisis del Proyecto de Ley Orgánica para la igualdad de mujeres y hombres a la luz de la Directiva 2004/113/CE', *La Ley,* 2006, pp. 1657–1667.

García Rubio 2007
García Rubio, M.P., 'Discriminación por razón de sexo y derecho contractual en la Ley Orgánica 3/2007, de 22 de marzo, para la igualdad efectiva de mujeres y hombres', *Derecho privado y Constitución,* 2007, pp. 131–166.

García Rubio 2008
García Rubio, M.P., 'De nuevo sobre la incidencia del principio de no discriminación por razón de sexo en la contratación privada', in E. Gómez Campelo & F. Valbuena González (coords.), *Igualdad de género: una visión jurídica plural,* Burgos: Universidad de Burgos, 2008, pp. 176–190.

García Rubio 2009
García Rubio, M.P., 'Restitución de beneficios obtenidos por intromisión en derecho ajeno, por incumplimiento contractual y por ilícito extracontractual', Contestación a la Ponencia presentada por Enrique Barros Bourié, in: E. Barros Bourié, M.P. García Rubio & A.M. Morales Moreno, *Derecho de daños*, Madrid: Fundación Coloquio Jurídico Europeo, 2009, pp. 79–133.

García Rubio 2011
García Rubio, M.P. 'La discriminación por razón de sexo en la contratación privada' in: M.P. García Rubio & M.R. Valpuesta Fernández, *El levantamiento del velo: las mujeres en el Derecho privado,* Valencia: Tirant lo Blanch, 2011, pp. 1073–1119.

García Rubio & Otero Crespo 2011
García Rubio, M.P. & Otero Crespo, M., 'Capacidad, incapacidad e indignidad para suceder' in: M.C. Gete-Alonso Calera, *Tratado de Derecho de sucesiones,* T.I, Madrid: Thomson-Civitas, 2011, pp. 261–308.

Gómez Pomar 2002
Gómez Pomar, F., *Previsión de daños, incumplimiento e indemnización,* Madrid: Civitas, 2002.

Jansen & Rademacher 2009
Jansen, N. & Rademacher, L., 'Punitive damages in Germany', in: H. Koziol & V. Wilcox (eds.), *Punitive Damages: Common Law and Civil Law Perspectives,* Vienna: Springer, 2009, pp. 75–86.

Jordano Fraga 1987
Jordano Fraga, F., *La responsabilidad contractual,* Madrid: Civitas, 1987.

Koch 2009
Koch, B., 'Punitive damages in European Law' in: H. Koziol & V. Wilcox (eds.), *Punitive Damages: Common Law and Civil Law Perspectives,* Vienna: Springer, 2009, pp. 197–209.

León González 2006
León González, J.M., 'De nuevo sobre el artículo 1107 del Código Civil: los daños previstos o previsibles' in: E. Llamas Pombo (coord.), *Estudios de derecho de obligaciones: homenaje al profesor Mariano Alonso Pérez,* Vol. 2, Madrid: La Ley, 2006, pp. 133–148.

López Jacoiste 1988
López Jacoiste, J.J., 'Intimidad, honor e imagen ante la responsabilidad civil', in: *Homenaje a Juan B. Vallet de Goytisolo,* Vol. IV, Junta de Decanos de los Colegios Notariales de España, Madrid: Consejo General del Notariado, 1988, pp. 537–619.

López Jacoiste 2002
López Jacoiste, J.J., 'Las filosofías de la responsabilidad civil', *Anales de la Real Academia de Jurisprudencia y Legislación,* 2002, pp. 137–186.

Lunney & Oliphant 2008
Lunney, M. & Oliphant, K., *Tort Law. Text and materials,* Oxford: Oxford University Press, 2008.

Magnus 2008
Magnus, U., 'Remedios. La indemnización', in: M. Martín Casals (coord.), *Principios de Derecho Europeo de la Responsabilidad Civil,* Cizur Menor, Navarra: Thomson-Aranzadi, 2008, pp. 201–226.

Mahé 2011
Mahé, C.B.P., 'Punitive Damages in the Competing Reform Drafts of the French Civil Code', contained in this book.

Marín García 2008
Marín García, I., 'Cláusula penal: la facultad moderadora del Juez', *InDret,* 2008, pp. 1–13.

Martín Casals 1989
Martín Casals, M., 'Notas sobre la indemnización del daño moral en las acciones por difamación de la LO 1/1982', in: *Centenario del Código Civil (1889–1989),* Vol 2., Madrid: Centro de Estudios Ramón Areces, 1989, pp. 1231–1274.

Martín Casals 1990
Martín Casals, M., 'Indemnizaciones de daños y otras medidas judiciales por intromisión ilegítima contra el derecho al honor', in: p. Salvador Coderch (dir.), *El mercado de las ideas,* Madrid: Centro de Estudios Constitucionales, 1990, pp. 382–409.

Mazeaud, Mazeaud & Tunc 1961
Mazeaud, H., Mazeaud, L., Tunc, A., *Tratado teórico y práctico de la responsabilidad civil delictual y contractual,* Tomo I, vols. 1 y 2, 5ª, Buenos Aires: Ediciones Jurídicas Europa-América, 1961.

Mesa Marrero 2011
Mesa Marrero, C., 'Consecuencias jurídicas de las conductas discriminatorias: ¿un resquicio para los punitive damages?', in: M.P. García Rubio & M.R. Valpuesta Fernández, *El levantamiento del velo: las mujeres en el Derecho privado,* Valencia: Tirant lo Blanch, 2011, pp. 1195–1217.

Miquel González 1993
Miquel González, J.Mª. (1993), 'La responsabilidad contractual y extracontractual: distinción y consecuencias', *Cuadernos de Derecho Judicial,* Madrid: CGPJ, 1993, pp. 61–78.

Navas Navarro 2007
Navas Navarro, S., 'Negativa a contratar y prohibición de discriminar (Derecho comunitario y Derecho español)', *Anuario de Derecho civil,* 2007, pp. 1619–1639.

Navas Navarro 2008
Navas Navarro, S., 'El principio de no discriminación en el Derecho contractual europeo', *Anuario de Derecho Civil,* 2008, pp. 1475–1490.

Navas Navarro 2009
Navas Navarro, S., 'Medidas en caso de discriminación por razón de sexo en la contratación privada (Derecho europeo y Derecho español), *Revista Crítica de Derecho Inmobiliario,* 2009, pp. 1467–1495.

Naveira Zarra 2003
Naveira Zarra, M.Mª., 'La Ley de Marcas de 2001: un punto de inflexión en el análisis funcional del Derecho de daños', *Revista de Derecho Privado,* 2003 (Id. vLex: VLEX-186754).

Pantaleón Prieto 1981
Pantaleón Prieto, F., *Del concepto de daño. Hacia una Teoría General del Derecho de daños (*doctoral thesis, unpublished), Universidad Autónoma de Madrid: Facultad de Derecho, Departamento de Derecho civil, 1981.

Pantaleón 1991
Pantaleón, F., 'El sistema de responsabilidad contractual: (materiales para un debate), *Anuario de Derecho Civil,* 1991, pp. 1019–1092.

Pantaleón 1993
Pantaleón, F., 'Comentario al art. 1902 Cc' in: C. Paz-Ares *et al.* (dirs.), *Comentario del Código civil*, T. II, Madrid: Ministerio de Justicia, 1993, pp. 1971–2003.

Pantaleón 1996
Pantaleón, F., 'La Constitución, el honor y unos abrigos', *La Ley*, 1996, pp. 1689–1695.

Pantaleón 2000
Pantaleón, F., 'Cómo repensar la responsabilidad civil extracontractual (también la de las Administraciones Públicas)' in: J.A. Moreno Martínez (coord.), *Perfiles de la responsabilidad civil en el nuevo milenio,* Madrid: Dykinson, 2000, pp. 439–468.

Pantaleón 2005
Pantaleón, F., 'Principles of European Tort Law: Basis of Liability and Defences. A critical view 'from outside'', *InDret*, 2005 (available at: www.indret.com), pp. 1–8.

Pérez González & Alguer 1950
Pérez González, B. & Alguer, J., *Derecho de Obligaciones* por L. Enneccerus, 11ª revisión por H. Lehmann, traducción de la 35ª edición alemana con estudios de comparación y adaptación a la legislación y jurisprudencia españolas, Vol. I, doctrinal especial, 2ª ed. al cuidado de J. Puig Brutau, Barcelona, 1950.

Polinsky & Shavell 1998
Polinsky, A.M. & Shavell, S., 'Punitive damages: an economic analysis', *Harv L Rev*, 1998, pp. 869–962.

Pomar & Ruiz 2001
Pomar, F., Luque, M. & Ruiz, J.A., 'STS, 4ª, 2.10.2000: recargo, indemnización de daños y sanciones administrativas laborales', *InDret* 2001, pp. 1–16.

Portalis 1999
Portalis, J.-E.-M., *Discours préliminaire au premier projet de Code civil,* préface de Michel Massenet, Collection 'Voix de la cité', París: Confluences, 1999.

Prosser 1971
Prosser, W.L., *Law of Torts,* St. Paul, Minnesota: West Publishing, 1971.

Reglero Campos 2008
Reglero Campos, L.F., 'Conceptos generales y elementos de delimitación', in: L. F: Reglero Campos (coord.), *Tratado de Responsabilidad civil,* T. I, Cizur Menor: Thomson-Aranzadi, 2008, pp. 47–246.

Requejo Isidro 1995
Requejo Isidro, M., 'Reconocimiento en España de sentencias extranjeras condenando al pago de punitive damages', *Iniuria*, 1995, pp. 83–112.

Requejo Isidro 1996
Requejo Isidro, M., 'Punitive damages y su notificación en el contexto del Convenio de la Haya de 15 de octubre de 1965', *Revista Española de Derecho Internacional (REDI)*, 1996, pp. 71–97.

Requejo Isidro 2009
Requejo Isidro, M., 'Punitive Damages from a Private International Law Perspective' in: H. Koziol & V. Wilcox (eds.), *Punitive Damages: Common Law and Civil Law Perspectives,* Vienna: Springer, 2009, pp. 237–255.

Requejo Isidro 2011
Requejo Isidro, M., 'Punitive Damages: how do they look when seen from abroad?', contained in this book.

Roca Trías 2004
Roca Trías, E., 'Resarcir o enriquecer: la concurrencia de indemnizaciones por un mismo daño', *Anuario de Derecho Civil*, 2004, pp. 901–928.

Salvador Coderch & Castiñeira Palou 1997
Salvador Coderch, p. & Castiñeira Palou, M.T., *Prevenir y castigar. Libertad de información y expresión, tutela del honor y funciones del derecho de daños,* Madrid: Marcial Pons, 1997.

Salvador Coderch 2000a
Salvador Coderch, P., 'Punitive damages', *InDret* 2000, pp. 1–17.

Salvador Coderch 2000b
Salvador Coderch, P., 'Punitive damages', in: F. Pantaleón (ed.), *La responsabilidad en el Derecho,* 4 Anuario de la Facultad de Derecho de la Universidad Autónoma de Madrid (AFDUAM), pp. 139–152.

Salvador Coderch & Azagra Malo 2004
Salvador Coderch, p. & Azagra Malo, A., 'Juan Ramón Romo v. Ford Motor Co.: Indemnización sancionatoria a la baja', *InDret,* 2004, pp. 1–4.

Santos Briz 1963
Santos Briz, J., *Derecho de daños,* Madrid: Revista de Derecho Privado, 1963.

Sebok 2009
Sebok, A.J., *'Punitive damages in the United States',* in: H. Koziol & V. Wilcox (eds.), *Punitive Damages: Common Law and Civil Law Perspectives,* Vienna: Springer, 2009, pp. 155–196.

Thüsin & Horler 2009
Thüsin, G. & Horler, S., 'Non-discrimination in the DCFR', in: G. Wagner, *The Common Frame of Reference: A view from Law & Economics,* Berlin: Sellier, 2009, pp. 207–224.

Viney & Jourdain 2006
Viney, G. & Jourdain, P., 'Les conditions de la reponsabilité' in: J. Ghestin (dir.), *Traité de Droit Civil*, Paris: L.G.D.J., 2006.

Wilcox 2009
Wilcox, V., 'Punitive damages in England' in: H. Koziol & V. Wilcox (eds.), *Punitive Damages: Common Law and Civil Law Perspectives,* Vienna: Springer, 2009, pp. 7–53.

Marta Requejo Isidro*

PUNITIVE DAMAGES: HOW DO THEY LOOK LIKE WHEN SEEN FROM ABROAD?

1. Introductory Remarks

Both because of their purpose and their extent, punitive damages are widely rejected in European civil law systems. This has been confirmed by the recent study *Punitive Damages: Common Law and Civil Law Perspectives*[1] – although the study also reveals how this kind of damages has slipped in some jurisdictions in hidden forms.[2]

But, is this rejection limited to domestic cases, or does it extend to private international relationships? There are at least three situations in which the authorities of a civil law system must face a private international law scenario with elements related to punitive damages: through the request for service to the defendant, domiciled in country A, of a lawsuit for punitive damages filed in country B; if recognition and/or enforcement of a foreign punitive damages award of country A is sought in country B; or if a claim including request for punitive damages is submitted in the forum, and a decision must be taken as to the applicable law.

There are reasons to believe that domestic and international situations may deserve a different treatment;[3] and also reasons to argue that the three cases described above are not identical.[4] I will try to justify these assertions in the following pages.

* Marta Requejo Isidro is Professor of Private International Law at the University of Santiago de Compostela, Spain.

1 Koziol & Wilcox, 2009.

2 A small opening towards punitive damages may be appreciated in Italy, where two domestic decisions of 2000 expressly awarded 'danni punitive': see Musy 2000, pp. 1121–1127. Non-compensatory goals have been identified in Germany in domestic moral damages awards: the so called *Caroline of Monaco* case (*judgment of the Bundesgerichtshof, BGH* 15 November 1994), where the German High Court expressly acknowledged that 'der Gedanke der Prävention' underlies the judgment, is frequently quoted as paradigmatic; the same idea had already appeared, if only implicitly, in previous decisions also involving personality rights. Linking the case with *punitive damages*: Rosengarten 1996; Körner 2000. For Spain, see Otero Crespo, contained in this publication.

3 Symeonides 2003, p. 3.

4 Especially as far as the public policy exception is concerned.

2. Service of Process Abroad

2.1. What's New in Germany?

The difficulties related to the service abroad of punitive damage claims have been widely studied in Europe, particularly in Germany, a country to where several requests from the United States have already been addressed.

In practice, authorities are reluctant to serve the documents when they suspect that the applicant's real interest is not to litigate, but to intimidate the other party, putting he or she under such pressure that he/she eventually agrees to settle. Obviously, this assumption has to be translated into legal terms. A request for cooperation from the United States to Germany[5] is channelled through the Hague Convention on the Service Abroad of Judicial and Extrajudicial Documents in Civil or Commercial Matters, of 15 November 1965. Denial of cooperation has been justified through characterization of punitive damages as a criminal matter, therefore falling outside the scope of the Convention;[6] and also through the possibility of refusal provided by its Article 13.

As a matter of fact, the first of these objections can be considered outdated by now: a generic qualification of punitive damages as pertaining to criminal law has been largely discarded, both in academic circles and in the practice of the courts. Opposing views, though existing, are really in minority.[7]

Once punitive damages are considered in the realm of civil law for the purposes of the Service Convention, the discussion focuses on the scope of its Article 13. Under this provision, 'Where a request for service complies with the terms of the present Convention, the State addressed may refuse to comply therewith only if it deems that compliance would infringe its sovereignty or security'. The rule is ordinarily seen as an international public policy clause, and, according to the prevailing writers' opinion and case law, it does not prevent service of documents concerning a punitive damages claim.[8]

This view had also been endorsed by the *Bundesgerichtshof* (*BGH* German Supreme Court), and even by the *Bundesverfassungsgericht* (*BVerfG*, Constitutional Court) after a first ruling where the opposite solution was preferred.[9] However, the trend took a sharp change in 2003 with the *BVerfG* decision of 25 July, where an interim order was granted to protect a German media company, Bertelsmann AG, from service of a complaint filed in the District Court for the Southern District of New York.[10] The *BVerfG* held that service could result in the violation of Article 2 (right to free development of personality), and

5 Or other European countries. Most of the EU Member States have signed the Hague Convention.

6 Requejo 2009, pp. 240–241.

7 See *judgment of the Oberlandsgerichtshof, OLG Koblenz,* 27 June 2005, *Praxis des Internationalen Privat- und Verfahrensrecht (IPRax)*, 2006, pp. 25–38; Piekenbrock 2006, p. 8; Merkt 2009, pp. 267–272.

8 See summary of views in Requejo 2009, pp. 243–244. Defending the opposite view, Merkt 1995, and Merkt 2009.

9 In 1994, the Federal Constitutional Court granted interim relief against the service of a writ related to a punitive damages suit. The order was lifted on December: *BVerfG*, 7 December 1994, *NJW*, 1995, pp. 649–651.

10 *IPRax*, 2004, pp. 61–64. See comments from Friedrich 2003; Hess 2003; Oberhammer 2004; Huber 2004; Prütting 2004. It is worth noting that Bertelmann AG did not claimed fear of execution of a

Article 14 (right of property) of the *Grundgesetz* (GG, Constitution), and accordingly suspended it issuing an injunction. The interim order was prolonged several times, though at the end Bertelsmann's request was unsuccessful, for the claim was served on one of the board's members during a stay at New York. The U.S. court recognized this as a valid alternative service, and Bertelsmann AG withdrew the constitutional complaint in Germany.

In 2007, the Federal Constitutional Court changed again its opinion and ruled that service of process of a claim for punitive damages does not violate 'essential principles of a free state governed by the rule of law'.[11] The Second Senate accepted that the scope of the public policy clause is not necessarily the same wherever it exists -service of process, applicable law, recognition and enforcement. It also held that Article 13 of the Hague Convention must rather have a convention-specific meaning, guided by the principles underlying the Convention as expressed in the Preamble ('Desiring to create appropriate means to ensure that judicial and extrajudicial documents to be served abroad shall be brought to the notice of the addressee in sufficient time'); and that, as far as service of process is concerned, the *ordre public* exception should be applied in a more restricted way than in other fields, such as applicable law – Article 40 III 2 of the German Conflict of Laws Act -, or when it comes to the recognition and enforcement of a foreign judgment – §328 (1) No. 4 of the Code of Civil Procedure.[12] The core of the *BVerfG* decision reads 'Despite the fundamental decision in favour of service of the foreign process the proviso of Article 13 of the Hague Convention is not meaningless. A limit is to be seen where the goal of the claim is manifestly contrary to essential principles of a democratic State (…). The fact that punitive damages might be imposed does not still violate any absolute rule of law (…). For claims of punitive damages of an amount that would endanger the existence of the appellant, (…) the incompatibility of service with the essential principles of a liberal constitutional State cannot simply be ruled out if these claims appear as a clear abuse of rights'.[13]

punitive damage award in Germany, but the execution of a possible sentence against their assets in the United States.

11 'Unverzichtbare Grundsätze eines freiheitlichen Rechtsstaats': *BVerfG*, 24 January 2007, *IPRax*, 2009, pp. 249–250. See also *BVerfG*, 14 June 2007, *NJW*, pp. 3709–3711; and *BVerFG*, 4 September 2008, *IPRax*, 2009, pp. 253–256.

12 The assessment in view of applying Article 13 should be made case by case. Rogler 2009, p. 228, analyses the arguments of the OLG Koblenz decision of 27 June 2005, against the correct understanding of Article 13.

13 'Trotz der grundsätzlichen Entscheidung zu Gunsten der Zustellung der ausländischen Klage is die Vorbehaltsklausel des Article 13 HZÜ nicht inhaltsleer. Eine Grenze muss dort als erreicht angesehen warden, wo das mit der Klage verfolgte Ziel *offentsichtlich gegen unverzichtbare Grundsätze einer freiheitlichen Rechtsstaats verstiesse.* Die Möglichkeit der Verhängung von Strafschadensersatz (punitive damages) verletzt noch nicht unverzichtbare rechtsstaatliche Grundsätze. Bei Forderungen von Strafschadensersatz in für einen Beschwerdeführer existenzgefährdender Höhe oder bie Sammelklagen mit einer unübersehbaren Anzahl von Klägern, einer esntsprechenden Klageforderung und einer begleitenden Medienkampagne scheint die Unvereinbarkeit einer Zustellung mit unverzichtbaren Grundsätzen eines freiheitlichen Rechtsstaates aber jedenfalls dann nicht schlechthin ausgeschlossen zu sein, wenn diese Forderungen als offensichtlich rechtsmissbräuchlich erscheinen'.

Such being also the most widespread scholarly opinion,[14] it may be asserted by now that the punitive nature of punitive damages does not violate the public policy clause as far as service of process is concerned. But, what about the – generally – big size of the awards?

The point of departure of a denial to comply with the request due to the expected amount is the assumption that the plaintiff will indeed be awarded punitive damages, and that he will attempt to enforce the decision in Germany; therefore, the grounds for refusing recognition are already considered at the time of service, and cooperation is denied. But operating on such a conviction – that is, anticipating the outcome of the claim – goes directly against the Taborda Ferreira Report on the 1965 Hague Convention, which expressly states that service does not prejudge recognition or subsequent enforcement.[15] Article 13, on the other hand, only allows taking into account the effects of complying with the service requested, and not the consequences of any future decision. In other words: compliance does not affect any principle or fundamental right (such as the prohibition of arbitrariness in Article 3 GG, or the right to property in Article 14 GG), for at the stage of service of process it is not possible to venture what the outcome of the foreign claim will be.

Finally, two practical considerations speak in favour of serving the documents concerning a punitive damages claim: even if service abroad fails due to the refusal of the requested State, the most likely is that proceedings will go ahead in the United States;[16] and, actually, notice of the claim protects the defendant, as it prevents him from being considered part of proceedings without even knowing that they are pending.[17]

2.2. Service of Process Request within the EU

What if the request for service of documents comes from an EU country, and is addressed to another? I am unaware of any actual case in which request for service of process concerning punitive damages claims has been made pursuant to the Community Regulation (EC) No. 1393/2007 of the European Parliament and of the Council, of 13 November 2007, on the service in the Member States of judicial and extrajudicial documents in civil or commercial matters (service of documents) – or its immediate predecessor, Regulation (EC) No. 1348/2000. As I already said somewhere else,[18] the conclusions regarding the Hague Convention are, to a great extent and despite the difference in context, also valid for a request from EU countries. Besides, reciprocal relations within the EU are marked by the principle of mutual trust, and there is no

14 See Bachmann 2005, pp. 7–13; Hopt, Kulms & Von Hein 2006, pp. 130–132; Rasmussen-Bonne, 2009. For the opposite view, *supra*, fn. 8. Obviously, the question now is what situations constitute an abuse of rights: Rogler 2009, p. 228.

15 Requejo 2009, p. 243.

16 See *Volkswagenwerk A.G. v. Schlunk*, 486 US 694 (1988) where service of process was 'nationalized' and documents served to a US-based subsidiary of the German society. See also the *Bertelsmann's* case – claim was served on a board member during a stay at New York.

17 The defendant will be usually interested in starting his or her strategy at the very beginning of the proceedings, for example through a motion to dismiss.

18 Requejo 2009, pp. 241–242.

provision parallel to Article 13 of the Hague Convention, enabling denial to comply with the request for service due to contrariety to the forum's *ordre public*.[19] Therefore, a punitive damage claim will certainly be served.

3. Applicable Law

The claim for punitive damages in international cases gives rise to several issues: characterisation, applicable law, and possible interference of devices – like the public policy exception – to correct the outcome of the conflict of laws rule.

3.1. Characterisation

When talking about 'punitive damages' we immediately think of torts and non-contractual obligations. The law applicable to such obligations in the EU (except Denmark) is set up in Regulation (EC) No. 864/2007 of the European Parliament and of the Council, on the law applicable to non-contractual obligations, of 11 July 2007, Rome II.[20] That the Regulation may provide coverage for punitive damages derives clearly from the allusion to them in Recital 32. Besides, Article 15 c) of the Regulation indicates that the law applicable to non-contractual obligations shall govern in particular 'the existence, nature and assessment of damages or the remedy claimed', thus corroborating the idea that repair is not modelled on damage. In other words, the Regulation does not assume *integral reparation* as the only possible philosophy; instead, it opens the door for damages based on principles other than compensation.[21]

This, however, is not enough to conclude that *any* claim for punitive damages is governed by the Rome II Regulation. In fact, the remedy sought is of no relevance when it comes to decide whether a particular claim falls within the scope of the Regulation. To begin with, what matters is the nature – contractual, non-contractual; but punitive damages have been also awarded in family claims -[22] of the issues raised by the claim.[23]

19 The absence of a public policy clause may lead to a stricter attitude when it comes to decide what matters are 'civil and commercial' within the meaning of regulation; see also Article 6.3: 'If the request for service is manifestly outside the scope of this Regulation or if non-compliance with the formal conditions required makes service impossible, the request and the documents transmitted shall be returned (...) to the transmitting agency (...)'.

20 *Official Journal of the European Union* (OJ), L 199, 31 July 2007. Any law specified by the Regulation shall be applied whether or not it is the law of a Member State. To our knowledge, the question of the applicability of a foreign law awarding punitive damages has not yet been raised in any European country.

21 Boskovic 2008, p. 189.

22 See for instance *Bailey v. Searles-Bailey*, 746 N.E.2d 1159 (2000). Family cases are excluded from both Regulations Rome II and Regulation (EC) No. 593/2008 of the European Parliament and the Council, on the law applicable to contractual obligations, Rome I. The particular claim underlying *Bailey* would also be excluded from Council Regulation (EC) no 2201/2003 of 27 November 2003 concerning jurisdiction and the recognition and enforcement of judgments in matrimonial matters and the matters of parental responsibility.

23 Scott 2009, pp. 75–76. See also ECJ, as. C-406/09, interpreting Regulation Brussels I, but also applicable to the Rome Regulations.

In this respect, characterisation of an obligation as non-contractual has to be autonomous, in order to provide uniformity in the Regulation's application. Moreover, definition of the substantive scope of Regulation Rome II and the instruments dealing with the law applicable to contractual obligations should be reciprocally consistent, and also consistent with Council Regulation (EC) No. 44/2001 of 22 December 2000 on jurisdiction and the recognition and enforcement of judgments in civil and commercial matters (Recital 7 of Rome II). Finally, once the nature of the issue at stake has been characterised as non-contractual, the application of the Rome II Regulation may still be excluded through Article 1.[24]

An overview of the national legal systems that allow the granting of punitive damages suggests, nonetheless, that application of the Rome II Regulation would be the most common outcome in the EU Member States. The award of punitive damages in non-tortious cases is controversial in Anglo-Saxon countries. Although different degrees of development may be appreciated,[25] the traditional position, seemingly still prevalent, is the one represented by the US Restatement (second) on Contract Damages 1981, par. 355: 'Punitive damages are not recoverable for a breach of contract unless the conduct constituting the breach is also a tort for which punitive damages are recoverable'. This link to a contract may have implications when determining the applicable law – see Article 4.3 Regulation Rome II -, but it does not change characterisation of the issue as non-contractual, *i.e.*, it does not compromise the applicability of the Rome II Regulation.

For tort matters excluded from the Rome II Regulation, the applicable law would have to be determined through conventional or autonomous conflict of laws rules. It is worth noting the radical exclusion of punitive damages in national conflict rules such as Article 40 III 2 of the German EGBGB, a provision specifically conceived 'gegen US-amerikasche punitive damages':[26] 'Claims that are subject to the laws of another State cannot be enforced if: 1. they go much further than necessary to adequately compensate the injured; 2. they manifestly seek other than a reasonable compensation of the injured (...)'.[27] The same pattern is found in Article 116 and Article 119 of the Romanian International Private Law Act,[28] or in par. 52 of the Estonian International Private Law Act.[29] Section 5 of the English Protection of Trading Interests Act, 1980, which

24 So far as punitive damages are concerned, an exclusion of interest is Article 1.2 *g*:'non-contractual obligations arising out of violations of privacy and rights relating to personality, including defamation'. See also Article 1.1 excluding 'the liability of the State for acts and omissions in the exercise of State authority (*acta iure imperii*)': does the first category of punitive damages in England after *Rookes v. Barnard* [1964] 1 All ER 367 ('oppressive, arbitrary or unconstitutional action by servants of the Government') fit the rule?

25 Tettenborn 2005, *passim*. For England *vid*. Wilcox 2009, pp. 21–22.

26 Hopt, Kulms & Von Hein 2006, p. 131.

27 'Ansprüche, die dem Recht eines anderen Staates unterliegen, können nicht geltend gemacht werden, soweit sie: 1. wesentlich weiter gehen als zur angemessenen Entschädigung des Verletzten erforderlich; 2. offensichtlich anderen Zwecken als einer angemessenen Entschädigung des Verletzten dienen'.

28 Law 105/1992.

29 27 March 2002. Par. 52: 'If a claim arising from unlawful causing of damage is governed by foreign law, compensation ordered in Estonia shall not be significantly greater than the compensation prescribed for similar damage by Estonian law'.

restricts the enforcement of judgments for multiple damages,[30] has been classified as mandatory rule of the forum – or even as part of public policy.[31] Still in Europe, but outside the EU, the Swiss Private International Law Act offers another example: see Article 135.2 ('Product liability: 2. If the claims based on a defect or defective description of a product are governed by foreign law, damages over those that would be allocated under Swiss law shall not be awarded in Switzerland'); Article 137.2 ('Obstruction to competition: 2. If the claims based on an impediment to competition are governed by foreign law, damages over those that would be allocated under Swiss law for such an obstruction shall not be awarded in Switzerland').[32]

3.2. *What Would Be the Law Applicable under the Rome II Regulation?*

As already said, following Article 15 'The law applicable to non-contractual obligations under this Regulation shall govern in particular (c) the existence, the nature and the assessment of damage or the remedy claimed'. Unless otherwise provided for in the Regulation, this shall be (Article 4.1) 'the law of the country in which the damage occurs irrespective of the country in which the event giving rise to the damage occurred and irrespective of the country or countries in which the indirect consequences of that event occur'.

The applicability of the law of the place where damage occurs to punitive damages, as if they were just another liability matter devoid of any specialty, is striking when contrasted with their treatment in common law countries such as the United States or England. To begin with, *dépeçage* is a regular practice there: that is, different issues of tort liability may be subjected to different conflict analysis. In this regard, punitive damages may be characterised as a procedural issue (therefore within the scope of the law applicable to procedure);[33] on the other hand, they may be considered as a substantive matter, but pertaining to a law different from the one applicable to compensatory damages[34] (something that seems perfectly reasonable in light of the purposes of each type of damages, though it has not been accepted in the Community Regulation).[35] Punitive damages themselves could be 'dépecés': actually, up to four different issues have been distinguished in punitive damages for the sake of the applicable law analysis.[36] Secondly – although this is not a unanimous answer[37] – the predominant approach in Anglo-

30 'A judgment for an amount arrived at by doubling, trebling or otherwise multiplying a sum assessed as compensation for the loss or damage sustained by the person in whose favour the judgment is given'.

31 Plender & Wilderspin 2009, p. 752; though see Rushworth 2009, p. 201.

32 Article 135.2: 'Responsabilité du fait d'un produit: 2. Si des prétentions fondées sur un défaut ou une description défectueuse d'un produit sont régies par le droit étranger, on ne peut en Suisse accorder d'autres indemnités que celles qui seraient allouées pour un tel dommage en vertu du droit suisse'. Article 137.2: 'Entrave à la concurrence: 2. Si des prétentions fondées sur une entrave à la concurrence sont régies par le droit étranger, on ne peut, en Suisse, accorder d'autres indemnités que celles qui seraient allouées pour une entrave à la concurrence en vertu du droit suisse'.

33 Rushworth 2009, pp. 199–200.

34 See Restatement (Second) Conflict of Laws, sec. 171, reporter's note to *comment d*.

35 See Article 15. In favour of such a solution Boskovic 2008, p. 189. Before, Boskovic 2006, p. 1585.

36 Borchers 2010, p. 541.

37 On the other hand, as already stated Article 4 gives way in numerous occasions to a specific rule.

Saxon systems takes as starting point the purpose of the remedy: in the case of punitive damages, punishing the defendant and deterring the conduct engaged by him. Connecting factors such as the place where the damage is experienced, the defendant's domicile, and above all, the place of the activity that has caused the damage, come therefore to the front.[38]

For the sake of completeness it has to be said that Article 4.1 of the Regulation does not always apply. Specific rules have been laid down for special torts where the general rule does not allow a reasonable balance between the interests at stake: claims of product liability, unfair competition and acts restricting free competition, environmental damages, infringement of intellectual property rights or an industrial action have therefore been accorded a special solution. Some of these rules are, however, just a clarification of the general provision, thus providing for the same result – and deserving (at least in a rough, first approach) the same critical comments.

Article 4 may also be excluded through parties' choice of law (Article 14: though a defendant's agreement to a deal that would subject him or her to punitive damages seems unlikely).[39] In addition, Article 4 will not be applied if both the person claimed to be liable and the person sustaining damage have their habitual residence in the same country at the time when the damage occurs; in such a case the law of that country shall apply. Finally, there is an escape clause: where it is clear from all the circumstances of the case that the tort/delict is manifestly more closely connected with a country other than that indicated in paragraphs 1 or 2 of Article 4, the law of that other country shall apply. When asked whether Article 4.3 could lead to substituting the law of the place where the damage occurs, in order to apply the law of the place of the harmful activity, academics have answered negatively.[40]

The Rome II Regulation establishes a classic *ordre public* clause in Article 26. The history of the provision is especially interesting when it comes to punitive damages.

Under Article 20 of the Commission Proposal for a Regulation of the European Parliament and the Council on the Law Applicable to Non-contractual Obligations, of 3 May 2002, application of the law designated pursuant to the Regulation could be rejected if said application was manifestly contrary to the forum's *ordre public*. In the following proposal, of 22 July 2003,[41] an article (Article 24) was added specifying that 'The application of a provision of the law designated by this Regulation which would have the effect of causing non-compensatory damages, such as exemplary or punitive damages, is contrary to the public policy of the Community'.

The Commission's text was quite a disturbing one. Two points were especially targeted with criticism: first, the exclusion of 'non-compensatory damages, such as exemplary or

38 Symeonides 2003, p. 15; Borchers 2010, p. 546, also speaks of the place in which the injury occurred, although he finally favours the place of the defendant's conduct (pp. 547–549). See Rushworth 2009, pp. 202, 216, for England.

39 The agreement must be entered after the event giving rise to the damage occurred – except when all the parties are pursuing a commercial activity –: the defendant is then perfectly aware of the threat of punitive damages.

40 Rushworth 2009, p. 202. See also Fentiman 2009, *passim*, for general doubts about the real utility of the clause.

41 COM (2003) 427 final, unpublished.

punitive damages', as it meant that some types of non-compensatory damages that are clearly non-exemplary were also left out;[42] second, the reference to a *Community public policy*. The European Parliament, in a Resolution of 6 July 2005,[43] suggested amendments of considerable interest: Article 24 should not refer to 'Community public policy', but to that of the forum; and 'is contrary' should be changed to 'could be contrary'. After the Parliament resolution, the Commission redrafted its proposal in February 2006,[44] in such a way that the law designated pursuant to the Regulation would not be applied if it was *contrary to the forum's public policy*; in particular, 'the application under this Regulation of a law that would have the effect of causing non-compensatory damages to be awarded that would be excessive may be considered incompatible with the public policy of the forum'. This paragraph was not included in the Common Position of the Council approved on 25 September 2006, which was limited to the reference to public policy;[45] neither does it appear in the final text of Article 26; but it has been included in the Regulation via Recital 32 ('Considerations of public interest justify giving the courts of the Member States the possibility, in exceptional circumstances, of applying exceptions based on public policy and overriding mandatory provisions. In particular, the application of a provision of the law designated by this Regulation which would have the effect of causing non compensatory exemplary or punitive damages of an excessive nature to be awarded may, depending on the circumstances of the case and the legal order of the Member State of the court seized, be regarded as being contrary to the public policy (*ordre public*) of the forum'.)

What is the real meaning of Recital 32? To start with, a mere recital has no normative effects.[46] But even if this fact is to be ignored, according to scholars' opinion the Recital would have little practical effect beyond that of making clear that exemplary damages may be subject to the public policy exclusion.[47]

In our view, another reading is nonetheless possible. Literally, the text does not reject all non-compensatory damages of punitive or exemplary function, but only those 'of an excessive nature'.[48] It does not rule out functions other than compensatory in the context of civil liability; correspondingly, the philosophy behind national rules such as Article 40 EGBGB, par. 52 of the Estonian International Private Law Act, etc, would have no significance where the Rome II Regulation is to be applied. In short, should the recital have legal effect, it would cut short the chance to appreciate incompatibility with public policy of each singular Member State, since it literally requires more than the non-compensatory nature of the remedy at stake. As a mere recital, devoid of legal force, it is still a hint in this direction.

The fact that rejection of punitive damages has been reduced to a recital – thus extracting it from the regulatory text – and the possibility of reading such recital in the above proposed form, could also have a meaning in terms of Community policy with

42 Plender & Wilderspin 2009, p. 751.
43 OJ C 157 E, 6 July 2006.
44 COM (2006) 83 final, OJ C 67, 18 March 2006.
45 OJ C 289 E, 28 November 2006.
46 Licari 2010, p. 1247, points out a different opinion.
47 Plender & Wilderspin 2009, p. 751.
48 Boscovik 2006, p. 1586; Requejo 2009, p. 254; Licari 2010, p. 1246.

regard to punitive damages.[49] There are some other evidences in this sense. In light of the jurisprudence of the ECJ, it can be concluded that there is no Community public policy contrary to the *function* that underlies punitive damages: ECJ affair C-180/95, *Draemphaehl,* of 1997, related to transposition of Directive 76/207/EEC by Germany, may be cited in this respect. The Directive establishes the obligation to sanction discrimination by reason of gender in the labour context, with the States being free to articulate such a sanction. However, the German option of using civil liability limited to a maximum overall amount was rejected as, according to the ECJ, 'such a consequence would not correspond to the effective legal protection required by the Directive and would not have the deterrent effect likewise required by the Directive' (No. 40 of the grounds and 3 of the ruling). Later on, in *Manfredi,*[50] concerning a breach of Community competition law, the ECJ specifically stated that in the absence of Community law, it is for the domestic legal system of each State to establish the criteria determining the scope of damages caused by collusive practice, always respecting the rule of equivalence, so that if 'particular damages such as exemplary or punitive damages can be granted in the context of national actions similar to those based on Community law on competition, this should also be the case for the latter' (No. 99 of the grounds and 3 of the ruling). The idea has been picked up by the Commission: in the *White Paper on Damages actions for Breach of the EC Antitrust Rules,*[51] it is said that 'there is no absolute principle of Community law that prevents victims of a competition law infringement from being economically better off after a successful damages claim than the situation they would be in *but for* the infringement'. No doubt these assertions will be of interest in case of a control of compatibility between domestic and EU rules.

3.3. *Meaning of 'Excessive'*

If the above stated position is accepted, a new controversy around it is bound to arise, for, what does 'excessive' mean?

It is interesting to note the trend already existing in England, and also in the United States, to correct the excesses and to rationalize and restrain the pronouncements of punitive damages. In England a judge's suggestion to the jury of guidelines, or maximum and minimum numbers (brackets), is not uncommon – though such hint is not binding. Moreover, since 1990, with the reform of the Courts and Legal Service Act 1990 and rule 11(4) of the Rules of the Supreme Court, Order 59, the Court of Appeal may substitute the verdict of the jury if the amount accorded is deemed to be excessive.[52]

49 For Licari, *loc. ult. cit.*, the fact that the reference to punitive damages has been moved to a recital of the text is reveling by itself: 'La réticence européenne vid-à-vis des dommages-intérêts punitifs a fortement pâli dans la version finale du règlement, puisqu'il n'est plus fait allusion à ceux-ci que dans un considérant, texte dénué de portée normative'. Our conclusion is not refuted by Koch 2009.

50 *Judgement of the European Court of Justice,* 13 July 2006, joined cases C-295/04 to C-298/04, *Manfredi;* already in *Judgement of the European Court of Justice,* 5 March 1996, joined cases C-46/93 and C-48/93 *Factortame III.*

51 COM(2008) 165 final, par. 190–192. The same statement appears in 'Staff Working Paper Accompanying the White Paper on Damages Actions for Breach of the EC Antitrust Rules', SEC(2008) 404, April, pp. 57–58.

52 Lloyd-Bostock & Thomas 1999, pp. 13–14.

The debate on the constitutionality of punitive damages has been a longstanding topic in the United States. The changes there are taking place under the 14th Amendment to the Constitution, or *due process* provision: substantive limits (that affect the size of the awards) and procedural safeguards (affecting for instance the burden of proof) hence result for punitive damages awards. The formula is articulated through judicial decisions of the Supreme Court reversing those of lower courts.[53] Several rulings appear as milestones in this path: *BMW of North America v. Gore* of 1996;[54] *State Farm Mutual Automobile Insurance Co v. Campbell et al.* of 2003;[55] and *Philip Morris v. Williams* of 2007.[56] In the first decision, the U.S. Supreme Court ruled that the sum of punitive damages was disproportionate, and that the defendant could not have foreseen it as a result of his conduct; on these grounds the award was contrary to the due process clause. The Supreme Court also proceeded to establish three criteria for the constitutional compatibility of punitive damages: the degree of reprehensibility of the defendant's misconduct; the disparity between the actual or potential harm suffered by the plaintiff and the punitive damages award; and the difference between the award and civil or criminal penalties in comparable cases.

In *State Farm v. Campbell* the Supreme Court refined the precedent, stating that as a rule punitive damages should be limited to less than ten times the size of the compensatory damages awarded (rule of 'single-digit multiplier'). The Supreme Court added that wealth of the defendant is not to be considered; and rejected the 'total harm approach', under which the reprehensibility of the conduct should be measured against the potential harm to everyone the defendant tried to harm, or exposed to injury through his or her reckless conduct.

The Supreme Court's criteria have not been accepted unanimously. Among other critics, they have been accused of reducing the effectiveness of punitive damages against large companies.[57] The saga *Philip Morris v. Williams* stands as a paradigmatic example of the hesitation to follow the restrictions outlined by the Supreme Court. The amount of damages fixed by the jury in 1999, ratified by the Oregon Supreme Court on two occasions (2002 and 2004),[58] was calculated ignoring the rule of single-digit multiplier on the grounds that the conduct of the tobacco trader had caused damage to all Oregonians, in addition to the specific victim. The Federal Supreme Court has been twice forced to withdraw the decision of the Court of Oregon.[59] The judgment of February 20, 2007, has served to clarify the guidelines of *State Farm*: jurors may punish a defendant only for the harm done to the person suing, and not to other smokers that could make similar claims.

53 On the other hand, from a legal perspective it is worth recalling President Clinton's veto, in May 1996, to a bill that would have imposed limits on punitive damages awards both before state and federal courts.

54 *BMW of North America v. Gore*, 517 US 559.

55 *State Farm Mutual Automobile Insurance Co v. Campbell et al.* 538 US 408.

56 *Philip Morris v. Williams* 127 S.Ct. 1057.

57 See for instance *Romo v. Ford Motor Co*, 113 Cal. App. 4th 738 (2003) where the California Court of Appeal reduced the sum imposed by the lower courts, which had not paid attention to the criteria set by the Supreme Court.

58 182 Ore. App. 44; 193 Ore. App. 527.

59 Finally, on 31 March 2009, the Supreme Court's judges said in a one-sentence order that they were not passing judgment on the legal issues presented.

It should be noted that this case law seriously questions the possibility of *punitive damages* in class actions.[60]

Would these movements towards limiting and rationalizing punitive damages have any impact in civil law systems' attitude, as far as the applicable law is concerned? Clearly, what is or is not considered excessive or proportionate in the United States (or what should the parameters of comparison be) is not binding in Europe. Also, recent events in the domain of recognition of foreign judgments point to perseverance in the non-acceptance of punitive damages, no matter how proportionate they are: in the U.S. decision underlying the recent ruling of the French *Cour de Cassation* (1 December 2010), the amount of compensatory damages was USD 1.39 million, and that of punitive damages USD 1.46 million – that is, the ratio was one to one. Still, the negative solution is not followed everywhere in Europe.[61] But, on the other hand, the following assertion does not seem unreasonable: the scope of the *ordre public* exception should be more reduced when it comes to the applicable law, in comparison with recognition and enforcement, because where public policy is used to refuse recognition the effect is limited to the requested State; on the contrary, when a Court uses the exception to refuse the application of foreign law, it 'essentially elevates its public policy to a pan-European level for the purposes of the particular case, as all other Member States will have to recognise that judgment'.[62] It also has been noted that a *quantitative* assessment of the compatibility of punitive damages to public policy 'may be admitted, but requires caution',[63] in order to prevent an undesirable result, such as considering that any amount exceeding the result of applying the domestic standards is contrary to public policy (in line with Article 40 EGBGB, or Article 135, Article 137 of the Swiss International Private Law Act). Finally, in the context of public policy exception only fundamental principles and basic rights should be taken into account; in this regard, the guidelines set by the ECHR may be useful when assessing incompatibility with the forum's public policy.[64]

Be it as it may, the inclusion of Recital 32 in the Rome II Regulation may help to close all debates on what 'excessive nature' is, for it provides the ECJ with a basis for interpretation: 'Perhaps the only real significance to Recital 32 is to provide some anchor for the European Court of Justice to operate from, should it wish to do so, in policing the boundaries of public policy in this area. Clearly different Member States will draw the line as to what amounts to an excessive non-compensatory award in different places and in the interests of at least broad uniformity the Court of Justice might be keen to intervene to define the limits of public policy'.[65]

60 Rather, the idea is that class actions that seek punitive damages would not be authorised.

61 See *infra* the Spanish case.

62 Rushworth 2009, pp. 201–202. The proposition is not unanimously accepted: for instance, in Germany *ordre public* is understood in the context of recognition as 'attenuated *ordre public*', meaning less intense than ordre public in the context of the conflicts of laws. See *BGH*, 4 June 1992, *NJW*, 1992, pp. 3096–3106; Bachmann 2005, p. 13.

63 Lopez de Gonzalo 2008, pp. 84–85.

64 See ECHR *Miloslavsky v. UK*, 13 July 1995, application no. 18139/91: an exemplary award so excessive that it infringes a fundamental right cannot be admitted. The ECHR estimated that an award of 1.5 million pounds was so high that it violated the right to freedom of expression.

65 Plender & Wilderspin 2009, p. 752.

4. Request for Recognition and Enforcement

4.1. Introduction

The application for recognition and enforcement of a punitive damages award in a Member State may come from outside the EU or from an EU country; the origin of the decision determines the regime to be applied. In the first case, the subject matter of the litigation will normally lead to Council Regulation (EC) No. 44/2001 of 22 December 2000 on jurisdiction and the recognition and enforcement of judgments in civil and commercial matters[66] – or Regulation (EC) No. 805/04 of the European Parliament and of the Council of 21 April 2004 creating a European Enforcement Order for uncontested claims.[67] In the second case, for countries like the United States[68] the judgment will be submitted to the autonomous system of the State where recognition is sought;[69] in the future, for the cases falling within its scope, the Hague Convention on Choice of Court Agreements, of June 30, 2005 will also have to be considered.[70] In all these instruments the public policy exception appears as an essential barrier to recognition and enforcement of foreign judgments, as shown by decisions in Germany,[71] Greece,[72] Italy,[73] or France.[74]

For any of the aforementioned schemes the public policy clause presents two possible contents: one procedural and one substantive. As punitive damages awards are concerned, the latter will usually be more relevant than the former. Although some doubts have been detected in the procedural framework,[75] due to lack of motivation of the decision, in the end they have not determined refusal to recognize;[76] or, the obstacle has been saved by

66 OJ L 12, 16 January 2001. On punitive damages and the scope of the Regulation see developments *supra* about the Rome II Regulation, whose interpretation must be consistent with Regulation No. 44/01.

67 OJ L 143, 30 April 2004.

68 Or other countries. It is interesting to note that several countries in Latin America have recently enacted statutes authorizing their courts to apply tort liability and damages law similar to that of the country in which an action was previously commenced by one of their residents, and dismissed on *forum non conveniens* grounds. As a matter of fact, such statutes are specifically conceived to counteract dismissals of transnational tort claims brought by citizens of those countries in the United States, against U.S. defendants. Therefore, punitive damages may also be awarded by these courts.

69 The failure of the proposed Hague Convention on jurisdiction and foreign judgments in civil and commercial matters is well known. The recent Commission Proposal for a Regulation of the European Parliament and of the Council on jurisdiction and the recognition and enforcement of judgments in civil and commercial matters, COM(2010) 748 final, leaves out the recognition and enforcement of third State judgments.

70 Not yet in forced, but signed by both the EU and the US.

71 *BGH,* 4 June 1992, *NJW,* 1992, pp. 3096–3106.

72 See Triadafillidis 2002.

73 *Corte di Cassazione*, n. 1183, 19 January 2007, *Riv. Dir. Int. Pr. Pr.*, 2007, 777–779.

74 *Cour de Cassation,* 1 December 2010, *Dalloz*, 2011, pp. 10–11.

75 Beyond the generic problems that may arise from the specialties of U.S. law regarding notification or discovery.

76 See *Corte d'Appello de Venecia*, 15 October 2001, *Riv. Dir. Int. Pr. Pr.*, 2002, 1021–1030. However, lack of motivation could have been a factor determining the classification of the damages as criminal: Lopez de Gonzalo 2008, at 81.

the display of other documents.[77] The lack of the safeguards surrounding criminal procedures has also been argued against recognition, but such objection has been dismissed recalling the position of the parties: both the defendant and the plaintiff are private parties; the plaintiff lacks the superior resources of a public prosecutor.[78]

4.2. *Recognition and Enforcement in a Community Framework*

A couple of things appear worth recalling when the relationship between the public policy exception and punitive damages awards is studied in the EU framework. To start with, there is no longer a clause of non-contrariety with the forum's *ordre public* in Regulation No. 805/04. However, the result of applying this Regulation and Regulation Brussels I (where the *ordre public* clause still exists) must be the same: the material scope of both Regulations coincides;[79] and according to Article 27 of Regulation No. 805/04, both instruments are interchangeable, meaning that recognition and enforcement of a judgment, a court settlement or an authentic instrument on an uncontested claim, may be sought either in accordance with Regulation No. 44/2001 or with Regulation No. 805/04.

Disappearance of the *ordre public* clause in Regulation No. 805/04 has been explained in terms of Community trust, reinforcing the idea of mutual recognition. The recent Commission Proposal for a Regulation on jurisdiction and the recognition and enforcement of judgments in civil and commercial matters[80] elaborates on this idea, with the exception of certain procedures which will transiently remain subjected to the same recognition requirements as before. From a Spanish perspective suppression of the public policy exception is no catastrophe as regards punitive damages awards. Other countries – Germany, Greece, Italy, France – may find the removal of the clause somewhat premature. But this does not allow it to resuscitate; not even in borderline areas like punitive damages.[81]

Could the same conclusion be reached for Regulation No. 44/01, in spite of its (still in force) Article 34.1? To date there have been no requests for the recognition in one Member State of punitive damages awarded in another; all developments are therefore speculative. As point of departure it must be recalled that there is no public policy exception of *community content*.[82] The *ordre public* clause includes the core principles of the country in which recognition or enforcement is sought, so that, in principle, to determine whether a punitive damages awarded in Member State A will be recognized in Member State B it would suffice to have a look at B's *ordre public*. However, the community framework has a weight in the working of the exception: first, the *ordre public* clause is formulated in a deliberately strict manner (*manifestly*); second, as we are reminded by the ECJ, the conditions of application of the public policy clause are certainly set by domestic law, but

77 *Cour d'Appel de Poitiers*, 26 February 2009, *JDI*, 2010, pp. 1230–1234.

78 Symeonides 2003, at 6.

79 See Article 1 of Regulation No. 44/01, and Article 2 of Regulation No. 805/04.

80 Commission Proposal for a Regulation of the European Parliament and of the Council on jurisdiction and the recognition and enforcement of judgments in civil and commercial matters, COM(2010)748 final, 14 December 2010.

81 Hay 2007, at I-290.

82 See supra, under 3.

under the scrutiny of the ECJ;[83] third, mutual trust has proven to be a quite elastic principle, as well as a fertile idea. Therefore, scholars' assertion that an English judgment awarding exemplary damages to an English plaintiff would not be denied recognition in another Member State on public policy grounds should not come as a surprise.[84] This solution is also said to be valid for the recognition/enforcement of a Member State's decision recognising itself a punitive damages award of another (third) country.[85]

4.3. *The Conventional Framework*

Under Article 11.1 of the Hague Convention on Choice of Court Agreements, of 30 June 2005, 'Recognition or enforcement of a judgment may be refused if, and to the extent that, the judgment awards damages, including exemplary or punitive damages, that do not compensate a party for actual loss or harm suffered'. The rule is severed from the general *ordre public* clause contemplated in Article 9 e). It may therefore be said that it is not possible any more to use the latter to deny recognition of punitive damages awards.[86]

In spite of the softness of the formula *may be refused*, Article 11 does not hide the mistrust against punitive damages, and the fear that a favourable attitude toward them thwart the success of a Convention meant to be accepted by as many States as possible. That is why Article 11 moves away from its predecessors, inspired by the negotiations for the (failed) Convention on jurisdiction and foreign judgments in civil and commercial matters, which contained a more generous provision for punitive damages: 'A judgment which awards non-compensatory damages, including exemplary or punitive damages, shall be recognized and enforced to the extent that a court in the requested State could have awarded similar or comparable damages. Nothing in this paragraph shall preclude the court addressed from recognising and enforcing the judgment under its law for an amount up to the full amount of the damages awarded by the court of origin'.[87] As commentators of the rule pointed out, its purpose was both '[to] introduce greater certainty' and 'reassure those States that might have been unwilling to sign the Convention if they had had to enforce awards they regarded as excessive'; but also, '[to] ensure that States would not use the public policy exception of the Convention to refuse to enforce an award of punitive damages if they could have awarded similar or comparable damages themselves'.[88]

4.4. *The National Framework*

In autonomous (national) systems of recognition/enforcement, the public policy obstacle against punitive damages awards is twofold: on the one hand, they are suspicious due to

83 See *Judgment of the European Court of Justice*, 28 March 2000 C-7/98, *Krombach*, at No. 23; *Judgment of the European Court of Justice*, 2 April 2009, C-394/07, *Gambazzi*, at No. 26.

84 This is the interpretation of some authors (*vid.* www.conflictoslaw.net) of Hay 2007, at I-293.

85 Requejo 2009, at 251, citing Hay 2007, at I-293.

86 See Nygh & Pocar 2000, at 117 (commenting on Article 33 of the Preliminary Draft Convention on Jurisdiction and Foreign Judgments in Civil and Commercial Matters).

87 Article 15 Draft on Exclusive Choice of Court Agreements, Work. Doc. 110 E Revised, distribution May 2004.

88 Dogauchi & Hartley 2004, par 144 and fn. 141.

their function, too close to criminal concerns; on the other hand, there is the question of their amount, which is routinely considered 'excessive' or 'disproportionate'. Some flexibility has been introduced recently in relation to the first difficulty: that is especially clear in Greece, France and Spain,[89] as evidenced by some recent decisions on the recognition and enforcement of punitive damages awards.

In Greece, the Efetio of Larissa granted exequatur to an American decision awarding US$ 1,359,578 USD, in 1996; around 650,000 corresponded to punitive damages.[90] The Efetio's resolution was revoked upon appeal: but it is worth noting that the reversal was not unanimous, and that denial of recognition was not based on the punitive nature of the damages but on the disproportionate sum awarded. The Areopag expressly stated that 'the award of an additional sum of money in excess of the actual damages in order to punish the defendant is not rejected in general…'; therefore, the decisive element was the amount involved. The Court reached its decision after analysing all the aspects of the case: an operation criticised in as much as it comes dangerously close to a forbidden *révision au fond*.[91]

The Spanish state of the art is represented by the *Auto del Tribunal Supremo*, 13 November 2001, concerning the recognition of a U.S. decision. The Spanish Supreme Court admits that some statements of the foreign decision do not pursue a compensatory purpose, but a punitive, preventive, and disciplinary one. However, the Court does not infer incompatibility with Spanish public policy; rather, it speaks literally in the opposite direction, stating that 'punitive damages cannot be referred to as an entity which attacks ordre public'.[92] The Supreme Court turns down the idea of incompatibility of punitive damages to Spanish system noting that '[the values] under which the mechanism of compensation of damages operates are not entirely alien to the idea of prevention, nor are they strangers to punitive instruments of coercion, both in the substantive (…) sphere, as in the judicial one'.[93] In the Court's view this is particularly clear when the damages at stake are moral: 'It is not always easy to distinguish among the compensatory concepts and to differentiate the amount respectively corresponding to sanction and to moral damages'.[94] The Supreme Court also alludes to the international nature of the case and its links with

89 Also, as far as the *Corte di Cassazione*, n. 1183, 19 January 2007, is concerned, it is hard to escape the feeling that what really scared the Court was the sum awarded: Lopez de Gonzalo 2008, at 84. The author argues that differences between countries in terms of the amount of the sentences encourage *forum shopping* (in this sense also Borchers 2010, at 532–538); but its correction should not come through the *ordre public* exception: *ibid.*, at. 89.

90 Triadafillidis 2002, at 236.

91 In this respect, Triadafillidis 2002, at 238.

92 Legal grounds, at 9: 'no puede hablarse de los daños punitivos como una entidad atentatoria contra el orden público'.

93 '[los valores] bajo los que se desenvuelve el mecanismo de la indemnización de los daños y perjuicios no son ajenos enteramente a la idea de prevención, y que tampoco les son extraños los instrumentos sancionatorios coercitivos, tanto en el ámbito material – contractual, específicamente – como en la esfera procesal'.

94 'No siempre es fácil, además, diferenciar los conceptos indemnizatorios y delimitar el quantum correspondiente a esa sanción coercitiva y el que responde a la reparación de daños morales'. In the US literature it is believed that continental moral damages reflect factors that the U.S. system takes into account when awarding punitive damages: Stephens 2009, pp. 523–524. Reciprocally, punitive damages were born to be applied to this kind of damage: Wells 2009, at 13.

Spain, in what (I think) is a reflection of the theory that modulates the intensity of the *public order* exception depending on the proximity between the forum and the case.

In France, the incompatibility of a punitive damages award with French public policy was declared in 2009 by the *Cour d'Appel de Poitiers*, relying on the purposes of the sentence.[95] The decision has been recently reversed by the *Cour de Cassation*. According to the Supreme Court, 'the principles underlying an award of punitive damages are not in themselves contrary to public policy';[96] nevertheless, incompatibility may result from the awarded sum, if it is 'disproportionate in relation with the injury suffered and the breach of the contractual obligations of the debtor'.[97] It is worth noting that in this point the French and the Spanish Courts reached opposite conclusions: in France the exequatur was finally refused on the grounds of a proportionality test. The French Supreme Court's exam has been criticized for several reasons, especially for the terms actually retained to draw the comparison – the loss and the compensatory damages granted -, and the total oblivion of others – for instance the wickedness of the defendant's misconduct.[98] A second criticism is directed against the assessment of damages, too close to a (forbidden) review of the merits of the foreign decision.[99]

Spanish case law provides some useful information when it comes to assessing the quantum of an award in civil liability sentences, both in respect to shortness and excess. In the event the amount is considered too small, recognition may be refused due to incompatibility with the constitutional mandate to respect the dignity of the person (Article 10.1 Spanish Constitution),[100] in relation to the fundamental rights affected by the act causing the damage (life, physical integrity …), when through a decision awarding an insufficient (or, directly, a symbolic amount), those rights are emptied of their essential content.[101] On the other hand, excess is also challenged. An interesting statement is found in this respect in the above mentioned Spanish *Auto* on punitive damages, where the Court said that 'the judgment (…) is not contrary to public policy (…). When assessing the proportionality (…) of trebling the amount accorded to patrimonial damages, the fact of its legal mandate, and therefore, its origin in the substantive applicable rules, cannot be obviated; [neither can be obviated] the importance of the interests protected and preserved [by these trebled damages] in the framework of a market economy, [an importance which is] not strictly local, but of general and universal appreciation by the States sharing similar legal, social and economic conceptions'.[102] Two elements seem to be

95 *Cour d'Appel de Poitiers*, 26 February 2009. See the in-depth analysis by Licari 2010, at 1230–1263.

96 'Le principe d'une condamnation à des dommages-intérêts punitifs n'est pas, en soi, contraire à l'ordre public'.

97 'Disproportionné au regard du préjudice subi et des manquements aux obligations contractuelles du débiteur'.

98 Licari 2011, at 426.

99 Licari 2011, at 426–427.

100 Though Article 10 Spanish Constitution cannot be used as an independent ground for an appeal before the Spanish *Tribunal Constitucional*, it is certainly part of the Spanish public policy.

101 *STC* (Sentencia del Tribunal Constitucional) *300/2006; STC 186/2001.*

102 '(…) el pronunciamiento de la sentencia (…) no resulta contrario al orden público (…) Lo mismo cabe decir del pronunciamiento referido a la violación del derecho de marca de la mercantil de la que la aquí actora trae su derecho, pues el juicio de proporcionalidad que pueda hacerse sobre el triple de las cantidades correspondientes a los daños materiales efectivamente causados no puede desconectarse del

relevant for the Spanish Supreme Court: the predictability of the award, and the nature of the interest protected. As for the first, the Court specifically refers to the *legal provisions* for damages: does it mean that other forms of predictability are not admitted (and therefore, recognition of the award would be denied)? In this regard it is worth noting that both in England and the United States the proverbial lack of predictability of punitive damages awards is in fact only relative: in England, thanks to the Guidelines that are being developed by the case law since *Rookes v. Barnard*.[103] In the United States studies support the assertion that 'the size of punitive damages awards, while not invariable fixed, is predictably determined by the size of the compensatory award'; 'Punitive damages awards are somewhat predictable (…) awarded much more often in certain types of torts than others. For example, in recent years, medical malpractice and product liability cases have exhibited the lowest frequency of punitive damages (…)', while 'The highest frequency of punitive damages awards have occurred in intentional torts (…), defamation, and what many refer to as *financial torts*'.[104]

The second element of the proportionality test retained by the Spanish Supreme Court – the nature of the interests at stake – permits to suppose that the recognition of punitive damages awards will be more or less straightforward, depending on the importance of the underlying right or principle. At this point it is worth recalling American punitive damages awards related to grave violations of human rights, under the Alien Tort Statute Act, of 1789:[105] that is, punitive damages *in defense* of human rights. ATS judgments have awarded compensation as well as punitive damages: prior to the Supreme Court's (so far) only ruling, *Sosa v. Alvarez Machain*,[106] and also post-Sosa. In *Filartiga v. Pena Irala*, the Court held that remedies should 'give effect to the manifest objectives of the international prohibition against torture'.[107] To do so, the Court took into consideration several sources: the law of the place where the injuries occurred, state law, international law and federal law. From this approach – a federal common law approach – the Court inferred that the vindication of the international rights concerns demands a punitive damage award.[108]

Punitive damages have also been awarded under the Torture Victim Protection Act of 1991, although the law speaks merely of damages, without going into details. In *Xuncax*

hecho de su previsión legal, y, por tanto, de su origen en la propia norma materialmente aplicable, ni, especialmente, de la trascendencia de los intereses a cuya tutela y salvaguardia están notoriamente orientados en el marco de una economía de mercado, relevancia no estrictamente local, sino de general y universal apreciación en los Estados que participan de similares concepciones jurídicas, sociales y económicas'.

103 Wilcox 2009, at 38–42.

104 Sebok 2009, at 156–158, and *supra*, the test established by the US Supreme Court.

105 28 U.S.C. § 1350. See also Wells 1996, at 864–870, for the so called 'constitutional torts'. Wilcox 2009, at 24: the ECHR does not grant punitive damages, neither do English judges under the Human Rights Act 1998.

106 542 U.S. 692 (2004); 331 F.3d 604, reversed.

107 577 F.Supp. 860, at 865.

108 On the contrary, the law of the country where the abuses occurred is mostly excluded, for different reasons: first, because it is usually the law of a developing country, and does not provide a remedy of quality, consistent with the importance of the damaged legal right. Second, because the application to the same fact -torture- of a local law, differently in different countries, would 'domesticate' the tort, darkening its international relevance. Stephens *et al.* 2008, at 525, citing *Xuncax v. Gramajo*, 866 F.Supp. 162.

v. Gramajo the District court concluded that TVPA was enacted 'with an eye toward eradicating the evil [of torture] altogether'.[109]

Finally, it is interesting to note that applications for recognition of punitive damages awards have raised the question of the boundaries between public policy control and the (forbidden) review of the merits of the foreign judgment. Article 15 of the Draft on Exclusive Choice of Court Agreements[110] had been criticized precisely for reinstating such review: '[it] specifically authorizes the court to reopen the damages determination made by the originating court, listing principles applicable in the recognizing court'.[111] The fact is that the practice has already been identified in Canada;[112] and it may also be reported in European countries.[113] When Greek, Italian, Spanish or French courts, as requested courts, asses the proportionality of the foreign award, they are actually reproducing an operation already carried out by the foreign jurisdiction; in other words, the foreign judgement is being reviewed as to its substance. This leads us to another point, for a logical consequence of accepting the *révision au fond* would be partial recognition carried out by the recognizing courts, on their own motion: 'When dealing with U.S. awards of punitive damages, judges operating in those countries in which punitive damages are deemed contrary to public policy should try to decipher the amount of compensatory damages and limit their enforcement to that portion of damages (...) Absent such a differentiation, it should be the enforcing judge's job to read between the lines and (...) extrapolate a number that would compensate (...) the plaintiff for the losses suffered'.[114]

5. Conclusive Remarks

What is to be inferred from the foregoing arguments? I would say that a tolerant attitude toward punitive damages is making its way in European countries when private international situations (as opposed to pure domestic ones) are at stake – and I believe that, actually, that is how it should be. To be sure, the degree of openness towards punitive damages varies depending on the issue under exam: it is complete as far as service of process is concerned; a less successful, still hesitant opening can be observed in the fields of both applicable law and recognition/enforcement of foreign awards. Some indulgence from the Community acts and case law helps.[115]

But should this come as a surprise? In 1986, the Spanish Constitutional Court denied legal protection (*amparo*) against an exequatur decree issued by the Supreme Court the 25 February 1985, in favour of an American judgment of the District Court State of Michigan (US), ordering a Spanish entity to pay US$ 137,537, plus interests. Before the Constitutional Court the appellants alleged the violation of the *due process* clause in order

109 *Xuncax v. Gramajo*, 866 F.Supp. 162, 199–200.

110 See fn. 87.

111 Brand 2005, at 194, 195.

112 *Beals v. Saldanha* [2003] 3 SCR 416, cited by Brand 2005, at 191–192.

113 Licari 2011, at 426–427.

114 Quarta 2008, at 755, 777. In France, Licari 2011, at 427.

115 An indulgence that may not be found in wider contexts, such as the Hague Conference on Private International Law.

to avoid the enforcement of a sentence of an amount 'extraordinarily high for their modest possibilities'; they also argued that the execution would inevitably lead to the end of the Company.[116] The Constitutional Court ruled against the appellants, stating that 'The applicant forgets that, when exporting his goods abroad, he himself established a connection with a system whose needs and requirements cannot be ignored, and that the Spanish authorities must respect for the sake of certainty of the international relations'.[117] In the international arena players can certainly choose among many different legal systems: but they must accept that their disadvantages (such as being sued in an action for punitive damages, or being sentenced to pay them) come along with their good things.

116 They were even prepared to argue that the granting of exequatur in circumstances such as those of the case would endanger all Spanish exports. Though the whole debate revolved around procedural items – it could not have been otherwise before the Constitutional Court –, the real problem was obviously the award and its size.

117 *STC 43/1986*: 'Pasa por alto, por lo demás, la solicitante de amparo que ha sido ella misma la que, al exportar sus mercancías al extranjero ha establecido un punto de conexión con un ordenamiento cuyas exigencias y requisitos no puede desconocer y que las autoridades españolas deben respetar en aras de la seguridad del tráfico internacional'.

Bibliography

Bachmann 2005
Bachmann, B., 'Neue Rechtsentwicklungen bei punitive damages?', in: B. Bachmann *et al.* (eds), *Festschrift für p. Schlosser zum 70. Geburtstag*, Tübingen: Mohr Siebeck, 2005, pp. 1–18.

Borchers 2010
Borchers, P., 'Punitive Damages, Forum Shopping and the Conflict of Laws', *La L Rev*, 2010, pp. 529–555.

Boskovic 2006
Boskovic, O., 'Les dommages et intérêts en droit international privé. Ne pas manquer une occasion de progrès', *JCP. La Semaine Juridique* 2006, I, n. 163.

Boskovic 2008
Boskovic, O., 'Le domain de la loi applicable', in: S. Corneloup & N. Joubert (eds.), *Le Règlement Communautaire Rome II sur la loi applicable aux obligations non contractuelles*, Paris: Litec, 2008, pp. 183–195.

Brand 2005
Brand, R., 'Punitive Damages Revisited: Taking the Rationale for Non-Recognition of Foreing Judgments Too Far', *J L & Com*, 2005, pp. 181–196.

Dogauchi & Hartley 2004
Dogauchi, M., Hartley, T., *Explanatory Report to the Preliminary Draft Convention on Exclusive Choice of Court Agreements*, Prel. Doc. no 25, March 2004.

Fentiman 2009
Fentiman, R., 'The Significance of Close Connection', in: J. Ahern & W. Binchy (eds.), *The Rome II Regulation on the Law Applicable to Non-Contractual Obligations*, Leiden, Boston: Martinus Nijhoff Publishers, 2009, pp. 85–112.

Friedrich 2003
Friedrich, B., 'Federal Constitutional Court Grants Interim Legal Protection against Service of a Writ of Punitive Damages Suit', *German Law Journal*, 2003, pp. 1233–1240.

Hay 2007
Hay, P., 'The Development of the Public Policy Barrier to Judgment Recognition within the European Community', *European Legal Forum*, 2007, I-289 to I-294.

Hess 2003
Hess, B., 'Transatlantischer Rechtsverkehr heute: von der kooperation zum Konflikt?', *JZ*, 2003, pp. 923–926.

Hopt, Kulms & Von Hein 2006
Hopt, K.J, Kulms, R. & Von Hein, J., *Rechtshilfe und Rechtsstaat*, Tübingen: Mohr Siebeck, 2006.

Huber 2004
Huber, P., 'Playing the Same Old Song- German Courts, the Napster Case, and the International Law of Service of Process', in: H.P. Mansel *et al.*, *Festschrift für E. Jayme*, vol. I, München: Sellier, 2004, pp. 361–370.

Koch 2009
Koch, H., 'Punitive Damages in European Law', in: H. Koziol, H. & V. Wilcox (eds), *Punitive Damages: Common Law and Civil Law Perspectives*, Vienna: Springer, 2009, pp. 197–209.

Körner 2000
Körner, M., 'Zur Aufgabe des Haftungsrechts- Bedeutunsgewinn präventiver und punitiver Elemente', *NJW*, 2000, pp. 241–246.

Koziol & Wilcox 2009
Koziol, H. & Wilcox, V. (eds.), *Punitive Damages: Common Law and Civil Law Perspectives*, Vienna: Springer, 2009.

Licari 2010
Licari, F.X., Note 'Cour d'Appel de Poitiers, 26.02.2009', *JDI*, 2010, pp. 1230–1263.

Licari 2011
Licari, F.X., Note 'Cour de Cassation, 1.12.2010', *Recueil Dalloz*, 10.02.2011, pp. 423–427.

Lopez de Gonzalo 2008
Lopez de Gonzalo, M., 'Punitive damages e ordine pubblico', *Riv Dir Int Pr Pr,* 2008, pp. 79–90.

Lloyd-Bostock & Thomas 1999
Lloyd-Bostock, S. & Thomas C., 'Decline of the *Little Parliament:* juries and jury reform in England and Wales', *Law & Contemp Probs*, 1999, pp. 7–40.

Merkt 1995
Merkt, H., *Abwehr der Zustellung von punitive damages-Klagen*, Heidelberg: Verlag Recht und Wirtschaft, 1995.

Merkt 2009
Merkt, H., 'Von Monstern und komischen Vögeln: Kritische Anmerkungen zur Zustellung US-amerikanisher punitive damages-Klagen in Deutschland', in: R. Stürner *et al.*, *Festschrift für Dieter Leipold zum 70. Geburstag*, Tübingen: Mohr Siebeck, 2009, pp. 265–280.

Musy 2000
Musy A.M., 'Punitive damages e resistenza temeraria in giudizio: regole, definizioni e modelli istituzionali a confronto (Tribunale di Torre Annunziata, Sez. stralcio, 24 febbraio 2000; Tribunale di Torre Annunziata, Sez. stralcio, 14 marzo 2000)', *Danno e responsabilità*, 2000, pp. 1121–1127.

Nygh & Pocar 2000
Nygh, P. & Pocar, F., *Report on the Preliminary Draft Convention on Jurisdiction and Foreign Judgments in Civil and Commercial Matters*, Prel. Doc. no 11, August 2000.

Oberhammer 2004
Oberhammer, P., 'Deutsche Grundrechte und die Zustellung US-amerikanischer Klagen im Rechtshilfweg', *IPRax*, 2004, pp. 40–45.

Otero Crespo (contained in this publication)
Otero Crespo, M., 'Punitive Damages under Spanish Law: a subtle Recognition?'.

Piekenbrock 2006
Piekenbrock, A., 'Zur Zustellung kartellrechtlicher treble damages-Klagen in Deutschland', *IPRax*, 2006, pp. 4–10.

Plender & Wilderspin 2009
Plender, R. & Wilderspin, M., *The European Private International Law of Obligations*, London: Sweet & Maxwell, 2009.

Prütting 2004
Prütting, H., 'Ein neues Kapitel im Justizkonflikt USA-Deutschland', in: H.P. Mansel *et al.*, *Festschrift für E. Jayme*, vol. I, München: Sellier, 2004, pp. 709–718.

Quarta 2008
Quarta, F., 'Recognition and Enforcement of US Punitive Damages Awards in Continental Europe: The Italian Supreme Court's Veto', *Hastings Int'l & Comp L R*, 2008, pp. 753–783.

Rasmussen-Bonne 2009
Rasmussen-Bonne, H.E., 'The Pendulum Swings Back: The Cooperative Approach of German Courts', in: P. Hay *et al.*, *Resolving International Conflicts Liber Amicorum Tibor Várady*, Budapest-New York: Central European University Press, 2009, pp. 231–253.

Requejo 2009
Requejo, M., 'Punitive Damages from a Private International Law Perspective', in: H. Koziol & V. Wilcox (eds.), *Punitive Damages: Common Law and Civil Law Perspectives*, Vienna: Springer, 2009, pp. 236–255.

Rogler 2009
Rogler, J., 'Die Entcheidung des BverfG vom 24.1.2007 zur Zustellung einer US-amerikanishen Klagen auf Strafschadensersatz: Ist das Ende des transatlantischen Justizkonflikts erreicht?', *IPRax*, 2009, pp. 223–230.

Rosengarten 1996
Rosengarten, J., 'Der Präventionsgedanke im deutschen Zivilrecht', *NJW*, 1996, p. 1935.

Rushworth 2009
Rushworth, A., 'Remedies and the Rome II Regulation', in: J. Ahern & W. Binchy (eds.), *The Rome II Regulation on the Law Applicable to Non-Contractual Obligations*, Leiden, Boston: Martinus Nijhoff Publishers, 2009, pp. 199–218.

Scott 2009
Scott, A., 'The Scope of *Non-Contractual Obligations*', in: J. Ahern & W. Binchy (eds.), *The Rome II Regulation on the Law Applicable to Non-Contractual Obligations*, Leiden, Boston: Martinus Nijhoff Publishers, 2009, pp. 57–83.

Sebok 2009
Sebok, A.J., 'Punitive Damages in the United States', in: H. Koziol & V. Wilcox (eds.), *Punitive Damages: Common Law and Civil Law Perspectives*, Vienna: Springer, 2009, pp. 158–196.

Stephens 2008
Stephens, B. *et al.*, *International Human Rights Litigation in U.S. Courts*, Leiden: Martinus Nijhoff Publishers, 2008.

Symeonides 2003
Symeonides, S.C., 'Resolving punitive-damages conflicts', *YPIL*, 2003, pp. 1–34.

Tettenborn 2005
Tettenborn, A., 'Punitive Damages for Breach of Contract: What's so special about Contract Claims?', 2005, SSRN: http://ssrn.com/abstract=938700.

Triadafillidis 2002
Triadafillidis, C.D., 'Anerkennung und Vollstreckung von *punitive damages* - Urteilen nach kontinentalem und insbesondere nach griechischem Recht', *IPRax*, 2002, pp. 236–238.

Wells 1996
Wells, M.L., 'Punitive Damages for Constitutional Torts', *La L R*, 1996, pp. 841–872.

Wells 2009
Wells, M.L., 'A Common Lawyer's Perspective on the European Perspective on Punitive Damages', *University of Georgia School of Law- Research Papers Series*, 2009, Paper no. 09–11.

Wilcox 2009
Wilcox, V., 'Punitive Damages in England', in: H. Koziol and V. Wilcox (eds.), *Punitive Damages: Common Law and Civil Law Perspectives*, Vienna: Springer, 2009, pp. 7–53.

Cedric Vanleenhove*

PUNITIVE DAMAGES AND EUROPEAN LAW: *QUO VADEMUS*?

1. The Concept of Punitive Damages

The availability of punitive damages has long been recognized in common law jurisdictions including the United States, New Zealand, Canada and Australia.[1] They are not intended to compensate for harm done but are awarded in excess of any compensatory or nominal damages.[2] Compensatory damages on the other hand provide reparation both for economic (e.g. medical costs) and for non-economic losses (e.g. pain and suffering). Punitive damages essentially serve four purposes: to punish the offender for uncivilized conduct, to deter the offender and others from similar conduct, to reward the plaintiff for enforcing the law and to supplement inadequate compensatory damages.[3] Although punitive damages are not intended to compensate the plaintiff, the plaintiff will in fact receive all or some portion of the punitive damages award.[4] Punitive damages are typically limited to tort actions where the defendant has engaged in exceptionally objectionable conduct and are consequently rarely awarded for breach of contract.[5]

In the European Union only the common law countries England, Wales, Ireland, Northern Ireland and the mixed system of Cyprus provide for this specific kind of damages in their respective legal systems.[6] The availability of punitive damages however is by no means without constraints. England for example restricts exemplary damages (as they are called there) to three specific circumstances.[7] In continental Europe and in

* Ph.D. Researcher at the Private International Law Department of Ghent University (Belgium), LL.M. (Cantab).

1 Gray 2009, pp. 111–112.

2 Nater-Bass 2003, p. 154.

3 This accurate enumeration ironically comes from the German Federal Supreme Court ('Bundesgerichtshof'): BGH, 4 June 1992, *BGHZ* 118, 312, English translation in 32 *ILM* 1320 (1993); Brand 2005, p. 185.

4 Ryan 2003, pp. 76 and 92.

5 Gotanda 1998, p. 193. Only Canada and the U.S. award punitive damages as a remedy in contract cases. In England and Australia punitive damages are not available for breach of contract (Gotanda 2003, p. 12, p. 19, pp. 44 and 51).

6 As a matter of fact, the concept of punitive damages in the US, Canada, Australia and New Zealand has its roots in 18th-century English law: Wilcox 2009, p. 8, nr. 3.

7 Lord Devlin in *Rookes v. Barnard* [1964] *AC* 1129, [1964] 1 *All ER* 367. The three categories are: oppressive, arbitrary or unconstitutional actions by government servants, torts committed for profit and exemplary damages expressly authorized by statute.

other civil law countries across the globe the concept of punitive damages is scarcely recognised in law. Generally, punitive damages are considered to be a penal sanction.[8] The indemnification obligation of civil law systems primarily has a compensatory purpose, *i.e.* restoring the injured party's former situation. The laws of the Continental European countries do not aim to punish the tortfeasor through damages but rather serve to compensate the victim for the damage sustained.[9]

As Europe consists of both civil and common law orientated countries, it is interesting to examine the position which European law takes on punitive damages. This article will try to establish that punitive damages do not – perhaps yet – play a significant role in European law. The author shares Koziol's view that Community law is inconsistent in reflecting the contrast between common law and continental civil law in Europe.[10]

2. Punitive Damages in European Law

2.1. Drafting History of the Rome II Regulation

The EU's attitude towards punitive damages has been described as ambivalent and self-contradictory.[11] The drafting history of the Rome II Regulation, although dealing with private international law situations, clearly demonstrates this. The original proposal from 2003 combined a general rule on public policy (*ordre public*) in its Article 22 with a more specific rule on non-compensatory damages in its Article 24. Article 24 read as follows:

> 'The application of a provision of the law designated by this regulation which has the effect of causing non-compensatory damages, such as exemplary or punitive damages, to be awarded shall be contrary to Community public policy'.[12]

The insertion of a separate article was inspired by a predominately German call for a rule corresponding to Article 40 paragraph 3(1) of the Introductory Act to the Civil Code (*Einführungsgesetz zum Bürgerlichen Gesetzbuche – EGBGB*) which, although not explicitly mentioning punitive damages, rejects the enforcement of any awards that 'substantially go beyond what is necessary for an adequate compensation of the injured party'. During the consultation phase, the German federal bar, along with other contributors, had expressed the concern that the absence of provisions limiting liability would be problematic. It found the mechanism of a general *ordre public* exception (as later set out in Article 22) insufficient to avoid exorbitant damages such as punitive damages.[13] The idea of applying

8 Nater-Bass 2003, p. 154.
9 Sein 2007, p. 46.
10 Koziol 2008, p. 748.
11 Wagner 2006, p. 69.
12 Proposal for a Regulation of the European Parliament and the Council on the law applicable to non-contractual obligations ('Rome II'), 22/07/2003, COM/2003/0427 final.
13 Position of the Bundesrechtsanwaltskammer (The German Federal Bar) on the Preliminary Draft Proposal for a Council Regulation on the Law Applicable to Non-Contractual Obligations (to be

the law of a third country providing for damages not calculated to compensate for damage sustained worried many contributors to the written consultation.[14]

The inclusion of the express rule of Article 24 suggested that punitive damages violate some kind of Community public policy.[15] The Commission however seemed to have forgotten how the legal systems of England and Ireland actually operate.[16] The original draft would have had illogical consequences for those Member States since an English court for instance would have had to refuse the application of a foreign law granting punitive damages and replace it by its own domestic law (*lex fori*) which awards such damages itself.[17] Article 24 would also have caught other non-compensatory damages such as the account of profits which have an important function and are fundamentally different from punitive damages. This was caused by the lack of specificity as to the types of non-compensatory damages Article 24 aims to exclude. In our view the Commission did not intend to outlaw such remedies.[18]

The Report on the proposal (also known as the Wallis report) dropped the reference to the Community public policy. Rapporteur Diana Wallis thought it beyond the scope of the Regulation to introduce this new concept and to remove the possibility of awarding punitive damages as the Commission proposed in Article 24.[19] Even though she felt sympathetic towards the proposed provision, she preferred to have Article 22 amended and made the suggestion to return to the mere possibility for the forum to refuse the application of a foreign law allowing for punitive damages.[20]

The Commission subsequently amended its proposal by deleting Article 24 and merging it with Article 23. In Article 23 it was stated that:

> 'The application of a rule of the law of any country specified by this Regulation may be refused only if such application is manifestly incompatible with the public policy ('*ordre public*') of the forum. In particular, the application under this Regulation of a law that would have the effect of causing non-compensatory damages to be awarded that would be excessive may be considered incompatible with the public policy of the forum'.[21]

Instead of automatically ruling out punitive damages as violating the public policy of the European Community, this new article leaves the national judge free to decide whether

found at http://ec.europa.eu/justice/news/consulting_public/rome_ii/contributions/bundesrechtsanwaltskammer_en.pdf), par. 8.

14 Explanatory Memorandum to the Proposal for a Regulation of the European Parliament and the Council on the law applicable to non-contractual obligations ('Rome II'), COM/2003/0427 final, p. 29.

15 Koch 2009, p. 198.

16 Tebbens 2009, p. 286.

17 Koch 2009, p. 199.

18 European Union Committee of the House of Lords, The Rome II Regulation, 8th Report of Session 2003–04, no. 169–170.

19 Draft Report on the proposal for a regulation of the European Parliament and of the Council on the law applicable to non-contractual obligations ('Rome II'), COD/2003/0168, p. 31.

20 Draft Report on the proposal for a regulation of the European Parliament and of the Council on the law applicable to non-contractual obligations ('Rome II'), COD/2003/0168, p. 33.

21 Amended proposal for a European Parliament and Council Regulation on the law applicable to non-contractual obligations ('Rome II'), 21/02/2006, COD/2003/0168.

punitive damages are acceptable in light of his own country's public policy. Furthermore, only 'excessive' punitive damages are deemed to fall under the umbrella of the public policy exception.[22]

However, this softened approach was not followed by the Council which in its Common Position deleted the rule due to difficulties in establishing a definition of public policy.[23] In the final version of the Rome II Regulation only the first sentence of Article 23 of the proposal was retained in current Article 26, which deals with the public policy of the forum. The Commission and Parliament managed to sneak a reminder of the discussion on punitive damages into the Regulation's Preamble.[24] The relevant part of Recital 32 reads:

> 'In particular, the application of a provision of the law designated by this Regulation which would have the effect of causing non-compensatory exemplary or punitive damages of an excessive nature to be awarded may, depending on the circumstances of the case and the legal order of the Member State of the court seized, be regarded as being contrary to the public policy (ordre public) of the forum'.

The wording of Recital 32 is similar to the second sentence of Article 23 of the proposal. The transfer of the reference to punitive damages from the main text to the Preamble makes little difference as a Member State court can still find punitive damages in violation of the public policy of the forum even though Article 26 does not mention this *expressis verbis*.[25] The inclusion of the Recital in the Regulation is meaningful because it enables the European Court of Justice (ECJ) to draw the line as to what amounts to an excessive non-compensatory award, thereby defining the boundaries of public policy.[26]

2.2. *Other Legislative Sources*

The European Union's attitude toward punitive damages is also unclear and inconsistent in other legal acts and decisions.[27] Wagner has argued that there is no EU legislation specifically authorizing courts to award punitive damages.[28] This is too strong an assertion. As Koch has already put forward, supporters of punitive damages could for instance point to Article 18 of Regulation No. 1768/95 as proof of the existence of punitive awards within European law. This Regulation contains rules which implement the agricultural exemption as provided for in Article 14 paragraph 3 of Regulation 2100/94 on Community plant variety rights. Article 18 deals with special civil law claims and reads (emphasis added):

22 Licari 2010, nr. 17.

23 Common Position adopted by the Council on 25 September 2006 with a view to the adoption of a Regulation of the European Parliament and of the Council on the law applicable to non-contractual obligations ('Rome II') No. 22/2006, OJ C 289/3, p. 68.

24 Koch 2009, p. 199.

25 Koch 2009, p. 199. In the same sense: Plender & Wilderspin 2009, p. 751.

26 Plender & Wilderspin 2009, p. 752.

27 Wagner 2006, p. 71.

28 Wagner 2011, p. 5.

> '1. A person referred to in Article 17 may be sued by the holder to fulfil his obligations pursuant to Article 14(3) of the basic Regulation as specified in this Regulation.
> 2. If such person has repeatedly and intentionally not complied with his obligation pursuant to Article 14(3) 4th indent of the basic Regulation, in respect of one or more varieties of the same holder, the liability to compensate the holder for any further damage pursuant to Article 94(2) of the basic Regulation shall cover at least *a lump sum calculated on the basis of the quadruple average amount charged for the licensed production* of a corresponding quantity of propagating material of protected varieties of the plant species concerned in the same area, without prejudice to the compensation of any higher damage'.

Under this provision of the Regulation the right holder is thus awarded a multiple of the actual loss incurred. This overcompensation of the victim therefore seems to be punitive in nature. The scope of this Regulation, however, is quite limited and restricted to the particular field of plant breeders' rights within intellectual property.[29]

There are also Community instruments that speak out against non-compensatory damages. Recital 26 of the preamble to the IPR Enforcement Directive of 2004 clearly rejects the establishment of punitive damages when it states (in its last sentence):

> 'The aim is not to introduce an obligation to provide for punitive damages but to allow for compensation based on an objective criterion (...)'.[30]

Article 340 TFEU (ex Article 288 ECT) equally seems to limit the extent of the liability of EU institutions to strict compensation. Any claims for exemplary damages by EU employees have been identified and treated by the European judiciary as requests for non-material relief, thereby avoiding giving their award a punitive effect.[31] Its second sentence reads that (emphasis added):

> '(...) the Union will (...) *make good* any damage caused by its institutions or by its servants in the performance of their duties'.

This phrase emphasises the compensatory nature of the indemnification.[32] Similarly, Article 29, second sentence of the Montreal Convention for the Unification of Certain Rules for International Carriage by Air, concluded by the European Community in April 2001, states that in any action for damages concerning the carriage of passengers, baggage or

29 Koch 2009, p. 208–209.

30 Directive 2004/48/EC of the European Parliament and of the Council of 29 April 2004 on the enforcement of intellectual property rights, OJ L 157, 30/04/2004, p. 45. It has been argued that although the Directive does not explicitly provide for the awarding of punitive damages, some provisions come quite close (Borghetti 2009, p. 58). This view seems inconsistent with the wording of Recital 26.

31 ECJ 17 March 1993, *Andrew Macrae Moat v. Commission of the European Communities, ECR* 1993, p. 287, par. 6 and 48; CFI 26 October 1993, *Renato Caronna v. Commission of the European Communities, ECR* 1993, p. 1129, par. 102 and 106.

32 Oliphant 2008, p. 244.

cargo, punitive, exemplary or any other non-compensatory damages shall not be recoverable.[33]

3. Punitive Damages in the Case Law of the ECJ

Not only the body of Community legislative acts but also the jurisprudence of the European Court of Justice is a useful tool in the search for the nature of the EU's stance on punitive damages.[34]

3.1. Von Colson

The case of *Sabine von Colson and Elisabeth Kamann v. Land Nordrhein-Westfalen* ('*Von Colson*')[35] concerned the correct interpretation of the Equal Treatment Directive.[36] Both women applied for two positions at the all-male Werl prison in North Rhine Westphalia (Germany). Due to the problems and risks attached to female employees working in a prison populated by men, the recruitment officials decided to engage two less well-qualified men to fill the vacancies. The applicants felt they were unlawfully denied employment on grounds of their sex and sought compensation in the German courts. The Hamm Labour Court ('Arbeitsgericht') referred several questions to the ECJ for a preliminary ruling. At that time only Article 6 of the Directive provided for sanctions. It imposed on Member States the obligation to introduce into their national legal systems such measures as are necessary to enable all persons who consider themselves wronged by a failure to apply to them the principle of equal treatment to pursue their claims by judicial process. The ECJ found the German transformation of the Directive to be inadequate. The Court held that:

> 'The principle of the effective transposition of the directive requires that the sanctions must be of such nature as to constitute appropriate compensation for the candidate discriminated

33 Convention for the Unification of Certain Rules for International Carriage by Air (the Montreal Convention), OJ L 194, 18/07/2001, p. 34. The European Union approved of this Convention by Council Decision 2001/539/EC of 5 April 2001 on the conclusion by the European Community of the Convention for the Unification of Certain Rules for International Carriage by Air (the Montreal Convention), *OJ L* 194, 18/07/2001, p. 33.

34 On a side note, the European Court of Human Rights does not award punitive damages. This follows from par. 9 of the Practice Direction on Just Satisfaction Claims from 28 March 2007 as well as from case-law (e.g. *Akdivar and Others v. Turkey*, 01/04/1998, no. 21893/93; *Ludescher v. Austria*, 20/12/2001, no. 35019/97; *B.B. v. the United Kingdom*, 10/02/2004, no. 53760/00, par. 36 and *Wainwright v. the United Kingdom*, 26/09/2006, no. 12350/04, par. 60). All EU Member States are Members of the Council of Europe and have ratified the European Convention for the Protection of Human Rights and Fundamental Freedoms.

35 ECJ 10 April 1984, *Sabine von Colson and Elisabeth Kamann v. Land Nordrhein-Westfalen*, *ECR* 1984, p. 1891. There is also a corresponding case of the same day: ECJ 10 April 1984, *Dorit Harz v. Deutsche Tradax GmbH*, *ECR* 1984, p. 1921.

36 Council Directive 76/207/EEC of 9 February 1976 on the implementation of the principle of equal treatment for men and women as regards access to employment, vocational training and promotion, and working conditions, L 039, 14/02/1976, p. 40.

against and for the employer a means of pressure which it would be unwise to disregard and which would prompt him to respect the principle of equal treatment. A national measure which provides for compensation only for losses actually incurred through reliance on an expectation ('Vertrauensschaden')[37] is not sufficient to ensure compliance with that principle'.[38]

The ECJ acknowledged that Member States are left free to choose appropriate measures to remedy violations of Article 6 of the Directive but called for higher damages than the costs of postage and other application expenses to be awarded in addition to requiring liability to go beyond mere symbolic payment[39]:

'If a Member State chooses to penalize breaches (...) by the award of compensation, then in order to ensure that it is effective and that it has a deterrent effect, that compensation must in any event be adequate in relation to the damage sustained and must therefore amount to more than purely nominal compensation such as, for example, the reimbursement only of the expenses incurred in connection with the application'.[40]

With this paragraph the ECJ muddied the waters even further and offered as Koch has astutely put it: '(...) a rollercoaster ride between compensatory and non-compensatory damages'. Koch takes the position that the Court in *Von Colson* decided to remain within the realm of classic tort law remedies, despite the use of confusing and contradicting language such as 'deterrent effect' and 'penalize'. He correctly believes the core message to be that '(...) compensation must (...) be adequate in relation to damage (...)'. The case should therefore have been (and should in the future be) classified as upholding the principle of compensation in relation to damage (*i.e.* damages should not exceed the full indemnification of the injured party) and thus as unfavourable toward punitive damages.[41] This view is not shared by authors such as Behr and Jansen & Rademacher, who argue that these damages for discrimination cannot be explained within the traditional compensatory framework but conversely fit into the concept of punitive damages.[42]

In 2002 an amendment to the original Equal Treatment Directive came into effect.[43] Under paragraph 2 of new Article 6 Member States have to 'introduce into their national legal systems such measures as are necessary to ensure real and effective compensation or reparation as the Member States so determine for the loss and damage sustained by a person injured as a result of discrimination, in a way which is dissuasive and proportionate

37 'Fidelty guarantee claim' – the term 'Vertrauensschaden' refers to damages restricted to the losses incurred when one believes that a valid contract is concluded (Behr 2005, p. 214, footnote 91).

38 ECJ 10 April 1984, *Sabine von Colson and Elisabeth Kamann v. Land Nordrhein-Westfalen*, *ECR* 1984, p. 1891, par. 14.

39 Jansen & Rademacher 2009, p. 85.

40 ECJ 10 April 1984, *Sabine von Colson and Elisabeth Kamann v. Land Nordrhein-Westfalen*, *ECR* 1984, p. 1891, par. 28.

41 Koch 2009, p. 204.

42 Behr 2005, pp. 215–216 and Jansen & Rademacher 2009, pp. 84–85.

43 Directive 2002/73/EC of the European Parliament and of the Council of 23 September 2002 amending Council Directive 76/207/EEC on the implementation of the principle of equal treatment for men and women as regards access to employment, vocational training and promotion, and working conditions, OJ L 269, 05/10/2002, p. 15.

to the damage suffered; such compensation or reparation may not be restricted by the fixing of a prior upper limit (...)'. Article 8d further requires Member States to (emphasis added) 'lay down the rules on sanctions applicable to infringements of the national provisions adopted pursuant to this Directive, and [to] take all measures necessary to ensure that they are applied. The sanctions, which may comprise the payment of compensation to the victim, must be *effective, proportionate and dissuasive*'.

This last phrase is nothing novel; it finds its origin in the *Commission v. Hellenic Republic* ('*Greek Maize*') judgment of the ECJ.[44] In that case the Court pointed out that, according to Article 5 of the EEC Treaty, Member States have to take all measures necessary to guarantee the application and effectiveness of Community law.[45] As was already said in *Von Colson*, the Member States are free to choose the penalties necessary to achieve this. They do, however, have to ensure that infringements of Community law are penalized under conditions, both procedural and substantial, which are analogous to those applicable to infringements of national law of a similar nature and importance and which, in any event, make the penalty *effective, proportionate and dissuasive*.[46]

Despite its 'boiler-plate'[47] character, this formula has ever since been pervasive throughout the various pieces of European legislation and EU case law.[48] Some of these sources also use the word 'penalties' which seems to imply that they do not wish to touch upon private law remedies, whereas others speak of 'sanctions' with some specifying that this is 'without prejudice to Member States' civil liability regimes'.[49] This would mean they wish to draw a distinction between private law remedies and administrative or other 'sanctions'.[50] In our view, however, it seems unlikely that any of these EU rules aim to encourage the granting of awards exceeding the amount of full compensation. Although admittedly a few pieces of legislation such as Article 28 of Directive 2004/109/EC[51] address civil law remedies as penalties, thereby suggesting the punitive nature of the sanction. Our view seems to find implicit support in the drafting of the Consumer Credit Directive which originally suggested 'the loss of interest and charges by the creditor and continuation of the right of repayment in instalments of the total amount of credit by the consumer' as an example of how Member States could lay down penalties for the infringements of the Directive.[52] The creditor's loss of interest and charges has nothing to do with actual damage incurred by the consumer but is a form of punishment for the

44 ECJ 21 September 1989, *Commission of the European Communities v. Hellenic Republic*, *ECR* 1989, 2965.

45 *Ibid.*, par. 23.

46 *Ibid.*, par. 24.

47 Koch 2009, p. 200.

48 *Ibid.*

49 See Koch 2009, footnotes 15–17 for an extensive list of each category.

50 Koch 2009, pp. 200–201.

51 Directive 2004/109/EC of the European Parliament and of the Council of 15 December 2004 on the harmonisation of transparency requirements in relation to information about issuers whose securities are admitted to trading on a regulated market and amending Directive 2001/34/EC, OJ L 390, 31/12/2004, p. 38, Article 28.

52 Proposal for a Directive of the European Parliament and of the Council on the harmonisation of the laws, regulations and administrative provisions of the Member States concerning credit for consumers, COM(2002) 443 final, OJ C 331, 31/12/2002, p. 200, Article 31.

creditor's misbehaviour and therefore arguably boils down to punitive damages.[53] However, this explicit reference was dropped in favour of the vague and well-known mantra of 'effective, proportionate and dissuasive [penalties]'.[54]

3.2. *The Post Von Colson Case Law*

The above-mentioned amendment to the Equal Treatment Directive was influenced by the *Von Colson* judgment and subsequent rulings of the ECJ. In these latter cases the Court elaborated on the measures Member States need to take to implement the Directive. *M. Helen Marshall v. Southampton and South-West Hampshire Area Health Authority* (*'Marshall II'*) concerned a discriminatory dismissal.[55] The applicant Miss Marshall felt she had been the victim of unlawful discrimination on grounds of sex as she had been dismissed because she had attained the qualifying age for a State pension, that age being different under national legislation for women than for men. Her claim was upheld by the Court of Appeal which remitted the question of compensation to the Industrial Tribunal. The English Sex Discrimination Act, however, provided for an *ex ante* cap on the damages an Industrial Tribunal could award.[56]

In his Opinion, Advocate-General Van Gerven took the view that compensation must be adequate in relation to the damage sustained but does not have to be equal thereto.[57] He did not find the imposition of an upper limit on the compensation payable an automatic failure to implement the Directive.[58] The ECJ however declined to follow the AG's reasoning and reaffirmed the principle of full compensation.[59] England's system use of an upper limit was therefore found to be in violation of the Directive.[60]

In the case of *Nils Draehmpaehl v. Urania Immobilienservice OHG* (*'Draehmpaehl'*) the ECJ had to deal with a case of discriminatory selection for employment. Mr. Draehmpaehl responded to a job advertisement in a Hamburg newspaper stating that defendant Urania was looking for 'an experienced female assistant'. He did not get a reply and sued Urania in the Hamburg Labour Court ('Arbeitsgericht') claiming that he was the best qualified applicant and that he had suffered from sex discrimination. He asked for compensation for three and a half months' wages based on §611a of the German Civil Code (the transformation of the Equal Treatment Directive into German

53 Kelliher 2008, p. 11, footnote 43.

54 Directive 2008/48/EC of the European Parliament and of the Council of 23 April 2008 on credit agreements for consumers and repealing Council Directive 87/102/EEC, OJ L 133, 22/05/2008, p. 66, Article 23.

55 ECJ 2 August 1993, *M. Helen Marshall v. Southampton and South-West Hampshire Area Health Authority*, *ECR* 1993, p. 4367.

56 Sex Discrimination Act 1975, section 65(2).

57 Opinion of Mr. Advocate General Van Gerven delivered on 26 January 1993, *ECR* 1993, p. 4367, par. 17.

58 Opinion of Mr. Advocate General Van Gerven delivered on 26 January 1993, *ECR* 1993, p. 4367, par. 29; Oliphant 2008, p. 251.

59 ECJ 2 August 1993, *M. Helen Marshall v. Southampton and South-West Hampshire Area Health Authority*, *ECR* 1993, p. 4367, par. 26; Oliphant 2008, p. 252.

60 ECJ 2 August 1993, *M. Helen Marshall v. Southampton and South-West Hampshire Area Health Authority*, *ECR* 1993, p. 4367, par. 32.

law) which restricts financial compensation to three months' earnings.[61] The Court ruled that Member States are not precluded from imposing a ceiling on the compensation payable where the applicant would not have obtained the position due to another candidate's superior profile.[62] Such upper ceiling is not allowed where the applicant would have gotten the job if the discrimination had not occurred.[63] However, as opposed to its *Marshall II* decision, the ECJ in *Draehmpaehl* nowhere mentions the need for 'full' compensation but accepts 'adequate' compensation as effective judicial protection.[64]

As Koch rightly concludes, the lesson to be drawn from both *Marshall II* and *Draehmpaehl* is that limits on damages are not acceptable in light of the Directive since they may discourage injured parties from bringing their case to court and therefore have no dissuasive effect on the employer. More importantly, the caps are criticized because they prevent victims from receiving compensation adequate to the losses sustained which in our opinion seems to be, at the very least, a statement unsupportive of punitive damages.[65] The core message seems to be that the European Court of Justice does not seek to impose punitive damages on the Member States but rather that they will sanction any deviations from the boundaries set out by community law.[66]

3.3. *Punitive Damages through the Backdoor via the Principle of Equivalence*

Even though the ECJ does not promote the granting of punitive damages, national courts are in certain instances required to awards such damages for breaches of EU law. According to the EU principle of equivalence remedies made available for the protection of EU rights by national law must not be less favourable than those available for similar domestic rights. In *Brasserie du Pêcheur SA v. Federal Republic of Germany and Reg. v. Secretary of State for Transport, Ex parte Factortame Ltd. (no. 4)* (*'Brasserie du Pêcheur and Factortame'*) it was therefore established that:

> '(...) it must be possible to award specific damages, such as the exemplary damages provided for by English law, pursuant to claims or actions founded on Community law, if such damages may be awarded pursuant to similar claims or actions founded on domestic law'.[67]

Similarly, in *Manfredi v. Lloyd Adriatico Assicurazioni SpA* (*'Manfredi'*) the Court held that national courts can award punitive damages for violations of Community law (in

61 The ECJ's judgment does not mention the facts of the case. A summary of the facts in German can be found in *Neue Juristische Wochenschrift* 1997, p. 1839. The English translation of these facts: Behr 2004, p. 213.

62 ECJ 22 April 1997, *Nils Draehmpaehl v. Urania Immobilienservice OHG, ECR* 1997, p. 2195, par. 37.

63 Kelliher 2008, p. 15.

64 Oliphant 2008, p. 253.

65 Koch 2009, p. 204. See also ECJ 8 November 1990, *Elisabeth Johanna Pacifica Dekker v. Stichting Vormingscentrum voor Jong Volwassenen (VJV-Centrum) Plus, ECR* 1990, p. 3941.

66 Koch 2009, p. 205.

67 Joined cases ECJ 5 March 1996, *Brasserie du Pêcheur SA v. Bundesrepublik Deutschland* and *The Queen v. Secretary of State for Transport, ex parte: Factortame Ltd and others, ECR* 1996, p. 1029, par. 90.

this case: an infringement of Article 81 ECT) if their national legal system awards such damages for domestic claims.[68] Following its ruling in *Brasserie du Pêcheur and Factortame* the ECJ affirmed that: '(...) first, in accordance with the principle of equivalence, if it is possible to award specific damages, such as exemplary or punitive damages, in domestic actions similar to actions founded on the Community competition rules, it must also be possible to award such damages in actions founded on Community rules'.[69] It is important to note that in both cases the non-compensatory part of the award is not founded in EU law but is treated as a purely national peculiarity respected at European level.[70]

The equivalence principle raises issues of a private international law nature. Under Section 14 (5) of the Irish Competition Act for instance, exemplary damages are available in actions for breach of national competition law. An Irish judge is thus bound to award punitive damages for violations of EU antitrust rules. When the enforcement of this decision is sought in another Member State, Community law becomes contradictory as it on the one hand obliges the granting of punitive damages and on the other does not prevent the requested court from invoking public policy to decline enforcement.[71] This a problem that the EU will need to address.

4. EU Proposals in the Pipeline

As already noted by Koch, the *Manfredi* judgment has been interpreted by the EU Commission in such a way as to give the impression that punitive damages are part of the *acquis communautaire*.[72] In an attempt to make private antitrust lawsuits more prominent within the EU, in 2005 the Commission published a Green Paper on Damages Actions for Breach of the EU antitrust rules.[73] This proposal called for the awarding of double damages for horizontal cartel cases and was seen as a means to provide for an incentive for private enforcement of competition law, inspired by the treble damages of U.S. antitrust law.[74] In 2008 the Commission continued its effort through the adoption of a White Paper. In this proposal, the mechanism of punitive damages in the form of double damages has disappeared. The Paper's primary objective is the improvement of the legal conditions for victims to exercise their right to reparation of all damage suffered as a

68 Joined cases ECJ 13 July 2006, *Vincenzo Manfredi v. Lloyd Adriatico Assicurazioni SpA, Antonio Cannito v. Fondiaria Sai SpA* and *Nicolò Tricarico and Pasqualina Murgolo v. Assitalia SpA*, *ECR* 2006, p. 6619; Koch 2009, p. 206.

69 Joined cases ECJ 13 July 2006, *Vincenzo Manfredi v. Lloyd Adriatico Assicurazioni SpA, Antonio Cannito v. Fondiaria Sai SpA* and *Nicolò Tricarico and Pasqualina Murgolo v. Assitalia SpA*, *ECR* 2006, p. 6619, par. 99.

70 Koch 2009, p. 206.

71 Cavalier & Quéguiner 2007, p. 9.

72 Koch 2009, p. 207.

73 Green Paper on Damages Actions for Breach of the EC antitrust rules, COM(2005) 672 final, 19 December 2005.

74 Gotanda 2007, p. 520; Sein 2007, p. 49.

result of a breach of the EC antitrust rules. It therefore takes the idea of full compensation as its first and foremost guiding principle.[75]

In the Working Paper accompanying the White Paper the Commission however changes its tone and includes punitive damages into the *acquis communautaire*. It correctly states that the ECJ did not consider punitive damages to be a violation of European public order but derives from this the idea that the opposite is true.[76] Moreover, although openly admitting elsewhere[77] in the Working Paper that the Green Paper's introduction of double damages has triggered a lot of opposition, the Commission claims that unjust enrichment of the injured party is not legally forbidden under Community law. The ECJ in *Manfredi* had ruled that:

> '(...) Community law does not prevent national courts from taking steps to ensure that the protection of the rights guaranteed by Community law does not entail the unjust enrichment of those who enjoy them'.[78]

As the Commission officials who wrote the Working Paper construed things, this means that punitive awards can only be reduced if they are deemed to be excessive and thus that such awards are a legitimate form of (unjust) enrichment.[79] This does not seem to be what the ECJ intended.[80] The Court sought to prevent the (unjust) enrichment of victims, a principle that the Commission itself in the White Paper attaches great importance to.[81]

In other legislative documents the Commission seems to take the opposite position. In the first proposal for a Regulation on the Community Patent punitive damages were explicitly excluded.[82] While disagreement over the language requirements surrounding such a unitary patent has blocked the establishment of the EU patent for over a decade, the outward rejection of punitive awards has never been under discussion. The latest draft leaves no doubt that punitive damages are not available, whether it be in an action for reasonable compensation for a breach of the rights conferred after publication[83] or in a normal action for damages.[84]

75 White Paper on damages actions for breach of the EC antitrust rules, COM/2008/0165 final, p. 3.

76 Commission Staff Working Paper accompanying the White Paper on damages actions for breach of the EC antitrust rules, SEC/2008/0404 final, p. 57, nr. 190; Koch 2009, p. 207.

77 Commission Staff Working Paper accompanying the White Paper on damages actions for breach of the EC antitrust rules, SEC/2008/0404 final, p. 55, nr. 182.

78 Joined cases ECJ 13 July 2006, *Vincenzo Manfredi v. Lloyd Adriatico Assicurazioni SpA, Antonio Cannito v. Fondiaria Sai SpA* and *Nicolò Tricarico and Pasqualina Murgolo v. Assitalia SpA, ECR* 2006, p. 6619, par. 99.

79 Commission Staff Working Paper accompanying the White Paper on damages actions for breach of the EC antitrust rules, SEC/2008/0404 final, p. 58, nr. 192.

80 Wagner 2011, p. 6.

81 Koch 2009, pp. 207–208.

82 Proposal for a Council Regulation on the Community patent, COM(2000) 412 final, *OJ* C 337E, 28/11/2000, p. 278, Article 44, par. 2.

83 Proposal for a Council Regulation on the Community patent, 8/03/2004, Article 11.2.

84 *Ibid.*, Article 44.2.

5. Soft Law Instruments

Finally, it can be useful to draw one's attention to the several harmonization projects at European level. It is clear that none of these instruments envisage punitive damages as part of the substantive body of law they aim to create.[85] The Principles of European Tort Law (PETL) emphasize in Article 10:101 that damages are intended to restore the injured party to the position he would have been in if the wrong had not been committed. Under the Principles punitive damages are therefore not available as they are always out of proportion to the victim's actual loss.[86] The commentary to the PETL also explicitly confirms that they are not a basis for punitive damages or for other payments that do not correspond to the actual harm suffered.[87] The Principles of the Study Group on a European Civil Code, the Swiss and the Austrian draft, equally does not accept punitive damages.[88] Article 2:101 of Book VI of the Draft Common Frame of Reference does not list punitive damages under the heads of legally relevant damages. Article 6:101 of the same Book addresses reparation as the key element of remedies. In our view it leaves no room for the granting of punitive awards. The Principles of European Contract Law (PECL) – unsurprisingly because the awarding of punitive damages as a contractual remedy is also less extensive in the U.S. and in Canada[89] – do not mention punitive damages in explicit terms. Article 9:509 (1) does, however, thereby acknowledging their existence in European civil law systems, accept the concept of penalty clauses which can be seen as a form of contractually agreed upon punitive damages for non-performance. Article 160 of the proposed Common European Sales Law also emphasises the compensatory nature of the remedy of damages.[90]

6. Conclusion and Recommendations

The availability of punitive damages is very rare under European law as it stands today. Although some phrases in EU documents refer to non-compensatory awards, the concept of punitive damages generally is absent from European law.

The core message to be understood from the ECJ's rulings in *Von Colson*, *Marshall II* and *Draehmpaehl* appears to be that neither the EU legislature nor the European Court of Justice want to impose punitive damages on the Member States but rather that they will sanction any deviations from the boundaries set out by community law.[91] Member States have the freedom to determine how to sanction breaches of EU law as long as the measures imposed are effective, proportionate and dissuasive. This formula found its way into several acts of the EU legislature.[92]

85 Wagner 2011, p. 6.
86 Magnus 2005, Article 10.101 nr. 4.
87 Koziol 2009, p. 298.
88 *Ibid.*, p. 287.
89 See also footnote 6.
90 Annex I to the Proposal for a Regulation of the European Parliament and of the Council on a Common European Sales Law, 11/10/2011, COM(2011) 635 final.
91 Koch 2009, p. 205; Oliphant 2008, no. 11/8, 11/26 and 11/64.
92 Wagner 2011, p. 5.

This however does not lead us to the conclusion that punitive damages cannot be awarded at all in a European context. The principle of equivalence may require punitive damages to be made available by the national court to the extent that they are available in domestic law for analogous actions.[93] In those circumstances the awarding of punitive damages is not granted on the basis of Community law but is nothing more than a national curiosity tolerated by the EU.

At EU level, there presently is no consensus about whether punitive damages are *a priori* in conflict with the principles of European law.[94] The absence of a clear stand is hardly surprising in light of the difference in approach between Europe's legal systems, as it would be analogous to asking a father to pick his favourite child.[95]

93 Kellner 2008, p. 581.
94 Sein 2007, p. 49.
95 Koch 2009, p. 208.

Bibliography

Behr 2004
Behr, V., 'Myth and reality of punitive damages in Germany', *J L & Com*, 2004, pp. 197–224.

Borghetti 2009
Borghetti, J.-S., 'Punitive Damages in France', in: H. Koziol & V. Wilcox (eds.), *Punitive Damages: Common Law and Civil Law Perspectives*, Vienna: Springer, 2009, pp. 55–73.

Brand 2005
Brand, R., 'Punitive damages revisited: taking the rationale for non-recognition of foreign judgments too far', *J L & Com*, 2005, pp. 181–196.

Cavalier & Quéguiner 2007
Cavalier, G. & Quéguiner, J.-S., *Punitive Damages and French Public Policy*, Lyon Symposium, Lyon, 4–5 October, 2007 (to be found at: http://papers.ssrn.com/sol3/papers.cfm?abstract_id=1174363).

Gotanda 1998
Gotanda, J., *Supplemental Damages in Private International Law*, The Hague: Kluwer, 1998.

Gotanda 2003
Gotanda, J., 'Punitive Damages: A Comparative Analysis', *Villanova University School of Law Working Paper Series*, no. 8, 2003 (to be found at: http://law.bepress.com/villanovalwps/papers/art8).

Gotanda 2007
Gotanda, J., 'Charting Developments Concerning Punitive Damages: Is the Tide Changing?', *Colum J Transnat'l L*, 2007, pp. 507–528.

Gray 2009
Gray, A., 'Enforcement of punitive damages awards in the Convention on Choice of Court Agreement', *Willamette J Int'l L & Disp Resol*, 2009, pp. 105–156.

Jansen & Rademacher 2009
Jansen, N. & Rademacher, L., 'Punitive Damages in Germany', in: H. Koziol & V. Wilcox (eds.), *Punitive Damages: Common Law and Civil Law Perspectives*, Vienna: Springer, 2009, pp. 75–86.

Kelliher 2008
Kelliher, D.N., 'Aims and Scope', in: H. Koziol & R. Schulze (eds.), *Tort Law of the European Community*, Vienna: Springer, 2008, pp. 1–22.

Kellner 2008
Kellner, M., 'Comparative Report', in: H. Koziol & R. Schulze (eds.), *Tort Law of the European Community*, Vienna: Springer, 2008, pp. 559–588.

Koch 2009
Koch, B.A., 'Punitive Damages in European Law', in: H. Koziol & V. Wilcox (eds.), *Punitive Damages: Common Law and Civil Law Perspectives*, Vienna: Springer, 2009, pp. 197–209.

Koziol 2008
Koziol, H., 'Punitive Damages – A European Perspective', *La L Rev*, 2008, pp. 741–764.

Koziol 2009
Koziol, H., 'Punitive Damages: Admission into the Seventh Legal Heaven or Eternal Damnation? Comparative Report and Conclusions', in: H. Koziol & V. Wilcox (eds.), *Punitive Damages: Common Law and Civil Law Perspectives*, Vienna: Springer, 2009, pp. 275–308.

Licari 2010
Licari, F.-X., 'Prendre les punitive damages au sérieux: propos critique sur un refus d'accorder l'exequatur à une decision californienne ayant alloué des dommages-intérêts punitifs', *JDI*, 2010, pp. 1230–1263.

Magnus 2005
Magnus, U., 'Article 10:101. Nature and Purpose of Damages', in: European Group on Tort Law, *Principles of European Tort Law. Text and Commentary*, Vienna: Springer, 2005, pp. 149–153.

Nater-Bass 2003
Nater-Bass, G., 'U.S.-Style Punitive Damages Awards and their Recognition and Enforcement in Switzerland and Other Civil-Law Countries', *DAJV Newsletter*, 2003, pp. 154–160.

Oliphant 2008
Oliphant, K., 'The Nature and Assessment of Damages', in: H. Koziol & R. Schulze (eds.), *Tort Law of the European Community*, Vienna: Springer, 2008, pp. 241–271.

Plender & Wilderspin 2009
Plender, R. & Wilderspin, M., *The European Private International Law of Obligations*, London: Sweet & Maxwell, 2009.

Ryan 2003
Ryan, P.S., 'Revisiting the United States application of punitive damages: separating myth from reality', *Ilsa J Int'l & Comp L*, 2003, pp. 69–93.

Sein 2007
Sein, K., 'Should Estonian Law Provide for an Award of Punitive Damages?', *Juridica International*, 2007, pp. 46–54.

Tebbens 2009
Tebbens, H.D., 'Punitive damages: towards a rule of reason for U.S. awards and their recognition elsewhere', in: G. Venturini & S. Bariatti (eds.), *Liber Fausto Pocar, Volume II – Nuovi strumenti del diritto internazionale private*, Milan: Giuffre, 2009, pp. 273–290.

Wagner 2006
Wagner, G., 'Neue Perspektiven im Schadenersatzrecht – Kommerzialisierung, Strafschadenersatz, Kollektivschaden, Gutachten für den 66. Deutschen Juristentag', in: *Verhandlungen des 66. Deutschen Juristentages Stuttgart 2006*, C.H. Beck, 2006, Vol. I, Part A.

Wagner 2011
Wagner, G., 'Punitive Damages in European Private Law', forthcoming in: J. Basedow, K. J. Hopt & R. Zimmermann (eds.), *Handbook of European Private Law*, 2011 (available at: http://ssrn.com/abstract=1766113).

Wilcox 2009
Wilcox, V., 'Punitive Damages in England', in: H. Koziol & V. Wilcox (eds.), *Punitive Damages: Common Law and Civil Law Perspectives*, Vienna: Springer, 2009, pp. 7–53.

PART III

SPECIAL THEMES

Robert Hardy*

PUNITIVE DAMAGES FOR CERTAIN CATEGORIES OF BREACHES OF CONTRACT?

1. Introduction[1]

Remedies for breach of contract might attempt to do one of several things. They might attempt to put the promisee into the position in which he would have been if the contract had never been made. But contract remedies in most legal systems typically go beyond the pursuit of this objective. Remedies for breach of contract normally seek to compensate, and put the promisee into the position in which he would have been if the contract had not been breached. As a general rule, in most legal systems, punitive (or exemplary) damages are not normally available for breach of contract. Punitive damages can be awarded in certain tort cases, but generally not in a purely contractual action. Punitive damages are awarded with reference to the conduct of the promisor to signify disapproval of the promisor's conduct – and perhaps to deter and to punish the promisor – (e.g., where the promisor has deliberately committed a wrong with a view to profit), but the purpose of such damages is not to compensate the promisee. In contract law, punitive damages are basically not available[2] even though the breach was committed deliberately and with a view to profit.

In the last decades, law and economic scholars, predominantly in the U.S., have subjected the system of remedies to an economic analysis: is the system of remedies supported by efficiency arguments? Starting in the 1970s, concurrent with the expansion of the law and economics movement, American legal scholars have reviewed efficiency justifications for the American system of remedies for breach of contract. Although the original reasons for the rule against punitive damages in contract law are perhaps somewhat unclear, law and economics scholars have found a contemporary justification in the theory of efficient breach.

This paper critically assesses whether punitive damages should be available for certain types of contract breaches. This paper is structured as follows. In Section 4, I

* Associate, Latham & Watkins LLP and Member of the Ius Commune Research School; J.D., Ph.D., Maastricht University; LL.M., Harvard Law School. The views expressed in this paper are the author's and do not reflect the views of Latham & Watkins LLP or any of its clients.

1 Parts of this Paper are based on Hardy 2008.

2 See, for instance, Asser 2008, no. 19 (for Dutch law), and Treitel 2007, par. 20-015 (for English law).

provide the reader with an overview of arguments made in law and economics literature both against and in favour of the award of punitive damages for breach of contract.[3] In particular, as arguments *contra* I discuss the theory of efficient breach (4.1.2) and post-breach negotiations costs (4.1.3). The argument *pro* punitive damages that I consider relate to the under-compensatory effect of damages (4.2.2). Section 4 is preceded by a brief explanation of the general economic theory of contracts (Section 2), and the (common law) system of remedies for breach of contract (Section 3). I believe these accounts enable the reader to better understand the point of departure in the law and economics literature. Finally, in Section 5, I discuss the different categories of breaches and apply the insights from law and economics to each of these categories.

2. The Economic Theory of Contracts

Each legal system recognizes a scheme of remedies for breach of contract. But why are these remedies necessary and what goal exactly should these remedies serve? In principle, economic theory, and in that light also the law and economics literature, purports that contractual remedies should help to achieve efficient contracting situations which enhance total welfare. The following paragraphs serve to introduce the reader to economic contract theory in order to enhance the understanding of the notion of an efficient contract and welfare maximization. As such, these paragraphs will also familiarize the reader with some basic principles underlying the school of law and economics.

A contract – in common law terminology – consists of the exchange of promises or the exchange of a promise for a performance or the exchange of performances. All other circumstances being equal, parties will usually commit to perform their promises. However, a change of circumstances may alter the advantages initially conferred upon a party through the conclusion of a contract, causing that party to regret its promise. In a perfect world, the contract will excuse performance upon occurrence of such a circumstance, whenever this non-performance will result in a greater joint wealth, *i.e.*, the wealth of both parties is increased when one of the parties fails to perform.[4] Economists call such a contract 'state contingent' or 'perfectly complete', indicating that the agreement optimally specifies parties' obligations and rights ('payments') to be rendered under each possible circumstance or contingency.[5] Strict adherence to the terms of such a contract leaves both parties best off; neither party has an incentive to depart from the contract.

3 It should be made clear from the outset that the limited length of this Paper does not allow me to provide a complete overview of the law and economics literature on this subject.

4 Shavell 1980, pp. 467.

5 See amongst others Hart & Moore 1999; Williamson 1985; Maskin & Tirole 1999. The economic definition of a complete or state contingent contract is distinct from the traditional legal definition of a complete contract. The latter refers to a contract which does not contain any gaps, *i.e.*, the contract covers every conceivable contingency. In contrast to the economic definition, this legal definition does not include any element of efficiency. The traditional distinction between the legal and economic definition of a complete contract is presently less sharp; see amongst others Van Bijnen 2005, p. 414.

The perfectly complete or state contingent contract can only be drafted in a perfect world or under the assumption of the perfect market. Such a market is characterized by many buyers and sellers who are perfectly and completely informed, as the sellers have equal access to resources and information, offer functionally identical (homogeneous) commodities, and face low entry and exit barriers. Absent any constraints, such as information asymmetries or transaction costs, allocative and productive efficiency are achieved in market equilibrium: the goods produced are those most highly valued by consumers and production of these goods is carried out at minimum cost. Allocative efficiency under perfect market conditions will constitute Pareto efficiency,[6] meaning it will be impossible to make at least one person better off without making another person worse off.[7] Conversely, a Pareto improvement occurs when it is possible to make at least one person better off by moving from one allocation to another, without making any other person worse off. Pareto efficiency occurs when no further Pareto improvements can be made. Under Pareto efficiency, consumer and producer surplus are maximized. Consumer surplus refers to the benefit that the consumer receives from the market transaction, *i.e.*, the value of the good to the consumer ('willingness to pay') minus the price of the good. Producer surplus refers to the benefit the seller attains from the market exchange, thus the price of the good minus its cost of production. The maximization of consumer and producer surplus implies that all the potential gains from trade are exploited. Consumer and producer surplus may be used to indicate a certain degree of welfare. For reasons of simplicity, I assume that the maximization of consumer and producer surplus in market equilibrium also implies a maximization of total welfare. State contingent or perfectly complete contracts, which are based upon the assumption of perfect markets, realise this maximization of welfare; the terms of the contract are efficient and there are no mutually beneficial changes that the parties can make in order to increase their wealth.

In the real world, however, market conditions are far from perfect: parties are boundedly rational and face information asymmetries and transaction costs.[8] More specifically, parties lack the rationality and information to foresee all possible (change of) circumstances, and the conclusion of contracts entails search and negotiation costs. Under the condition of imperfect markets, contracts are incomplete or not state contingent. Therefore, parties have an incentive to depart from their contract terms when they feel that adherence would not be in their best interest and as such does not maximize their welfare.

The economic function of a system of contract remedies is to alter the incentives in respect of a party who regrets the conclusion of the contract. In the real world of imperfect

6 Birmingham 1970, p. 280: 'Although Pareto optimality is a characteristic of any equilibrium which maximizes community utility, this characteristic is shared by an infinite set of economic states'.

7 In practice, however, it is almost impossible to make a change without making at least one person worse off. Presently, economists often refer to the Kaldor-Hicks criterion rather than Pareto efficiency. Under the Kaldor-Hicks criterion, the market outcome is efficient if those that are made better off ('the winners'), gain enough such that, in theory, they can compensate those that are made worse off ('the losers'). It is not also required that compensation actually takes place.

8 See amongst others Coase 1937; Williamson 1985.

markets, courts must supplement incomplete contracts with damages measures that induce behaviour that a party would exhibit under a state contingent contract.[9]

3. Remedies for Breach of Contract (in Common Law Jurisdictions)

Generally, there are two types of remedies available to the injured party in case of breach of contract: monetary damages and a decree for specific performance.[10] Damages accord the promisee a right to monetary compensation for the loss caused by the breach, aiming to place the promisee in the position in which he would have been had the contract been performed, and specific performance assigns the promisee an absolute entitlement to the goods or services from the moment the contract is made.[11] In the following paragraphs these two types of remedies will be discussed in greater detail from a common law perspective, and within this category, particularly from the point of view of American contract law.

In common law jurisdictions, every contract is treated as containing a warranty for performance. In other words, every contractual term, express or implied, is in law a warranty. If a term is broken, the innocent party is entitled to claim damages for breach of contract.[12] This liability is strict, in the sense that the claim for damages is not dependent on whether or not the promisor is at fault. In order for a claim for damages to succeed, however, a causal link must exist between the contractual breach and the damages. In other words, the breach must have caused the harm suffered by the promisee.

In assessing the amount of monetary damages to be awarded, three different interests may be considered: restitution interest, reliance interest, or expectation interest.[13] First, a party may have relied on a promise and in that light bestowed some value on the counterparty to the contract. If the latter subsequently fails to perform, the court may compel the defaulting party to re-assign the value received to the non-breaching party. The restitution interest prevents any gain of the defaulting promisor at the expense of the promisee and thus aims to prevent unjust enrichment. Second, a promisee may have changed its position in reliance on the promise, in the sense that it has made some preparatory investments or not pursued any opportunities with third parties. In light of the reliance interest, a court will award damages to the innocent party in the amount necessary to place the plaintiff in its pre-contractual position. Damages based on the reliance interest seek to compensate for any harm the plaintiff has suffered in reliance on the promise of the defendant. Finally, damages based on the expectation interest aim to place the innocent party in the position in which he would have been had the contract

9 Mahoney 2000, p. 120; Kornhauser 1986, p. 697: 'The economic analysis of remedies seeks to identify the measure of damages that leads to efficient outcomes, ones in which neither promisee nor promisor can be made better off without making the other worse off'; Cooter & Ulen 2003, pp. 237–239.

10 Another remedy which may be considered is rescission or termination of the contract, but this possibility will not be discussed in this Paper. It may be noted, however, that a claim for termination is often accompanied by a claim for monetary damages.

11 See *Robinson v. Harman* (1848) 1 Exch. 850, p. 855. On the distinction between property and liability rules, see also Calabresi &Melamed 1972.

12 The innocent party must, however, continue to uphold his own side of the bargain.

13 Fuller & Purdue 1936. See also Ulen 1984.

been performed. These damages seek to award to the promisee the net benefit it would have received had performance been effected.[14]

The standard damage measure in most legal systems – whether common law or civil law – equates to compensation based on the injured party's expectation, placing the promisee in the position in which he would have been had the contract been performed:

> 'In fixing the amount of (...) damages, the general purpose of the law is, and should be, to give compensation: that is, to put the plaintiff in as good a position as he would have been in had the defendant kept his contract'.[15]

In common law, this rule was first enunciated in *Robinson v. Harman*.[16] That the expectation interest is the standard for damages in contracts in most continental European legal systems is reflected in instruments such as the so-called 'Principles of European Contract Law',[17] the 'Draft Common Frame of Reference',[18] and the 'Feasibility study for a future instrument in European Contract Law':

> 'The general measure of damages for loss caused by non-performance of an obligation is such sum as will put the creditor as nearly as possible into the position in which the creditor would have been if the obligation had been duly performed. Such damages cover loss which the creditor has suffered and gain of which the creditor has been deprived'.[19]

In principle, expectation damages are measured in relation to the actual value that performance of the specific contract would have conferred upon the injured party and not the value that performance of the contract might have had to some hypothetical reasonable person. In measuring the expectation damages, the court will therefore attempt to take account of the specific circumstances of the case.[20] In the end, the

14 See Fuller & Purdue 1936; Fuller & Purdue, 1937. Damages based on the expectation interest are often referred to in civil law jurisdictions as 'positive damages'.

15 Williston 1936, § 1338 cited by Birmingham 1970, p. 281. See also Restatement (Second) of Contracts § 344 in which expectation interest is defined as the party's 'interest in having the benefit of his bargain by being put in as good a position as he would have been in had the contract been performed (...)'.

16 The court ruled: '[W]here a party sustains a loss by reason of breach of contract, he is, so far as money can do it, to be placed in the same situation, with respect to damages, as if the contract had been performed' (154 Eng. Rep. 363, p. 365 (Ex. 1848). See also Scott & Triantis 2004, p. 1446, who indicate that the adoption of Article 2 UCC in the 50 States has elevated recovery of the expectation interest as a default and overarching norm: 'The remedies provided in this Act shall be liberally administered to the end that the aggrieved party may be put in as good a position as if the other party had fully performed (...)' (UCC § 1-305(a)). See also Restatement (Second) of Contracts § 347: 'Subject to the limitations stated in §§ 350–51, the injured party has a right to damages based on his expectation interest as measured by (a) the loss in the value to him of the other party's performance caused by its failure or deficiency, plus (b) any other loss, including incidental or consequential loss, caused by the breach, less (c) any cost or other loss that he has avoided by not having to perform'.

17 Available at http://frontpage.cbs.dk/law/commission_on_european_contract_law.

18 Available at http://ec.europa.eu/justice/contract/files/european-private-law_en.pdf.

19 Article 164 of the Feasibility Study, available at www.ec.europa.eu/justice/contract/files/feasibility-study_en.pdf. The other instruments have provisions similar to Article 164 of the Feasibility Study.

20 Farnsworth 2000, § 12.8.

expectation measure is expected to grant full compensation to the injured party. However, as will be especially shown in Subsection 4.2.2 below, several limitations may cause the expectation remedy to fall short of full compensation.

Thus, in principle, breach of contract in common law entitles the plaintiff to a claim for damages. However, rules in equity may, under special circumstances, allow the plaintiff to resort to a claim for specific performance instead of damages. A court order for specific performance is an order requiring a party to perform a specific act, in this case the completion of the transaction. Generally, a claim for specific performance may be made if the plaintiff can show that the remedy available at law – damages – is inadequate or that the sought interest in performance of the contract cannot be translated into money terms.[21] Whether or not a claim for specific performance will be awarded lies within the discretion of the court. Traditionally, damages have been considered inadequate, and claims for specific performance justified, as far as regards contracts for the transfer of land or real rights[22] or unique goods.[23] It is submitted that where no substitute performance is attainable, it will be difficult to estimate the amount of damages with any degree of accuracy and full compensation cannot then be achieved. In contrast, damages are likely to be an adequate remedy when the claimant is able to obtain the promised performance from another source and the damages serve to cover the difference in cost of the alternative performance.[24] It is important to note that the inadequacy of the damages measure is very important but not determinative for an order of specific performance to be made.[25] Developments in case law have led the courts to consider a broader range of factors to decide whether or not to grant an order for specific performance, e.g. the degree of hardship that realisation of specific performance would cause the defendant; whether consideration for the defendant's promise to perform is inadequate; the conduct of the plaintiff, in the sense that if the plaintiff has acted unfairly or improperly this may be used as a basis for denying the remedy on the ground that the plaintiff does not have 'clean hands'; whether performance is still possible; and whether execution of a judgment for damages would cause grave inconvenience in general.[26] Cases in which the courts have rejected a claim for specific performance include

21 *Co-operative Insurance Society Ltd. v. Argyll Stores (Holdings) Ltd.* A.C. 1 (ENG); *cf.*, Restatement (Second) of Contracts § 359(1): 'Specific performance or an injunction will not be ordered if damages would be adequate to protect the expectation interest of the injured party (…)'.

22 Historically, real property has been held in special esteem by English courts and, therefore, singled out for special treatment. Each plot of land was considered unique and its value difficult to assess. As such, monetary compensation was not considered an adequate means to enable the promisee to secure a substitute, and thus specific performance would be granted. See also Farnsworth 2000, § 12.8.

23 *Cf.*, *Hoffman v. Boone*, 708 F. Supp. 78 (S.D.N.Y. 1989) and UCC § 2-716.

24 See also Restatement (Second) of Contracts § 369: '[In] determining whether the remedy in damages would be adequate, the following circumstances are significant: (a) the difficulty of proving damages with reasonable certainty, (b) the difficulty of procuring a suitable substitute performance by means of money awarded as damages, and (c) the likelihood that an award of damages could not be collected'.

25 *Cf. Van Wagner Advertising Corp v. S & M Enters*, 492 N.E.2d 756 (N.Y. 1986), where a claim for specific performance concerning the lease of a unique outdoor advertising space was not granted, because ' 'uniqueness' is not a magic door to specific performance' and 'at some level all property may be interchangeable with money'. See also Farnsworth 2000, § 12.8.

26 Nevertheless, the majority of the courts will refuse a claim for specific performance where damages would be adequate and the aforementioned developments seem to be less dramatic than they appear.

construction contracts because of the difficulty of framing and enforcing orders, contracts that are too vague, and contracts sought to be enforced in part only.[27] In addition, specific performance will not usually be granted where it concerns the performance of a personal service.[28] This includes employment contracts, but also applies to other 'contracts involving personal service even though they are not strictly contracts of service'.[29] The foregoing is based on the understanding that the defendant would be forced into involuntary servitude and the fact that it will be difficult for the court to establish whether the level of service is in accordance with the contract.

4. Some Arguments Against and in Favour of Punitive Damages as Remedy for Breach of Contract

4.1. *Arguments Against*

4.1.1. General Arguments Against Punitive Damages

A first general argument against the availability of punitive damages as a remedy in contract law relates to the boundary between private (in particular: contract) and criminal laws. It may be argued that punitive damages, the purpose of which perhaps is to punish and deter the promisee, are more characteristic of the criminal law than of the private law. The inclusion of punitive damages in private law would usurp the function of criminal law and imports an alien public law function into private law.[30] Criminal law allows for the prosecution and punishment of acts which are regarded as morally reprehensible and as damaging to society as a whole, not merely to the individual.[31] In contrast, private law is generally described as having the function of regulating relationships between individuals and dispensing justice as between the parties to a case, without regard to the wider interests of society.[32] Deterrence is also associated with criminal sanctions rather than private ones.

A number of arguments may also be made which highlight the impracticability of including punitive damages awards in contract law. It may be argued that the promisee is to be subjected to punitive damages (*i.e.* punitive sanctions) only if he has the benefit of the procedural safeguards which are available in the criminal courts but not in the civil. The criminal law's imposition of penal sanctions is justified, *inter alia*, by the fact

27 In both the U.S. and England, rules concerning a decree for specific performance have also been provided by statute, e.g., Article 2 of the Uniform Commercial Code (UCC) and Section 52 of the Sale of Goods Act 1979.

28 See, e.g., *Johnson v. Shrewsbury and Birmingham Ry.* (1853) 3 d.M. & G. 358; *Brett v. East India and London Shipping Co. Ltd.* (1864) 2 H & M. 404. Especially under English law, specific performance is only impeded in case of a contract concerning a personal service; there is no general rule against the award of specific performance merely because the contract concerns the provision of a service in general.

29 Gordley & Von Mehren 2006, p. 530.

30 The Law Reform Commission Ireland, p. 6 ff.

31 *Ibid.*

32 *Ibid.*

that only a narrow range of acts are criminal offenses, by the strict procedural safeguards, and by the high standard of proof in such trials. Comparable safeguards do not exist where punitive damages are imposed in private law cases. Thus public law elements are being introduced into an area of law which, arguably, is not equipped to deal with them.[33]

Another argument against punitive damages is that the promisee will benefit from an award of punitive damages, resulting in an unjust enrichment of the promisee. The award of punitive damages is namely assessed with reference only to the promisor and his conduct, and does not aim to compensate the promisee. The promisee, who will already have been fully compensated for his loss by an award of compensatory damages, may become the fortunate beneficiary of the promisor's (morally bad) behaviour.

4.1.2. The Theory of Efficient Breach

One of the first theories in law and economics to address the choice of remedies for breach of contract is efficient breach. Proponents of efficient breach theory such as Birmingham and Posner[34] argue that parties to a contract should be able to forego performance and breach a contract when this would be efficient from an economic point of view, *i.e.* in those situations where a state contingent contract would excuse performance based on welfare justifications:

> '[I]n some cases a party [to a contract] would be tempted to breach the contract simply because his profit from breach would exceed his expected profit from completion of the contract. If his profit from breach would also exceed the expected profit to the other party from completion of the contract, and if damages are limited to the loss of expected profit, there will be an incentive to commit a breach. There should be'.[35]

One can also frame efficient breach as an opportunity for one of the parties to obtain a Pareto improvement, because non-performance will make the breaching party better off, without making the non-breaching party worse off (both parties move to a new equilibrium in which Pareto efficiency is obtained). This condition only holds true, however, if the injured party is compensated in full for its expectation interest. Let me illustrate this with a simple example.[36] Imagine a contract for the sale of a machine concluded by a seller and buyer 1 at US$ 100. The seller's production cost is US$ 70 and, therefore, the seller will make a profit of US$ 30 (US$ 100 – US$ 70) upon completion of the contract. Before delivery of the machine, however, buyer 2 offers to buy the machine at

33 *Ibid.*

34 Birmingham 1970; Posner 1972.

35 Posner 1972, p. 57, cited in Eisenberg 2005, p. 997. Likewise Birmingham 1970, p. 284; Farnsworth 1979, pp. 247–248.

36 This example concerns a breach by the seller where the buyer is able to secure substitute performance on the market. Different situations, however, are possible. For example, the transaction may concern unique performance for which no substitute is available, or the buyer rather than the seller may breach the contract. See for a more elaborate differentiation of cases, e.g., Cooter & Ulen 2003, pp. 237–295.

US$ 150.[37] Subsequently, the market price rises to US$ 125. According to efficient breach theory, the seller will have an incentive to breach his contract with buyer 1 in order to deal with buyer 2, as this non-performance will increase not only the seller's expected profit, but also total welfare. How? The seller will be able to make a profit from the contract with buyer 2 of US$ 80 (US$ 150 – US$ 70), which is higher than the profit the seller would make under the contract with buyer 1 (US$ 30). In contrast, breach will make buyer 1 worse off by US$ 25 (US$ 125 – US$ 100). However, the seller will be able to compensate buyer 1 for his loss and still retain a profit of US$ 55 (US$ 80 – US$ 25) for himself – almost twice as much as under the first contract. The seller is thus made better off without making buyer 1 worse off. Pareto improvement is possible and total welfare is increased when the seller breaches the contract with buyer 1.[38]

In accordance with efficient breach theory, the traditional debate on remedies for breach of contract in the law and economics literature has taken the view that expectation damages equate to the most efficient remedy. This view also justifies the position that awarding punitive damages is not a normal or presumptive remedy for breach of contract.

Efficient breach theory, however, is not without its shortcomings. Several authors have argued that the premises on which the economic theory of contracts in general and efficient breach theory in particular are based are closely associated with over-simplifications of the competitive market model, which falls short of perfection. Economic contract theory, for example, assumes that renegotiations are always successful, parties are able to achieve efficient outcomes and neither party will exhibit opportunistic behaviour.[39] Yet, in practice, parties are faced by numerous constraints such as transaction costs, information asymmetries and bounded rationality, which may affect the efficiency outcome of the different remedies. Related to the foregoing is the assumption that the court can adequately calculate the amount in expectation damages, making the promisee indifferent between a claim for (specific) performance and damages. In the real world, however, the aforementioned constraints may prevent an accurate estimation of damages, thereby failing to provide the plaintiff with full compensation.[40] If courts systematically underestimate damages, then just as punitive damages would lead to over-performance, expectation damages may lead to excessive breach.[41] Furthermore, several legal scholars indicate that the economic perspective obscures the traditional notions in contract

37 This may be referred to as a fortunate contingency, which makes non-performance even more profitable than performance, *i.e.*, a third party, buyer 2, values the product even more than buyer 1. Another situation is the occurrence of an unfortunate contingency, *i.e.*, a circumstance which will increase the cost of performance. In this case, for example, the seller's production cost may rise to US$ 110, which would make non-performance more profitable for the seller than performance. See also Cooter & Ulen 2003, pp. 254–261 and Posner 2003, pp. 118–120.

38 See, e.g., *Patton v. Mid-Continent Sys.*, 841 F.2d 742 (7th Cir. 1988) in which Judge Posner states: 'Even if the breach is deliberate, it is not necessarily blameworthy. The promisor may simply have discovered that his performance is worth more to someone else. If so, efficiency is promoted by allowing him to break his promise, provided he makes good the promisee's actual losses'. See also Farnsworth 2000, § 12.3, n. 3.

39 Kornhauser 1986, p. 707.

40 Friedman 1965, p. 20.

41 Mahoney 2000, pp. 125–126; Birmingham 1970, p. 285.

theory such as sanctity of contract and the moral obligation to keep one's promises.[42] Moreover, some authors assert that the (narrow) focus of efficient breach theory on allocative efficiency undermines the importance of distributive efficiency.[43] Finally, allowing a promisor to breach and pay only expectation damages is perhaps not the most efficient way to avoid inefficient performance.[44] Subjecting a promisor who wishes to escape his contract to the threat of punitive damages will not require an inefficient performance. Such threat will perhaps lead the promisor to negotiate with the promisee for a release rather than making a unilateral decision to breach. The foregoing may be efficient if one assumes that the costs of negotiation will be lower on average than the costs of litigation necessary to establish expectation damages.

4.1.3. Post-breach Negotiation Costs

Another argument advanced in the literature to justify compensatory damages as the normal or presumptive remedy is the existence of post-breach negotiation costs.[45] A punitive sanction – similar to specific performance – seeks to deter breach absolutely. In order for punitive damages/specific performance to have that effect, however, the assumption must be made that renegotiation over the award for punitive damages/ specific performance is costly. Below, I explain the so-called concept of post-breach negotiation costs. For the sake of simplicity and because the literature has focused primarily on the remedy of specific performance, I discuss the concept from the perspective of specific performance. Note however that were I speak of 'specific performance' below, one can and should also read 'an award for punitive damages'.

Take once more the example of the contract for the sale of the machine.[46] Buyer 1 contracts with the seller to buy the machine for US$ 100. Prior to delivery, however, demand increases and buyer 2 comes along and offers a price of US$ 150 for the same machine. Subsequently, the equilibrium price rises to US$ 125. If available as a remedy, buyer 1 will demand specific performance, unless the seller pays US$ 25 in substitution damages plus US$ 15 profit. This premium is higher than what buyer 1 would have received under normal damages (US$ 125 – US$ 100 = US$ 25). The seller can sell to buyer 2 at US$ 150, compensate buyer 1 and still make a profit. Whenever the offer made by buyer 2 is higher than the market price, the seller will thus have an incentive to breach and buyer 1 will have an incentive to threaten with the enforcement of specific performance, in order to capture some of the profit the seller stands to gain from breach. More specifically, the seller, under a decree for specific performance, will negotiate with buyer 1 the surrender of the latter's right to specific performance in exchange for a sum of money. These post-breach negotiations, however, represent a deadweight loss, as they only serve to redistribute wealth between the seller and buyer 1 and do not generate

42 Farnsworth 2000, § 12.3. See also Birmingham 1970, p. 281. *Cf.* Ulen 1984 p. 345: 'At least with regard to remedies in contract law, we believe it to be the case that widely held notions of fairness and morality argue for the same sort of conclusions as emerge from an efficiency analysis'.

43 See, e.g., Friedman 1989, p. 5.

44 Dodge 1999, p. 651 ff.

45 See also Schwartz 1979, pp. 284–285; Varadarajan 2001, p. 739.

46 A comparable example is also used by Schwartz 1979, p. 285.

additional wealth: buyer 1 accrues part of the profit otherwise collected by the seller. If society is indifferent as to whether sellers or buyers profit from an increase in demand, and this is the case if society attempts to increase total welfare, then the law should eliminate such efficiency loss. Apparently, expectation damages eliminate this loss by foreclosing post-breach negotiations. Under an award of expectation damages, the seller in the example set out above would be able to make a larger profit, and compensate buyer 1 according to the expectation interest, without incurring any post-breach negotiation costs. This *ex post* efficiency argument is the cornerstone of the efficient breach theory espoused by Posner.[47]

Absent transaction costs, however, either remedy should achieve similar efficiency results, albeit with a different wealth distribution among parties.[48] In particular, absent post-breach negotiation costs and assuming that negotiations are successful, the promisor will be able to buy his way out of the specific performance without incurring any cost. If we mirror reality and add transaction costs to our model,[49] why should it be assumed that post-breach negotiation costs are higher in the case of specific performance than in the case of an award of expectation damages? The efficiency of each remedy depends on the transaction costs associated with each individual situation. Proponents of expectation damages presume, however, that in case of an award of expectation damages, post-breach negotiation costs are zero, and post-breach negotiation costs in case of specific performance are so high that this will force a promisor to buy its way out of performance and subsequently lead to over-performance.

In my opinion, Schwartz correctly argues that the foregoing analysis is erroneous. Designating expectation damages as the routine remedy would only be more efficient if post-breach negotiation costs under expectation damages were smaller than under a decree for specific performance. It might indeed seem easy to assume that this is the case. The difference between the market price and the contract is easily determined, inducing the seller to pay promptly and reap the additional profits of selling to buyer 2. However, Schwartz illustrates that this conjecture is based upon the assumption that buyer 1 has access to the market at a significantly lower cost than the seller, *i.e.*, buyer 1 is assumed to easily attain another offer with the amount of money awarded as expectation damages.[50] If both buyer 1 and the seller have similar access to the market, however, the seller would have an incentive to sell to buyer 1 at US$ 100 and buy a new machine on the market for US$ 125 to sell to buyer 2 for US$ 150. This implies that the seller can cover as easily as the buyer, which would result in three transactions taking place. None of the aforementioned transactions involve post-breach negotiation costs. If sellers are able to cover as well as buyers, specific performance will not lead to post-breach negotiation costs. The question is whether similar cover costs exist in practice. Schwartz assumes that this is indeed the case and counters the arguments which might indicate that cover

47 Posner 2003, p. 133.

48 Mahoney 2000.

49 See also Kornhauser 1986, p. 708, who indicates that proponents of monetary damages as the routine remedy wrongly assume that that costs of initial contract negotiation and dispute resolution amount to zero.

50 Schwartz 1979, p. 285, n. 46 defines cover costs as 'the costs incurred in locating the substitute and making a second transaction'.

costs differ, thereby subsequently undermining the assumption of higher post-breach negotiation costs in case of specific performance.[51]

Schwartz puts forward and counters the following arguments. A first argument is that dissimilar cover costs may encourage a buyer to breach the contract in order to redistribute part of the gains from breach through post-breach negotiations. Schwartz indicates, however, that underlying this argument is the erroneous assumption that the cover costs of both parties exceed the buyer's litigation costs.[52] The second argument made against similar cover costs is that in some cases the seller may not be able to cover at all (say, if the seller is a monopolist), and specific performance may lead to excessive post-breach negotiations. However, in such a case, the buyer will most likely face the same problem; thus post-breach negotiations will generally not differ for either remedy.[53] The third objection refers to the fact that buyer 1 and buyer 2 have different uses for performance, for example buyer 1's use is fungible while buyer 2's is not. Since cover costs for buyer 1 are then low, specific performance will generate high(er) post-breach negotiation costs as buyer 1 attempts to capture some of the gains from breach. In these cases, the exception should therefore be made for specific performance. However, Schwartz counters this argument by stating that the litigation and uncertainty costs of such an exception are likely to exceed the efficiency gains associated with suspending specific performance.[54] Finally, an argument against the assumption of similar cover costs and consequently post-breach negotiation costs is that upon occurrence of changed circumstances, post-breach negotiation costs will be higher under an order for specific performance than under expectation damages. However, Schwartz shows that specific performance and expectation damages 'create identical incentives for the parties to engage in costly post-breach negotiations in the event of (e.g.) unexpected inflation'.[55]

Ulen substantiates the arguments made by Schwartz on similar cover costs, and makes two additional arguments to undermine the assumption of high post-negotiation costs in case of specific performance. First of all, parties may have taken their relative access to the market advantages into account in their contract price. The party with superior access abilities may have used this advantage to offer the counterparty more attractive terms: 'If so, then the matter of who should bear liability for covering in the event of breach becomes a matter of determining parties' implicit assignment of the risk of a particular contingency'.[56] Second, it is an overstatement to call post-breach negotiation costs a deadweight efficiency loss in so far as they serve only to redistribute wealth. While this might be the case in some situations, these short term efficiency losses may also lead to a superior exchange of mutually beneficial promises in the future and so pay for themselves:

> 'The short-term efficiency losses that occur are transitory and should not form the basis of a general argument in favor of money damages. That is, these losses should be balanced against

51 Schwartz 1979, pp. 287–290.

52 Schwartz 1979, pp. 287–288; Ulen 1984, p. 386.

53 Schwartz 1979, pp. 288–289; Ulen 1984, pp. 386–387.

54 Schwartz 1979, pp. 289–290; Ulen 1984, p. 387.

55 Schwartz 1979, p. 291; Ulen 1984, pp. 387–388.

56 Ulen 1984, p. 388.

the present discounted value of the resulting increases in the efficiency of exchanging promises in the future plus the present discounted value of the savings from reduced uncertainty about and from litigation over the terms of future exchanges'.[57]

Several other arguments may be made against the disposition of higher post-breach negotiation costs under an order for specific performance. Ulen argues that in general, post-breach negotiation costs should never be high, as parties are engaged in, and have built up a relationship; if they have not yet provided for relief in case of breach, the costs of doing so post-breach should be low.[58] Ulen states additionally that under specific performance, the costs of determining parties' valuations of performance are borne by those parties in voluntary negotiations.[59] Finally, Ulen contends that if contractual parties are on aware that valid promises will be specifically enforced, they will exchange reciprocal promises more efficiently at the time of formation. In particular, they will have a stronger incentive than currently exists under the dominant legal remedy of expectation damages to allocate efficiently the risks of loss from breach rather than leave that task, in whole or in part, to the court or to post-breach negotiations conducted under the threat of a potentially inefficient legal remedy. In contrast, in case of expectation damages, parties may incur high post-breach negotiation costs relative to specific performance: under an order for specific performance, the inquiry of the court ends with the determination that breach has occurred; in case of expectation damages, the court must also establish the amount of damages that will efficiently compensate the innocent promisee.[60] Indeed, Eisenberg and Schwartz indicate that post-breach negotiation costs are also incurred in case of expectation damages, as the plaintiff will incur costs related to the determination of the value of the loss, the employment of experts to aid in that determination, the negotiations conducted in order to recover the losses and the legal fees and costs of litigation.[61]

In contrast, Bishop indicates that even when no empirical evidence has been found, there is sound theoretical reason to believe that the post-breach negotiation costs generated by specific performance are higher than those generated by the expectation damages rule.[62] In his analysis, Bishop refers to a concept that is wider than unique goods, namely non-substitutable contracts, indicating that the seller cannot substitute his performance with an act or object different from the original one. Bishop identifies two critical components of the post-breach negotiation costs: information costs (the costs of transmitting information), and bargaining costs (the costs generated by a bilateral monopoly). According to Bishop, negotiations are successful when parties are able to avoid both excessive performance and breach. Consider the example mentioned earlier with buyer 1 and 2 and the seller. As far as regards expectation damages, only the value of buyer 1's expectancy under the contract is of importance; the seller's expectancy of the second sale is relevant, but only for the seller. In contrast, as far as specific performance

57 *Ibid.*, p. 389.
58 *Ibid.*, p. 370.
59 Ulen 1984, pp. 365–366.
60 *Ibid.*, p. 365.
61 Schwartz 1979, p. 288; Eisenberg 2005.
62 Bishop 1985, pp. 311–314. See also for more elaborate criticism Yorio 1982.

is concerned, the value of the seller's expectancy on buyer 2 is also of relevance to buyer 1, as buyer 1 will want to reap part of the profits from breach. Thus, contends Bishop, more time is spent acquiring information in light of post-breach negotiations under a specific performance award than under a expectation damages rule, which increases information and subsequently post-breach negotiation costs. This is especially the case since information is asymmetric between buyer 1 and the seller: the seller will want to make buyer 1 believe that the expectancy value of buyer 2 is low, an assertion which buyer 1 will distrust, demanding more evidence. In the second place, post-breach negotiation costs will also be higher due to the fact that the bargaining game will be extended under a specific performance award, even when parties agree on a value at the time of breach.[63] The bilateral monopoly situation under a specific performance award poses a problem because the value of the seller's payment to buyer 1 can range from buyer 1's expectancy value under the original contract to the seller's expectancy value from breach. Thus, the bilateral monopoly induces an extra cost of strategic behaviour between buyer 1 and the seller. Each will attempt to capture the largest part of the pie. In contrast, under an expectation damages rule the result would be determinate, *i.e.* the seller pays an amount in damages and reaps profits of buyer 2, but the foregoing illustrates that under a specific performance award, the game is indeterminate.[64]

Finally, Bishop argues that the analysis by Schwartz in relation to cover costs is too simplistic. The analysis is based on the distinction between unique and non-unique goods, but Bishop, as mentioned before, argues that a distinction should instead be made between unique and non-unique uses: '[a] particular good may be unique in [buyer 1's] use and non-unique in [buyer 2's] use, and vice versa',[65] while in addition the seller's performance may or may not be substitutable. Bishop illustrates that expectation damages will be superior in the case where buyer 1's use is non-unique and buyer 2's use is unique. For example, Schwartz argues that specific performance will be inefficient in the case where the seller has higher cover costs than the buyer, but that these cases are rare. Bishop indicates that Schwartz does not consider the reverse case where expectation damages may be inefficient under higher cover costs for buyer 1 '[b]ecause [buyer 1's] damages will always include his cover cost, [and the seller] has an automatic incentive under a damages rule to cover himself whenever he has a cover cost advantage'.[66] Expectation damages then are always efficient in this case, in contrast to specific performance.

4.2. *Arguments in Favour of Punitive Damages*

4.2.1. General Arguments in Favour of Punitive Damages

The proposition that punitive damages usurp the function of criminal law to contract law (see above under Section 4.1) can be disputed. The boundary between private law and criminal law needs not be viewed as unbreakable; functions, such as deterrence, which

63 Bishop 1985, p. 313.
64 *Ibid.*, p. 314.
65 *Ibid.*
66 Bishop 1985, p. 316.

have traditionally been identified with criminal law are not necessarily excluded from private law. An argument may also be made that a punitive purpose is not unknown to private law (tort law in particular). When subjected to close inspection, the distinction between compensation and punishment in monetary sanctions is difficult to distinguish. The tort/crime distinction may be called into question by developments which import more private and compensatory elements into criminal law. For instance, in some jurisdictions, a range of measures has been introduced which are aimed at expanding the role of the victim in criminal law. These measures include a victim's statement and the payment of compensation to the victim by the offender.

Objections to punitive damages on the basis of the lack of procedural safeguards in private law may also be contested. The absence of such procedural safeguards, as well as the lower burden of proof in civil cases, can be justified by reference to the different consequences of a finding of responsibility in private law as opposed to criminal law. Conviction of a criminal offence may in principle result in loss of liberty; whereas the liberty of the individual is not threatened in a claim for punitive damages.

It may be true that a promisee in a case in which punitive damages are awarded is 'overcompensated'. However, he is also probably the most appropriate person to benefit. It is the promisee who has been the victim of the non-performance and it is also the promisee who has brought the action against the promisor (perhaps at considerable financial risk to himself). Finally, if it is considered that the enrichment of the promisee through the receipt of punitive damages is unjust, damages, or a portion of them, can go to the State or to a public fund (as is the case in some States in the United States).

4.2.2. The Under-compensatory Effect of Expectation Damages

The primary goal of remedies for breach of contract is compensation. The injured party should be fully compensated for its loss. Proponents of the routine availability of expectation damages argue that expectation damages are in principle fully compensatory, making the promisee indifferent between actual performance and breach coupled with an award of damages. This is referred to as the 'indifference principle'.[67] If damages are indeed fully compensatory and the indifference principle holds true, the general introduction of punitive damages would lead to over-performance, since the promisor would be required to perform even in cases where non-performance would actually increase total welfare.

However, even advocates of the routine availability of monetary damages recognize that the amount in damages awarded by the court may fall short of full compensation, leading to under-compensation.[68] Kronman, in this light, argues that the risk of under-compensation depends on the completeness and reliability of the information available to the court on which it bases the amount of damages to be awarded. On the one hand, there exists the well-developed market which encompasses complete and reliable information on substitutable goods, meaning products which are similar to the

67 *Cf.*, Schwartz 1979, p. 274; Eisenberg 2005, pp. 989–996; Ulen 1984, p. 365; Kornhauser 1986, p. 708; and Varadarajan 2001, pp. 737–738.

68 See, e.g., Kronman 1978, p. 363.

performance under the contract and which can replace the performance under the contract.[69] On the other hand, a court may be faced with the existence of an undeveloped market for unique goods (goods without a substitute or equivalent)[70] in which information on substitutes or comparable goods is thin and unreliable. It is precisely in case of transactions concerning unique performance or goods that are embedded in an undeveloped market that the court cannot acquire at reasonable cost sufficient information on substitutes which will allow it to calculate the amount in damages without an inappropriately high risk of under-compensation. In contrast, when courts are able to rely on a well-developed market that generates abundant and highly dependable information on available substitutes, the risk of under-compensation in awarding damages for breach of contract is negligible. Proponents of expectation damages, amongst whom Kronman, generally argue that it is, therefore, precisely in the case of unique goods or services that the court should award a decree for specific performance – or in my opinion similarly: punitive damages (which have an effect similar to a decree for specific performance, namely to deter non-delivery of the unique good or non-performance of the service) – instead of expectation damages, since the risk of under-compensation in these specific cases exceeds the risk of over-performance mentioned above.[71] The common law rules regarding remedies for breach of contract reflect this 'uniqueness-test'.

According to Kronman, there is a second reason why expectation damages are under-compensatory in the case of unique goods. When a party seeks to buy a good on the market, it will incur a certain level of pre-contractual search costs (the costs of locating the object, obtaining information about it, et cetera). These pre-contractual search costs, while incurred, are generally not compensated for by way of a monetary award of expectation damages. In the case of non-unique goods, however, a party can largely 're-use' the obtained information in search of a substitute. In the case of unique performance on the other hand, the undeveloped market will usually necessitate a new search for each alternate product. Pre-contractual search costs are then likely to be higher in transactions concerning unique performance.

By contrast, advocates of specific performance indicate that specific performance – and similarly: punitive damages – is the most accurate manner in which to achieve the goal of compensation. The promisee is able to get precisely what it contracted for, without over-compensation or under-compensation (ever) taking place, and the very fact that a promisee will request specific performance reflects in essence a shortfall in the award of

69 Kronman 1978 indicates that there is a difference between the economic substitutability of a good and the common uniqueness of a good, like its properties. With regard to the substitutability of goods, economists refer to the cross-elasticity of demand. The cross-elasticity of demand measures the degree to which alteration in the relative price of one good affects the demand for another good, *i.e.*, the degree of substitutability of two goods. In essence, under economic theory all goods are ultimately commensurable.

70 Kronman 1978, pp. 358–359.

71 Kronman 1978 indirectly remarks that even in a developed market the exact value of performance to the buyer may be difficult to calculate as the buyer may prefer certain qualities of goods or know certain things about goods which are not reflected in the market price. An example is the knowledge that a particular good may last longer than others. In other words, the objective value of the good on the market does not always reflect the subjective value of a good to a buyer.

expectation damages.[72] In addition, proponents of a broader availability of specific performance – and similarly: punitive damages – such as Schwartz argue that under-compensation is not only a risk associated with unique goods, but is also built into the structure of expectation damages in general. In the first place, the subjective preferences of promisees are often not reflected in the market price, and therefore damages based on the difference between the contract price and the constructed market price will regularly fail to satisfy the indifference principle. Indeed, Goetz and Scott indicate that the achievement of full compensation is particularly difficult when there is a developed market for the promised performance, 'but the promisee attaches an additional idiosyncratic value to the performance' – idiosyncratic value meaning any subjective or fanciful appraisal which varies considerably from the market value.[73] Ulen adds that the costs of ascertaining any subjective value to a court are very high.[74] Secondly, the general reluctance of courts to award damages which are uncertain, difficult to measure, unforeseeable, or compensate for emotional harm associated with contractual breach, may also hinder full compensation.[75] First, the amount in damages is reduced when a proportion of the promisee's loss is attributable to circumstances that could not have been foreseen at the time of formation of the contract.[76] The degree of foreseeability is traditionally quite high.[77] Second, the amount of damages is reduced when a portion of the promisee's loss is attributable to the promisee's failure to take actions that would have minimized losses subsequent to the promisor's breach (mitigation rule). Third, the amount in damages is reduced to the extent that the promisee cannot show that the loss was reasonably certain. The level of certainty is set at a higher level under contract law than tort:[78] it is not sufficient that it is probable that the plaintiff suffered a loss as a result of breach, but the plaintiff must prove the amount of this loss with sufficient certainty. Fourth, the amount in damages is reduced to the extent that the loss consists of emotional distress.[79] It has also been contended that to make the promisee indifferent between a claim for specific performance and an award of damages, the promisee should be able to

72 See also Schwartz 1979, p. 274.

73 Goetz & Scott 1977, p. 570. See also n. 47 on p. 570, in which the authors refer to the tort case of *Thomanson v. Hackney & Moale Co.*, 159 N.C. 299, 305, 74 S.E. (1912), p. 1024 where the court defined this idiosyncratic value as 'an imaginary value placed upon a thing by the fancy of its owner, growing out of his or her attachment for the specific article, its associations and so forth, which, perhaps, may not inaptly be called its sentimental value'.

74 More specifically, Ulen 1984, pp. 361–365 argues that the problem with expectation damages is measuring lost profit; a promisee has an incentive to exaggerate the gain he expected from performance, while the promisor will assert that the gain could never have been that large. Ulen argues that the court's best shot is to determine the relative magnitude of surplus *vis-à-vis* the costs to the seller of completing the contract. This can, however, go wrong, see, e.g., *Peevyhouse v. Garland Coal & Mining Co.*, 382 P.2d 109 (Okla.), *cert. denied*, 375 U.S. 906 (1963).

75 See, e.g., Schwartz 1979, p. 276; Scott & Triantis 2004, p. 1434; Goetz & Scott 1977, pp. 570–572; Eisenberg 2005, pp. 991–995; Posner 2000, p. 163.

76 See *Hadley v. Baxendale, Court of Exchequer*, 1854, 9 Exch. 341.

77 Hesen & Hardy 2006.

78 See also the comment under Restatement (Second) of Contracts § 352 and *Kenford Co v. County of Erie* 493 N.E.2d 234 (N.Y. 1986).

79 See also Restatement (Second) of Contracts §§ 350–53 on avoidability, unforeseeability, uncertainty and loss due to emotional disturbance respectively.

recover the time value of its lost gains during the period between the date of breach and the date on which judgment is rendered, measured by the compound interest rate that he pays for borrowed funds.[80]

5. Conclusion: Punitive Damages for Certain Types of Breaches of Contract

5.1. *Categories of Breaches*

Contract breaches can be divided into different categories.[81] Two basic categories are: (i) involuntary and (ii) wilful (*i.e.*, deliberate). Involuntary breaches are contract breaches that do not involve a deliberate decision by the promisor to breach (e.g., breaches because of mere oversight, or because the promisor refuses to perform in the good faith (though mistaken) belief that performance is excused by a certain defence). Wilful breaches can be further subdivided into two categories: (iia) efficient and (iib) opportunistic. A breach is efficient if it makes the promisor so much better off that he could compensate the promisee for his losses and still come out ahead (see Section 4.1.2. above). A breach is opportunistic if the promisor attempts to get more than he bargained for at the expense of the promisee. An opportunistic breach does not increase the size of the economic pie; the promisor gains simply by capturing a larger share of the pie at the expense of the promisee.[82] For instance, a promisor who withholds payment in bad faith after the promisee has performed in the hope of obtaining a reduction in the contract price is breaching opportunistically.[83]

5.2. *No Punitive Damages for Involuntary Breaches*

There are several reasons why involuntary breaches should not be subjected to punitive damages.

A first reason for not awarding punitive damages in the case of involuntary breaches is that such breaches simply do not involve the level of culpability traditionally required for punitive damages. In torts, for instance, punitive damages are awarded where the defendant acted wilfully or with reckless disregard for the injured party's rights; they are not awarded for mere negligence.

According to some authors, the reason for allowing punitive damages for contract breach is to encourage negotiations for a release because the parties can establish the value of the contractual entitlement more efficiently than a court.[84] Negotiation is not possible, however, if the decision to breach is not deliberate. Punitive damages might even discourage the promisee from agreeing to a modification that would avert breach in the hopes of collecting punitive damages. Punitive damages might perhaps even give the

80 Eisenberg 2005, p. 996 in reference to the case of *Patton v. Mid-Continent Systems, Inc.* 841 F.2d 742, 751 (7th Circuit 1988).

81 Dodge 1999, p. 651 ff.

82 *Ibid.*

83 *Ibid.*

84 *Ibid.*

promisee an incentive to induce the promisor to breach. Therefore, imposing punitive damages for involuntary breaches would not serve to encourage negotiations.

Imposing punitive damages for involuntary breaches might encourage promisors to take additional precautions against such breaches, but such additional precautions would likely not be efficient. Precautions are efficient if they cost less than the amount of the loss they are designed to prevent, discounted by the probability of that loss occurring. Investing in precautions beyond that amount is inefficient. Punitive damages for involuntary breaches would encourage promisors to take an inefficient amount of precautions in order to avoid the possibility of punitive damages. Moreover, making punitive damages available for involuntary breaches might also discourage promisor's from raising legitimate defences to performance.

5.3. *Punitive Damages for Opportunistic Breaches of Contract*

Most authors would *not* allow punitive damages for efficient breaches (again: on efficient breach, see Section 4.1.2. above). Although it is perhaps not always easy for judges (and parties to a contract) to assess correctly whether a breach is efficient, in general I do agree with this majority view. In the words of Posner:

> 'Even if the breach is deliberate, it is not necessarily blameworthy. The promisor may simply have discovered that his performance is worth more to someone else. If so, efficiency is promoted by allowing him to break his promise, provided he makes good the promisee's actual losses. If he is forced to pay more than that, an efficient breach may be deterred, and the law doesn't want to bring about such a result. '[85]

Although Posner would not allow punitive damages to discourage efficient breaches of contract, it seems he would allow punitive damages to discourage opportunistic breaches of contract:

> 'It makes a difference in deciding which remedy to grant whether the breach was opportunistic. If a promisor breaks his promise merely to take advantage of the vulnerability of the promisee in a setting (the normal contract setting) where performance is sequential rather than simultaneous, we might as well throw the book at the promisor. An example would be where A pays B in advance for goods and instead of delivering them B uses the money in another venture. Such conduct has no economic justification and ought simply to be deterred. '[86]

Opportunistic behaviour does not create wealth but simply redistributes wealth from the promisee to the promisor. Indeed, opportunism perhaps actually consumes existing wealth because potential opportunists and victims spend resources perpetrating and protecting against opportunism. The opportunist may expend resources looking for loopholes in a contract or trying to make his cheating more difficult to detect.[87] The

85 *Patton v. Mid-Continent Sys.*, 841 F.2d 742 (7th Cir. 1988).

86 Posner 1998, p. 130.

87 Dodge 1999, p. 651 ff.

victim, on the other hand, may try to guard against opportunistic behaviour by investigating its prospective contractual partners more carefully, by drafting a more detailed contract, or by spending more resources monitoring the other party's performance.[88] None of these expenditures increases society's total welfare.

Compensatory damages are perhaps not always sufficient to discourage opportunism. An opportunistic promisor will sometimes escape liability, either because the promisee fails to detect the breach or because the latter cannot afford to bring suit to enforce his rights. If an opportunistic promisor needs only to pay compensatory damages when he is held liable and can keep his opportunistic gains when he is not, then opportunism may be a profitable strategy.

In his discussion of opportunistic breaches, Posner suggests that the opportunistic promisor should pay restitution of any benefits received from the breach:

> 'We can deter this kind of behavior by making it worthless to the promisor, which we do by making him hand over all his profits from the breach to the promisee; no lighter sanction would deter. '[89]

Because there is at least some chance that the opportunistic promisor will not be held liable at all, however, restitution alone is not sufficient to deter opportunistic breaches. Perhaps for this reason, Posner approves of what he sees as a judicial trend towards awarding 'punitive damages (…) as a sanction for opportunistic breaches'.[90]

I am of the opinion that punitive damages in the case of certain categories of opportunistic behaviour should be (more broadly) available. Especially in the case of two types of breaches, I see a role for punitive damages in contract: (i) when a promisor's bad faith failure to perform could threaten the promisee's survival (e.g. in the case of a contract with a vital supplier), and (ii) when contractual surplus would be maximized if the promisee makes relation-specific investments and the promisor's bad faith breach occurs after the promisee's has made the investments (e.g. after the production of something that only the promisor can use).[91] These opportunistic breaches of contract in particular likely are inefficient. They not only fail to create wealth, but actually consume it. Compensatory damages are likely not sufficient to deter these breaches, and thus sometimes punitive damages may be necessary. A punitive sanction – similar to specific performance – seeks to deter breach absolutely. The two types of opportunistic breaches I just described generally deserve to be deterred absolutely. Currently, in the absence of an independent tort, however, many legal system's traditional rule shields opportunistic promisors from punitive damages, thus sometimes encouraging inefficient opportunism.

88 *Ibid.*

89 Posner 1998, pp. 130–131.

90 *Ibid*, p. 142.

91 Schwartz & Scott 2003, p. 546.

Bibliography

Asser 2008
Hartkamp, A. & Sieburgh, C., Mr. C. Asser's handleiding tot de beoefening van het Nederlands burgerlijk recht, Verbintenissenrecht, Volume 6-II, *De verbintenis in het algemeen, tweede gedeelte*, Deventer: Kluwer, 2008.

Birmingham 1970
Birmingham, R., 'Breach of Contract, Damage Measures, and Economic Efficiency', *Rutgers L Rev*, 1970, pp. 273–292.

Bishop 1985
Bishop, W., 'The choice of remedy for breach of contract', *J Legal Stud*, 1985, pp. 299–320.

Calabresi & Melamed 1972
Calabresi, G. & Melamed, D., 'Property Rules, Liability Rules, and Inalienability: One View of the Cathedral', *Harv L Rev*, 1972, pp. 1089–1128.

Coase 1937
Coase, R., 'The Nature of the Firm', *Economica*, 1937, pp. 386–405.

Cooter & Ulen 2003
Cooter, R. & Ulen, T., *Law & Economics*, Boston: Addison Wesley, 2003.

Dodge 1999
Dodge, W., 'The Case for Punitive Damages in Contract', *Duke L J*, 1999, pp. 629–699.

Eisenberg 2005
Eisenberg, M., 'Actual and Virtual Specific Performance, the Theory of Efficient Breach, and the Indifference Principle in Contract Law', *Cal L Rev*, 2005, pp. 975–1050.

Farnsworth 1979
Farnsworth, A., 'Damages and Specific Relief', *Am J Comp L*, 1979, pp. 247–253.

Farnsworth 2000
Farnsworth, A., *Farnsworth on Contracts*, New York: Aspen Publishers, 2000.

Friedman 1989
Friedman, D., 'The Efficient Breach Fallacy', *J Legal Stud*, 1989, pp. 1–24.

Friedman 1965
Friedman, L., *Contract Law in America: A Social and Economic Case Study*, Madison: University of Wisconsin Press, 1965.

Fuller & Purdue 1936
Fuller, L. & Purdue, W., 'The Reliance Interest in Contract Damages I', *Yale L J*, 1936, pp. 52–96.

Fuller & Purdue 1937
Fuller, L. & Purdue, W., 'The Reliance Interest in Contract Damages II', *Yale L J*, 1937, pp. 373–420.

Goetz & Scott 1977
Goetz, C. & Scott, R., 'Liquidated Damages, Penalties and the Just Compensation Principle: Some Notes on an Enforcement Model and a Theory of Efficient Breach', *Colum L Rev*, 1977, pp. 554–594.

Gordley & Von Mehren 2006
Gordley, J. & Von Mehren A. (eds.), *An Introduction to the Comparative Study of Private Law. Readings, Cases, Materials*, Cambridge/New York: Cambridge University Press, 2006.

Hardy 2008
Hardy, R., 'Is the System of Contract Remedies in the Netherlands Efficient from a Law and Economics Perspective?', in: J. Smits, D. Haas, & G. Hesen (eds.), *Specific Performance: National and Other Perspectives*, Antwerpen: Intersentia, 2008, pp. 287–326 (with Hesen, G.).

Hart & Moore 1999
Hart, O. & Moore, J., 'Foundations of Incomplete Contracts', *Review of Economic Studies*, 1999, pp. 115–138.

Hesen & Hardy 2006
Hesen, G. & Hardy, R., 'Hadley v. Baxendale: 'perhaps the best-known of all English contract cases'', *NTBR*, 2006, pp. 326–331.

Kornhauser 1986
Kornhauser, L., 'An Introduction to the Economic Analysis of Contract Remedies', *U Colo L Rev*, 1986, pp. 683–725.

Kronman 1978
Kronman, A., 'Specific Performance', *U Chi L Rev*, 1978, pp. 351–382.

Mahoney 2000
Mahoney, P., 'Contract Remedies: General', in: B. Bouckaert & G. De Geest (eds.), Encyclopedia of Law and Economics, Volume III, *The Regulation of Contracts*, Cheltenham: Edward Elgar, 2000, pp. 117–140.

Maskin & Tirole 1999
Maskin, E. & Tirole, J., 'Unforeseen Contingencies and Incomplete Contracts', *Review of Economic Studies*, 1999, pp. 83–114.

Posner 2000
Posner, E., 'Contract Remedies: Foreseeability, Precaution, Causation and Mitigation', in: B. Bouckaert & G. De Geest (eds.), Encyclopedia of Law and Economics, Volume III, *The Regulation of Contracts,* Cheltenham: Edward Elgar, 2000, pp. 162–178.

Posner 1972
Posner, R., *Economic Analysis of Law*, New York: Aspen Publishers, 1972.

Posner 1998
Posner, R., *Economic Analysis of Law*, New York: Aspen Publishers, 1998.

Posner 2003
Posner, R., *Economic Analysis of Law*, New York: Aspen Publishers, 2003.

Scott & Triantis 2004
Scott, R. & Triantis, G., 'Embedded Options and the Case against Compensation in Contract Law', *Colum L Rev*, 2004, pp. 1428–1491.

Schwartz 1979
Schwartz, A., 'The Case for Specific Performance', *Yale L J*, 1979, pp. 271–306.

Schwartz & Scot 2003
Schwartz, A. & Scott, R., 'Contract Theory and the Limits of Contract Law', *Yale L J*, 2003, pp. 541–619.

Shavell 1980
Shavell, S., 'Damage Measures for Breach of Contract', *The Bell Journal of Economics*, 1980, pp. 466–490.

The Law Reform Commission Ireland 1998
The Law Reform Commission Ireland, *Consultation Paper on Aggravated, Exemplary and Restitutionary Damages*, 1998, p. 6 ff., available at: www.lawreform.ie.

Treitel 2007
Treitel, G., *The Law of Contract*, Londen: Sweet & Maxwell, 2007.

Ulen 1984
Ulen, T., 'The Efficiency of Specific Performance: Toward a Unified Theory of Contract Remedies', *Mich L Rev*, 1984, pp. 341–403.

Van Bijnen 2005
Van Bijnen, R., *Aanvullend contractenrecht*, Den Haag: Boom Juridische uitgevers, 2005.

Varadarajan 2001
Varadarajan, D., 'Tortious Interference and the Law of Contract: the Case for Specific Performance Revisited', *Yale L J*, 2001, pp. 735–760.

Williamson 1985
Williamson, O., *The Economic Institutions of Capitalism*, New York: Free Press, 1985.

Williston 1936
Williston, S., *A Treatise on the Law of Contracts*, New York: Baker, Voorhis & co., 1936–38.

Yorio 1982
Yorio, E., 'In Defense of Money Damages for Breach of Contract', *Colum L Rev*, 1982, pp. 1365–1424.

Sara Matthé*

ENFORCEMENT IN FAMILY LAW BY MEANS OF PRIVATE PENALTIES

1. Abstract

Under Common Law, private penalties are being used to facilitate the enforcement of family law obligations. The traditional continental European Civil Law perspective on private penalties rejects such fines. The public authorities are thought of as having a monopoly over the punishing of wrongful behaviour, through criminal law. Since the introduction of the French *Code civil* of 1804, the autonomy of parties in family law has increased significantly. Questions now arise on the respective roles of the state and the family with regard to the enforcement of an individual's rights in family law. This article explores whether the arguments under the traditional continental European Civil Law perspective on private penalties resist the increasing role of family members in enforcing their family law obligations. To answer that question, I will first examine whether criminal law effectively serves the purpose of enforcement in family law. Next, I will investigate the existence of private penalties in family law and the desirability of expanding the use of these as a means of enforcing rights in family law. While answering these questions, attention will be focused on a case-study with relation to the enforcement of the parents' right to contact with their child, comparing Belgian and Dutch law. This study shows that, in the Netherlands, private penalties are an established phenomenon both in the domain of private law in general and in family law. Belgium, on the other hand, still concurs with the traditional continental European Civil Law perspective on private penalties. Nonetheless, the Belgian legislator is also developing private measures whose potential, or at the least partial punitive nature, can no longer be doubted, as a consequence of the legislator's growing awareness of the public enforcement measures' ineffectiveness. The results suggest that there are no arguments to obstruct the continually increasing autonomy in family law to result in a growing role for family members in enforcing family law obligations. Enforcement of family law obligations should be made possible by means of penalty clauses. Family members should be given the possibility to agree on a penalty in the case of violation of a family law obligation, with a power for the court to modify the agreed amount in case of noncompliance, when fairness manifestly so requires, taking

* Sara Matthé (Sara.Matthe@ua.ac.be) is a research assistant and PhD student at the University of Antwerp. She is currently working on a doctoral dissertation concerning the application of the general theory on contracts to family law, under promotership of professor dr. Frederik Swennen.

into account all circumstances from the entering into the contract until the judge's decision. The public order will determine the limits of such a penalty's validity. Only when the principal obligation does not harm the public order will a penalty clause be valid. This allows the penalty clause's validity to evolve in the same way as the concept 'public order' and consequently to follow the increasing autonomy in family law.

2. Introduction

A private penalty can be defined as a sanction imposed on a wrongdoer that entirely benefits the victim of the offensive behaviour. The penalty is related to the offender's conduct and has no relation with the loss suffered by the victim. Consequently this legal concept holds both a private, and a punitive aspect. The private aspect is related to the fact that the penalty comes entirely to the victim, whereas its relation to the wrongdoer's conduct is characteristic of its punitive nature. A private penalty has a repressive and preventive function. It is intended to cause distress to the offender and influence his way of behaving. It can therefore be utilized to advance the enforcement of an individual's rights.[1]

In several Common Law countries,[2] private penalties are being used to deter undesirable conduct. The most extensive practice of private penalties is punitive damages. Tort actions can give rise not solely to the award of compensatory damages. In cases of truly outrageous behaviour, as a result of which the award of compensatory damages does not adequately reach punishment and deterrence, they can additionally lead to a conviction to pay punitive damages to the victim.[3] While compensatory damages redress the actual loss to the plaintiff, punitive damages are mainly[4] awarded to punish the wrongdoer and to deter similar conduct in the future.[5] Punitive damages serve the purpose of both specific and general deterrence. They not only give an incentive to the defendant not to repeat the same misconduct, but they also prevent others from acting in a similar way.[6]

Even in proceedings involving family law, punitive damages have been awarded. A majority of states in the United States uses tort law – including the possibility to award punitive damages – for instance to influence parents' behaviour in cases of interference by one parent with the other parent's parent-child relationship by not complying with a

1 Slok & Van 1990, p. 1827; Weyts 2005, p. 1650, n. 27; Cauffman 2007, p. 802, 854 and 857, ns. 1, 94 and 99; Adriaanse *et al.* 2008, p. 275.

2 For example by means of punitive damages in Australia, Canada, England, New-Zealand, United States; Gotanda 2003, pp. 391–444.

3 Ghiardi 1965, p. 282; Slok & Van 1990, p. 1824; Dobbs 2000, p. 2, 1062 and 1064; O'Connell 2000, p. 875; Gotanda 2003, p. 395; Garner 2004, p. 418; Goldberg, Sebok & Zipursky 2004, p. 470; Cauffman 2007, p. 831, n. 49; Brooke 2009, p. 1, n. 1; Sebok 2009, p. 155, n. 1; Galligan 2009, p. 411.

4 Some authors have mentioned supplementary functions like to vent the indignation of the victimized, to discourage the injured party from engaging in self-help remedies, extra compensation, to reimburse the plaintiff for litigation expenses that are not otherwise recoverable, e.g., Gotanda 2003, p. 396; O'Connell 2000, p. 876.

5 Ghiardi 1965, p. 283; Jowitt, Walsh & Burke 1977, p. 1467; Garner 1987, p. 452; Slok & Van 1990, p. 1824; Dobbs 2000, p. 1063; Gotanda 2003, p. 396; Garner 2004, p. 419; Murphy 2007, p. 637.

6 O'Connell 2000, p. 877; Sebok 2009, pp. 178–180, ns. 52–58.

custody and visitation order.[7] Although criminal sanctions and judicial[8] remedies generally are the first steps the victimized parent takes, tort actions are seen as an additional remedy to deter parental abductions and noncompliance with custody and visitation orders.[9] Punitive damages serve as an additional deterrent[10] and therefore improve enforcement in family law.

The traditional continental European Civil Law perspective on private penalties consists of a rejection of all the above. The recognition of private penalties is believed to be contrary to the division between public and private law. Punishment is outside of the private law. It is assumed that only the government punishes wrongful behaviour through criminal law. Furthermore, private penalties are supposed to lead to unjust enrichment of the victim. Criminal law rather than private law is appropriate, if there are no arguments for awarding an advantage to the victim, but only for punishing or deterring the wrongdoer.[11]

In case these arguments are refuted, even then accepting private penalties in family law will not be the definite consequence. Family law is believed to occupy an exceptional position within private law. Whereas the principle of self-determination is the point of departure in private law,[12] family law is traditionally believed to be of public order. As a consequence, the autonomy of parties in family law is the exception.[13]

3. Presentation of the Question

The question arises whether these arguments can, in our current society, persuade to reject private penalties in family law. On the one hand, it can be stated that the dividing line between public law and private law is becoming blurred.[14] A privatization of criminal law is taking place. The punishment of criminal acts is not purely seen as a task of the government any longer. Criminal law more and more involves the victim in actions of investigation,[15]

7 § 700 Restatement of the Law of Torts; *Wood v. Wood*, 338 N.W.2d 123 (Iowa 1983); Wentzel 1990, pp. 264–266; Dobbs 1991, pp. 1166–1169; Dobbs 2000, pp. 1249–1252; Krause & D.D. Meyer 2003, p. 201.

8 The majority of judicial remedies are coercive civil contempt remedies. Enforcement is reached by conviction to a serial fine payable to the court or jail sentence which continues until the contemnor satisfies conditions set out in the contempt order. These conditions typically require compliance with the terms of the initial custody and visitation order; Mahoney 2006, p. 861 and 866–871.

9 Goldman 1986, p. 324; Dobbs 1991, p. 1177, 1187 and 1189.

10 *Wood v. Wood*, 338 N.W.2d 123 (Iowa 1983); Wentzel 1990, p. 275; Dobbs 1991, p. 1189; Feinberg & Loeb 1994, pp. 278–279.

11 Slok & Van 1990, p. 1827; Piedelièvre 2001, pp. 68 and 71–72, ns. 1 and 21–22; Weyts 2005, p. 1650, ns. 28 and 29; Cauffman 2007, pp. 803, 852 and 854, ns. 3, 89 and 94; Koziol 2007, pp. 751–753.

12 Van Oevelen 1991, pp. 98–112, ns. 4–13; Van Gerven & Covemaeker 2006, p. 71; Dekkers & Verbeke 2007, p. 18, n. 30.

13 Swennen 2010, pp. 30 and 74, ns. 51 and 121.

14 Slok & Van 1990, p. 1827.

15 E.g. Article 61*quinquies*, § 1 of the Belgian Code of Criminal Procedure (Sv.) assigns to the civil party a right to ask the performance of additional investigation deeds.

prosecution[16] and in some degree even of punishment.[17, 18] In addition, private law is encroaching on criminal law.[19] This applies, for example, to liability law. If wrongdoers are held liable, the damages awarded to the victims are not allowed to exceed their losses. As a consequence, most authors state that punishment is outside the scope of liability law. Nevertheless, they ascribe a deterrent effect to the awarded compensation.[20] Yet, punishment and deterrence are closely linked.[21] When damages are limited to pure compensation, the preventive function often cannot be fulfilled. This is, for example, true for lucrative faults. By way of compensating this failure, courts sometimes award large sums for moral damages. In practice, this comes down to awarding punitive damages.[22] This approach between criminal law and private law results in increasing attention on the enforcement of rights in private law by means of private penalties.[23]

On the other hand, one can question the exceptional position of family law as a part of private law. Since the implementation of the *Code Civil*, society has developed in a way that focuses more on an individualistic perspective. The autonomy of parties in family law has increased significantly.[24] In such a society, a question regarding the respective roles of either the state or the family with regard to the enforcement of an individual's rights in family law, presents itself.

With a view towards answering these questions, I will conduct a case-study concerning the enforcement of the parents' right to have contact with their child. The growing number of recomposed families causes an increase in disputes in this regard. In this case-study, I will first examine whether criminal law serves the purpose of enforcement in family law. Next, I will investigate the existence of private penalties in family law and the desirability of expanding the use of private penalties as a means of enforcing rights in family law. Since an evolution towards the enforcement by means of private penalties in private law in general can, contrary to Belgian law, already be found in the Netherlands, a comparison is made between Belgian and Dutch law.[25] I will then conclude by discussing in general the desirability of the enforcement of family law obligations by means of private penalties.

16 E.g. Article 64 of the Belgian Code of Criminal Procedure (Sv.) assigns to the victim of a misdemeanor offence the right to directly summon the wrongdoer before the correctional court.

17 Altough the main principle still is that the victim does not have actual saying in the criminal punishment of a wrongdoer, Article 37*ter* of the Belgian Criminal Code states that the criminal court can take the victim's interests into account while deciding to convict the wrongdoer to a community service; Verhelst 2010, p. 40.

18 Hutsebaut 2001, pp. 311–325; Cauffman 2007, p. 853, n. 92.

19 Slok & Van 1990, p. 1827.

20 Cornelis 1989, p. 12; Van Gerven & Covemaeker 2006, p. 324.

21 Weyts 2005, p. 1649, n. 26; Cauffman 2007, pp. 853–854, n. 93.

22 Weyts 2005, pp. 1645–1646, n. 14.

23 Slok & Van 1990, pp. 1823–1829; Piedelièvre 2001, pp. 68–72; Weyts 2005, pp. 1641–1652; Cauffman 2007, pp. 799–865.

24 Heyvaert 2001, pp. 165–195; Renchon 2005, pp. 269–332; Gallus 2009b, p. 231 and following.

25 For example Article 6:94 of the Dutch Civil Code (NBW) accepts both coercive and compensatory penalty clauses. By contrast Article 1226 of the Belgian Civil Code only accepts a penalty clause's compensatory function.

4. Enforcement in Family Law by means of Private Penalties: a Case Study with Relation to the Enforcement of the Parents' Right to Contact with their Child

This case study will focus its attention on the contact rights between parents and their child. Belgian family law, as well as Dutch family law, gives the court the authority to impose a regulation on the parents concerning this contact right, either as a part of custody,[26] or as the realisation of the visitation rights of a noncustodial parent.[27] This regulation can be based on an agreement between the parents, or can be ordered by the court. In both cases, the child's best interests are taken into account.[28]

Deteriorating relations between partners can result in both their separation and the interference in each other's right to have contact with their child. Even in the case of divorce by mutual consent, problems of noncompliance arise, particularly when one parent enters into a relationship with a new partner.[29] Given the fact that the regulations concerning the contact between parents and their child are based on the child's best interests, it is necessary to guarantee their enforcement effectively.[30]

4.1. Public Enforcement of the Parents' Right to Contact by means of Criminal Sanctions

4.1.1. Article 8 of the European Convention on Human Rights

According to Article 8 of the European Convention on Human Rights, states have a positive obligation to take all the necessary steps that could reasonably be demanded to enforce these regulations.[31] In *Zawadka v. Poland*, the European Court of Human Rights (ECHR) stated that 'article 8 includes the right of a parent to have measures taken with a view to him or her being reunited with the child, and an obligation for the national authorities to take such measures'.[32] The ECHR clarified that 'this applies not only to cases dealing with the compulsory taking of children into public care and the implementation of care measures, but also to cases where contact and residence disputes

26 Belgian law; Article 374, § 1, section 5 and 374, § 2 Civil Code; Dutch law; Article 1:253 a, section 2, a Civil Code.

27 Belgian law; Article 374, § 1, section 4 Civil Code (BW); Dutch law; Article 1:377 a, section 2 Civil Code (NBW).

28 Belgian law; Article 374, § 2 and 387*bis* Civil Code (BW); Article 1290, section 2 and 5, 1293, section 5 and 1298 Judicial Code (Ger.W.).

29 Wetsvoorstel tot het waarborgen van het omgangsrecht tussen ouders en kinderen en tussen grootouders en kleinkinderen, *Parl.St.* Kamer 2003–04, n. 51 0976/001, 5.

30 De Smet 2008, p. 185.

31 Wetsontwerp tot het bevoorrechten van een gelijkmatig verdeelde huisvesting van het kind van wie de ouders gescheiden zijn en tot regeling van de gedwongen tenuitvoerlegging inzake huisvesting van het kind, *Parl.St.* Kamer 2004–05, n. 51 1673/001, p. 9; ECHR 26 June 2003, *Maire v. Portugal*, case n. 48206/99, § 69; ECHR 23 June 2005, *Zawadka v. Poland*, case n. 48542/99, § 53 and 56; Vlaardingerbroeck *et al.* 2008, p. 462; De Boer 2010, p. 894.

32 ECHR 23 June 2005, *Zawadka v. Poland*, case n. 48542/99, § 55. See also ECHR 26 June 2003, *Maire v. Portugal*, case n. 48206/99, § 70.

concerning children arise between parents and/or other members of the children's family'.[33]

Although the ECHR takes the view that in this area 'the use of sanctions must not be ruled out in the event of manifestly unlawful behaviour',[34] states are not obliged to impose criminal sanctions.[35] In *Reigado Ramos v. Portugal*, the ECHR observed that states are given wide discretion as to their legislative choices, especially with regard to their criminal policy. The use of criminal law is not necessarily the only solution in enforcing the parents' right to contact with their child.[36]

4.1.2. The Ineffectiveness of Criminal Sanctions

Despite the lack of an obligation under Article 8 of the European Convention on Human Rights to penalise noncompliance with a custody and visitation order, some countries have nevertheless chosen to enforce such orders by means of criminal sanctions. The Act of 15 May 1912 on child protection e.g. has introduced Article 369*bis* into the Belgian Criminal Code, with the purpose of assuring the parents' respect for civil[37] decisions with regard to their children.[38] This penalization can currently be found in Article 432 of the Criminal Code. It is directed against a parent who, in violation of an enforceable court order, intentionally fails to hand over the child to the person to whom the court order has granted a right to contact. Such a parent can be sentenced to imprisonment or a fine.[39]

In theory, Article 432 of the Criminal Code meets the obligation to enforce regulations concerning the parent-child relationship. However, the public prosecutor usually does not bring an action against a parent.[40] Even supposing a parent is brought before the criminal court, the judge frequently hesitates in deciding that parent's guilt.[41] In practice, this criminal law commonly leaves the recalcitrant parent unpunished. This could be solved by making the prosecution of this crime a top priority. However, criminal prosecution and conviction imposing criminal sanctions appear to be ineffective for

33 ECHR 23 June 2005, *Zawadka v. Poland*, case n. 48542/99, § 55.

34 ECHR 26 June 2003, *Maire v. Portugal*, case n. 48206/99, § 76.

35 Vlaardingerbroek 2009, p. 108; De Boer 2010, p. 895. *Contra*: De Smet 2008, p. 208.

36 ECHR 22 November 2005, *Reigado Ramos v. Portugal*, case n. 73229/01, § 56.

37 The Act of 20 July 1927 (*Pasin.* 1927, no. 344, 354–357) introduced a fourth paragraph to Article 369*bis* Criminal Code to fill a loophole in the original Act. The text of the original Act only named decisions ordered with regard to the law on child protection, while it was the intention of the legislator to penalize the parents' noncompliance with all civil decisions concerning the custody of their child; See Tulkens 1982, pp. 374–376, and the references there.

38 Rigaux & Trousse 1968, p. 260; Screvens 1972, p. 424, n. 6093; Trousse 1978, p. 649; Tulkens 1982, p. 378; De Nauw 2005, p. 205, n. 284.

39 Article 432 Belgian Criminal Code (Sw.); See for a more detailed exposition on this subject; Rigaux & Trousse 1968, pp. 257–268; Screvens 1972, pp. 424–429, ns 6092–6139; Tulkens 1982, pp. 371–401; Messine & Hirsch 1986, pp. 633–645; De Nauw 2005, pp. 204–209, ns. 284–291; De Smet 2007; De Smet 2008, pp. 185–209; De Smet 2010, pp. 200–202.

40 Wetsvoorstel tot het waarborgen van het omgangsrecht tussen ouders en kinderen en tussen grootouders en kleinkinderen, *Parl.St.* Kamer 2003–04, n. 51 0976/001, p. 6; De Wit 2006, p. 5.

41 Wetsvoorstel tot het waarborgen van het omgangsrecht tussen ouders en kinderen en tussen grootouders en kleinkinderen, *Parl.St.* Kamer 2003–04, n. 51 0976/001, p. 7; Trousse 1978, p. 652.

the following reasons.[42] Firstly, criminal proceedings threaten to increase conflict between the parents.[43] A criminal conviction, which mostly results in imprisonment,[44] stigmatizes the convicted parent. Moreover, the imprisonment will cause the latter to lose physical custody of his or her child.[45] The increase in conflict risks causing a decrease in the prospect of complying with the contact regulation after a conviction.[46] Secondly, enforcement by means of criminal sanctions threatens to be contrary to the child's best interests.[47] A criminal procedure has a duration from a few months[48] up to a few years.[49] The granting of a delay frequently occurs in these criminal actions.[50] During this period, the child risks becoming the victim of manipulation by the prosecuted parent. The latter has a long period during which he or she can try to make the child and the victimized parent drift apart.[51] The damage thereby caused to the parent-child relationship is often irreparable.[52] In case of detention of the recalcitrant parent either as preventive custody, or as a result of a jail sentence, the child will have to be separated from the detained parent. He or she will be obliged to live with the victimized parent, a reliable family member or in an institution. Consequently, the relationship between the victimized

42 *Kamerstukken* II, 2002–03, 28600 VI, n. 105, https://zoek.officielebekendmakingen.nl, p. 11; Hiernaux 2007, p. 44. *Contra*: De Nauw 1978, p. 646; Prinsen 2003, pp. 16 and 19; they both plead for the penalization in criminal law because of its deterrent effect.

43 Verslag namens de subcommissie familierecht over het wetsontwerp tot het bevoorrechten van een gelijkmatig verdeelde huisvesting van het kind van wie de ouders gescheiden zijn en tot regeling van de gedwongen tenuitvoerlegging inzake huisvesting van het kind, *Parl.St.* Kamer 2005–06, n. 51 1673/014, p. 320; Hiernaux 2007, p. 44; De Smet 2008, p. 206; Gallus 2009a, p. 210.

44 Wetsvoorstel tot het waarborgen van het omgangsrecht tussen ouders en kinderen en tussen grootouders en kleinkinderen, *Parl.St.* Kamer 2003–04, n. 51 0976/001, p. 6.

45 De Smet 2008, p. 206.

46 Tweede Kamer 11 februari 2000, *Kamerstukken* II, 1999–2000, 25451, n. 5, https://zoek.officielebekendmakingen.nl, p. 5.

47 Tweede Kamer 11 februari 2000, *Kamerstukken* II, 1999–2000, 25451, n. 5, https://zoek.officielebekendmakingen.nl, p. 5; Tulkens 1982, p. 399; Gallus 2009a, p. 210.

48 Wetsontwerp tot het bevoorrechten van een gelijkmatig verdeelde huisvesting van het kind van wie de ouders gescheiden zijn en tot regeling van de gedwongen tenuitvoerlegging inzake huisvesting van het kind, *Parl.St.* Kamer 2004–05, n. 51 1673/001, p. 9.

49 Verslag namens de subcommissie familierecht over het wetsontwerp tot het bevoorrechten van een gelijkmatig verdeelde huisvesting van het kind van wie de ouders gescheiden zijn en tot regeling van de gedwongen tenuitvoerlegging inzake huisvesting van het kind, *Parl.St.* Kamer 2005–06, n. 51 1673/014, p. 7 and 109.

50 Wetsvoorstel tot het waarborgen van het omgangsrecht tussen ouders en kinderen en tussen grootouders en kleinkinderen, *Parl.St.* Kamer 2003–04, n. 51 0976/001, p. 7.

51 Wetsvoorstel tot het waarborgen van het omgangsrecht tussen ouders en kinderen en tussen grootouders en kleinkinderen, *Parl.St.* Kamer 2003–04, n. 51 0976/001, p. 8; Wetsontwerp tot het bevoorrechten van een gelijkmatig verdeelde huisvesting van het kind van wie de ouders gescheiden zijn en tot regeling van de gedwongen tenuitvoerlegging inzake huisvesting van het kind, *Parl.St.* Kamer 2004–05, n. 51 1673/001, p. 9; Verslag namens de subcommissie familierecht over het wetsontwerp tot het bevoorrechten van een gelijkmatig verdeelde huisvesting van het kind van wie de ouders gescheiden zijn en tot regeling van de gedwongen tenuitvoerlegging inzake huisvesting van het kind, *Parl.St.* Kamer 2005–06, n. 51 1673/014, p. 109; De Smet 2007, n. 63; Hiernaux 2007, p. 44; Pire 2007, p. 212.

52 Wetsvoorstel tot het waarborgen van het omgangsrecht tussen ouders en kinderen en tussen grootouders en kleinkinderen, *Parl.St.* Kamer 2003–04, n. 51 0976/001, p. 6.

parent and the child will only too often deteriorate.[53] This counts all the more in case a strong emotional bond exists between the child and the convicted parent.[54] What is more, the criminal conviction of a parent stigmatizes the child.[55]

4.2. *Enforcement of the Parents' Right to Contact by means of Private Penalties*

Because of the ineffectiveness of criminal penalties, states have frequently developed means, outside of criminal proceedings, to achieve compliance with custody and visitation orders. In the Netherlands, the enforcement of the regulation concerning the contact between a child and a noncustodial parent can only be reached by means of civil measures.[56] The Dutch government refuses to use criminal sanctions to prevent the frustration of this right because of the abovementioned ineffectiveness.[57] Both Belgian[58] and Dutch family law enforce custody and visitation orders through the compulsory taking of a child,[59] the civil judicial penalty payment *(astreinte)*,[60] modification of the custody[61] or residence[62] order and through guidance[63] or mediation.[64] Under Dutch family law, the noncompliance by a parent with the custody or visitation order can also cause the reduction or even the dismissal of the recalcitrant parent's maintenance.[65] Ultimately, the enforcement in the Netherlands can also be reached by the personal arrest of the parent who frustrates the other parent's parent-child relationship, which

53 De Smet 2007, n. 61; De Smet 2008, pp. 206–207.

54 De Smet 2007, n. 63; De Smet 2008, p. 208.

55 Wetsvoorstel tot het waarborgen van het omgangsrecht tussen ouders en kinderen en tussen grootouders en kleinkinderen, *Parl.St.* Kamer 2003–04, n. 51 0976/001, p. 7.

56 Vlaardingerbroek 2009, p. 108.

57 Tweede Kamer 11 februari 2000, *Kamerstukken* II, 1999–2000, 25451, n. 5, https://zoek.officielebekendmakingen.nl, p. 5; *Kamerstukken* II, 2002–03, 28600 VI, n. 105, https://zoek.officielebekendmakingen.nl, p. 11; De Boer 2010, p. 895; Frustration with the right to contact of a custodial parent on the other hand is penalized in Article 279 Dutch Criminal Code (Sr.), even in case of joint custody; HR 15 February 2005, LJN AR8250, www.rechtspraak.nl; Rb. Leeuwarden 5 February 2009, *FJR* 2010, 58; Vlaardingerbroek 2009, pp. 106–110.

58 Belgian law: Article 387*ter* Civil Code (BW).

59 Dutch law: Article 812, section 2 Dutch Code of Civil Procedure (Rv.); De Boer 2010, p. 896.

60 Dutch law: Article 611a-611i Dutch Code of Civil Procedure (Rv.); Benelux Court of Justice 11 May 1982, *NJ* 1983, nr. 613; HR 1 October 1982, *NJ* 1983, nr. 614, note WHH; HR 26 January 1996, *NJ* 1996, n. 355; Van der Burght & Doek 2002, p. 592; De Boer 2010, p. 896.

61 Dutch law: Hof Amsterdam 27 January 2005, LJN AS6020, www.rechtspraak.nl; Hof 's-Gravenhage 31 August2005, LJN AU2003, www.rechtspraak.nl; Van Der Burght & Doek 2002, p. 593; De Boer 2010, p. 897.

62 Dutch law: HR 15 December 2000, *NJ* 2001, n. 123, note S. Wortmann.

63 Dutch law: Guidance is believed to be a useful tool. It is offered by the Contacthouses (omgangshuizen). A judge cannot make the Board on Child Protection (Raad voor Kinderbescherming) responsible for it; HR 29 June 2001, *NJ* 2001, n. 598, note S. Wortmann; Van der Burght & Doek 2002, p. 593; Vlaardingerbroek 2009, p. 109; De Boer 2010, p. 898.

64 Dutch law: Article 818, section 2 Dutch Code on Civil Procedure (Rv.); De Boer 2010, p. 898.

65 Dutch law: Article 1:157, section 1 and 1:401 Dutch Civil Code (NBW); Rb. Den Bosch 10 November 2000, *FJR* 2001, 86; Rb. Leeuwarden 9 July 2008, LJN BD6634, www.rechtspraak.nl; De Boer 2010, p. 897.

operates as a coercive measure that can only be enforced on the victimized parent's explicit request and thus has a private nature.[66]

Among these civil measures, an evolution towards enforcement by means of private penalties can be seen. As demonstrated hereafter, the civil judicial penalty payment (4.2.1), the modification of the order to the advantage of the victim (4.2.2) and the reduction or dismissal of the recalcitrant parent's maintenance (4.2.3) all have a (potential) (partial) punitive nature.

4.2.1. The Civil Judicial Penalty Payment (*Astreinte*)

Belgian, as well as Dutch law, contains the possibility for a court to pronounce a principal sentence subject to a civil judicial penalty payment (hereafter also abbreviated to penalty payment). According to Article 1385*bis* of the Belgian Judicial Code and Article 611*a* of the Dutch Code of Civil Procedure, a judge can condemn a party, convicted in the judge's principal sentence to comply with an obligation to the benefit of the opposite party, to pay to the latter a sum of money in case of noncompliance with the principal sentence. Both statutory regulations are parallel, since either one finds its origin in the Benelux Treaty containing a Uniform Law on Penalty Payments (hereafter Benelux Treaty).[67]

The notion 'civil judicial penalty payment' is used in two senses. It can firstly refer to the additional and suspended sentence to pay a fine to the other party, in case of noncompliance with the obligation as stipulated in the principal sentence. Secondly, it indicates the sum of money a convicted person has to pay, because he failed to comply with the principal sentence.[68]

The preparatory acts of the Benelux Treaty state that the civil judicial penalty payment is no punishment.[69] Firstly, I will examine whether this means: 'no criminal charge'. If the answer is positive, I will subsequently research whether the preparatory acts' statement means that the idea of sanctioning is totally unknown to the penalty payment. An affirmative answer to this question would mean that this civil enforcement measure cannot be seen as a private penalty, as defined earlier in this article.

66 Dutch law: Articles 585–590 Dutch Code of Civil Procedure (Rv.); HR 5 December 1986, *NJ* 1987, n. 527; KG Rb. Groningen 21 juni 2007, LJN BB9198, *www.rechtspraak.nl;* Lenters 1999, pp. 96–99; Snijders, Ynzonides & Meijer 2002, pp. 408–409; De Boer 2010, p. 897.

67 Benelux Treaty 26 November 1973 containing a Uniform Law on Penalty Payments, *http://wetten.overheid.nl/BWBV0003371/geldigheidsdatum_16-12-2009*; Wagner 1999, n. 2; M. B. Beekkhoven van den Boezem 2006, p. 413.

68 Ballon 1980, p. 2, n. 3; Jongbloed 1991, p. 2; Wagner 2003, p. 1, n. 2.

69 Gemeenschappelijke memorie van toelichting van de Benelux Overeenkomst houdende eenvormige wet betreffende de dwangsom als bijlage bij Wetsontwerp houdende goedkeuring van de Benelux-Overeenkomst houdende eenvormige wet betreffende de dwangsom, en van de Bijlage (eenvormige wet betreffende de dwangsom), ondertekend te 's-Gravenhage op 26 november 1973, *Parl.St.* Kamer 1977–78, n. 353, 16.

4.2.1.1. *Not a Criminal Charge*

Belgian and Dutch law do not internally qualify a penalty payment as a criminal sanction.[70] Nor can the conviction to or the recovery of a penalty payment be seen as a criminal charge in the sense of Article 6 ECHR. Firstly, it is doubtful whether or not a penalty payment is 'criminal'. When an infringement internally is not qualified as 'criminal', the infringement's nature and the severity of the sanction are of overriding importance.[71]

According to the infringement's nature, a penalty payment is not 'criminal'. The forfeiture of a penalty payment is, contrary to what some doctrine has defended, not caused by the breach of the general rule to obey a judgment.[72] As an additional sentence, the penalty is linked to the obligation, as determined in the principal sentence.[73] This obligation is made specific by the judge in the sentence and only affects the parties involved. It is the violation of this specific obligation that causes the forfeiture of the penalty payment.[74]

The severity of the sanction as well, does not seem to lead to the conclusion that a penalty payment is 'criminal'. The penalty payment as an additional suspended sentence is purely preventive. It is intended to cause the convicted party to voluntarily comply with the obligation as defined in the principal sentence. The penalty payment is not intended to be forfeited.[75] Only in case of noncompliance the sum of money payable could conceivably, depending on the amount, be qualified as 'criminal'.

Even if the severity of the sanction would lead to the conclusion that the penalty payment is 'criminal', this would not mean that the safeguards of Articles 6.2 and 6.3 ECHR are applicable. The applicability of these provisions demands not only that the penalty payment is 'criminal', but also that the requirement of a 'charge' is met.[76] In none of both senses in which the notion 'penalty payment' can be used, is the requirement of a 'charge' satisfied. In *Deweer v. Belgium* the ECHR defines a charge as: 'the official

70 Guldix 1980, p. 130, n. 3; Moreau-Margrève 1982, pp. 43–44; Jongbloed 1991, p. 3; Wagner 2003, p. 16, n. 15.

71 ECHR 8 June 1976, *Engel v. The Netherlands*, case ns. 5100/71; 5101/71; 5102/71; 5354/72; 5370/72, § 82; ECHR 21 February 1984, *Oztürk v. Germany*, case n. 8544/79, § 50; De Smet, Lathouwers & Rimanque 2004, pp. 410–414, ns. 65–72; Cauffman 2007, p. 850, n. 86.

72 Glansdorf 1980, p. 313; Gras 2007, p. 2006; Gras emphasizes that the High Court (Hoge Raad) explicitly ruled that a penalty payment is aimed at the compliance with a judicial order. Yet the High Court has in the arrest in question also referred to the concrete obligation as stated in the specific judicial order. The High Court wrote that the penalty payment is due not because of the noncompliance with the purchase agreement, but because of the noncompliance with the judicial order as given in the summary procedure. This judicial order consists in an obligation to collaborate on the legal delivery of the immovable property (HR 22 December 1989, *NJ* 1990, n. 434, 1695). Consequently a penalty payment is aimed at the compliance with the obligation as stipulated in the judicial order in question.; Kortmann & C. Sieburgh 2009, n. 2.5, in fine.

73 Ballon 1980, p. 20, n. 49; Jongbloed 1991, p. 17; Wagner 2003, p. 8, n. 8.

74 Moreau-Margrève 1982, p. 43; Beekhoven van den Boezem 2006, p. 67.

75 Planiol & Ripert 1931, p. 95, n. 793; Jongbloed 1991, pp. 19 and 21–24; Wagner 2003, p. 8, n. 7.

76 Boot 2008, p. 205; Cauffman seems to have lost sight of this second requirement to fall under the scope of Articles 6.2 and 6.3 ECHR. She only demands a private penalty to be 'criminal' to conclude the applicability of the guaranties of these articles; Cauffman 2007, pp. 849–850, n. 86.

notification given to an individual by the competent authority of an allegation that he has committed a criminal offence'.[77] The Court further clarifies that a charge comes into being from the moment 'the situation of the suspect is substantially affected'.[78] The conviction of a penalty payment has to be requested by the civil party and the latter also recovers the sum of money due in case of noncompliance. When a civil court pronounces a penalty payment, there is no prosecuting *authority*.[79]

4.2.1.2. A Private Penalty

Although not a criminal sanction, the doctrine attributes a punitive nature to a penalty payment next to a private nature. This legal concept is repeatedly described as a private penalty or civil fine.[80]

Wagner nuances this assertion by making a distinction between a penalty payment as an additional and suspended sentence, and a penalty payment as a sum of money payable. He is right not to question a penalty payment's private nature.[81] To justify this private nature, he correctly points out the fact that a judge can only order a penalty payment in case of an explicit request thereto by a private party[82], and that the forfeited penalty payment entirely falls to the party who obtained the conviction.[83] According to Wagner however, only the second sense in which the notion 'penalty payment' can be used has a punitive nature.

He argues that a penalty payment as an additional and suspended sentence is entirely unrelated to punishment, since the penalty payment is a means of applying pressure aimed at obtaining the voluntarily fulfilment of an obligation in kind, as a result of which the convicted party can always escape its forfeiture by complying with the principal sentence.[84] Nonetheless, in my opinion this argument does not suffice to reject the punitive nature altogether. The judge who pronounces a principal sentence subject to a penalty payment already lays down the amount due in case of noncompliance in the

77 ECHR 27 February 1980, *Deweer v. Belgium*, case n. 6903/75, § 46.

78 ECHR 27 February 1980, *Deweer v. Belgium*, case n. 6903/75, § 46.

79 Boot 2008, p. 205.

80 Cass. 24 January 1924, *Pas.* 1924, I, 151; Van Mullen 1977, pp. 42–43, ns. 38, 44 and 45; Ballon 1980, p. 24, n. 60; Glansdorf 1980, p. 312; Guldix 1980, pp. 130, 150 and 160, ns. 2, 33 and 45; Malengreau 1981, p. 2, n. 6; Moreau-Margrève 1982, p. 44; Fettweis 1987, p. 600; Vandermersch 1995, p. 236; Dirix & Broeckx 1996, p. 1402, n. 10; Dirix 1999, p. 49, n. 23; Chabas & Deis-Beauquesne 2005, n. 64.

81 Wagner 2003, p. 16, n. 15.

82 Belgian law; Article 1385*bis,* section 1, first sentence Judicial Code (Ger.W.); Dutch law; Article 611*a*, section 1, first sentence Code of Civil Procedure (Rv.); Guldix 1980, p. 148, n. 30; Malengreau 1981, p. 3, n.14; Moreau-Margrève 1982, p. 20; Fettweis 1987, p. 600, n. 950; Jongbloed 1991, p. 33; Wagner 2003, p. 21, n. 20.

83 Belgian law; Article 1385*quater* Judicial Code (Ger.W.); Dutch law; Article 611*c* Code on Civil Procedure (Rv.); Gemeenschappelijke memorie van toelichting van de Benelux Overeenkomst houdende eenvormige wet betreffende de dwangsom als bijlage bij Wetsontwerp houdende goedkeuring van de Benelux-Overeenkomst houdende eenvormige wet betreffende de dwangsom, en van de Bijlage (eenvormige wet betreffende de dwangsom), ondertekend te 's-Gravenhage op 26 november 1973, *Parl. St.* Kamer 1977–78, n. 353, p. 19; Guldix 1980, p. 153, n. 37; Moreau-Margrève 1982, p. 27; Wagner 1999, n. 84.

84 Wagner 2003, p. 17, n. 15.

additional and suspended sentence. He fixes this amount taking into account the expected resistance. Hereby the convicted party's earlier behaviour that signals this party's malicious intent, as well as his or her financial capacity, is at the centre.[85] The estimated damage the other party will suffer in case of noncompliance is not taken into account.[86] It is precisely the lack of any relation between the sanction's amount and the loss suffered by the victim that is characteristic of the punitive nature of a private penalty. The fact that the first notion in which a penalty payment can be used, as a consequence of its suspended character, only potentially ascribes an advantage to the victim of a wrongful conduct to the detriment of the wrongdoer, does not undermine this punitive nature in every respect. To point out the conditional nature of the advantage's attribution without denying its punitive character, a penalty payment as an additional and suspended sentence can best be described as a private measure with a potential punitive nature.

Evidently, the penalty payment as the sum of money due in case of noncompliance with the principal sentence, has a punitive nature. It is the wrongful conduct of the convicted party not to comply with the obligation as stipulated in the principal sentence that gives rise to the forfeiture of the penalty payment.[87] As described above, the amount due is unrelated to the damage the opposite party suffers. Accumulation of a penalty payment and compensatory damages is explicitly allowed by law.[88] It cannot be doubted that a penalty payment used in this sense has the nature of a private penalty.[89]

4.2.1.3. The Penalty Payment and the Enforcement of the Parents' Right to Contact

In 1982, the Benelux Court of Justice had already removed all possible doubts concerning the applicability of the penalty payment in family law. The Court clarified that in the case where a principal sentence concerns a family law obligation, a conviction applying a penalty payment is possible.[90] As mentioned above, the penalty payment is used in family law, among others,[91] to protect the parent-child relationship. It can be used

85 Gemeenschappelijke memorie van toelichting van de Benelux Overeenkomst houdende eenvormige wet betreffende de dwangsom als bijlage bij Wetsontwerp houdende goedkeuring van de Benelux-Overeenkomst houdende eenvormige wet betreffende de dwangsom, en van de Bijlage (eenvormige wet betreffende de dwangsom), ondertekend te 's-Gravenhage op 26 november 1973, *Parl.St.* Kamer 1977–78, n. 353, p. 16; Malengreau 1981, p. 3, n. 19; Moreau-Margrève 1982, p. 24 and 54; Jongbloed 1991, p. 36; Wagner 2001, p. 337; Wagner 2003, p. 23, n. 23.

86 Ballon 1980, p. 25, n. 61; Malengreau 1981, pp. 2 and 3, ns. 9 and 18; Moreau-Margrève 1982, p. 24; Fettweis 1987, p. 600, n. 950; Pouleau 1987, p. 202, n. 10; Wagner 2003, p. 12, n.12.

87 Van Mullen 1977, p. 42, n. 45.

88 Belgian law; Article 1385*bis*, section 1, first sentence, in fine Judicial Code (Ger.W.); Dutch law; Article 611*a*, section 1, first sentence Code of Civil Procedure (Rv.); Gemeenschappelijke memorie van toelichting van de Benelux Overeenkomst houdende eenvormige wet betreffende de dwangsom als bijlage bij Wetsontwerp houdende goedkeuring van de Benelux-Overeenkomst houdende eenvormige wet betreffende de dwangsom, en van de Bijlage (eenvormige wet betreffende de dwangsom), ondertekend te 's-Gravenhage op 26 november 1973, *Parl.St.* Kamer 1977–78, n. 353, p. 17; Van Mullen 1977, p. 42, n. 38; Ballon 1980, p. 23, n. 56; Guldix 1980, p. 150, n. 33; Malengreau 1981, p. 4, ns. 20 and 21; Wagner 1999, n. 83.

89 Moreau-Margrève 1982, p. 27; Wagner 2003, p. 17, n. 17.

90 Benelux Court of Justice 11 May 1982, *RW* 1982–1983, 290, concl. F. Dumon, note M. Storme.

91 See for other examples; Jongbloed 1991, pp. 82–89; Pouleau 1987, pp. 203–206; Senaeve 1999, pp. 85–98; Senaeve 2003, pp. 150–157; Wagner 2003, pp. 189–194, ns. 217–221; Compagnion 2005, pp. 70–73; Bunkens 2010, pp. 139–156, ns. 43–79.

posterior, as a means to empower a court order that obliges a parent to stop interfering with the other parent's parent-child relationship.[92] A preventive conviction of a penalty payment to guarantee compliance with the court regulation concerning the parents' right to contact with their child is possible as well.[93]

Contrary to criminal sanctions, the penalty payment is valued as a very effective means of enforcing the parents' right to contact with their child for the following reasons. Interference with the parent-child relationship is ended in the short-term, since the criminal procedural safeguards do not apply.[94] Consequently, the risk of manipulation of the child by the recalcitrant parent is, in comparison to the enforcement by means of criminal sanctions, significantly smaller. As well, the child suffers less financial consequences, than in the case of a conviction to pay a criminal fine to the government. A penalty payment's private character only results in a shift of capital from the recalcitrant parent to the victimized parent.[95] Both are responsible for raising the child, who has the right to participate in his or her parents' standard of living. Furthermore, the emotional burden a penalty payment causes to the child is limited. Contrary to a situation of the compulsory removal of a child, the penalty payment does not involve the latter directly in the conflict.[96] Finally, the possibility to convict preventively using a penalty payment gives the opportunity to prevent interference in the parent-child relationship.[97]

Only in cases where the recalcitrant parent has a low income could the effectiveness of the penalty payment be questioned.[98] The Belgian legislator was not indifferent to this criticism. Since the Act of 18 July 2006, a judge can grant a parent who obtains a conviction of the other parent to end the existing interference in the parent-child relationship under the punishment of a penalty payment, a permit to attach the convicted parent's entire earnings in case he refuses to pay the forfeited penalty payments.[99]

4.2.2. The Modification of the Violated Decision to the Advantage of the Victimized Parent

In cases where a parent interferes with the other parent's parent-child relationship through noncompliance with an existing custody and visitation order, the latter can request the competent civil court to modify the violated decision to his or her advantage.

92 Belgian law; Article 387*ter* Civil Code (BW); Pouleau 1987, p. 203, n. 14; Senaeve 1999, pp. 88–91; Bunkens 2010, p. 128, n. 17.

93 Pouleau 1987, p. 203, n. 14; Senaeve 1999, pp. 94–98; Pire 2007, p. 226, n. 65; Vanbockrijck 2007, p. 161, n. 274; Vanbockrijck 2008, p. 45, n. 27; Vanbockrijck 2009, p. 224, n. 290; Bunkens 2010, p. 128, n. 17.

94 Senaeve 1999, p. 88; Vanbockrijck 2007, p. 106, n. 273; Senaeve 2010, p. 127, n. 62.

95 Wagner 2003, pp. 189–190, n. 217.

96 Jongbloed 1991, p. 88; Senaeve 1999, p. 97; Wagner 2003, p. 189, n. 217; Vanbockrijck 2007, p. 161, n. 273; Bunkens 2010, p. 127, n. 14.

97 Pouleau 1987, p. 201, n. 3.

98 Vanbockrijck 2005, pp. 94–95, n. 4; De Boer 2010, p. 896.

99 Belgian law; Article 387*ter* Civil Code (BW); Martens 2006, p. 448; Aps 2006–07, p. 1432, n. 21; Dandoy & Reusens 2007, p. 187; Hiernaux 2007, pp. 56–57; Pire 2007, pp. 225–227, ns. 63–65; Vanbockrijck 2007, pp. 161–165, ns. 276–286; Vasseur 2007, p. 18, n. 18; Vanbockrijck 2008, p. 45, n. 28; Mareschal 2008, p. 71; Gallus 2009a, p. 219; Senaeve 2009, pp. 69–71, ns. 168–172; Vanbockrijck 2009, pp. 224–225, ns. 291–292; Senaeve 2010, pp. 128–130, ns. 66–71; Bunkens 2010, pp. 135–136, ns. 35–36.

This measure is considered to be a very effective means of coercion. The recalcitrant parent knows that the regulation concerning the parent's right to contact with their child could be reversed to his or her disadvantage in case he or she prevents all contact between the child and the other parent. This knowledge is believed to cause parents to reconsider their point of view concerning their willingness to comply with custody and visitation orders.[100]

The private character of this civil enforcement measure cannot be doubted. An explicit request of the victimized parent is needed for the court to be able to change the violated decision.[101] If requested, the court can reverse the regulation concerning the parent's right to contact with the child to the advantage of the victimized parent.[102]

On the other hand, this measure is only partially punitive. It is indeed wrongful behaviour not to comply with the custody and visitation order that triggers the possibility of modifying the violated court order. Nevertheless, Article 8 ECHR requires that the child's best interests are at the basis of the actual decision to reverse the existing regulation.[103] This measure can therefore best be described as a private one with a partially punitive nature. Hence, the fact that it is the wrongdoer's behaviour that instigates the possibility to change the violated decision is not being denied. Besides, it is made clear that defending this measure's purely[104] punitive nature would imply a violation of Article 8 ECHR.

4.2.3. The Reduction or Dismissal of the Recalcitrant Parent's Maintenance

Under Dutch law, a third civil enforcement measure that implies the attribution of an advantage to the victimized parent has become established. The noncompliance with a custody and visitation order can, as a non-financial factor, lead to the reduction or dismissal of the recalcitrant parent's alimony. In case of interference with the parent-child relationship by noncompliance with a court regulation, the court examines whether this wrongful behaviour is so serious as to justify in all reasonableness the reduction or

100 Wetsvoorstel tot wijziging van het Burgerlijk Wetboek en het Gerechtelijk Wetboek om de afdwingbaarheid van de persoonlijke omgang met de kinderen bij de echt- of feitelijke scheiding te verbeteren, *Parl.St.* Senaat 2003–04, n. 3–833/001, p. 4; Wetsvoorstel teneinde de afdwingbaarheid van de persoonlijke omgang met de kinderen naar aanleiding van een echt- of feitelijke scheiding te verbeteren, *Parl.St.* Kamer 2004–05, n. 51–1288/001, p. 5; Verslag namens de subcommissie familierecht over het wetsontwerp tot het bevoorrechten van een gelijkmatig verdeelde huisvesting van het kind van wie de ouders gescheiden zijn en tot regeling van de gedwongen tenuitvoerlegging inzake huisvesting van het kind, *Parl.St.* Kamer 2005–06, n. 51 1673/014, p. 30.

101 Hiernaux 2007, p. 50; Senaeve 2010, p. 124, n. 49.

102 Belgian law; Article 387*ter* BW; Dutch law; De Boer 2010, p. 897.

103 ECHR 28 September 2004, *Sabou and Pircalab v. Romania*, case n. 46572/99, § 47; Van Der Burght & Doek 2002, p. 593; Dandoy & Reusens 2007, p. 187; Hiernaux 2007, p. 51; Vanbockrijck 2007, p. 176, n. 312; Vasseur 2007, p. 17, n. 16; Vanbockrijck 20008, p. 48, n. 34; Vanbockrijck 2009, pp. 227–228, n. 298; De Boer 2010, p. 897.

104 Massager seems to defend that the noncompliance with a custody and visitation order should as a general rule lead to the change of the violated decision in the advantage of the victimized parent; Massager 2006, p. 499.

dismissal of the recalcitrant parent's maintenance.[105] Outlining the fact that it is the wrongdoer's behaviour which underlies this civil measure, at the same time bearing in mind that not every noncompliance will lead to the dismissal or reduction of the recalcitrant parent's maintenance, this measure can best be described as a potential private penalty.

Although under Belgian law changed circumstances can cause a judge to revise the amount of the parent's maintenance,[106] misconduct is usually not classed as changed circumstances.[107] Nevertheless, such an interpretation would be preferable.

Both the penalty payment as well as the reduction or dismissal of the recalcitrant parent's maintenance affect the latter's financial capital. The revision of the parent's maintenance has the advantage that the victimized parent is not dependent on the recalcitrant parent's willingness to pay, or his or her quantity of attachable goods. The victimized parent can simply deduct a part of the other parent's maintenance. However, this civil enforcement measure could only be used in case the victimized parent is under the obligation to pay maintenance to the other parent. Consequently, other effective measures remain indispensable.

4.3. *Desirability to Expand the Use of Private Penalties as a means of Enforcing the Parents' Right to Contact*

4.3.1. The Penalty Clause

4.3.1.1. Definition and Functions

A penalty clause can be defined as a stipulation in a contract, holding an accessory obligation in case of noncompliance with the principal commitment. Such an undertaking can be made by a debtor for the sake of two causes. Firstly, a penalty clause can avoid future disputes concerning the existence and the dimensions of the damage suffered in consequence of contractual breach. It consists in a previously fixed determination of the damage and therefore alleviates the creditor's burden of proof. In that case, the penalty clause has a compensatory function. Subsequently, the penalty clause can be used to encourage the debtor to voluntarily comply with the principal obligation. The prospect of a sanction in case of contractual breach, urges the debtor to fulfil his or her principal commitment; hence, the penalty clause functions as a coercive clause.[108]

105 Article 1:157, section 1 and 1:401 Dutch Civil Code (NBW); Rb. Den Bosch 10 November 2000, *FJR* 2001, 86; Rb. Leeuwarden 9 July 2008, LJN BD6634, *www.rechtspraak.nl*; De Boer 2010, p. 897.

106 Belgian law; Article 301, § 7 Civil Code (BW).

107 Only Swennen and Weyts qualify misconduct as a new circumstance; Swennen 2010, p. 475, n. 809; Swennen & B. Weyts 2010, p. 129, n. 60.

108 Toelichting bij het wetsvoorstel tot wijziging, wat het strafbeding en de moratoire interest betreft, van het Burgerlijk Wetboek, *Parl.St.* Kamer 1997–98, n. 49 1373/1, pp. 1–2; Goegebeur 2001, p. 401, ns. 2–3; Stijns 2001–02, p. 1270, nr. 28; Schelhaas 2004, p. 5; Hartkamp & Sieburgh 2008, p. 319.

4.3.1.2. *Divergence between the Belgian and the Dutch System*

Belgian law has always been very averse towards a penalty clause's coercive function. Before the Act of 23 November 1998,[109] a penalty clause was, according to the Court of Cassation's decree of 17 April 1970,[110] exclusively allowed to consist in a compensation for the damage caused by a breach of contract. In case the stipulated obligation exceeded the damage predictable at the time of the entering into the contract and made noncompliance more attractive to the creditor then the fulfilment of the contract, the clause was believed to harm the public order. Pure coercive, as well as mixed coercive and compensatory penalty clauses, were therefore null and void. While evaluating the exclusive compensatory nature of a stipulated clause, the parties' intention was not essential. The judge's objective finding that the agreed amount went beyond the damage predictable at the time of entering into the contract was sufficient to make the clause invalid.[111] The Court of Cassation's decree provoked criticism, both on the basis of an exegetic study of the provisions of the civil code concerning the penalty clause,[112] as well as by virtue of the denial of the idea that private penalties are contrary to the public order.[113] In spite of this, the legislature perpetuated the aversion to the penalty clause's coercive function by the Act of 23 November 1998.[114] Since then, a penalty clause is defined as 'a stipulation holding an obligation in case of noncompliance with the principal commitment, to pay a fixed compensation for the damage the creditor could suffer as a result of the noncompliance with the principal obligation'.[115] By contrast, the Act of 23 November 1998 substituted the nullity of an illicit penalty clause, as introduced by the Court of Cassation's decree of 17 April 1970, with a judge's power to moderate the agreed compensation. In case the accessory obligation manifestly exceeds the damage predictable at the time of the entering into the contract, a judge has the obligation[116] to moderate the agreed sum of money. Hereby he or she is not allowed to attribute a compensation award lower than the actual damage suffered.[117] There is some uncertainty about the interaction

109 Act 23 November 1998 towards a change of the civil code concerning the penalty clause and the moratory interest, *BS* 13 January 1999, 00901.

110 Cass. 17 April 1970, *Arr. Cass.* 1970, 754, concl. E. Krings and *RCJB* 1972, 454, note I. Moreau-Margrève; confirmed in among others Cass. 24 November 1972, *Arr. Cass.* 1973, 302; Cass. 8 February 1974, *Arr. Cass.* 1974, 624; Cass. 2 December 1983, *Arr. Cass.* 1983–84, 398; Cass. 21 November 1985, *Arr. Cass.* 1991–92, 404; Cass. 28 November 1991, *Arr. Cass.* 1991–92, 282; Cass. 3 February 1995, *Arr. Cass.* 1995, 130.

111 Moreau-Margrève 1972, pp. 462–463 and 472–478; E. Wymeersch 1982, pp. 428–429; Delforge 1999, pp. 598–599; Schelhaas 2000, pp. 303-306; Samoy 2001, p. 351, n. 17; Goegebeur 2001–02, p. 404, ns. 11–12.

112 Moreau-Margrève 1972, pp. 479–481; Van Ryn 1980, pp. 557–558, ns. 1–5; Vansweevelt 1984, pp. 2470–2474, ns. 6–9. *Contra*: E. Wymeersch 1982, pp. 430–431.

113 Moreau-Margrève 1972, pp. 496–498; Moreau-Margrève 1976, p. 641.

114 Act 23 November 1998 towards a change of the civil code concerning the penalty clause and the moratory interest, *BS* 13 January 1999, 00901.

115 Article 1226 Belgian Civil Code (BW) (translation).

116 Article 1231, § 1 Belgian Civil Code states that a judge *'can'* moderate. However, since a private penalty is still considered to be contrary to the public order, a judge has the obligation to moderate in case he finds a penalty clause excessive. In that sense see; Delforge 1999, p. 610; Goegebeur 2001, p. 408, n. 24. *Contra*: Cornelis 2000, p. 14, n. 25; Moreau-Margrève 2000, p. 204.

117 Article 1231, § 2 Belgian Civil Code (BW).

between the definition given in Article 1226 of the Belgian civil code and the judge's power to moderate. Goegebeur even states that moderation is never possible. This author defends his statement, by the fact that the analysis of the penalty clause's validity always precedes the evaluation of its excessive character. Either the agreed amount exceeds the damage predictable at the time of the entering into the contract, as a result of which the clause is invalid, or there is no overrunning of the predictable damage, in which case there is no reason to moderate.[118] To overcome this deadlock, Samoy distinguishes clauses with some compensatory aim from clauses completely foreign to compensation. According to Samoy, both pure compensatory as well as mixed compensatory and coercive penalty clauses, fall under the scope of a penalty clause's definition. By contrast, pure coercive clauses do not answer to the definition of a penalty clause. They still are believed to harm the public order, as a result of which they are, according to Article 6 of the Belgian civil code, null and void. The author sees the power to moderate as a particular application of this article. She believes the moderation amounts to the partial nullification of the penalty clause. Only the part that holds a private penalty will be declared null and void. The penalty clause will be reduced to the damage predictable at the time of the entering into the contract.[119] Since the coercive function is still believed to be contrary to the public order, this position is preferable to Goegebeur's ineffective statement.

Under Dutch law, a penalty clause is considered to be valid, regardless of the clause's function.[120] Since parties usually do not pay the same attention to a penalty clause as to the principal stipulation's content and the penalty clause is often the result of an unequal negotiation position, excesses are considered to be likely.[121] To counteract these excesses, the legislature has given judges the power to moderate and supplement the agreed amount on the parties' explicit request, when fairness manifestly so requires.[122] Whereas the judicial review under Belgian law presupposes an *ex ante* comparison with the damage predictable at the time of the entering into the contract, under Dutch law a judge has to make an *ex post* comparison. Numerous factual circumstances,[123] which can be located at the time of entering into the contract, as well as from the breach of contract until the judge's intervention, will lead the judge in his decision to moderate or to supplement. To prevent the *de facto* undermining of a coercive penalty clause's fundamental validity, the court should, however, be cautious when assessing the necessity to moderate or supplement the agreed amount. The agreed amount can at the most be supplemented till the actual damage suffered. With regard to the moderation, Article 6:94 of the Dutch civil code states that the same limit applies. However, the actual damage

118 Goegebeur 2001, pp. 408 and 410, ns. 23 and 32.

119 Samoy 2001, pp. 352–353, ns. 19–22; in the same sense see; Baeck 2004, pp. 23–24, n. 28; Schelhaas 2004, pp. 184–187.

120 Article 6:91 Dutch Civil Code (NBW); under the civil code of 1838 a penalty clauses double function was affirmed by the High Court (Hoge Raad); HR 2 February 1922, *NJ* 1922, 379.

121 Schelhaas 2004, p. 69.

122 Article 6:94 Dutch Civil Code.

123 Among others: the ratio between the actual damage suffered and the agreed penalty, the contract's nature, the clause's purpose and the circumstances surrounding the appeal to the clause, the debtor's behaviour, the way the contract came about, the financial position of the parties, the relation between the parties, the coercive or compensative function, the advantage and disadvantage experienced as a consequence of the breach of contract.

suffered only limits the moderation in case of a pure compensatory penalty clause. A pure coercive penalty clause does not affect the right to compensation of the damage suffered and could therefore theoretically be moderated to zero. However, a systematic moderation of this kind of penalty clause would erode the recognition of a penalty clause's coercive function. The same opposes the automatic moderation of a mixed compensatory and coercive penalty clause to the actual damage suffered. Consequently, the right way is to moderate till the amount no longer conflicts with the evident fairness.[124]

4.3.1.3. Refutation of the Belgian Arguments against a Penalty Clause's Coercive Function

The Belgian resistance to a penalty clause's coercive function is threefold.

Firstly, coercive penalty clauses are believed to impinge upon the legislature's monopoly to punish and therefore are considered to harm the public order.[125] This legislature's monopoly, also referred to as '*nullum crimen, nulle poena sine lege*', is incorporated in Article 7§1 ECHR,[126] as well as in Article 14 of the Belgian Constitution.

The terms 'criminal offence' and 'penalty' used in Article 7§1 ECHR, ought to be interpreted in the same way as the term 'criminal charge' used in Article 6 ECHR.[127] By no means does a coercive penalty clause answer to the definition of a 'criminal charge' in the sense of Article 6 ECHR.[128] Like a penalty payment, a penalty clause does not meet the requisite of a 'charge'. The penalty clause's accessory obligation is agreed by the parties. In no way can one argue that there is a prosecuting authority. Nor can a penalty clause be qualified as 'criminal'. As to the nature of the offence, the ECHR confirmed in *Blake v. United Kingdom*, that when an obligation to pay a sum of money is directly based on a breach of contract, the cause of action is civil by nature.[129] The agreed penalty is not due because of the violation of a rule with a general scope. It is the noncompliance with the principal obligation as stipulated in the contract that gives rise to the owing of the accessory obligation. This principal commitment is only directed towards the parties involved. With regard to the severity of the penalty, it should be mentioned that a penalty clause's accessory obligation is mainly intended to encourage the debtor to voluntarily comply with the principal stipulation. However, this preventive function requires that

124 Schelhaas 2004, pp. 80–105; Hartkamp & Sieburgh 2008, pp. 318–331.

125 Amendement (Landuyt) bij het wetsvoorstel tot wijziging, wat het strafbeding en de moratoire interest betreft, van het Burgerlijk Wetboek, *Parl.St.* Kamer 1997–98, n. 49 1373/2, p. 2; Concl. E. Krings along with Cass. 17 April 1970, *Arr. Cass.* 1970, (755) 756, n. 3; Goegebeur 2001, p. 405, n. 14.

126 ECHR 25 May 1993, *Kokkinakis v. Greece*, case n. 14307/88, § 52.

127 ECHR 8 June 1976, *Engel and Others v. Netherlands*, case ns. 5100/71; 5101/71; 5102/71; 5354/72; 5370/72, § 81; ECHR 7 July 1989, *Tre Traktörer Aktiebolag v. Sweden*, case n. 10873/84, § 46; ECHR 9 February 1995, *Welch v. United Kingdom*, case n. 17440/90, § 27; Cromheecke & Dhont 2004, p. 667, n. 15.

128 In the same sense see Schelhaas 2004, p. 440; Cauffman 2007, p. 847, n. 78.

129 ECHR 26 September 2006, *Blake v. United Kingdom*, case n. 68890/01, § 98; In this case the sum of money payable were restitutionary damages. Such damages are measured by reference to the profits gained by the wrongdoer, and are like coercive penalty clauses foreign to the loss suffered by the victim.

the penalty agreed by the parties is due, in case the penalty clause fails in its coercive function.[130] When debtors agree to coercive penalty clauses, and they themselves decide not to fulfil the principal obligations they agreed to as well, the severity of the sanctions cannot, in my opinion, make the coercive penalty clauses 'criminal'.[131] This counts all the more when a judge has the power to moderate the penalty due, taking into account the factual circumstances from the moment of the breach of contract until the court's decision, till the penalty no longer conflicts with the evident fairness. Article 7§1 ECHR therefore does not prevent a coercive penalty clause.

Despite the fact that a coercive penalty clause does not imply a criminal penalty, it can be qualified as a private measure with a potential punitive nature. In cases where the contractual penalty is due, it is payable to the creditor. Consequently, its private nature is indisputable. Due to its coercive nature, the penalty agreed to in the contract exceeds the damage suffered by the creditor. It is fear of the penalty that should discourage a breach of contract.[132] Therefore a coercive penalty clause also has a punitive nature. However, the penalty is merely 'provisionally' forced upon the debtor. Only in case prevention fails, the agreed penalty will be due.[133] As a (potential) private penalty, a coercive penalty clause does not harm the constitutionally established legislature's monopoly to punish. Article 14 of the Belgian Constitution is intended to protect individuals against arbitrary actions taken by the executive or judicial power. It is in no way aimed at a contract between two private individuals.[134]

Secondly, only the legislature is to determine the rules concerning the enforcement of an individual's rights.[135] This argument is not convincing. A coercive penalty clause limits itself to encouraging the debtor to voluntarily comply with the principal stipulation. It does not give the creditor a right to the compulsory execution of the principal commitment. Consequently, a penalty clause does not detract from the laws concerning the enforcement of contractual rights.[136]

Finally, a coercive penalty clause is believed to be contrary to the *bona mores* principle, for in cases of noncompliance the penalty is payable to the creditor, as a result of which he enriches himself. The creditor is deemed to have a larger interest in a breach of contract than in compliance with the principal obligation. Consequently, there would be a risk that the creditor speculates on the debtor's breach of contract and encourages him or her not to fulfil the principal obligation.[137] The creditor's enrichment is considered to be

130 Schelhaas 2004, pp. 440–441.

131 The voluntarily acceptance of the penalty in the contract is also highlighted by Schelhaas 2004, p. 439.

132 Moreau-Margrève 2000, pp. 199–200.

133 Delforge 1999, p. 623; Moreau-Margrève 2000, pp. 199–200; Schelhaas 2004, p. 441; Schelhaas calls the punitive nature a necessary consequence of its preventive function.

134 Moreau-Margrève 1972, p. 496; Moreau-Margrève 2000, pp. 194–195; Goegebeur 2001–02, p. 410, n. 30.

135 Concl. E. Krings along with Cass. 17 April 1970, *Arr. Cass.* 1970, (755) 756, n. 3.

136 Moreau-Margrève 1972, pp. 496–497.

137 Amendement (Landuyt) bij het wetsvoorstel tot wijziging, wat het strafbeding en de moratoire interest betreft, van het Burgerlijk Wetboek, *Parl.St.* Kamer 1997–98, n. 49 1373/2, p. 3; Concl. E. Krings along with Cass. 17 April 1970, *Arr. Cass.* 1970, (755) 757, n.6.

unjustified[138] and to be contrary to the principle that contracts ought to be executed.[139] However, it should be underlined that the precise aim of a coercive penalty clause is the punctual execution of the contract. It leaves the debtor's choice to comply with the principal obligation untouched.[140] Besides, the penalty will not be due in cases where the breach of contract is caused by an act the creditor is accountable for.[141] Accordingly, a coercive penalty clause does not harm the principle that contracts ought to be executed. Furthermore, the enrichment does find a justification in the preventive function a coercive penalty clause strives for.[142] In order for the penalty clause to have a preventive effect, it is necessary that the debtor is under the obligation to pay the agreed amount in case of noncompliance with the principal obligation. Moreover, the attribution of the amount to the creditor is needed. Otherwise most creditors will not be inclined to include a coercive penalty clause in a contract, as a result of which this legal concept will lose its effectiveness. Finally, the creditor's enrichment finds its cause in the contract itself.[143]

4.3.1.4. *The Desired Penalty Clause in Private Law in General*

The potential punitive nature cannot be put forward as an argument against a coercive penalty clause's validity. Self-determination is the point of departure in private law. Therefore, in principle parties should be allowed to encourage the punctual execution of their contractual obligations, by holding out the prospect of a penalty in case of noncompliance.[144] The acceptance of such a penalty clause comes in fact down to the privatisation of the penalty payment. Given that an increased possibility for excesses is intrinsic[145] to a penalty clause's coercive function, the granting of a power to moderate or supplement after the Dutch model, is preferable. Such *ex post* comparison has the advantage of being a solution tailored to all the factual circumstances of the breach of contract. A judicial review preceding the entering into the contract is therefore, unlike Delforge[146] suggested, not by any means indispensable. In addition, the Dutch system has the advantage of working with one regulation for both the compensatory, as well as the coercive penalty clause. It is often not clear which of the two functions is intended; frequently parties strive for both.[147] It is therefore preferable to use the same system for both kinds of penalty clauses. Consequently, the accumulation of the penalty payment on the one hand and the principal commitment's forced execution should as a general rule of permissive law be prohibited. In case parties intend the compensatory function,

138 Delforge 1999, p. 595.
139 Schelhaas 2004, p. 448.
140 Moreau-Margrève 1972, p. 493; Schelhaas 2004, p. 448.
141 Van Gerven & Covemaeker 2006, p. 171.
142 Moreau-Margrève 1976, p. 641.
143 Cauffman 2007, pp. 854–855, ns. 95 and 97.
144 Toelichting bij het wetsvoorstel tot wijziging, wat het strafbeding en de moratoire interest betreft, van het Burgerlijk Wetboek, *Parl.St.* Kamer 1997–98, n. 49 1373/1, p. 3; Moreau-Margrève 1976, p. 641; Cornelis 2000, pp. 13–14, n. 24.
145 Schelhaas 2004, pp. 431–436.
146 Delforge 1999, pp. 600–601.
147 Goegebeur 2001, p. 401, n. 4.

this prohibition applies, whereas parties purposing a coercive penalty clause contractually agree on the allowance of the abovementioned accumulation. An exception to the general rule should, however, be made for a penalty clause directed at the delayed execution, as well as for an on-going contract involving a series of obligations.[148]

4.3.1.5. The Penalty Clause in Family Law

Also in family law, a penalty clause could be very advantageous. Concerning the right to contact between parents and their child, only the penalty payment is currently apt to prevent interference by one parent with the other parent's parent-child relationship by noncompliance with a custody and visitation order. Nevertheless, judges are rather cautious when confronted with a parent's request to preventively convict the other parent with a penalty payment to guarantee compliance with the court regulation.[149] They require a well-founded fear of interference in the parent-child relationship.[150] This fear will not be present, in case the court regulation is based on an agreement between the parents. However, even in the case of divorce by mutual consent, problems of noncompliance have been found to occur.[151] When parents are given the opportunity to agree on custody and visitation under the condition that their agreement does not manifestly harm the child's best interests,[152] they should also have the opportunity to agree on a penalty in case of noncompliance with their understanding. In fact, the agreement consists of a series of successive obligations to respect the other parent's parent-child relationship. Accessory to each of these separated obligations, the penalty clause is added. In case of noncompliance with one of these obligations, the penalty is due. This does not end the victimized parent's right to demand execution of the successive obligations. Regardless of the penalty's largeness, a penalty clause can, at the time of entering into the contract, not be contrary to the child's best interests. When the regulation itself respects the child's best interests, its enforcement also does.[153] However, it is possible that the penalty's largeness could cause unfair consequences for the recalcitrant parent or the child after noncompliance. In that case, moderation is appropriate. Obviously, accepting the coercive function's validity does not end the possibility of modifying the custody and visitation regulations, when required by the child's best interests.[154]

Also, to reach enforcement of other family law obligations, a coercive penalty clause could be an effective means. For instance, when a former husband and wife agree on the

148 Dutch law; Articles 6:85 and 6:87 Civil Code (NBW); Schelhaas 2004, pp. 265–266.

149 Seneave 1998, n. 29; Senaeve 1999, p. 95.

150 Bergen 22 June 1999, *TBBR* 2001, 53; refusal to convict to a penalty payment because of the lack of any fear; Senaeve 2003, pp. 151–153, ns. 6 and 9; Bunkens 2010, pp. 126–127, n. 14.

151 Wetsvoorstel tot het waarborgen van het omgangsrecht tussen ouders en kinderen en tussen grootouders en kleinkinderen, *Parl.St.* Kamer 2003–04, n. 51 0976/001, p. 5.

152 Belgian law; Articles 374, § 2 and 387bis Civil Code (BW); Articles 1290, section 2 and 5, 1293, section 5 and 1298 Judicial Code (Ger.W.).

153 See in the same way concerning the child's best interests and the penalty payment; Senaeve 2003, pp. 152–153, n. 7.

154 Belgian law; Article 387*bis* Civil Code (BW); Article 1288 Judicial Code (Ger.W.).

maintenance one has to pay to the other, an amount of interest owing in case of delayed payment could form an effective means of convincing the debtor to correctly execute his or her obligation. There are no convincing arguments to deal with such a penalty clause in a different way than a penalty clause holding an obligation to pay a sum of money, as is done under current Belgian law.[155] Consequently, a high interest rate should be valid. Factors, such as the deliberate failure to correctly comply with the obligation, the intended function and the financial consequences, could in case the interest is due, all possibly lead to moderation.

Accepting the coercive penalty clause's validity does not however mean family members are entirely free to contract no matter which family law obligation. As a consequence of a penalty clause's accessory character, its validity is subordinated to the principal stipulation's legitimacy. For that reason, cohabiting partners can for instance not agree on a penalty in case of adultery. An obligation to be faithful consists in a restriction of these partners' individual freedom and is therefore contrary to the public order.[156] By contrast, husband and wife can indeed agree on a penalty in case of adultery. The mutual obligation to be faithful is incorporated in the law.[157] The penalty is in no way contrary to the generally accepted prohibition to use physical force.[158] It is in first instance directed to make the husband and spouse voluntarily abandon adultery. In case the penalty clause's preventive effect fails, the possibility to divorce is left untouched. In the same way, an obligation to pay a penalty in case a spouse petitions for a divorce without prior counselling, seems valid. The couple maintains its right to divorce. Yet, the obligation to present the dispute to a third person before suing for a divorce may not include the commitment to obey that person's remarks. The spouses' marital state is as a consequence of its public order character not at their disposal.[159] On the contrary, an obligation to pay a penalty in case of divorce is not valid. Such a penalty clause would harm the husband's and wife's right to end their marriage.[160]

5. Conclusion on the Enforcement in Family Law by means of Private Penalties

In the Netherlands, a clear evolution towards the enforcement by means of private penalties can already be found in the domain of private law in general. A penalty clause is in principal valid, irrespective of its function. In the domain of family law, private penalties are an established phenomenon as well. Both the penalty payment, and the reduction or dismissal of the recalcitrant parent's maintenance are common measures, used to end and/or prevent interference in the parent-child relationship. Although there

155 Belgian law; Article 1153 Civil Code (BW); Wéry even calls the distinction made an *inelegatia iuris,* that escaped the legislature's attention; Wéry 2001, n. 56.

156 Rb. Brugge 9 April 2001, *RW* 2002–03, 1552; Herbots 1992, p. 104, n. 153; Swennen 2010, p. 502, n. 862.

157 Belgian law; Article 213 Civil Code (BW).

158 Swennen 2010, p. 427, n. 713.

159 Tilleman *et al.* 2000, pp. 330 and 334, ns. 679 and 689.

160 Verslag namens de subcommissie familierecht bij het wetsontwerp betreffende de hervorming van de echtscheiding, *Parl.St.* Kamer 2005–06, n. 51 2341/007, p. 9.

are no convincing reasons why a penalty clause should not be used for the purpose of enforcing family law obligations, the Dutch case law shows that the penalty clause does not yet seem to be used frequently in the enforcement of family law obligations. Only marriage settlements with regard to the division of the matrimonial property, or other property law contracts between spouses, include penalty clauses.[161]

Belgium, on the other hand, still concurs with the traditional continental European Civil Law perspective on private penalties. Nonetheless, the state's role in enforcing family law rights is being questioned. Public enforcement measures are considered to be ineffective. Consequently, the Belgian legislator is also developing private measures, of which the potential, or at the least the partial punitive nature, can no longer be doubted.

There are by no means arguments to obstruct the continually increasing autonomy in family law to result in a rising role for family members in the enforcement of their family law obligations. Family members should be given the possibility to agree on a penalty in case of violation of a family law obligation. The public order will determine the limits of such a penalty's validity. Only in case the principal obligation does not harm public order will a penalty clause be valid. This allows the penalty clause's validity to evolve in the same way as the concept 'public order' and consequently to follow the increasing autonomy in family law.

161 HR 2 March 2001, LNJ AB0382, *www.rechtspraak.nl*; HR 16 November 2001, LNJ AD3990, *www.rechtspraak.nl*.

Bibliography

Adriaanse *et al.* 2008
Adriaanse, P.C., Barkhuysen, T., den Houdijker, E.M.J. & Zippro, E.J., 'Het EVRM-kader voor invoering van *punitive damages* in mededingingszaken. Europese toestanden in het schadevergoedingsrecht?', *NTBR*, 2008, pp. 274–286.

Aps 2006
Aps, F., 'De wet van 18 juli 2006: promotie van het gelijkmatig verdeeld verblijf voor kinderen van gescheiden ouders en optimalisering van de uitvoeringsmaatregelen tegen de onwillige ouder(s)', *RW*, 2006, pp. 1422–1433.

Baeck 2004
Baeck, J., 'Strafbedingen', in: I. Claeys (ed.), *Contractenrecht in beweging*, Mechelen: Kluwer, 2004, pp. 1–33.

Ballon 1980
Ballon, G.L., 'Dwangsom' in: *APR*, Gent: Story-Scientia, 1980.

Beekhoven van den Boezem 2006
Beekhoven van den Boezem, M.B., *De dwangsom in het burgerlijk recht*, Deventer: Kluwer, 2006.

Boot 2008
Boot, J., 'Privaatrecht & boete', *Ars Aequi*, 2008, pp. 200–208.

Brooke 2009
Brooke, H., 'A Brief Introduction: The Origins of Punitive Damages', in: H. Koziol & V. Wilcox (eds.), *Punitive Damages: Common Law and Civil Law Perspectives*, Vienna: Springer, 2009, pp. 1–3.

Bunkens 2010
Bunkens, M., 'Ontwikkelingen inzake de dwangsom in het personen- en familierecht 2000–2010', in: p. Senaeve & J. Du Mongh (eds.), Brugge: die Keure, 2010, pp. 119–157.

Cauffman 2007
Cauffman, C., 'Naar een punitief Europees verbintenissenrecht? Een rechtsvergelijkende studie naar de draagwijdte, de (grond)wettigheid en de wenselijkheid van het bestraffend karakter van het verbintenissenrecht', *TPR*, 2007, pp. 799–873.

Chabas & Deis-Beauquesne 2005
Chabas, F. & Deis-Beauquesne, S., 'Astreintes', in: E. Savaux (ed.), *Répertoire de droit civil*, II, Paris, Dalloz, 2005.

Compagnion 2005
Compagnion, B., 'L'astreinte et le droit de la famille', *Divorce*, 2005, pp. 69–74.

Cornelis 1989
Cornelis, L., *Beginselen van het Belgische buitencontractueel aansprakelijkheidsrecht*, Antwerpen: Maklu, 1989.

Cornelis 2000
Cornelis, L., 'Lief zijn voor het verbintenissenrecht (over het virtuele strafbeding)', *TBH*, 2000, pp. 5–22.

Cromheecke & Dhont 2004
Cromheecke, M. & Dhont, F., 'Art. 7. Geen straf zonder wet', in: J. Vande Lanotte & Y. Haeck (eds.), *Handboek EVRM*, II, *Artikelsgewijze Commentaar*, I, Antwerpen: Intersentia, 2004, pp. 653–703.

Dandoy & Reusens 2007
Dandoy, N. & Reusens, F., 'L'hébergement égalitaire', *JT*, 2007, pp. 177–188.

De Boer 2010
De Boer, J., 'Personen- en familierecht' in: *Mr. C. Assers Handleiding tot de beoefening van het Nederlands Burgerlijk Recht*, Deventer: Kluwer, 2010.

Dekkers & Verbeke 2007
Dekkers, R. & Verbeke, A., *Handboek burgerlijk recht*, III, *Verbintenissen-Bewijsleer-Gebruikelijke contracten*, Antwerpen: Intersentia, 2007.

Delforge 1999
Delforge, C., 'Entre prudence et audace... Réflexions sur la récente modification des dispositions du Code civil relatives à la clause pénale et aux intérêts moratoires', *Rev Not b*, 1999, pp. 594–624.

De Nauw 1978
De Nauw, A., 'Bedenkingen over de hiërarchie van de waarden in het bijzonder strafrecht', *RW*, 1978, pp. 626–654.

De Nauw 2005
De Nauw, A., *Inleiding tot het bijzonder strafrecht*, Mechelen: Kluwer, 2005.

De Smet 2007
De Smet, B., 'Niet-afgifte van kinderen', in: A. Vandeplas *et al.* (eds.), *Strafrecht en strafvordering. Artikelsgewijze commentaar met overzicht van rechtspraak en rechtsleer*, Antwerpen: Kluwer, 2007.

De Smet 2008
De Smet, B., 'Niet-afgifte van kinderen door vader of moeder', in: CBR (ed.), *Verblijfsregeling*, Antwerpen: Intersentia, 2008, pp. 183–209.

De Smet 2010
De Smet, B., *Jeugdbeschermingsrecht in hoofdlijnen*, Antwerpen: Intersentia, 2010.

De Smet, Lathouwers & Rimanque 2004
De Smet, B., Lathouwers, J. & Rimanque, K., 'Artikel 6, §1 EVRM', in: J. Vande Lanotte & Y. Haeck (eds.), *Handboek EVRM*, II, *Artikelsgewijze Commentaar*, I, Antwerpen: Intersentia, 2004, pp. 386–518.

De Wit 2006
De Wit, J., 'Omgangsrecht wordt beter afdwingbaar', *Juristenkrant*, 2006, nr. 127, p. 5.

Dirix 1999
Dirix, E., 'Executieproblemen met betrekking tot de dwangsom', in: Jura Falconis Libri (ed.), *De Dwangsom*, Leuven: Jura Falconis V.Z.W., 1999, pp. 37–60.

Dirix & Broeckx 1996
Dirix, E. & Broeckx, K., 'Overzicht van rechtspraak beslagrecht 1991–1996', *TPR*, 1996, pp. 1391–1552.

Dobbs 2000
Dobbs, D.B., *The law of torts*, St. Paul: West Group, 2000.

Dobbs 1991
Dobbs, S.M., 'Tort Recovery for Intentional Interference with Custodial Rights in Minnesota', *Wm Mitchell L Rev*, 1991, pp. 1159–1189.

Feinberg & Loeb 1994
Feinberg, J. M. & Loeb, L. S., 'Custody and Visitation Interference: Alternative Remedies', *J Am Acad Matrimonial Law*, 1994, pp. 271–284.

Fettweis 1987
Fettweis, A., *Manuel de procédure civile*, Liège: Faculté de droit de Liège, 1987.

Galligan 2009
Galligan, T.C., 'Foreword: Punitive Damages Today and Tomorrow', *La L Rev*, 2009, pp. 411–420.

Gallus 2009a
Gallus, N., 'L'exécution forcée en nature des obligations de faire (art. 387*ter* C. civ.)', in: F. Georges (ed.), *Actualités en droit de l'exécution forcée*, Liège: Anthemis, 2009, pp. 207–226.

Gallus 2009b
Gallus, N., *Le droit de la filiation. Rôle de la vérité socio-affective et de la volonté en droit belge*, Brussels: Larcier, 2009.

Garner 1987
Garner, B.A., *A dictionary of modern legal usage*, Oxford: Oxford University Press, 1987.

Garner 2004
Garner, B.A., *Black's Law Dictionary*, St. Paul: Thompson West, 2004.

Ghiardi 1965
Ghiardi, J.D., 'Should punitive damages be abolished? – A statement for the affirmative', *ABA Sec Ins Negl & Comp L Proc*, 1965, pp. 282–291.

Glansdorf 1980
Glansdorf, F., 'La légalisation de l'astreinte en droit belge: la loi du 31 janvier 1980 portant approbation de la Convention Benelux du 26 novembre 1973', *JT*, 1980, pp. 312–313.

Goegebeur 2001
Goegebeur, A., 'Schade- en strafbedingen in rechtshistorisch en rechtsvergelijkend perspectief', *RW*, 2001, pp. 401–411.

Goldberg, Sebok & Zipursky 2004
Goldberg, J.C.P., Sebok, A.J. & Zipursky, B.C., *Tort Law. Responsibilities and Redress*, New York: Aspen Publishers, 2004.

Goldman 1986
Goldman, L. A., 'Tortious interference with visitation rights: a new and important remedy for non-custodial parents', *J Marschall L Rev*, 1986, pp. 307–324.

Gotanda 2003
Gotanda, J. Y., 'Punitive Damages: A Comparative Analysis', *Colum J Transnat' l L*, 2003, pp. 391–444.

Gras 2007
Gras, E., 'De dwangsom als sanctie op tegenover de overheid verboden eigenrichting', *NJB*, 2007, pp. 2004–2009.

Guldix 1980
Guldix, E., 'De dwangsom eindelijk legaal', *T Vred*, 1980, pp. 129–162.

Hartkamp & Sieburgh 2008
Hartkamp, A.S. & Sieburgh, C.H., 'Verbintenissenrecht' in: *Mr. C. Assers Handleiding tot de beoefening van het Nederlands Burgerlijk Recht*, Deventer: Kluwer, 2008.

Herbots 1992
Herbots, J., 'Concubinaat in het verbintenissenrecht', in: P. Senaeve (ed.), *Concubinaat. De buitenhuwelijkse tweerelatie*, Gent: Story Scientia, 1992, pp. 73–115.

Heyvaert 2001
Heyvaert, A., 'De contractualisering van verhoudingen van staat', in: X (ed.), *Liber Amicorum Yvette Merchiers*, Brugge: die Keure, 2001, pp. 165–195.

Hiernaux 2007
Hiernaux, G., 'La loi du 18 juillet 2006 tendant à privilégier l'hébergement égalitaire de l'enfant dont les parents sont séparés et réglementant l'exécution forcée en matière d'hébergement d'enfant', *RTDF*, 2007, pp. 9–60.

Hutsebaut 2001
Hutsebaut, F., 'Rechten voor slachtoffers: het spanningsveld tussen de private en de publieke ruimte', in: L. Dupont & F. Hutsebaut (eds.), *Herstelrecht tussen toekomst en verleden. Liber amicorum Tony Peters*, Leuven: Universitaire pers, 2001, pp. 311–325.

Jongbloed 1991
Jongbloed, A.W., *De dwangsom in het Nederlandse privaatrecht*, Lelystad: Koninklijke Vermande BV, 1991.

Jowitt, Walsh & Burke 1977
Jowitt, E., Walsh, C. & Burke, J., *Jowitt's dictionary of English law*, II, London: Sweet & Maxwell Limited, 1977.

Kortmann & Sieburgh 2009
Kortmann, J. & Sieburgh, C., 'Handhaving door Nederlands privaatrecht', in: A. Scheltema *et al.* (eds.), *Preadviezen 2009: Toezicht op de financiële markt en de energiemarkt, Staatsgeheimen en het strafproces, Rechtshandhaving door het privaatrecht*, Den Haag: Boom Juridische uitgevers, 2009, www.stibbe.co.uk/upload/c66bd26012a6585ce54015fa.PDF.

Koziol 2008
Koziol, H., 'Punitive Damages – A European Perspective', *La L Rev*, 2008, pp. 741–764.

Krause & Meyer 2003
Krause, H. D. & Meyer, D. D., *Family Law in a nutshell*, St. Paul: Thompson West, 2003.

Lenters 1999
Lenters, H., 'Tenuitvoerlegging van lijfsdwang', *FJR*, 1999, pp. 96–99.

Mahoney 2006
Mahoney, M.M., 'The enforcement of child custody orders by contempt remedies', *U Pitt L Rev*, 2006, pp. 835–877.

Malengreau 1981
Malengreau, X., 'L'introduction de l'Astreinte en Droit belge', *RGAR*, 1981, nr. 10348, pp. 1–6.

Mareschal 2008
Mareschal, M., 'L'article 387*ter* du Code civil ou le renforcement de la complexité procédurale en matière familiale', *Act dr Fam*, 2008, pp. 69–81.

Martens 2006
Martens, I., 'Diverse innovaties inzake verblijfs- en omgangsregeling voor kinderen van niet-samenlevende ouders', *TvW*, 2006, pp. 443–448.

Massager 2006
Massager, N., 'Autorité parentale et hébergement', in: X (ed.), *Droit des personnes et des familles*, Brussel: Larcier, 2006.

Messine & Hirsch 1986
Messine, J. & Hirsch, M., 'Propos sur le délit de non-représentation d'enfant', in: X (ed.), *Mélanges offerts à Raymond Vander Elst,* Brussels: Nemesis, 1986, pp. 633–645.

Moreau-Margrève 1972
Moreau-Margrève, I., 'Une institution en crise: la clause pénale' (note under Cass. 17 April 1970), *RCJB*, 1972, pp. 459–504.

Moreau-Margrève 1976
Moreau-Margrève, I., 'Pour un certain pouvoir de révision des clauses pénales', *JT*, 1976, pp. 637–643.

Moreau-Margrève 1982
Moreau-Margrève, I., 'L'astreinte', *Ann Fac Dr Liège*, 1982, pp. 11–96.

Moreau-Margrève 2000
Moreau-Margrève, I., 'Variations sur un thème récurrent: la clause pénale', in: X (ed.), *Mélanges offerts à Pierre Van Ommeslaghe*, Brussels: Bruylant, 2000, pp. 191–219.

Murphy 2007
Murphy, J., *Street on torts*, New York: Oxford University Press, 2007.

O'Connell 2000
O'Connell, L. W., 'The case for continuing to award punitive damages', *Tort Ins L J*, 2000, pp. 873–897.

Piedelièvre 2001
Piedelièvre, S., 'Les dommages et intérêts punitifs: une solution d'avenir?', *Res civ et ass*, 2001, pp. 68–72.

Pire 2007
Pire, D., 'La nouvelle loi sur l'hébergement égalitaire' in D. Pire (ed.), *Droit des familles*, Liège: Anthemis, 2007, pp. 187–230.

Planiol & Ripert 1931
Planiol, M. & Ripert, G., *Traité pratique de droit civil français*, VII, *Obligations*, II, Paris: Librairie Générale de droit & de jurisprudence, 1931.

Pouleau 1987
Pouleau, V., 'Astreinte et droit familial', *JT*, 1987, pp. 201–206.

Prinsen 2003
Prinsen, P., 'Een kantiaanse benadering van het familierecht', *FJR*, 2003, pp. 13–19.

Renchon 2005
Renchon, J.-L., 'Indisponibilité, ordre public et autonomie de la volonté dans le droit des personnes et de la famille', in: A. Wijffels (ed.), *Le Code civil entre ius commune et droit privé européen*, Brussel: Bruylant, 2005, pp. 269–332.

Rigaux & Trousse 1968
Rigaux, M. & Trousse, p. E., *Les crimes et les délits du Code pénal*, *V*, Brussel: Bruylant, 1968.

Samoy 2001
Samoy, I., 'De geoorloofdheid van schadebedingen na de wet van 23 november 1998: de figurantenrol van de werkelijk geleden schade en van de nietigheidssanctie', *R Cass*, 2001, pp. 342–354.

Schelhaas 2000
Schelhaas, H.N., 'Het boetebeding in Nederland en België', in: J. Smits & S. Stijns (eds.), *Remedies in het Belgisch en Nederlands contractenrecht*, Antwerpen: Intersentia, 2000, pp. 295–325.

Schelhaas 2004
Schelhaas, H. N., *Het boetebeding in het Europese contractenrecht*, Utrecht: Kluwer, 2004.

Screvens 1972
Screvens, R., *Droit pénal*, III, in *Les Novelles*, Brussel: Larcier, 1972.

Sebok 2009
Sebok, A. J., 'Punitive Damages in the United States', in: H. Koziol & V. Wilcox (eds.), *Punitive Damages: Common Law and Civil Law Perspectives*, Vienna: Springer, 2009, pp. 155–196.

Senaeve 1998
Senaeve, P., 'Commentaar bij art. 1385*bis*-1385*nonies* Ger.W'., in: H. Casman, *et al.* (eds.), *Personen- en familierecht: artikelsgewijze commentaar met overzicht van rechtspraak en rechtsleer*, Antwerpen: Kluwer, 1998.

Senaeve 1999
Senaeve, P., 'De dwangsom in het personen- en familierecht', in: Jura Falconis Libri (ed.), *De Dwangsom*, Leuven: Jura Falconis V.Z.W., 1999, pp. 83–115.

Senaeve 2003
Senaeve, P., 'Overzicht van rechtspraak (1995–2003) – de aanwending van de dwangsom inzake huwelijk en echtscheiding', *EJ*, 2003, pp. 150–159.

Senaeve 2009
Senaeve, P., 'De rechtspleging voor de jeugdgerechten in civielrechtelijke zaken', *CABG*, 2009, pp. 1–84.

Senaeve 2010
Senaeve, P., 'Drie jaar toepassing van artikel 387*ter* BW (Wet van 18 juli 2006)', *T Fam*, 2010, pp. 114–132.

Slok & Van 1990
Slok, W.M.K. & Van, A.J., 'De privaatrechtelijke boete en artikel 6:106 Nieuw BW', *NJB*, 1990, pp. 1823–1829.

Snijders, Ynzonides & Meijer 2002
Snijders, H.J., Ynzonides, M. & Meijer, G.J., *Nederlands burgerlijk procesrecht*, Deventer: Kluwer, 2002.

Stijns 2001
Stijns, S., 'Contractualisering van sancties in het privaatrecht, inzonderheid bij contractuele wanprestatie', *RW*, 2001, pp. 1258–1286.

Swennen 2010
Swennen, F., *Het personen- en familierecht*, Antwerpen: Intersentia, 2010.

Swennen & Weyts 2010
Swennen, F. & Weyts, B., 'Fouten tussen echtgenoten. Een tocht doorheen het echtscheidings- en aansprakelijkheidsrecht', in: G. Verschelden (ed.), *XXXVIste Postuniversitaire Cyclus Willy Delva. Echtscheiding 2009–2010*, Mechelen: Kluwer, 2010, pp. 87–145.

Tilleman *et al.* 2000
Tilleman, B., Claeys, I., Coudron, C. & Loontjens, K., 'Dading' in: *APR*, Antwerpen: Story Scientia, 2000.

Trousse 1978
Trousse, P.E., 'Les sanctions pénales du droit de la famille', in: Centre de Droit de la Famille (ed.), *Famille, Droit et changement social dans les sociétés contemporaines*, Brussel: Bruylant, 1978, pp. 638–681.

Tulkens 1982
Tulkens, F., 'Lorsque l'enfant ne paraît pas. Analyse critique du délit de non-présentation d'enfant dans l'article 369*bis* du Code pénal', *RTDF*, 1982, pp. 371–401.

Vanbockrijck 2005
Vanbockrijck, H., 'Moeilijkheden bij de uitoefening van het omgangsrecht', *EJ*, 2005, pp. 94–96.

Vanbockrijck 2007
Vanbockrijck, H., 'Sanctionering van de niet-naleving van beslissingen aangaande verblijf en omgangsrecht', in: P. Senaeve, F. Swennen & G. Verschelden (eds.), *Verblijfsco-ouderschap. Uitvoering en sanctionering van verblijfs- en omgangsregelingen. Adoptie door personen van hetzelfde geslacht*, Antwerpen: Intersentia, 2007, pp. 147–197.

Vanbockrijck 2008
Vanbockrijck, H., 'Evaluatie na één jaar toepassing van de wet van 18 juli 2006 aangaande het verblijfsco-ouderschap en de tenuitvoerlegging van uitspraken inzake verblijf en omgang', in: P. Senaeve (ed.), *Personen- en Familierecht*, Brugge: die Keure, 2008, pp. 31–56.

Vanbockrijck 2009
Vanbockrijck, H., 'Twee jaar toepassing van de wet van 18 juli 2006 inzake het verblijfsco-ouderschap en de uitvoering en sanctionering van verblijfs- en omgangsregelingen', in: P. Senaeve, F. Swennen en G. Verschelden (eds.), *Knelpunten echtscheiding, afstamming en verblijfsregelingen*, Antwerpen: Intersentia, 2009, pp. 189–240.

Van der Burght & Doek 2002
Van der Burght, G. & Doek, J.E., *Personen- en familierecht* in *Pitlo Het Nederlands Burgerlijk Wetboek*, Deventer: Kluwer, 2002.

Vandermersch 1995
Vandermersch, M., 'Incidence sur l'astreinte de la réformation en appel de la décision entreprise' (note under Brussels 4 November 1993), *TBBR*, 1995, pp. 234–245.

Van Gerven & Covemaeker 2006
Van Gerven, W. & Covemaeker, S., *Verbintenissenrecht*, Leuven: Acco, 2006.

Van Mullen 1977
Van Mullen, J., 'Vers une législation de l'astreinte en droit belge?', *JT*, 1977, pp. 37–43.

Van Oevelen 1991
Van Oevelen, A., 'Algemene rechtsbeginselen in het verbintenissen- en contractenrecht', in: M. Van Hoecke (ed.), *Algemene rechtsbeginselen,* Antwerpen: Kluwer, 1991, pp. 95–157.

Van Ryn 1980
Van Ryn, J., 'Nature et fonction de la clause pénale selon le Code civil', *JT*, 1980, pp. 557–559.

Vansweevelt 1984
Vansweevelt, T., 'Het strafbeding en de redactie van de code napoleon', *RW*, 1984, pp. 2467–2474.

Vasseur 2007
Vasseur, R., 'De verblijfsregeling van kinderen van gescheiden ouders: een verruimd wettelijk kader', *TJK*, 2007, pp. 11–20.

Verhelst 2010
Verhelst, S., 'Is er nood aan privatisering van het straf(process)recht? Een aanzet vanuit tot reflectie vanuit rechtseconomische invalshoek', *NC*, 2010, pp. 13–49.

Vlaardingerbroeck *et al.* 2008
Vlaardingerbroeck, P., Blankman, K., Heida, A., Van der Linden, A.P., Punselie, E.C.C. & Van Raak-Kuiper, J.A.E., *Het hedendaagse personen- en familierecht*, Deventer: Kluwer, 2008.

Vlaardingerbroek 2009
Vlaardingerbroek, P., 'Omgang moet, maar tot welke prijs?', *FJR*, 2009, pp. 106–110.

Wagner 1999
Wagner, K., 'Commentaar bij art. 1385*bis* Ger.W'., in: R. De Corte *et al.* (eds.), *Gerechtelijk recht: artikelsgewijze commentaar met overzicht van rechtspraak en rechtsleer*, Antwerpen, Kluwer, 1999.

Wagner 2001
Wagner, K., 'Dwangsom en omgangsregeling' (note under Antwerp 8 February 2000), *AJT*, 2001, pp. 336–337.

Wagner 2003
Wagner, K., 'Dwangsom' in: *APR*, Mechelen: Story-Scientia, 2003.

Wentzel 1990
Wentzel, K. A., 'In the Best Interests of the Child? Minnesota's Refusal to Recognize the Tort of Intentional Interference with Custodial Rights', *Hamline L Rev*, 1990, pp. 257–276.

Wéry 2001
Wéry, P., 'La clause pénale', in: P. Wéry (ed.), *Les clauses applicables en cas d'inexécution des obligations contractuelles*, Namur: La Charte, 2001, pp. 249–324.

Weyts 2005
Weyts, B., 'Lucratieve fouten in het aansprakelijkheids- en verzekeringsrecht. The winner takes it all', *RW*, 2005, pp. 1641–1652.

Wymeersch 1982
Wymeersch, E., 'De betwistingen rond het strafbeding: Een stand van zaken', *BRH*, 1982, pp. 428–454.

Emily Nordin
Daily Wuyts*

THE INSURABILITY OF PUNITIVE DAMAGES UNDER BELGIAN LAW

1. Introduction

The research into the insurability of punitive or exemplary[1] damages has been a subject to debate in the common law of torts for more than three decades.[2] With the discussion on the introduction of punitive damages into the continental law systems, comes inevitably the same problem. However, the first issue in debating whether or not awards for punitive damages are or should be insurable under Belgian law, is the fact that the legal concept of exemplary damages is to date not generally[3] recognised.[4] The finding that part of the legal doctrine has established that the European and Belgian contract and tort law contain certain punitive elements, does not diminish this traditional point of view.[5]

Thus, a hypothetical situation has to be created in order to enable this research. Therefore, we assume the introduction of punitive damages under Belgian tort law as they are defined and recognized in the common law. This also means this article will not cover possible arguments against punitive damages.[6] Before discussing the main problem of the insurability of punitive damages, the concept of punitive damages as it exists under common law will be clarified (§2). After this short introduction to punitive damages, the question of the insurability of punitive damages will be elucidated (§3). First we discuss the public policy issues against the insurability of punitive damages (3.1), followed by an overview of some practical arguments on the matter (3.2). Secondly, the contractual provisions and the legislative restrictions which might prevent or allow

* Emily Nordin and Daily Wuyts are PhD Candidates at the University of Antwerp.

1 These terms have the same meaning and can be used interchangeably: Goldberg *et al.* 2004, p. 469 and McGregor 2009, p. 420, par. 11-001.

2 See already Fisher 1957, pp. 144–153 and the contributions at the beginning of the eighties which fuelled the debate, e.g.: Ellis, 1982, pp. 71–78 and Rosenhouse, 1982, pp. 11–47.

3 It has been argued that some Belgian judges in certain cases award a high amount of moral damages as compensation for the fact that they are unable to award punitive damages. In those cases the compensatory damages, at least for some part, obtain a punitive character: Weyts 2006, pp. 1645–1646.

4 Vansweevelt & Weyts 2009, p. 10, par. 13.

5 See the inventory provided by: Cauffman 2007, pp. 804–841, par. 6–66.

6 For these arguments, see: Beever, 2003, pp. 87–110; Cauffman 2007, pp. 841–863, par. 67–105 and Wilcox, 2009, 32, par. 65 *et seq.*

coverage, will be examined (3.3). Lastly, all of these findings will be summarized in a conclusion (§4).

2. The Concept of Punitive Damages in the Common Law

First of all, it is important to note that punitive damages form a special category of damages that stands apart from damages compensating a tort victim for lost wages, medical expenses, pain and suffering etc.[7] This also means that exemplary damages do not have a specific stand alone status, but co-exist with the classic compensatory damages.[8] Though this seems self-evident, the recognition of punitive damages enforces the dormant functions of tort law. Where only compensatory damages exist, the main function of the law of torts is chiefly limited to the indemnification of tort victims.[9] Without punitive damages the repressive and preventive function of tort law is very restricted. This is, for example, the case with Belgian tort law. Especially in the presence of liability insurance the direct bond between the tort-feasor and the person indemnifying the victim is often weakened. In those cases the insurer will compensate the victim directly and thus the preventive function of tort law is reduced to a minimum.[10] However, insurers providing incentives under the form of cancellations, the raising of premiums and exclusion of certain behaviour as to stimulate cautious behaviour, preserve some of this preventive function.[11] With the introduction of punitive damages the repressive function of tort law which has been entrusted to criminal law[12] and the preventive function which has been weakened by liability insurance, are revived. This is because the two main functions of punitive damages are to punish the wrongdoer and deter him from similar conduct in the future.[13] Since the nature of punitive damages comes so close to criminal law, not every tortuous conduct will lead to the awarding of punitive damages.[14]

In English law there is little scope for an award of punitive damages.[15] Although exemplary damages are not bound to a specific tort, they may only be awarded in cases of oppressive, arbitrary or unconstitutional action by the servants of the government, where the defendant's conduct has been calculated by him to make a profit for himself which may well exceed the compensation payable to the claimant or where it is authorised by statute.[16] In *Broome v. Cassel & Co* punitive damages were awarded to a naval officer who brought actions for libel against the publishers and author of a book which described

7 Goldberg *et al.* 2004, pp. 469–470 and Sebok 2009, p. 155, par. 1.
8 Deakin *et al.* 2008, p. 944.
9 Lunney & Oliphant 2008, pp. 854–855.
10 Fontaine 2011, p. 473, par. 666.
11 Vansweevelt & Weyts 2009, pp. 5–8, par. 6–9.
12 Cauffman 2007, p. 803, par. 4.
13 Dobbs 2000, p. 1063 and Murphy 2007, p. 637, par. 8.
14 McGregor 2009, pp. 420–421, par. 11-001.
15 The first leading case to recognise punitive damages was the famous case: *Rookes v. Barnard* [1964] ALL ER 367.
16 Dugdale 2006, p. 1884, par. 29–140 *et seq*; Deakin *et al.* 2008, p. 946 *et seq.*; McGregor 2009, p. 429, par. 11-017 *et seq.* and Murphy 2007, p. 638 *et seq.*

how he, as commander of a convoy destroyer, was partly responsible for a wartime disaster in 1942. There were documents showing that the publishers and the author knew from an early stage that the naval officer objected to the passages describing his conduct and threatened with libel. It was held that this kind of behaviour is to be considered as calculated since the publisher and the author made the assumption that the economic advantage probably exceeded the damages at risk.[17]

In the United States, the exact mode of expressing the requirements for the awarding of exemplary damages has varied somewhat from court to court, but in general the courts demand sufficiently outrageous conduct to merit punishment by disclosing malice, fraud, cruelty, intent to injure or flagrant indifference to the safety of others.[18] A well known example of a case where punitive damages were awarded is the case of *Philip Morris USA v. Williams*. Mr Williams was a heavy smoker of Marlboro who died of lung cancer. After his death his widow sued Philip Morris, the manufacturer of Marlboro, for negligence and deceit because Philip Morris had deliberately led Mr Williams to believe that smoking was safe.[19]

Although traditionally punitive damages serve two central functions, namely deterrence and punishment,[20] some authors have argued that there is only one main punitive function to this kind of damages.[21] The other rationales for punitive damages can all be considered as derivates from this main function.[22] This distinction seems to be based on the variety of effects that punishment can induce. First of all, deterrence flows from punishment. It is only in the perception of possible punishment that at least some measure of the deterrent for possible (repeated) offenders lays.[23] Secondly, punishment can lead to education for both the individual and society. It teaches society's disapproval of serious misconduct and the importance that the law attaches to the invaded rights. Thirdly, adequate punishment can also serve as a form of retribution and compensation.[24] Punishment can be construed as an institutionalised form of revenge which also offers a form of moral compensation to the victim. Even though the inability of compensatory damages to fully indemnify the victim should not be masked by adding a new purpose to the introduction of punitive damages, it is sometimes argued that the obtained punitive damages can even compensate the victim for actual losses which are hard to prove or for which the rules of compensatory damages do not provide relief, like the expenses of bringing a suit.[25] When the injury is intangible an award for compensatory damages may fall short. For example, if a person would spit on another person and this would be considered outrageous conduct, it would cause an injury that is extremely

17 *Broome v. Cassel & Co. Ltd* [1972] AC 1027.
18 Dobbs 2000, pp. 1062–1064.
19 *Philip Morris USA v. Williams* [2007] 549 U.S. 346, 127 S. Ct. 1057, 166 L. Ed. 2d 940.
20 Sebok 2009, p. 171, par.35.
21 Thompson *et al.* 2002, p. 136.
22 Owen 1994, p. 363 *et seq.*
23 The discussion of all the factors related to punishment that influence the deterrent effect, lie well beyond the scope of this paper.
24 Cauffman 2007, pp. 856–857, par. 98.
25 Dobbs 2000, p. 1063 and Owen 1994, p. 363 *et seq.*

difficult to quantify.[26] This has led to the conclusion that punitive damages indirectly serve a 'third' but secondary purpose in the compensation of the victim.[27]

3. The Insurability of Punitive Damages

Since punitive damages have no stand alone status and are considered a form of damages, their insurability is *prima facie* possible. Article 77 of the insurance contract law (*Wet Landverzekeringsovereenkomsten*, hereafter WLVO) states that a liability insurance covers all claims for damages arising from an established liability. According to this provision no distinction is made as to the form of the damage.[28] Holding this in mind, two approaches of the discussion on the insurability of punitive damages are possible.[29] One possibility is to first make an insurance technical examination of the insurance policy in light of insurance contract law to determine whether there is coverage for punitive awards. This implies studying the text of the policy, judicial and legislative limitations on coverage, possible exclusions *etc.* A second approach is to determine whether or not public policy prohibits insurance coverage of punitive awards before studying the individual insurance contract itself. Most American courts prefer the pragmatic approach by first examining the insurance policy. In an individual case it makes no difference on which grounds coverage can be denied. If coverage can be denied on grounds of the insurance policy, the judge can avoid the more complex and abstract question whether or not public policy prohibits coverage.[30] From an academic point of view it is more interesting to first examine public policy relating to the insurability of punitive damages, before studying which legislative provisions or contractual constructions can limit coverage.

3.1. *Public Policy and Insurability*

The examination of public policy[31] is important, because a court can decide that the interest of freedom of contract is outweighed by some overriding interest of society, in which case it can refuse to enforce a contract for reasons of illegality.[32] Therefore, one must verify whether or not the insurance of punitive damages is per definition against public policy.

As cases of punitive damages in the United Kingdom are comparatively rare, the courts have had little opportunity to discuss this matter.[33] Therefore, it is not surprising

26 Shulman *et al.* 2010, p. 508.
27 Sebok 2009, pp. 171–173, par. 36–40.
28 Fontaine 2011, pp. 479–480, par. 672–673 and Schuermans 2008, p. 447, par. 607.
29 Ostrager 2009, p. 651.
30 Seyferth 1990, p. 75.
31 For a definition of public policy under Belgian Law see: Cass. 9 december 1948, *Arr. Cass.* 1948, 615; De Page 1967, p. 111; Van Gerven & Covemaeker 2006, p. 79.
32 Second Restatement on Contract Law, RES. 2d CONTR 8 IN NT.
33 Merkin 2006, p. 689, par. 20–12.

that there is only one judgement[34] on the subject considered to be the leading case.[35] The situation in the United States is slightly different since there is no unilateral voice that states whether or not the insurance of punitive awards comes into conflict with public policy. Judging the same arguments, some courts conclude that there is a conflict of interests, while others enforce the insurance. More interesting than giving an overview of these conflicting decisions is the analysis of the provided arguments in those cases.

3.1.1. Legal Status of Punitive Damages

If we accept the general traditional proposition that punitive damages serve two functions, punishment and deterrence, then punitive damages are in nature very closely linked to criminal law. In civil law as well as in common law it is generally accepted to be contrary to public policy to allow an individual to enforce an insurance policy which indemnifies him against a fine or other punishment imposed for committing a criminal offence.[36] In Belgian law this principle flows from Article 6 Belgian Civil Code (*Burgerlijk Wetboek*) which states that no contract can detract from any legislative provision relating to public order (like the penalties under the penal code) and is made explicit under Article 91 WLVO.[37] The ratio of this provision is that the personal and individual character of a punishment prohibits that its burden be transferred to an insurer.[38] Although this provision only applies to insurance for legal aid *(rechtsbijstandverzekering)*, it can be considered as an expression of a general rule of insurance law.[39]

The core problem with exemplary damages is that they strive towards some of the same objectives as criminal law, but they do not share the same formal status. In the United States this lack of penal status may be enough to close this debate, since it was considered a sufficient argument to discard the possible problem that may arise from the *ne bis in idem*-principle.[40] However, the lack of a formal penal status on a national level does not necessarily exclude the qualification of punishment on an European level. Since the *Engel v. The Netherlands* judgement, the ECHR applies a autonomous definition of the term 'criminal charge' or punishment.[41] According to the ECHR three alternative[42] criteria are determinant to define a sanction as criminal. First there is a criminal sanction where the national law system qualifies it as such. This, as shown above, is not the case for punitive damages as they only fall under the civil category of 'damages'. Secondly, even in the absence of a national qualification, a sanction can be considered criminal because of its repressive or punitive nature and because it sanctions a general rule which

34 *Lancashire County Council v. Municipal Mutual insurance ltd* [1996] 3 WLR 493.

35 Clarke 2006, p. 757, par. 24–4b and Wilcox 2009, p. 50, par. 11.

36 Law Commission, *Report on aggravated, exemplary and restitutionary damages*, 1997, p. 90, par. 1.192; Colle 2005, p. 300, par. 434; Clarke 2006, p. 757, par. 24–4b; Burrows 2007, p. 990, par. 13.26; Fontaine 2011, p. 162, par. 174; Merkin 2006, p. 119, par. 5–37 and Schuermans 2008, pp. 261–263, par. 354.

37 Fontaine 2011, p. 162, par. 174.

38 Colle 2005, p. 300, par. 434.

39 Fontaine 2011, p. 337, par. 412.

40 *Hevering v. Mitchel* [1938] 303 U.S. 391, 58 S. Ct. 630.

41 ECHR 8 June 1976, *Engel t. Nederland*; EHRM 27 August 1991, *Demicoli v. Malta*.

42 ECHR 24 September 1997, *Garyfallou AEBE v. Griekenland*.

can be imposed on anyone. Thirdly a criminal sanction exists as a result of the seriousness of the sanction. Although punitive damages most certainly can be regarded as meeting some of these criteria – for instance the name itself refers to its punitive nature – it does not seem like the case is this clear cut. For example, in the United Kingdom this element has never been a big issue in the debate on the insurability of punitive damages.[43] When confronted with the question whether damages based on the profit an offender gained from his breach of contract, the ECHR stated that 'The fact remains that the ultimate decision of the House of Lords to order an account of profits against the applicant was based on his breach of contract, a cause of action clearly civil in character'.[44] A flexible approach towards the concept of punitive damages is argued, since the impact a criminal sanction can have on an individual cannot be equalised with the impact punitive damages can have. For one, punitive damages are more stigmatizing than compensatory damages, but they still do not have the same moral consequences as a criminal sanction resulting in a fine. No separate judicial organ is organized to prosecute; no separate register exists where the offence is mentioned; no criminal investigation is conducted to establish the unwanted conduct.[45] In Belgium a similar reasoning has also been applied to the insurance against administrative sanctions (*administratieve sancties*), *i.e.* sanctions imposed not by a judge but by the administration of the government. The Belgian Court of Cassation initially held that the national qualification should stand strong.[46] Later, in two judgements on 5 January 1999 it recognized that certain administrative sanctions can be considered a punishment even though nationally they are attributed an administrative nature. Administrative sanctions are also not considered to enforce fundamental values in society. Nevertheless, the amount of the damages can result in such a serious sanction that it can be qualified as criminal.[47] Colle, however, emphasizes the national qualification and argues that even though these sanctions were construed to efficiently punish minor infractions which were of no priority to the public prosecutors, their insurability could not be rejected on the sole consideration that they have a similar function as the criminal law, since they lack a formal penal status.[48]

Since it is unclear whether punitive damages should be regarded as criminal despite their lack of penal status, we will now discuss what would happen if they would not be qualified as such. This situation after all does not prohibit a judge to find the insurance against punitive damages to be contrary to public policy on other grounds. Public policy contains more than the prohibition of insurance against criminal offences. When refusing the enforcement he will, therefore, be obliged to bring forward other arguments to demonstrate the irreconcilability with public order. This leaves us with two important questions. Does the insurance of exemplary damages diminish its functions and reasons of existence and does this devaluation form enough legal ground to refuse coverage?

43 Compare Cauffman 2007, p. 842, par. 69.

44 Decision of the ECHR 25 October 2005, *Blake v. United Kingdom*.

45 Cauffman 2007, pp. 845–847, par. 71–78.

46 Cass. 27 september 1991, *RW* 1991–92, 708.

47 Mast *et al.* 2006, pp. 10–11, par. 11.

48 Colle 2005, p. 300, par. 434: who rejects the insurability of administrative sanctions on description of the coverage and not on public policy grounds.

3.1.2. The Effect of the Insurance on the Functions of Punitive Damages

One of the main reasons to refuse the insurability of punitive damages lies in the fact that they would diminish the main and thereof derived functions of punitive damages. In general, it is argued that the punitive and deterrent character of the exemplary damages is annihilated when the burden of the punishment is transferred to the insurer. Therefore, there seems to be an inevitable conflict between the nature of insurance as a shifting of risk and the nature of punitive damages as the deprivation of something the wrongdoer values.[49] The payment of an insurance premium does not significantly restore this balance, as the premium is but a fraction of the possible punitive damages.

First of all, irrespective of the portrayal of man, the insurance of punitive damages conflicts with the deterrent and educational factor. A calculating wrongdoer, who makes a cost-benefit analysis, will highly value the global financial outcome of his tortious act. By insuring, he can pass off an important negative cost and will get rid of an important impediment. For the more conformist wrongdoer who holds morally accepted conduct in high regard, the educational factor might be less impeded, because an abstract condemnation of his conduct, will still exist in the ruling of the judge.[50] However, the norm projection will become less evident because the connection between the awarded damages and the norm imposition is cut.

Secondly, when punitive damages are construed as a form of punishment and retribution, it can hardly be debated that insurance for these damages undercuts these justifications, because the hurting of the perpetrator under the form of financial loss is diverted towards an insurer.[51] The question arises whether the decrease in availability, the rising cost of future insurances combined with the loss of good-will of these economic entities, will restore the retributive function.[52] This will probably not be the case, because these perceived costs do not measure up to the costs for the perpetrator in absence of insurance.

Thirdly, as stated above, the rationales of punitive damages can be stretched so far that they incorporate a compensatory function.[53] Solely from that point of view the insurability of these damages does not interfere with this purpose. As far as these damages are aimed at the indemnification of the victim, it makes no difference who compensates them.[54] The moral culpability of the wrongdoer becomes irrelevant and only the amount of damages suffered by the victim becomes the central *crux*.[55] Even though it may be the insurer who pays, this goal is still achieved. Since the compensatory function of punitive damages is only a secondary and much debated effect[56], a strict comparison cannot be pursued.[57]

49 Baker 1998, pp. 103–104.
50 Sebok 2009, p. 179, par. 55–56.
51 Priest 1989, p. 1012.
52 Baker 1998, p. 112; See the opinion of Simon Brown in *Lancashire County Council v. Municipal Mutual insurance ltd*, [1996] 3 WLR 493 and Markel 2009, p. 1469.
53 Widiss 1994, p. 477.
54 Fontaine 2011, p. 473, par. 666.
55 Vansweevelt & Weyts 2009, pp. 5–7, par. 6–7 and p. 271, par. 391.
56 Sebok 2009, pp. 171–172, par. 37 and Ebert 2009, p. 214, par. 4.
57 Baker 1998, p. 108.

A similar discussion regarding the functions of punitive damages was held when the question arose whether or not punitive damages could be awarded for vicarious liability.[58] The main problem lays in the fact that a third person, the principal, is held liable for punitive damages caused by the wrongful conduct of another. Like the insurer (who on the other hand acts on contractual grounds), the principal will be paying the punitive damages resulting from the wrongful act of a third person. The burden is thus transferred.[59] Since the parallel with the insurance against punitive damages is striking,[60] the question arises if the same public policy reasons are evoked. A distinction can be made between two situations.

Firstly, when this liability is based on a highly morally rejectable shortcoming of the principal, one could argue that the principal also deserves punishment for his own behaviour.[61] This is for instance the case when the principal authorised, approved or ratified the actions of his agent/employee thus participating in the wrongful act.[62] Here the deterrent and punitive function of exemplary damages can be upheld. This explains why many United States courts demand evidence hereof before awarding punitive damages under vicarious liability.[63] Some states picked up this tendency and even adopted statutory provisions requiring proof of this high degree of culpability.[64] This does however not detract from the fact that it is strange to hold a third person liable for the punitive damages calculated on the basis of someone else's wrongdoing. If one is to punish the vicariously liable person, should the amount of exemplary damages not be based on his own morally culpable behaviour and not on that of his agent or employee?

Secondly, when vicarious liability amounts to a form of strict liability[65] (like the liability of the principal under Article 1384, §3 Belgian Civil Code)[66] based on the *respondeat superior*-doctrine, the situation becomes even more grim. The purpose of this kind of vicarious liability is found in an extra certainty for compensation of the victim and is again not based upon the conduct of the principal. Therefore this does not undermine the alleged compensatory character of the punitive damages, but definitely puts a strain on its deterrent and retributive facet.[67] Even more remarkable is that the public policy reasons for denying the insurability of punitive damages do sometimes not suffice for the English[68] and some American Courts[69] to reject punitive damages under

58 McGregor 2009, p. 449, par. 11–047 and Goldberg *et al.* 2004, p. 487.

59 Thompson *et al.* 2002, p. 147.

60 Law Commission, Report on aggravated, exemplary and restitutionary damages, 1997, p. 174, par. 1.266 www.lawcom.gov.uk/docs/lc247.pdf.

61 See the opinion of Moore-Bick L.J. in *Rowlands v. Chief constable of Merseyside Police* [2006] EWCA Civ. 1773, 47.

62 Widiss 1994, p. 455.

63 Corpus Juris Secundum, 2A C.J.S. Agency, § 443, May 2010.

64 This is for instance the case in California (*College Hospital Inc. v. Superior Court,* 8 Cal. 4t 704 (1994)) and Montana (*Daniels v. Dean*, 253 Mont. 465 (1992).

65 Third Restatement of Agency, Rest. 3d Agen. § 7.07; Sebok 2009, p. 155, par. 1.

66 Vansweevelt & Weyts 2009, p. 425, par. 640.

67 Beever 2003, p. 96.

68 *Kuddus v. Chief constable of Leicestershire Constabulary* [2002] 2 AC 122 and *Rowlands v. Chief constable of Merseyside Police* [2007] 1 W.L.R. 1065 CA.

69 Corpus Juris Secundum, 2A C.J.S. Agency, § 443, May 2010.

strict vicarious liability. Some scholars put forward that by imposing this liability upon employers an incentive is provided to control the ways in which their employees operate, thereby recreating a certain preventive and deterrent effect.[70] Yet dissenting opinions put forward that it is against the principle of punitive damages to punish a person not blameworthy[71] and who is punished on the sole basis of his capacity.[72] The same reasoning was applied in *Manley v. Commissioner of Police of the Metropolis* where it was upheld that despite the insulting, malicious and oppressive conduct of the police officers there was no room for punitive damages under vicarious liability against the Commissioner in charge, since he was not the actual perpetrator.[73]

Two remarkable things have to be retained from the discussion above. First of all, the courts who maintained punitive damages under vicarious liability can be expected to enforce the insurability of exemplary damages on these public policy grounds. Apparently, in their opinion the lack of functionality is not considered sufficient enough. In their defence they will argue that a small portion of the deterrent and preventive function is still present.[74] This is however questionable and has been rebutted by the majority of American courts[75] who consider the functions of punitive damages to be annihilated in such cases and thus refuse to award punitive damages under vicarious liability. The same goes for the 'compensatory argument', since punitive damages do not serve as a safety net for the insufficiency of compensatory damages.[76] Secondly, it has to be noted that there was an important resemblance between insurance of punitive damages and exemplary damages under vicarious liability as far as in both cases a third person will carry the financial burden caused by the wrongful conduct of another. If we limit our vision to these facts, the logical conclusion would be that the courts will also refuse to enforce insurance against punitive damages.[77] The reality is very different since the English leading case (although limited to vicarious liability)[78], the Law Commission,[79] and slightly more than half of the American courts[80] accept the insurability of punitive damages. Therefore the questions arises what sets aside these two situations. It seems that the main distinguishing argument is based on the grounds on which the burden is

70 *Kuddus v. Chief constable of Leicestershire Constabulary* [2002] 2 AC 122 and *Rowlands v. Chief constable of Merseyside Police* [2007] 1 W.L.R. 1065 CA. See on this matter also: McGregor 2009, pp. 449–451, par. 11–047 - 11–049.

71 See the dissenting opinion of Lord Scott in *Kuddus v. Chief constable of Leicestershire Constabulary* [2002] 2 AC 163.

72 *Briner v. Hislop* 337 N.W. 2d 858.

73 *Manley v. Commissioner of Police of the Metropolis* [2006] EWCA Civ 879.

74 *Rowlands v. Chief constable of Merseyside Police* [2007] 1 WLR 1065 CA. See also the concurring opinion of: McGregor 2009, p. 451, par. 11–049.

75 For a recent overview: Ostrager 2009, p. 660 *et. seq.* Compare also the older overviews: Ryan & McCullough 1997, p. 198 *et. seq.* and Posner 1993, pp. 404–406.

76 Ebert 2009, p. 214, par.4.

77 Wilcox 2009, p. 50, par. 110 and Ebert 2009, p. 214, par.4.

78 *Lancashire County Council v. Municipal Mutual insurance ltd* [1996] 3 WLR 493: Here the court allowed the insurance against punitive damages for vicarious liability. Until to date there are no other leading cases deciding the insurability against punitive damages.

79 Law Commission, *Report on aggravated, exemplary and restitutionary damages*, 1997, p. 167, par. 1.236 www.lawcom.gov.uk/docs/lc247.pdf.

80 Ebert 2009, p. 213 and Jerry 1999, p. 475, par. 65.

transferred. Regarding vicarious liability this was the sole capacity of the principal. On the contrary, the obligation of the insurer to pay is based on a contractual relation between the insurer and the insured.

3.1.3. Sanctity of Contract

When considering the public policy reasons for (dis)allowing the insurance against punitive damages, an important factor is the contract concluded with the insurer.[81] There is a general policy underlying the law of contracts that commercial contracts are not to be lightly interfered with by courts.[82] The freedom of contract should only be barred on public policy grounds in very plain cases where there is no room for doubt,[83] for instance where a person seeks to insure himself against the penal consequences of any criminality.[84] In absence of any form of criminal behaviour the case is less plain. When weighing the importance of the freedom of contract against the decrease of functions of punitive damages, most courts hold the sanctity of contract in higher regard. This is probably the correct interpretation, since punitive damages lack any penal status[85] and the public policy case is far from clear.[86]

Moreover, the principle of sanctity of contract is not just confined to freedom of contract[87], but contains the important principle of *pacta sunt servanda*. This generally means that whenever an insurer accepts a premium to cover a certain risk, he should meet it,[88] especially when presuming that the insurer believed the premium to be sufficient for such coverage.[89] Like with the freedom of contract, this general rule must yield when the agreement is inconsistent with public policy, but as we have seen the existence of such a policy is far from clear. Moreover, one could wonder whether the non-enforcement of insurance against punitive damages puts more of a strain on public policy, as it sets aside the binding force of the contract.[90] The trust of the insured that the contract will be honoured also deserves a certain degree of protection.[91] Since insurance contracts are 'form contracts', construed by the insurer, it is the insurer who is in the best position to clarify if coverage for punitive damages is intended. This point of view is only fortified by the knowledge that insurers are aware of the on-going debate concerning the insurability of punitive damages. Nevertheless, insurers mostly use a broad and general

81 Seyferth 1990, p. 75.

82 *Printing & Numerical Registering co v. Sampson* [1875] LR 19 Eq 462.

83 Law Commission, Report on aggravated, exemplary and restitutionary damages, 1997, p. 168, par. 1.242. Ebert 2009, p. 214, par. 4.

84 See the opinion of Simon Brown L.J. in *Lancashire County Council v. Municipal Mutual insurance ltd* [1996] 3 WLR 493.

85 Cfr. Colle 2005, p. 300, par. 434.

86 Law Commission, *Report on aggravated, exemplary and restitutionary damages*, 1997, p. 169, par. 1.244 www.lawcom.gov.uk/docs/lc247.pdf;.

87 Jerry 1999, p. 473, par. 65.

88 Law Commission, *Report on aggravated, exemplary and restitutionary damages*, 1997, p. 169, par. 1.246 www.lawcom.gov.uk/docs/lc247.pdf.

89 *Harrel v. Travelers Indem. Co.* [1977] 567 p. 2d 1013, pp. 1021–22.

90 Jerry 1999, p. 473, par. 65.

91 Merkin 2006, p. 690, par. 20–12.

definition of the scope of coverage by using terms like 'all sums' or 'compensation for damages'.[92] Therefore, the insured, who cannot be considered an expert, may well expect that coverage applies to all amounts of damages that may be awarded by the courts including punitive damages. This trust is fuelled by the increasing number of rulings allowing coverage[93], which only increases the expectance of the insured that coverage will be allowed by courts.[94] The insurer's reluctance to clarify the scope of coverage, should not have consequences for the insured. On the contrary, as the stronger party, it is the insurer who should bare the risk.[95] It seems unfair to let an insurer collect the premiums and pretend to extend coverage to 'all sums', but later on allow him to escape his responsibility.[96] An unclear public policy should not be a windfall for the insurer. However, since the sanctity of contract does not only mean that the contract should be honoured, but also that the contracting parties have enough freedom to negotiate their obligations, we will later[97] discuss which possibilities are available to the insurer for defining the scope of coverage.

Since this article explores the insurability of punitive damages under Belgian law, research needs to be done whether the arguments based on the doctrine of sanctity of contract can be transposed. Like the common law, Belgian contract law is familiar with the two important principles of freedom of contract and the binding force of contract (Article 1134 Belgian Civil Code).[98] These two rules are not absolute, but are bound by the general principle of Article 6 Belgian Civil Code.[99] This article states that no agreement can take away from the laws governing public order and public morality. Applied to insurance law this means that the performance of the insurer cannot be contrary to public order.[100] Since the starting hypothesis was that punitive damages as they exist in common law, are allowed under Belgian law, we have to ascertain whether payment by the insurer of these damages is contrary to Article 6 Belgian Civil Code. It is beyond doubt that parties cannot transfer the burden of penal consequences resulting from a criminal offence to an insurer.[101] This would interfere with the individual character of a punishment, which does concern public order.[102] Any civil consequences, even if they result from criminal conduct, can be insured as long as the insurance is not aimed at maintaining or creating an illegal situation.[103] If the insurer refuses to pay damages in cases of criminal conduct, this will be based upon insurance law (Article 8 WLVO) or the insurance policy, which can provide exclusions for intentional or highly culpable

92 Merkin 2006, p. 689, par. 20–12 and Widiss 1994, p. 455; *Lancashire County Council v. Municipal Mutual insurance ltd* [1996] 3 WLR 493.

93 For an overview of these majority rulings see: Ostrager 2009, p. 652 and Seyferth 1990, p. 76.

94 E.g. *Skyline Harvestore Sys., Inc. v. Centennial Ins. Co.*, 331 [1983] N.W. 2d 106, 107; Ebert 2009, p. 214, par.4.

95 Priest 1989, p. 1019.

96 Seyferth 1990, p. 81.

97 *Infra* 19.

98 Van Gerven & Covemaeker 2006, p. 72 *et. seq.*

99 For a definition of public policy see: Cass. 9 December 1948, *Pas.* 1948, I, 699.

100 Colle 2006, p. 26, par. 28 and Cornelis 2000, par. 106.

101 Schuermans 2008, p. 262, par. 354.

102 Colle 2005, p. 300, par. 434.

103 Schuermans 2008, p. 263, par. 354.

behaviour.[104] The sole fact that exemplary damages are punitive in nature does not give them a penal status. What is more, the insurability of other punitive elements of damages, like interests for late payment (*moratoire interest*) or penalty clauses,[105] is already a reality.[106]

3.1.4. Public Policy and the Insurability of Vicarious Liability

Until now we have mainly addressed the case of the insurability of punitive damages without making a distinction between punitive damages awarded for personal conduct and those awarded on the basis of someone else's conduct. Yet, there seems to be a difference between these two situations in the American jurisprudence. Some States that do not enforce insurance against punitive damages for one's own conduct, waive their objections when the insurance covers exemplary damages under vicarious liability.[107] This might be understandable in the case of strict vicarious liability where punitive damages cannot fulfil their main functions anyway. When punitive damages are awarded under vicarious liability because it is deemed necessary to punish the principal for his misconduct, the insurability seems less consistent.[108] There is no reasonable justification why a principal whose actions are deemed equal, should be treated differently from the agent. If the principal deserves a form of punishment, he should be treated the same as the agent.[109]

3.2. Non-Public Policy Related Objections

Although there are, in our opinion, no decisive public policy reasons for rejecting the insurability of punitive damages, other practical arguments can emerge.

First, it has been argued that the plaintiff will be reluctant to pursue a claim for punitive damages when the wrongdoer does not have the financial capacity to pay them.[110] Allowing the insurability of punitive damages could remove this obstacle. This argument is derived from the function of liability insurance in cases of compensatory damages.[111] Nevertheless the main focus of punitive damages is wrongdoer-orientated, and not aimed at compensating the victim.[112]

Secondly, the insurability of punitive damages can prevent the wrongdoer from bankruptcy.[113] It is doubtful whether this is an argument in favour of insurability of punitive damages. Rather it seems an argument concerning the awarding and the amount

104 *Infra* 20.

105 Cauffman 2007, pp. 804–810, par. 6–14. See also: Schuermans 2008, pp. 461–462, par. 623–626.

106 Ebert 2009, p. 216, par.8.

107 Ebert 2009, p. 216, par. 7, footnote 9 and the overview in Ostrager 2009, p. 660 *et. seq.*

108 Ostrager 2009, p. 656 and the cited case law.

109 Jerry 1999, p. 476, par. 65.

110 Jerry 1999, p. 474, par. 65 and Law Commission, *Report on aggravated, exemplary and restitutionary damages*, 1997,p. 167, par. 1.237, www.lawcom.gov.uk/docs/lc247.pdf.

111 Vansweevelt & Weyts 2009, p. 6, par. 6.

112 Beever 2003, p. 96 and Jerry 1999, p. 474, par. 65.

113 Ebert 2009, p. 214, par.4 and Jerry 1999, p. 474, par. 65.

of punitive damages as such and linked to their civil nature.[114] Punitive damages are allowed to hurt the wrongdoer. Moreover, if private law is allowed to award 'punishment', then should the civil judge not be allowed to consider mitigating circumstances?

Thirdly, permitting insurance against punitive damages may minimise conflict between the insurer and the insured.[115] If the wrongdoer is only insured for the non-punitive part of an award, the obligation of the insurer to take control of the litigation ends there.[116] This is also valid under Belgian law. According to Article 79 WLVO the insurer takes control of the procedure, but only as far as his interests and those of the insured coincide and as far as they fall within the scope of coverage.[117] Alternately, this obligation of the insurer does not extend to litigations concerning an uninsured liability.[118]

Fourthly, the deep-pocket argument might function as an argument against the insurability of punitive damages as it could lead juries to award a higher amount of punitive damages, knowing that it is the insurer who will be paying.[119] A possible solution for this problem was suggested by Justice Compton in *Shane*. He proposed to split the trail into two phases. In the first phase that jury has to decide whether or not to award punitive damages. Any evidence of insurance is excluded until the second phase where the jury determines the proper amount of the punitive damages award.[120] This criticism seems to be typical of a jury system and can therefore not be transposed to the Belgian situation. If the decision-making is left to a professional judge it may be expected that he will make abstraction of the existence of insurance.

Fifthly, in its report on aggravated, exemplary and restitutionary damages the British Law Commission made a comparison between the insurance of punitive damages and other alternative ways in which this liability can be met. According to some consul tees a bar on insurance could be objectionable because it produces inequality between organisations and persons who are wealthy enough to self insure and those who cannot. Moreover, there is no objection in allowing another person or organization to meet one's liability to punitive damages by way of gift.[121] In Belgium the same reasoning can be applied, since Article 1236 Belgian Civil Code allows payment of a debt by a third party. In the authors' opinion this seems irrelevant. In reality it is never excluded that a third party pays the debt of someone else. By way of gift it is even possible to pay someone's penal fine. However, this fact has never been an argument in favour of the insurability of penal fines. It is not because someone is willing to pay based upon his goodwill, that the legislator should allow coverage of these costs under contract of insurance. There is a big difference in degree of uncertainty between the first and second hypothesis.

114 See: Ostrager 2009, p. 647.
115 Ostrager 2009, p. 657.
116 Law Commission, *Report on aggravated, exemplary and restitutionary damages*, 1997, p. 169, par. 1.248, www.lawcom.gov.uk/docs/lc247.pdf.
117 Colle 2006, pp. 167–168, par. 230 and Schuermans 2008, p. 459.
118 Fontaine 2011, p. 501, par. 716.
119 Ebert 2009, p. 215, par. 5 and Seyferth 1990, p. 71 *et seq.*
120 See the concurring opinion of Justice Compton in *Shane v. Rhines* [1983] 672 P 2d 895.
121 Law Commission, *Report on aggravated, exemplary and restitutionary damages*, 1997, p. 169, par. 1.247, www.lawcom.gov.uk/docs/lc247.pdf.

Finally, the general problem of moral hazard, which inevitably is linked to liability insurance,[122] is sometimes seen as an argument against the insurability of punitive damages. Knowing he will not be carrying the burden of his misconduct, the insured might be stimulated to embark on risky behaviour.[123] Although the existence of moral hazard cannot be denied, this argument has to be put into perspective. As regards liability insurance there is little ground for this concern.[124] Few insured will commit strategic negligence, those who do can be dissuaded by adequate contractual provisions, for instance by exclusions (for deliberate misconduct), franchises, and other policy provisions.[125]

3.3. *Contractual Regulation*

Even though the above reasoning supports the case for the insurability against punitive damages, it is still important to verify how insurers can deal with the coverage of these damages. The main problem is that in most liability insurances the definition of coverage is often very broad and contains no specific reference to punitive damages.

The scope of coverage in most insurance contracts is linked to the kind of liability that is insured.[126] As a general rule no distinction is made between different categories of damages the insured becomes legally obliged to pay.[127] Therefore, the coverage is mostly defined as a promise to pay 'all sums (obliged to pay as damages/compensation)'.[128] In Belgium a reference to the coverage of 'all sums' has become redundant, as Article 82, sect 1 WLVO already obliges the insurer to pay the total sum resulting from the liability covered, without making a further distinction. It thus falls within the competence of the courts to determine whether or not this terminology includes coverage for punitive damages. Most common law courts in applying general rules of interpretation[129] conclude that these general terms cover compensatory damages as well as punitive damages.[130] For example, the *contra proferentem*-rule, as formulated by Article 1162 Belgian Civil Code,[131] is often used to extend general terms as 'compensation' to all forms of damages payable by the insured.[132] In the cases where there is a reference to exclusion for a specific kind of punitive damages in a limited context of a strictly defined liability, a restricted or

122 Baker 1996, pp. 237–292; Parsons 2009, pp. 448–471 and Faure & Van Boom 2008, p. 309, par. 2.3.

123 Ebert 2009, p. 215, par.5.

124 Jerry 1999, pp. 475–476, par. 65.

125 Clarke 2005, p. 254.

126 Baker 1998, p. 115 and Fontaine 2011, pp. 480–481, par. 674.

127 Colle 2006, pp. 171–172, par. 233–234 and Schuermans 2008, p. 461, par. 623–624.

128 Merkin 2006, p. 689, par. 20–12.

129 For an overview of these rules applied to insurance law see: Schuermans 2008, pp. 281–283, par. 380–383.

130 Jerry 1999, p. 472, par. 65, footnote 131; Merkin 2006, p. 689, par. 20–12 and Widiss 1994, p. 474.

131 The rule of *contra proferentem* is a rule of interpretation which states that in case of doubt concerning the meaning of a term or stipulation, the clause will be interpreted against the contractual party who stipulated the specific obligation: Fontaine 20011, p. 372, par. 484. For some common law examples see: Widiss 1994, pp. 475–476.

132 *Lancashire County Council v. Municipal Mutual insurance ltd* [1996] 3 WLR 493.

a contrario reasoning can be used to include other forms of punitive damages.[133] Another problem emerges when the judge does not make a clear distinction between the part of the damages that is compensatory and the part that is punitive. In this case the rules of interpretation serve no useful purpose. In such a case the judge will decide that the insurer should pay the entire amount of damages awarded.[134]

Even when the coverage is broadly defined, the insurer has the possibility to appeal upon the general rule that deliberate damages or deliberate injury are never insurable.[135] Thus, in consistency, punitive damages awarded for these actions are not insurable.[136] In Belgian law this principle flows from Article 8 WLVO, which states that intentionally caused damages are excluded from insurance. It is important to note that the Belgian Supreme Court (*Hof van Cassatie*) gave a new definition of intentionally caused damages in a recent judgement. According to this judgement it is now required that not only the act causing the damages was intentional, but that the perpetrator also had the intention to damage.[137] This aligns the Belgian definition with the one used by the majority under common law, which also requires not only a deliberate action, but also a deliberate loss/ damage.[138]

However, punitive damages are not just awarded when there is intentional harm, but can also be awarded in other cases of outrageous or malicious conduct which do not meet the applicable insurance law standard for intentional harm.[139] For this kind of behaviour the insurer cannot solely rely on public policy which excludes deliberate loss, but will have to stipulate exclusions aimed at that specific behaviour. Damages resulting from a severely culpable act (*grove schuld*) are covered under Article 8, sect 2 WLVO. That same article offers the insurer the possibility to stipulate exclusions for those actions as far as they are explicitly and restrictively defined in the insurance policy. This means generally defined exclusions for severely culpable behaviour are not allowed.[140] The question arises if a general exclusion for punitive damages is explicit and restrictive enough, since punitive damages are being awarded for an ever expanding range of severely culpable behaviour. This is especially the case, when the line between the amount of damages that are compensatory and the amount that is punitive is not always made by the court. Therefore, it is safer for the insurer not to generally exclude punitive damages, but to exclude, depending on the specific field of insurance, specific kinds of highly culpable behaviour.

Another possibility for the insurer to avoid coverage is to introduce caps (monetary limits) in the contract.[141] This flows from the principle doctrine of freedom of contract.

133 *Lancashire County Council v. Municipal Mutual insurance ltd* [1996] 3 WLR 493 and Fontaine 2011, p. 372, par. 483.

134 Merkin 2006, p. 689, par. 20–12.

135 Clarke 2005, pp. 255–256.

136 Widiss 1994, p. 462.

137 Cass. 24 april 2009, *NJWB* 2009, 635, noot G. Jocqué *TBH* 2010, 56 noot H. Cousy, *T.Verz.* 2010, 38, noot J-L. Fagnart. See about this evolution: Wuyts 2010, pp. 1313–1324.

138 Clarke 2006, pp. 576–577; Jerry 1999, pp. 403–404, par. 63C (b) and Merkin 2006, pp. 125–126, par. 5–44.

139 Baker 1998, p. 121 and Widiss 1994, pp. 478–479.

140 Schuermans 2008, p. 657, par. 888, footnote 84.

141 Baker 1998, pp. 118–119 and Ebert 2009, p. 216, par. 10.

However, empirical research by Baker has shown that in most professional and business classes in the United States most limits well exceed the amount of awarded punitive damages. Only in the large commercial insurance market policy limits seem effective as a way of avoiding coverage. On the other hand most large commercial entities will negotiate higher limits in exchange for a higher premium.[142] This is a clear example of a case where the sanctity of contract will be regarded as a strong argument for allowing coverage.[143]

An insurer should bear in mind that in some legislation the legislator might have imposed a minimum coverage for certain types of insurance contracts. Under Belgian law this is, for example, the case in the statute on family insurance (*BA privéleven*[144]) and the statute on motor insurance (*WAM-wet*[145]).[146] This limits the possibility of the insurers to introduce caps on coverage. Since these minimum coverages imposed by the legislator are often very high,[147] it remains questionable whether the eventual limits are of any use to the insurer as most awarded sums for punitive damages do not exceed the boundaries of minimum coverage.[148] Another question that arises is how an award for punitive damages should be qualified. The height of the minimum coverage in the Belgian legislation depends on the type of damage (immaterial or material). Therefore, it is important to establish under which category, if any, punitive damages can be placed.

4. Conclusion

Since punitive damages as a legal concept do not exist under Belgian law, inspiration has been found in the common law approach to this concept. However, we have found that the common law does not provide a clear cut answer to the question whether or not punitive damages should be insurable. We argued that since punitive damages do not have a standalone status and it remains questionable whether they should be regarded as 'criminal' in the sense of Article 6 ECHR, they should be approached as would the insurability of any kind of damages.

The first question we faced was whether or not public policy can be used as an argument to put a ban on the insurability of punitive damages. We have seen that the courts do not uphold a uniform conclusion concerning the content of public policy. As Clarke remarked the content of public policy depends on the decision the court wants to reach: 'The court that wants to enforce cover usually stresses the importance of compensation. The court against cover stresses the seriousness of the act of the insured

142 Baker 1998, p. 118.

143 See *supra* 3.1.3.

144 See Article 5 KB 12 januari 1984 tot vaststelling van de minimumgarantievoorwaarden van de verzekeringsovereenkomsten tot deking van de burgerrechtelijk aansprakelijkheid buiten overeenkomst met betrekking tot het privé-leven, *BS* 31 januari 1984.

145 See Article 3, § 2 Wet 21 november 1989 betreffende de verplichte aansprakelijkheidsverzekering inzake motorrijtuigen, *BS* 8 december 1989.

146 For more examples see: Schuermans 2008, p. 640, par. 870.

147 For instance in the statute of family insurance minimum coverage for physical damages exceeds €12 million, whereas the coverage for material damages exceeds €600,000. Both are per loss.

148 Baker 1998, p. 118.

and the importance of discouraging that kind of behaviour. Clearly, the court's perception of public policy has a role, but that role is not clearly defined or articulated'.[149] This debate usually results in a trade off between the importance of the discouraging functions of punitive damages and the sanctity of contract. Applying the Belgian general rules of contract we have argued that since punitive damages have no undisputed penal status and given the fact that other punitive elements of damages like interests or penalty clauses are insurable, there is no clear conflict with public policy. Thus, the sanctity of contract should prevail.

Next to the public policy issue, we also discussed more practical problems related to the insurability of punitive damages. These problems, like for instance the deep-pocket argument, the prevention of bankruptcy and the conflict between insurer and insured etc., never seem to touch the core problem, and could therefore not lead to a different conclusion.

Once uncertainty about the arguments against the principle of insurability had been established, the contractual possibilities and legislative limitations concerning insurability could be examined. As a general rule of Belgian and common law, we ascertained that no distinction is made between different categories of damages in liability insurance. Therefore, if no further specification has been made the insurer will be obliged to cover punitive damages. However, we also determined that insurers who want to exclude coverage for punitive damages are adequately equipped. On the one hand there is the legislative prohibition of coverage for deliberate damage; on the other hand there is the freedom of contract which allows the insurer to specify his obligations.

In conclusion, considering the legal status of punitive damages, we see no compelling obstacles in the recognition of the insurability of punitive damages.

149 Clarke 2005, p. 255.

Bibliography

Baker 1996
Baker, T., 'On the genealogy of moral hazard', *Tex L Rev*, 1996, pp. 237–292.

Baker 1998
Baker, T., 'Reconsidering insurance for punitive damages', *Wis L Rev*, 1998, pp. 101–130.

Beever 2003
Beever, A., 'The structure of aggravated and exemplary damages', *Oxford J Legal Stud*, 2003, pp. 87–111.

Burrows 2007
Burrows, A., 'English private law', in *Oxford principle of English law*, Oxford: Oxford University Press, 2007.

Cauffman 2007
Cauffman, C., 'Naar een punitief Europees verbintenissenrecht? Een rechtsvergelijkende studie naar de draagwijdte, de (grond)wettigheid en de wenselijkheid van het bestraffend karakter van het verbintenissenrecht', *TPR*, 2007, pp. 799–873.

Clarck 2005
Clarke, M.A., *Policies and perceptions of insurance law in the twenty-first century*, Oxford: Oxford University Press, 2005.

Clarke 2006
Clarke, M.A., *The law of insurance contracts*, Londen: Informa, 2006.

Colle 2006
Colle, P., *Algemene beginselen van het Belgisch verzekeringsrecht*, Antwerpen: Intersentia, 2006.

Colle 2010
Colle, P., *Handboek bijzonder gereglementeerde verzekeringscontracten*, Antwerpen: Intersentia, 2010.

Cornelis 2000
Cornelis, L., *Algemene theorie van de verbintenis*, Antwerpen: Intersentia, 2000.

Deakin *et al.* 2008
Deakin, S. *et al.*, *Markesinis and Deakin's Tort Law*, Oxford: Clarendon Press, 2008.

De Page 1967
De Page, H., *Traité élémentaire de droit civil belge*, III, *Les obligations*, Brussel: Bruylant, 1967.

Dobbs 2000
Dobbs, D.B., *The Law of Torts*, St. Paul: West Group, 2000.

Dugdale 2006
Dugdale, A., *Clerk & Lindsell on Torts*, Londen: Sweet & Maxwell, 2006.

Ebert 2009
Ebert, I., 'Punitive damages and liability insurance', in: H. Koziol & V. Wilcox (eds.), *Punitive damages: common law and civil law perspectives*, New York: Springer, 2009, pp. 213–218.

Ellis 1982
Ellis, D.D., 'Fairness and efficiency in the law of punitive damages', *S Cal L Rev*, 1982, pp. 71–78.

Goldberg *et al.* 2004
Goldberg, J.C.P. *et al.*, *Tort Law. Responsibilities and Redress*, New York: Aspen Publishers, 2004.

Faure & Van Boom 2008
Faure, M. & Van Boom, W.H., 'Hoe houdbaar zijn gedragsveronderstellingen in verzekeringsrecht en economie?', in: W.H. Van Boom, I. Giesen & A.J. Verheij (eds.), *Gedrag en privaatrecht*, Den Haag: Boom juridische uitgevers, 2008.

Fisher 1957
Fisher, T. D., 'Insurance coverage and the punitive award in the automobile accident suit', *U Pitt L Rev*, 1957, pp. 144–153.

Fontaine 2011
Fontaine, M., *Droit des assurances*, Brussel: Larcier, 2011.

Jerry 1999
Jerry, R.H., *Understanding insurance law*, New York: Matthew Bender, 1999.

Lunney & Oliphant 2008
Lunney, M. & Oliphant, K., *Tort Law*, Oxford: Oxford university Press, 2008.

Markel 2009
Markel, D., 'How should punitive damages work?', *U Pa L Rev*, 2009, pp. 1383–1684.

Mast *et al.* 2006
Mast, A. *et al.*, *Overzicht van het Belgisch administratief recht*, Mechelen: Kluwer, 2006.

McGregor 2009
McGregor, H., *McGregor on damages*, Londen: Thomson Reuters, 2009.

Merkin 2006
Merkin, R., *Collinveaux's law of insurance*, Londen: Sweet and Maxwell, 2006.

Murphy 2007
Murphy, J., *Street on Torts*, Oxford: Oxford University Press, 2007.

Ostrager 2009
Ostrager, B.R., *Handbook on insurance coverage disputes, vol.2*, Aspen: Kluwer, 2009.

Owen 1994
Owen, D., 'A punitive damages overview', *Vill L Rev*, 1994, pp. 363–413.

Parsons 2009
Parsons, C., 'Moral hazard in liability insurance', *The Geneva papers on risk and insurance*, 2009, pp. 448–471.

Posner 1993
Posner, K.B., 'Coverage for punitive damages: choice of law 'Shell game', *Int ILR*, 1993, pp. 402–407.

Priest 1989
Priest, G.L., 'Insurability and punitive damages', *Ala L rev*, 1989, pp. 1009–1035.

Rosenhouse 1982
Rosenhouse, A., 'Liability insurance coverage as extending to liability for punitive or exemplary damages', *ALR*, 1982, pp. 11–47.

Ryan & McCullough 1997
Ryan, R.R. & McCullough, J.W., 'The insurability of punitive damages in the United States', *Int I L R*, 1997, pp. 196–205.

Schuermans 2008
Schuermans, L., *Grondslagen van het Belgisch verzekeringsrecht*, Antwerpen: Intersentia, 2008.

Sebok 2009
Sebok, A. J., 'Punitive damages in the United States' H. Koziol & V. Wilcox (eds.), *Punitive damages: common law and civil law perspectives*, New York: Springer, 2009, pp. 155–176.

Seyferth 1990
Seyferth, P. D., 'The construction and admissibility of insurance policies that provide coverage for punitive damage awards', *Alaska L Rev*, 1990, pp. 75–86.

Shulman *et al.* 2010
Shulman, H. *et al.*, *Law on torts cases and materials*, New York: Foundation Press, 2010.

Thompson *et al.* 2002
Thompson, R.S. *et al.*, *Remedies: Damages, Equity and Restitution*, Newark: LexisNexis, 2002.

Van Gerven & Covemaeker 2006
Van Gerven, W. & Covemaeker, S., *Verbintenissenrecht*, Leuven: Acco, 2006.

Vansweevelt & Weyts 2009
Vansweevelt, T. & Weyts, B., *Handboek buitencontractueel aansprakelijkheidsrecht*, Antwerpen: Intersentia, 2009.

Weyts 2006
Weyts, B., 'Lucratieve fouten in het aansprakelijkheids- en verzekeringsrecht. The winner takes it all', *RW*, 2006, pp. 1641–1652.

Widdis 1994
Widdis, A.I, 'Liability Insurance coverage for punitive damages? Discerning answers to the conundrum created by disputes involving conflicting public policies: pragmatic considerations and political actions', *Vill L Rev*, 1994, pp. 455–503.

Wilcox 2009
Wilcox, V., 'Punitive damages in England', in: H. Koziol & V. Wilcox (eds.), *Punitive damages: common law and civil law perspectives*, New York: Springer, 2009, pp. 7–54.

Wuyts 2010
Wuyts, D., 'De definiëring van het opzettelijk veroorzaakt schadegeval in de zin van artikel 8 WLVO', *RABG*, 2010, pp. 1313–1324.

A. Ortega González*

PUNITIVE DAMAGES FOR CARTEL INFRINGEMENTS: WHY DIDN'T THE COMMISSION GRASP THE OPPORTUNITY?

1. Introduction

In stark contrast to the United States where private antitrust lawsuits are most prevalent, private damages actions in the European Union (EU) are not very common and have never played a central enforcement role. The debate on 'private enforcement' of competition law in Europe[1] was reopened by the decision in *Courage v. Crehan* 2001,[2] in which the European Court of Justice explicitly recognised a right to damages for breaches of EU competition law. Subsequently, the European Commission (hereinafter 'the Commission') has put forward various proposals to facilitate and encourage the private enforcement of competition law. In 2005, the Commission published its Green Paper on Damages Actions for Breach of the EU antitrust rules, which was followed in 2008 by a White Paper on the same topic. In these policy documents, the Commission identifies the main obstacles to more efficient private enforcement in the Member States and proposes measures to promote it. These measures would enable aggrieved parties to obtain compensation for damages suffered as a result of a breach of competition rules. One of the proposals of the Green Paper was the introduction of double damages, a form of punitive damages, for horizontal cartel cases. This option was very controversial and was consequently dropped in the 2008 White Paper.

This article will analyse the Commission's approach regarding the adoption of punitive damages for competition law infringements. First, the developments leading to the White Paper will be reviewed (par. 2). Following that, it will be examined whether the introduction of double damages in the case of hard-core cartels can be justified (par. 3). The reasons underlying the Commission's decision to finally abandon this proposal will also be explored (par. 4). In this context it will be demonstrated that the desirability

* PhD candidate and teaching assistant of European Economic Law/European Competition Law at the University of Antwerp. The author would like to thank Professor Anne-Marie Van den Bossche for her helpful comments and suggestions.

1 The first discussions on private enforcement date back to the early years of the EC. See Commission de la CEE, Collection; Etudes Série Concurrence No.1, 'La Réparation des conséquences dommageables d'une violation des articles 85 et 86 du Traité instituant la CEE' (1966).

2 Judgment of the Court of Justice of 20 September 2001, Case C-453/99, *Courage Ldt v. Bernard Crehan*, ECR 2001, I-6297. Hereinafter '*Courage v. Crehan*'.

of the introduction of multiple damages depends significantly on the Commission's enforcement priorities. The legal traditions of the Member States regarding the nature of damages awards and the interference with public enforcement are also important factors to take into account in assessing the suitability of punitive damages as an enforcement instrument. This analysis will clarify whether the Commission made the correct choice when it decided to no longer pursue the adoption of exemplary damages, or whether, on the other hand, it should have grasped the opportunity (par. 5).

2. Developments in Europe Leading to the White Paper

2.1. Specifics in the EU Context

Provisions of EU law that are directly effective can be invoked by individuals before national courts in private litigation. National courts are bound to apply the directly effective provisions, to give them precedence over conflicting principles of national law and to protect the rights which derive from EU law. The concrete level of protection given to EU rights and the availability of remedies for breach of those rights will depend on the procedural, evidential, and substantive rules applicable in each particular Member State. These rules have to be compatible with the general principles of EU law.[3]

The direct effect of Articles 101 and 102 TFEU,[4] *i.e.* the competition law provisions, was confirmed by the European Court of Justice in *BRT v. SABAM*.[5] In this case, the Court stated that 'as the prohibitions of Articles 85 and 86 [now 101 and 102 TFEU] tend by their very nature to produce direct effects in relations between individuals, these Articles create rights in respect of the individuals concerned which the national courts must safeguard. To deny [...] the national courts' jurisdiction to afford this safeguard, would mean depriving individuals of rights which they hold under the treaty itself'.[6]

Private parties may use the competition law rules in national courts as a 'shield' or as a 'sword'.[7] The former refers to the use of competition rules as a part of a defence claim, normally through the application of the nullity sanction of Article 101(2) against claims for breach of contract. The use of competition rules as a sword is more proactive and frequently involves damage claims to obtain compensation for loss suffered as a result of an infringement of competition law.[8]

3 Jones & Sufrin 2004, p. 1304. The main principles of EU law that should be considered in this context are the principle of effectiveness, requiring that national laws does not render the exercise of EU rights excessively difficult, and the principle of equivalence, which demands that the national remedies for the protection of EU rights are no less favourable than those concerning similar domestic actions.

4 They were Articles 81 and 82 EC prior to the Lisbon reform. In this article, when referring to Treaty provisions, I will only be referring to the Treaty on the Functioning of the European Union, except when Articles are mentioned in direct quotations.

5 Judgment of the Court of 30 January 1974, Case 127/73, *Belgische Radio en Televisie v. SV SABAM* and *NV Fonior* [1974] ECR 313.

6 *Ibid.*, par. 16–17.

7 See also Komninos 2008, p. 3.

8 It is also important to point out that this particular use of competition law includes a broader set of remedies than the right to damages, ranging from injunctive to declaratory relief. See also Ezrachi 2008, p. 118.

As observed, the EU antitrust rules have long been there for individuals and companies to rely on in private litigation. However, they have rarely been used for such a purpose, and if they were, they mainly represented a 'shield' rather than a 'sword'.[9] In this context, the European Commission and the Court of Justice have taken various initiatives to encourage this more proactive use of antitrust law in national courts.

2.2. *The CJEU Case Law*

2.2.1. The *Courage* Case

The European Court of Justice has played an essential role in the initial shaping and further development of private antitrust enforcement in Europe. The pioneering decision in this context was *Courage v. Crehan,* which led to the establishment of a *European* right to damages in competition cases.[10]

As regards the possibility of seeking compensation for loss caused by an anti-competitive contract, the Court stressed the important role of national courts in applying the EU law provisions. National courts should ensure that these rules take full effect and protect the rights they confer on individuals. It further stated that 'the full effectiveness of Art 81 [now 101 TFEU] of the EC-Treaty and, in particular, the practical effect of the prohibition laid down in Article 81(1) [now 101(1) TFEU] would be put at risk if it were not open to any individual to claim damages for loss caused to him by a contract or by conduct liable to restrict or distort competition'.[11] The Court acknowledged that 'the existence of such a right strengthens the working of the Community competition rules and discourages – frequently covert – agreements or practices, which are liable to restrict or distort competition. From that point of view, actions for damages before the national courts can make a significant contribution to the maintenance of effective competition in the Community'.[12]

The judgment is also particularly remarkable because the claimant in this case was not a victim of the anticompetitive agreement but a party to the illegal cartel. Under English law there was a rule establishing that a party cannot obtain compensation from another party if they are both equally responsible for the damage. The Court's point of view is that there should not be an absolute bar to that effect, and that the possibility of recovery of damages must in principle be open to any individual.[13]

9 See Libertini & Maugeri 2005, p. 250.

10 *Courage v. Crehan.* In this case, Mr. Crehan a leaseholder in two Inntrepreneur pubs was contracted to purchase most of his beer from the brewer Courage. Courage sued Crehan in the English High Court for unpaid debt. In his defense Crehan, challenged the lawfulness of agreement claiming that it violated art 101 TFEU. Crehan also launched a counterclaim for damages, arguing that the illegal agreement caused the failure of his business. The case reached the Court of Appeal, which in turn referred it to the ECJ, asking among other things, whether a co-contractor has a right to damages. See also Ezrachi 2008, p. 120.

11 *Courage v. Crehan*, par. 25–26.

12 *Ibid.*, par. 27.

13 *Ibid.*, par. 28.

It is difficult to overlook the relevance of this case. On the one hand, it established a clear European right to damages for antitrust violations. This right is essential in order to provide an adequate level of judicial protection in the form of compensation, and aggrieved parties should be completely aware of this possibility. On the other hand, the Court positively valued and recognized the deterrent effects of private actions in the general EU context. Its favourable view towards damage claims represents in general an important encouragement to enforce competition law in national courts.[14]

2.2.2. The *Manfredi* Case

The Court's ruling in the case of *Vincenzo Manfredi v. Lloyd Adriatico Assicurazioni*[15] confirmed the judgment in *Courage*. In its ruling, the Court reiterated that the full effectiveness of Article 101(1) required that 'any individual can claim compensation for the harm suffered where there is a causal relationship between that harm and an agreement or practice prohibited under Article 81 EC [now 101 TFEU]'.[16]

As to the award of damages and the possibility of punitive damages as a remedy, the Court found that 'in the absence of Community rules governing the matter, it is for the domestic legal system of each Member State to set the criteria for determining the extent of the damages, provided that the principles of equivalence and effectiveness are observed'. Therefore, punitive damages should be available if they are also available for similar domestic claims. The Court further stated that injured persons must be able to seek compensation not only for actual loss (*damnum emergens*) but also for loss of profit (*lucrum cessans*) plus interest.[17]

The *Manfredi* judgment reiterates the need for an effective redress for the victims of competition law infringements. Aggrieved parties are entitled to damages, and it is for the particular Member States to define their extent. This should, however, not lead to the conclusion that the Court considers punitive damages to be appropriate in all competition cases, or that they should be available in all jurisdictions. As it will be examined, the adoption of multiple damages gives rise to numerous issues, and should therefore be assessed in the light of the concrete circumstances and context of the case. However, the fact that the Court left the door open for the Member States to make use of this possibility, can be seen again as an attempt to enhance private enforcement.

14 For an interesting study on the primary rationale of the Courage judgement see Nebbia 2008, pp. 23–43.

15 Judgment of the Court of 13 July 2006, C-295 to 298/04, *Vincenzo Manfredi v. Lloyd Adriatico Assicurazioni* 2006 [ECR], I-6619, (hereinafter '*Manfredi*'). The case concerned a follow-on damages action in the Italian courts regarding a price-fixing cartel agreement in the car insurance sector. Manfredi and other applicants claimed they had suffered economic damage and brought actions against their respective insurers to obtain compensation. A number of questions were referred to the Court for a preliminary ruling. These questions related to the right to claim damages, the right to obtain interests, the time limitations, the reservation of competence and the award of punitive damages to remove the illegal gain. For a general analysis of the *Manfredi* case and its impact on the Commission's initiatives see De Smijter & O'Sullivan 2006, pp. 23–26.

16 *Manfredi*, par. 60–61. It should be noted that the Court does not establish any requirement regarding fault, besides the proof of the infringement.

17 *Manfredi*, par. 91–95.

2.3. The Commission's Initiatives

2.3.1. The Modernisation Package

Despite the fact that the European Courts had confirmed the direct effect of the competition law provisions more than 30 years ago,[18] national courts have not often been invited by particulars to enforce the competition rules. The previous enforcement system based on Regulation 17[19] can partially explain this situation. This Regulation established a system of centralized application,[20] in which the Commission was the main actor and the only competent authority to grant exemptions under Article 101(3) EU.[21]

The adoption of Regulation 1/2003,[22] entailing the modernization and decentralization of competition law enforcement, led to significant changes in the traditional enforcement system, including the role of national courts, which created great expectations for the field of private competition law enforcement. The new Regulation not only highlighted the role of national courts by stating that they have an essential part to play in applying the competition rules and that 'when deciding disputes between private individuals, they protect the subjective rights under Community law, for example by awarding damages to the victims of infringements'.[23] In addition, as a result of the transformations, the national courts were empowered to directly apply Articles 101 and 102 EU, including the exception under Article 101(3) TFEU.[24] Consequently, they became full players in the new enforcement system, together with the national competition authorities and the Commission. This profound reform was expected to have a very positive impact on private enforcement of the EU competition rules.[25]

In addition to the greater expectations for private enforcement, the transformations and the enhanced role of national courts and competition authorities also illustrated the growing necessity for coherence and uniformity in the application of competition law throughout the EU. Regulation 1/2003 established in Article 15 innovative cooperation

18 See *supra*, note 5 and 6.

19 Council Regulation No 17 of 6 February 1962, First Regulation implementing Articles 85 and 86 of the Treaty, in *Official Journal of the European Communities (OJEC)*, 21 February 1962, p. 204/62.

20 See Gerber 1998, p 386. According to Gerber 'the lack of private suits for enforcement in Community courts and their rarity in Member State courts means that the Commission makes most decisions regarding objectives to be pursued, conduct to be challenged, resources to be used and the arguments to be employed in justifying decisions'.

21 The Commission exemption monopoly was generally considered to be an obstacle to more private enforcement, see Komninos 2006, p. 7 with further references.

22 Council Regulation No. 1/2003 of 16 December 2002 on the implementation of the rules on competition laid down in Articles 81 and 82 of the Treaty, [2003] OJ L1/1. Hereafter 'Regulation 1/2003'. Regulation 1/2003 replaced Regulation 17/1962. For a discussion of the main reforms and areas of concern see Wils 2004, pp. 661–736.

23 Regulation 1/2003, recital 7.

24 Under 101(3) TFEU certain agreements were, and still are, entitled to exemptions where they contribute to improving the production or distribution of goods, promote technical and economic progress or ensure that consumers reaped considerable benefits.

25 See Jones 1999, p 112. See also Komninos 2006, p. 7 with further references. National courts would then be able to 'address the full range of competition law for the first time'. They would no longer be obliged to suspend their procedures pending a commission decision on the applicability of 101(3).

mechanisms between national courts and the Commission, and Article 16 ensures a uniform application of EU competition law. These provisions need to be read in conjunction with the 2004 Cooperation Notice, which clarifies important aspects of the national courts' position in the enforcement of Competition law, and is of special importance for private enforcement.[26]

While it was expected that the radical transformations would lead to much greater private enforcement, the reforms conversely showed that the Commission's efforts were still not enough to achieve a much higher level of private enforcement. The modernization package was undoubtedly favourable and even necessary to stimulate private enforcement in Europe. In this sense, the innovative measures did promote private enforcement, but at a much slower pace than was anticipated.[27] Despite the removal of some of the obstacles, the reforms did not lead to a significant surge in competition litigation. As a result, the Commission continued taking initiatives to solve the remaining issues and to further encourage private enforcement.

2.3.2. The Ashurst Report

A first step to take was to identify the main obstacles hindering private enforcement, and to find possible solutions. With this aim the Commission ordered a study, known as the Ashurst Report,[28] which was published in August 2004. The report showed that, notwithstanding all the initiatives taken by the Commission, private damages actions in EU Member States were in a state of 'astonishing diversity and total underdevelopment'.[29] The report found only 60 or so cases leading to a judgment on damages, 28 of which had effectively led to a damages award. Although these figures might misrepresent the actual number of private actions,[30] it can hardly be disputed that the national private enforcement systems posed numerous impediments to a more efficient and successful (private) enforcement of EU competition law.

In contrast with the situation prior to the *Courage* case, the uncertainty of the existence of a right to damages no longer seemed to be the main impediment. Potential claimants had mostly been discouraged by unfavourable elements of this remedy, a lack

26 European Commission, Notice on Cooperation between National Courts and the European Commission in Applying Articles 81 and 82 of the EC Treaty, [1993] OJ C39/6. It details the mechanism which governs the cooperation between Commission and courts and reiterates the relevant case law. For a more detailed overview of the cooperation issues and mechanism, see Gerber & Cassinis 2006, pp. 10–18 and 51–57.

27 See Commission 34th Report on Competition Policy – 2004, Brussels/Luxembourg, 2005, p. 15, referring to Regulation 1/2003 as 'a first step in strengthening private enforcement before national courts by giving the latter the power to apply Article 81(3)'.

28 Study on the conditions of claims for damages in case of infringement of EC competition rules (Ashurst, Brussels, 2004). Hereafter 'Ashurst Report', available at: http://ec.europa.eu/competition/antitrust/actionsdamages/comparative_report_clean_en.pdf, visited on 12 March 2011.

29 Ashurst Report, p. 1.

30 It is argued in this sense that the report does not take into account the settled cases. See Rodger 2008, p. 96. Some damages claims had also been settled between pharmaceutical producers and the department of health, the paying by British airways Virgin Atlantic etc.

of clarity as to its application, and a general reluctance to make use of it.[31] Logically, victims of competition law violations remain often uncompensated for their losses.[32]

2.3.3. The Green Paper

On the basis of the Ashurst Study, the Commission published a Green Paper[33] and a Commission Staff Working Paper[34] on antitrust damages actions in December 2005. The documents address the conditions for bringing damages claims for infringement of EU antitrust law. Their objective was to 'identify the obstacles to a more efficient system for bringing such claims and propose options for solving these problems'.[35]

The measures proposed by the Green Paper would ensure that companies and consumers were compensated for their losses, while avoiding claims instituted without sufficient grounds and serving only to cause annoyance to the defendant.[36] In addition, at the time the Green Paper was published the Competition Commissioner, Neelie Kroes stressed that the right of businesses and individuals to see their damage compensated, was often only theoretical because too many obstacles to exercising this right existed in practice. The Green Paper was meant to set out options for making that right a real possibility.[37]

The main issues identified were, amongst others, access to evidence and documents,[38] the need for a fault requirement or the sufficiency of the proof of the infringement,[39] the definition of damages,[40] the availability of passing-on defence and indirect purchaser standing,[41] the possibility for bringing collective actions,[42] and the existence of special rules on the payment of costs of actions.[43] For each of the obstacles, several options were

31 See Eilmansberger 2007, p. 434. 'The Green Paper on damages actions for breach of the EC antitrust rules and beyond: reflections on the utility and feasibility of stimulating private enforcement through legislative action'.

32 Commission Staff Working Paper, Annex to COM(2005) 672 final, Green Paper – Damages actions for breach of the EC antitrust rules, SEC(2005) 1732, par. 37.

33 Commission Green Paper on Damages Actions for Breach of the EC Antitrust Rules, par. 1.1, COM (2005) 672 final (19 December 2005) (hereinafter 'Green Paper'). In the EU, green papers are documents published by the European Commission to stimulate discussion on given topics at European level. They invite the relevant parties to participate in a consultation process and debate on the basis of the proposals they put forward. The proposals included in green papers and their subsequent discussion may give rise to legislative developments that are then outlined in White Papers. See European Union, Glossary: Green Paper, available at: http://europa.eu/scadplus/glossary/green_paper_en.htm.

34 Commission Staff Working Paper (*supra* note 32).

35 Green Paper, par. 3.

36 Commission's press release from 20th Dec 2005. Available at: http://europa.eu/rapid/pressReleasesAction.do?reference=IP/05/1634&format=HTML&aged=0&language=EN&guiLanguage=en (last visited on 20 March 2010).

37 Commission's press release from 20 December 2005, *supra*, note 37.

38 Green Paper, par. 5–6.

39 *Ibid.*, par. 6–7.

40 *Ibid.*, par. 7.

41 *Ibid.*, par. 7–8.

42 *Ibid.*, par. 8–9.

43 *Ibid.*, par. 9.

put forward for debate. The Commission invited all interested parties to comment on the issues and the suggested measures

The majority of the responses to the Green Paper acknowledged the complementary role and the significance of private damage actions for the enforcement of competition rules. The consultation process also revealed a general consensus on the fact that victims of competition law infringements should be compensated and, consequently, are entitled to damages.

2.3.4. The White Paper

The next step was taken in April 2008, when the Commission adopted the White Paper[44] on private damages actions for breach of the EC Antitrust Rules,[45] along with a Staff Working Paper[46] and an Impact Assessment.[47] The White Paper's primary objective is 'to improve the legal conditions for victims to exercise their right under the Treaty to reparation of all damage suffered as a result of a breach of the EC antitrust rules'.[48]

In the light of the reactions to the Green Paper, the White Paper put forward various proposals, which would help ensuring that any victim of competition law infringements can have access to appropriate enforcement instruments and be effectively compensated.

Compared to the Green Paper, the measures proposed in the White paper were more conservative and have been considered by some as disappointing.[49] It is obvious that the Commission tried to encourage more balanced reforms, rooted in European legal culture and traditions, and which would consequently face less resistance at a national level.

44 A Commission White Paper is a document containing policy proposals for EU actions in a specific area. As it does in this case, it often follows a Green Paper published to launch a consultation process on EU level. A White Paper does not have any binding effect but it can lead to an action programme for the EU in the area concerned, if it is favourably received. See European Union, Glossary: White Paper, available at: http://europa.eu/scadplus/glossary/white_paper_en.htm.

45 White Paper on damages actions for breach of the EC antitrust rules, COM(2008) 165 final. Hereafter 'White Paper'.

46 Commission staff working paper accompanying the White Paper on damages actions for breach of the EC antitrust rules, SEC(2008) 404 final.

47 Commission staff working paper accompanying the White Paper on damages actions for breach of the EC antitrust rules – Impact assessment, SEC(2008) 405 final. The White Paper should be read in conjunction with the aforementioned documents, the former offering a relevant overview of the existing *acquis communautaire*, and the latter analysing the benefits and costs of the various policy options.

48 White Paper, p. 3.

49 Ezrachi 2008, p. 125.

3. Punitive Damages for Antitrust Violations

3.1. *The Commission's Proposals*

3.1.1. The Green Paper: Double Damages in Horizontal Cartel Cases

The 2005 Green Paper addressed various issues concerning the actual scope of damages. As regards the definition of the damages award, the Commission made different proposals. Damages could be awarded with reference to the loss suffered by the claimant (compensatory damages), with reference to the illegal gain made by the infringer (recovery of illegal gain), and most notably, double damages for horizontal cartels.[50] Under this last option, such awards would be granted either at the discretion of the court, automatically or conditionally.[51] The Green Paper also considered that prejudgment interest should be available from the date of the infringement or from the date of the injury.[52]

In effect, Option 16 proposing the award of double damages for horizontal cartels was the most controversial suggestion in the Green Paper. The responses and reactions to the Green Paper demonstrated that the compensatory principle for the recovery of damages was strongly supported by a great majority, which was completely opposed to any other proposal that would depart from this principle.

3.1.2. The White Paper: Single Damages and Interest

The Commission did not incorporate the Green Paper option of double damages for horizontal cartel cases into the White Paper. Instead, the Commission opted for a definition of damages reflecting the loss suffered by the claimant.[53] It should be stressed that this proposal does not exclude the possibility of a Member State to offer multiple damages. The option of full compensation of the real value of the loss suffered contained in the White Paper should be seen as a minimum and basic right of the victim. This right to full compensation includes the actual loss due to an anti-competitive price increase, the loss of profit as a result of any reduction of sales, and a right to interest.[54]

3.2. *The U.S. Model: Treble Damages for Antitrust Infringements*

In the United States, the Clayton Act authorizes private persons and entities injured by violations of the antitrust laws to sue and 'recover threefold the damages by him

50 Green Paper, par. 2.3; see also OECD: Private remedies 270 (2007), available at: www.oecd.org/dataoecd/ 24/62/39892177.pdf ('The Commission does not see double damages as punitive, but 'merely a required financial incentive to support the purpose of compensation').

51 Green Paper, par. 2.3.

52 *Ibid.*

53 White Paper, par. 2.5.

54 *Ibid.*

sustained'.[55] The Clayton Act gives standing to any person who is injured in his business or property by reason of anything forbidden by the antitrust laws.[56] Treble damages were designed to deter illegal conduct, deprive antitrust violators of the fruits of their illegal activities and provide compensation to victims of wrongdoing.[57]

The Clayton Act's treble damages provision has been often considered as central to the private enforcement of U.S. antitrust law.[58] While it represents an important incentive for plaintiffs to litigate, the risk for firms of facing a considerable sanction will discourage future violations. The supporters of treble damages argue that plaintiffs would not be motivated to sue for only a small amount of damages, especially if they are not financially equipped to cover their costs.[59] Furthermore, they suggest that treble damages provide for the perfect amount of deterrence.[60]

In contrast, this provision has also been criticized for various reasons. Some practitioners and policy makers maintain that trebling damages creates an excessive incentive for plaintiffs to sue, which can result in a windfall to claimants. Additionally, higher fines or criminal sanctions can also provide an additional deterrent effect.[61] Some others believe that it encourages settlement on inadequate grounds because of the fear of paying a tremendous damage award.[62] There is also concern that treble damages, certainly in combination with large class actions, produce unjustifiably large damage awards,[63] which ultimately leads to overdeterrence and has a chilling effect on competition.

4. Justifying the Commission's Approach

4.1. *The Nature of Cartels*

In Europe, the common understanding is that the objective of damages should be to compensate losses, and should therefore be limited to single damages. Consequently, in stark contrast to the United States, there seems to be an overall agreement that punitive damages are only appropriate in very rare exceptions.

55 The Clayton Act of 1914, 15 U.S.C. par. 15.

56 *Ibid.*

57 See case US Supreme Court, *Blue Shield of Virginia v. McCready*, 457 US 465, 472 (1982), decided on June 21, 1982. Available at: http://supreme.justia.com/us/457/465/.

58 See Sittenreich 2010, p. 2733.

59 See Eisen 1990, p. 268 ('Antitrust suits are expensive to prosecute for all but the most well-heeled plaintiffs, making the availability of treble damages almost mandatory for a plaintiff to be able financially to proceed'.).

60 See further Ginsburg 2005, p. 437.

61 See Wils 2003, p. 12. See also Comments of the Section of Antitrust Law and the Section of International Law of the American Bar Association in Response to the Request for Public Comment of the Commission of the European Communities on Damage Actions for Breaches of EU Antitrust Rules (ABA Response), April 2006, at 26–27. The validity of treble damages continues to be a topic of conversation in the US legal community and was the subject of an Antitrust Modernisation Committee hearing in July 2005.

62 See Sittenreich 2010, p. 2734, referring to Ysewyn 2006, p 15.

63 OECD, 'Private remedies' 270 (2007) (available at: www.oecd.org/dataoecd/24/62/39892177.pdf), p. 16 ('A frequently expressed view of U.S. antitrust litigation is that treble damage awards, combined with the possibility of suits of multiple groups of plaintiffs suits against a single cartel could frequently lead to excessive damage awards that were not justified under a theory of compensation or as a deterrent'.).

Cases in which undertakings take part in the most damaging forms of anti-competitive activity, such as hard-core cartels,[64] undoubtedly provide convincing reasons which can justify the award of damages at a higher rate.

In essence, cartels are secret horizontal agreements that divide markets, fix prices, limit output and prevent new competitors from entering the market. This illegal conduct is unique within competition law. Unlike other forms of anti-competitive behaviour, cartels have been primarily designed to work in the interests of their members and not the consumer or the overall well-functioning of the economy. They serve the only purpose of reducing or eliminating competition. Since they can never be viewed favourably from an economic standpoint, they have no possible (legal) justification and are categorically condemned.

Such infringements have a significantly damaging impact on their victims.[65] They lead to less choice for consumers, higher costs and reduced competitiveness for industry, delays in firms making essential adjustments, and less innovation.[66] Furthermore, taking part in a cartel agreement allows the companies involved to enjoy higher profits, which are extracted directly from their customers. The low chances of being detected,[67] in addition to the high profitability and the damaging nature of cartels, are factors that may indeed justify the need to impose sanctions in excess of actual harm, like punitive damages, without risking overdeterrence.[68]

4.2. *Enforcement Priorities and the Role of Punitive Damages*

4.2.1. Evolving Policy Goals

The benefits of the adoption of punitive damages for the enforcement system in general may justify in certain situations a departure from the principles that normally apply in civil litigation. Whether this is the case in the EU context can only be assessed in the light of the policy objectives and priorities pursued by the Commission and the Member States.

64 For an overview of the main characteristics of cartels and their damaging effects see Monti, 'Cartels Why and How? Why should we be concerned with cartels and collusive behaviour?', speech delivered to *3rd Nordic Competition Policy Conference*, Stockholm. September 2000, available at: www.kkv.se/upload/filer/eng/publications/3rdnordic010412.pdf.

65 See for economic impact of cartels, for example, Connor & Boltova 2005, p. 22.

66 European Commission, 34th Competition Policy Report (2001). See also the facts of the decision of the Commission of 21 October 1998 (COMP IV/35.691/E.4 – Pre-insulated pipes, OJ L 24, 30 January 1999, p. 1).

67 Combe, Monier, & Legal 2008, p. 1.

68 For an interesting discussion as regards the adequate level of liability see Polinsky & Shavell 1994, pp. 427–437. In particular they argue that in a world were legal errors are possible, 'the gain-based measure would result in a pronounced chilling effect on socially desirable behaviour,' while harm-based liability does not have such effect. For actions that are easily observed and whose legality is determined by the 'rule of reason,' punitive damages would offer excessive deterrence, *i.e.* deter some socially desirable actions.

Already as early as 1983 the Commission stressed the idea that private enforcement was a complimentary tool to its traditional enforcement arsenal.[69] However, the goals pursued by the Commission when encouraging private enforcement appear to have changed. In this context, one may wonder what the Commission intends to achieve by taking initiatives to facilitate antitrust damages claims.

In the Green Paper, the Commission clearly stated that damages actions for the infringement of competition law serve several purposes, namely to compensate those who have suffered a loss as a consequence of anti-competitive behaviour, and to ensure the full effectiveness of the antitrust rules by discouraging anti-competitive behaviour, thus contributing to the maintenance of effective competition in the EU (deterrence).[70]

The White Paper, in contrast, focused only on the need to improve the legal conditions for victims to exercise their right to reparation for all damage suffered. Full compensation was clearly established as the first and foremost guiding principle.

The Commission did acknowledge that improving compensatory justice would naturally entail other benefits. It would, for instance, create additional deterrence of future infringements and greater compliance with EU antitrust rules. Nonetheless, it was clear that in its new approach, deterrence was no further an objective to achieve, but rather an inevitable collateral consequence of the proposed measures.[71]

This policy document further emphasized that the reforms would follow a 'genuinely European approach'.[72] The proposals would consist of balanced measures, rooted in European legal culture and traditions. Unsurprisingly, in line with this new approach, the White Paper suggested a single measure of damages instead of the U.S. Clayton Act's treble damages system.

In 2009, the Commission proposed a directive on rules governing damage actions[73] in which it reiterated that the main goal of damages actions is compensation and that deterrence is merely a side effect.[74] However, the Commission withdrew its proposal in early October of that same year.

4.2.2. The Role of Punitive Damages in Context

The desirability of the introduction of punitive damages not only depends on the nature of the infringement. As observed, such controversial remedy may indeed be acceptable when dealing with the most deliberate violations of competition law. But it also appears necessary to assess the role of this particular remedy in the light of the Commission's policy. The suitability of the adoption of punitive damages will also depend on the role it plays in achieving the Commission's goals.[75]

69 European Commission, 13th Report on Competition Policy (1983), p. 135.

70 *Ibid.*, par. 1.1.

71 White Paper, par. 1.2.

72 *Ibid.*

73 See Alfaro & Reher 2010, pp. 44–45; see also, in general Donald 2009.

74 See Alfaro & Reher 2010, p. 43: 'The Commission now clarifies: The proposed Directive takes a compensatory approach: its aim is to allow those who have suffered damage caused by an infringement of the EC competition rules to recuperate that loss from the undertaking(s) which infringed the law'.

75 See also Sittenreich 2010, pp. 2743–2744.

4.2.2.1. *Deterrence*

Punitive damages serve various objectives.[76] By its very nature, one of the primary aims of this remedy is deterrence. This objective consists in discouraging or preventing future conduct similar to that presently being punished. It is generally accepted that awarding punitive damages serves to deter future conduct.[77] Deterrence is normally achieved when the defendant has to pay multiple damages. The higher the damages award, the greater deterrent effect it will cause.

Accordingly, if deterrence is one of the Commission's objectives when encouraging damage claims, as it stated in the Green Paper, the concession of multiple damages will in effect contribute to achieve this objective and can be considered a logical, and eventually adequate, measure. Allowing individuals to recover multiple damages can compensate for low probabilities of detection of hard-core cartels, and at the same time act as a disincentive for firms that are considering taking part in such agreements. The approach taken by the Commission in the Green Paper clearly reflects this point of view.

On the other hand, one should also keep in mind that as the European Court of Justice recognized in the *Courage* judgment, damage claims inevitably entail deterrent effects. The question now is which level of deterrence is necessary and what is the most adequate method to achieve it. In terms of deterrence, one should keep in mind that the superiority of public enforcement is practicably undeniable.[78] For this reason, if additional monetary sanctions are required for deterrence purposes, this objective could be properly achieved, eventually in a cheaper manner by increasing the level of fines imposed through administrative enforcement.[79] This approach would avoid overcompensation of victims, which could possibly lead to excessive private litigation.

4.2.2.2. *Compensation*

The ability to compensate victims for the antitrust harm they have suffered is one of the functions of private antitrust that cannot be achieved through public enforcement.[80]

76 For an overview of the different objectives of punitive damages see Owen 1994, pp. 363–413.

77 On the deterrent effect of damages awards see for example Mestmäcker 2000, p. 422; Jones & Sufrin 2004, p. 1192.

78 See Wils 2003, p. 12. Wils argues that public enforcement is inherently superior over private enforcement, for three sets of reasons: 'Firstly, public enforcement benefits from more effective investigative and sanctioning powers. Secondly, as private enforcement is driven by the private profit motive, it systematically diverges from the general interest. Thirdly, private enforcement is more costly than public enforcement'.

79 It should be noted that, in any case, Article 23(1) Regulation 1/2003 provides that the maximum level of fines is limited to 10% total turnover of the business year preceding the infringement. This provision, which objective is to maintain the proportionality of fines, will be problematic in order to impose higher fines.

80 See also Komninos 2006, pp. 5–26. This author notes that it is not correct to exclude any role for public enforcement in this area: 'there are cases where the public agency enforcing the competition rules may take into account the injury to specific victims of an anti-competitive practice and impose on the perpetrator the obligation to compensate those persons. Indeed, the public agency may pursue this

Compensation awards can logically also have deterrent effects, but as explained, in this case deterrence would just be a consequence or a side effect.

If by facilitating private damages actions, the Commission only aims at assuring full compensation of loss, the introduction of multiple damages awards would inevitably be excessive. It is certain that punitive damages do have compensatory benefits. The problem is that since this remedy affords by definition a higher award than the value of the loss suffered, the victims are *over*compensated. The additional award incorporated in the 'punitive element' of the remedy, would at the same time result in a 'not pursued' deterrent effect. Full compensation can in all cases be effectively achieved by just awarding single damages, which are more adequate, as long as the final award for the victims is properly aligned with the size of the harm actually suffered.[81] This brings us to the conclusion that there is no need for awarding double damages according to the new enforcement priority. The choice of the Commission not to include that option in the White paper appears thus to be coherent and in line with its more recent approach.

4.2.2.3. Incentive to Sue

The Commission has also seen punitive damages as a mechanism to motivate victims of antitrust infringements to bring damages claims.[82] In effect, the fact that victims can only claim a compensating amount of damages is not very encouraging to sue, particularly if we take into account the high costs that private litigation commonly involves and its unpredictable character. In this context, punitive damages can act as an (economic) incentive: plaintiffs will obviously be more likely to bring damage claims when the potential awards are higher.

One should note, however, that the damages award in Europe is likely to be coupled with prejudgment interest, as granting interest is usually the norm in European jurisdictions.[83] In contrast, in the United States, the Sherman Act does not provide for a similar pre-judgment interest.[84] Comparing these situations, one can conclude that the inclusion of the pre-judgment interest in the EU can result in a comparable level of

informally, for example through an informal settlement. In addition, some competition regimes also provide for a role for the public authority in claiming damages, acting on behalf of the victims.

81 Given the diverse types of damage that cartels produce, there are numerous economic and also legal obstacles for the quantification of harm in these cases. See Friederiszick & Röller 2010, pp. 595–618.

82 See N. Kroes 'More private antitrust enforcement through better access to damages: an invitation for an open debate'. Speech delivered at the *Academy of European Law conference Private enforcement in EC competition law: the Green Paper on damages actions*, Brussels, 9th March 2006. The former competition commissioner specially referred to cartel infringements when she stated that by increasing the benefits of damages actions, victims can be more motivated to bring damages claims. 'It is with this point in mind that the Green Paper considers the option of double damages'.

83 For detailed discussion on the impact of pre-judgment interest see Jones 2004, p. 422. In the case of an infringement of competition law, pre-judgment interest is available in the United Kingdom, in Germany and in France.

84 Although there is a limited right to pre-judgment interest (s. 4 Clayton Act) for the period between commencement of the action and the date of final judgment. Interest is available to compensate the claimant for delays by the defendant.

compensation as the US-style treble damages remedy provides.[85] In view of that, the lack of multiple damages (double or treble) should not be translated into disincentives to sue. In addition, the Commission has demonstrated that it is aware of the risks that excessive incentives entail, when it stated that its final objective is to encourage a competition culture, rather than a litigation culture.[86]

The jurisprudence of the European Court of Justice has also confirmed that the provision of pre-judgment interest, in accordance with national rules, is an essential element of compensation for loss and damage sustained.[87] Therefore, while the award of treble damages can potentially act as an incentive for unmeritorious claims in the United States, this is not as important as it might appear at first sight. In the EU and the Member States, pre-judgment interest can effectively achieve a similar effect without the potential drawbacks.

4.3. The Legal Traditions of the Member States

As observed, in the Member States the nature of damages is traditionally compensatory.[88] The Commission has also recognized in its Working Paper that most Member States exclude exemplary or punitive damages, since they are contrary to their public policy.[89]

In Germany, for instance, the *Bundesgerichtshof*[90] refused to enforce a US court judgment awarding punitive damages, in part due to its 'incompatibility with the state's monopoly on punishment'.[91] In addition, the Federal Cartel Office,[92] in its Discussion Paper from 2005, described different methods to determine adequate compensatory damages to victims of a cartel. All these methods aimed at establishing the difference between a claimant's financial position on a market with and without the occurrence of the competition law infringement. Furthermore, the discussion paper clearly stated that the introduction of multiple damages should be rejected in all forms, since it would be contrary to the equalization function of the right to damage compensation, which is one of the main principles of the law on damage compensation in Germany. Damage compensation serves to compensate for losses that have occurred and it does not have a punishing or deterrent role.

85 The extent to which prejudgment interest increases the final award also depends on the date from which interest is calculated. See Lande 1993, p. 118. According to this study treble damages without prejudgment interest would fall between single and double damage awards with prejudgment interest.

86 Neelie Kroes, Dinner Speech at the Harvard Club: Enhancing Actions for Damages for Breach of Competition Rules in Europe (September 22, 2005), available at: http://europa.eu/rapid/pressReleasesAction.do?reference=SPEECH/05/533&format=HTML&aged=0&language=EN&guiLanguage=en.

87 Judgment of the Court of 2 August 1993, Case C- 271/91, *M. Helen Marshall v. Southampton and South-West Hampshire Area Health Authority* [1993] ECR I-4367 at par. 31; cited at par. 122, note 86 of the Working Paper. This judgement was confirmed in *Manfredi*, par. 97–100.

88 See different comments on the Green Paper available at: http://ec.europa.eu/competition/antitrust/actionsdamages/green_paper_comments.html.

89 Working paper published with the Green Paper, par. 121.

90 The Federal Court of Justice, Germany's highest court in the field of ordinary jurisdiction.

91 *Bundesgerichtshof*, Judgment of 4 June 1992, *Neue Juristische Wochenschrift* 1992, 3096, 3103 ff.

92 Bundesverband der Deutschen Industrie, *i.e.* the Federal Cartel Office.

Also under French (tort) law, damages are in no event punitive in nature, and aim at compensating the damage sustained and not at punishing certain behaviour.[93] The notion of punitive double damages for horizontal cartels was consequently dismissed since victims should not obtain any compensation that is greater than the actual loss incurred. This would also transform the French civil liability compensation system into a tool to prevent and repress anti-competitive practices.[94]

The legal systems of a minority of Member States like the United Kingdom and Ireland[95] do, on the other hand, recognize punitive damages.[96] However, actually awarding punitive damages is something that rarely happens. In the United Kingdom, multiple damages may be awarded in very limited and exceptional cases. One of such cases concern competition law infringements, more precisely when a defendant calculates that the profit will outweigh the damages and therefore decides to proceed with the infringement. Nevertheless, as the Commission recognized in its Working Paper, this will only apply in very extreme antitrust cases.[97] To date, punitive damages have not been awarded in a competition law case.[98]

4.4. *Influence on the Effectiveness of Public Enforcement*

One of the main concerns about the introduction of punitive damages was the potential impact that it could have on public enforcement, and especially on the effectiveness of the leniency programme.

According to the Leniency Notice undertakings that participate in or have participated in secret horizontal cartels can obtain a fine reduction, or immunity from fines in exchange of cooperation with the Commission in the detection and in the collection of evidence of the cartel.

93 *Avis du 21 septembre 2006 relatif à l'introduction de l'action de groupe en matière de pratiques anticoncurrentielles*, par. 70.

94 '(...) il convient tout particulièrement de veiller à la cohérence globale du système car les risques de neutralisation de l'action publique par l'action privée ne sont pas négligeables, tout particulièrement dans le domaine des programmes de clémence ', Secrétariat Général des affaires Européennes de la République Française, *Note à la Commission Européenne, in the context of the Consultation about the Green Paper*, available at: http://ec.europa.eu/comm/competition/antitrust/others/actions_for_damages/058.pdf. See also Réponse de l'AFEC au livre vert sur les actions en dommages et intérêts pour infraction aux règles communautaires sur les ententes et abus de position dominante, available at: http://ec.europa.eu/comm/competition/antitrust/others/actions_for_damages/101.pd.

95 In Ireland, punitive damages are 'rarely awarded... and are usually, relatively modest'. See Commission Staff Working Paper (*supra* note 32) par. 119.

96 Commission Staff Working Paper, *supra*, note 32, par. 118–119.

97 Commission Staff Working Paper, *supra*, note 32, par. 118. See also Davey & Holmes 2007, p. 945.

98 However the Competition Appeal Tribunal (CAT) has considered this question in a number of recent cases. In the case *Healthcare at Home v. Genzyme Ltd*, Court of Appeal – United Kingdom Competition Appeals Tribunal, 15 November 2006, [2006] CAT 29, the CAT awarded a substantial interim award to a claimant, indicating that it would have thoroughly examined the claim put forward for exemplary damages, had the case not been settled before it came to a ruling. This unusual case will remain a rather isolated and unique example and should not be misunderstood as a general way forward to the introduction of the US concept of punitive damages into Europe.

The Commission's Notice states explicitly that the fact that immunity or reduction in respect of fines is granted cannot protect an undertaking from the civil law consequences of its participation in an infringement of Article 101 EU.[99] The introduction of punitive damages as an enforcement instrument could have a negative impact on the effectiveness of the European Commission's and the Member States' leniency programmes. Undertakings involved in a cartel infringement may indeed decide not to go down the cooperation path, as long as there is no guarantee of leniency for successful immunity applicants, or at least a reduction in civil damages liability. This is an issue that has also been recognized and addressed by law enforcement in the United States, where a detrebling of civil damages for immunity applicants has been introduced into the law. Also the European Commission is aware of this issue and made proposals in the Green and White papers to avoid that damage claims could undermine the success of the Leniency Notice.

Accordingly, the Green Paper studied two possibilities as regards to civil liability of whistle-blowers. One option was to grant a successful immunity applicant a rebate on any damages claim in return for helping claimants bring damages claims against all cartel members.[100] The claims against the other infringers who are jointly and severally liable for the entire harm would in this case remain unchanged. The granting of rebate would depend on the scope of the damages, and would lead to four possible outcomes: compensatory damages (the actual scope of the damages suffered), restitutionary damages (the amount of the illicit gain) and/or double damaged for hard-core cartels with or without prejudgment interest.[101] The second option was to remove joint and several liability for a successful immunity applicant and limit it to the harm corresponding to its share in the cartelized market only for the direct and indirect contractual parties.[102]

Although these measures could indeed safeguard the efficiency of the Leniency Notice, one can also question whether granting leniency recipients immunity from damages or any reduction of their liability in private claims would indeed be necessary and, more importantly fair.[103] It is of course true that the incentives to apply for leniency would be increased by granting leniency recipients immunity or a reduction in private claims. Nevertheless, granting immunity from administrative sanctions, certainly taking into account the increasing levels of fines imposed in the last years, is on its own a great

99 Commission Notice on Immunity from fines and reduction of fines in cartel cases, [2006] OJ C298/17, par. 39.

100 Green Paper, option 29.

101 Green Paper, option 14–17. It should be stressed that the Commission's concerns do not particularly relate the effects of punitive damages on the Leniency system, but the whole effect of enhanced damage actions. The White paper chooses only compensatory damages encompassing actual loss and loss of profit with the right to pre-judgment interest. However, in order to safeguard the efficiency of the Leniency system, although for successful immunity recipient civil liability will be limited to direct and indirect contractual partners together with removal of joint and several liability. The successful immunity recipient will bear the burden of proving the extent to which its liability must be limited.

102 Green Paper, option 30.

103 See also Association of European Competition Law Judges, 'Comments on the Commission's White Paper on damages actions for breach of the EC antitrust rules' (2008), accessible at: http://ec.europa.eu/comm/competition/antitrust/actionsdamages/white_paper_comments/judges_en.pdf, at 6–7.

incentive which is able to maintain the effective functioning of the leniency system. If there was a need to enhance the attractiveness of leniency,[104] it has been argued that this could be done by other means, like increasing the level of fines or other public penalties from which leniency recipients are granted immunity or reductions.[105] As Wils observes, 'In the absence of any necessity in the public interest, it would also be unjust to deprive, wholly or in part, the victims of antitrust infringements of their subjective right to claim compensations for the harm caused to them by the antitrust offenders'.[106]

5. Did the Commission Make the Right Choice?

The 21st century fight against cartels has resulted in the adoption of numerous and innovative enforcement instruments, which ultimately aim at deterrence. The Commission has often referred to cartels as its main enforcement priority,[107] and it is aware of the fact that, despite the high fines and new enforcement tools, cartels continue to exist and are becoming more sophisticated and difficult to detect. The Commission, submerged in and totally focused on this fight, proposed to introduce punitive damages in the Green Paper, which would not only provide a remedy for the victims, but would also contribute to combat cartels increasing deterrence considerately.

At the time the Green Paper was published, the Commission seemed to overlook the fact that the primary aim of private damage actions should be compensation, and rather focused on cartel deterrence. The award of damages to compensate the harm is in effect what significantly distinguishes private from public enforcement. It is unquestionable that private enforcement can also accomplish other objectives like punishment and deterrence. However, if these were also main goals, the added value of private enforcement to public enforcement, and the stability of the system could be undermined. Accordingly, compensation for the harm suffered should be the central driving force for private actions, and any measure proposed to enhance its operation should take this priority into account. This was finally acknowledged by the Commission in the White Paper. The general adoption of an enforcement instrument like punitive damages, which primary aims at achieving punishment and deterrence, although it would also provide compensation benefits, does not seem to be adequate in the EU context.

It appears that the Commission needed some time and input to effectively recognize that while an adequate level of juridical protection necessarily involves offering full compensation, the question of 'extra punishment' is not as essential and could be left to the respective Member States, as the Court of Justice stated in *Manfredi*. In this sense, the Commission also demonstrated its will to be respectful for European legal traditions, and more notably, for the individual legal systems.

104 As Wils notes, 'it is important to keep in mind that leniency is not an objective in itself, but an instrument to facilitate the public enforcement of the cartel prohibition so as to achieve deterrence and punishment. Leniency has both positive and negative effects for deterrence and punishment, and the most attractive leniency programme is thus unlikely to be the optimal one'; for a detailed analysis see Wils 2008.

105 Wils 2009, pp. 31–32.

106 *Ibid.*

107 See for example A. Italianer, 'Priorities for Competition Policy', speech delivered at St. Gallen International Competition Law Forum, (2010) St. Gallen, Switzerland.

As regards the possible impact of punitive damages on the efficiency of the leniency programme, it is certain that the introduction of multiple damages would inevitably result in a risk of higher damages liability, which might be a disincentive to apply for leniency. However, since the Commission found possible solutions for these problems, it appears that they were not too relevant for deciding whether or not to pursue punitive damages.

It is obvious that the EU context is different from the model used in the United States, and although the experiences under this latter model can be of a particular use for the European Union, this does not mean that vital components of the US-system, like punitive damages, can just be absorbed in Europe. Considering the main objectives that private actions should pursue in the EU, the legal context of the Member States, and the impact that the general introduction of multiple damages would have on the whole balance of the enforcement system, it can be concluded that the Commission definitely made the right choice.

Bibliography

Alfaro & Reher 2010
Alfaro, J. & Reher, T., 'Towards the Directive on Private Enforcement of EC Competition Law: Is the Time Ripe?', *European Antitrust Review*, 2010, pp. 44–45.

Combe, Monier, & Legal 2008
Combe, E., Monier, C. & Legal, R., 'Cartels: the probabilities of getting caught in the European Union', *European Economic Reseach Papers*, 2008, pp. 1–26. Available at: www.coleurop.be/eco/publications.htm.

Connor & Boltova 2005
Connor, J.M. & Boltova, Y., 'Cartel Overcharges: Survey and Meta-Analysis', *Purdue University Paper*, 2005, available at: www.agecon.purdue.edu/staff/connor/papers/META-ANALYSIS_03-10-05_1_.pdf.

Davey & Holmes 2007
Davey, L. & Holmes, M., 'The United Kingdom', in: L. Davey, & M. Holmes (eds.), *A Practical Guide to National Competition Rules Across Europe,* The Hague: Kluwer Law International, 2007.

De Smijter & O'Sullivan 2006
De Smijter, E. & O'Sullivan, D., 'The Manfredi Judgment of the ECJ and how it relates to the Commission's initiative on EC antitrust damages actions', *Competition Policy Newsletter,* 2006, pp. 23–26.

Donald 2009
Donald, R., 'Lawyers React to Withdrawal of EU Private Litigation Directive', *GCR*, 2009, available at: www.globalcompetitionreview.com/news/article/18952/lawyers-react-withdrawal-euprivate- litigation-directive/.

Eilmansberger 2007
Eilmansberger, T., 'The Green Paper on damages actions for breach of the EC antitrust rules and beyond: reflections on the utility and feasibility of stimulating private enforcement through legislative action', *CMLR*, 2007, pp. 431–478.

Eisen 1990
Eisen, J.B., 'Antitrust Reform for Joint Production Ventures', *Jurimetrics J.*, 1990, pp. 253–270.

Ezrachi 2008
Ezrachi, A., 'From Courage v. Crehan to the White Paper – The changing landscape of European private enforcement and the possible implications for Article 82 litigation', in: M.O. Mackenrodt, B. Conde Gallego, S. Enchelmaier (eds.), *Art. 82 EC: New Interpretation, New Enforcement Mechanisms?* Dordrecht: Springer, 2008, pp. 117–135.

Friederiszick & Röller 2010
Friederiszick, H. & Röller, L.H., 'Quantification of Harm in Damages Actions for Antitrust Infringements: Insights from German Cartel Cases', *JOCLEC*, 2010, pp. 595–618.

Gerber 1998
Gerber, D., *Law and Competition in Twentieth Century Europe: Protecting Prometheus,* Oxford: OUP, 1998.

Gerber & Cassinis 2006
Gerber, D. & Cassinis G., 'The modernization of European Community competition law: achieving consistency in enforcement: part I and II', *ECLR*, 2006, pp. 10–18 and 51–57.

Ginsburg 2005
Ginsburg, D., 'Comparing Antitrust Enforcement in the United States and Europe', *JOCLEC*, 2005, pp. 427–439.

Jones & Sufrin 2004
Jones, A. & Sufrin, B., *EC Competition Law, Text, Cases, and Materials,* Oxford: OUP, 2004.

Jones 1999
Jones, A., *Private Enforcement of Antitrust Law in the EU, UK and USA,* Oxford: OUP, 1999.

Jones 2004
Jones, A., 'Exporting Antitrust Courtrooms to the World: Private Enforcement in a Global Market', *Loy Consumer L Rev,* 2004, pp. 409–430.

Komninos 2006
Komninos, A.P., 'Public and Private Antitrust Enforcement in Europe: Complement? Overlap?', *CLR,* 2006, pp. 5–26.

Komninos 2008
Komninos, A.P., *EC Private Antitrust Enforcement: Decentralised Application of EC Competition Law by National Courts,* Portland: Hart Publishing, 2008.

Lande 1993
Lande, R.H., 'Are Antitrust 'Treble' Damages Really Single Damages?', *Ohio St L J,* 1993, pp. 115–118.

Libertini & Maugeri 2005
Libertini, M. & Maugeri, M., 'Infringement of Competition law and invalidity of contracts', *ERCL,* 2005, pp. 250–272.

Mestmäcker 2000
Mestmäcker, E.-J., 'The EC Commission's Modernization of Competition Policy: A Challenge to the Community's Constitutional Order', *EBOLR*, 2000, pp. 401–444.

Nebbia 2008
Nebbia, P., 'Damages actions for the infringement of EC competition law: compensation or deterrence?' *E L Rev*, 2008, pp. 23–43.

Owen 1994
Owen, D.G., 'A Punitive Damages Overview: Functions, Problems and Reform', *Vill L Rev*, 1994, pp. 363–413.

Polinsky & Shavell 1994
Polinsky, M. & Shavell, S., 'Should Liability Be Based on the Harm to the Victim or the Gain to the Injurer?', *J L Econ & Org*, 1994, pp. 427–437.

Rodger 2008
Rodger, B., 'Private enforcement of competition law, the hidden story: Competition law litigation settlements in the UK 2000–2005', *ECLR*, 2008, pp. 96–116.

Sittenreich 2010
Sittenreich, M.A., 'The Rocky Path for Private Directors General: Procedure, Politics, and the Uncertain Future of EU Antitrust Damages Actions', *Fordham L Rev*, 2010, pp. 2701–2749.

Wils 2003
Wils, W.P.J., 'Should Private Antitrust Enforcement Be Encouraged in Europe?', *WC*, 2003, pp. 473–488. Available at: http://ssrn.com/abstract=1540006.

Wils 2004
Wils, W.P.J., 'The reform of competition law enforcement' in: D. Cahill (ed.), *The Modernisation of EU Competition Law Enforcement in the EU – FIDE 2004 National Reports*, Cambridge: Cambridge University Press, 2004, pp. 661–736.

Wils 2008
Wils, W.P.J., 'Leniency in Antitrust Enforcement: Theory and Practice', in: W.P.J Wils (ed.), *Efficiency and Justice in European Antitrust Enforcement,* Oxford and Portland, Oregon: Hart Publishing, 2008, pp. 113–153.

Wils 2009
Wils, W.P.J., 'The Relationship between Public Antitrust Enforcement and Private Actions for Damages', *WC*, 2009, p 3–26. Also available at: http://papers.ssrn.com/sol3/cf_dev/AbsByAuth.cfm?per_id=456087.

Ysewyn 2006
Ysewyn, J., 'Private Enforcement of Competition Law in the EU: Trials and Tribulations', *INT'L L Practicum,* 2006, pp. 14–22.

J.L. Smeehuijzen*

SOME TENTATIVE THOUGHTS ON PUNITIVE DAMAGES IN CASE OF BAD FAITH CLAIM HANDLING BY INSURERS

1. Introduction

The case where an insurer refuses to pay a claim that is not reasonably debatable – so called 'bad faith settlement' – would seem to be the paradigm candidate for punitive damages. In the absence of a punitive instrument, the insurer is left in a 'no-lose situation'. He may attempt to shake off the creditor by unfair conduct. If his bad faith tactics succeed, he pays less or nothing at all. If his bad faith tactics fail, he pays the interest he received anyway by keeping the money. Adding a serious downside to the equation – making, in other words, the insurer pay for his bad faith behaviour – appears to be no more than logical. The profitable tort becomes a liability; the insurer loses his motive for bad faith settlement; he will from now on pay duly what he owes.

Indeed, there are jurisdictions where substantial punitive damage awards are rendered against insurance companies engaging in unfair claims practices. The prime example is the United States, where the tort of bad faith was established in the 1950s and has since 'grown from infancy as a compensable action in contract law into a major source of litigation'.[1] It has been claimed there are many hundreds of thousands bad faith claimants.[2] The amounts awarded may amount to millions of dollars. Scholarly attention goes beyond traditional legal writing; a growing body of empirical studies on the limits and scope of bad faith laws' utility is evolving.[34]

* Associate professor civil law Vrije Universiteit Amsterdam.

1 Schwarts & Appel 2009, p. 1478.

2 The process is ongoing: 'For example, in the past two years, Colorado, Maryland, Minnesota, and Washington have each significantly amended their bad-faith laws. A number of other states have also considered legislatively expanding their bad-faith laws' (Schwarts & Appel 2009, p. 1480).

3 Asmat & Tennyson 2010; Hyman, Black & Silver 2010; Frank & Gryphon 2009; Browne, Pryor & Puelz 2004; Levine 1978.

4 There are materials for the general public as well; *Delay, deny, defend* (Feinman 2010) for example, a 248-pages book, aims to show the claimant 'how to fight back, explaining how to choose a carrier that won't take advantage of you, how to file a claim so that your provider can't avoid paying you, and what to do when your insurer disputes your claim'.

In Europe, by contrast, punitive damages for unfair claim handling play no role of significance. Two causes for this reluctance may be distinguished. First, in Europe, civil law traditionally is supposed to compensate and not to punish; to inflict deterrent and punitive penalties is found to be the function of criminal law, not of civil law. Secondly, the unequal bargaining power of insurers and claimants has not been considered to be an issue of large social importance; the claimant having little recourse against an insurer that treated him unfairly in the claim settlement process, was a status quo that for decades did not provoke much controversy.

Currently, both these causes appear to be fading. The principle of non-punitive civil law is in decline or is at least questioned[5]; perhaps, we are now ready to wonder, as an instrument for reinforcement, raising the 'punitive level' of our civil law is an option. Additionally, there is a growing awareness that insurance plays a key role in our society, and that the insurer having an interest in the claim and deciding on its validity at the same time, may be a cause for concern – the threat of abuse of bargaining power must be taken seriously. Insurer's behaviour, in other words, is under increasing societal scrutiny.[6]

In view of these two developments, the matter comes in our sight quite naturally: we no longer *a priori* think punitive damages are not an option and we do consider it important bad faith settlement is banned. Therefore: what are we to think of punitive damages in insurance bad faith actions? This question will be central in the pages to come.

An article at the crossroads of two emerging doctrines can do no more than scratch the surface. My observations will not go into technicalities[7]; I thought it best to focus on principles rather than legal detail, primarily because of the subject matter but also because differences in Europe's substantive laws require a fair degree of abstraction.

2. Punitive Damages versus Consequential Damages in the Context of Bad Faith

As a preliminary comment, the relation between punitive damages and consequential damages in the context of bad faith requires specific attention. An example: in 1993 a Texas jury assessed compensatory damages of US$ 2,170,000 and punitive damages of US$ 100,000,000 against an insurer that denied a US$ 20,000 claim.[8] A distinction is made here between damages as a consequence of the wrongful claims practices and damages that do not result from the wrongful claims practices. The former aims to bring the claimant in the position where he had been if the wrongful claims practices had not taken place and the latter aims to 'punish' the insurer in order to deter him (and other insurers) from misbehaviour in the future. All is clear so far.

5 This very book serves as an illustration. See also Koziol & Wilcox, 2009.

6 Van Boom, 2011, p. 78.

7 I do not, for example, put the question what the appropriate form of action is (does bad faith settlement provide ground for an action for breach of fiduciary duty, an action in contract, an action in tort or a hybrid action?), nor will I distinguish between first-party and third-party liability.

8 *Hedrick v. Sentry Insurance Co.*, No 96–128100–90 (Terrant County, Tex. Dist. Ct. 1993).

Now if we start focusing on punitive damages straight away, we might be deluded into assuming that consequential damages require no special attention; that bringing the claimant in the position where he had been if the wrongful claims practices had not taken place is well taken care of by our traditional comparative (hypothetical position minus actual position) approach. But this is not the case. On the contrary, the primary matter of discussion in current European practice appears to be whether the law permits us to simply bring the claimant 'back to zero' or that he should be kept under this level.[9] This is due to the fact that a debate regarding wrongful claims practices often takes the shape of a debate about late payment. In case of late payment, the claimant in many jurisdictions is entitled only to (statutory) interest. (Statutory) interest may well be a mere fraction of the damages actually suffered.

This phenomenon is illustrated by the recent joint report of the Law Commission and the Scottish Law Commission titled 'Damages for Late Payment and the Insurer's duty of Good Faith'[10] of which the opening paragraphs reads:

> 'In this Issues Paper we consider whether a policyholder should be entitled to damages where the insurer has refused to pay a valid insurance claim, or has paid only after considerable delay. In England and Wales, a policyholder who has not been paid a valid claim is entitled to sue the insurer for the money owed, plus interest. However, the policyholder is not entitled to damages for any further loss suffered through the delay in receiving the money. (...) This has proved controversial. By contrast, in Scotland (and in most other common law jurisdictions) damages are payable, provided that the loss is considered foreseeable at the time the contract is made'.

The decision that provoked this discussion was *Sprung v. Royal Insurance (UK) Ltd*[11], where Mr Sprung bought an insurance policy to protect his factory against 'sudden and unforeseen damage'. Vandals broke into the factory causing considerable damage, the insurer rejected the claim, Mr Sprung lacked financial resources to carry out repairs and went out of business as a consequence. Loss: £75,000 for the lost opportunity to sell his business. The Court of Appeal held that Mr Sprung was entitled to no more than simple interest and costs, as a claim for further loss was not recognised in law.

This debate '(statutory) interest *versus* damages for further loss' is less controversial than the issue of punitive damages. Victory of 'damages for further loss' over 'mere interest' could be implemented in most jurisdictions without any radical changes of the law; it does not require the introduction of a concept that is alien in terms of legal culture.[12] In the Joint Report, for example, it is argued that *Sprung* is out of line with the

9 Van Boom, 2011, gives a comparative legal analysis of wrongful claims handling by insurance companies in the United Kingdom, Germany, France and in the Principles of European Insurance Contract Law. The central matters of discussion are the percentage of interest and the question whether the insured can claim additional damages exceeding the interest (England and Wales: no, but rule under criticism; Germany: yes; France: no, unless insurer acted in bad faith, PEICL: yes). Punitive damages do not seem to be an issue.

10 Joint Law Commission, 2010.

11 [1999] 1 Lloyd's Rep IR 111; [1997] CLC 70.

12 In part 2.

principles of ordinary contract law. The action to be taken would simply be to bring the law in line with the principles of ordinary contract law. Moreover, from an ethical point of view allowing damages actually suffered hardly is problematic, whereas punishing the insurer financially may not be as readily in line with our intuition.

Separate issues as they may be – '(statutory) interest *versus* damages for further loss' on the one hand and punitive damages on the other –, there may be close interconnections. The main one is the following: the more realistic the possibilities are for an insured to recover his actual loss, the less we need punitive damages. If there were a 100% score for the insured – effortless, free and certain reimbursement –, there would be no need for punitive damages. Yet if it proves to be difficult to recover actual damages, the need for an instrument that is triggered in case of a mere infringement of the norm (such as punitive damages) gains relevance.

The above implies thinking about compensation should precede thinking about punitive damages.

3. Shortcomings of Compensation

If conventional civil law guarantees, in theory but also in practice, an effortless, free and certain reimbursement of any costs and damages (both pecuniary and non-pecuniary) arising from insurers' bad faith, there is no need for punitive damages. But is there such a thing? Even if the insured were entitled not only to statutory interest but also to damages for further loss, various obstacles still stand in the way of perfect remedy.[13]

First, it will in general be hard to establish the insurer acted in bad faith. The mere rejection of a claim that is later judged to be valid does not as such constitute bad faith; where there is 'reasonable disagreement', there is no bad faith. Any lawyer knows that few positions exceed the realm of the arguable; plausible arguments, with the exception of the simplest cases, are seldom far away. Furthermore, from a procedural point of view, the malicious elements that do amount to bad faith – e.g. the insurer deliberately refuses to investigate, or advances spurious defences, or deliberately delays payment on a claim it knows to be valid – will not always be easy to prove.

Not only does the insurers' misconduct have to be established, the insured will also have to prove the causal relation between the insurers' conduct and his damages; Mr Sprung, for example, had to refute the allegation that his business was no longer viable anyway and prove he went out of business as a consequence of the insurers' refusal to pay. This prove of *conditio sine qua non* is another hurdle in legal proceedings.

Additionally, the aspects of unfair settlement that trouble the insured perhaps most, may provide no ground for damages. I am referring to the distress over of a battle against an insurer that spans years. Insurance aims to bring the insured peace of mind. With bad faith settlement, the insurer provokes the very opposite. In most European jurisdictions however, compensation for such discomfort – which by definition does not translate into monetary loss – is absent or modest. Bearing in mind the ambition to

13 Sketching the 'shortcomings of traditional European civil law' in one page requires a high degree of generalisation. I have tried, at a basic level, to find the common core, but I do not pretend to adequately cover all individual jurisdictions.

completely compensate the insured, insufficient remedy on a non-pecuniary level is a crucial flaw.

Finally, we are faced with the following paradox. The insurer who readily admits his own misconduct over the past years of legal action, is probably an obscurity. Out of court settlement of a bad faith action is possible, but not feasible in most cases. In order for the insured to be compensated for the insurers' bad faith conduct, he will have to engage in precisely what was aimed to avoid: legal action against his insurer. Ironically, this may take years too, involve financial risk, cause distress.

In conclusion, traditional weaponry against bad faith settlement has serious shortcomings: it may be problematic, (i) both materially and (ii) procedurally, to argue the insurer acted in bad faith; (iii) it may likewise be problematic to prove conditio sine qua non; (iv) mental distress is insufficiently compensated and (v) a bad faith action requires the type of action we set out to avoid.

4. The Utility of Punitive Damages

Let us for the moment assume further thinking leads to conclude there is need for a superior alternative – mere compensation is not enough to counter bad faith claim handling. What would support punitive damages' candidacy?

Punitive damages' appeal in bad faith claims practices is primarily empirical. In the absence of a punitive instrument, the insurer is left in a 'no-lose situation'. He may attempt to shake off the creditor by unfair conduct. If his bad faith tactics succeed, he pays less or nothing at all. If his bad faith tactics fail, he pays the interest he received anyway by keeping the money. Adding a serious downside to the equation – making, in other words, the insurer pay for his bad faith behaviour – appears to be no more than logical. The profitable tort becomes a liability; the insurer loses his motive for bad faith settlement; he will from now on pay duly what he owes.

Punitive damages thus primarily serve a general interest. The individual claimant will be happy to receive sums in excess of his actual damages, but this is not punitive damages' objective. On the contrary, the 'unfair windfall to the plaintiff' is often viewed as an argument against punitive damages. It is all about the social desirability of reforming unfair insurance claim practices.

The pivotal question therefore is whether punitive damages are indeed likely to bring us closer to this goal. One cannot take a stance either against or in favour of punitive damages without an understanding of their empirical effects. These effects should not be perceived too narrowly. It is not just about the successfulness in improving claims processing by insurers; matters such as the effects on premiums and expansion in litigation[14] ('satellite litigation') should also be looked at. As European research on the

14 The Californian Supreme Court, e.g., considered that: ' It seem (...) that attorneys who handle policy claims against insurance companies are no longer interested in collecting on those claims, but spend their wits and energies trying to maneuver the insurers into committing acts which the insureds can later trot out as evidence of bad faith'. (*White v. W. Title Ins. Co.*, 710 P.2d 309, 328 n.2 (Cal 1985).

subject is far from mature[15], it is too early to express any strong views on punitive damages' utility in bad faith cases.

What could be said about future research? Looking at studies from the United States is an obvious first step. Bad faith laws in the United States have existed for a number of decades. An increasing body of empirical research into their effectiveness is evolving.[16]

Initially, the imposition of punitive damages signalled concern, because they were said to increase the cost of insurance and are unnecessarily passed on to the consumers in the form of higher premiums.[17] But it was also argued that these 'costs' might be one of the best 'purchases' in the history of common law. An author in the nineteen seventies, for example, claimed to 'illustrate the social desirability of the punitive damages doctrine by demonstrating its efficacy in reforming unfair insurance claims practices'.[18]

In recent years, academic writing is increasingly based on the analyses of large amounts of data. The abstract of a study from May 2010 for example[19], reads as follows:

> 'Economic theory predicts that policyholders in states that recognize a private cause of action for insurer bad faith should receive more favorable claim settlements if bargaining is undertaken with the bad faith regime in mind. (...) We find that tort liability for insurer bad faith increases claim settlements, and that this increase is statistically significant even after accounting for changes in claimed loss amounts when bad faith liability is expanded. We find further that the impact of tort liability on settlement amounts is greatest for small claims, and that tort liability reduces the likelihood of claims being underpaid. These results provide supporting evidence that tort liability for first-party insurer bad faith has real consequences for claim settlement outcomes'.

Yet the authors continue:

> 'These findings notwithstanding, normative inferences regarding the consequences of bad faith laws on claim settlements are not possible from our analysis. Higher claim settlements under tort bad faith may be evidence of beneficial effects of bad faith liability if in its absence insurers would underpay valid claims. Alternatively, higher claim settlements may indicate that tort liability creates insurer reluctance to challenge suspicious claims, which would create efficiency losses. Additional research on the relationship between bad faith regimes and other important aspects of the claim settlement process, such as the likelihood of fraud and the determinants of insurers' denials of claims, would help to shed light on the welfare consequences of bad faith liability'.

Surely findings such as these do not provide a sufficient basis for empirical expectations of punitive damages' performance in a European context. The above is a mere fraction of

15 See in this book: Louis Visscher, The Law and Economics of Punitive Damages.
16 See note 3.
17 Levine 1978, p. 614.
18 *Ibid.*
19 Tennyson & Asmat 2010, p. 26.

American writing on the subject. What is available should be properly analysed – we should be aware, for example, that many studies do not focus exclusively on punitive damages, but deal with tort liability for bad faith settlement in general. Furthermore, it should be borne in mind the outcome of empirical research is deeply affected by the precise features of the regime we choose. It is, for example, unlikely that if punitive damages were introduced in Europe, the stakes would be as high as in the United States. This supposed European modesty will affect the deterrent power of punitive damages. Transposing American results to the European setting therefore has serious limitations. For European policy-making, further research with a specific European focus appears to be required.

Having said that, postponing any policy-decisions until definitive empirical findings are presented may not be realistic. The American case tells us empirical studies are not likely to give any certain answers about the effects of punitive damages at short notice. After decades of research in the United States, results are still not conclusive, even though the Americans have databases covering decades of bad faith laws. We have no such resources, which makes finding solid proof even harder. We initially may have to rely on mere economic theory and assumptions. A deeper understanding will probably grow along the way.

5. 'Bad Faith Settlement': an Exclusive Criterion

I will not go into economic theory in this article, nor will I develop any specific thoughts on the empirical effects of bad faith rules. But I will in this paragraph try to shed some light on the type of cases a bad faith doctrine can be expected to cover.

This of course *in abstracto* is a matter of definition. In the United States, it has been observed that 'The term 'bad faith' (...) is not self-defining, nor has it historically been a recognized, independent basis of culpability in tort law. (...) Consequently, its use has caused definitional problems from the outset'.[20] The European debate will have to take its own course[21], yet it seems reasonable to expect that at the core of any bad faith definition lies the refusal of a claim without a reasonable basis for its refusal.

My expectation is that relatively few cases will fall under this category. I would like to illustrate this by referring to two personal experiences over the last two years.

20 Henderson 1992, p. 4. Schwartz & Appel (2009) illustrate this definitial discussion may last for decades. See http://apps.leg.wa.gov/wac/default.aspx?cite=284-30-330 for a bad faith definition comprising 19 subsections.

21 The following quotation from the Joint Report serves as an example of how such a discussion might evolve:
'Should legislation include guidelines for the content of the insurer's duty to act in good faith?
If so, should it specify that:
(1) An insurer should investigate claims fairly;
(2) An insurer should assess claims in a way which is free from bias, taking into account relevant circumstances, and not taking into account irrelevant ones;
(3) If an insurer considers a claim to be invalid, it should give the insured reasons for its decisions;
(4) If the insurer considers the claim to be valid, it should pay it within a reasonable time?
Do consultees agree that this should be a non-exhaustive list?'

In 2009, I published an article on bad faith settlement in the Netherlands.[22] This was read by a number of lawyers who were convinced their clients were treated unfairly by insurers. They contacted me and asked whether in my view the insurers' behaviour amounted to bad faith. I looked at some of those cases.

What struck me, was that even in those instances where there was every reason for the claimant to feel deeply frustrated about the insurers' unwillingness to duly pay, a close, detailed reconstruction of the insurers' conduct made the bad faith claim fall apart. Yes, it did seem obvious the medical error was an error indeed, but the insurer has a legitimate right to have an expert heard. Yes, after it was established an error had been made, his further request to hear an expert on the causal relation between the error and your loss of sight was most annoying, but, yet again, he was entitled to have an expert heard. Yes, it will have caused mental distress to provide the insurer with highly privacy-sensitive material, but from a legal point of view he is entitled to know whether any complaints were pre-existent. Yes, six weeks for a response is a long time, but your own lawyer sometimes needed rather a long time to answer any letters as well.

Now: did the insurer refuse of a claim without a reasonable basis for its refusal? Probably not; he simply exercised his procedural rights. He did refuse a claim where he should have paid, but the claim was fairly debatable in law and/or in fact.

Second example. I am a deputy justice in a Dutch Court of Appeal. In my experience, and I can only speak for myself, it is often very hard to find out what *really* happened between parties. Judges have techniques enabling them to reach a decision, but there are a number of mechanisms obscuring their view on real life: (i) there may be loss of information when the claimant tells his lawyer what happened; (ii) there may be loss of information when the lawyer tells the court what happened; (iii) relevant facts may have taken place, but cannot be proven. In addition to this uncertainty about the facts, the judge will have to weigh the case and come to a decision that seldom is incontrovertible; it generally requires a fair amount of rather subjective appreciation – of law, but also morally. In my experience, judges are well aware of these obstacles in the way of perfect, indisputable judgment. If we ask a judge to decide not only whether a claim should be awarded or not, but also to speak out whether the insurer acted inappropriately in the settlement process, he is in fact required to decide 'a battle within a battle'. For this second battle to be won by the insured, the judge will feel he needs to have an extremely high degree of certainty about his decision in the first battle. In fact, 'this is as well as I can do given the facts as presented to me' does not suffice; he will have to feel there can be no doubt about the facts and his appreciation of these facts; in his perception there should be no room for reasonable disagreement. I would expect this level of certainty to be rather exceptional.

In conclusion, I think procedural and judicial dynamics are such that in legal practice only cases of rather extreme misconduct will fall under the 'bad faith' heading. This takes us to the next paragraph.

22 Smeehuijzen, 2009.

6. The Limited Potential of Punitive Damages in Promoting Neutral Claim Assessment by Insurers; the Need for Additional Instruments

A bad faith definition along the lines of 'refusal of a claim without a reasonable basis for its refusal' in practice leaves the insurer a large room for manoeuvre. It will not force the insurer to assess the claim neutrally, but will instead allow it to take a 'negative approach' – he denies coverage, unless no plausible argument for rejection can be made.

I imagine this negative approach to be much more effective economically than actual bad faith settlement. If an insurer aims to make more profit by paying less out in claims, he does not have to argue the unarguable. He simply needs to take a reluctant stance on every aspect of the case. In the hands of a skilled lawyer, little is self-evident. With the exception of the simplest cases, there is a good change the insurer will find a handful of plausible arguments why the claim should be (partly) rejected or more closely investigated. The insurer may loose the odd case that is taken to court, but this is no serious downside to these kinds of tactics; there will be no bad faith consequences and a single failure represents a whole range of cases where the claimant is less persistent and settles for less or gives up altogether. Still a 'no-lose' position, thus, for the insurer.

This observation does not imply discouraging bad faith tactics by means of punitive damages is futile. But it does give reason to believe that punitive damages have limited potential to solve the problem. In aiming to restore the balance of power between insurer and claimant, a broader range of instruments should be looked at. I will give two examples.

First, in the above, punitive damages were presented as an alternative for compensation. But if punitive damages fall short, compensation may prove to be a welcome companion; both actions may well exist side by side. Punitive damages could be awarded in case of bad faith; compensation could be awarded in case the insurer fails to pay a valid claim, also if he had reasonable grounds for its initial rejection – irrespective, thus, of its good or bad faith. The joint Law Commission writes on this 'strict liability':

> We prefer the approach of the law in Scotland and in most other common law jurisdictions, which considers the insurer to be under a primary contractual obligation to pay valid claims. If the insurer fails in this primary obligation, then under normal contract principles, the insurer should be liable for any foreseeable losses which result. The test is an objective one. If the insurer refused a claim later held to be valid, the insurer would be liable, even if it had reasonable grounds for its original refusal.[23]

This type of action from a practical perspective is not without problems. With the exception of the fact that no bad faith needs to be established, all the obstacles as mentioned in paragraph 2 apply. But it may bring relief in some cases and, compensation may, as well as punitive damages, serve purposes of deterrence – albeit less forcefully.

23 Joint Report, nr 9.4.

Compensation is not the only remedy besides punitive damages. In France, for example, interest rates increase over time as an incentive for swift claim handling. This, too, is an option worth considering.

Secondly, if it is recognised insurance is a matter of the public interest, regulatory law and self-regulation may be brought into play.[24] And further steps may be required. I personally think a close analysis of the dynamics of claim handling within the insurance industry would be useful.[25] We know little about the (dis)incentives for insurers' personnel to judge a claim swiftly and truly neutrally. In-depth knowledge of the claim handling process enables the design of measures stimulating fair claim handling, to be implemented in insurance organisations.

7. Conclusion

The principle of non-punitive civil law being subject to reconsideration combined with an increasingly critical attitude towards insurers' claims handling, puts the question whether punitive damages are a suitable instrument to counter bad faith settlement by insurers. Because mere compensation does not seem to provide sufficient recourse against bad faith, punitive damages may well serve a useful purpose.

Since punitive damages primarily serve a general interest – the social desirability of reforming unfair insurance claim practices – punitive damages' ability to actually achieve societal improvement, is all-decisive. This essentially is an empirical matter. Insufficient research has yet been done into the factual workings of punitive damages in European to come a stance either against or in favour of punitive damages.

There is however reason to assume procedural and judicial dynamics are such that in legal practice, only cases of rather extreme misconduct will fall under the bad faith heading. This gives reason to believe that punitive damages have limited potential to restore the balance of power between insurer and claimant. A broader range of instruments should be considered.

24 Van Boom, 2011, p. 72: '(...) it seems that it could be beneficial to stimulate 'competition' between the ordinary redress offered by civil courts and that offered by other, more flexible instruments such as Branch Codes and ADR'.

25 Feinman, 2010, paints a rather bleak picture of the American market in chapter 4; 'McKinsey Redefines the Game: Claims as a Profit Center'. Whether there is truth in this image for (parts of) the European market I do not know, but it does show that the management of claim adjusters affects the quality of the claims handling process.

Bibliography

Asmat, D.P. & Tennyson, S.L. 2010
Asmat, D.P. & Tennyson, S.L., 'Bargaining in the Shadow of the Law: How do 'Bad Faith' Laws Affect Insurance Settlements?', 2010, available at SSRN: http://ssrn.com/abstract=1520882.

Browne, Pryor & Puelz 2004
Browne, M.J., Pryor, E.S. & Puelz, R., 'The Effect of Bad-Faith Laws on First-Party Insurance Claims Decisions', 2004, available at SSRN: http://ssrn.com/abstract=1604979.

Feinman 2010
Feinman, J.M. *Delay, Deny, Defend*, New York: Penguin Group, 2010.

Frank & Gryphon 2009
Frank, T.H. & Gryphon, M., 'Negotiating in the Shadow of 'Bad Faith' Refusal to Settle: A Game Theory Model of Medical Malpractice Pre-Trial Settlements and Insurance Limits' 2009, available at SSRN: http://ssrn.com/abstract=1463655.

Henderson 1992
Henderson, R.C., 'The Tort of Bad Faith in First-Party Insurance Transactions: Refining the Standard of Culpability and Reformulating the Remedies by Statute', *U Mich J L Reform*, 1992, pp. 1–68.

Hyman, Black & Silver 2010
Hyman, D.A., Black, B.S. & Silver, C.M., 'Settlement at Policy Limits and the Duty to Settle: Evidence From Texas', 2010, available at SSRN: http://ssrn.com/abstract=1134202.

Joint Law Commission 2010
Law Commission and the Scottish Law Commission, Joint Report *Damages for Late Payment and the Insurer's duty of Good Faith*, 2010, available at www.lawcom.gov.uk/insurance contract.htm.

Koziol & Wilcox 2009
Koziol, H. & Wilcox, V., *Punitive Damages: Common Law and Civil Law Perspectives*, Vienna: Springer, 2009.

Levine 1978
Levine, H.R., 'Demonstrating and Preserving the Deterrent Effect of Punitive Damages in Insurance Bad Faith Actions', *USF L Rev.* 1978, pp. 613–638.

Schwarts & Appel 2009
Schwarts V., & Appel, C.E., 'Restoring the Good Faith in Bad Faith', *Am U L Rev*, 2009, pp. 1477–1531.

Smeehuijzen 2009
Smeehuijzen, J.L. 'Schadevergoeding wegens onzorgvuldige afwikkeling van letselschadevorderingen', *NTBR* 2009, pp. 328–340.

Van Boom 2011
Van Boom, W.H., 'Do Insurers Have to Pay for Bad Behaviour in Settling Claims? Legal Aspects of Insurers' Wrongful Claims Handling', *JETL*, 2011, pp. 77–102 (available at: SSRN: http://ssrn.com/abstract=1829868.)

Louis Visscher*

THE LAW AND ECONOMICS OF PUNITIVE DAMAGES

1. Introduction

There are many possible issues related to the overall topic of 'Punitive Damages', as already became clear from reading the call for papers of the Liability & Insurance workshop of the 15th Ius Commune congress, and I have chosen the topic 'A Law and Economics Approach to Punitive Damages'. In my chapter, however, I will also pay attention to several of the other topics mentioned, because many of them are relevant in the economic approach to punitive damages.

One of the topics mentioned is 'Debunking the Myth' and in my view it is indeed necessary to do this. It is important to realize that the enormous amounts of punitive damages sometimes awarded by juries are often reduced by the court.[1] Moreover, empirical research shows that punitive damages are awarded in less than 5% of the cases in which the plaintiff prevailed.[2] Incorporating the fact that only very few claims result in trial and that plaintiffs win in about half of the cases, this implies that only very few claims result in punitive damages. They are not awarded more often nowadays than in the past.[3] Punitive damages generally speaking are not very high.[4] In a research regarding punitive damages in the 75 largest American counties in 2001, the median award was about US$ 50,000 (US$ 25,000 for torts cases and US$ 83,000 for contract cases) while it was US$ 63,000 in 1992. Punitive damages exceeded compensatory awards in 39% of the

* Louis Visscher is Associate Professor in Law and Economics at the *Rotterdam Institute of Law and Economics* (RILE) of the Erasmus School of Law. E-mail: visscher@law.eur.nl.

1 Vidmar & Wolfe 2009, p. 180.

2 Eisenberg *et al.* 2006, p. 268. Langton & Cohen 2008, p. 6 also find that in 5% of the general civil trials in 2005, punitive damages were awarded (http://purl.access.gpo.gov/GPO/LPS108623). Eaton, Mustard & Mustard 2005, p. 344 state that only 2–5% of the successful plaintiffs receive punitive damages. Sebok 2007, p. 964 mentions 2–9%, 'and an average of the studies suggests a rate on the low end of the range'. Eisenberg *et al.* 2002, p. 749 mentions a figure of 4%, as do Ostrom, Rotteman & Goerdt 1996, pp. 238–239.

3 Vidmar & Wolfe 2009, p. 189.

4 The US Supreme Court in *Exxon Shipping Co. et al. v. Baker et al.* (2008) states that 'most accounts show that the median ratio of punitive to compensatory awards remains less than 1:1'.

civil trials involving punitive damages.[5] In an older research (of the period 1981–1985) covering fewer counties, the median award in fifteen of the twenty counties with more than ten punitive verdicts was below US$ 40,000 (for thirteen of those counties it was even below US$ 30,000).[6] Finally, punitive damages are positively correlated with compensatory damages.[7]

This empirical research in my view suggests that the fear for 'American situations', that many European lawyers have when it comes to the topic of punitive damages, is unwarranted. The debate whether or not to introduce punitive damages in Europe therefore should not be cut off by using urban legends about American excesses.

In fully analysing the possible role of punitive damages, arguments from Law and Economics should be included. This paper serves to provide these arguments. I will spend most of my attention on punitive damages in tort law, but I will also discuss the possible role of such damages in contractual settings.

Section 2 briefly sketches the economic approach to tort law and damages in general. This is necessary so set the stage for the specific topic of punitive damages in tort law, because the question 'Why Punitive Damages?' (which is the first topic suggested in the call for papers) regards the goals of tort law and the law of damages. A discussion of the goals of law is very important in Law and Economics. Especially the goals of deterrence and punishment will be emphasized, because in legal literature they are generally regarded as the paramount goals of punitive damages.

After having provided this general overview, section 3 describes the specific function which punitive damages in tort law have from an economic perspective. It will become clear that both the topic of public versus private enforcement, as well as possible problems resulting from the divide between private law and penal law (again two topics mentioned in the call) are relevant here.

Section 4 analyses some specific issues relating to punitive damages in tort law, being intentional torts, the question whether potential tortfeasors should be able to insure against such damages, and basing damages on gains of the tortfeasor rather than on loss of the victim.

Section 5 discusses the economic analysis of punitive damages in contract law, which is relevant for the topic 'contract law: deliberate breach and punitive damages' from the call for papers. Some of the arguments are comparable to those in tort law, for example a too low probability of being held liable. However, given that contract law fulfils a different function than tort law, the role of punitive damages also is somewhat different. In this section I will first briefly discuss the role of contract law and contractual damages from an economic perspective, before turning to the question whether punitive damages should be granted for deliberate breach.

Section 6 concludes.

5 Cohen 2005, p. 1, 2. Note that due to incidental large punitive damage awards, the mean award is much higher, e.g. in 1992 it was US$ 481,000 for tort cases (median: US$ 36,000) and US$ 1,003,000 for contract cases (median: US$ 52,000). See DeFrances *et al.* 1995, p. 8.

6 Daniels & Martin 1990, p. 41, 42.

7 Vidmar & Wolfe 2009, p. 189; Sebok 2009, p. 158.

2. The Economics of Tort Law and the Law of Damages

2.1. Deterrence and Risk Distribution/Spreading

Many lawyers regard compensation of losses as the most important goal of tort law. In the Law and Economics literature, this view is challenged. If mere compensation would be the primary goal, it is difficult to understand why the behaviour of the injurer is such an important factor in establishing liability. After all, a rule of strict liability would result in compensation of losses in many more cases. Furthermore, *if* compensation would be the paramount goal, it could be achieved by a much less costly system: insurance. And one should not forget that the rules of tort law may also lead to the conclusion that the injurer in a specific case is not liable, so that there will be no compensation for the victim. Hence, tort law is not about compensation as such, but it is about deciding in which cases compensation is required and in which cases not.[8] The losses of the victim are only shifted to the tortfeasor if there are good reasons to do so. These 'good reasons' are the goals of tort law. Viewed in this way, compensation is not a goal in itself, but it is the means with which the goals of tort law are striven for.

What are the goals of tort law from an economic perspective? Briefly stated, the central objective is the minimization of total accident costs. These costs, according to Calabresi,[9] consist of:

- *Primary* accident costs: these are the expected accident losses (*i.e.* the probability of an accident multiplied by the losses which occur if an accident happens) plus the costs of precautionary measures which are taken to reduce the expected accident losses. The primary accident costs are influenced by the level of care (and of activity) taken by the actors. By inducing them to take care measures which cost less than the reduction in expected accident losses they cause, primary accident costs are reduced. This is the goal of optimal deterrence or prevention;
- *Secondary accident costs*: these costs are the costs of having to bear the expected losses. These costs may be reduced by shifting the losses to an actor who can better bear them (e.g. because he is wealthier or because he has better opportunities to insure himself), or by spreading them over a larger group. This is the goal of optimal risk spreading and distribution;
- *Tertiary accident costs*: these are the costs made in order to reduce primary and/or secondary accident costs (e.g. through the tort system). The costs incurred in order to reduce the primary and secondary accident costs, should not outweigh that reduction. Tertiary costs are also known as 'system costs' or 'administrative costs'.

The accident losses in economic terms are 'negative externalities', *i.e.* costs caused by an actor who is engaged in a certain activity, but which fall on someone else. The economic solution to externalities is 'internalization', meaning that the actor who causes the losses should incorporate them in his decision whether or not to act, how often to act, and how

8 See e.g. Keeton *et al.* 1984, p. 20; Fleming 1992, p. 3; Kötz 2001, p. 17; Rogers 2006, p. 4.
9 Calabresi 1977, p. 24 ff.

much care measures to take in order to reduce the losses. Tort liability is such an internalization device. Under strict liability, the injurer is always liable, so he will incorporate the expected accident losses into his decision and hence he will take the desired care measures and reduce his activity to the desired level.[10] After all, any costs caused by him are, through tort liability, channelled back to him. As long as the additional costs ('marginal costs') of reducing the activity level and/or increasing the care level are lower than the additional benefits ('marginal benefits') in the sense of a reduction in expected accident losses, it is desirable that the injurer takes the additional measure. As soon as the marginal costs start to exceed the marginal benefits, it is desirable that he does not take the measure. The optimal care and activity level are found there where the marginal costs equal the marginal benefits. Under negligence, an injurer who did not behave careful enough is liable, while an injurer who was careful enough is not. If the court bases the due care level on a correct weighing of the costs of care measures and the reduction in expected accident losses caused by these measures (in other words, if due care is equal to optimal care), negligence can give the correct behavioural incentives to the injurer.

Hence, tort law primarily aims at providing optimal care and activity incentives ('deterrence'). Not all accident costs will be avoided, because that is too expensive. The accidents of which the marginal costs of deterrence outweigh the marginal benefits are, in economic terms, too expensive to avoid. The optimal amount of accident losses therefore is higher than zero. The costs that still occur should be distributed and spread optimally, to lower the impact of these losses. Finally, the system costs should not outweigh the reduction in primary and secondary costs.

The instrument with which tort law provides the behavioural incentives, is damages.[11] In order to fully internalize the externalities, damages under a rule of strict liability should in principle encompass all losses caused by the tortfeasor.[12] If damages would be lower, the injurer would not be confronted with all costs caused by his activity, so that he would choose a too high activity level and would take inadequate care measures. After all, he would then weigh the full costs of reducing his activity level and/or increasing his care level against only a fraction of the benefits thereof. Under negligence, damages need not necessarily encompass all losses. There the injurer will decide to take due care as long as the damages are high enough to make taking due care more attractive than being negligent and hence liable.

2.2. *Punishment*

Much legal literature expresses the view that punishment is not a goal of tort law, among other reasons because there need not be any correlation between the reprehensibility of the behaviour which caused the losses and the magnitude of those losses and hence of the

10 This is, of course, a simplification. Many problems exist which hinder this perfect functioning of tort law. The rich Law and Economics literature deals with those problems, see e.g. Faure 2009.

11 In this paper I will not discuss injunctions. For an economic account of injunctions, see Ogus & Visscher 2010, pp. 32–47.

12 See e.g. Posner 2003, p. 192; Shavell 2004, p. 236 and Cooter & Ulen 2008, p. 339.

damages. A slight mistake may result in large damage while reckless behaviour might not cause any losses. Also the existence of liability insurance makes punishment problematic as goal of tort law. I will return to the insurance issue in section 4.3 below.

In Law and Economics, punishment is regarded as a goal of tort law neither. What is more, even in criminal law the primary goal is not punishment as such, but deterring wrongdoing.[13] This implies that tort law and criminal law in principle both serve the goal of deterrence. Criminal law is regarded as an *ultimum remedium*, which may become necessary as a result of possible problems with the working of tort law. If, for instance, the probability that an injurer is held liable is below 100%, tort damages do not adequately deter. Below I will argue that this is a possible reason for applying punitive damages, but it is an economic *raison d'être* for criminal law as well. Insolvency of the injurer (so that he cannot pay the damages) and rational apathy of the victim (so that he does not bring a tort claim) are other reasons why criminal law may be required alongside tort law in order to deter wrongdoing.

Polinsky and Shavell discuss the separate goal of punishment in their analysis of punitive damages.[14] The punishment goal is then derived from the desire of individuals to have blameworthy parties appropriately punished. I will return to this issue in section 3.6 below.

2.3. *Conclusion*

Tort damages serve the goals of optimal deterrence (by providing incentives to the parties involved to internalize the externalities they cause) and optimal loss distribution and loss spreading (by distributing and/or spreading the losses in such a way that the impact they have on social welfare is reduced). Compensation as such is not a goal. It is the instrument with which the abovementioned goals are aimed for. Punishment is not regarded as a goal of tort law either.

3. The Economics of Punitive Damages in Tort Law

3.1. *Introduction*

If one reads legal literature on the topic of punitive damages, it quickly becomes clear that deterrence and punishment are often regarded as the most important goals.[15] In this section, I will discuss the role of punitive damages from an economic perspective. Given the above-written, it will come as no surprise that in the economic literature, deterrence-based

13 See e.g. Becker 1968, pp. 169–217; Posner 2003, p. 217 ff; Shavell 2004, p. 543 ff.; Cooter & Ulen 2008, p. 510.

14 Polinsky & Shavell 1998a, p. 948 ff.

15 See e.g. many of the country reports in Koziol & Wilcox 2009. Also see Duggan 2006, p. 308, 309; Geistfeld 2008, p. 269; Vidmar & Wolfe 2009, p. 186 and the US Supreme Court decision *Exxon Shipping Co. et al. v. Baker et al.* (2008), where it considers that 'regardless of the alternative rationales over the years, the consensus today is that punitives are aimed not at compensation but principally at retribution and deterring harmful conduct'.

arguments are the most important.[16] Punitive damages are primarily analysed in their potential to ameliorate problems which are caused by the fact that tort law and tort damages in reality do not function as assumed in the simple model described in section 2.1.

The fact that punishment is regarded as a goal of the private law instrument of damages introduces the question whether this form of private enforcement is an alternative for public enforcement (again, one of the topics from the call for papers). There is a rich Law and Economics literature on the question under which circumstances private enforcement is better and when public enforcement is to be preferred.[17] A discussion of that literature lies beyond the scope of this paper, but a few remarks are in place.

As I have already mentioned in section 2.2, both criminal law and tort law serve the goal of deterrence. Given that tort law has lower system costs than criminal law (due to the latter's procedural safeguards, high social costs of its sanctions et cetera), criminal law is regarded as an *ultimum remedium* which should only be utilized if tort law cannot adequately deter wrongful behaviour. A first reason why this could be the case, is the fact that not all wrongdoers will face liability in all cases (also see section 3.2 below, as this is an economic reason for imposing punitive damages). The expected liability therefore is too low to provide the correct incentives. Criminal sanctions may ameliorate this problem. Second, the injurer may have too few assets to pay the full damages, so that the financial incentives from tort law do not fully reach him. Non-financial sanctions from criminal law could then be required to provide adequate behavioural incentives. The fact that criminal sanctions may stigmatize the convicted wrongdoer adds to this deterrent function of criminal sanctions. Finally, there are several reasons why a victim may not start a lawsuit against the wrongdoer (also see section 3.2 below). Criminal law, with the action being brought by the public prosecutor rather than the victim, can overcome this problem.

Punitive damages may be able to solve some of the aforementioned problems, without shifting from private law to penal law. The economic arguments for punitive damages, both from a deterrent and from a punishment perspective, will be discussed in the remainder of this section.

3.2. *Too Low Probability of Being Held Liable*

The first, and in my view most important Law and Economics argument for punitive damages, is that they may correct the problem that the injurer does not face a 100% probability of being held liable. The correct weighing of costs and benefits of precautionary measures assumes that the injurer compares his (private) costs of reducing his activity level and/or increasing his care level, with the (social) benefits of a decrease in expected accident losses. However, the injurer does not compare his costs with the social benefits of taking such measures, but with the private benefits thereof. These private benefits

16 See Schwartz 1982, p. 135.

17 See e.g. Landes & Posner 1975, pp. 1–46; Polinsky 1980, pp. 105–127; Shavell 1984, pp. 357–374; Shavell 1986, pp. 43–58; Shavell 1993, pp. 255–287; Polinsky & Shavell 2000a, pp. 223–237; Polinsky & Shavell 2000b, pp. 307–344; Innes 2004, pp. 29–48.

consist of a reduction in expected liability, rather than in expected accident losses. If an injurer would be certain that victims would not bring a tort claim, he would not receive behavioural incentives from the tort system, even if there would be a rule of strict liability. After all, if the victim does not bring a suit, the injurer does not pay. As soon as the probability of being held liable falls below 100%, the injurer does not fully internalize the externality and will not act optimally.

Several reasons exist why the probability of being held liable indeed will lie below 100%. If a victim-plaintiff does not succeed in proving a prerequisite of liability of which he has the burden of proof, the injurer will not be held liable. It might be, for example, impossible to prove causation between exposure to asbestos and lung cancer, especially if the plaintiff was a smoker. Injurers therefore may escape liability in cases where they should have been liable. It is also possible that the victim does not know the identity of the injurer, so that he cannot bring a tort claim to start with. It might even be that the victim does not know that he was the victim of a tort in the first place. Even if none of the above-mentioned problems exist, the victim might decide not to bring a claim because the costs attached to this outweigh the expected benefits. This might also be true if the victim is certain to prevail. In economic terms, the victim remains 'rationally apathetic', because bringing the claim would result in a worse outcome than not bringing it. This situation may especially occur if the losses are scattered over many victims, so that for none of the individual victims, bringing a claim makes sense. The total losses caused by the injurer may however be substantial, so that from a societal point of view it would have been desirable that the injurer would have been held liable. A last reason why the probability of being held liable may lie below 100% is that the injurer might actively try to escape liability. This is most likely in cases where he intentionally committed the tort. He then may take action to reduce the probability of being detected.[18]

Punitive damages are a way to solve the problem of a too low probability of being held liable.[19] The potential injurer weighs his costs of precautionary measures against the reduction in expected liability they cause. Expected liability consists of the probability of being held liable, multiplied by the damages he has to pay if he is held liable. If the probability decreases, but the damages increase proportionally, it is still possible to provide the correct behavioural incentives. This implies that total damages should be determined by multiplying the amount of the losses with the reciprocal of the probability of being held liable. Hence, if this probability is 50%, damages should be doubled to provide the correct incentives. If the losses of the victim would be €10,000, total damages would then consist of compensatory damages of €10,000 and punitive damages of €10,000. Expected liability of the injurer would then be 50% × €20,000, hence €10,000. Tort law can then still provide the correct incentives. It is interesting to see that according to several writers (and according to the U.S. Supreme Court), there has to be a ratio of the punitive award to the compensatory award.[20] The fact that the Supreme Court in principle

18 For the arguments mentioned in this paragraph, also see Polinsky and Shavell 1998a; Polinsky & Shavell 1998b; Landes & Posner 1987, p. 160.

19 See e.g. Ellis 1982, pp. 25, 26; Cooter 1989, p. 1148 ff; Polinksy & Shavell 1998a, p. 887 ff; Polinksy & Shavell 1998b, pp. 193, 194.

20 Eisenberg *et al.* 1997, pp. 638, 639; Sebok 2009, p. 158; Vidmar & Wolfe 2009, pp. 182, 190, 191.

wants to restrict the punitive damages multiplier to 'single digits'[21] in itself does not make economic sense, if the probability of being held liable would lie below 10%.[22]

The function of punitive damages to correct a too low probability of being held liable is consistent with the fact that punitive damages are often awarded in cases of intentional torts. Especially in such cases, the injurer might try to avoid being caught. Punitive damages may also serve as an instrument to overcome rational apathy, because the expected benefits from suing increase due to the higher damages award.[23]

3.3. *Too Low Compensatory Damages*

The second possible economic argument for punitive damages is the fact that compensatory damages may not cover all losses of the victim. In such cases, even if there is a 100% probability of being held liable, the injurer again does not internalize the full externality he causes. By adding punitive damages to the compensatory damages, this problem (at least in theory) can be solved. The problem of too low compensatory damages is realistic if damages are difficult to assess, e.g. due to the immaterial or subjective nature of the losses. Defamation cases are an example of this, and it turns out that punitive damages frequently occur in such cases.[24]

However, in order to determine how high punitive damages should be, one needs to assess by which amount compensatory damages fall short of their ideal magnitude. If it would be possible to assess this, the problem of too low compensatory damages would not occur in the first place, because one would then already have made a correct assessment of compensatory damages.[25] Polinsky and Shavell explain that it is better to try to include such difficult-to-measure losses in compensatory damages than in punitive damages, because punitive damages are awarded much less often and because the rules for calculating punitive damages are not so fine-tuned.[26] Furthermore, if certain types of losses are deliberately excluded from compensatory damages, it is questionable if it would be desirable to include them in punitive damages, because the exclusion then becomes illusory.

3.4. *Socially Illicit Costs or Benefits*

In deciding the optimal care level and the optimal activity level, so far all costs and benefits were included in the analysis, also the benefits which the injurer derives from his

21 See e.g. *State Farm v. Campbell* (2003) and *Exxon Shipping Co. et al. v. Baker et al.* (2008).

22 Also see Hylton 1998, pp. 454, 455 and Sharkey 2009, p. 29.

23 See e.g. Wils 2003, p. 476 on the issue of 'treble damages' in American antitrust law. Also see Sebok 2009, p. 171 on punitive damages in the U.S. generally; Wilcox 2009, p. 37 and Menyhárd 2009, p. 89. Schwartz 1982, p. 140, however, argues that it is better to revise the rules on damages so that they e.g. include the legal costs of the plaintiff directly, than to resort to punitive damages. He provides the example of Connecticut, where victims of intentional or wanton violation of their rights can recover additional damages, which cannot exceed their litigation expenses.

24 Sebok 2009, p. 158.

25 Ellis 1982, p. 31; Polinsky & Shavell 1998a, p. 940.

26 Polinsky & Shavell 1998a, pp. 940, 941; Polinsky & Shavell 1998b, p. 194.

activity and the costs he bears from taking precautionary measures. The optimal levels were found where the marginal costs equal the marginal benefits.

It is conceivable that some costs and benefits are regarded as socially illicit, so that we do not want to include them in the analysis. Think about the pleasure an injurer derives from deliberately hurting someone else, or an exceptionally large thrill he gets when driving at excessive speed and which he has to forego when keeping to the speed limit. The gains of the injurer may be higher than the losses this person causes to others, but given that they are labelled as socially illicit, we do not want to include them in our analysis. Due to their illicit nature, we want these acts to be deterred completely, but compensatory damages do not suffice to reach this goal. After all, after having paid compensatory damages, the injurer still has received his unacceptable gains. Punitive damages may solve this problem, because by imposing such damages, the injurer is forced to pay for more than the mere losses of the victim. Punitive damages should make committing the act so expensive, that the injurer rather refrains from it.[27] The same line of reasoning holds if the specific injurer incurs exceptionally high care costs.

Cooter stresses this rationale for punitive damages.[28] Given that it is (much) cheaper for most potential injurers to take due care than to be liable (Cooter speaks about fault liability), noncompliance often will be unintentional. According to Cooter, neither the deterrence goal nor the punishment goal requires punitive damages then (but above it already became clear that there are other rationales, which Cooter apparently does not consider). However, in case of socially illicit costs or benefits, the injurer may intentionally commit the tort and then probably will significantly fall short of the due care standard. Hence, punitive damages should be restricted to intentional fault, which often will manifest itself as gross negligence. The magnitude should be based on the illicit benefits or exceptional costs, because they trigger the intentional fault.

The value of this third rationale in my view is limited. First, Schwartz rightfully argues that behaviour that is regarded as socially illicit is often considered criminal, so that there are already deterrent incentives in place which go beyond compensatory damages.[29] Second, Polinsky and Shavell state that much socially undesirable behaviour is not aimed at causing harm, so that the issue of socially illicit gains is only rarely relevant.[30] Third, it is difficult to decide which acts are regarded as socially desirable. From an economic point of view, a weighing of costs and benefits would determine if an act is desirable or not. *A priori* excluding certain costs or benefits from this weighing influences the conclusion whether or not an act is socially desirable. It actually assumes the conclusion of undesirability rather than proving it.[31] However, with intentional torts the possible gains are often smaller than the losses caused by the tortfeasor, so that a full weighing of costs and benefits would often result in the conclusion that such acts are socially undesirable anyway.[32] I will spend more detailed attention to intentional torts in section 4.1.

27 Ellis 1982, p. 32; Cooter 1982, p. 89; Polinsky & Shavell 1998b, p. 194.

28 Cooter 1982, pp. 79, 80, 86 ff.

29 Schwartz 1982, p. 138.

30 Polinsky & Shavell 1998b, p. 194.

31 Friedman 1989, p. 1128 ff; Haddock 1990, p. 12; Marks 1996, p. 215 ff; Hylton 1998, p. 464 ff.; Friedman 2000, p. 230 ff.

32 Ellis 1983, p. 50.

3.5. *Stimulating Voluntary Transfers*

An important strand of literature in Law and Economics regards the so-called 'property rule – liability rule framework', which originates from the famous article of Calabresi and Melamed in 1972.[33] In this article, the authors discuss the issue of how entitlements may be protected by law. They distinguish between *property rules* (where the entitlement can only be transferred in a voluntary transaction, hence with consent of the owner), *liability rules* (where also involuntary transactions can take place, provided that the person who takes the entitlement subsequently pays an objectively determined amount for it, hence damages) and *inalienability rules* (where the entitlement cannot be transferred at all). In settings of low transaction costs, parties can negotiate with each other, so that a voluntary transaction is preferred there. After all, in case of voluntary transactions, welfare increases because all parties involved in the transaction agree. This implies that in settings of low transaction costs, property rule protection is preferred. In settings of high transaction costs, however, parties may not be able to reach an agreement. Property rule protection then could effectively bar transactions, also if this transaction would have been welfare increasing. Liability rules may be better then, because they do not require consent of the owner, but they do provide him with an (objectively determined) price for his entitlement.

A potential problem with liability rule protection is that the objectively determined price does not encompass all subjective valuations of the parties involved. Hence, if a potential 'taker' values the entitlement of the owner higher than the objectively determined price, but lower than the subjective valuation of the owner, the involuntary transfer actually decreases joint welfare of both parties involved. Therefore, as long as transaction costs are low enough for voluntary transfers to be possible, entitlements should be protected by property rules, also because they avoid the costs of having to determine an objective price.

Punitive damages may induce a potential injurer to refrain from tortious behaviour in settings of low transaction costs, and to seek a voluntary transfer instead. As long as compensatory damages (which are an objectively determined price) fall short of the gain which an injurer receives from his behaviour, it is profitable for him to commit the tort, even if the probability of being held liable would be 100%. In settings of low transaction costs, we prefer him to reach a voluntary transaction with the owner of the entitlement, because only then are we certain that also the subjective valuations of the owner are taken into account. In addition, the administrative costs of voluntary transactions (via the market) are lower than those of involuntary transactions (via lawsuits). Punitive damages increase the costs of an involuntary transfer, thereby inducing a voluntary transfer instead. So, in order to stimulate voluntary transactions, the sanction on involuntary transactions should outweigh the mere value of the entitlement, because otherwise a potential taker could simply convert a property rule into a liability rule.[34]

33 Calabresi & Melamed 1972, pp. 1089–1128. Also see e.g. Krier & Schwab 1995, pp. 440–483; Kaplow & Shavell 1996, pp. 713–790.

34 See Calabresi & Melamed 1972, p. 1126; Klevorick 1985, pp. 289–309; Coleman 1985, pp. 311–328.

Polinsky and Shavell explain that in situations where compensatory damages fall short of true losses, potential injurers may seek out such opportunities and potential victims invest in avoiding such acts. Both expenditures are socially undesirable. Here again, punitive damages may ameliorate the problem. The authors provide the example of copyright infringements,[35] which exactly is an area in which damages are relatively often increased to above-compensatory levels.[36]

3.6. *Punishment*

As I have already noted above, according to the Law and Economics view, both tort law and criminal law serve the aim of deterrence. Punishment is not regarded as a goal in itself, but as a means to deter wrongdoing. The addition of punitive damages serves to correct the above-discussed problems, which make compensatory damages inadequate to deter the wrongdoer.

Notwithstanding the principal focus on deterrence, Polinsky and Shavell discuss punishment as a possible goal in itself (hence, punishment as an end, not as a means to deterrence).[37] This goal is derived from the desire of individuals to see blameworthy parties appropriately punished. The level of the sanction should then depend on the reprehensibility of the behaviour. This is in accordance with the fact that punitive damages are often connected to behaviour which goes beyond mere negligence (intent, gross recklessness, malice, et cetera). The authors explain that this is difficult if the defendant is a firm, because the sanction might not be borne by the blameworthy individuals. It might be difficult for the firm to identify the wrongdoers; the internal sanction that the firm applies if it is able to identify the wrongdoers might not be influenced by imposing punitive damages; there may not be a culpable employee to start with (due to dispersed responsibilities or because the person does not work for the firm anymore); in the end the shareholders and customers often are the ones who bear the consequences of the punitive damages, although they often do not influence the decision making process. In conclusion, it is very doubtful if punitive damages are able to punish blameworthy individuals if the defendant is a company.

It should be clear that the punishment goal results in different conclusions as to when and how much punitive damages should be awarded than the deterrence goal. For example, reprehensible behaviour which will very likely lead to liability does not require large punitive damages from a deterrence perspective (the multiplier is low), while the punishment objective does warrant them. The *Exxon Valdez* case can be regarded as an example of this.[38] On the other hand, irreprehensible behaviour with a low probability of

35 Polinsky & Shavell 1998b, p. 195.

36 See several of the country reports in Koziol & Wilcox 2009.

37 Polinsky & Shavell 1998a, pp. 948–954.

38 See e.g. the following quotes of the Supreme Court in this case: 'Regardless of culpability, however, heavier punitive awards have been thought to be justifiable when wrongdoing is hard to detect (increasing chances of getting away with it), (...) or when the value of injury and the corresponding compensatory award are small (providing low incentives to sue)' (p. 2622); 'We know, for example, that Congress devised the treble damages remedy for private antitrust actions with an eye to supplementing official enforcement by inducing private litigation, which might otherwise have been too rare if nothing

liability requires punitive damages from the deterrence point of view, but not from the punishment point of view. If the reprehensibility of the behaviour is based on the illicitness of the gains of the injurer, then the goals of punishment and deterrence both point in the direction of punitive damages.

Diamond analyses the optimal level of punitive damages when incorporating both the deterrence and the punishment goal in the social welfare function. He does this by introducing social costs which are caused by having a total magnitude of sanctions (compensatory damages, civil and criminal fines and punitive damages) which differs from the sanction which is ideal for retribution purposes only. Hence, if the total sanction differs from the optimal retributive sanction, this lowers social welfare, irrespective of its impact on deterrence.[39] In situations where risk taking is considered as outrageous, even though it is based on a full weighing of costs and benefits of precautions, choosing the optimal sanction for retribution lowers social welfare due to inefficient precautions, while choosing the optimal amount for deterrence lowers the social welfare because the total sanction differs from the optimal retributive sanction. This implies that both goals have to be balanced against each other: in cases where there is no deterrence-based reason for punitive damages, imposing them on the basis of retribution-reasons will result in over deterrence. The social optimum is found when the gains from further increasing punitive damages towards the optimal retributive magnitude are exactly offset by the costs of moving farther away from the optimal deterrent magnitude.[40] In situations where the injurer takes too much risk because he does not bear the full social costs of his activity and this behaviour is regarded as outrageous, both goals warrant punitive damages. Depending mainly on the probability of being held liable, the optimal amount for deterrence may be smaller than, equal to, or larger than the optimal amount for retribution.[41]

For the punishment goal, also the wealth of the defendant matters. The wealthier the defendant, the larger a sanction has to be in order to result in an appropriate utility loss of the wrongdoer.[42] This implies that punitive damages in principle should increase with the wealth of the defendant.[43] For the deterrence goal, wealth of the defendant is not relevant, because optimal compensatory damages are determined by the size of the externality, not

but compensatory damages were available at the end of the day. (...) That concern has no traction here, in this case of staggering damage inevitably provoking governmental enforcers to indict and any number of private parties to sue. (...) In a well-functioning system, we would expect that awards at the median or lower would roughly express jurors' sense of reasonable penalties in cases (...) (again like this one) without the modest economic harm or odds of detection that have opened the door to higher awards.' (pp. 2632, 2633). Note that the Court does not regard the fact that the captain of the tanker regularly was drunk while on duty as exceptionally blameworthy within the punishable spectrum, because he did not act intentionally or maliciously.

39 Diamond 2002, p. 124.

40 Diamond 2002, p. 127.

41 Diamond 2002, p. 132, 133.

42 This is caused by the decreasing marginal utility of wealth, which entails that the more wealth an individual already has, the less utility an additional amount of wealth will add to the overall utility of this individual. After all, he will satisfy his needs in the order of urgency, so that the first euros someone acquires will yield more utility than subsequent euros.

43 Polinsky & Shavell 1998a, p. 953.

by the wealth of the wrongdoer.[44] Optimal punitive damages are subsequently determined on the basis of the factors which were discussed in sections 3.2–3.5.

4. Specific Topics on Punitive Damages in Tort Law

In this section, I will discuss several specific topics related to punitive damages. I will start with the issue of intentional torts, because a large fraction of punitive damages is awarded in intentional tort cases. Subsequently I will analyze whether basing liability on gains rather than losses could be an alternative for imposing punitive damages. Finally I will treat the question whether potential injurers should be able to insure against punitive damages.

4.1. Intentional Torts

From an economic point of view, it is understandable why punitive damages are relatively often awarded in cases of intentional torts. First, the injurer may take measures to lower the probability of being detected. In section 3.2. it became clear that a probability of being held liable which lies below 100% is an economic reason to introduce punitive damages. Second, intentional torts often take place in a setting of low transaction costs.[45] In such situations, punitive damages can induce voluntary transfers (see section 3.5). Third, intentional torts have a few characteristics which make them, almost by definition, undesirable, so that the risk of over deterrence does not exist. Increasing the expected sanction by using punitive damages strengthens the deterrent effect of tort law. These characteristics are first the fact that intentional torts are often used to bring the victim in a worse position, not primarily to bring the injurer in a better position.[46] In those cases, the losses of the victim will outweigh the gains to the injurer (if these exist at all) so that the tort lowers social welfare. Second, intentional torts are characterized by so-called 'negative care costs'.[47] This means that the injurer does not incur costs to *avoid* the tort, but he rather spends resources to *enable* the tort. This lowers welfare, irrespective of the fact that the tort will also cause relatively high expected losses, now the accident probability will be relatively high due to the intent. Finally, if the utility which the injurer derives from his intentional tort is regarded as socially illicit, the line of reasoning explained in section 3.4 provides an additional reason to impose punitive damages in such cases.

4.2. Liability Based on Gains Rather Than on Losses

The arguments presented in section 3 show that there are several reasons why tort damages in certain situations should outweigh the losses to the victim. An alternative to

44 Cooter 1989, pp. 1176, 1177. Note that if the injurer is risk averse and cannot insure against punitive damages, the lower his wealth is, the lower the punitive damages can be in order to provide the correct deterrent incentives.

45 Arlen 2000, p. 696; Posner 2003, p. 205.

46 Ellis 1983, p. 50.

47 Landes & Posner 1981, p. 128 ff; Posner 2003, p. 206.

punitive damages could be to base the damages on the gains of the wrongdoer rather than on the losses of the victim, if those gains are higher than the losses.[48]

As a starting point, in absence of the problem of underestimating the victim's losses, Law and Economics favors basing damages on losses rather than gains. After all, the externality which has to be internalized consists of the costs. If these are not underestimated, basing damages on losses exactly internalizes the externality. If the gains outweigh the costs, in principle the act increases social welfare and should be allowed, unless the victim's entitlement is protected by a property (or inalienability) rule or the gains are regarded as socially illicit. In addition, if the gains to the injurer are underestimated, he will still benefit from committing the tort if damages are based on these underestimated gains.[49]

If the losses of the victim may be underestimated, we already saw above that damages based on the losses provide inadequate behavioural incentives to the injurer. In those cases, it could be better to base damages on the injurer's gains, because they remove the benefits of the wrongful behaviour (assuming that the gains are not underestimated) so that he will refrain from the tort. The need to introduce punitive damages is then avoided, while the deterrence goal is better attained.

Hylton challenges the view that in principle, damages should be based on losses, unless there is a risk of underestimating them.[50] If gains exceed the losses and damages are based on the latter, one should not forget that the damaging behaviour may entail more social costs than only the losses to the victim (e.g. losses to others, costs of enforcement and litigation). In such cases it could be desirable to base the damages on the gains to deter the behaviour, even though the gains of the injurer outweigh the costs of the victim. This holds especially in situations of low transaction costs, where the potential injurer can seek a voluntary transfer.

To summarize: if the main goal is to induce the injurer to take a correct level of care and to choose a correct activity level, basing damages on the losses is preferred. If it is more important to deter the behaviour altogether, gain-based damages are preferable.

4.3. *Insurability of Punitive Damages*

The answer to the question whether one should be able to insure against punitive damages depends to a large extent on the goal which one attributes to punitive damages: punishment or deterrence. If punitive damages serve to punish the wrongdoer, insurance should not be allowed, because then it is not the wrongdoer who bears the sanction, but all insured.[51]

According to Cooter and Ulen, insurance against criminal fines (but their analysis is also applicable to punitive damages) can make economic sense if the injurer does not

48 Koziol & Wilcox 2009 shows that several countries which do not know the figure of punitive damages do accept the idea of basing damages on gains of the wrongdoer, even if they outweigh the losses of the victim, so that these damages are supra-compensatory.

49 Polinsky & Shavell 1994, pp. 427–437.

50 Hylton 1998, p. 423ff.

51 Schwartz 1982, p. 136. Also see Ebert 2009, p. 215.

have enough assets to pay the fines so that there is a need for non-monetary sanctions such as imprisonment. Insurance would allow him to pay the fine, which would avoid the need for the expensive non-monetary sanctions. In order to combat moral hazard, the insurance company would monitor the behaviour of the insured. This private enforcement by insurance companies would then supplement public enforcement by the police.[52] It is important to see that the argument of Cooter and Ulen is based on the deterrence goal of criminal law, not on the goal of punishment as such. The same holds for the line of reasoning of Faure and Heine, who argue that insurability against fines as such is not undesirable if the insurance company can monitor the insured, because the preventive function is then shifted to the insurer.[53]

Focusing on the deterrence goal of punitive damages, insurability of punitive damages makes sense from an economic point of view, provided that the problems of moral hazard and adverse selection can be addressed. Liability insurance increases the utility of risk averse injurers and if moral hazard and adverse selection can be adequately tackled, it does not decrease the utility of victims. Cooter even argues that victims who receive punitive damages may be better off, now the damages they receive (which they might not have received if the injurer was not insured, because his assets may be limited) exceed their losses.[54] Ellis and Ebert argue that exactly moral hazard will be problematic, among other reasons because there are too few cases on punitive damages to make a correct risk estimation.[55] This latter problem may be ameliorated if punitive damages are awarded on a more systematic and better predictable basis, as is advocated by Law and Economics scholars.

5. Punitive Damages in Contract Law

5.1. The Economic Functions of Contract Law

In section 2 above I explained that tort law seeks to enhance social welfare by letting parties internalize the externalities they cause. Contract law is also aimed at increasing social welfare, by facilitating voluntary transfers between parties in settings of low transaction costs. Contract law is more concerned with property rules, whereas tort law focuses more on liability rules.

A voluntary transfer between parties increases social welfare, because the entitlement that was transferred is worth more to the buyer than to the seller. After all, the parties were able to negotiate a price which was high enough for the previous owner to sell, but low enough for the new owner to buy. According to the Coase theorem, in absence of transaction costs, welfare increasing transactions will take place until entitlements end up with the party who values them highest.[56] Of course, in reality transaction costs do

52 Cooter & Ulen 2008, p. 514.
53 Faure & Heine 1991, p. 47.
54 Cooter 1982, p. 96.
55 Ellis 1982, p. 74; Ebert 2009, p. 215.
56 Coase 1960, pp. 1–44. Obviously, information asymmetry may frustrate this line of reasoning. If, for example, the seller knows of certain hidden defects but the buyer does not, the transaction may actually

exist, such as the costs involved in finding a transaction partner, acquiring information about the entitlement, negotiating over the price, writing down the agreement, enforcing it, et cetera. These costs, if high enough, may hinder voluntary transactions.

From an economic point of view, contract law serves the goal of facilitating voluntary transfers by lowering transaction costs. In the absence of transaction costs, parties would write a so-called 'complete contract' in which they reach agreement on *all* possible situations which may occur. Assuming that parties act rational, *i.e.* that they act the way they think is best for them, a complete contract contains only optimal clauses, so that the contract maximizes the joint benefits of the contracting parties. Given that in reality transaction costs do exist, parties will *not* draft a complete contract, because they do not think of certain contingencies or because they think that a situation is so unlikely that it is not worthwhile to include it in the contract. Contract law enables parties to save on transaction costs, because it offers them a set of default rules which applies if they do not choose a different set of rules in the contract. After all, only if parties want to depart from the default rules, they have to include a clause in their contract.[57] The use of standard terms can also lower transaction costs, because parties no longer have to include everything in their contract.[58] Good faith can fulfil a comparable role, and it also decreases the possibilities of strategic behaviour.[59]

Besides lowering transaction costs, contract law also makes the voluntary agreements enforceable. This is especially important if the creditor and the debtor in the agreement do not act simultaneously. If for instance the buyer first has to pay and only after a certain period the seller has to deliver, the problem may arise that the seller, who already has received his money, does not want to perform anymore. Or if the seller first delivers and only after a certain period the buyer has to pay, the problem may arise that the buyer does not want to pay anymore, because he already has received what he has bought. If the 'first mover' in such a sequential game cannot act against the non-cooperative behaviour of the second mover, he may decide not to engage in the transaction in the first place. That would lower social welfare in comparison to the situation where both parties would have performed. The different remedies against breach of contract, *i.e.* specific performance and damages, provide the second mover with incentives to perform his contractual duties. After all, by performing, the second mover will receive his part of the contractual surplus, whereas by not performing, he faces the risk of a sanction. The question which is most relevant for the current paper is whether punitive damages should be part of the arsenal of contractual sanctions. Before addressing that question, in section 5.2 I will discuss the choice between specific performance and damages, and the topic of 'efficient breach'.

lower social welfare, because the buyer acquires something which he might not have acquired if he would have had full information.

57 See e.g. Craswell 2000, p. 2ff.

58 For possible problems, see e.g. Van Wijck & Theeuwes 2000, pp. 73–89; Korobkin 2003, pp. 1203–1295 and Luth 2010.

59 See e.g. Sepe 2010.

5.2. *Damages, Specific Performance and Efficient Breach*

In the theoretical complete contract, parties would also agree on the situations in which the debtor does not have to perform, e.g. because his costs of performance have increased since the contract was closed. If they would have agreed that the debtor still would have to perform, even if his costs of performance have increased, the price the debtor would have asked would be higher to cover this risk. It is, however, possible that the creditor would have preferred a lower price whereby he accepts that in certain situations the debtor would not have to perform. Such an agreement would have increased the contractual surplus and the contracting parties would have both benefited from it. Hence, in a complete contract, parties agree on the circumstances under which the debtor still has to perform and when he does not have to perform.[60]

However, given that in reality contracts are not complete, a situation may occur where performance is still in the interest of one party, but not of the other, while parties did not include a clause in the contract which deals with this situation. It may be difficult or impossible for the parties to reach a new agreement given the situation that has arisen, because the interests of the parties are opposed. The remedies for breach of contract in essence determine the price which has to be paid for non-performance. The higher the price, the larger the incentive for the debtor to still perform will be.

From an economic point of view, performance is desirable as long as the costs of performance to the debtor are lower than the benefits of performance to the creditor, because in such cases, performance increases joint welfare.[61] This implies that performance is undesirable if the costs outweigh the benefits. In a complete contract, parties would have agreed that the debtor would not have to perform in such a situation. The remedies of contract law should provide similar incentives in the situation where parties did not agree on this.[62] Hence, contract law should allow 'efficient breach', *i.e.* non-performance if the costs of performance to the debtor outweigh the benefits of performance to the creditor. In order to provide the potentially breaching debtor with the correct incentives, he should bear the negative consequences of his breach. His decision to breach then maximizes joint welfare of the parties involved, and that was the goal to start with. The costs of breaching to the creditor consist of him not yielding the benefits which he expected to derive from the contract. These forgone benefits form the correct basis of damages for breach of contract and are labelled 'expectation damages'. If the debtor pays expectation damages to the creditor, the latter is brought into the same (financial) position as he would have reached after performance. If it is less costly for the debtor to pay expectation damages than to perform, joint welfare is increased by allowing this efficient breach and subsequently letting the debtor pay expectation damages. *Ex*

60 See e.g. Shavell 2004, p. 308; Shavell 2006, p. 441.

61 See e.g. Edlin 1998, p. 174 ff.; Mahoney 2000, p. 245 ff.

62 If transaction costs after the breach are low, parties can of course renegotiate regarding the price the debtor has to pay in order not to have to perform, so that parties can solve the problem themselves, see e.g. Ulen 1998, p. 482. However, the creditor may behave strategically if he knows he can force the debtor to perform, so that the former can try to collect a large share of the cooperative surplus. It is therefore questionable if parties indeed would be able to solve the problem.

ante the creditor even benefits, because by allowing efficient breach the contractual surplus increases and the creditor receives a share of this.[63]

So, expectation damages in theory provide incentives for the debtor to behave optimally. If the costs of performance outweigh the benefits (which are reflected in the expectation damages), he will breach and pay the damages. If the benefits outweigh the costs, though, the debtor will perform. In practice, damages will depart from perfect expectation damages, e.g. because subjective elements are relevant but cannot be assessed perfectly. This will generally lead to too low damages.[64] Also the fact that the benefits arising from the contract are influenced by uncertain factors will likely result in too low damages. Hence, expectation damages may result in excessive breaching whereas ordering specific performance may lead to excessive performance. The more difficult it is to assess expectation damages, the more attractive specific performance becomes. On the other hand, the more monitoring is required in case an unwilling debtor has to perform, the more attractive damages are.

5.3. *Punitive Damages for Deliberate Breach*

In the Second Restatement of Contracts, it is argued that the traditional goal of contract remedies is not to compel the promisor to perform, but to compensate the promisee for the loss resulting from breach. It is then irrelevant whether the breach was wilful. 'In general, therefore, a party may find it advantageous to refuse to perform a contract if he will still have a net gain after he has fully compensated the injured party for the resulting loss'.[65] This nicely fits the Law and Economics line of reasoning. As long as the remedy equals the harm, the correct incentives are provided. In that line of reasoning, deliberate breach does not have to be deterred, as long as the non-performing party pays expectation damages to the other party. This implies that punitive damages for wilful breach have to be rejected.

Craswell argues that as long as the definition of 'wilful' would exclude all breachers who behaved efficiently, the penalty on inefficient behaviour (including inefficient breach, but also e.g. inefficient precautions in an earlier stage of executing the contract) could be increased without a problem, because inefficient breach should be deterred so that the problem of over deterrence does not exist. After all, by behaving efficiently breachers can escape the higher sanction. This implies that if it would be possible to define wilful breach in such a way that it excludes efficient behaviour (hence, also efficient breach), punitive damages could be applied for wilful breach.[66] However, given that it will not be possible for courts to perfectly identify efficient behaviour and for potential defendants to be able

63 Two other forms of damages would provide inadequate incentives to the debtor, inducing him to breach too often. Under 'reliance damages' the debtor compensates the creditor for the costs he has incurred in the expectation that the contract would be executed, but not for the benefits he expected to receive out of the contract. Under 'restitution damages' the debtor only has to compensate the creditor for what he already did in order to fulfill his own obligations (e.g. refunding a payment, returning delivered goods, et cetera), which is even less than under reliance damages.

64 See e.g. Schwartz 1979, p. 276 and Ulen 1998, p. 482.

65 Restatement (Second) 1981, Chapter 16.

66 Craswell 2009, p. 1501, 1507 ff.

to assess in advance which types of behaviour will be deemed inefficient, too high damages may induce excessive care, because parties run a risk of having to pay (punitive) damages also in cases where they should not. Punitive damages for wilful breach then are not desirable.

Punitive damages may be desirable if there is a possibility that an (inefficient) breacher escapes having to pay damages. This line of reasoning is comparable to the argument in tort law, where the too low probability of being held liable can be offset by multiplying compensatory damages with the reciprocal of this probability.[67] According to Polinsky and Shavell, parties often do not want damages for breach to include a punitive element, because 'the breach is obvious, the nature of the breach is such that it easily can be proven in court, and the amount at stake is large enough to justify suit'.[68] Punitive damages in such situations would lead to excessive performance, which is sub-optimal. Also the fact that contractual damages may not fully compensate the creditor, an issue which is discussed above, could be used as an argument in favour of punitive damages.[69] However, the same problems which were listed in section 3.3 hold here, so that it is better to try to improve the assessment of compensatory damages than to introduce punitive damages.

So, the general conclusion in the Law and Economics literature is that expectation damages in principle provide adequate incentives so that punitive damages are not desirable.[70] Deliberate breaches which are efficient should not be deterred. Inefficient breaches should be deterred, but expectation damages suffice for that goal. Bar-Gil and Ben-Sharah, however, have recently argued that also from a Law and Economics point of view, punitive damages for wilful breach may be justified after all. In their view, wilful breach reveals that the contracting partner has an opportunistic nature. Such a person will likely have committed other opportunistic acts as well, which may have gone undetected. Increasing the penalty in cases where such a person is 'caught' also penalizes him for the cases in which he was not caught.[71] This line of reasoning resembles the idea of the too low probability of being caught, combined with the idea of socially illicit costs or benefits. Of course, the probability of being caught for the wilful breach is relatively high, so punitive damages are not required there. However, they intend to correct for the fact that *other* wrongful behaviour was not detected. In my view, it would be very problematic to assess the proper magnitude of punitive damages, because they do not relate to the wilful breach under consideration. Furthermore, in section 3.4 I already explained the problems of the idea of socially illicit costs and benefits. I therefore think that the scope of Bar-Gils and Ben-Shahars argumentation is limited.

67 See e.g. Farber 1980, pp. 1443–1484; Chapman & Trebilcock 1989, p. 818; Perlstein 1992, p. 885 ff.; Polinsky & Shavell 1998a, p. 936 ff. Also see Craswell 2009, p. 1514, who argues that in most cases, calculating the optimal damages is more complicated than merely applying a multiplier.

68 Polinsky & Shavell 1998a, p. 938.

69 It could also be used as an argument in favor of upholding liquidated damages clauses or penalty clauses in a contract, because they avoid the problems which occur if the court *ex post* has to assess the losses. With liquidated damages and penalty clauses, the parties *ex ante* agree on the amount of damages to be paid in case of breach. For an introduction into the economic approach to these topics, see De Geest & Wuyts 2000, pp. 141–161.

70 Bar-Gill & Ben-Shahar 2009, p. 1483.

71 Also see Cooter 1982, p. 97.

6. Conclusions

Law and Economics views tort damages in their capacity to achieve the goal of the reduction of total accident costs. An important aspect of this goal is to provide deterrent incentives to potential wrongdoers. Punitive damages are regarded in the same light. They serve to improve the deterrent function of tort law in situations where compensatory damages are inadequate.

The most important topic in this respect is the fact that punitive damages may offset the too low probability of being held liable. Other arguments are the risk of underestimation of losses, the problem of socially illicit costs or benefits and the desire to induce voluntary transfers in settings of low transaction costs. All these arguments relate to the deterrent function of tort law and damages.

Criminal law is analysed in a similar fashion: it provides incentives to actors to refrain from unlawful behaviour. This implies that according to Law and Economics, the primary goal of criminal law is deterrence as well. As a result, punishment as such is not given much weight. The same holds for the possible punishment goal of punitive damages. Many punishment arguments turn out to be deterrence arguments. In as far as punishment is regarded as a goal in itself, reprehensibility of the behaviour is the most important factor in determining the appropriate sanction. For the answer to the question whether an actor should be able to insure against punitive damages, the goal again is important: if punitive damages serve to punish the wrongdoer, he should not be able to insure against such damages. If the goal is deterrence, insurance should be allowed.

The analysis of punitive damages for deliberate breach of contract differs from that of punitive damages in tort law. Whereas Law and Economics literature in principle regards punitive damages in tort law favourably because they may correct certain problems, in contract law there are less economics reasons to allow punitive damages. The most important problem is that punitive damages may lead to excessive performance. After all, in cases where the costs of performance to the debtor outweigh the benefits of performance to the creditor, the concept of efficient breach suggests that the debtor should be allowed to breach, as long as he compensates the creditor on the basis of expectation damages. Given that punitive damages outweigh this measure, they may induce inefficient, excessive performance.

The Law and Economics approach to punitive damages has turned out to encompass many of the questions mentioned in the Introduction. I hope that my contribution has shown how these separate questions relate to each other, and what answers the Law and Economics literature provides.

Bibliography

Arlen 2000
Arlen, J., 'Tort Damages', in: B. Bouckaert & G. De Geest (eds.), *Encyclopedia of Law and Economics. Volume II. Civil Law and Economics*, Cheltenham: Edward Elgar, 2000, pp. 682–734.

Bar-Gill & Ben-Shahar 2009
Bar-Gill, O. & Ben-Shahar, O., 'An Information Theory of Willful Breach', *Mich L Rev*, 2009, pp. 1479–1500.

Becker 1968
Becker, G.S., 'Crime and Punishment: An Economic Approach', *JPE*, 1968, pp. 169–217.

Calabresi 1977
Calabresi, G., *The Costs of Accidents. A Legal and Economic Analysis*, New Haven: Yale University Press, 1977.

Calabresi & Melamed 1972
Calabresi, G. & Melamed, A.D., 'Property Rules, Liability Rules, and Inalienability: One View of the Cathedral', *Harv L Rev*, 1972, pp. 1089–1128.

Chapman & Trebilcock 1989
Chapman, B. & Trebilcock, M., 'Punitive Damages: Divergence in Search of a Rationale', *Ala L Rev*, 1989, pp. 741–828.

Coase 1960
Coase, R.H., 'The Problem of Social Cost', *JLE*, 1960, pp. 1–44.

Cohen 2001
Cohen, T.H., 'Punitive Damage Awards in Large Counties, 2001', *Bureau of Justice Statistics Selected Findings, NCJ 208445*, 2005.

Coleman 1985
Coleman, J.L., 'Crime, Kickers and Transaction Structures', in: J.R. Pennock and J.W. Chapman (eds.), *Criminal Justice*, NOMOS XXVII, New York: New York University Press, 1985, pp. 311–328.

Cooter 1982
Cooter, R.D., 'Economic Analysis of Punitive Damages', *S Cal L Rev*, 1982, pp. 79–102.

Cooter 1989
Cooter, R.D., 'Punitive Damages for Deterrence: When and How Much?', *Ala L Rev*, 1989, pp. 1143–1196.

Cooter & Ulen 2008
Cooter, R.D. & Ulen, T.S., *Law and Economics*, Boston: Pearson Addison Wesley, 2008.

Craswell 2000
Craswell, R., 'Contract Law: General Theories', in: B. Bouckaert & G. De Geest (eds.), *Encyclopedia of Law And Economics, Volume III. The Regulation of Contracts*, Cheltenham: Edward Elgar, 2000, pp. 1–24.

Craswell 2009
Craswell, R., 'When is a Willful Breach "Willful"? The Link Between Definitions and Damages', *Mich L Rev*, 2009, pp. 1501–1516.

Daniels & Martin 1990
Daniels, S. & Martin, J., 'Myth and Reality in Punitive Damages', *Minn L Rev*, 1990, pp. 1–64.

DeFrances *et al.* 1995
DeFrances, C.J. *et al.*, 'Civil Jury Cases and Verdicts in Large Counties', *Bureau of Justice Statistics Special Report, NCJ 154346*, 1995.

De Geest & Wuyts 2000
De Geest, G. & Wuyts, F., 'Penalty Clauses and Liquidated Damages', in: B. Bouckaert & G. De Geest (eds.), *Encyclopedia of Law and Economics, Volume III. The Regulation of Contracts*, Cheltenham: Edward Elgar, 2000, pp. 141–161.

Diamond 2002
Diamond, P., 'Integrating Punishment and Efficiency Concerns in Punitive Damages for Reckless Disregard of Risks to Others', *JLEO*, 2002, pp. 117–139.

Duggan 2006
Duggan, A., 'Exemplary Damages in Equity: A Law and Economics Perspective', *Oxford J Legal Stud*, 2006, pp. 303–326.

Eaton, Mustard & Mustard 2005
Eaton, T.A., Mustard, D.B., & Mustard, S.M., 'The Effects of Seeking Punitive Damages on the Processing of Tort Claims', *JLS*, 2005, pp. 344–370.

Ebert 2009
Ebert, I., 'Punitive Damages and Liability Insurance', in H. Koziol & V. Wilcox (eds.), *Punitive Damages: Common Law and Civil Law Perspectives*, Vienna: Springer, 2009, pp. 213–217.

Edlin 1998
Edlin, A.S., 'Breach Remedies', in: P. Newman (ed.), *The New Palgrave Dictionary of Economics and the Law*, Londen: MacMillan Reference Limited, 1998, pp. 174–178.

Eisenberg *et al.* 1997
Eisenberg, T. *et al.*, 'The Predictability of Punitive Damages', *JLS*, 1997, pp. 623–662.

Eisenberg *et al.* 2002
Eisenberg, T., *et al.*, 'Juries, Judges, and Punitive Damages: An Empirical Study', *Cornell L Rev*, 2002, pp. 743–782.

Eisenberg *et al.* 2006
Eisenberg, T. *et al.*, 'Juries, Judges, and Punitive Damages: Empirical Analyses Using the Civil Justice Survey of State Courts 1992, 1996, and 2001 Data', *JELS*, 2006, pp. 263–295.

Ellis 1982
Ellis, D.D., 'Fairness and Efficiency in the Law of Punitive Damages', *S Cal L Rev*, 1982, pp. 1–78.

Ellis 1983
Ellis, D.D., 'An Economic Theory of Intentional Torts: A Comment', *Int Rev Law & Econ*, 1983, pp. 45–57.

Farber 1980
Farber, D.A., 'Reassessing the Economic Efficiency of Compensatory Damages for Breach of Contract', *Va L Rev*, 1980, pp. 1443–1484.

Faure & Heine 1991
Faure, M.G. & Heine, G., 'The Insurance of Fines: The Case of Oil Pollution', *The Geneva Papers on Risk and Insurance – Issues and Practice*, 1991, pp. 39–58.

Faure 2009
Faure, M.G. (ed.), *Tort Law and Economics. Volume 1. Encyclopedia of Law and Economics, Second Edition*, Cheltenham: Edward Elgar, 2009.

Fleming 1992
Fleming, J.G., *The Law of Torts*, Sydney: The Law Book Company, 1992.

Friedman 1989
Friedman, D.D., 'An Economic Explanation of Punitive Damages', *Ala L Rev*, 1989, pp. 1125–1142.

Friedman 2000
Friedman, D.D., *Law's Order: What Economics Has to Do with Law and Why it Matters*, Princeton, New Jersey: Princeton University Press, 2000.

Geistfeld 2008
Geistfeld, M., 'Punitive Damages, Retribution, and Due Process', *S Cal L Rev*, 2008, pp. 263–310.

Haddock, McChesney & Spiegel 1990
Haddock, D.D., McChesney F.S., & Spiegel, M., 'An Ordinary Economic Rationale for Extraordinary Legal Sanctions', *Cal L Rev*, 1990, pp. 1–52.

Hylton 1998
Hylton, K.N., 'Punitive Damages and the Economic Theory of Penalties', *Geo L J*, 1998, pp. 421–472.

Innes 2004
Innes, R., 'Enforcement Costs, Optimal Sanctions, and the Choice Between Ex-post Liability and Ex-ante Regulation', *Int Rev Law & Econ*, 2004, pp. 29–48.

Kaplow & Shavell 1996
Kaplow, L. & Shavell, S., 'Property Rules versus Liability Rules: An Economic Analysis', *Harv L Rev*, 1996, pp. 713–790.

Keeton *et al.* 1984
Keeton, W.P. *et al.*, *Prosser and Keeton on the Law of Torts*, St. Paul, Minnesota: West Publishing Co., 1984.

Klevorick 1985
Klevorick, A.K., 'On the Economic Theory of Crime', in: J.R. Pennock & J.W. Chapman (eds.), *Criminal Justice*, NOMOS XXVII, New York: New York University Press, 1985, pp. 289–309.

Korobkin 2003
Korobkin, R., 'Bounded Rationality, Standard Form Contracts, and Unconscionability', *U Chi L Rev*, 2003, pp. 1203–1295.

Kötz 2001
Kötz, H., *Deliktsrecht*, Neuwied: Luchterhand, 2001.

Koziol & Wilcox 2009
Koziol, H. & Wilcox, V. (ed.), *Punitive Damages: Common Law and Civil Law Perspectives*, Vienna: Springer, 2009.

Krier & Schwab 1995
Krier, J.E. & Schwab, S.J. 'Property Rules and Liability Rules: The Cathedral in Another Light', *NYU L Rev*, 1995, pp. 440–483.

Landes & Posner 1975
Landes, W.M. & Posner, R.A., 'The Private Enforcement of Law', *JLS*, 1975, pp. 1–46.

Landes & Posner 1981
Landes, W.M. & Posner, R.A., 'An Economic Theory of Intentional Torts', *Int Rev Law & Econ*, 1981, pp. 127–154.

Landes & Posner 1987
Landes, W.M. & Posner, R.A., *The Economic Structure of Tort Law*, Cambridge, Massachusetts: Harvard University Press, 1987.

Langton & Cohen 2008
Langton, L. & Cohen, T.H., 'Civil Bench and Jury Trials in State Courts, 2005', *Bureau of Justice Statistics Special Report, NCJ 223851*, 2008.

Luth 2010
Luth, H.A., *Behavioural Economics in Consumer Policy. The Economic Analysis of Standard Terms in Consumer Contracts Revisited*, Antwerp: Intersentia, 2010.

Mahoney 2000
Mahoney, P.G., 'Contract Remedies: General', in: B. Bouckaert & G. De Geest (eds.), *Encyclopedia of Law and Economics, Volume III. The Regulation of Contracts*, Cheltenham: Edward Elgar, 2000, pp. 117–140.

Marks 1996
Marks, S., 'Utility and Community: Musings on the Tort/Crime Distinction', *B U L Rev*, 1996, pp. 215–240.

Menyhárd 2009
Menyhárd, A., 'Punitive Damages in Hungary', in: H. Koziol & V. Wilcox (eds.), *Punitive Damages: Common Law and Civil Law Perspectives*, Vienna: Springer, 2009, pp. 87–102.

Ogus & Visscher 2010
Ogus, A. & Visscher, L.T., 'A Law and Economics Perspective on Injunctive Relief', *MJECL*, 2010, pp. 32–47.

Ostrom, Rotteman & Goerdt 1996
Ostrom, B.J., Rotteman, D.B., & Goerdt, J.A., 'A Step Above Anecdote: A Profile of the Civil Jury in the 1990s', *Judicature*, 1996, pp. 233–241.

Perlstein 1992
Perlstein, B., 'Crossing the Contract-Tort Boundary: An Economic Argument for the Imposition of Extracompensatory Damages for Opportunitistic Breach of Contract', *Brook L Rev*, 1992, pp. 877–912.

Polinsky 1980
Polinsky, A.M., 'Private Versus Public Enforcement of Fines', *JLS* 1980, pp. 105–127.

Polinsky & Shavell 1994
Polinsky, A.M. & Shavell, S., 'Should Liability Be Based on the Harm to the Victim or the Gain to the Injurer?', *JLEO*, 1994, pp. 427–437.

Polinsky & Shavell 1998a
Polinsky, A.M. & Shavell, S., 'Punitive Damages: An Economic Analysis', *Harv L Rev*, 1998, pp. 869–962.

Polinsky & Shavell 1998b
Polinsky, A.M. & Shavell, S., 'Punitive Damages', in: P. Newman (ed.), *The Palgrave Dictionary of Economics and the Law*, London: MacMillan Reference Limited, 1998, pp. 192–198.

Polinsky & Shavell 2000a
Polinsky, A.M. & Shavell, S., 'The Fairness of Sanctions: Some Implications for Optimal Enforcement Policy', *ALER*, 2000, pp. 223–237.

Polinsky & Shavell 2000b
Polinsky, A.M. & Shavell, S., 'Public Enforcement of Law', in: B. Bouckaert & G. De Geest (eds.), *Encyclopedia of Law and Economics. Volume V. The Economics of Crime and Litigation*, Cheltenham: Edward Elgar, 2000, pp. 307–344.

Posner 2003
Posner, R.A., *Economic Analysis of Law*, New York: Aspen Publishers, 2003.

Restatement (Second) 1981
Restatement (Second) of Contracts, 1981, Chapter 16.

Rogers 2006
Rogers, W.V.H., *Winfield & Jolowicz on Tort*, London: Sweet and Maxwell, 2006.

Sharkey 2009
Sharkey, C.M., 'The Exxon Valdez Litigation Marathon: A Window on Punitive Damages', *U St Thomas L J*, 2009, pp. 25–54.

Shavell 1984
Shavell, S., 'Liability for Harm Versus Regulation of Safety', *JLS*, 1984, pp. 357–374.

Shavell 1986
Shavell, S., 'The Judgment Proof Problem', *Int Rev Law & Econ*, 1986, pp. 43–58.

Shavell 1993
Shavell, S., 'The Optimal Structure of Law Enforcement', *JLE*, 1993, pp. 255–287.

Shavell 2004
Shavell, S., *Foundations of Economic Analysis of Law*, Cambridge, Massachusetts: The Belknap Press of Harvard University Press, 2004.

Shavell 2006
Shavell, S., 'Is Breach of Contract Immoral?', *Emory L J*, 2006, pp. 439–460.

Schwartz 1979
Schwartz, A., 'The Case for Specific Performance', *Yale L J*, 1979, pp. 271–307.

Schwartz 1982
Schwartz, G.T., 'Deterrence and Punishment in the Common Law of Punitive Damages: A Comment', *S Cal L Rev*, 1982, pp. 133–154.

Sebok 2007
Sebok, A.J., 'Punitive Damages: From Myth to Theory', *Iowa L Rev*, 2007, pp. 957–1036.

Sebok 2009
Sebok, A.J., 'Punitive Damages in the United States', in: H. Koziol & V. Wilcox (eds.), *Punitive Damages: Common Law and Civil Law Perspectives*, Vienna: Springer, 2009, pp. 155–196.

Sepe 2010
Sepe, S.M., 'Good Faith And Contract Interpretation: A Law And Economics Perspective', *Arizona Legal Studies Discussion Paper No. 10-28* 2010, available at papers.ssrn.com/sol3/papers.cfm?abstract_id=1086323.

Ulen 1998
Ulen, T.S., 'Specific Performance', in: P. Newman (ed.), *The Palgrave Dictionary of Economics and the Law*, London: MacMillan Reference Limited, 1998, pp. 481–484.

Van Wijck & Theeuwes 2000
Wijck, P.W., van, & Theeuwes, J.J.M., 'Protection against Unfair Contracts: An Economic Analysis of European Regulation', *EJLE*, 2000, pp. 73–89.

Vidmar & Wolfe 2009
Vidmar, N. & Wolfe, M.W., 'Punitive Damages', *Ann Rev L & Soc Sci*, 2009, pp. 179–199.

Wilcox 2009
Wilcox, V., 'Punitive Damages in England', in: H. Koziol & V. Wilcox (eds.), *Punitive Damages: Common Law and Civil Law Perspectives*, Vienna: Springer, 2009, pp. 7–53.

Wils 2003
Wils, W.P.J., 'Should Private Antitrust Enforcement Be Encouraged in Europe?', *World Competition*, 2003, pp. 473–488.

Vanessa Wilcox*

PUNITIVE DAMAGES IN THE ARMOURY OF HUMAN RIGHTS ARBITERS

1. Introduction

Various adjectives attach to the noun 'damages': 'compensatory', 'nominal', 'contemptuous', 'aggravated', 'restitutionary', 'exemplary', 'punitive', 'vindicatory', 'vindictive', 'retributory', etc, to mark the different purposes for which damages may be awarded. Some are ambiguous; some are synonymous with others; and some overlap in function. We are concerned here with a form of damages whose story is best illustrated by a fable: In an evil day the common law, like the hospitable Arab, who permitted the camel to shelter his head within the domestic tent, gave shelter to a new form of damages – punitive damages, seemingly of much promise though of precarious nature and precarious tenure of life. Punitive damages have repaid the hospitality of the law, even as the camel rewarded his master – by making the legal household permanently uncomfortable. The law, awakening to the peril of housing so sturdy a species, has smiled uneasily and then apparently on the principle of Christian Science, has tried to ignore its anomalies. But its anomalies will not be ignored. Nor, it seems will the law ignore the beast. As a convenient factor of legal redress, he emerges uncannily from every attempt at extinction, much after the fashion of Antaeus, who, cast to earth, renewed his vitality.[1]

The following pages chart the recourse to extra-compensatory damages as a strategic element in the law's armoury against breaches of fundamental rights. Specifically, the paper assesses the influence the jurisprudence of the European Court of Human Rights has had on contracting states whose tradition it is to award punitive or exemplary damages in their development of the relevant cause of action at domestic level. In particular, the position in England and Wales on the one hand and Ireland on the other is examined with emphasis on their varying constitutional contexts. Finally, an analysis of recent authorities on 'vindicatory damages' – the latest conception of members of the House of Lords sitting as the Privy Council – confirms that the appetite for damages in excess of compensatory damages to mark the infringement of a right still remains. The

* Vanessa Wilcox, LL.B., LL.M. (Cantab) is based at the Austrian Academy of Sciences' Institute for European Tort Law in Vienna, Austria. She wishes to acknowledge her very substantial obligation to Eoin Quill for valuable advice in the drafting of this paper.

1 Adapted from Deiser 1908, pp. 131–132.

paper concludes – in line with the 2011 UK Supreme Court decision of *Lumba and Mighty v. Secretary of State for the Home Department*[2] – that there is no justification for awarding vindicatory damages (in this sense) under the laws of England and Wales.

2. The European Court's Approach to Punitive Damages

The recurring theme of studies on the European Court of Human Rights' application of Article 41 ECHR has centred on the Court's notoriously flexible and seemingly unprincipled basis for assessing just satisfaction.[3] So it has been said that '[t]he Student of the Court's practice is left wondering whether the process by which the Court arrives at its judgments is anything more sophisticated than sticking a finger in the air or tossing a coin.'[4] In respect of the synonymously termed punitive or exemplary damages, however, the Court's position is clear and unequivocal. That such damages – once labelled 'a monstrous heresy...an unsightly and unhealthy excrescence, deforming the symmetry of the body of law...out of place, irregular, anomalous, exceptional, unjust, unscientific, not to say absurd and ridiculous when classed among civil remedies'[5] – do not form part of the existing jurisprudence of the Strasbourg Court is confirmed by the Court's consistent stance against them in its case law[6] and latterly in its Practice Direction on Just Satisfaction Claims.[7] This exclusory approach rests on the purpose of the Court's awards under Article 41 ECHR; that is, 'to compensate the applicant for the actual harmful consequences of a violation.'[8] Therefore, the Court has said that they are 'not intended to punish the contracting state responsible.'[9]

That punishment is not the object of the Court's awards is unsurprising given the Court's inclination to take guidance from domestic standards in awarding just satisfaction and given the absence of punitive damages in the majority of those standards.[10] In fact, if one concedes that the entire business of awarding damages is of *secondary* import to the Court's chief concerns of marking the infringement of the applicant's right – as is evidenced by its routine recourse to finding a violation as sufficient just satisfaction – and bringing the violation to an end, one begins to appreciate how far removed the punitive option is from the Court's weaponry. This is so as punitive damages, under English law at least, are only available if, but only if, the sum which the court has in mind to award as

2 [2011] UKSC 12.

3 See among others, The Law Commission and the Scottish Law Commission 1998, par. 3.4; Shelton 1999, p. 2; Lester & Pannick 2004, par. 2.8.4; Simor & Emmerson 1999, par. 19.063 ff; Clayton & Tomlinson 2009, par. 21.30; Fenyves *et al.* 2011. See, however, The Law Commission and the Scottish Law Commission 1998, par. 3.4 ff.

4 Grosz, Beatson & Duffy 1999, p. 145.

5 *Fay v. Parker*, 53 NH 342, 382, (1873).

6 See, among other authorities, *BB v. the United Kingdom*, 10 February 2004, no. 53760/00, § 36; *Wainwright v. the United Kingdom*, 26 September 2006, no. 12350/04, § 60. See also Wilcox 2011.

7 Practice Direction, Just Satisfaction Claims, 28 March 2007, par. 9.

8 Ibid.

9 Ibid. See *Varnava and Others v. Turkey*, 18 September 2009, nos. 16064/90, 16065/90, 16066/90, 16068/90, 16069/90, 16070/90, 16071/90, 16072/90 and 16073/90, § 223.

10 Ibid, par. 3. See Koziol & Wilcox 2009 and Carnwath 2000, pp. 517–527.

compensation is not itself sufficient to punish the wrongdoer.[11] As a 'topping-up' award, their application is thus dependant on compensatory damages playing a more prominent role than they do in Strasbourg.

In addition to upholding those rights and freedoms which the Convention perceives warrantable of international guarantee at the present time, it is equally true that the Court is concerned to see that similar breaches are avoided. Punitive damages – or vindicatory damages if one prefers to distance them from the punitory connotation – with their propensity to deter would, as other international human rights courts see it, 'do the job'. But the Human Rights Court in Strasbourg has rejected their competency and rightly so. If one looks behind the Court's judgments to the structure of the entire human rights machinery under the aegis of the Council of Europe one is better placed to appreciate the Court's approach to securing observance of the Convention by member states, to preventing systematic violations and the fuller picture as regards remedies generally.

For a contracting state, a finding of a violation and/or the payment by way of just satisfaction of the sums due to those concerned does not necessarily bring the case to an end. To suggest this would be to go against the state's moral and legal obligation under Article 1 ECHR to correct the infringement. Consequently, as part of their undertaking to abide by the final judgment of the Court,[12] states are free to choose, subject to supervision by the Committee of Ministers (CoM), the individual and/or, if appropriate, general measures to be adopted in their domestic legal systems in order to put an end to the violation found.[13] Individual measures relate to the applicant *per se* and are, where applicable, taken in order to ensure *restitutio in integrum*. Encompassed within this notion is the payment of just satisfaction including, as the case may be, default interest. Where the violation is not adequately remedied by the Court's pecuniary award or a finding of a violation, the individual measure in question may require further actions, e.g. re-opening of proceedings at national level, destroying information gathered in breach of the right to privacy, striking-out of criminal records, etc. It is because this aspect of the Strasbourg system is very rarely pronounced in the Court's judgments that it is less celebrated.[14]

11 *Rookes v. Barnard* [1964] 1 All ER 367, 412. See also *Cassell & Co Ltd v. Broome and Another* [1972] AC 1027, 1089 per Lord Reid and *Thompson v. Commissioner of Police of the Metropolis* [1998] QB 498, 517.

12 Article 46(1) European Convention on Human Rights (ECHR).

13 Article 46(2) ECHR.

14 The original intentions of the founding fathers of the Convention was for the scope of the Court's powers to be broadly drawn. Article 50 ECHR in its preparatory stages originally read thus: The verdict of the Court shall order the state concerned: (1) to annul, suspend or amend the incriminating decision; (2) to make reparation for damage caused; (3) to require the appropriate penal, administrative or civil sanctions to be applied to the person or persons responsible. The current and more restricted wording was as a result of a later modification by the Committee of Experts for Human Rights. Therefore, very rarely will the Court pronounce on the domestic measures that the state concerned should use in discharging its obligation under Article 46 ECHR to abide by the Court's final judgment. Exceptionally, however, and with a view to helping the respondent state fulfil its obligations under Article 46 ECHR, the Court may propose various options though leaving the choice of measure and its implementation to the discretion of the state concerned. This is particularly so in the case of systemic breaches: *Broniowski v. Poland* [GC], 22 June 2004, no. 31443/96, § 194. In even more exceptional cases, the nature of the violation found may be such as to leave no real choice as to the measures required to remedy it

More germane to the present paper is that unlike the remedial role played by individual measures, general measures serve a preventative purpose – one of the stated goals of punitive damages. They seek to avoid new similar violations of the Convention. General measures are distinguishable from punitive damages firstly in that their aim is not to punish the recalcitrant state or make an example of it and secondly, no 'windfall' accrues to the victim. With general measures, the avoidance of repeated violations may entail constitutional, legislative or regulatory amendments, a change in administrative practice or in case-law, the refurbishment of a prison, etc.[15] Accordingly, rather than taking from the public purse to put into the applicant's pocket, with general measures a state is in a position to concentrate its resources on a broader public cause with a view to avoiding comparable breaches. It is not until the CoM is satisfied that the Contracting Party concerned has taken all the necessary measures to abide by the judgment or that the terms of a friendly settlement have been executed, that it adopts a final resolution concluding that its functions under the Convention have been exercised.[16]

The subsidiary character of the Convention and hence the subsidiary character of intervention on the part of the Strasbourg Court is reflected, *inter alia*, in the choice of means afforded to states to achieve the object and purpose underlying the Convention. It is primarily for the respondent states themselves, as set out in Article 1 ECHR, to move change. To expect the Court to order extravagant awards of damages as an inducement to states to observe the legal standards set out in the Convention would be to subvert the principle of subsidiarity and to invert the relationship between national courts and the Court. Rather, the terms of the Convention are pursued through a tripartite alliance between the Court, state and the close and systematic monitoring by the other states through their representation in the CoM. If one concedes to this 'principle of solidarity', one must also concede that imposing punitive measures on states – who unlike citizens at national level, voluntarily commit themselves to the jurisdiction of the Court – would not be the best way of encouraging cooperation. In addition, it is to be remembered after all that the clout of the Statute of the Council of Europe lies in the possibility to suspend or terminate Council membership for serious failures to uphold the principles of the rule of law and to protect human rights and fundamental freedoms.[17]

As to the efficacy of the supervisory role of the CoM, the Committee revealed in its forth Annual Report issued in April 2011 that almost 10,000 cases were pending before it, including ones dating from as far back as the early 1980s. That the CoM must exert more pressure to ensure the rapid and effective execution of judgments has been acknowledged and it is thought that the implementation of proposals ushered in by the Interlaken Action Plan from 1 January 2011 should accelerate the process.[18]

and the Court may decide to indicate only one such measure: *Assanidze v. Georgia* [GC], 8 April 2004, 71503/01, § 202 f.

15 See Rule 6 of the Rules of the Committee of Ministers for the supervision of the execution of judgments and of the terms of friendly settlements. The CoM may also adopt interim measures to prevent similar violations pending the adoption of more comprehensive and definitive measures: Rule 16.

16 Ibid. Rule 17.

17 s. 8 and 3 Statute of the Council of Europe.

18 A twin-track supervisory system now classifies cases for examination under either a standard procedure or an enhanced procedure freeing up the CoM's resources to give priority to the latter. Judgments

3. Impact of the European Court's Stance on Domestic Courts

Although the Human Rights Court has ruled against them, it has not precluded those of its constituent states which recognise punitive damages – notably Cyprus, the United Kingdom (more specifically, England and Wales)[19] and Ireland – from imposing them in domestic actions based on Convention violations. Recent authorities in England and Wales, however, have decided to follow in the shadows of the Strasbourg Court. We turn now to consider the position in England and Wales and Ireland in greater detail.

3.1. England and Wales

The United Kingdom, one of few states in the vanguard in drafting the European Convention on Human Rights, was the first to ratify it on 8 March 1951 with effect from 3 September 1953. It was not until 14 January 1966,[20] however, that alleged victims of human rights infractions could take their cases to Strasbourg, albeit via 'the long and costly road', in pursuit of recourse against the United Kingdom.[21] The right to petition the Strasbourg Court directly continues to exist today. For decades, however, the campaign persisted for parliament to give British judges a mandate, through incorporation, to enforce Convention rights 'at home'. As, it was said towards the end of that century, 'Britain's dirty laundry has been washed slowly, expensively and inefficiently in Strasbourg, much of the fabric still stained afterwards or cleaned far too late to be of value to the customer.'[22] Victory came on 2 October 2000 when the Human Rights Act 1998 entered into force. Since then, the question of the nature of the cause of action under the Act and the appropriate quantum of damages awardable under it has attracted much attention.

R (on the application of Greenfield) v. Secretary of State for the Home Dept is the leading authority on the subject. There, Lord Bingham (with whom the remaining members of the House of Lords concurred) ruled that it is the Strasbourg Court's awards,

raising structural or complex problems, *inter alia*, are dealt with under the enhanced procedure though specific and general measures are retained under both tracks. A further feature of the new execution process is its handing over of primary responsibility to states – in line with the principle of subsidiarity – to draw up action plans (setting out measures they intend to take to implement the Court's judgment) and action reports (setting out measures taken to implement the Court's judgment, and/or explanations otherwise). The latter necessarily precedes a proposal by the CoM to close the case.

19 For an overview on exemplary damages under English law see Wilcox 2009, p. 7 ff. For Cyprus see Michaelides-Mateou on p. 163 ff. of this publication.

20 As Mole writes, this right to petition was prudently delayed to ensure the statutory reversal (by the War Damage Act 1965) of the House of Lords' decision in *Burmah Oil v. Lord Advocate* [1965] AC 75 so as to deprive Burmah Oil of its right to compensation for damage caused during WWII. The date chosen – 14 January 1966 – fell outside the six-month limitation period for challenges to the 1965 Act thus ensuring that Burmah Oil could not bring its case before the Strasbourg Court: See Mole 2004, p. 18.

21 The delay can be explained by the fact that although the final version of the Convention owed much to British ideas and drafting as far as the definition of rights was concerned, the enforcement mechanism, including the right of individual petition and the creation of a supranational human rights court, owed little to British thinking and had been opposed by British representatives on the drafting committee. See the House of Commons, Library Research Papers, The Human Rights Bill [HL] Bill 119 of 1997–98, No: 98/24, February 1998, p. 7.

22 HL Deb, 25 January 1995, vol. 560 col. 1137.

and not those of English courts in tort cases, that should provide the appropriate comparator for damages.[23] This was so despite several voices that English courts should be free to depart from the comparatively low amount of compensatory damages awarded by the European Court.[24] Lord Bingham then proceeded to elaborate several reasons for his preferred approach: first, he said, 'the 1998 Act is not a tort statute. Its objects are different and broader.' He gave as a second and third reason that the very wording of s. 8 of the Human Rights Act 1998 on Judicial Remedies dictated reference to Strasbourg. Modelled on Article 41 of the European Convention, s. 8(3) of the Act allows for an award of 'just satisfaction' if necessary.[25] Significantly, s. 8(4) requires a domestic court to take into account the principles applied by the European Court under Article 41 ECHR not only in determining: (a) whether to award damages, but also in determining; (b) the amount of the award. The purpose of incorporating the Convention into domestic law through the 1998 Act, he explained, was not to give people better remedies. To do this would be to contradict the White Paper 'Rights Brought Home: The Human Rights Bill' whose par. 2.6 specifically provided that incorporation sought to enable people to receive compensation from a domestic court 'equivalent to' what they would have received but without the delay and expense of resort to Strasbourg.[26] In awarding damages therefore, English judges should not be cast adrift from their international mooring.

Naturally then, when the question whether punitive damages should be available for Convention breaches before English courts arose in *Watkins v. Secretary of State for the Home Department and Others*, the answer came that as exemplary damages form no part of the existing jurisprudence of the Strasbourg Court it would be wrong to award them in equivalent proceedings for a breach of the relevant Convention rights.[27] Granted that in so doing, English judges aim not to be significantly more generous than the Human Rights Court might be expected to be, but if that is indeed so, one could legitimately argue that ordinary rights enjoy better advantages than fundamental rights – from the claimant's perspective at least. Indeed, following the abolition of the 'cause of action' test

23 *R (on the application of Greenfield) v. Secretary of State for the Home Dept* [2005] UKHL 14, at [19] f.

24 See, for example, *R (Bernard) v. Enfield LBC* [2002] EWHC 2282 (Admin) per Sullivan J, at [45]; *R (KB) v. South London and South and West Region Mental Health Review Tribunal* [2003] EWHC 193 (Admin), at [47] and [53] per Stanley Burnton J; *Anufrijeva v. Southwark London Borough Council* [2003] EWCA Civ 1406, at [73] and [74]. See also The Law Commission and the Scottish Law Commission 1998, par. 4.6 f.

25 Specifically, s. 8 (3) reads: No award of damages is to be made unless, taking account of all the circumstances of the case, including:
(a) any other relief or remedy granted, or order made, in relation to the act in question (by that or any other court); and
(b) the consequences of any decision (of that or any other court) in respect of that act, the court is satisfied that the award is necessary to afford just satisfaction to the person in whose favour it is made.

26 Per Lord Bingham in *R (on the application of Greenfield) v. Secretary of State for the Home Dept* [2005] UKHL 14, at [19]. See also HL Deb, 3 November 1997, vol. 582 col. 1232 per Lord Irvine.

27 *Watkins v. Secretary of State for the Home Department and Others* [2006] UKHL 395, at [64] per Lord Roger. Although not expressly referred to in the case, this decision was consistent with the then Lord Chief Justice, Lord Woolf's view in *Anufrijeva v. Southwark London Borough Council* [2003] EWCA Civ 1406 and his extra-judicial writings on exemplary damages under the 1998 Act, in Lord Wolf 2000, p. 434.

by the House of Lords in *Kuddus v. Chief Constable of Leicestershire Constabulary*[28] there was nothing to suggest that punitive damages could not, in principle, be awarded for a violation of the 1998 Act.[29]

Since *Greenfield*, several commentators have levelled criticism at the notion of 'equivalency' of redress which was invoked by Lord Bingham to justify the weight of Strasbourg jurisprudence.[30] Without rehearing their arguments here, it is clear that there is a case to be made for looking to domestic law on the question of quantum 'as a starting point, but subject to any true principle which emerges from the jurisprudence and consistent practice of the ECtHR…'.[31] It follows from this that as the Strasbourg Court has a clear and constant principle on exemplary damages, it is right that the latter should not be available under the Act. That no role would be given to them was clearly not the view taken by some in the course of debating the precursor to the Act, the Human Rights Bill, however. Lord Lester, a leading proponent of human rights and tireless campaigner for the incorporation of the Convention into domestic law, having opined that it would be quite wrong to fetter or clog the discretion of the English, Scottish and Northern Irish courts in deciding upon the appropriate principles for the award of compensation continued that: 'It would be absurd, if, for example, domestic law concepts such as that of exemplary damages in an appropriate case, which is not a concept that has been developed by the European court, were to be excluded. It would be absurd if our courts were not able, in developing the common law, to stick to our own principles…'.[32]

Lord Mackay's response to this – one that was later taken up by the Law Commission in its recommendation that damages under s. 8 should not be exemplary or punitive[33] – was that in light of the absence of such damages within the powers of the Scottish courts,[34] to read the then Clause 8 as allowing exemplary damages would lead to different results in different jurisdictions within the United Kingdom.[35] In fact, however, it is respectfully submitted, that that in itself is scarcely a decisive argument: different results in different jurisdictions exist anyway and arguments that claimants in England, Wales

28 *Kuddus v. Chief Constable of Leicestershire Constabulary* [2002] 2 AC 122. The position under English law today is that punitive damages can only be awarded if the facts can be brought within one of three categories enumerated by Lord Devlin in the seminal case of *Rookes v. Barnard*: (a) oppressive, arbitrary or unconstitutional action by servants of the government; (b) conduct calculated by the defendant to make a profit for himself which may well exceed the compensation payable to the claimant; and (c) express statutory authorisation. Before 2002, it was thought that punitive damages were limited to torts (or causes of action) in respect of which it could be established that they had already been awarded prior to 1964 when *Rookes* was decided. This 'cause of action' test, introduced by the Court of Appeal in *AB v. South West Water Services Ltd* [1993] QB 507, was abolished by the House of Lords in *Kuddus v. Chief Constable of Leicestershire Constabulary*.

29 In *Kuddus*, the question of the availability of exemplary damages for a breach of the 1998 Act in respect of the common law categories was specifically left open: See Lord Mackay, at [46] and Lord Hutton, at [92].

30 Among others, Steele 2008, Varuhas 2009 and Burrows 2011.

31 McGregor 2009, par. 43–035.

32 HL Deb, 29 January 1998, vol. 585 col. 386 f. Emphasis added.

33 The Law Commission and the Scottish Law Commission 1998, par. 5.5. See also *Watkins v. Secretary of State for the Home Department and Others* [2006] UKHL 395, at [64] per Lord Roger.

34 *Black v. North British Railway Co* 1908 SC 444, 453 f per Lord President (Dunedin); *Watkins v. Secretary of State for the Home Department*, at [30] f per Lord Hope and [64] per Lord Roger.

35 HL Deb, 29 January 1998, vol. 585 col. 386 f.

or Ireland should for that matter not be entitled to exemplary damages in tortious proceedings because their neighbours in Scotland are not, have never held ground. The Law Commission's other case against exemplary damages is today redundant following their Lordships' ruling in *Kuddus*. It had been said that 'the preconditions for an award of punitive damages under English law include the principle that, in the absence of specific statutory provision, they will only be awarded if the tort in question is one for which punitive damages had been awarded prior to *Rookes v. Barnard*. As an action under the HRA does not satisfy this requirement, and no provision for punitive damages is made in the Act itself, there seems no basis for such awards.'[36] The need to satisfy the 'cause of action' criterion has now been abolished so that exemplary damages can in principle be extended to fresh torts.[37] Hence as Fairgrieve wrote after the decision in *Kuddus* was handed down: 'In light of the surreptitious practice of the Strasbourg court, it might be argued that the English courts should be allowed to include a penal element in damages awards under the HRA. If exemplary damages serve a purpose in stigmatising, punishing and deterring oppressive conduct by public servants, then they should be available in the cases of breaches of fundamental rights. The serious breach of human rights would seem to be an example *par excellence* of the need to single out egregious behaviour for particular censure.'[38]

That said, if due weight is given to the words 'just and appropriate' under s. 8(1) and 'necessary to afford just satisfaction' under s. 8(3) one cannot but accept that an award of exemplary damages would not be appropriate. Second, the various arguments proffered to undermine s. 8(4), along the lines that the Strasbourg Court has no discernible principles,[39] simply do not apply to exemplary damages. Thus, as Fairgrieve continued, 'there are arguments for excluding punitive damages in this sphere. The language of the HRA instructs the English courts to take account of the "principles" of the ECtHR. And whatever the surreptitious practice of the ECtHR might be, it has made it clear that in principle it will not award punitive and aggravated damages.' Third, if indeed it where the intention of parliament to allow such damages, it would have expressly so provided. This is particularly the case as the Human Rights Bill was drafted post-*AB v. South West Water Services Ltd*[40] when it was clear that punitive damages would not have been available under the Act without their express mention as an action under it was not one in which exemplary damages had been awarded pre-*Rookes*. Finally, if, as Lord Bingham has said, it is incorrect to classify a cause of action under the Human Rights Act as a tort – despite the previously held views[41] – then the question on the availability of exemplary damages is redundant as their Lordships remarks in *Kuddus* on the application of such damages are believed to be confined to categories of tort. In *Mosley v. News Group*

36 The Law Commission and the Scottish Law Commission 1998, par. 4.72.

37 See fn. 19 and 28 above.

38 Fairgrieve 2001, p. 705 ff.

39 See fn. 2 above.

40 *AB v. South West Water Services Ltd* [1993] QB 507.

41 See, for example, The Law Commission and the Scottish Law Commission 1998, par. 4.20; Dugdale & Jones 2000, par. 1–04, 12–75 ff; Lester & Pannick 2000, p. 382; Stanton, Skidmore & Harris 2003, p. 144 and Burrows 2004, p. 16. So also McGregor 2009, par. 43–006, who writes that the analogy is not perfect as the remedy is discretionary but otherwise the analogy is a useful one.

Newspapers Ltd Eady J thought this to be significant and having considered the authorities before him, refused to award punitive damages for breach of privacy which in his view was not a tort.[42] The view taken in *Watkins* seems appropriate therefore.

The Act aside, it is clear that where a claim under it arises collaterally with a cause of action in tort, a claimant can bring concurrent proceedings in tort alongside a claim for breach of human rights and he may, if appropriate, recover exemplary damages under the former mode of redress.[43] In this sense it can be said that while the power of English courts to award relief to victims of human rights abuses is, in Lord Bingham's words, 'different and broader', the functions of damages under the Human Rights Act 1998 are more tapered than those under tort law.[44] Baroness Hale in *Lumba and Mighty v Secretary of State for the Home Department* similarly confirmed that the power to award damages under s. 8(3) and (4) of the Human Rights Act 1998 is 'narrowly drawn'.[45]

3.2. *Ireland*

The position in Ireland is different. Ireland signed the European Convention on Human Rights on 29 June 1953 with effect from 3 September 1953. Like England, however, it is a dualist state requiring domestic legislation to incorporate international treaties into domestic law. The European Convention on Human Rights Act 2003, which is similar but not identical to its English counterpart, became law as recently as 1 January 2004.

S. 2 of the 2003 Act imposes an obligation on Irish courts to interpret Irish law in accordance with the Convention.[46] Under s. 3(2), a person who has suffered injury, loss or damage as a result of a contravention of s. 3(1)[47] may institute proceedings to recover damages. This is subject to the proviso that 'no other remedy in damages is available'. S. 3(2) goes on to state that a court may award to the person such damages (if any) as it considers appropriate. The Act, like the Human Rights Act 1998 Act, is also silent on exemplary damages. Unlike s. 8(4) of the 1998 Act, s. 3 of the 2003 Act does not specifically refer courts, in determining whether and if so the quantum of damages to be awarded, to Strasbourg jurisprudence under Article 41 ECHR. However, s. 4 of the 2003 Act clearly consolidates elements of s. 2 and s. 8(4) of the 1998 Act insofar as it directs courts adjudicating under the Act 'to take notice of the Convention provisions and of – (a) any declaration, decision, advisory opinion or judgment of the European Court of Human Rights…and shall, when interpreting the Convention provisions, take due account of the principles laid down by those declarations, decisions, advisory opinions, opinions and

42 Cf McGregor 2009, par. 42–015 ff, who has criticised the case as Lord Nicholls in *Campbell v. MGN Ltd* [2002] EMLR 30, p. 617 had classified breach of privacy as a tort.

43 See McGregor 2009, par. 42–017 ff.

44 See Steele 2008, p. 615 f.

45 [2011] UKSC 12, at [216].

46 The Act does not apply retrospectively: see s. 2(2). See also *Dublin City Council v. Jeanette Fennell* [2005] I IR 604.

47 The provision states that 'Subject to any statutory provision (other than this Act) or rule of law, every organ of the State shall perform its functions in a manner compatible with the State's obligations under the Convention provisions.'

judgements.'[48] It is thus unambiguous that in awarding damages Irish courts, by reason of the provisions of s. 4, must have regard to the emerging principles of the Strasbourg Court on damages. In a recent High Court decision, *Pullen & Ors v. Dublin City Council*, Irvine J referred to the aforementioned report by the Law Commission on 'Damages under the Human Rights Act 1998' and proceeded to summarise the principles urged by the Strasbourg Court including the fact that punitive damages are not awarded as a matter of practice.[49] No punitive damages were sought on the facts. If they were however, it is unlikely – in light of the Irish courts' recognition of the principle against such damages in Strasbourg – that they would be available under the 2003 Act.

Notwithstanding so, the scope for an award of exemplary damages for breaches of fundamental rights is much broader in Ireland than it is in England. Ireland, unlike England, has a written constitution and Irish jurisprudence recognises the significance of compensatory, aggravated and exemplary damages under tort law and for breaches of constitutional rights.[50] In *Kennedy v. Ireland*, three claimants were awarded a total of £30,000 for deliberate, conscious and unjustifiable interference by the state, through its executive organ, with their telephonic communications. Though the 'right to privacy' is not specifically guaranteed under Article 40 (on Fundamental Rights) of the Irish Constitution the court held that the right is 'one of the fundamental personal rights of the citizen which flow from the Christian and democratic nature of the State'. In determining the appropriate amount of damages, Hamilton P stated that: 'The action of the executive in this case in "tapping" the telephones of the plaintiffs without any lawful justification and in interfering with and intruding upon the privacy of the plaintiffs constituted an attack on their dignity and freedom as individuals and as journalists and cannot be tolerated in a democratic society such as ours is and our Constitution requires it to be and the injury done to the plaintiffs has been aggravated by the fact that it has been done by an organ of state which is under a constitutional obligation to respect, vindicate and defend their rights. The plaintiffs are in my opinion entitled to substantial damages and it is, in the circumstances of this case, irrelevant whether they be described as "aggravated" or "exemplary" damages.'[51]

In *Conway v. INTO*,[52] the Irish Supreme Court in line with *Kennedy*[53] confirmed the propriety of an award of exemplary damages for breach of constitutional rights. Significantly, none of the defendants in the case were agents of the executive or of the

48 Interestingly, s. 5(5) is clearly modelled on s. 8(4). Following a declaration of compatibility under s. 5(1), a party may under s. 5(4) seek compensation for damage as a result of the incompatibility concerned and the Government may discretionarily make an *ex gratia* payment of compensation. Any advisor appointed for the purpose of advising the Government of the appropriate amount of such compensation (if any) is directed under s. 5(5) to 'take appropriate account of the principles and practice applied by the European Court of Human Rights in relation to affording just satisfaction to an injured party under Article 41 of the Convention.'

49 *Pullen & Ors v. Dublin City Council* [2009] IEHC 452, at 5.7 ff.

50 See The Law Reform Commission, 2000, par. 1.31 ff.

51 *Kennedy v. Ireland* [1987] IR 587.

52 *Conway v. INTO* [1987] IR 587.

53 In *Kennedy*, Hamilton P has distinguished punitive damages from exemplary damages. This distinction was, it is submitted, rightly overruled by the Supreme Court in *Conway v. INTO*. See Hogan, Whyte & Kelly 2003, par. 7.1.133 ff.

government. In allowing punitive damages against private individuals who violated constitutional rights, *Conway* thus also unanimously rejected the categories propounded by Lord Devlin in *Rookes v. Barnard*, for actions under the Constitution at least, and in so doing ensured that where constitutional rights are violated with impunity, the courts' power to deter would be wide.

Conway was applied in *Shortt v. Commissioner of an Garda Síochána and others*; an appeal confined to the quantification of damages before the Supreme Court. The plaintiff in the case was a victim of disreputable conduct and of shocking abuse of power by two Garda officers who concocted false evidence against him. He was said to have been 'sacrificed in order to assist the career ambitions' of the officers. In awarding Shortt a total of €4,623,871 including €1,000,000 in exemplary damages, Murray CJ held that '[a]lthough the grounds of the plaintiff's claims were not laid as, or characterised as, breaches of constitutional rights *per se*, the conduct of the Garda officers involved set at nought core constitutional rights of the plaintiff to due process and a fair trial. However they are characterised he is entitled to such damages.'[54] It can thus fairly be concluded, reflecting the view of Irish courts' (and as will be seen below other jurisdictions on the question of the parameters of constitutional claims), that constitutional rights enjoy more generous (fiscal) protection both against private actors and the state in Ireland than they do in England.[55]

4. Vindicatory Damages as Constitutional Redress in the Commonwealth Caribbean

Against the preponderance of authority in England, the House of Lords, with its Privy Council hat on, has repeatedly ruled that substantial awards of damages may be appropriate where executive action has infringed fundamental rights and freedoms. *Attorney General of Trinidad and Tobago v. Ramanoop* was the first case in point. The proceedings were instituted by Siewchand Ramanoop who had been unjustifiably roughed up by a police officer, arrested, taken to the police station and locked up for a few hours. His appeal to the Privy Council raised the question whether exemplary damages could be awarded for a violation of rights enshrined in the Constitution of Trinidad and Tobago. In *Harrikissoon v Attorney-General of Trinidad and Tobago* the Privy Council – through Lord Diplock's pen – had already ruled that s. 14(2) of the Constitution of Trinidad and Tobago which provides that the court 'may' make such orders, etc, as it may consider appropriate for the purpose of enforcing a constitutional right should not be used unless the circumstances of the complaint include some feature which makes it appropriate to take that course.[56] Giving the judgment of the Board in *Ramanoop* Lord Nicholls who, it might be remembered, sat in *Kuddus* and said of punitive damages that they 'played a significant role in buttressing civil liberties, in claims for false imprisonment and wrongful arrest', said that: 'An award of compensation will go some distance towards

54 *Shortt v. Commissioner of an Garda Síochána and others* [2007] IESC 9, at [105]. See Quill 2008, p. 354 ff and Binchy 2007, p. 20 ff.

55 For the position in the U.S. see Lord Scott, Holland & Varner 2006.

56 [1980] AC 265.

vindicating the infringed constitutional right. How far it goes will depend on the circumstances, but in principle it may well not suffice. The fact that the right violated was a constitutional right adds an extra dimension to the wrong. An additional award, not necessarily of substantial size, may be needed to reflect the sense of public outrage, emphasise the importance of the constitutional right and the gravity of the breach, and deter further breaches. All these elements have a place in this additional award. "Redress" in section 14 [of the Constitution] is apt to encompass such an award if the court considers it is required having regard to all the circumstances. Although such an award, where called for, is likely in most cases to cover much the same ground in financial terms as would an award by way of punishment in the strict sense of retribution, punishment in the latter sense is not its object. Accordingly, the expressions "punitive damages" or "exemplary damages" are better avoided as descriptions of this type of additional award.'[57]

On that basis, the Board remitted the case back to the lower courts for consideration of whether, and if so, the extent to which the appellant was entitled to an additional award. *Ramanoop* was thus consistent with the 'enlightened approach' adopted by the Privy Council in earlier cases, marked by an expansion of the scope of constitutional redress clauses for the purpose of securing the effective protection of fundamental rights.[58] It was also consistent with, and indeed influenced by, New Zealand jurisprudence on constitutional infringements.[59]

57 *Attorney General of Trinidad and Tobago v. Ramanoop* [2005] UKPC 15, at [19]. Before setting out the principles for the assessment of damages, including exemplary damages, as constitutional relief their Lordships trawled through earlier authorities which like the authorities pre-*Rookes* were in an unsettled state: In *Maharaj v. The Attorney General of Trinidad & Tobago (No 2)* [1979] AC 385, a case in which the claimant was deprived of his liberty, the Board found it unnecessary to express a view on the applicability of an award of exemplary or punitive damages as none were sought. *Attorney General of St Christopher, Nevis & Anguilla v. Reynolds* [1980] AC 637 was taken as restricting courts' ability to award exemplary damages for constitutional breaches as the Board there upheld a small sum as exemplary damages for wrongful imprisonment (a common law action) but did not fully express a view on their availability for an action under the constitution. Encouraged by the dictum of the court in *Jorsingh v. The Attorney General* (1997) 52 WIR 501 – where de la Bastide CJ opined in dissent that the power to award damages conferred by the Constitution of Trinidad and Tobago was a very wide one indeed – punitive damages were awarded for claims for constitutional relief by the courts in *Ramesar v. The Attorney General of Trinidad & Tobago* HCA S-895 of 1992 (20 January 1999) and *Abraham v. The Attorney General of Trinidad and Tobago* HCA 801 of 1997 (26 February 1999) but not in *Jones v. The Attorney General of Trinidad and Tobago* HCA 19 of 1998. In *Jorsingh* Sharma JA, in holding that the remedies under s. 14(2) of the Constitution expanded beyond the common law principles, also added that: 'The court is mandated to do whatever it thinks appropriate for the purpose of enforcing or securing the enforcement of any of the provisions dealing with the fundamental right...*Not only can the court enlarge old remedies; it can invent new ones* as well, if that is what it takes or is necessary in an appropriate case to secure and *vindicate* the rights breached.' Emphasis added. See McGregor (2009) par. 11–018.

58 See *Maharaj v. Attorney-General of Trinidad and Tobago* (No 2) [1979] AC 385 and *Jennifer Gairy v. The Attorney General of Grenada* [2001] UKPC 30, among other examples. See also Ventose 2009, p. 247. Cf *Director of Public Prosecutions v. Nasralla* [1967] 2 AC 238 and *Jaundoo v. Attorney General* (Guyana) [1971] AC 972.

59 New Zealand has no written constitution but a Bill of Rights. Their Lordships in *Ramanoop* were assisted by Cooke P and Thomas J's observations in *Simpson v. Attorney-General (Baigent's case)* [1994]

The principles set out in *Ramanoop* were said to equally apply to claims for redress under comparable provisions of other Commonwealth Caribbean constitutions.[60] In *Merson v. Cartwright and the Attorney General*, a case against Sergeant Cartwright, an officer of the Bahamian police, and the Attorney General of the Bahamas, Lord Scott stated that the appropriate sum would depend upon the nature of the particular infringement and the circumstances relating to that infringement.[61] On the facts the Board upheld an award of $100,000 as vindicatory damages for the victim of an assault, battery, false imprisonment and malicious prosecution said to have been subject to such callous, high handed and insulting behaviour for the sole reason of forcing her father, who had been named in a search warrant, to return to the Bahamas to check on her welfare. Unlike *Ramanoop*, where only constitutional damages were claimed despite the existence of several torts, in *Merson* the $100,000 was in addition to two awards of $90,000 for tortious damages for the above wrongs.[62] The Board accepted that the three awards taken together in *Merson* included aggravated and exemplary damages but nevertheless restored the vindicatory award set aside by the Court of Appeal.[63] Lord Scott justified the entire award on the basis that 'there was some special feature' that necessitated the additional award *i.e.* the wholesale contempt shown by the authorities. The possibility of duplication in the damages awarded for the nominate torts and vindicatory damages was, on balance, unlikely. The success of the case if appealed today is doubtful following their Lordships' ruling in *Atain Takitota v. The Attorney General & Others (Bahamas)* on the impropriety of an award both by way of exemplary damages and an award of vindicatory damages.[64]

Ramanoop was also followed in *Horace Fraser Appellant v. Judicial and Legal Services Commission and the Attorney General of Saint Lucia* and *Inniss v. Attorney General of Saint Christopher and Nevis*, which bore similar facts to the latter case. It was in *Inniss* that the scope of the remedy was further expanded. The rights infringed in *Ramanoop* and *Merson* were fundamental rights. *Inniss* involved the wrongful dismissal of a public service lawyer whose contract fell within constitutional protection but outside the section on fundamental rights and freedoms. The applicant was nonetheless awarded $50,000

3 NZLR 667, 678 and *Dunlea v. Attorney General* [2000] 3 NZLR 136, 152 respectively. After *Ramanoop*, *Taunoa v. Attorney General* [2008] 1 NZLR 429 was delivered. There the Supreme Court of New Zealand embraced vindicatory damages with Tipping J stating that the interests of the victim require the court to consider what compensation is due, but society is a victim also, and the court must consider what compensation is necessary by way of vindication to protect fundamental rights and freedoms, at [317]. See also Elias CJ, at [109], Blanchard, at [258] and McGrath, at [370]. The decision of the Supreme Court of Canada in *Vancouver (City of) v. Ward* [2010] 2 SCR 28 is also noteworthy. There McLachlin CJ held that the Canadian Charter of Rights and Freedoms had the function of compensation, vindication and deterrence. See also Pilkington, 1984, who predicted that damages under s. 24(1) of the Charter ought in an appropriate case to deter or punish unacceptable behaviour or reward those who expose it.

60 The relevant constitutional provisions include Article 28(1) for the Bahamas; s. 96(1) for Saint Christopher and Nevis; and s. 105(1) and (3) for Saint Lucia.

61 *Merson v. Cartwright and the Attorney General*, [2005] UKPC 38, at [18].

62 $8,160 was also awarded as special damages.

63 According to their Lordships, a reading of the judgments suggested that the judge formed a view of the totality of the damages that Ms. Merson should receive and then divided the sum, in round figures, between the three heading under which the awards were made.

64 *Atain Takitota v. The Attorney General & Others (Bahamas)* [2009] UKPC 11, at [13].

for breach of contract and $50,000 as constitutional relief to deter the executive from 'resorting to similar breaches in the future to further its own interest'.[65] Lord Hope explained that entitlement to such damages does not hinge on the violation of a fundamental right or freedom. It is sufficient that the provision in question is to be found somewhere in the constitution. Having said that, allowance was made for the importance of the right and the gravity of the breach in the assessment of the award.[66] Since *Inniss*, 'the beckoning finger that invites victims who have suffered abuse of their constitutional rights' has led to further successful claims, *inter alia*, in *Alphie Subiah v. The Attorney General of Trinidad and Tobago* (where it was said that the quantum of the compensatory award and again that the gravity of the constitutional violation were relevant to whether and if so the quantity of vindicatory damages to be awarded)[67] and *Durity v. Attorney General of Trinidad and Tobago*.[68] However, there have been instances were their Lordships have refused to overstretch the boundaries of this exceptional remedy as was the case in *Kenneth Suratt and others v. The Attorney General of Trinidad and Tobago*,[69] *James v. Attorney General of Trinidad and Tobago* (No 2)[70] and *Daniel v. Attorney General of Trinidad and Tobago*,[71] where it was held that declaratory relief sufficed.

5. Assessing the Nature of Vindicatory Damages

The phrase 'vindicatory damages' has now become fossilised as an accepted term for this new species of damages; their nature cannot but raise suspicion, however. They are available if, but only if, the compensatory sum (including aggravated damages) which the judge has in mind to award is insufficient to do the job.[72] So are punitive damages. They aim to mark the excitement of public outrage. So do punitive damages. To emphasise the gravity of the breach.[73] As do punitive damages. To deter further breaches. Punitive damages alike. It appears too that such damages should be specifically pleaded.[74] As Burrows put it, '[i]t is immediately apparent, once one has rigorously unpacked the functions in this way, how very similar those functions are to those which are offered as

65 *Inniss v. Attorney General of Saint Christopher and Nevis* [2008] UKPC 42, at [28] per Lord Hope.

66 *Inniss v. Attorney General of Saint Christopher and Nevis* [2008] UKPC 42, at [27] per Lord Hope.

67 *Alphie Subiah v. The Attorney General of Trinidad and Tobago* [2008] UKPC 47, at [11] per lord Bingham.

68 *Horace Fraser Appellant v. Judicial and Legal Services Commission and the Attorney General* [2008] UKPC 25 and *Durity v. Attorney General of Trinidad and Tobago* [2008] UKPC.

69 *Kenneth Suratt and others v. The Attorney General of Trinidad and Tobago* [2008] UKPC 38.

70 *James v. Attorney General of Trinidad and Tobago* (No 2) [2010] UKPC 23.

71 [2011] UKPC 31.

72 *Alphie Subiah v. The Attorney General of Trinidad and Tobago* [2008] UKPC 47, at [11] and [13] per Lord Bingham.

73 *Inniss v. Attorney General of Saint Christopher and Nevis* [2008] UKPC 42, at [27] per Lord Hope and *Alphie Subiah v. The Attorney General of Trinidad and Tobago* [2008] UKPC 47, at [11] per Lord Bingham.

74 *Greenwood-Henry v. The Attorney General of Jamaica*, Claim No CL G 116 OF 1999. Had vindicatory damages been claimed, Sykes J of the Supreme Court of Jamaica said, at [20], that there was ample evidence to support such an award.

justifying punitive or exemplary damages in tort law.'[75] Although not Christened 'punitive damages', that vindicatory damages have 'much the same object as the common law award of exemplary damages...'[76] is supported by Lord Carswell's view in *Atain Takitota v. The Attorney General & Others* that it would not be appropriate to make an award both by way of exemplary damages and an award of vindicatory damages: 'When the vindicatory function of the latter head of damages has been discharged, with the element of deterrence that a substantial award carries with it,' Lord Carswell held, 'the purpose of exemplary damages has largely been achieved.'[77] To impose both would be to introduce duplication into the calculation.

The employment of the adjective 'vindicatory' implies a distinction from 'punitive' or 'exemplary' damages. Although the latter two terms are 'considered as eventually meaning the same thing', as Finlay CJ rightly, it is submitted, said 'in the assessment of punitive or exemplary damages the element of punishment may be foremost in one case and the element of example may be somewhat greater in another.'[78] The authorities have laid down that it is neither the object of vindicatory damages to punish the executive nor to teach him not to behave as before *i.e.* make an example of him. Rather, vindicatory damages, it is said, seek to vindicate the constitutional right of the complainant. With respect, however, this seems a play on words. As Burrows has said, it is difficult to capture the essence of such damages given that all judicial remedies, both monetary and non-monetary, have a subsidiary function – or a primary function in the case of a declaration and nominal damages – of vindicating the right infringed.[79] Hence the notion that all remedies are bound, to some extent at least, to act as a deterrent against further breaches.

In fact, however, in some awards under English law e.g. for defamation, vindication has long been recognised as an express component[80] and an element of it may be contained, although seldom, in other torts such as false imprisonment.[81] Further, 'vindication' as an object of damages has been creeping into the law in other quarters. In *Mosely v News Group Newspaper Ltd*, Eady J – citing the House of Lords in *Ashley v Chief Constable of Sussex*[82] and *Chester v Afshar*[83] – felt that vindication was a legitimate factor that ought 'probably' to be taken into consideration in an award of damages for breach of privacy. He went on to stress that vindication in this sense was different from vindication

75 Burrows 2011.

76 *Atain Takitota v. The Attorney General & Others (Bahamas)* [2009] UKPC 11, at [13].

77 Ibid, at [15].

78 *Conway v. INTO* [1987] IR 587.

79 Burrows 2011. As Lord Scott put it in *Merson*, at [18], 'the nature of damages awarded may be compensatory but should always be vindicatory'.

80 See *Rooke v. Fairrie* [1941] 1 KB 507. See also McGregor (2009) par. 39–032 and 37–070 ff and Price, Duodu & Cain 2010, par. 20–03.

81 *Hook v. Cunard S.S. Co.* [1953] 1 WLR 682. See also McGregor (2009) par. 1–002, 37–013 ff and 39–032. In the case of defamation, McGregor writes that the object of the award is to show publicly that the claimant's reputation has been wrongly attacked. In the case of false imprisonment, Lawrence LJ in *Walter v. Alltools* (1944) 61 TLR 39 CA 40 held that it does not merely affect a man's liberty but also his reputation and therefore, vindicatory damages are warranted here too.

82 [2008] 2 WLR 975, at [21]–[22].

83 [2005] 1 AC 134, at [87].

of reputation. The object here is 'to mark the fact that either the state or a relevant individual has taken away or undermined the right of another – in this case taken away a person's dignity and struck at the core of his personality.'[84] A large sum was then awarded. As McGregor rightly put it, however, it 'cannot be said to be established that the infringement of a right can in our law lead to an award of vindicatory damages.' Neither of the two House of Lords' decisions cited in *Mosely* were proper authority on vindicatory damages.[85] This approach was at least supported by some of their Lordships in *Lumba and Mighty v. Secretary of State for the Home Department.*[86]

The truth of the matter is that vindicatory damages (apart from in the tradition application) are wolves dressed in sheep's clothing. Given the great deal of overlap between them and punitive/exemplary damages, the difference is clearly one of emphasis, not substance.[87] It is no wonder then that having espoused the purpose of vindicatory damages for constitutional breaches, Lord Nicholls in *Ramanoop* continued that such damages will '...in most cases... cover much the same ground in financial terms as would an award by way of punishment...'.

To this extent, it appears that the Irish valour in calling a spade a spade is to be commended. In *Shortt v. Commissioner of an Garda Síochána and others* discussed above, the Irish Supreme Court emphasised that in addition to all the above functions discharged by an award of punitive damages, such damages may in an appropriate case be used to fully vindicate the rights of the plaintiff. In Murray CJ's words: 'Indeed in exercising its constitutional function to defend and vindicate the rights of individuals the power of the court to award exemplary or punitive damages against the State in appropriate circumstances is, as the decisions of this court demonstrate, of fundamental importance.'[88] Murray CJ went on to clarify that the aim of vindicating constitutional rights could be achieved through punitive or exemplary damages though with less emphasis on the desire to punish the state: 'In their purely punitive dimension the means of a defendant may be relevant in order to ensure that the punishment is proportionate. However the purely punitive element of these damages is hardly relevant where the state is the defendant since no individual, let alone those persons who have actually committed the wrong, will bear responsibility for paying any of the damages. The liability of the state to pay arises from its vicarious responsibility for its servants or agents and the payment of damages is made out of public funds. This of course does not relieve the State from its liability for such damages...'.[89]

Admittedly, however, the fact that punishment *per se* is not the intended outcome is neither here nor there, from the defendant's perspective at least.

Extra judicially, Lord Scott has also sought to capture the subtle terminological distinction between 'punitive' and 'exemplary' damages. While the former speaks for

84 [2008] EMLR 20, at [216].

85 McGregor (2009) par. 42–007 ff.

86 [2011] UKSC 12, per Lord Dyson, at [99] ff and per Lord Collins, at [234] ff.

87 See de la Bastide 2010.

88 *Shortt v. Commissioner of an Garda Síochána and others* [2007] IESC 9, at [119].

89 At [109] f. The means of the parties (invariably the defendant's) were one of three considerations enumerated by Lord Devlin that ought to be borne in mind in awarding exemplary damages. See Wilcox 2009, p. 25 ff.

itself, the latter, he found less descriptive and concluded that the synonymous uses of the terms were unhelpful and confusing: 'In the pre *Rookes v. Barnard* days the expression "exemplary damages" was sometimes used as describing what we today might call "aggravated" damages *i.e.* damages where extra compensation is due because of aggravating conduct on the part of a wrongdoer that has increased the degree of damage suffered by the victim. But, nowadays, damages are described as "exemplary" in contrast to, and not as a sub-division of, compensatory damages. But if damages are neither aggravated damages awarded for the purpose of compensation nor punitive damages for the purpose of punishment, what is left? Today, I suggest, vindicatory damages, exemplified by two recent Privy Council cases, *A-G of Trinidad v. Ramanoop*...and... *Merson v. Cartwright*, cover all the remaining ground that might formally have been occupied by "exemplary" damages *i.e.* extra-compensatory damages that are substantial (as opposed to nominal) but are not punitive in intent.'[90]

While Lord Scott is correct in equating vindicatory damages to exemplary damages, the need for the latter to now acquire a separate and distinct meaning from punitive damages – and in so doing, overturn what has been accepted since *Rookes* and as reiterated in *Broome v. Cassell & Co*[91] in 1972 as interchangeable terms – is unnecessary. As Finlay CJ put it 'as a matter of common sense it is almost impossible to award damages for the purpose of making an example of a person without, to some extent, at least, punishing that person. It is equally impossible to award damages for the purpose of punishing a person without, to some extent, making an example of him.'[92]

Whatever their designation, it is clear that vindicatory damages would not be available under the Human Rights Act 1998. This is so despite Lord Scott's view that 'just satisfaction' within the meaning of s. 8(3) 'may, in an appropriate case, require a vindicatory award in order to demonstrate that the complainant does indeed have the right contended for and/or to emphasise that the defendant's conduct was unlawful and should not be repeated.'[93] This is because the same reasons on the propriety of punitive damages under the 1998 Act apply. In particular, vindicatory damages do not form part of the language or practice of the Strasbourg Court.

Alternatively, it has been suggested that English courts should take the lead from the Privy Council's authorities so that vindicatory damages can be awarded in addition to tort damages where the overlap between common law damages and damages under the Human Rights Act is incomplete and the authorities have show a wholesale contempt of the rule of law.[94] Again, one would caution against inviting a further anomaly into the law. Another yet unexplored scenario is a case in which exemplary damages are inappropriate under the common law for some reason or other. Could vindicatory damages bridge the gap?

90 Lord Scott 2006, p. 6. Indeed, Lord Scott's advocacy of vindicatory damages is surprising given his scathing dislike for punitive damages as displayed in *Kuddus*.

91 *Broome v. Cassell & Co* [1972] AC 1027 per Lord Hailsham LC's, 1073.

92 *Conway v. INTO* [1987] IR 587.

93 Lord Scott 2006, pp. 6 and 7. See also *Ashley and Another v. Chief Constable of Sussex Police* [2008] UKHL 25, at [22].

94 Clayton & Tomlinson 2009, par. 21.53.

This question was decided by the UK Supreme Court in *Lumba and Mighty v. Secretary of State for the Home Department*. The case was one on false imprisonment whereby the applicants suffered no loss or damage as a result of the unlawful exercise by the Secretary of State of the power to detain. The appellants were thus awarded nominal damages only. Having refused to award punitive damages, as the conduct in question was not sufficiently outrageous, the court went on to consider whether it would be appropriate for there to be 'a middle course between compensatory and exemplary damages' ie vindicatory damages; not to compensate the claimants for harm, nor to punish the defendant but simply to mark the law's recognition that a wrong was done.[95]

Citing McGregor, who wrote that the appeals to the Privy Council from Caribbean countries in which the courts sanctioned the award of vindicatory damages for infringement of a right are far removed from tortious claims under the common law as the right infringed in each case was a constitutional right guaranteed by the constitution of the particular country,[96] Lord Dyson ruled firstly that the reference by Lord Nicholls to reflecting public outrage showed 'how closely linked vindicatory damages are to punitive and exemplary damages.'[97] He then went onto state that: 'The implications of awarding vindicatory damages in the present case would be far reaching. Undesirable uncertainty would result. If they were awarded here, then they could in principle be awarded in any case involving a battery or false imprisonment by an arm of the state. Indeed, why limit it to such torts? And why limit it to torts committed by the state? I see no justification for letting such an unruly horse loose on our law. In my view, the purpose of vindicating a claimant's common law rights is sufficiently met by: (i) an award of compensatory damages, including (in the case of strict liability torts) nominal damages where no substantial loss is proved; (ii) where appropriate, a declaration in suitable terms; and (iii) again, where appropriate, an award of exemplary damages. There is no justification for awarding vindicatory damages for false imprisonment to any of the FNPs.'[98]

Lord Hope, Lord Walker[99] and Baroness Hale were sympathetic to vindicatory damages. Lord Hope opined that notwithstanding the absence of special damage, the conduct of the officials was serious abuse of power and it was deplorable.[100] The vindicatory award, he felt, should not be more than a modest one and on the facts, he concurred with Lord Walker that £1,000 to each appellant was appropriate. While preferring to award the applicants £500, Baroness Hale agreed that the right to be free from arbitrary imprisonment by the state is one which the law should be able to vindicate in some way, 'irrespective of whether compensatable harm has been suffered or the conduct of the authorities has been so egregious as to merit exemplary damages.'[101] Referring to the concept of a conventional sum awarded in *Rees v. Darlington Memorial*

95 [2011] UKSC 12, at [213] per Baroness Hale.
96 McGregor 2009, par. 42–009.
97 [2011] UKSC 12, at [100].
98 At [101].
99 At [195].
100 At [176].
101 At [217].

Hospital NHS Trust,[102] '[t]he common law', she said, 'has shown itself capable of growing and adapting to meet new situations.'[103]

Lord Collins on the other hand was rightly concerned that a separate award for vindicatory damages would confuse the *purpose* of damages awards with the nature of the award stating, as Burrows did (supra), that a declaration, or an award of nominal damages, may itself have a vindicatory purpose and effect. For this reason, he considered there was no basis in the present law for the creation of a head of vindicatory damages at common law.[104] Lord Kerr's words are to be read with care and seem to be limited to the facts of the case at hand: 'If there is any scope for the award of vindicatory damages where exemplary damages are not appropriate, it must be, in my opinion, very limited indeed. Such an award could only be justified where the declaration that a claimant's right has been infringed provides insufficiently emphatic recognition of the seriousness of the defendant's default. That situation does not arise here.' Lords Phillips,[105] Brown and Rodger dissented on the central aspect of the case. On vindicatory damages, however, all three agreed that they were objectionable to those conceded to have been rightly detained.[106]

The case was not one on damages under s. 8(3) and (4) of the Human Rights Act 1998 thus it remains to be seen in a case precisely on the point whether vindicatory damages will stand. Further, in *Lumba and Mighty*, although 6 out of 9 judges objected to them, one of the judge's decision was based on the facts of the case and three of the decisions were obiter so the question cannot be put to sleep though it is unlikely, given the strong sentiments against them that vindicatory damages will (in the modern sense) ever form part of English law, scope for vindicatory damages which are contrary to the principles of Scots law and are incompetent. The same goes for exemplary damages.[107]

6. Conclusion

What emerges following this examination is that in respect of extra-compensatory damages, English judges sit uncomfortably between their Commonwealth relatives on the one hand and their European neighbours on the other. Being one of the progenitors of the European Convention on Human Rights, it is easy to see how parliament in Britain sought to be loyal to Strasbourg principles in drafting what became the Human Rights Act 1998 and in so doing sought to be in close harmony with the will of the majority of Strasbourg judges on their stance on damages.[108] Ireland followed in the same vein

102 [2004] AC 309. See also Lord Hope's dictum, at [179] and that of Lord Kerr's, at [236].

103 [2011] UKSC 12, at [216].

104 At [236] ff.

105 At [335].

106 At [361]. See also *Queen on the Application of NAB v. Secretary of State for the Home Department* [2011] EWHC 1191, at [6] per Lord Irwin, R (*Kambadzi v. Secretary of State for Home Department* [2011] UKSC 23, at [74] per Baroness Hale and *Queen on the Application of Amin Sino v. Secretary of State for Home Department* [2011] EWHC 2249, at [79] and [89] Per John Howell QC.

107 *S v. Secretary of State for Home Department* 2011 STL 297, at [26] per Lord Menzies.

108 The ECJ has ruled that 'it must be possible to award specific damages, such as the exemplary damages provided for by English law, pursuant to claims or actions founded on Community law, if such damages

though with more latitude to give credibility to it policies on the protection of fundamental rights where actions are brought under the Constitution. It went further, as several Commonwealth jurisdictions have done, in rejecting the curbs placed on the availability of exemplary damages by *Rookes v. Barnard*[109] in respect of such violations.

Where the wording permits, however, it is clear as the House sitting in Privy Council have shown that English judges are eager to retain their tradition of maximising deterrence for flagrant breaches through an award of extra-compensatory damages. It remains difficult to see, however, why a change in terminology was thought necessary especially given that 'exemplary damages' are awarded in some Commonwealth jurisdictions as relief for breach of constitutional rights and are so called.[110] As it has been said: 'The development of a coherent legal theory of extra-compensatory damages should be an important task for judges and lawyers…in the coming years.'[111] The recent decision in *Lumba and Mighty* is therefore a welcome one in this respect. There is simply no room for vindicatory damages in the Arab's tent.

7. Recommendations

It can almost confidently be assumed that the panorama of the world of remedies in future Continental Europe will be one without punitive damages – at least not formally. As the study by Koziol & Wilcox reveals,[112] several attempts (some successful) have been made to introduce such or similar damages both at national and European level (both openly and covertly). However, the tide against them by some of the greatest minds is strong and broad and lawmakers have proved unhurried, in opposition to such names, to lay down otherwise. It is to be remembered that though an ancient remedy 'modern' punitive, or exemplary damages as the English prefer, are rooted in and peculiar to English law and to English traditions and have endured a long history of germination and budding and pruning and dormancy in those soils. So far, they have escaped uprooting with Parliament content to leave it to judges to develop the remedy as they see fit. Today, they are confined to a narrow category of wrongs which though anomalous must reluctantly be accepted. Other Commonwealth countries have attempted to fashion the contours of punitive damages in their respective jurisdictions less artificially – the U.S. model tending to prove the most divisive. It seems right that countries with no historical underpinning of such damages should not now seek to graft them into their legal systems. In Lord Kilbrandon's words, 'I do not suppose that anyone now sitting down to draft a civil code would include an article providing for punitive damages.'[113] The grass is not always greener.

may be awarded pursuant to similar claims or actions founded on domestic law' They are yet to be successfully invoked for a breach of Community law, however. The effect of *Kuddus* in this area of law is yet to be seen. See Wilcox 2009, p. 23 f.

109 In real terms, however, the significance of this rejection is paled by the fact that most cases for breach of the Constitution fall within Lord Devlin's first category (Oppressive, arbitrary or unconstitutional action by servants of the government) anyway.

110 See Clayton & Tomlinson 2009, par. 21.50 f.

111 Per Lord Scott, Holland & Varner 2006, p. 500.

112 Koziol & Wilcox 2009.

113 *Cassell & Co. Ltd v. Broome and Another* [1972] AC 1027, 1134.

Bibliography

Binchy 2007
Binchy, W., 'Damages Awards after *Shortt v An Garda Síochána*: New Questions', *QRTL*, 2007, pp. 20–27.

Burrows 2004
Burrows, A., *Remedies for Torts and Breach of Contract*, Oxford: Oxford University Press, 2004.

Burrows 2011
Burrows, A., 'Damages and Rights', in: A. Robertson & D. Nolan (eds.), *Rights and Private Law*, Oxford: Hart Publishing, 2011 forthcoming.

Carnwath 2000
Carnwath, R., 'ECHR Remedies from a Comparative Perspective', *ICQL*, 2000, pp. 517–527.

Clayton & Tomlinson 2009
Clayton, R. & Tomlinson, H., *The Law of Human Rights*, New York: Oxford University Press, 2009.

Deiser 1908
Deiser, G. F., 'The Juristic Person I', *UPaLRev*, 1908, pp. 131–142.

de la Bastide 2010
de la Bastide, M., 'Developments in Judicial Protection of Human Rights in the Commonwealth Caribbean', *CLB*, 2010, pp. 223–233.

Dugdale & Jones 2000
Dugdale, A. & Jones, M., *Clerk and Lindsell on Torts*, London: Sweet & Maxwell, 2000.

Fairgrieve 2001
Fairgrieve, D., 'The Human Rights Act 1998, Damages and Tort Law', *PL*, 2001, pp. 695–716.

Fenyves *et al.* 2011
Fenyves, A. *et al.* (eds.), *Tort Law in the Jurisprudence of the European Court of Human Rights*, Boston: De Gruyter Verlag, 2011.

Grosz, Beatson & Duffy 1999
Grosz, S., Beatson J. & Duffy, P., *Human Rights Act 1998*, London: Sweet & Maxwell, 1999.

Hogan, Whyte & Kelly 2003
Hogan G.W., Whyte, G.F. & Kelly, J.M., *The Irish Constitution*, Dublin: LexisNexis Butterworths, 2003.

Koziol & Wilcox 2009
Koziol, H. & Wilcox, V. (eds.), *Punitive Damages: Common Law and Civil Law Perspectives*, Vienna: Springer, 2009.

Lester & Pannick 2000
Lester, A.P. & Pannick, D., 'The Impact of the Human Rights Act on Private Law: The Knight's Move', *LQR*, 2000, pp. 380–285.

Lester & Pannick 2004
Lester, A.P. & Pannick, D., *Human Rights Law and Practice*, London: LexisNexis Butterworths, 2004.

McGregor 2009
McGregor, H., *McGregor on Damages*, London: Sweet & Maxwell, 2009.

Mole 2004
Mole, N., 'International Law, the Individual and AW Brian Simpson's Contribution to the Defence of Human Rights', in: K. O'Donovan & G.R. Rubin (eds.), *Human Rights and Legal History*, Oxford: Oxford University Press, 2004, pp. 13–28.

Pilkington 1984
Pilkington, M.L., 'Damages as a Remedy for Infringement of the Canadian Charter of Rights and Freedoms' 62 *CBR*, 1984, pp. 517–576.

Price, Duodu & Cain, 2010
Price, D., Duodu, K. & Cain, N., *Defamation Law Procedure and Practice*, London: Sweet & Maxwell, 2010.

Quill 2008
Quill, E., 'Ireland', in: H. Koziol & B.C. Steininger (eds.), *European Tort Law 2007*, Vienna; Springer, 2008, pp. 352–372.

Lord Scott, Holland, R.J. & Varner, S.D. 2006
Lord Scott, Holland, R.J. & Varner, S.D, 'The Role of "Extra-Compensatory" Damages for Violations of Fundamental Human Rights in the United Kingdom and the United States', *VaJInt'lL*, 2006, pp. 475–500.

Shelton 1999
Shelton, D., *Remedies in International Human Rights Law*, New York: Oxford University Press, 1999.

Simor & Emmerson 1999
Simor, J. & Emmerson, B., *Human Rights Practice*, London: Sweet & Maxwell, 1999.

Stanton, Skidmore & Harris 2003
Stanton, K.M., Skidmore, P. & Harris, M., *Statutory Torts*, London: Sweet & Maxwell, 2003.

Steele 2008
Steele, J., 'Damages in Tort and under the Human Rights Act: Remedial or Functional Separation', *CLJ*, 2008, pp. 606–634.

Varuhas 2009
Varuhas, J.N.E, 'A Tort-Based Approach to Damages under the Human Rights Act 1998', *MLR*, 2009, pp. 750–782.

Ventose 2009
Ventose, E.D., '"Vindicatory Damages" for Infringements of Constitutional Rights in the Commonwealth Caribbean', *LQR*, 2009, pp. 247–252.

Wilcox 2009
Wilcox, V., 'Punitive Damages in England', in: H. Koziol & V. Wilcox, *Punitive Damages: Common Law and Civil Law Perspectives*, Vienna: Springer, 2009, pp. 7–53.

Wilcox 2011
Wilcox, V., 'Punitive Damages and Nominal Damages', in: A. Fenyves *et al.* (eds.) *Tort Law in the Jurisprudence of the European Court of Human Rights*, Boston: De Gruyter Verlag, 2011, 725–737.

Lord Wolf 2000
Lord Wolf, 'The Human Rights Act 1998 and Remedies', in: M. Andenas & D. Fairgrieve (eds.), *Judicial Review in International Perspective*, 2000, pp. 429–436.

The Law Commission and the Scottish Law Commission, 'Damages under the Human Rights Act', LC266, 1998.

The Law Reform Commission, 'Report on Aggravated, Exemplary and Restitutionary Damages', LRC60–2000, 2000.

Lord Scott, Lecture Given at the Chancery Bar Association Conference, 20 January, 2006.

Lotte Meurkens

EPILOGUE

The main question asked in this book is whether Europe is missing out by not recognizing punitive damages as a penal remedy in tort law. The authors give their viewpoints on different approaches towards punishment in private law, punitive damages in particular. Now, what has this brought us? This epilogue will first reflect on the author's findings, thereby paying attention to the pros and cons, applicability, aims, and limitations of punitive damages. This will be done in the following order: 1) reluctance or opposition to punitive damages, 2) neutrality or prudence – usually based on experience with the legal remedy – with a positive approach and resulting in practical ideas, and 3) curiosity and enthusiasm. This categorization may be based on the subjective opinions of the authors, but also on more objective viewpoints that are brought forward by them on the basis of certain (European) developments. In other words, the placing of an author's contribution in a certain category does not necessarily mean that the author has made clear that he or she is personally in favour or against the introduction of punitive damages in Continental Europe. Second, an attempt to answer the main question will be made.

1. The Power of Punitive Damages...?

Perhaps the most important conclusion that should be derived from this book is that there clearly are problems relating to law enforcement, prevention of damage, compensation or satisfaction of victims etc., for which a solution *should* be found. Although there is a lot of opposition in Europe, the option of a penal remedy in private law deserves fair consideration. After all, it is not only trouble and affliction that punitive damages have caused. The positive side of it is that the legal remedy has served many Americans and other common law systems well, as an instrument to prevent damage, to punish wrongdoing, to vindicate victims and to enforce the law. These advantages should be kept in mind when assessing the value of punitive damages. Europeans should be careful with suspicion of and mistrust for so-called 'American situations', induced by fear for a claim culture with exorbitant damages awards. Fear is a bad counsellor. That does however not mean that the question whether Europe is missing out is an easy question. Punishment in private law is still a very controversial issue. Also the authors of this book are divided on the issue whether or not punitive damages should play a role in the European debate. In general, most authors are rather hesitant, or at least prudent to some extent. Some are in favour, whereas others are clearly against the introduction of punitive damages in private law. All of them show that there are numerous suggestions and questions that should be considered.

1.1. Reluctance

Some of the authors show reluctance or even opposition to introducing punitive damages into Continental European legal systems. Among them are Vanessa Wilcox, Angela Ortega González, Ulrich Magnus and Danuta Mendelson.

Vanessa Wilcox has the final word in part three of this book. In her contribution concerning the important issue of punitive damages for human rights violations, she looks into 'the recourse to extra-compensatory damages as a strategic element in the law's armoury against breaches of fundamental rights'. She first examines the ECHR's approach to punitive damages, after which she goes into the impact of the Court's position on domestic courts in countries that recognise punitive damages, particularly England, Wales and Ireland. As a final point, the concept of vindicatory damages (a recent idea of the House of Lords sitting as the Privy Council) is assessed. According to Wilcox, 'English judges are eager to retain their tradition of maximising deterrence for flagrant (human rights) breaches through an award of extra-compensatory damages'. Wilcox however concludes by taking a reluctant stance towards the general introduction of punitive damages in Continental Europe.

The contribution by Angela Ortega González concerns a development which was appointed in my introduction as the immediate cause for the increased European attention for punitive damages, namely private enforcement of EC competition law. Ortega González gives an extensive overview of the European Commission's approach with regard to the possible use of punitive damages for competition law infringements. She explains that the introduction of punitive damages depends largely on enforcement priorities of the Commission, the legal traditions of the Member States with regard to the nature of damages awards, and the interference with public enforcement. According to Ortega González, the Commission made the right choice by deciding no longer to strive for the adoption of punitive damages within EC competition law.

It follows from the contribution of Ulrich Magnus on punitive damages and German law that he is not in favour of introducing punitive damages in European law, mainly because this is inconsistent with the criminal-private law divide. Magnus does however suggest to strengthen the preventive function of tort law by 'raising the level of damages until a noticeable deterrent effect is reached', as is in line with the Principles of European Tort Law and principles prepared by the study group on a European Civil Code.

In her contribution 'Punitive Damages *Sensu Stricto* in Australia', Danuta Mendelson explains the position of common law punitive damages in Australian law. Mendelson not only discusses punitive damages, but also aggravated damages, which is a form of monetary compensation for harm involving 'injury to the plaintiff's feelings caused by insult, humiliation and the like' that is awarded particularly in cases of intentional torts. Australian courts evidently failed to draw a clear line between these two forms of damages, and legislatures responded to that failure by either abolishing or placing limitations on both remedies. Instead, Australian legislators developed a way of deterring and punishing violators of statutory prohibitions through a system of (fixed amounts of) civil penalties that are to be collected by the Crown. Mendelson concludes by stating that Europe would be wise to forget the idea of punitive damages and recommends to look further into the Australian idea of civil penalties instead.

To conclude, Sophia Michaelides-Mateou from Cyprus is not so much against punitive damages herself, but – after having provided an overview of a number of specific legal situations relating to punitive damages, namely trespass to land, defamation, contract law, products liability, competition law, patent law and employment law – she does determine that Cypriot courts do not readily award punitive damages and are probably also reluctant to do so in for example future competition and patent cases.

1.2. Neutrality or 'Positive' prudence

To start with, attention should at this point be paid to a more general problem that is often brought forward as an argument against (the introduction of) punitive damages, *i.e.* the insurability for punitive damages. Emily Nordin and Daily Wuyts give their opinion on this difficult point, which is so controversial because it is questionable what the consequences of insurance are for the deterrent function of punitive damages. An often heard argument is that insurance deprives punitive damages of their deterrent effect. Nordin and Wuyts look into this subject from a Belgian law perspective, and particularly discuss public policy arguments as well as practical objections against insurability. Furthermore, they look into contractual provisions and legislative restrictions that might prevent or allow coverage in the hypothetical situation that punitive damages exist in Belgian law. The authors clearly explain why they see no compelling obstacles in the recognition of insurability for punitive damages. First of all, they find that there is no conflict with public policy arguments, as according to Belgian contract law other punitive elements like penalty clauses are insurable as well. Furthermore, other practical problems such as for example the prevention of bankruptcy also do no hinder the insurability of punitive damages. Even though these authors do not plea for *the* introduction of punitive damages as such, they do conclude that Belgian insurance law as it exists today would not prohibit their insurability.

The authors from the United States and England actually tell us to be prudent and to get the theory right before introducing it. This is a wise suggestion that should be kept in mind by legislators and policymakers on the road ahead. The Americans offer practical ideas based on their long experience with the legal remedy.

To start with, Anthony Sebok gives a profound explanation of the constitutional theory of punitive damages as developed by the U.S. Supreme Court from the 1980s, by which courts were obliged to review punitive damages awards thoroughly. He first described the eight cases[1] in which the Court has tested state common law punitive

1 *Browning-Ferris Industries of Vermont v. Kelco Disposal, Inc.*, 493 U.S. 257 (1989); *Pacific Mutual Life Insurance Co. v. Haslip*, 499 U.S. 1 (1991); *TXO Production Corp. v. Alliance Resources Corp.*, 509 U.S. 443 (1993); *Honda Motor Co. v. Oberg*, 512 U.S. 415 (1994); *BMW of North America, Inc. v. Gore*, 517 U.S. 559 (1996); *Cooper Industries, Inc. v. Leatherman Tool Group, Inc.*, 532 U.S. 424 (2001), 121 S. Ct. 1678; *State Farm Mutual Automobile Insurance Co. v. Campbell*, 538 U.S. 408 (2003); *Philip Morris USA v. Williams*, 127 S. Ct. 1057 (2007).

damages verdicts against the limits set out by the Constitution, *i.e.* the excessive fines clause (Eight Amendment) and the due process clause (Fourteenth Amendment). In these cases, the Court 'simply' reviewed what state courts had done (wrong). Then, in its most recent case,[2] the Court for the first time had to decide the content of a federal common law theory of punitive damages. As explained by Sebok, this has resulted in different levels of judicial punitive damages theories in the United States, and the gap between them is significant. He therefore recommends the Europeans to get the theory right, before adopting any kind of punitive damages.

Concerning the theory, David Owen has a somewhat different opinion on the functions of punitive damages, thereby deviating from the 'mainstream'. In his contribution 'Punitive Damages as Restitution', Owen advocates that in addition to punishment and deterrence, restitution should be viewed as *the* important pillar of punitive damages law. Restitution, which is grounded in compensation, should be required from the grave wrongdoer in order to restore what has been stolen from the victim. According to Owen, the focus of punitive damages should not so much be on the public's interest in retribution and deterrence, but rather on private law interests of the victim such as compensation and restitution. In this way, courts can also prevent 'results that look suspiciously like they sprang from a public-law scheme for inflicting punishment that has masked itself in a regime marked 'private''. Most value should therefore be attached to '*private* retribution and *private* deterrence in pursuit of restorative goals'.

Mark Geistfeld also gives his opinion on the theoretical approach to punitive damages. In his contribution 'Due Process and the Deterrence Rationale for Punitive Damages', he gives his opinion on the limitation of punitive damages to individual deterrence by the U.S. Supreme Court.[3] According to the Court, 'the Constitution's Due Process Clause forbids a State to use a punitive damages award to punish a defendant for injury that it inflicts upon non-parties or those whom they directly represent, *i.e.*, injury that it inflicts on those who are, essentially, strangers to the litigation'.[4] This underestimates the value that should be attached to the *general* deterrence purpose of punitive damages, which according to Geistfeld is 'of much greater practical importance'. Geistfeld's contribution shows that punitive damages awards that vindicate the individual tort can also further the social interest in punishment and general deterrence, at least when 'the individual tort right is situated in a mass market', for example products liability situations.

Jim Gash has looked into the Multiple Punishments Problem. He analyses the situation 'where a defendant, who has injured multiple potential plaintiffs by a single act or course of conduct, faces multiple punitive damages awards for that conduct'. This is a topic of great concern in the American punitive damages debate. The problem has been addressed twice by the U.S. Supreme Court,[5] which – according to Gash – have been largely ineffective attempts. A possible solution to the problem, as Gash suggests, lies in the creation of a National Punitive Damages Registry. Such a system could also be helpful

2 *Exxon Shipping Co. v. Baker,* 554 U.S. 471 (2008).
3 *Philip Morris USA v. Williams*, 549 U.S. 346 (2007).
4 *Ibid.*, at 353.
5 *State Farm Mut. Auto. Ins. Co. v. Campbell*, 538 U.S. 408, 423 (2003); *Philip Morris USA v. Williams*, 549 U.S. 346 (2007).

for European countries, so to anticipate difficulties in light of multiple punishment. The idea is that the defendant files a registration in case punitive damages have been awarded against him, which will release him from any future punitive damages awards based upon the conduct as described in the registration. The multiple punishment problem as well as the registry system are extensively explained.

The final contribution in part one is that of Jonathan Morgan from England, who shows the difficulty that the English have in getting the punitive damages, or the English term 'exemplary damages', theory right. He asserts that as the English Courts have shown ambivalence with regard to punishment through tort law, legislative intervention is needed, and that the Law Commission for England and Wales issued a report on punitive damages including proposals for their reform. Morgan discusses not only the background of the judicial disagreement, but also the Law Commission report (one conclusion is that punitive damages retain their value in some situations). Furthermore, he pays attention to punitive damages in relation to vicarious liability and liability insurance – stating that particularly in these areas, empirical research into the impact of (potential) liability on defendants is needed –, as well as to the English costs of litigation system which already has a punitive element in it and therefore forms an argument against punitive damages.

1.3. *Curiosity and Enthusiasm*

The contribution of Louis Visscher concerns the economic approach to punitive damages, and the role that such damages could play in both tort law and contract law. One of the objectives that Visscher has with his contribution is to debunk the myth surrounding the punitive damages remedy. Thus, by providing several empirical data, he suggests that the 'fear for 'American situations' that many European lawyers have is unwarranted'. Then, after an overview of the goals of tort law and the law of damages, the specific function that punitive damages in tort law plays from an economic perspective is described. Specific themes such as intentional torts, insurance and disgorgement of profits are also explained in an understandable law and economics manner. Lastly, the subject of punitive damages in contract law is discussed. According to Visscher, based on law and economics theories, punitive damages can play an important role in tort law, but rather as an instrument to serve deterrence goals than punishment goals. Furthermore, he argues that in contract law there are less economic reasons to allow punitive damages than in tort law. The most important problem, he writes, is that punitive damages may lead to excessive performance.

Robert Hardy specifically focuses on the subject of punitive damages in contract law, and 'assesses whether punitive damages should be available for certain types of contract breaches'. He first describes the general economic theory of contracts and the system of remedies for breach of contract, after which law and economics arguments against and in favour of punitive damages for breach of contract are given and applied to different categories of breaches. Hardy is of the opinion that punitive damages should especially be available in two categories of opportunistic behaviour, as compensatory damages do not sufficiently deter these opportunistic breaches of contract. The following two situations are mentioned: '(i) when a promisor's bad faith failure to perform could threaten the promisee's survival (e.g. in the case of a contract with a vital supplier), and

(ii) when contractual surplus would be maximized if the promisee makes relation-specific investments and the promisor's bad faith breach occurs after the promisee's has made the investments (e.g. after the production of something that only the promisor can use)'.

Also in relation to contracts, Lodewijk Smeehuijzen gives us some insights into the issue of punitive damages in case of bad faith claim handling by insurers. This is an important point, as victims of such bad faith insurers may suffer serious (additional) material and immaterial damage when 'an insurer refuses to pay a claim that is not reasonably debatable'. According to Smeehuijzen, the bad faith insurer is a 'paradigm candidate for punitive damages', as has been the situation in the United States for over fifty years now. Furthermore, he asserts that the main objections to punitive damages in such a situation seem to be fading.

Evelien de Kezel looks into the limits and opportunities of protecting and enforcing private interests via punitive damages in Belgian law. Her contribution is clearly focused on the instrumental view of tort law as well as the law enforcement function of punitive damages. She thereby pays attention to developments in the areas of competition law, environmental law, consumer protection and health. De Kezel especially compares the Belgian way of addressing physical loss with the American approach, and examines whether the Belgian practice leaves room for awarding punitive damages and for enforcing American punitive damages awards. She makes clear that 'a mix of public and private law enforcement provides for the most effective enforcement of legal rules'. As regards the differences between the United States and Europe in approach to civil litigation and enforcing private interests, she is of the opinion that the goals underlying both systems seem to be the same and that different approaches underlying both systems seem to be converging. Furthermore, de Kezel asserts that private enforcement mechanisms should not only play a compensatory, but also a regulatory and punitive role.

In her contribution concerning the 'Enforcement in Family Law by means of Private Penalties', Sara Matthé makes a legal comparison between Belgian and Dutch law. Also in family law, there is discussion on the increasing role of family members in enforcing their family law obligations. According to Matthé, the Americans do award punitive damages in family law proceedings, for example 'to influence parents' behaviour in cases of interference by one parent with the other parent's parent-child relationship by not complying with a custody and visitation order'. Punitive damages are thereby seen as an additional deterrent to improve enforcement in family law, as criminal sanctions are normally considered to be the first step. Matthé describes the Belgian and Dutch situation on the basis of a case-study regarding the enforcement of the parents' right to contact with their child, and asserts that 'enforcement of family law obligations should in principle be made possible by means of penalty clauses'.

Marta Requejo Isidro provides an overview of developments from a private international law perspective, which is an interesting angle as it says something about the *communis opinio* with regard to the recognition and enforcement of foreign punitive damages awards. The current point of view in Europe is that punitive damages violate the *ordre public*. Requejo Isidro explains 'three situations in which the authorities of a civil law system must face a private international law scenario with elements related to punitive damages'. She concludes by supporting a tolerant attitude toward punitive damages when private international situations are at stake.

To end with, the following three authors describe interesting developments taking place in Europe which show that there is less opposition to punitive damages. These contributions give a clear idea of the curiosity for the legal remedy that lives in Europe.

Chantal Mahé discusses three reform drafts of the French civil code and the role that punitive damages play therein. The French in fact have a rather open attitude towards punitive damages, which not only follows from the drafts, but also from a recent decision of the Cour de Cassation,[6] and it surely is interesting to see what the reasons for this 'cautious admission', as Mahé puts it, are. She first gives a profound overview of the different drafts, after which a detailed description of the punitive damages provisions that have been included in the drafts follows.

The Spanish situation is extensively described by Marta Otero Crespo in her contribution 'Punitive Damages under Spanish Law: a Subtle Recognition?'. As regards the *status quo* of punitive damages in Spain, Otero Crespo assesses 'a certain openness towards their recognition'. Like in France, the Spanish supreme court not so long ago issued a decision favouring an American punitive damages award.[7] Furthermore, she asserts that although punitive damages are not expressly mentioned, there seems to be a 'subtle presence' of punitive-deterrent awards in Spanish substantive law. Several examples that support this view are given.

The final contribution of part two, by Cedric Vanleenhove, is titled 'Punitive Damages and European Law: *Quo Vademus*?'. Vanleenhove discusses the role that punitive damages play in European substantive law and European Court of Justice decisions. According to Vanleenhove, punitive damages do not (yet) play a significant role in European law. However, the Member States' freedom to sanction breaches of EU law in an effective, proportionate and dissuasive manner might leave room for interpretation.

2. … Is Europe missing out?

The contributors to this book have all dived into the subject of punitive damages, which has resulted in more than a lot of food for thought on the question whether Europe is missing out by not making use of this private law remedy. Some of the authors are, because of their legal background, familiar with the legal remedy, whereas most of them give their viewpoints from a relative distance. It is interesting to have both sides of the story included in this book. What is striking is that it does not matter whether the author lives in a country where punitive damages are (frequently) awarded or not: all authors have written profound and critical contributions, some being enthusiastic, others being more reticent about punitive damages.

Although punitive damages awards are controversial, they are still considered an important remedy in American law, primarily aiming at punishment. Furthermore, punitive damages serve the (instrumental) functions of law enforcement, deterrence and

6 Cass. 1e civ., 1 December 2010, no. 09-13303, (Epoux X – Rejet pourvoi c/CA Poitiers, 26 February 2009).

7 'Auto' of the Supreme Court, 13 November 2001, JUR 2002, 608.

compensation. Despite criticism on their frequency, size and predictability, punitive damages awards appear to be relatively uncommon and are normally awarded by the American courts with caution. Several safeguards to control punitive damages awards have been created. For example, aggravating circumstances relating to the conduct and state of mind of the wrongdoer are needed for punitive damages to be awarded. Moreover, the plaintiff must have suffered actual damage, and must at least be entitled to a nominal or compensatory damages award. The Americans have nevertheless become aware of the inherent precariousness of awarding punitive damages, and have therefore done efforts relating to both legislative reforms and judicial review so to constringe the use of it. This might already take away some of the mistrust that Europeans have for the above mentioned 'American situations', which is more often than not based on unfounded stories (*cf.* the contribution of Louis Visscher). However, my guess is that there is still a long road ahead before the majority of Europeans can really familiarize with the strange legal remedy that puts a powerful incentive in the hand of the civil judge and the citizen. In the meantime, several developments do show that policy makers, legal scholars and legislators throughout Europe are in search for a powerful legal instrument to deter grave misconduct and to enforce private law interests. Examples can be found in the area of competition law, tort law itself, but also other more specific fields of the law as has particularly been explained by the contributors to part three of this book, dealing with punitive damages and certain special themes.

More and more, tort law is pin-pointed as a possible instrument to solve several problems that citizens and society have to deal with. As stated in my introductory contribution, it is not unwise to at least consider the advantages that punitive damages may bring in this regard. In so doing, it is important to strive for an open and flexible approach rather than a conservative stand that often seems to be based on 'fear for the unknown' arguments, by which I do not wish to suggest that these arguments come totally out of the blue. It is completely understandable that European lawyers see great obstacles to introduce punitive damages, because this legal remedy is simply not consistent with our legal tradition. The main hurdles relate to the mere compensatory function of tort law, the strict public-private law divide, and the role of government. With regard to the first two points, these seem to be losing ground. Compensation is no longer the sole purpose of tort law: more and more attention is paid to other functions such as prevention and law enforcement. Furthermore, also in civil law countries the public-private law distinction is becoming less strict. In my opinion, and with reference to my introduction, the most serious impediment to incorporation of punitive damages lies in the latter point, *i.e.* the role of government. When compared to the American situation, the government has a rather active role in the lives of Europeans. This is a political, cultural and societal difference that is demonstrated, for example, by the reliance on social security laws or regulatory governmental authorities. However, we have to keep in mind that also in this regard changes are taking place. In recent years, Western Europeans have noticed a retreat of the Welfare State. Another example lies in the area of competition law, *i.e.* European competition law authorities lack capacity to do all the work and look into the possibility to make an appeal to citizens in terms of law enforcement. Again, punitive damages pop up, and no matter how uninviting this option might seem, it still deserves serious consideration.

At this point, there are no definite answers yet as to what exact role punitive damages or penal remedies in private law could and should play in Continental Europe. In a study on the common law and civil law perspectives on punitive damages launched by the Institute for European Tort Law ('ETL') in 2009, one of the editors professor Koziol ended his concluding chapter with the following words:[8]

> 'Punitive damages don't have to be admitted into the seventh legal heaven but neither would eternal damnation be appropriate. I think they should be condemned to purgatory and after quite some purefication some may graciously be admitted to the first legal heaven'.

Although Koziol is prudent, he does not close the door. I hope that this book has brought the debate another step further, and that it has shown that the European punitive damages debate is still alive. Questions in this regard that spring to mind are: How urgent is the need for powerful private enforcement instruments in Europe? To which legal areas does this apply? What role can punitive damages play in this, or are there other options, *i.e.* better instruments, available? Are the European and American enforcement systems really converging, as suggested by De Kezel in this book? What about the influence of the role of government, how does this affect private law enforcement theories? For which specific (tort) situations can punitive damages be helpful? Can punitive damages for example enhance general public safety, if made available in class actions? Is the public-private law divide still an impediment? How important has the preventive function of tort law become? In light of 'getting the theory right': which functions should punitive damages fulfill? Questions of insurability, as dealt with by Nordin and Wuyts, also come to mind. Another important question is: where should the punitive damages award go to? To the victim? To the treasury? Or perhaps to a State fund, such as a general victim fund.

In my opinion, there is plenty of room for more debate on the matter. It is however too early to conclude that Europe is missing out. I personally attach value to further research into the subject being carried out, from a positive starting point and flexible attitude to the legal remedy and with fair consideration of the pros and cons, so that this important question can eventually be answered in a more concrete manner.

8 Koziol 2009, p. 328 (see the bibliography in my introductory contribution).

IUS COMMUNE EUROPAEUM

A peer-reviewed book series in which the common foundations of the legal systems of the Member States of the European Community are the central focus.

The *Ius Commune Europaeum* series includes horizontal comparative legal studies as well as studies on the effect of treaties within the national legal systems. All the classic fields of law are covered. The books are published in various European languages under the auspices of METRO, the Institute for Transnational Legal Research at Maastricht University.

Recently published:
Volume 90: *Evolutie van de basisbeginselen van het contractenrecht*, I. Samoy (red.)
Volume 91: *Recidive in België en Nederland. Een analyse van 200 jaar rechtspraak en rechtsleer*, M. Dams
Volume 92: *An EU-wide Letter of Rights. Towards Best Practice*, T. Spronken (ed.)
Volume 93: *The Costanzo Obligation. The Obligations of National Administrative Authorities in the Case of Incompatibility between National Law and European Law*, M. Verhoeven
Volume 94: *The Effect of a Change of Circumstances on the Binding Force of Contracts. Comparative Perspectives*, R. Momberg Uribe
Volume 95: *The Landscape of the Legal Professions in Europe and the USA: Continuity and Change*, A. Uzelac and C.H. van Rhee (eds.)
Volume 96: *Constitutional Constraints on Ad Hoc Legislation. A Comparative Study of the United States, Germany and the Netherlands*, A. Jasiak
Volume 97: *The Social Security Position of Irregular Migrant Workers. New Insights from National Security Law and International Law*, K. Kapuy
Volume 98: *Educating European Lawyers*, A.W. Heringa and B. Akkermans (eds.)
Volume 99: *The Draft Common Frame of Reference: A National and Comparative Perspective*, E. Terryn, V. Sagaert and M.E. Storme (eds.)
Volume 100: *Does Law Matter? On Law and Economic Growth*, M. Faure and J. Smits (eds.)

www.ingramcontent.com/pod-product-compliance
Ingram Content Group UK Ltd.
Pitfield, Milton Keynes, MK11 3LW, UK
UKHW051925100926
8556IPUK00022B/1366

9 781780 680477